Glencoe

Speech

Mc
Graw
Hill
Education

SPEECH

Randall McCutcheon

James Schaffer

Joseph R. Wycoff

McGraw Hill Education

CONTENTS IN BRIEF

TABLE OF CONTENTS

(t) U.S. Air Force photo by Master Sgt. Val Gempis; (b) Hybrid Images/Getty Images

TABLE OF CONTENTS

TABLE OF CONTENTS

TABLE OF CONTENTS

Randall McCutcheon, former Director of Forensics, Albuquerque Academy, Albuquerque, New Mexico, and member of the National Forensic League Hall of Fame, has over 25 years of experience teaching speech. He has authored eight other books, including *Journalism Matters*, an introductory high school journalism textbook; *Can You Find It?*, a guide to teaching research skills to high school students (it received the Ben Franklin Award for best self-help book of the year in 1990); *Get Off My Brain*, a survival guide for students who hate to study (it was selected by the New York Public Library as one of 1998's Best Books for Teenagers); *It Doesn't Take A Genius: Five Truths to Inspire Success in Every Student*, written with Tommie Lindsey (a MacArthur Foundation "Genius Grant" recipient); and four ACT and SAT preparation guides (co-written by Jim Schaffer).

Nationally recognized by the U.S. Department of Education for innovation in curriculum, Mr. McCutcheon was selected Nebraska Teacher of the Year, 1985, and the National Forensic League's Coach of the Year, 1987. He holds memberships in the Speech Communication Association, the National Forensic League, and the Catholic Forensic League. He completed his undergraduate work at the University of Nebraska with emphasis in speech and theater. His graduate-level work was in the study of rhetoric, persuasion, and interpersonal communication. After nearly a decade of working in radio and television, he has taught in public and private schools in Nebraska, Iowa, Massachusetts, and New Mexico, and coached his speech teams to 25 state and five national championships (NFL and CFL).

James Schaffer, a journalism professor and publications advisor at Nebraska Wesleyan University, earned a Ph.D. in English from the University of Virginia.

A strong interest in the space program led Schaffer to apply for the Teacher in Space contest. He became a national semi-finalist and was named State Aerospace Educator of the Year. He also won a Christa McAuliffe Fellowship from the U.S. Department of Education that enabled him to give over 400 programs on space travel to school and community groups.

As a high school teacher for 15 years at Lincoln East High School, he advised award-winning publications, including a newspaper, a magazine, and a yearbook. He and his wife Mary Lynn, also an educator, have three children—Suzanne, Sarah, and Stephen—who all love to speak.

Joseph R. Wycoff is currently the Administrator of Arts and Activities at Apple Valley High School in Apple Valley, Minnesota. He is also actively involved with the Speech and Debate Program. Before moving to Minnesota, Mr. Wycoff taught at Chesterton High School (Indiana) for 31 years. He retired from Indiana in 1989 and moved to Minnesota, where he continued teaching English and coaching Speech. At Chesterton, he taught Language Arts and was the Coach/Director of Speech and Debate for twenty years. During that time, his teams won fifteen Indiana State Speech championships and three consecutive National Forensic League titles (1989, 1990, and 1991). He is a member of the Indiana Coaching Hall of Fame, and in 1992 he was inducted into the National Forensic League National Hall of Fame—the youngest member ever so honored. As an educator and as a coach, he has won numerous awards. In teaching, he has been named Teacher of the Year by his students, Professional of the Year by the faculty, and Educator of the Year by the administration. He was an Indiana Teacher of the Year finalist, and in 1989 he received a Creative Endowment Grant from the Eli Lilly Grant Foundation. He received his Masters of Arts from Valparaiso University (Indiana).

Mr. Wycoff has traveled to over 35 states, giving over 100 instructional/ motivational seminars to both students and adults on "burnout," leadership, ethics in competition, and effective communication; and has taught summer speech sessions at Bradley University (Illinois), Longwood College (Virginia), and the University of Iowa. Mr. Wycoff has three adult sons—Jeff, Jon, and Joe—and six grandchildren. His wife, Pam Campbell Cady Wycoff, is the current Director of Speech and Debate at Apple Valley High School.

REVIEWERS

The authors would like to thank the following high school teachers for their comments and suggestions during the development of the text.

Joni Anker
Eagan High School
Eagan, Minnesota

Antonette Aragon
Thompson Valley High School
Loveland, Colorado

Cindy Bomboske
Monacan High School
Richmond, Virginia

Barbara J. Evans
Mayo High School
Rochester, Minnesota

Kim Falco
Franklin High School
El Paso, Texas

Karen S. Finch
Blacksburg High School
Blacksburg, Virginia

Tommie Lindsey, Jr.
James Logan High School
Union City, California

Lou Ann Mahlandt
Lafayette High School
St. Joseph, Missouri

Connie McKee
Amarillo High School
Amarillo, Texas

Debbie Nicholas
Woodrow Wilson High School
Dallas, Texas

Jane Saunders
Travis High School
Austin, Texas

Patricia Smith
Connally High School
Austin, Texas

Michael Tile
John F. Kennedy High School
Silver Spring, Maryland

Bryan Waltz
North High School
Evansville, Indiana

John Weddendorf
Westland High School
Galloway, Ohio

UNIT

1

The Person

UNIT CONTENTS

BUILDING RESPONSIBILITY

Few things can help an individual more than to place responsibility on him, and to let him know that you trust him.

—Booker T. Washington

Learning Objectives

After completing this chapter, you will be able to do the following.

- Identify and analyze the ethical and social responsibilities of communicators.
- Identify the components of the communication process and their functions.
- Explain the importance of effective communication skills in personal, professional, and social contexts.
- Recognize your audience as an important element in building responsible communication skills.
- Realize the importance and impact of both verbal and nonverbal communication.

Chapter Outline

Following are the main sections in this chapter.

1. What Is Communication?
2. Laying the Proper Foundation
3. Building the Proper Motivation

Speech Vocabulary

In this chapter, you will learn the meanings of the speech terms listed below.

ethics
communication
sender
message
receiver
feedback
communication
  barrier
written
  communication
oral (or verbal)
  communication
nonverbal
  communication

symbol
intrapersonal
  communication
interpersonal
  communication
oratory/rhetoric
orator
logical appeal
emotional appeal
ethical (personal)
  appeal
dialogue
motivation
stereotyping

Academic Vocabulary

Expanding your academic vocabulary will help you become a more effective communicator. Listed below are some words appearing in this chapter that you should make part of your vocabulary.

responsible
epitomize
mesmerized

flippant
reciprocal

Francis Horn, a past president of the University of Rhode Island, said, "Never before has it been so essential to learn to separate the true from the false. We have come to put great emphasis on education in science and engineering. But speech, rather than science or engineering, may actually hold the key to the future of the world."

Horn is telling us that before we turn to test tubes and computers for all of the world's solutions, we had better get in touch with each other. Very simply, we need to master the art of talk and meaningful communication. There is a world of difference between random, meaningless talk—and responsible talk.

In this chapter, you will learn what communication is and, more specifically, what speech communication is. Next, you will learn the role that responsibility plays in the communication process. Finally, you will learn that effective speech communication can be better accomplished when the building of character comes before the building of speech content and skillful delivery.

Introduction

Unit 1 of this book deals with "The Person" and Chapter 1 with "Building Responsibility." To understand how these two titles are connected, let's examine a few of the key words.

Ethics can be a dangerous word to use because it can mean different things to different people. However, most people would agree that ethics refers to a person's sense of right and wrong. If you are an ethical person, you work to do what's right. You have a sense of conscience and a personalized code of conduct that you feel is important in the building of character. An ethical judge strives to be impartial when hearing a case. An ethical police officer always follows the law. Likewise, an ethical communicator puts a high premium on using his or her words constructively and promoting what's right.

Responsibility goes hand in hand with ethics, but what does it mean to be responsible? Quite simply, being responsible means that you will be accountable for your actions and that you will get done what you say you will. Responsible citizens vote, responsible drivers wear seat belts, and responsible speakers pay attention to the words that they use and the way that they use them.

You can be responsible by volunteering for projects that help improve and renovate areas in your city.

When you combine ethical with responsible, you take the first step in building successful oral communication.

Before dealing with ethics or responsibility in any more detail, though, let's examine exactly what communication means and how the speech communication process works.

What Is Communication?

When the author Robert Louis Stevenson said, "There can be no fairer ambition than to excel in talk," he was speaking about the art of effective oral communication. **Communication** is the process of sending and receiving messages, and it occurs whenever we express ourselves in a manner that is clearly understood.

The Communication Process

Sam and Lynette are discussing basketball. Sam believes that David Robinson and Tim Duncan of the San Antonio Spurs are the best two players of all time in the National Basketball Association. He points to the facts that San Antonio won an NBA championship under the leadership of Robinson and that Duncan was named Most Valuable Player in the playoffs. Lynette, on the other hand, favors John Stockton and Karl Malone of the Utah Jazz. She lists that team's overall record and the numerous awards that both Stockton and Malone won. Both Sam and Lynette are communicating a message, listening to what the other has to say, and then responding. Consequently, they are actively involved in the communication process, which consists of the sender, the receiver, the message, and feedback.

The **sender** is the one who transmits the **message**: what is sent or said. The sender starts the communication process by using words. Words are the symbols you use to convey your ideas. Your words must clearly communicate to your listener the exact message you are trying to convey. The **receiver** is the person who intercepts the message and then decodes, or interprets, it. **Feedback** includes the reactions that the receiver gives to the message offered by the sender.

Every day, when you talk on a phone, write letters, check e-mail, or watch television, you are either sending messages or receiving them. Teachers communicate with students when they give clear

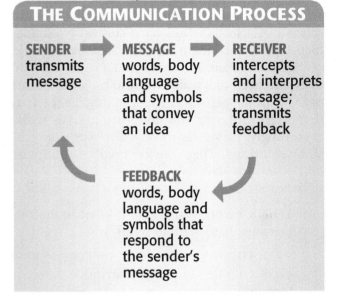

THE COMMUNICATION PROCESS

SENDER transmits message → **MESSAGE** words, body language and symbols that convey an idea → **RECEIVER** intercepts and interprets message; transmits feedback

FEEDBACK words, body language and symbols that respond to the sender's message

directions for taking an exam. Students communicate when they accurately explain an assignment to a classmate who had been absent. Parents communicate when they leave specific instructions for a baby-sitter. When words are clearly put together, they build a solid communication system intended to express a specific message.

In a perfect world, meaningful communication would always occur. The sender would send a clear message that would be accurately picked up by the receiver—who would then provide positive feedback that the words have been understood. However, sometimes problems arise. The messages might be blocked by certain communication barriers. A **communication barrier** is any obstacle that gets in the way of effective communication. These obstacles might be . . .

- Attitudinal—("I really don't *like* what we're talking about here!")
- Social—("This person is *not* one of my friends!")
- Educational—("I'm far too *smart* to listen to this stuff!")

- Cultural—("This person's *heritage* isn't like mine at all!")
- Environmental—("I'm too *hot* in this room to even think!" or "There's too much *noise* to concentrate!")

Each obstacle can prevent the receiver from correctly interpreting the words being spoken by the sender. How can we remove these oral communication obstacles? The answer is simple, yet sound: focus! Communication experts advise us to get rid of our distractions and try to find a common field of experience—or a realistic way to be "on the same page" with the person who is speaking. They tell us that the process of communicating takes work. Accordingly, they offer three action words as possible solutions. Their advice involves both the sender and the receiver.

To the sender:

1. THINK before you speak. ("What is the real message that I want to send?")

2. ARTICULATE your words. ("Am I enunciating each syllable, or am I slurring my words together?")

3. WATCH the receiver of your words to make sure that you are getting the correct nonverbal signals. ("She isn't responding correctly. I had better say this a different way.")

To the receiver:

1. ASK questions; make polite requests. ("Could you turn down the heat, please? I can't concentrate in a hot room.")

2. LEARN more about issues and people. They can both make you smarter. (Say to yourself, "I need to listen. It's good to hear an opinion or voice other than my own.")

3. RELATE to the background and experiences of those speaking. They're speaking for a reason. It's worth your time to listen and try to understand their world. ("I should try to understand what they've gone through and what message they're trying to convey.")

The above advice applies to both the social and the professional worlds. You shouldn't tune out possible friends, nor should you tune out your boss, your colleagues at work, or customers. Apply some CPR, or Communication for Positive Results, by allowing the communication process to help you build relationships. Participate actively in the communication process.

Any communication that must be read is called **written communication**. When the communication is spoken, it's often called oral or **verbal communication**. Your ability to put words together effectively, either in written or verbal form, will

A responsible communicator works to eliminate communication barriers.

Image Source

Communicating with People Who Have Disabilities

The Americans with Disabilities Act, enacted in 1990, has improved building access, created job opportunities, and ensured realistic portrayals of people who have a variety of disabling conditions. But there is still work to be done to help everyone communicate with people who have disabilities. Affirmative phrases such as "developmental disability" or "person who uses a wheelchair" can go a long way toward integrating persons who have disabilities.

Here are some suggestions of etiquette and general tips on communicating with people with disabilities.

If the person . . .

. . . is blind or visually impaired: Say who you are in a clear, calm tone of voice, and never reach out for the person's service dog without first asking the owner. And tell the person when you are leaving.

. . . is deaf or hard of hearing: Get the person's attention with a physical touch before speaking. Then, talk clearly and slowly, directly to the person.

. . . is in a wheelchair: Sit at eye level before speaking, if possible. Don't touch the chair or the person, and ask first if you can help before moving the individual to another location.

. . . has a cognitive disability: Move to the side if you're in a public space, and realize that you might have to repeat yourself.

. . . has a speech impediment: Resist the urge to finish the person's speech, and ask the individual to repeat what he or she said if you don't understand it.

The best way to converse with a person in a wheelchair is eye-to-eye.

help determine your impact as a communicator. In this book, you will be learning specifically how to become a more effective oral communicator, a more persuasive speaker.

Let's now take a look at nonverbal communication and symbols. Both are important elements in communication and are further discussed in later chapters, where they can be seen in action.

Nonverbal Communication

While the verbal message involves the actual words being spoken, the nonverbal message might be relayed through facial expressions or body movements. Thus, **nonverbal communication** expresses your attitudes or moods about a person, situation, or idea. The person who is cheerful and sitting up straight communicates through "body language" one sort of message. The person who frowns and slouches communicates another sort.

Nonverbal signals may mean different things to different people. For instance, giving someone the thumbs-up sign is a compliment in America but is considered rude and offensive in Australia. In the United States, nodding the head means "yes," but in Greece it means "no." The book *Do's and Taboos Around the World* goes on to add that waving the entire hand means "goodbye" in America, but in Europe, where only the fingers are used to say farewell, it means "no." The book's editor, Roger Axtell, suggests that we all need to realize the impact that nonverbal communication can have on the receiver.

Symbols

Another way people communicate is through symbols. A **symbol** is anything that stands for an idea and is used for communication. Since symbols represent something else by association, they include both nonverbal and verbal communication.

In a nonverbal manner, the "peace" sign calls for nonviolence. Tangible objects such as a flag can stand for freedom, and a bald eagle can stand for America. A letter jacket can represent your school. In the award-winning play *A Raisin in the Sun* by Lorraine Hansberry, a small plant signifies a family's

THE "V" SIGN IN HISTORY

In the 1940s, British Prime Minister Winston Churchill used the "V" sign to rally the British against German aggression.

In the 1960s, the "V" sign stood for peace and nonviolence.

In some countries, athletes use the "V" sign to symbolize victory."

hopes and determination. Nonverbal symbols are powerful, for they speak visually and appeal to people's imaginations and emotions.

Words—verbal symbols—can also be powerful. Advertisers often use key words that symbolize desirable qualities, hoping that you will associate the word with their product. Words such as trust, honesty, heritage, family, and America might be used to arouse your sense of community. Words can even *epitomize* the spirit of an entire nation. When Martin Luther King, Jr., said, "I have a dream," his dream eloquently stood for the hope that someday all Americans would stand together with dignity.

As a sender of messages to receivers, you must pay attention to the nonverbal communication and the symbols that you use if you wish to be taken seriously as a conscientious communicator.

Sharing Ideas Worth Spreading

You might imagine a "speech" as a dour lecture delivered in monotone on a tedious subject. But if the presentation is a riveting story told with a singular point of view that challenges your intellect (and lasts 18 minutes or less), then you likely are listening to a TED talk.

TED is a speaker's conference that has turned into a global phenomenon of sharing "ideas worth spreading." The TED franchise includes global conferences, localized confabs of a similar framework, and+D65 an expansive series of online videos of 18 minutes or less. And they're taking the world's collective consciousness to a new level.

TED conferences ("TED" stands for Technology, Entertainment/Design) are held twice yearly in Canada and are run by a nonprofit group with the mission to make excellent ideas accessible and to spur conversation. Major figures such as Bill Gates, former President Bill Clinton, and numerous Nobel Prize winners have presented their ideas on a plethora of subjects. Proceeds go toward making TED videos accessible to the world via the Internet, community-focused projects, and organizational staffing needs.

Being asked to present at one of the two annual TED conferences is almost as rare as being a finalist on American Idol. So there's a franchised version of TED, called TEDx. These local events are held around the world using local organizers "to spark conversation and connection through local TED-like experiences." There is a wide variety of TEDx types, including youth events, internal events for companies or groups, and university events.

Ted Talks, available for free viewing on ted.com, are a series of video essays by the rich, famous, intellectual, and just plain interesting on a variety of topics as wide as the imagination. Especially in the information technology industry, being asked to present a TED Talk is akin to creating an intellectual calling card. The format is part of the popularity. Ted Talks are limited to 18 minutes, enough time to capture the audience's attention but not long enough to lose it. Presenters don't stand at a podium. Rather, they move about an open stage in full view of the audience. They can present material or just go without props, but they're likely to be filmed from a variety of angles for the videos that will soon be posted online.

When TED started in 1984, it was a conference set up to share ideas in the areas of Technology, Entertainment, and Design. The conferences began to be held annually six years later. As access to video streaming became practical, organizers put the conference online for free beginning in 2006, and the public responded. TED is now a global media channel for sharing ideas. People from all walks of life now have a chance to share ideas in the video format, 18-minute nuggets of wisdom, advice, humor, and heartfelt inspiration. More than 1,700 videos are available, and viewership has topped 1 billion.

Some examples of the most-watched TED Talks are:

• *How schools kill creativity,* by Sir Ken Robinson, is a look at creating a new type of education system that celebrates the creative mind.

• *Your body language shapes who you are,* by Amy Cuddy, examines how posing for power can impact one's success.

• *Underwater astonishments,* by David Gallo, examines recorded underwater footage of amazing sea creatures.

Like social media, Ted Talks are designed to spark conversation. Typical TEDx events consist of 90 minutes of content with several half-hour breaks in between so attendees can talk about what they've just heard. You might hear people talk about the secrets to happiness, or winning the Super Bowl, or how our brains can fool our bodies. Many of the talks have a common form. They begin with a direct statement or challenge for the audience, then continue with a personal story, followed by data backing up the theme. The speaker then summarizes some of the ways that the topic can be applied and provides testimony to emphasize the point. The ending is commonly an invitation for the audience to do something good based on their own abilities.

Since TED-style events can be set up locally, it might be interesting to create one at your school, with students and staff invited to share their experiences and outlooks. What would you talk about if you had 18 minutes and an open microphone? When you plan a talk, consider half of the message is for the live audience, and the other half is for the audience that will watch it after it's recorded.

SECTION 1 REVIEW

Recalling the Facts

1. The four major parts of the communication process are the _____, the _____, the _____, and _____.
2. A responsible communicator works to eliminate communication barriers. One communication barrier is attitudinal. Name the other four, as given in your reading.
3. Another name for oral communication is _____ communication.

Thinking Critically

Nonverbal communication often refers to the attitude you give off to others. What are five positive nonverbal characteristics? Five negative nonverbal characteristics? Write out your lists. (Example: alert eye contact versus a "Get real!" look while someone is talking.) For each of your ten total items, be ready to say what each communicates. What nonverbal characteristics might help you in school? List them.

Taking Charge

Bring in an item from home, school, the community, or work that symbolizes something special. Be prepared to share with the class what your symbol means and what it should communicate to others who see it. Could it send different messages to different people? Explain.

Laying the Proper Foundation

eople building a house don't begin by putting up the walls or decorating the rooms. They begin by establishing a solid foundation that will anchor the rest of the structure. Similarly, you build the ethics of communication and responsibility when you anchor your oral communication to a solid value structure. Command of language, posture, eye contact, gestures, and other speech basics are certainly important and will be covered later in the book, but the "pouring" of your "value structure foundation" must come first. It consists of three essential elements: (1) working to be a good person, (2) communicating constructively, and (3) caring about your audience. Let's look at each separately.

Working to Be a Good Person

The nineteenth-century statesman and orator Daniel Webster said that if all of his talents and abilities except one were taken away, he would ask to keep his ability to speak. "With the ability to speak," he added, "I could regain all that I had lost." Here Webster is telling people of the vital role that speaking can play in their lives. However, he would also likely say that being a polished speaker isn't enough. He would promote the idea that those who speak should work to make the world a better place.

Some prominent speakers have worked to advance humankind. Some have worked to harm humankind. All of us would agree that Adolf Hitler was a powerful speaker, yet his words led to the deaths of millions of people during World War II. The minister and cult figure Jim Jones *mesmerized* his followers in Guyana, South America, in the late 1970s; hundreds died when he commanded them to commit suicide by drinking cyanide-laced Kool-Aid. Unfortunately, we don't have to look far to see what's wrong in our twenty-first-century world. The news is full of people who use speech to take advantage of unsuspecting victims. It is difficult to ignore

Planning a speech is a lot like constructing a building. You should start with a strong foundation.

people whose words have exhibited a less than desirable value structure. However, it would be negligent not to be optimistic and promote positive examples and role models.

For instance, contrast the previous two examples with the words of the Polish freedom fighter Lech Walesa, who said to the U.S. Congress in 1989:

> The world remembers the wonderful principle of the American democracy: "government of the people, by the people, for the people." I too remember these words; I, a shipyard worker from Gdansk, who has devoted his entire life . . . to the service of this idea: "government of the people, by the people, for the people." Against privilege and monopoly, against contempt and injustice . . . I do what I must do.

In his speech, Walesa is telling the world that he is driven by his sense of conscience, his sense of right and wrong—and his words still ring true today.

Design Pics / Kelly Redinger

Sometimes the most important speaking you do is the speaking you do with yourself. This ability to conduct an inner dialogue with yourself and to assess your thoughts, feelings, and reactions is known as **intrapersonal communication**. Many of our actions begin with these silent conversations. You must be honest and positive in your self-communication. A noted presidential speechwriter and political consultant once stated that every speaker must go through some personal "leveling." He or she should have an individual heart-to-heart talk to decide exactly what message the spoken words should convey. This is the type of personal "grounding" that can make a speaker's ideas real and believable to the audience.

For instance, when you have done something right, compliment yourself; when there is room for improvement, silently note what you can do better the next time. Negative intrapersonal communication occurs when you cloud your thoughts with self-doubt. Saying to yourself, "I can't do this. I'm too stupid!" or "I'm not popular enough for anyone to listen to me!" is counterproductive and doesn't give your talents a chance to work. Be honest but be positive and give yourself the benefit of the doubt.

Michael Jordan, the ex-basketball star, says that he loves to be a positive role model for children because "it's the right thing to do." Perhaps his belief is a result of intrapersonal communication. Because this type of communication affects the kind of person you are,

In the fire service, positive role models shape behavior and learning. Young firefighters look up to and often model their behaviors after senior leaders that they respect and admire.

what you communicate to yourself should exhibit a solid work ethic, a sense of integrity, compassion for others, and personal honesty. Most would agree that these are some of the qualities that make up a good person.

You should give a priority to being a good person, then; but the second element of our value structure foundation is just as important.

INSTANT IMPACT

The "Right" Stuff

Being a responsible communicator and using your words well is certainly a goal shared by many. Country singers George Strait and Clint Black have said that their music is dedicated to their audiences. They feel that the words to their songs should be meaningful and, most of all, honest.

Shaukat Qadir, a retired solider who is now a news analyst, asserts that there is no room in responsible journalism for "wrong facts." Every reporter, even those who express their views, need to have their facts right. If the writer draws conclusions from those facts, those conclusions need to be as objective as possible. Qadir also believes that journalists should present reasoning, but leave it to readers to agree or disagree. Only then have journalists responsibly communicated the news.

Communicating Constructively

Besides being able to talk to yourself (intrapersonal communication), you need to be able to talk effectively to others. This form of one-on-one communication is called **interpersonal communication**. This type of communication, which is specifically discussed in Chapter 5, takes place any time messages are transmitted between two or more people. Interpersonal communication is not limited to formal speaking situations. Your conversations in the hallway with other students, after class with teachers, at the dinner table with your family, or on the job with fellow workers are all examples of interpersonal communication. You have an opportunity to build good feelings and trust between and among people. Your job in communicating in this way is to realize that the spoken word should build, inspire, and motivate others, and never belittle or deceive them. Thus, when comedians use words to insult, when politicians use words to distort, when teachers use words to condemn, when businesspeople use words to justify ruining the environment, or when students spread rumors about other students, they are doing an injustice to what speech should do.

Oratory, or **rhetoric**, is the art or study of public speaking. An **orator** is a person who delivers oratory and uses words effectively. The Roman teacher Quintilian called the perfect orator "a good person speaking well." The young AIDS victim Ryan White was certainly a Quintilian-type orator. White spent the final years of his life speaking at schools to educate others about facts and myths regarding AIDS. After his mother was diagnosed with breast cancer, Jon Wagner-Holz, 17, of California, created a national hot line for children whose parents have cancer. He wanted to use his experience both to help others and to allow other young people to have a communication outlet for their words and feelings. These examples should remind us that people have special talents that need to be voiced.

How do you use your words? You must be willing to build up others if you wish to become the effective communicator that this book promotes. This idea carries through to the third and final element that makes up the foundation of your value structure: a genuine concern for the audience.

Interpersonal Communication

© Paul Bradbury / age fotostock

Caring About Your Audience

The noted actor and director Sir Laurence Olivier once said that performers can bring creative life to a play only if they respect the audience enough to think that the audience will understand the play. This lesson can also be applied to speaking. The speaker must respect the members of an audience and show a genuine concern for their thoughts and feelings.

INSTANT IMPACT

Speaking Out for Hispanics

According to the U.S. Census Bureau, the estimated population of Hispanic people in the United States was more than 44 million in 2006. This represented a 3.4 percent increase from 2005 to 2006. With this in mind, several companies around the nation have taken a leadership role in creating job opportunities for Hispanics. *Hispanic Magazine* compiled a list called the Hispanic Corporate 100 that named the top 100 companies providing opportunities and educational training for Hispanics. Among the companies listed on the 2006 list were American Airlines, Burger King, Ford Motor, General Motors, Marriott, Nordstrom, Toyota, Wal-Mart, and Washington Mutual.

The companies in the Hispanic Corporate 100 contribute not only jobs and training programs but also their voices. As corporate officials travel around the nation and the world, they speak to audiences on the positive contributions the Hispanic community can make to the corporate world. The Hispanic 100 are not only training the workforce for the future, they are building the reputation and esteem of an important segment of the U.S. population.

Before speaking, consider questions such as these:

- Is this material appropriate for this group?
- How would I feel if I were asked that question?
- Am I giving my audience new information?
- Is my material too difficult or too easy for my audience?

Also, pay attention to audience feedback and then adapt. You might be doing something wrong. If you are *flippant* in your presentation, you might nonverbally convey the attitude that your audience isn't very important to you. Or, if you are speaking in a dull monotone, you might convey the attitude that you are bored with your audience.

As Olivier implied, the most effective communication occurs when there is reciprocal respect between the performer and the audience—or the sender and the receiver.

You can show audience members you care about them by paying attention to the ideas of the Greek scientist and philosopher Aristotle. Aristotle said that there are three major methods for appealing to an audience: logical, emotional, and ethical. (These methods will also be discussed in Chapter 14, "Speeches to Persuade.")

A good speaker draws his audience into his performance by respecting them.

Dave and Les Jacobs/Blend Images LLC

- You offer a **logical appeal** when you provide your audience both with sequence and analysis in your organization and factual evidence to prove your point.
- You offer an **emotional appeal** when you "strike a chord" in your audience and appeal to their sense of patriotism, family, or justice, for example.
- You offer an **ethical** (or **personal**) **appeal** when you show your audience that you have a natural honesty about you, a strong constitution regarding right and wrong, and a no-compromise approach to values.

Remember, **dialogue**, or conversation, that doesn't begin with each person respecting the other often ends in hurt feelings and fractured communication. Taking the time to lay the proper foundation should help alleviate this problem.

The Greek philosopher Aristotle (right) stated three methods for appealing to audiences—logical, emotional, and personal.

SECTION 2 REVIEW

Recalling the Facts

1. This section talked about the value structure foundation. What are the three essential elements that make up this foundation?
2. What type of communication involves your having a conversation with yourself? What type is a "one-on-one" with someone else?
3. What is the name given to "the art or study of public speaking"?
4. Which of Artistotle's appeals draws an audience because of sound logic and reasoning?

Thinking Critically

1. A university professor wants to teach his theater survey course by e-mail. However, university officials frown on his plans, saying that students need to be taught by a "live" instructor giving "live" instruction. What might be the harm of teaching by e-mail? What part of the communication process is lost when teaching is totally technological?
2. Audiences can often make things tough for a speaker. How can an audience often make or break a person's ability to be a responsible speaker? What can you do (as the speaker) to get off to a good start with your audience?

Taking Charge

1. Where in school or at work can we all be better listeners and audience members? Why is this important? How can an audience make a speaker feel more at ease? Make a chart with headings for school, home, and work at the top. For each heading, list how and where you can become a better listener or audience member.
2. Tell of a time when you were in an audience that didn't listen well. Describe the results.

SECTION 3

Building the Proper Motivation

To this point, we have examined what communication is and how a solid value structure is the speaker's foundation. Now we need to take a look at what should be the driving force behind a speaker's words—the motivation.

Motivation is something, such as a need or a desire, that causes a person to act. Two internal forces should be responsible for motivating words: (1) the desire to treat both people and situations fairly and to avoid stereotyping others and (2) the desire to set a good example for others.

Stereotypes

Stereotyping means labeling every person in a group based on a preconceived idea as to what that group represents. To believe that all football players lack intelligence or that all straight-A students are "nerds" is unfair. Even though many people lack confidence in those responsible for leading and representing them, don't fall into the "stereotype trap" and say, for example, that all politicians or lawyers are dishonest or are only out for themselves.

It is possible to form very broad stereotypes—not only about people but about situations, too. For example, the ideas that all people are dishonest and that nothing is right are stereotypes. You must realize that forming an awareness of your world means seeing more than "doom and gloom." Every individual must be evaluated on his or her own merit and every instance must be evaluated for its own impact.

However, because so many leaders and heroes have been disappointing and so many con artists have lied to the public, many people have become skeptical about trusting anyone. For example, look at this article from a prominent Midwestern newspaper:

A company that said its pills could "blast away" pounds off customers without any exer-

When you look at the photos on this page, do you automatically fall into a "stereotype trap"?

cise or dieting must pay more than $48 million in penalties, the Federal Trade Commission said recently. The FTC charged *Slim America* with deceptive advertising. The SuperFormula diet product was billed as the "New Triple Medical Breakthrough." It claimed that you could lose 49 pounds in just 29 days.

It is difficult to become motivated to communicate effectively when we hear how often words can work to tear down or deceive. Too often, words are empty and promises are broken. So where do you go? Where is your motivation? The answers can be found in you. Your motivation to use the spoken word correctly should come from a desire to provide solutions that will make the world a better place. You can do this by working to set a positive example for others.

Setting an Example

Every day you may communicate with your parents, your brothers and sisters, the bus driver, friends and neighbors, and with your teachers and the community.

You are making an impression.

You have the opportunity to prove that your words can promote what is good in both ideas and people. Set a positive example for others to follow.

Using your "voice" is not only what you say. Your voice can also be heard by what you "build" by your actions. For example, America mourned the tragic death of John F. Kennedy, Jr., in the summer of 1999 when he was killed in a plane crash, along with his wife and her sister. Kennedy believed in responsibility, and he communicated this by both his speech and his actions. He initiated Reaching Up, a program to assist health care workers who work with the mentally handicapped. In addition, he formed the Robin Hood Foundation to help those in need living in the inner city.

Teacher and astronaut Christa McAuliffe (back row, second from left) set a positive example for others.

The classic rock group Led Zeppelin once released an album, *In Through the Out Door*, that had six different covers. The albums were wrapped in brown paper so that buyers wouldn't know which cover they were getting until they bought the album, took it home, and unwrapped it. This was a clever marketing tactic for a rock band trying to gain attention.

However, an effective oral communicator does not operate this way. You must work to be a "known quantity," a speaker and a person worthy of respect, and a role model for others to follow.

The job isn't easy, but the teacher and astronaut Christa McAuliffe was such a person. She died in the tragic explosion of the space shuttle *Challenger*. A poem she took with her on that final flight should serve as inspiration to everyone. It said: "Move over sun and give me some sky. / I've got some wings and I'm ready to fly. / World, / You're going to hear from me!"

Isn't it time that the rest of the world hears from you? Remember: When people believe in you, they will believe what you have to say.

SECTION 3 REVIEW

Recalling the Facts

1. What is the word that means "the desire that causes a person to act"?
2. When you label people without first getting to know them, you are unfairly _____ing them.
3. In the play *A Raisin in the Sun*, "a small plant," or a nonverbal _____ signified a family's hopes and determination.

Thinking Critically

At the age of twelve, Ishmael Beah fled from attacking rebels in his homeland. By thirteen, he'd been picked up by the government army and forced to be a soldier. Although Beah was a gentle boy, he soon had to do terrible things. When he left the army, he was rehabilitated in a UNICEF center. It took a long time for him to reenter the world of civilians, where people viewed him with fear and mistrust. Beah is one of many child soldiers, but one of the first to tell about his journey from refugee to soldier to an inspirational writer and speaker. Now 26 years old, Beah shares his story of redemption and hope with school and community groups.

1. What do you think motivated Beah to want to talk to school kids and community groups? Is he a "good person speaking well"? Explain.
2. Think of a celebrity you admired who you no longer look up to because of something he or she said. What do you think motivated that person to say what he or she did? Then give an example of someone in the public eye you did not respect who you now admire because of something he or she said or did. Explain what happened.

Taking Charge

Stereotyping is a problem that affects all of society. Make a poster, and through both words and pictures, indicate how people can unfairly stereotype others. What is the answer to the problem of stereotyping? Include the answer on your poster.

Looking Back

Listed below are the major ideas discussed in this chapter.

- A good speaker is aware that she or he has an ethical obligation to use the spoken word responsibly.
- The four parts of the communication process are the sender, the receiver, the message, and feedback.
- A good speaker is aware of communication barriers and works to eliminate them.
- Effective communication can be built through writing or the spoken word.
- A key component in communication is nonverbal communication.
- Symbols can project a meaningful message.

- The foundation for effective oral communication must be firmly laid before any content or delivery work is done.
- The foundation for effective oral communication consists of working to be a good person, using communication constructively, and valuing the audience.
- Aristotle said that a speaker could use logical, emotional, and ethical appeals.
- Intrapersonal communication involves the talking that you do with yourself.
- Interpersonal communication is one-to-one or one-to-many communication.
- You should work to avoid stereotypes and to set a good example for others.

Speech Vocabulary

For each speech vocabulary word, state the definition as given in the text.

ethics	intrapersonal communication
communication	interpersonal communication
sender	oratory
message	rhetoric
receiver	orator
feedback	logical appeal
communication barrier	emotional appeal
written communication	ethical (personal) appeal
oral (or verbal) communication	dialogue
nonverbal communication	motivation
symbol	stereotyping

Academic Vocabulary

Use context clues to determine the meaning of each academic vocabulary word. Then use a print or online dictionary to check the accuracy of your definition.

responsible	flippant
epitomize	reciprocal
mesmerized	

To Remember

Answer the following based on your reading of the chapter.

1. The sender can send the message to the receiver. However, without _____ the sender doesn't know if the message was truly understood.
2. Some advice for elimininating communication barriers was given to the "sender." What are the three action words for eliminating communication barriers?
3. What are the three verbs suggested to the "receiver"?
4. Another word for body language is _____ communication.
5. What are the three essential elements of a value structure foundation?
6. The ability to conduct an inner dialogue with yourself and to assess your thoughts, feelings, and reactions is called _____.
7. What is one-to-one communication called?
8. Aristotle said that an audience is influenced by someone with _____ appeal.

To Do

1. Interview a teacher, a professional club member, or someone in business and find out why communication is important to this person. What qualities does he or she try to promote when speaking?
2. Find an article in the newspaper that exhibits "a good person speaking (or doing) well." Now find an article that shows the opposite. Be ready to share your thoughts with the class.

To Talk About

1. It has been said that "nice guys finish last." What evidence can you find to prove or disprove this statement? What conclusions can you draw? Why do we need ethical and responsible people in society?
2. Only about 34 percent of Americans questioned in a Vanderbilt University survey said that the press has "too much freedom." However, 60 percent said that they did not think that the media in the United States tries to report without bias. More than 60 percent said that the media has a problem with "making up stories." Regardless, all First Amendment rights were deemed to be very important by those questioned. Nearly all Americans in the survey (97 percent) said that the right to practice one's own religion was essential, as was the right to speak freely (98 percent) and the right to protest or petition the government (94 percent). However, those questioned found it difficult to name the five freedoms protected by the First Amendment. Speech was the only freedom named by a majority of those surveyed (64 percent), followed by religion (19 percent), press and assembly (each 16 percent), and petition (3 percent).
   - Why is it not responsible to value the First Amendment but not know exactly what it says?
   - Why do you believe so many Americans think that the press is biased? Why do Americans believe that the media regularly reports stories that are not true?
   - Regardless, why is freedom of the press essential in a democracy?

3. Language is often used to manipulate. In advertisements language is used to influence people to buy particular items. Sometimes advertisements promise things they can't deliver. Sometimes the ads aren't ethical. Bring some newspaper or magazine ads to class. Work in a group to analyze the ads. Discuss the following questions.
   • What type of language is used to convince the reader that he or she needs the product being advertised?
   • Do you think the ad is ethical? Why or why not?
   • Does it make claims that the product can't fulfill?
   • Would you buy the product advertised based on the advertisement? Why or why not?

To Write About

1. Write a brief biography of one or more of the people discussed in this chapter. What contribution to speaking or society did each make? Was the contribution for good or ill?
2. A popular movie of the late 1980s, directed by Spike Lee, was titled *Do the Right Thing*. Why is doing the right thing sometimes so difficult? Give at least two reasons, and provide a documented or personal example for each.
3. Certain individuals in your school are leaders. What makes people follow others? A poll taken stated that the trait students valued most in a friend was honesty. Why do you believe this to be true?

Related Speech Topics

Find research to prove that people are taking positive stands regarding the following issues:

The environment
Education (local and national)
The homeless
Child abuse
Equal rights
Farmers/agriculture
School programs (academic, athletic, and social)

Sexual harassment in the workplace
Consumer protection
Entertainment/the media
Politics
The family
Sports and academics

BUILDING CONFIDENCE

Public speaking is no more difficult than breathing, using chopsticks, or tying a bow tie.

—Charles Osgood, news commentator and author

Learning Objectives

After completing this chapter, you will be able to do the following.

- Discuss what confidence means and how it is a vital element in effective speaking.
- Recognize the realities of stage fright and how you can appropriately deal with the problem.
- Realize the value of perception as it applies to confidence in your speaking.
- Implement the planks of confidence in your speaking.

Chapter Outline

Following are the main sections in this chapter.

1. Understanding Stage Fright
2. Establishing an Accurate Perception
3. Examining the Planks of Confidence

Speech Vocabulary

In this chapter, you will learn the meanings of the speech terms listed below.

confidence	notes
stage fright	friendliness
fear	impression
phobia	dedication
performance anxiety	empathy
perception	common ground
self-esteem	newness
content	conviction
organization	enthusiasm

Academic Vocabulary

Expanding your academic vocabulary will help you become a more effective communicator. Listed below are some words appearing in this chapter that you should make part of your vocabulary.

irrational	allegory
eulogy	assertion
synonymous	prioritizing
innovation	mannequin

It doesn't matter what you do in life—your chances of succeeding are improved when you are confident in yourself and in your abilities. This is particularly important when it comes to oral communication. It's tough to be confident as a speaker when you believe that you have little to offer.

Having confidence in speaking is closely related to having confidence about anything that you do in life. It has been said that you're confident when you feel that you are good at something. A construction contractor doesn't worry about a difficult job because he knows that he has the correct equipment and the intellectual know-how to do the job well. A computer programmer faced with a heavy workload and a detailed technical assignment doesn't quit because she knows that her training will prepare her to face any task.

Military strategists often say that "forewarned is forearmed." In other words, if you know what's coming, then you can adequately prepare for the challenge. For our purposes, the challenge is effective speaking. With this message in mind, the purpose of this chapter is to warn you of some apparent obstacles that speakers face, and then to arm you with the necessary tools that it takes for a "confidence victory." In Chapter 2 we will examine what the word *confidence* means, how fear is a real-world enemy, how perception plays a key role in speaking success, and why the "planks of confidence" are a necessary first line of defense against stage fright.

Introduction

Confidence is not a trait that you're born with. It is, however, a trait that anyone can develop. The confidence that great athletes like quarterback Peyton Manning or tennis players Serena and Venus Williams depend on to help them perform their best is the same attribute that will help you to succeed. So, if you're not born with confidence, then how do you get it? You begin by understanding exactly what it means to have confidence.

What does confidence mean? Simply put, **confidence** is the feeling you have when you believe that you are capable of handling a situation successfully. This attitude is a result of ongoing preparation and practice. The more times that you try something, the more likely you are to improve and to gauge what it takes to be successful in a given situation.

You may be asking, "How does this apply to oral communication? To the job world? To my social life?" Let's return to the example started in Chapter 1 stating that the construction of a house begins with the pouring of a solid foundation and that a solid value structure is the foundation that anchors the spoken word.

Carpenters next build the shell of the house by bolting the outside framework to the foundation. This framework is essential. It provides stability. Similarly, confidence is the internal framework of effective oral communication. Anchored to a solid value system, it gives stability to the speaker and makes her or his message believable. Thus, confidence is the attitude of assurance that causes an audience to take a speaker seriously.

But not everyone can speak with confidence, even if they understand its importance. Why? Stage fright is one reason.

Understanding Stage Fright

Stage fright, also referred to as *communication apprehension*, means that a person is afraid to speak, usually in public situations. Surveys indicate that 80 to 90 percent of Americans admit feeling extremely uncomfortable about any form of public speaking. Before we examine the "fear of speaking," however, let's take a look at the nature of fear itself.

What Is Fear?

According to Dr. William Guys, professor of speech communication at Western Michigan University, **fear** is a "biological process by which animals, including humans, secure the necessary energy to do a job that really matters—one that might potentially result in physical and/or psychological injury." Therefore, keep in mind that fear is normal! It's designed to protect us from harm. Fear activates our emergency energy system so that we can cope with danger.

We have two sources of energy in our bodies. The "regular" energy system is based on the food we eat, the air we breathe, and the sleep we get. All of this contributes to our ability to function on a basic level. However, when we're confronted with danger, our "emergency" energy system kicks in. This source of energy is mainly in the form of adrenaline. Think about it. When you're alone and you hear a mysterious noise in the house, your heart may immediately begin to beat faster. This is because your body is preparing to deal with the potential danger.

Understanding the nature of fear can help you in any situation. For some, the fear may be in the form of test anxiety; for others, it might be standing on a free-throw line with all eyes on them; and for many of us, it's the possibility of messing up a big job interview. Yet, in every situation, we have a choice of dealing with it—or running from it. Biologists call this the "fight or flight syndrome." Keep in mind that to "fight" does not mean literally to punch out

Have you ever felt fear while you were participating in a sporting event?

an opponent, but rather to confront a problem situation head-on. Granted, there are times when "flight" is the smart thing to do. When the train is coming and you're standing on the tracks, move! However, too many times, we think that an upcoming speech is as dangerous as an oncoming train. When our concern reaches this level, it becomes what is known as a **phobia**—or a persistent, *irrational* fear. When it comes to speaking, we need to remember that it is beneficial to confront our fears—and *fight* to make our ideas known.

Who Gets Frightened in Front of an Audience? Studies show that many people fear the thought of giving a speech more than they do the thought of dying. Comedian Jerry Seinfeld put this in perspective when he stated, "What this means is that if we are at a funeral, we would rather be the person in the casket—rather than be the one who is supposed to deliver the *eulogy*!" Yes, the fear of speaking is universal and can affect anyone, regardless of background or professional training. Barbara Tannenbaum is a senior lecturer in the Theater, Speech, and Dance Department at Brown University, who also teaches the "art of public speaking" and is a popular communications consultant. She notes that some of her most timid, shy, and apprehensive clients include doctors, bankers, judges, business executives, and politicians. She adds that the one trait they all have in common is that they're "frozen in terror" when it comes to speaking in front of others. So, if you're "scared stiff" about speaking, you're in good company. It doesn't matter whether you are:

- interviewing for a job,
- meeting people for the first time,
- answering a question in class,
- speaking at a community function,
- explaining a task to coworkers.

If a receiver of your message is present, you may suffer varying degrees of stage fright.

What Are the Symptoms? A popular radio and television commercial for a motel chain ended with a very down-home-style voice offering the memorable line, "We'll leave the light on for ya."

Did you know that the speaker was so nervous while taping the original commercial that he forgot some of the words and was left with some time to fill? The result was that he ad-libbed this now-famous ending. However, forgetting the words isn't the only symptom that accompanies a fear of speaking.

Have you ever experienced an upset stomach, a flushed face, dizziness, a fast heartbeat, shortness of breath, excessive perspiration, or wobbly legs either before or during a speech? If so, you're quite normal. These are common physical signs of communication apprehension, and they usually occur right before we speak and during the first 30 seconds or so after we have actually opened our mouths.

But why do we get these symptoms? The first reason is that our bodies are being flooded with energy because they're preparing for what they perceive to be an emergency situation. Another reason, though, is that most of us don't like to be evaluated or judged. We dislike the thought of opening up to an audience or of having others examine us or our thoughts too closely. The truth of the matter is that often we don't think our ideas are worth listening to, we doubt we can say our ideas well, or we fear the audience won't like us while we are speaking. Because we simply don't feel prepared to face all of these potential obstacles, we're certain that the worst will happen!

Some people experience stage fright when they have to give a presentation in front of their classmates.

Even Those on Stage Get Stage Fright

Winston Churchill

In an article titled "Stage Fright? Don't Collapse—Confront It," columnist Frank James gives a humorous account of his first major communication disaster. He notes that while a seventh grader in the Bronx, he tried to impress Janet Bing, a girl he had a crush on. When he finally mustered up the courage to talk to her face to face, his courage suddenly left him. So, he thought he would go to his second plan of action and impress her by athletically running down the stairs two at a time. He adds, "I tripped and wound up taking at least a dozen steps at once, head first. My body escaped unhurt, but my ego didn't."

His stage fright put him in very good company. When British Prime Minister Winston Churchill was a young politician, he became so frightened while delivering a memorized speech to Parliament that he totally blanked. From that point on, Churchill always had a copy of his speech with him and refused to speak publicly without it.

Entertainers, public officials, and media personalities can also experience **performance anxiety,** or an extreme fear of audiences. This is a type of stage fright. Singer Carly Simon had millions of people listen to her records and tapes during the 1970s and 1980s, but she virtually disappeared from the music scene because of her fear of performing in front of live audiences. In California, a 44-year-old San Diego municipal judge was placed on permanent disability because he couldn't face speaking in front of his courtroom. Finally, one of the most popular TV weathermen in the country, Willard Scott, developed stage fright and hyperventilated in front of millions.

Questions

1. Sometimes in social situations we try too hard to be impressive. In the first paragraph, what were two ways that seventh grader Frank James tried too hard? What were the negative consequences?

2. Communication apprehension can really be a problem when it involves our jobs. Winston Churchill found a way to solve his stage fright. He used detailed, accurate notes when he spoke. But what about the singer, the judge, and the weatherman? How did stage fright affect their careers? Analyze why it's ironic that they would suffer this condition.

Well, maybe it's time that we step back and see things a little differently. The Greek philosopher Socrates said that before we can move the world, we first have to move ourselves. But where do we get the confidence to start moving? How can we make our "internal frameworks" solid enough to withstand the strong winds and powerful rains of stage fright? Let's start by making sure that we have an accurate perception of our audience, of our speech, and of ourselves.

SECTION 1 REVIEW

Recalling the Facts

1. Define the term *stage fright*.
2. As discussed in this section, what word means "the feeling you have when you believe that you're capable of handling a situation successfully"?
3. As has been explained, what is the definition of the word *fear*?
4. Many people experience physical symptoms when they know that they are going to speak. What are the two reasons given that explain the reasons *why* these symptoms occur?

Thinking Critically

1. Many people find that they lose much of their speaking fear as the speech progresses. Why do you think that this might happen? Write at least two reasons and offer your thinking for each.
2. Sometimes an individual is called a "people person." This means that he or she is relaxed and friendly around others. How could this type of person be a benefit at the workplace or at a social activity? What prevents some of us from becoming a "people person"? Discuss your responses with a partner or in a small group.

Taking Charge

1. Take a class inventory (of at least ten other students) and find out what they consider the most outstanding traits of a confident person (intelligence, an outgoing personality, and so on). Why is being confident important in the business world? Can confidence ever be taken too far? Analyze how confidence can be a positive factor when used the right way, but a negative factor when used the wrong way. Be ready to discuss your answers with the class.
2. Regardless of your job, you will have to be confident in your abilities and in your oral communication skills. Talk to someone who is employed and ask him or her why exhibiting confidence is important in what he or she does—and how confidence is an important factor in the impact that he or she might have on others.

Establishing an Accurate Perception

As we will use the term here, **perception** refers to how you see things. To perceive means to gain an awareness and understanding of a person, an idea, or a situation. Obviously, an accurate perception is a tool that helps us learn more about ourselves, our objectives, and other people. In contrast, an inaccurate perception can cause us to blow things out of proportion, make a problem greater than it really is, and become our own worst enemies.

In constructing a house, carpenters often use a main support beam. This beam runs from one side of a room to another and works to make the internal structure stable. Establishing an accurate, realistic perception is the "main support beam" in building speaking confidence. It is this internal mind-set that allows you to say with a confident attitude, "I see things as they are, not as my fears might lead me to see them."

Nervousness can cause us to blow things out of proportion.

INSTANT IMPACT

The "Deer" Theory of Stage Fright

Charles Osgood, who offered the quotation at the beginning of this chapter, has an interesting theory on stage fright that compares it to a deer frozen in the beam of your car's headlights. "Here's my theory. The deer thinks the lights are spotlights, and what has it paralyzed is stage fright. It imagines the worst: It has to give a speech."

To Be Confident, Be Prepared

Ross and Patty Pangere are an American success story. The owners of RossCo, a multimillion-dollar construction-contracting business in the Midwest, this husband and wife team has experienced communication apprehension. For example, even though Ross had given hundreds of presentations to current and potential clients, he never felt totally at ease.

Being a perfectionist, Ross Pangere took charge of his oral communication: he sought a confidence boost. He attended speech workshops, brought in communication consultants, and listened to audiotapes on effective speaking. He learned the value of "being yourself," of having a clear message, and of developing a simple yet substance-oriented organizational plan. But the greatest lesson that he learned, he summed up in one word: *practice!* Ross became "confident" when he knew that he was so absolutely in charge of his material that he could speak effectively regardless of the situation. He concluded, "In today's world, those who can't confidently communicate and speak with poise simply can't compete."

Patty Pangere also built her confidence in business dealings when she took the time to sharpen her technological skills. In charge of a complicated computer system, she stated that after she became "technologically prepared," her apprehension decreased. Like Ross, because she thoroughly understood her subject matter, she could talk confidently with anyone.

Ross and Patty Pangere would like for students to learn from their experiences. Whether it's successful speaking or a successful life, you'll feel more "in charge" if you'll take the time to "do your homework." And if they can do it, then you can, too. Together, Ross and Patty understand that confidence and competence are directly linked, and because of this, they accomplished an oral communication breakthrough.

Questions

1. Do you think this lesson about confidence and being prepared applies only to business owners, or could it also apply to any worker?

2. Ross Pangere, who has been legally blind for over 20 years, and his wife have built a thriving business. What challenges in oral communication has he had to overcome that the rest of us might not ever have to face?

Your Perception of the Audience

People too often think that giving a speech is a life-or-death situation. They visualize passing out or feeling sick. They might think, "I know the audience sees my legs shaking" or "Everyone in the room is staring at the bead of sweat that's running down my forehead."

However, research proves that many speaking fears are simply unwarranted. Michael T. Motley, writing for *Psychology Today*, stated:

> Studies on how well an audience perceives anxiety should comfort nervous speakers. Researchers have found that most report noticing little or no anxiety in a speaker. Even when individuals are trained to detect anxiety cues and are instructed to look for them, there is little correlation between their evaluations and how anxious speakers actually felt.

This encouraging quote shows that audiences are often unaware of a speaker's nervousness. Remember, your audience will ignore or forgive any type of mistake or awkwardness if audience members feel that you are genuinely interested in them and trying to share with them.

Your Perception of the Speech

Part of the problem with giving a speech is the perception of what exactly the word *speech* should mean.

You should see speaking as an opportunity to share something you consider valuable—your message—with your audience. Thus, the word *speech* should not be viewed as being *synonymous* with performance. Instead, a speech should be viewed as a chance that you've been given to say something meaningful to others.

Speaking is not putting on a show. Too many times people seem to think of a speaking assignment as a Hollywood screen test. When this happens, they make the assignment more difficult than it needs to be. They believe that their words and actions have to be extraordinary. Don't fall into this trap!

Studies have shown that audiences often cannot perceive nervousness in speakers.

If you remember that a speech should be seen as a tremendous opportunity to share, an opportunity to enjoy a meaningful moment, an opportunity to communicate verbally with people you care about (your audience), then you can reduce feelings of stage fright.

The speech is an extension of you. It is an extension of your personality and of your feelings, likes, and dislikes. Have confidence, and see your speech as a potential beacon to guide others, not as a performance that your audience will judge by holding up score cards as judges do in the Olympics.

Steve Bair proves this point nicely. He was competing in Tulsa, Oklahoma, in the final round of the Original Oratory category of the National Forensic League championship. Only 6 contestants remained out of the over 180 contestants that had started in his category. Thousands of people in the audience had come to see the most talented high school speakers in the United States. Three microphones were on the stage, and there were television cameras and spotlights visible.

Suddenly, it was Steve Bair's turn to speak. Even though he had spoken hundreds of times before, his legs began to shake. He became warm, and his mouth felt like cotton.

He was suffering stage fright.

The Audience Isn't a Monster

Antonio Louw is founder and chairman of Louw's Management Corp. in New Jersey. His company helps both executives and key employees to improve their communication and business skills.

He has worked with companies around the world and notes that Americans are the most petrified about speaking. One of the major reasons for our fears, he believes, is that in our minds, we turn our audiences into monsters that are ready to pounce on our imperfections. "There's this fear of making a mistake or making a fool of yourself," he says. "I teach people to remember that the purpose of a public speech is to entertain, inform, or persuade. It's certainly not to avoid making a mistake!"

He gives an example of a young Chicago woman, an advertising executive, who was terrified of public speaking and audiences. She was intelligent and insightful, but she suffered stage fright. Louw took her out to the streets of Chicago during rush hour. He directed her to go up to strangers on the street and ask them the time. He said she was scared, but after asking people over and over, She realized that she had overcome her fear. He concludes by saying that audiences are simply people, and that most people are supportive and want speakers to succeed.

Steve started talking to himself (remember the discussion of intrapersonal communication in Chapter 1). He said, "I'm just a person who cares about people, and I also care about this speech. I care what it has to say. I'm happy that I now have the chance to say it in front of so many people!"

Steve Bair went on to win the national championship.

This true account might show you that your speech is not some alien creature to be feared or an enemy that you should run from. Your perception of the speech should include an awareness of how powerful words can be and a vision of how your words can make that power a reality.

Your Perception of Yourself

It is sometimes difficult for people to accept who they are. The media have created so many "beautiful people" that, in comparison, the rest of us may feel we stand little chance. The singer Madonna urged people to "strike a pose," and tennis star Andre Agassi once stated that "image is everything."

A speaker can build confidence by recognizing personal worth and not fearing failure.

Consequently, it is easy for us to perceive ourselves as not being pretty enough, handsome enough, intelligent enough, or witty enough. The book *One Hundred Percent American* by Daniel E. Weiss states that 99 percent of all women in the nation would change at least one thing about their looks. If you lack confidence in yourself, doesn't it stand to reason that you will also lack confidence in your spoken words?

Of course, in speaking, you should strive for excellence; but you should not think you always have to be perfect. Don't equate making a mistake with being a total failure. If you do, you might not even allow your oral communication the opportunity to succeed. How do you change this sort of negative perception of yourself?

First of all, recognize your own individual worth and like who you are. Consider the following story:

> Once upon a time, an unhappy horse wished for longer, thinner legs, a neck like a swan, and a saddle that would grow on his back as part of his body. He thought all of these things would bring him great happiness, because they would make him more beautiful. Well, it so happened that the horse's wishes were granted and he was given all the things he wished for. But when the horse went to a reflecting pond to admire his improved image, he was horrified. The things that had seemed so desirable individually had become totally undesirable collectively—he had been changed into a camel!
>
> Moral of the story: It is better to improve what you have than to wish for the things you don't have.

This moral also applies to perception and confidence in speaking. First, if you see yourself as an individual and unique rather than being different or inadequate, then you can start to build a confidence that stresses your uniqueness and emphasizes your own personal potential.

Second, don't fear being human. Don't be afraid to acknowledge the fact that you don't do everything perfectly. Politicians, company executives, movie stars—everyone makes mistakes. While it is true that you can make errors and sometimes fail, set out to learn from those failures.

Did you know that a professor at the University of Houston developed a course that became known as "Failure 101"? The object of the course was to convince students that failure should be seen as an opportunity for *innovation* instead of immediate defeat. His students loved the class. It showed them that not always being right the first time can, ironically, lead to discovery. For example, the inventor Thomas Edison faced many failures before he discovered the electric light.

The psychologist John Rosemond adds that confidence, or **self-esteem**, is often the result of this discovery process. He says that no one is born with confidence. On the contrary, confidence is built. When you can face your fears, your frustrations, and even your failures—and still come out standing on your own two feet—then confidence is being nurtured. Remember, you gain confidence every time that you face adversity and come out on top.

How does this apply to communication?

Very simply, it means that you shouldn't be afraid to fail. Don't worry that you are going to mess up in your speech. Suppose you make a mistake and realize:

- that your notes are shaking uncontrollably in your hands,
- that your eye contact is only with the back wall,
- that your knees are shaking,
- that you're opening your mouth but no words are coming out,
- that you are sweating.

Don't panic! Remember that this isn't brain surgery. It's sharing a truth and delivering a message. So smile . . . remember that you're human . . . take a deep breath . . . and think about how you're going to correct these problems when you speak the next time. And there will be a next time.

Sometimes the greatest therapy for stage fright is to laugh at your own mistakes in your speech. Your audience will probably laugh with you.

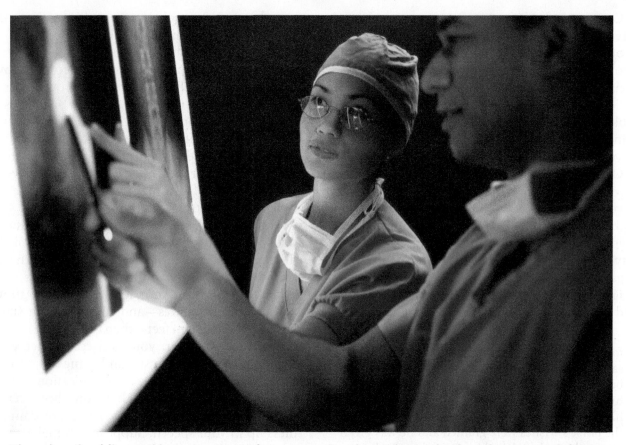

The rules of public speaking may not apply to every situation. Why might the rules not work for a doctor or a surgeon?

What Have You Learned about Perception?

One of the main points that you have learned about perception is that it is a key element in building confidence in speaking. Why? Because an accurate perception of things can help you to overcome stage fright. It will allow you to deal with what is real as opposed to what you might imagine to be real.

To illustrate, let's examine a story from the philosophical past. In *The Republic*, written in the fifth century B.C., Plato offers the famous *allegory* of the cave. This allegory describes people as prisoners in a cave, facing away from the opening of the cave and thus away from the light. Unable to see themselves or anyone else because they are shackled, they see only the shadows on the wall in front of them. Since they are never allowed to turn around and see the light, their perception is that the shadows are what is real.

What's the connection of this allegory to speaking? The answer is this: If you believe that:

- your audience is aware of everything that you do wrong in your speech,
- your speech is a performance rather than a sharing, or that

- you have little to offer as either a person or a speaker . . .

then you are being victimized by the "shadows" of stage fright and fear. Isn't it time that you "see the light"? The truth is that

- your audience doesn't see everything that you do wrong,
- your speech is a worthwhile sharing of good ideas and information, and that
- you have a lot to offer.

Let your perception work for you. Firmly implant the "main support beam"—an accurate perception—that is essential in the overall construction of building confidence.

Next, let's examine some of the specific planks that make up the confidence framework.

Don't let the "shadows of stage fright" victimize you!

SECTION 2 REVIEW

Recalling the Facts

1. How you see things is known as _____.
2. A speech should not be viewed as a performance. Instead, how would you define a speech?
3. Psychologist John Rosemond states that *confidence* is often the result of a discovery process. Another term for confidence, he notes, is self-_____.

Thinking Critically

1. This section mentions that the media have created the "beautiful people"—or those people who seem to look perfect and lead perfect lives. However, this perception is not always true. Many "superstars," representing different professions, have had their own share of problems. List some of those people. After you have made your list, analyze why we perceive their lives to be great. Finally, after describing the positive aspects of these people's lives, discuss the problems that they have had to face.
2. Socially, why is it sometimes difficult for us just to "be ourselves"?

Taking Charge

It's important for us to make the "right" impression on other people. With this in mind, interview a teacher, a coach, or an employer—and ask the following question: "Based on your perception, what qualities does a good student, a good performer, or a good employee possess?" Keep a list of the responses and be prepared to share this list with the class.

Examining the Planks of Confidence

Once again, think of a house. When you see the shell of a house being put up, you can't help but notice the individual pieces of wood, usually two-by-fours of varying lengths, that make up the walls and the roof. These individual pieces of wood might be referred to as planks.

Let's now take the word *confidence* and use each letter in the word as a figurative "plank." In the process, you will "nail down" some of the major ingredients of confidence. These are ten components that can help you build self-confidence.

Content	**D**edication
Organization	**E**mpathy
Notes	**N**ewness
Friendliness	**C**onviction
Impression	**E**nthusiasm

As you read about each plank, keep in mind that your confidence level will grow with each one you develop.

Content *Have something worthwhile to say.* You can't be confident as a speaker if you are not confident in your content. It is a good feeling to know that you have researched your topic.

High school students are often unfairly portrayed as having little academic promise or real-world awareness. Show that intellectually you have credibility and deserve attention. Audiences respect a person who shares a message that contains facts and pertinent evidence. Build a relevant message with solid content by going to the library or browsing the Internet, reading newspapers or current magazines, interviewing someone who is knowledgeable about your topic, or watching news or educational programs.

Remember, don't base your speaking on *assertions* or emotional appeals only. Spend time building an evidence file that shows appropriate documentation for the research you did.

Interviewing an expert on your speech's topic can be an excellent method to gather valuable information.

Lisa F. Young/Alamy

Referring to key words or phrases on notecards can help a speaker stay on track.

INSTANT IMPACT

Letterman Gets Serious

Late-night talk show host David Letterman gave the following statements about his experience taking a public speaking class in high school: "For the first time, I felt *confident*. It came easily to me— at least it was easier than algebra. So it was clear to me that this course was something to take *seriously*."

Organization *Have some type of an outline that is easy for both you and your audience to follow.* Operate from a format that is logical. Every speech needs **organization** and must have a main idea or main point being addressed, clear areas of analysis, and supporting evidence that fits. An introduction that leads to the thesis statement and a conclusion that summarizes the areas of analysis and provides some ending emotional appeal are also important.

Mark McCormack, a businessman and author, states that he gains confidence in his business dealings by dividing part of his day into five one-hour blocks. Each block has a specific purpose. For instance, one of his one-hour blocks involves *prioritizing* his phone calls and determining exactly how much time, on the average, he can spend on each. He says that this approach gives sequence to his business day and helps the day make sense.

This message can also apply to confidence in speaking. Don't be scatterbrained—don't always rely on "the spontaneity of the moment." Offer clarity and sequence to your audience. Your audience members will appreciate your guiding them, and you will feel confident that they are getting your point.

Notes *Jot down your ideas in a brief, directed (preferably outlined) form.* A notecard can be a comforting "security net" in case you are nervous about losing your place in the speech. However, be sure to avoid the two greatest problems regarding notes: (1) having too many words on a single notecard and (2) having too many notecards.

Notes are not supposed to be a substitute for preparation. They are not for you to read to your audience. Instead, notes should provide you with a memory springboard. Seeing a key word or phrase should remind you of where you are and where you should be going in your speech. Used correctly, notes can be the training wheels of oral communication, keeping you confidently on course and, most importantly, on topic.

Friendliness *Be congenial.* You can gain confidence if you express **friendliness** and see that your audience is giving you positive feedback. This positive feedback is often the result of your conveying a warm, friendly attitude. Roger Ailes, a noted author and communication consultant, says that being likable is the "magic bullet" in speaking. He writes in *Management Digest* that, "With [friendliness], your audience will forgive just about everything else you do wrong. Without it, you can hit every bull's-eye in the room and no one will be impressed."

So don't be afraid to smile and to talk to individuals in the room. Don't view your audience as a collective mass of faceless people.

Like a musician, a speaker needs to practice to feel confident while giving a speech.

Let both your words and your nonverbal communication work for you. Remember, an audience that likes you is more likely to be receptive to your message.

Impression *Getting off to a good start is essential in building confidence.* How your audience perceives you right from the beginning is very important. Do you, for instance, convey a positive attitude on your way to the front of the room? This text has already referred to a study that showed that 55 percent of what others think of you is determined before you ever open your mouth. If this is true, you should telegraph to your audience, "I'm really glad to be here today," before you begin to speak. This, in turn, should raise your confidence level.

Impression also refers to the way you are dressed and groomed. Use common sense and appropriate judgment in choosing your attire. If you expect to be taken seriously as a speaker, then never allow your clothing, hair, makeup, or jewelry to get in the way of your message. These things should not draw attention away from your main purpose: effective communication. While it is true that "clothes don't make the person," it is certainly also true that they can help. Showing the audience members that you took the time to look good for them means that you respect them. Build confidence by setting a good example and offering a solid first impression.

Dedication *Practice. Practice. Practice.* Too many times a student adequately researches a speech and prepares a catchy introduction and a dynamic conclusion, only to forget a basic part of speech presentation—orally practicing the actual delivery of the speech. Confidence does not come about as a result of going over the material mentally in the corner of your room while listening to music through your headphones; it requires **dedication.** You must get used to the sound of your own voice and speak as often as you can. You should often try to simulate the real thing.

Professionals in both sports and entertainment speak of the countless number of hours that they spend on basics: a simple exercise on the piano, covering first base on a bunt, a basic tennis stroke, or a routine dance step. These professionals know the value of practice.

Speaking is no different. Take the time to actually say the words you've worked so hard to create on paper. Gain command of your information. Practice looking at people while speaking. Practice your gestures. Practice moving to see how your body feels while taking a step. Be dedicated so that when the time comes to speak before an audience, you will feel more confident because you will already have been there!

Empathy *Know how it feels to feel the same way others feel.* The term **empathy** means a sincere understanding of the feelings, thoughts, and motives of others. You shouldn't assume that you are the only person with problems and challenges to face. Other people face these same difficulties.

In the novel *To Kill a Mockingbird* by Harper Lee, the character Atticus Finch tells his daughter, Scout, that you never truly understand a man until you "climb into his skin and walk around in it."

As speakers, learn from this advice. You can feel much more at ease if you will take a few minutes to get to know how your audience members are feeling. What are they thinking? Could they be facing problems at home? With boyfriends or girlfriends? Once you empathize, not only will you understand your audience better, you will understand feedback better. For instance, keep in mind that when audience members are looking out the window, slouch-ing in their seats, or not paying attention, it might simply mean that they are having a bad day.

If you have ever had a bad day, then you will understand and not take things personally. Keep speaking and working for **common ground.** When you establish common ground with your audience, you are saying with both verbal and nonverbal communication, "We're *all* in this together." You might become a more confident speaker as a result.

Newness *Apply some originality.* We often feel confident if we have something new and original to say. **Newness** could mean taking a different approach to discussing your topic in a unique way. A clever anecdote might make an original way to start your speech. A meaningful quotation that you've discovered could add an original punch to your conclusion. Charts, graphs, or artwork, if appropriate and well done, can offer an innovative means of uniquely reinforcing your point.

One of the best ways to put some originality in your speech is to tell a personal story. In his article "We Must Rediscover Our Stories," Richard Louv says that Americans have lost sight of the impact their personal stories can have. Somehow people assume that if a story isn't at the video store or on television, it must be worthless. However, Louv notes that personal stories and family stories are "real gold."

So tell your story! No one has one quite like yours. Your originality can show your audience that you are a creative, intelligent speaker. It can also help to establish the necessary common ground spoken of earlier and, in the process, add to your confidence in speaking.

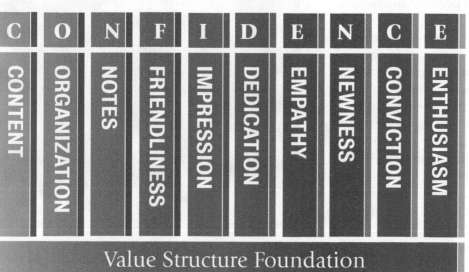

C O N F I D E N C E

CONTENT · ORGANIZATION · NOTES · FRIENDLINESS · IMPRESSION · DEDICATION · EMPATHY · NEWNESS · CONVICTION · ENTHUSIASM

Value Structure Foundation

Guides need to rediscover their stories every time they tell them to keep them fresh for each group.

Conviction *Believe in what you say.* Mahatma Gandhi, the Hindu spiritual leader, once said, "One needs to be slow to form convictions, but once formed they must be defended against the heaviest of odds." Even though most of our lives are not as dramatic as this quotation, the message is clear: Know what your principles are, and have the courage to stand up and voice those principles. Confidence can be greatly magnified when you have a strong belief in what your spoken words are conveying.

Some speech topics can be boring unless you add your own special dimension of personal **conviction.** For example, giving a speech on "My Summer Vacation" can come across as lifeless and monotonous. But what if on your summer vacation you saw a work by Michelangelo, the sixteenth-century painter and sculptor, that made you realize something about people or art that you passionately wish to share?

Similarly, a speech about "My Job" or "My Friends" could be tedious. But what if your job promotes hard work, and you believe that hard work and a strong work ethic are important for success? And what if your friends are the elderly couple down the street, and you have seen firsthand the value of kindness, touch, a smile, and compassion?

Suddenly, each of these "ordinary" topics takes on a new, more vital meaning that you can relate directly to your audience. Your conviction will tell your audience that you take your topic seriously.

Your audience will, in turn, take you and your speech more seriously.

Conviction can also allow you to take your mind off your fears, gestures, and facial expressions and let you focus on your speech content.

The main point about conviction is this: If you are confident about the importance of your message, then your audience is more likely to be persuaded.

Enthusiasm *Get fired up!* The character Spock of *Star Trek* fame is well known for relying on logic and reason and for exhibiting little emotional involvement. This might work in science fiction, but it probably won't work with your audience. No one wants to listen to an unemotional *mannequin*, standing lifelessly at the front of the room. You need energy and **enthusiasm.** You need to inspire your audience by showing them that you are fired up in two ways: intellectually, so

Mahatma Gandhi personified conviction.

that your mind is sharp and alert, and physically, so that your body is actively involved.

The most ordinary speech can become entertaining if you share your enthusiasm with your audience. Enthusiasm is directed energy. So if you feel energized, others in the room will feel that same electricity.

In addition, enthusiasm is often a convenient outlet for much of the nervous energy that public speaking might bring. However, nervous energy must be controlled. When you are about to make a speech, take a few deep breaths and relax. Have your body release some of the tension that might develop right before you speak.

Many great thinkers have given us advice on the value of enthusiasm. Ralph Waldo Emerson, the American essayist and poet of the mid-nineteenth century, said that nothing great was ever achieved without enthusiasm. The motivational speaker and businessman William McFee declared that the world belongs to the enthusiast who can "keep his cool." As a speaker, if you can keep your cool, yet show your audience members that you are excited about sharing your message, then you are sure to become a more confident communicator.

Lincoln was a powerful speaker because he prepared for each speech.

So where does this bring us?

Abraham Lincoln was once asked how he would cut down a tree if he were given eight hours to complete the job. He responded by saying that he would sharpen the blade on his axe for seven hours—so that he could easily cut down the tree in one hour. In other words, he would spend most of his time preparing so that his job would be easier.

Chapter 2 (as well as Chapter 1) has worked to teach you the same type of lesson regarding directed preparation, a lesson that will be extended in later chapters. Remember, a speech is built in much the same way a house is built—from the foundation up. You are ensuring success with your spoken words when you build a solid confidence framework that exhibits a responsible, ethical approach to communication.

Conviction that you are doing a worthwhile activity lets you focus your speech.

Recalling the Facts

1. Which of the ten planks of confidence might be a convenient outlet for much of the nervous energy that your body might feel prior to and during your speech?
2. A notecard can be a comforting "security net" for a speech. What are the two greatest problems regarding notes?
3. Businessman and author Mark McCormack outlines his day by dividing it into how many blocks of time? How long is each? What procedure does he use to organize his phone calls?

Thinking Critically

1. This chapter listed ten planks of confidence. Can you think of at least two other traits that might be commonly viewed as "confidence" but may actually be negative qualities? What is your reasoning behind each choice? Write your responses.
2. Why is practice essential for success at any undertaking? What problems might develop without it? How could failing to practice particular skills hurt you at work? Could this also damage your confidence? How?

Taking Charge

1. Conviction is certainly an important plank of confidence. Name two issues that you feel very strongly about. They may be personal, school, community, national, or world issues. What points would you stress about each if you had to give a speech? Share your views in small groups.
2. Item 1 above deals with your conviction about an issue. However, you need to have evidence (facts) to be smart about your position. Interview an adult who is knowledgeable on one of your issues and give his or her information to your group. In addition, bring in one article from a magazine or newspaper that proves your point. Be prepared to summarize the article for your small group.

Looking Back

Listed below are the major ideas discussed in this chapter.

- Confidence is the feeling you have when you know that you can accomplish a certain task successfully.
- Confidence in speaking is the internal skeletal framework that is anchored to the solid value foundation described in Chapter 1.
- Confidence is the motivating factor behind the power and believability of your words and is an essential element in your being taken seriously by an audience.
- Stage fright often threatens a speaker's confidence. We can think of it as a strong wind that works to blow down a confidence structure.
- Fear is a biological process that allows you to deal with potentially dangerous situations.
- People are often victimized by phobias, or fears that get out of hand.
- Everyone is potentially susceptible to performance anxiety (or stage fright), even profes-

sionals. The symptoms range from a rapid heartbeat to excessive perspiration to an upset stomach.
- One way to overcome this fear is to establish an accurate perception of your audience, your speech, and yourself.
- Perception is the main support beam of confidence. It challenges you to see things as they really are, not as your fears might lead you to believe they are.
- A second way to deal with performance anxiety and build your speaking confidence is by examining the ten planks of confidence: content, organization, notes, friendliness, impression, dedication, empathy, newness, conviction, and enthusiasm.
- Confidence is a consequence of preparation and hard work and is the driving force behind speaking effectiveness.

Speech Vocabulary

1. For each speech vocabulary word, give the definition as it appears in the text. Underline the word. Make sure that you can spell each word.

confidence
phobia
fear
performance anxiety
stage fright
perception
self-esteem
content
organization

notes
friendliness
impression
dedication
empathy
common ground
newness
conviction
enthusiasm

2. For each of the ten planks of confidence, copy the phrase or sentence from the chapter discussion that best describes what the plank is promoting. Do this in addition to writing down the short descriptive phrase that is given immediately beside each plank.

Academic Vocabulary

1. Define each academic vocabulary term by using a dictionary. Include the part of speech, the definition of the word as it is used in the chapter, and an original sentence of your own. Make sure that you can spell each word.
   irrational
   eulogy
   synonymous
   innovation
   allegory
   assertion
   prioritizing
   mannequin

2. Write an original story about "The Day I Overcame My Fear" or "The Day It Was My Turn to Perform!" Use at least twelve words from the combined speech and general vocabulary lists. Underline and number each word.

3. Are there any other words in Chapter 2 that you aren't familiar with or don't know how to spell? Find at least three, and add them to your lists.

To Remember

Answer the following based on your reading of the chapter.

1. Confidence is the feeling you have when you know that you can get the job done well. Confidence is the _____ of effective oral communication.

2. What is the name of the major type of energy that is released by the body in fear situations?

3. A persistent, irrational fear can be referred to as a _____.

4. Another name for performance anxiety is _____.

5. Perception refers to how we see things. Perception is the _____ in building speaking confidence.

6. What percentage of American women would change at least one thing about their looks?

7. A university course known as _____ works to prove the value of effort. The course shows people that they can learn from their mistakes.

8. Roger Ailes calls what word the "magic bullet" in speaking?

9. Richard Louv states that our real impact in speaking can come from our personal _____, which he refers to as "real gold."

10. When you establish _____ with your audience, you are forming a bond that says, "We're all in this together."

To Do

1. Wilma Rudolph was a world-class runner who captured three gold medals for the United States at the 1960 Olympics. However, it is a wonder she could even walk. A series of childhood illnesses had so crippled her that she was unable to walk until she was eight years old. It was through sheer determination and commitment that she overcame the odds. Research a figure from history who also had the confidence to overcome the odds. Show how something great was accomplished by this person. Also, interview someone in your family or community

who has exhibited the confidence to do something admirable in the face of adversity.
2. Compile a self-improvement chart. On it, list the things about you that you can't change. In another column, list the things about you that you *can* change and that you would like to improve. For each item that you can change, jot down how you are going to improve. Be sure to include areas of speaking in which you know that you can improve.

To Talk About

1. The science fiction writer Ray Bradbury once said that Americans, particularly young people, should never watch the evening news. He believed that the news too often erodes our sense of confidence in the future. Was he right? What problems might arise if we don't watch the news? How does what we see on the news affect our personal confidence?
2. It has been said that some people "die with potential." This means that some people never work hard enough to actualize all of their talents or abilities. How can each of us prevent this from happening in our lives?

To Write About

1. The things that might give us stage fright as a child are different from the things we could be frightened by later. Explain the stage fright that a child could feel. What about a teenager? A parent? An employer? An elderly person? How can you help others when you know that they are experiencing stage fright?
2. Denice Barsich, whose good-Samaritan action resulted in the loss of her right leg, didn't lose her zest for life. She was hit by a car while helping a fellow motorist out of a snow-filled ditch. She says that one of her goals is to "dance at my husband's Christmas party." Denice Barsich has one other objective: not to be bitter and to teach her children about the sanctity of life. What does she teach us by her words? Do we often take things for granted?
3. Organization is always an important element in clear communication. Make a list titled "Three Things I Must Get Done in School." Describe not only what your three objectives are but also how, where, and when you plan to accomplish each. Make another list titled "Three Things I Must Accomplish at Home or at Work." Do the same with these.

Related Speech Topics

Sexual harassment
Censorship
Phobias
Cooperative learning in education
Cheating in the United States
Peer pressure

Creativity
A strong work ethic
Law enforcement
Advancements in technology

UNIT

2

Person to Person

UNIT CONTENTS

Squaredpixels/Getty Images

CHAPTER 3
LISTENING

Image Source

Nobody ever listened himself out of a job.

—President Calvin Coolidge

Learning Objectives

After completing this chapter, you will be able to do the following.

- Explain the difference between hearing and listening.
- Identify the components of the listening process.
- Describe four different kinds of listening.
- Explain why good listening habits are important.

Chapter Outline

Following are the main sections in this chapter.

1. Listening Is More Than Hearing
2. Roadblocks to Good Listening
3. Effective Listening Strategies

Speech Vocabulary

In this chapter, you will learn the meanings of the speech terms listed below.

passive listening
active listening
listening spare time
appreciative listening
discriminative listen-
   ing
empathic listening
critical listening
filter
testimonial
false comparison
jump on the band-
   wagon
stack the deck
name calling
paraphrase
summarize

Academic Vocabulary

Expanding your academic vocabulary will help you become a more effective communicator. Listed below are some words appearing in this chapter that you should make part of your vocabulary.

excursion
disintegration
sounding board
vulnerable
gluttony
avarice
sloth
peripheral
bias
propaganda
rhetorical
retention
acronym

In one of Shakespeare's most famous lines, Mark Antony calls on his fellow Romans to "lend me your ears." In this chapter, we will ask you to lend us your ears for some retooling.

Most of us, it seems, are poor listeners—an unfortunate situation that can often lead to mistakes, misunderstandings, and even disaster. Yet listening is a skill that you can master if you are willing to adopt the right attitude and practice a few simple techniques. As good listeners, we not only can help ourselves gain knowledge and success, but we can also help the speaker. He or she will be encouraged by our attention and will gain confidence from our interest.

In a sense, the message of this chapter is, "What you get out of listening depends on what you put into it." Here you will learn how to evaluate yourself as a listener and how to recognize communication barriers that keep us from listening. You will also learn how to develop good listening habits such as paraphrasing, summarizing, and note-taking.

Introduction

You don't know how it happened. You think you were paying attention when your friend started to tell you about an argument she had with her father. But at some point, your eyes glazed over, and her voice became a dull hum. When you finally shook yourself out of your trance, she was asking, "So what should I do?" Poor listening has gotten you in hot water.

As listeners, we tend to think that the responsibility for successful communication lies with the person doing the talking. This attitude causes us to become lazy or **passive listeners**. We let the talker do all the work while we go along for the ride. We tolerate distractions—putting up with a noise in the hall, for instance, instead of getting up to shut the door. We pay more attention to how someone looks or talks than to what she or he has to say. And we generally fail to respond to the talker's message by asking questions or remembering things that were said.

Effective listeners, by contrast, play an active role by guiding the talker toward common interests. *Active listening* is a valuable skill. *Fortune* magazine rates listening as the top management skill needed for success in business. Employers constantly say that what they want most are employees who listen, understand, and follow directions.

Listening is also critical to a healthy family life and among friends. Good listeners do well in school—they follow directions better and don't waste time finding out what the assignment was. Put another way, good listening helps you keep things in perspective: "Nature has given us one tongue, but two ears," wrote the Greek philosopher Epictetus, "that we may hear twice as much as we speak."

Effective listeners are active listeners.

Design Pics/Don Hammond

Listening Is More Than Hearing

Listening is the "receiving" part of the communication process, but simply sensing what was said is just the beginning. We receive a message from someone talking when sound waves set off vibrations in our ears. Hearing, however, is only an automatic reaction of the senses and nervous system. By contrast, listening is the vastly more complicated process of understanding what was said.

When you listen, according to Webster's *New World Dictionary*, you "make a conscious effort to hear." Clearly, listening takes effort—it's a voluntary act in which we use our higher mental processes.

Some people think listening is not a skill at all, but something we do naturally. Unfortunately, we don't do it very well. Studies show that we remember only about 25 percent of what we hear; in other words, we forget, ignore, distort, or misunderstand the great majority of incoming messages. Are we hard of hearing or hard of listening?

The cost of poor listening is high. Poor listening may keep you from doing well on an exam, but it can cost all of us much more. One researcher put it this way: "If each of America's more than 100 million workers prevented just one $10 mistake by better listening, their organizations would save $1 billion."

Do workers make many $10 mistakes? You bet. A $10 mistake is as simple as missing a meeting (by not listening when the boss mentioned the time), putting an item of stock in the wrong place (daydreaming), or having to retype a letter (thinking about the weekend).

Have you ever heard people say they don't have time for something—taking a walk, visiting a sick friend, or writing someone a note? Not true. We all have the same 24 hours each day; what they mean is that something isn't important enough to make time for.

The same is true for listening. We will be poor listeners until we make up our minds to change. Listening keeps you informed, up to date, and out of trouble. It also increases your impact when you speak. It gives you an edge and power and influence. It makes other people like or even love you. But you have to train yourself to listen well.

Poor listeners do not play an active role in communicating or learning.

Chris Ryan/age fotostock

Listening with Time to Spare

One reason listening can be troublesome is that our minds and mouths work at different rates. Although most people speak about 120–180 words per minute, we can listen about six times as fast. Our brains simply work faster than our mouths. This "rate gap" helps explain why our minds sometimes start to wander while we listen.

At the rate a speaker normally talks, you can sandwich many thoughts between her words, and still not miss a thing she says. In other words, most of us find ourselves with a little **listening spare time** on our hands.

Stray thoughts may take you away from the speaker briefly, but they don't keep you from grasping her meaning. So you continue jumping back and forth, tuning in, tuning out, tuning in as you think some of your own thoughts, and then turning back to the speaker—a bit like the way a computer can do multitasking.

These private *excursions* away from the speaker can be troublesome. Let's imagine that you are speaking with a teacher and the teacher mentions your best friend. For just a moment, you start thinking about what you and your friend are planning to do this weekend. You follow that thought longer than you intended and then suddenly remember the teacher. "Whoops! What did he just say?"

Unfortunately, you discover you've missed a critical part of the message. The *disintegration* of your listening has begun. Eventually you give up; it's simply too hard to catch up. You nod your head occasionally for the sake of courtesy, but this is not listening. You've switched over to cruise control.

Fortunately, spare listening time can also be a listener's best friend. We can train ourselves to use it to improve our listening skills. Think of yourself as the rabbit in the fable of the tortoise and the hare. The tortoise represents the speaker, who moves down a path at a steady pace without ever speeding up, stopping, or taking a detour. The hare represents you, the listener, who can dash ahead, stop awhile, fall behind, and then catch up again.

The hare loses the race in the fable, but you'll be a winner if you can make the most of listening opportunities. In a later section, we'll show you how to do just that.

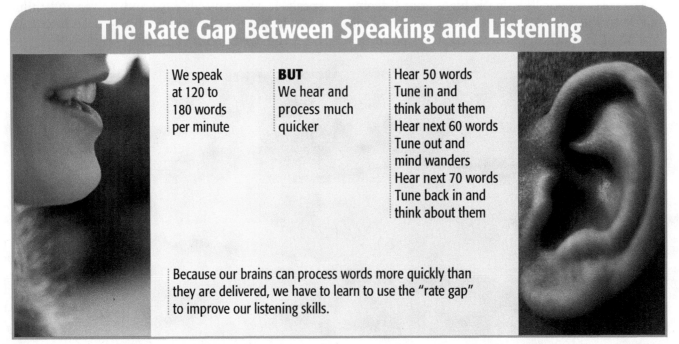

The Rate Gap Between Speaking and Listening

We speak at 120 to 180 words per minute

BUT We hear and process much quicker

Hear 50 words
Tune in and think about them
Hear next 60 words
Tune out and mind wanders
Hear next 70 words
Tune back in and think about them

Because our brains can process words more quickly than they are delivered, we have to learn to use the "rate gap" to improve our listening skills.

Four Ways to Listen An air-traffic controller straining to hear a "Mayday" call from a plane in trouble isn't listening the way you are when your Aunt Bessie calls from Des Moines to chat. We listen most carefully to what we feel is important to us.

We say we're "all ears" when the coach announces the starting lineup or the music teacher names soloists for a big performance, but somehow our ears jam up when Mom or Dad wants to talk about household chores. The fact is, we have different listening styles for different occasions. How successful we are as listeners may depend in part on choosing the right listening style for the situation.

Perhaps the most basic listening style is **appreciative listening**. We listen appreciatively when we enjoy music, a bird's song, or the murmur of a brook. We need a different style, one called **discriminative listening**, when we want to single out one particular sound from a noisy environment. You discriminate, for example, when you listen for a friend's voice in a crowded room.

The third listening style is more complex. **Empathic listening**, the style practiced by counselors, psychiatrists, and good friends, encourages people to talk freely without fear of embarrassment. Friends act as our *sounding boards* when we just want someone to listen. The empathic listener in a conversation with a troubled friend accepts what is said, tries hard to understand, and, above

Appreciative Listening

INSTANT IMPACT

The Ship That Couldn't Be Sunk

One of the greatest tragedies in the history of sea travel occurred on the night of April 12, 1912, when the crew of the *Titanic* refused to listen to repeated warnings of icebergs. The crew had been led to believe that this brand-new passenger liner was "unsinkable," and few doubted that boastful claim. Even after the ship struck an iceberg and was slowly sinking, some of the passengers ignored the captain's orders to get into the lifeboats.

When the ship finally began tilting dangerously, it was too late. There weren't enough lifeboats for all the passengers and, worse still, the *Californian*, the only other ship in the area (about ten miles away), made no attempt to reach the wreck. Her radio operator had gone off duty. As a result, more than a thousand people needlessly lost their lives.

all, makes no judgments. He listens without offering any solutions.

The fourth style, **critical listening**, is the one we will examine most closely. Critical listeners evaluate what they hear and decide if another person's message is logical, is worthwhile, or has value. We need to be critical listeners when someone wants us to buy something, vote a certain way, or support a particular idea. We also need to be critical listeners in school, where *listening* and *thinking* are closely linked.

Why Listening Matters Good listeners are popular everywhere. You will make more friends by listening than by speaking. Good listeners encourage speakers to do their best. Listening is a way of saying to the talker, "You are important, and I am interested in what you have to say." And after a while, good listeners actually get to know something.

Empathic Listening

Effective listening involves not only tuning in to others, but tuning in to ourselves as well. Listening carefully to what we say and how we say it can teach us an immense amount about ourselves. Statements we make often reflect our own self-concepts. If, for example, you heard yourself making the following statements, what would you conclude?

- "I can't handle angry people."
- "Someday I'm going to get organized."
- "I'd like to tell my boss how I feel, but I can't."

Listening is, in the final analysis, a thinking skill, because it requires us to be selective with our attention, to classify and categorize information, and to sort out important principles and concepts from a stream of facts, jokes, and stories.

Good listening skills are especially important in a society that grants freedom of speech to all people, whatever their views or causes. In the remainder of this chapter, we will focus on how to get rid of bad listening habits and how to acquire good ones.

Recalling the Facts

1. What is the difference between active and passive listening?
2. Name and briefly identify four listening styles.

Thinking Critically

1. Give descriptions of well-known people—perhaps people you are studying in other classes—and have your classmates guess their names.
2. Consider the empathic role of listening. Why would nonjudgmental listening be so valuable? Why is it that we can sometimes share our feelings freely with a stranger (someone we sit next to on the bus, for instance) but have difficulty being open with close friends or family?

Taking Charge

1. Record a portion of a radio talk show or call-in program. Play back what you have recorded several times so that you know it well, and make a list of specific questions about the information presented. Then play the segment for your classmates and ask your list of questions to check for understanding. Next, ask your classmates what feelings they remember being expressed in the segment. Have they listened better for facts or feelings? What do feelings sound like?

2. How many times have you heard a student ask a question and then the next student with her or his hand raised asks the very same question? To help your classmates listen to each other more attentively, stage a class discussion on some controversial topic. Each speaker must restate the previous speaker's point (to that speaker's satisfaction) before giving his or her own opinion. For example, you might say, "I understand you believe that watching TV can be a good way to learn about history. Let me explain why I disagree."

Roadblocks to Good Listening

Even Shakespeare, whose words have been heard by millions all over the globe, regretted poor listening. He had one of his characters lament, "It is the disease of not listening." Part of the reason listening is difficult is that we spend so little time working on it. Most of the communication instruction we get in school is geared toward reading, despite the fact that we listen about three times as much as we read. Are we paying more attention to what reaches our eyes than to what reaches our ears?

A Small Price to Pay

Good listening costs us something. To really listen we must *pay* attention. In listening, we pay out our most personal assets—our time, interest, and effort—to receive something in return: information, entertainment, and perhaps even comfort. Listening is hard work, which is why we do not give our attention easily.

1. Tune out dull topics.
2. Fake attention.
3. Yield to distractions.
4. Criticize delivery or physical appearance.
5. Jump to conclusions.
6. Overreact to emotional words.
7. Interrupt.

But while we are paying attention, we must also exercise judgment; as listeners, we risk being deceived. The spoken word seems to affect us much more powerfully than the written word. Researchers say that many of our most deeply held convictions come from things we hear, not things we read. A committee of the National Council on the Teaching of English concluded that students' "political ideals and ethical standards are influenced, if not largely determined, by their listening."

Unfortunately, professional persuaders such as politicians, advertisers, and con artists of every kind know this too. They have learned that people are most *vulnerable* when they are listening. Remember that while you should be willing to listen to almost anything, you must not give up your ability to think for yourself.

Why Is Listening Difficult?

Among the biggest hurdles to good listening is the very human desire to speak. Most of the time when someone is speaking to us, we're thinking of what we want to say next, not listening at all. We prefer speaking to listening. Good listeners must learn to let go of their egos. Train yourself not to worry about what you want to say until the other person has finished talking.

Our very busy lives (not to mention MTV, the Internet, and video games) have also caused us to develop extremely short attention spans. Our tiny attention spans and impatience sometimes lead us to assume we know what someone will say next. This is an especially poor habit because you're likely to shape what you do hear to fit what you expect. You will only hear, in other words, what you want to hear.

Bad Habits Make for Bad Company

During the Middle Ages, people worried about committing the seven deadly sins—*gluttony*, anger, greed, lechery, envy, *avarice*, and *sloth*. Today we should learn to avoid seven habits of bad listening. Any one of them will keep you from becoming an effective listener.

1. *Tuning out dull topics*
   Many listeners decide early on that a topic is simply not interesting—"Class, let's review our procedures for a fire drill." This decision rapidly leads to the MEGO syndrome ("My Eyes Glaze Over").

   Don't let yourself become a lazy listener if what you are listening to doesn't seem appealing. Instead, listen for something you can use yourself—an idea, a quote, a story, or even a joke. An energetic listener can nearly always find something of value in what another person is saying.

2. *Faking attention*
   It's no sin to be courteous, but sometimes we take good manners to an unfortunate extreme. When we find someone's conversation boring but are too polite (or too afraid) to risk offending him, we pretend to pay attention, though our minds are a thousand miles away. Don't assume that all a speaker really wants from us is that we look as if we're listening.

   To help yourself stay on track, create a mental paraphrase of what the speaker is saying—that is, translate the speaker's thoughts into your own words. And repeat key points to yourself periodically throughout the conversation. Both steps will help you maintain an attitude of genuine interest.

3. *Yielding to distractions*
   Peripheral noises or movements often can affect our concentration. A window drops shut, someone sneezes, a book falls to the floor. All too often, we give our attention to the hubbub around us instead of to the speaker. How often have you failed to hear your parents' words while you were busy playing a video game? The truth is that we

INSTANT IMPACT

Gender Talk

While it's clear there are differences between how men and women act, you might be surprised to know there are inherent differences in the ways they speak.

Linguistics professor Deborah Tannen addresses this phenomenon in her book, *You Just Don't Understand: Men and Women in Conversation.* She says that because they grow up so differently, speech between women and men is "cross-cultural communication."

What are these differences? Tannen says women are brought up to believe that conversation is a way to connect with others, thus she describes their speech as "rapport talk." Men learn to communicate through activity. Thus, conversation for them is a contest, which Tannen describes as "report talk."

Men tend to interrupt more often, jump into conversations rapidly and reply in a pattern of one-upmanship in order to maintain their pride. This means that men sometimes have to work harder to be good listeners.

Women tend to use language to create intimacy with whomever they're addressing. Tannen says that girls are raised to comprehend conversation as "glue" that binds a relationship. Thus, they more often seek consensus rather than allow their speech to stand on its own merits.

Tannen believes that if men and women become aware of the varying ways that they communicate, they could avoid many conflicts in their day-to-day dealings with each other.

can block out almost any distraction when we concentrate.

4. *Criticizing delivery or physical appearance*
   Many people abandon their good listening habits when they become preoccupied with a speaker's physical appearance ("He must have

found that shirt in his dad's closet") or delivery ("Let's count how many times she says 'like'"). Regardless of who the speaker is, the content of his message is what counts. Don't use poor physical appearance or speaking style as an excuse for not listening. And don't let yourself be put off by someone's manner, accent, or clothing. Be generous enough to overlook lisps, slurs, and mumbles.

5. *Jumping to conclusions*
Be patient. Occasionally, personal *biases* against a speaker's background or position ("Does this old man really know anything about hip hop?") interfere with listening. Such biases may cause a listener to ask too many questions, interrupt too often, or try to pick an argument. Again, withhold judgment until you're sure you know the speaker's position.

6. *Overreacting to emotional words*
We all react from time to time to certain words or phrases that push our "hot buttons." If a speaker says, for example, "liberal," "abortion," or, even worse, "grade point average," you might experience a strong emotional reaction that can either block out or perk up your ability to listen. In such cases, you need to make an extra effort to remain objective. Your memory of key facts or arguments may be wiped out by the first rush of hot blood.

COMMUNICATION *BREAKDOWN*

Thoughts During a College Lecture

College students may look as if they're listening to the day's lecture, but their minds may be elsewhere, says Paul Cameron, an assistant professor of psychology at Wayne State University. To prove his point, Cameron fired a gun (blanks) from time to time during a lecture and then asked students what they were thinking when they heard the shot. He found that

- About 20 percent of the students were thinking about someone of the opposite sex.

- Another 20 percent were thinking of a memory.

- Only 20 percent were actually paying attention to the lecturer (just 12 percent described themselves as active listeners).

- Of the rest, some were worrying, some daydreaming, some thinking about lunch, and 8 percent were thinking about religion.

Cameron obtained these results in a nine-week course in introductory psychology for college sophomores. The gun was fired 21 times at random intervals, usually when Cameron, who was himself the lecturer, was in the middle of a sentence. We would guess no one speaks out of turn in his class!

Questions
1. How well do you listen to classroom instructions or lectures?
2. What other things do you think about while you're listening?
3. What could you do to help focus your listening skills during class time?

Our emotions have a lot to do with our ability to listen. At times, they act as filters to screen out things we don't want to hear. If we hear something that attacks our deepest feelings or convictions, for example, our ears go temporarily deaf. Instead of listening, we make plans to trap the speaker or think of a question that will embarrass her. Perhaps we simply turn to thoughts that support our own feelings and tune the speaker out.

In any event, listening comes to a screeching halt. When you feel your emotional barriers begin to rise, stay calm. Wait until the speaker has finished. Then, and only then, review the speaker's main ideas and make up your mind how to respond.

7. *Interrupting*

"We never listen when we are eager to speak," wrote the French philosopher François La Rochefoucauld. Try to find out if you spend most of your listening time thinking about what you want to say. The natural result of this habit is for you to interrupt—an almost certain sign that you don't know or care about what the other person is saying.

Filters That Distort

Information goes through many **filters** when it passes from speaker to listener. Listeners filter what they hear based on their backgrounds and personalities. Just as sunlight becomes weaker as it passes through a tinted window, communication can become distorted when it passes through personal filters. When you tell your father that you totaled the car, his reaction will be affected by whether he ever had a bad accident himself. Or, when you listen to a coworker's decision to quit, your own attitudes about work will influence your reaction.

Filters become a problem when they interfere with good listening habits. For example, you may have trouble listening to older people. You may lose patience with their style of speech or perhaps you just think to yourself, "This person was young so long ago, she can't possibly understand what I'm going through." In this case your age acts as a filter to prevent communication from taking place.

Improving your ability to listen is largely a matter of mental conditioning. Anytime you feel your emotional barriers or filters start to rise, make a conscious effort to:

- Refrain from judging or evaluating the speaker.
- Focus your attention on the message (make the problem under discussion the enemy; that way you and the speaker are on the same side).
- Search for areas where you agree.
- Keep an open mind. (If someone says something that bothers you, write it on a slip of paper.

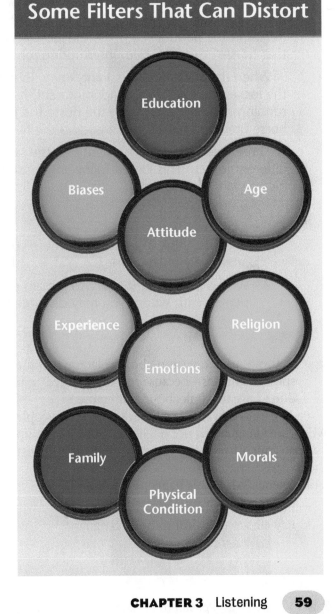

Some Filters That Can Distort

Education

Biases

Age

Attitude

Experience

Religion

Emotions

Family

Morals

Physical Condition

COMMUNICATION *BREAKTHROUGH*

Keep Emotions in Check

Specialists say that strong emotions can be powerful obstacles to good listening. When we become too emotionally involved in a situation, we tend to hear what we *want* to hear—not what is actually being said. Our emotions keep us from focusing on the real message.

Race horse trainer Phil Johnson discovered how much of a problem emotions can be when he gave his jockey last-minute instructions before the start of an important race at New York's Belmont Park. Johnson told the rider to hang back at the beginning of the race and then make a run for the front in the home stretch. But as he talked, he noticed that the jockey wasn't looking at him. Instead, the jockey kept staring at one of the other horses in the paddock, a horse the jockey had ridden in a previous race. "I have to beat that horse," the rider said, interrupting Johnson.

When the starting gate sprang open, Johnson quickly learned he had not been heard by the jockey. Much to his disappointment, he watched as his jockey dashed to the front, running neck and neck with the horse the jockey had ridden before. Eventually Johnson's horse tired and finished well back in the field.

Three weeks later Johnson entered the same horse in another race but this time with a different jockey. This jockey followed Johnson's instructions carefully and won, earning a nice reward for less than two minutes of listening.

Questions

1. Can you think of a situation where your emotions might keep you from listening attentively to someone?

2. Why is it important to try to remain objective and open-minded when listening to people with whom you may disagree?

You can ask a question about it later when the speaker finishes—because it's safely stored, you don't have to think about it anymore.)

People from different ethnic backgrounds or people whose first language is not English can also bump up against your filters, and you can bump up against theirs. Again, special care must be taken to be a responsible listener. When this happens, you should:

- Be patient.
- Pay closer attention to body language.
- Hold your temper when you disagree.
- Put yourself in the speaker's position.

To become successful in life and work, you should learn as much about your own filters. The more you recognize them, the more you will be able to listen carefully when you hear something that you might usually ignore. But no matter how much your filters affect your listening, you should always show respect for others' point of view.

Ingram Publishing

Try to keep an open mind as you listen to others.

SECTION 2 REVIEW

Recalling the Facts

1. List two reasons why listening is difficult.
2. Name and briefly describe five bad listening habits.

Thinking Critically

1. Many people accept the failure of poor listening. "I can look at a person and never hear a word he says," they say with little or no embarrassment. Could part of the reason be that we never practice? Stephen Covey, author of *The Seven Habits of Highly Effective People*, notes that "we spend years learning how to read, write, and speak, but we hardly get any training in listening." How could we train people to listen well?

2. Make a list of all the different kinds of distractions—both internal and external—that can interfere with good listening. What strategies can you suggest to overcome these distractions?

Taking Charge

Try an experiment in your classroom with distractions. Arrange with your teacher to have several distractions occur sometime during a class presentation—have a classmate deliver a pass from the office, "plant" a classmate who will drop a book, and so on. Ask one of your classmates to monitor what happens to the class's attention during each distraction. Discuss how these distractions affected attentiveness.

Effective Listening Strategies

You can learn to be a good listener. Studies have shown that a little bit of knowledge and a lot of practice can lead to improved listening. To practice well, however, takes the attitude that you will make the effort to become a better listener.

To become a good listener, you must stay alert on several fronts at once, working with ears, eyes, and your whole being. Total body listening means, for starters, adopting the right posture for listening: Face the speaker, establish eye contact, and block out distractions. Lean forward and nod occasionally. Good listening requires all of our senses and plenty of mental energy.

Listening to a Speech

Just as there are times to bear down and times to ease up, you should listen more carefully at some times than others. Your attention may lag in driver's education class, for example, as the teacher explains a formula for converting the safe following distance from seconds to feet. When it comes time to listen for directions on your driver's test, though, you will summon your most intense concentration.

Listening to speeches and presentations works the same way. Knowing how speeches are usually organized, for example, can make us smarter listeners because we will be sure to listen most intently when it matters the most. The following discussion illustrates how to listen during each of the three major parts of a speech. (A thorough discussion of how to organize a speech appears in Chapter 9.)

The Beginning Many people with good intentions try to listen hardest at the beginning of a speech. Actually, this is not the best strategy. The beginning may be the most entertaining part of the speech—because the speaker is doing her utmost to gain your attention—but it is usually not the most important. Often, listeners get so caught up in the

Good listeners use not only their ears but also their other senses.

Hero/Corbis/Glow Images

speaker's jokes, stories, and examples that they forget to be alert for the key idea.

Somewhere shortly after the beginning of a speech, the speaker will state the main idea of her talk. Once you find the main idea, your listening job becomes much easier. Now you will recognize the facts and details in the rest of the speech as strengthening or reinforcing the main idea. If you miss the main idea, these facts and details will keep you asking yourself, "Now how does this connect to what was said before?"

Rather than hanging on every word as a speech begins, you should think about the title of the speech and make a few guesses about what direction the speaker might take. This is a key to good listening. You should constantly try to figure out what the speaker's main point is and test hypotheses until you pounce on the main idea when it pops up. This approach differs from that of someone who assumes he knows what the speaker will say and, on that assumption, stops listening.

The Middle Be a critical listener during the body of the speech. Your main goal, of course, is to understand the speaker's message and intent. But this is also the time to test the strength of the speaker's message. Question the support that the speaker uses to defend assertions. How recent are the speaker's examples? How relevant are his quotes? What is the source for his statistics—or has he even given a source? In other words, evaluate the accuracy and fairness of what you hear.

Another part of evaluating the accuracy and fairness of what you hear is determining any bias in a speech. You may hear bias when a speaker defends a point of view without giving any support for his opinions. A speaker may use emotional approaches to argue against another point of view. The speaker may also show prejudice toward a person or a group of people. Listen carefully to what the speaker says to be sure he is approaching the topic in a fair and evenhanded way as well as properly supporting his point of view throughout the speech.

The End During the last part of a speech, the listener must be on guard for emotional appeals and *propaganda*, or material designed to distort the truth or deceive the audience. You can tell that a speech is nearly over when the speaker repeats the main idea, summarizes her most important support, or says "in conclusion" or words to that effect. Speakers often end their speeches by trying to appeal to the listener's feelings. Your job as a listener is to recognize whether the speaker is trying to mislead you.

This is when to be most alert for *rhetorical* devices, that is, tricks of language. Such techniques might include **testimonials** ("You should agree with me because many famous celebrities do"), **false comparisons** (comparing unlike things such as apples with oranges), or suggestions to **jump on the bandwagon** ("Everyone's doing it—don't be left out"). As a speaker ends her speech, ask yourself whether she has earned whatever acceptance or support she is asking you to give.

Use Your Listening "Spare Time" to Advantage

As mentioned earlier, you can listen much faster than anyone can speak. This means that during a speech you can easily fall victim to what listening expert Sally Scobey calls the "meandering mind menace." As our minds race ahead of the speaker, we may begin to daydream—fretting over old worries or thinking about other projects. But we can train ourselves to use this extra time more usefully. For example, here are four ways to keep your mind fully engaged.

Explore One way to use your spare listening time is to explore what lies ahead in the speech by asking, "What does this person want me to believe?" If you guess correctly, your understanding and *retention* will be strengthened. If you guess wrong, you can quickly compare the point you expected with the one the speaker actually made, and then consider why the speech surprised you. Bad listeners guess what the speaker is going to say and stop paying attention; good listeners guess too, but they listen intently to find out if their guess was correct.

The Silent Listener

Once when President Calvin Coolidge was in the White House, he had a visitor from his home state of Massachusetts. The visitor, Channing Cox, had succeeded Coolidge as governor and had come to ask him a question about the business of government. Cox asked Coolidge how he had been able to see so many visitors each day as governor.

"I've heard you always left the office at 5 P.M.," Cox said. "I never leave that early, and often I'm there 'til 9. Why the difference?"

Coolidge thought for a moment and then replied in his usual abrupt manner: "You talk back."

Analyze Another way to spend your listening spare time is to analyze the speaker's message. As the speaker makes arguments and defends assertions, ask yourself, "Are these reasons, examples, and facts convincing? Are things exactly as he says they are? Does this information match what I already know? Is he leaving anything out?"

Many clever speakers may try to mislead you with deceptive reasoning. They may **stack the deck** against a particular person or idea by giving only one side of the story. They may use **name calling** (giving someone a negative label without any evidence) or many other unbalanced arguments to convince you. But a good listener is a hard sell.

Review Every so often you should review what you have heard. Speakers usually allow time for listeners to catch their breath. They may pause, for example, to make a transition: "Now let me talk about . . . " These moments give you a perfect opportunity to review.

Mentally run over the points already made, stopping a split second to examine each. Reviewing helps you remember. Tell yourself that you will have to give a report on this speech sometime, and begin mentally preparing your report while the speech is still going.

Planning to share what you have heard with others is a great way to motivate yourself to remember.

Search for Hidden Meanings Throughout a speech, lecture, or presentation you should "listen between the lines" in search of hidden meanings. Are there shortcomings the speaker should admit but doesn't? Pay attention to any cues the speaker might give, such as changes in the pace of his or her speech. Does the speaker's silence on something indicate it might be a sore point? A speaker's body language and nonverbal behavior can offer big clues to what he is really thinking. (We will take a close look at body language in Chapter 4.) Often what a person doesn't say may be as important as what she does say.

Here is a handy *acronym* that might help you remember these suggestions. Think EARS:

- **E** for explore. Think ahead of the speaker.
- **A** for analyze. Consider carefully what's being said; look at it from several angles.
- **R** for review. Take advantage of your spare listening time to review.
- **S** for search. Be alert for hidden meanings.

Ask for Explanations

In many situations, you will find you need more information. When you ask for an explanation, you help the speaker make his message more understandable. To get additional information, you might say something like, "Would you please clarify that?" Other useful comments include

- "Would you say that again?"
- "I don't understand what you mean."
- "Could you be more specific?"

People are usually happy to help, but if you suggest that they *need* help, they may get angry. When you are confused, be sure to say something like "Maybe I misunderstood," and not "You aren't being very clear."

Paraphrase the Message

You can also help others by trying to **paraphrase** a message, or repeat in your own words what you think you heard. Your boss, for example, may give you detailed instructions on how to close the store for the evening or describe several errands you must run. In either case, paraphrasing goes a step beyond just asking for a further explanation.

Paraphrases often begin like this:

- "What I hear you saying is . . ."
- "Correct me if I'm wrong, but . . ."
- "In other words, your view is . . ."

When you paraphrase, you restate the speaker's message as a way of checking its accuracy. When you paraphrase someone, try to capture only the essence or main points of the message. Be selective rather than exhaustive. Try, too, to focus on the content of

By asking for explanations or paraphrasing, you can be sure you understand what your manager and others want you to do.

what was said rather than any feelings expressed. This can help defuse a potentially emotional situation.

Summarize the Message

You can go one step beyond a paraphrase by trying to **summarize** what you see as the main idea in a speech or conversation. Summaries are especially important when you need to relay a message from one person to another. The manager may ask you, for example, to convey her instructions to your coworkers.

When you summarize something, you condense the important points into a brief comment. Some typical summary statements might begin this way:

- "What the manager said so far is . . ."
- "Your key ideas, as I understand them, are . . ."
- "Recapping what you have been saying . . ."

Summaries are useful anytime a speaker becomes especially long-winded or confusing. Suppose a customer of long standing has come to complain about your company's service. This is what he says:

"Two out of the last six shipments have arrived at least a week overdue. I hope you realize that costs us $1,000 a day. The last time we ordered parts from you, they were late too—and that's never happened before. The agents I've spoken with have been rude. What's happening around here?"

A good listener will do the following:

✓ 1. Provide encouragement.
✓ 2. Ask for explanations.
✓ 3. Paraphase the message.
✓ 4. Summarize the message.
✓ 5. Put it down on paper.

Robert Nicholas/age fotostock

How Well Do You Listen?

Think about your responses to the following statements about your listening skills.

1. I often interrupt people to interject what I need to say.	Y N
2. I anticipate what someone is about to say and finish the statement.	Y N
3. During a conversation, I am easily distracted by what is happening around me.	Y N
4. I feel uncomfortable when I look directly at a speaker for more than a few seconds.	Y N
5. I "tune out" speakers I don't agree with.	Y N
6. I like to focus on a speaker's clothes and hair instead of what is being said.	Y N
7. I am turned off by a speaker who uses words I don't know.	Y N
8. Sometimes I daydream while people are talking to me.	Y N
9. During conversations, while the other person is speaking, I like to plan what I want to say.	Y N
10. I often pretend to be interested in what a speaker is saying even when I'm not.	Y N

How did you do? If you answered "no" to each statement, you are an excellent listener. If you answered "yes" one to three times, your listening skills could stand a little improvement. If you answered "yes" to more than three statements, you need to work hard on developing better listening habits for greater success at school, at work, or with your friends and family.

You summarize this conversation to your coworkers and manager as follows:

"Mr. Brown feels that we are letting him down all around—shipments, parts, and now service. He wants an explanation."

Summarizing is especially useful in situations involving conflicts or complaints or when some kind of problem solving is needed. Summarizing is also helpful at the close of a telephone conversation, especially when a variety of points have been discussed or one of the parties is expected to do something.

Put It Down on Paper

Memory alone can't guarantee that we will remember an important conversation a week or even a few days later. That's why note-taking is usually considered a listening skill. It seems that just making the effort to take notes will almost always help improve our listening. Those who take notes understand more and remember more.

For one thing, taking notes improves our attentiveness. "It helps you focus on the highlights of what is being said," notes Germaine Knapp, a communications consultant. Note-taking also increases the chances that you will review what has been said.

From time to time, a good note-taker looks back on his notes to see if they are complete. Such review is crucial to good listening. And, surprisingly, note-taking often helps the speaker. Speakers feel flattered when people write down things they say. They usually try to be as accurate as possible if they know someone is keeping track.

Keep these tips in mind when you take notes on important meetings or conversations:

- Be prepared. Try to carry a small notepad and pen with you whenever you think you might need to take notes.
- Get it down. Don't take the time to be neat. You can always recopy your notes later. The important thing is to work quickly—writing just clearly enough so that you can remember what you wrote and why.

- Don't try to write everything. Avoid complete sentences. Draw lines to connect ideas; omit vowels. Develop your own system of shorthand using symbols, pictures, punctuation, and abbreviations. For example, this note:

Glenna, lnch w/HP client, FRI 11:30 @ Macaroni's

means that you and Glenna Douglas (a colleague) have a lunch meeting scheduled with a Hewlett-Packard client on Friday at 11:30 a.m. at Macaroni's restaurant.

SECTION 3 REVIEW

Recalling the Facts

1. When are the most important times to listen carefully during a speech?
2. How can you use your listening "spare time" to best advantage?
3. Explain the difference between asking for an explanation, paraphrasing a message, and summarizing a message.

Thinking Critically

The average person spends 9 percent of his daily communication time writing, 16 percent reading, 30 percent speaking, and a whopping 45 percent listening. Students spend even more time listening—up to 60 percent during school hours, according to some studies. Do these percentages seem accurate? Which classes require the most listening? Which the least?

Taking Charge

1. Listen to a three-minute presentation by your teacher or a classmate. Use the strategies from this section to help you evaluate the speaker's intent. What are the main points of the presentation? What techniques did the speaker use to get those points across?
2. Watch one of the courtroom shows on television. Arrange to tape-record the judge's decision and comments, but don't listen. Instead, draw your own conclusions about the case based on what you've heard during the trial. Then compare your ruling with the judge's.
3. Listen to a recorded speech. Note any instances of bias, prejudice, or propaganda that you hear. How do these instances affect how you feel about the speaker's message?
4. Watch a short video or listen to a recording about a subject you're interested in. As you watch or listen, take notes and write down your own comments or observations about what you're hearing. What did you learn from the presentation? What can you take away from it to synthesize with other projects you are working on?

Looking Back

Listed below are the major ideas discussed in this chapter.

- Hearing is an automatic reaction of the senses and nervous system to sound. Listening, on the other hand, is a voluntary act.
- Poor listening costs us millions of dollars in lost business, mismanaged time, and waste. In places such as construction sites, poor listening could cause accidents or deaths.
- Because we can listen faster than anyone can speak, we have some "spare time" to use to our advantage. We can use this time to explore, analyze, review, and search for hidden meanings.
- Success in listening depends on choosing the right listening style for the situation.

- Seven habits of poor listening are tuning out dull topics, faking attention, yielding to distractions, criticizing a speaker's delivery, jumping to conclusions, overreacting to emotional words, and interrupting.
- Strong emotions can sometimes prevent us from being good listeners.
- Knowledge of how a typical speech is organized can be helpful to listeners, because different sections of a speech call for different kinds of listening.
- Note-taking can help improve our listening habits.

Speech Vocabulary

Fill in the blank with the correct term from the list below.

passive listening
active listening
listening spare time
appreciative listening
discriminative listening
empathic listening
critical listening
false comparison

paraphrase
summarize
filter
testimonials
stack the deck
name calling
jump on the
    bandwagon

1. We use _____ when we listen to someone relate her problems, hopes, or dreams, especially when the person doesn't want our approval or advice.
2. We can use our _____ to explore, analyze, and review a speaker's message.
3. When we recognize sounds, we are only hearing. If we pay little attention to those sounds, we are using _____. But if we try energetically to make sense of those sounds, we are using _____.

4. If you buy a CD to enjoy, you use _____ but if you intend to write a review of the CD for the school newspaper, you use _____.
5. _____ is the kind of listening that enables you to hear a friend across a crowded room.
6. Some of the propaganda techniques that professional persuaders use are _____ (using the name of a celebrity), _____ (holding up one candidate against a much older one),_____ ("Don't be left out!"), _____ (presenting only favorable evidence), and _____ (mudslinging).
7. Our personal biases may cause us to _____ out certain messages.

CHAPTER ③ Review and Enrichment

Academic Vocabulary

Match each of the following terms on the left with a definition on the right that helps explain its meaning.

___ A. excursion
___ B. disintegration
___ C. sounding board
___ D. vulnerable
___ E. peripheral
___ F. rhetorical

___ G. retention
___ H. acronym
___ I. bias
___ J. gluttony
___ K. avarice
___ L. propaganda
___ M. sloth

1. ability to remember
2. extreme desire to gain wealth
3. excessive eating or drinking
4. on the outside
5. fall into fragments
6. a person who gives feedback
7. laziness

8. tricks of language
9. trip or journey
10. unprotected
11. word formed from the initial letters of several words
12. words designed to distort the truth
13. a settled or prejudiced outlook

To Remember

Answer the following based on your reading of the chapter.

1. What is the difference between hearing and listening?
2. What are the four basic listening styles?
3. What are three reasons why listening is difficult?
4. Name the seven deadly habits of bad listening.
5. What should your listening strategy be when you feel strongly moved by what a speaker says?
6. What does a good listener look like? In other words, what is the right posture and bearing for a person who wants to listen well?
7. At what point in a formal speech is it important to listen most intently?
8. Give an example of a situation where paraphrasing would be useful. Do the same for summarizing.

To Do

1. To find out how well or poorly you listen, try this simple exercise. The next time someone begins a conversation, ask yourself, "Am I really listening or am I just waiting my turn to talk?" Pay attention to your own mental processes. Are you:
   - Easily distracted?
   - Faking attention?
   - Interrupting frequently?
   - Daydreaming?
   - Jumping to conclusions?
   - Finding fault with the speaker?
   - Thinking of what you want to say?
   If your answer is yes to any of the items on this list, you have fallen victim to a habit of bad listening. What remedies can you suggest?
2. Make a list of listening skills and habits, both good and bad. For example, "Do I listen attentively without interrupting?" "Do I listen carefully for main ideas and supporting points?" or "Do I keep my emotions under control?" Then grade yourself on a recent conversation, discussion, or lecture.

3. How well do students listen to each other? Appoint an observer. After a student has given a speech to the class, ask the observer to rate the class on its listening skills. What was the typical posture? How attentive were the listeners? Did they give encouragement? Have students form groups to discuss how they could improve their listening skills.
4. Ask several students to prepare short talks. Tell them that they may have to speak under very difficult circumstances but that they should continue no matter what happens.

Ask the speakers to leave the room and then instruct the class to listen very carefully to what each speaker says until a secret signal is given. At that point the students are to stop paying attention, perhaps by reading books or looking out the window. Call the student speakers back, one at a time, and ask them to give their talks. When they are finished, ask them to discuss how they felt when the class withdrew its attention and what changes they made in their speeches as a result.

To Talk About

1. What role does listening play in our everyday lives?
2. Certain people seem to naturally command our attention. Researchers say we listen quite willingly to those who have status (celebrities), those with seniority (parents and teachers), those who can do something for us, and members of the opposite sex. Do you agree with this conclusion? Are there other categories of people to whom you pay special attention? Is that attention warranted?
3. How well do we listen in different settings—for instance, at a family meal, in class, at a party, or on the job? Discuss the differences you notice in listening styles.

To Write About

1. Compile a list of occupations where listening is vital. Examples might include psychologist, counselor, and social worker. Interview someone in your community who works at one of those careers and write a report based on that person's definition of "professional" listening.
2. Examine what topics might cause you to "hear only what you want to hear." Examples might include either side of an issue like abortion or gun control. What ideas do you have about getting someone to listen to the other side of an issue?
3. Write about the teacher whose lectures you find easiest to understand. Explain what techniques that teacher uses to be successful.

Related Speech Topics

Silence is (or is not) golden.

Poor listening habits can lead to major problems in business and many other areas of life.

If we spend 60 percent of every school day listening, why aren't we learning more?

We are vulnerable to professional persuaders such as politicians and advertisers.

Females are better listeners than males (or vice versa).

It's not what we say but what we don't say that counts.

How to take notes well.

CHAPTER 4
NONVERBAL COMMUNICATION

Watch out for the man whose stomach doesn't move when he laughs.

—Chinese proverb

Learning Objectives

After completing this chapter, you will be able to do the following.

- Distinguish between verbal and nonverbal communication.
- Use body language to reinforce your verbal message.
- Recognize when someone is not telling the truth.
- Explain how the same gesture can have different meanings in different cultures.

Chapter Outline

Following are the main sections in this chapter.

1. Body Basics
2. Interpreting Nonverbal Messages
3. Multicultural Messages

Speech Vocabulary

In this chapter, you will learn the meanings of the speech terms listed below.

nonverbal message   personal space
body language   intimate distance
eye contact   personal distance
tone of voice   social distance
gesture   public distance

Academic Vocabulary

Expanding your academic vocabulary will help you become a more effective communicator. Listed below are some words appearing in this chapter that you should make part of your vocabulary.

sympathetic   suppress
diverse   anthropologist
distal   comparative
proximal   intimacy
timbre   stoic

Looking Ahead

We speak only with our mouths, but we communicate with our whole bodies. In fact, experts say that more than half of all communication is nonverbal. To truly understand other people, then, you must learn how to read their body language as well as interpret their words. You must learn what their facial expressions, hand gestures, and other signals mean. Even people's body temperature can be significant, as it reveals itself in the color of their faces or the moisture on their palms.

In this chapter, you will learn how to interpret body language, how body language varies from culture to culture, and how to use body language to make your own communication more effective and convincing.

Introduction

You can communicate even when you don't say a word. In 1990 a photographer for *National Geographic* magazine lined up the members of the U.S. Supreme Court for their official photograph. Justice Sandra Day O'Connor found herself standing directly behind Justice Byron White. According to news reports, O'Connor quietly formed a V with her fingers and held them just above White's head, making the old "rabbit ears" sign.

O'Connor was sending a nonverbal message to everyone who saw the photograph—a message that said, "We don't take ourselves quite as seriously as it looks." Nonverbal messages play an enormous and often unappreciated role in all of our communication.

"You *see*," says the detective Sherlock Holmes to his somewhat dim-witted assistant Dr. Watson, "but you do not *observe*." What Holmes means is that the best way to understand people is to watch them—to notice what they do as well as what they say.

Nonverbal messages often say as much or more than spoken words.

Albert Mehrabian, a professor of psychology at UCLA, claims that talking is the least important way we communicate. What counts most, he says, are our nonverbal messages. These messages include the way we sit or stand, how we tilt our heads, our facial expressions, our gestures, and our tone of voice.

Body Basics

Understanding nonverbal communication is vital in many ways. It helps us understand, for example, how others react to us and to our ideas. If someone you are speaking to crosses his arms or legs, you may suspect that he feels threatened by what you are saying or disagrees with you. If your listener opens his hands toward you, you may expect agreement or at least a *sympathetic* ear.

People from different cultures may attach different meanings to the same gestures. For example, consider the "hook 'em, horns" sign, made famous by fans of the University of Texas football team. To make the sign, hold up your index and pinky fingers. In Texas this signifies support for the team, but beware: in Italy, this sign is an insult. In Brazil, it means good luck; and among Hindus, it means a cow. Being sensitive to the way different people interpret nonverbal messages can help you communicate more effectively wherever you are.

Knowing something about nonverbal communication can also be helpful when you send messages. Your physical actions can either reinforce or contradict what you say. If you feel nervous about speaking to a group, for instance, you may avoid looking at your listeners, lean on the podium, or drop your voice to a low mumble.

With a little practice, however, you can master a different set of nonverbal habits—mannerisms that will convey confidence and authority. Eventually, by learning to look confident, you begin to feel confident.

Body Language

Also called the "silent language," **body language** is the way we use our bodies to send messages. A speaker for Toastmasters International once found an effective way to demonstrate to an audience how body language works. He asked his listeners to place their thumbs and forefingers together (as in the OK sign) and then told them to place their

Body language indicates that these people are friends.

hands on their chins. But while he was saying this, he did something different—he placed his own thumb and forefinger on his cheek.

Typically, 90 percent of his listeners followed his *actions*, not his words. Despite his instructions, they put their hands on their cheeks just as he did. "In business," notes Susan Bixler, president of Professional Image, "body language always wins out over verbal communication."

Why is body language important? First, because people usually remember more of what they see than what they hear, and second, because we have learned that it helps us recognize the truth. When a person's words and body language are consistent, we tend to believe that person. When their words and body language say different things, we tend to believe the body language and doubt the words.

Often, complicated feelings spill out in the form of body language. If a speaker is having difficulty controlling her anger, for example, she might raise her voice or turn away. "No mortal can keep a secret," noted Sigmund Freud. "If his lips are silent, he chatters with

PhotoAlto

Walk the Walk

One of the most interesting body movements is the walk. Some have called the way we walk a "second signature," because each person's walk is distinct. The way we walk results partly from body structure, of course, but pace and length of stride seem to change with our emotions. If you are happy, you may move more quickly and seem lighter on your feet. If you're unhappy, your shoulders may droop, and you may walk as though your shoes were made of lead.

Studies show that people tend to like men and women who have a bounce to their walk, swing their arms, and take long, strong strides. In fact, some psychologists say a long stride is such a positive body movement that you can improve your disposition—and make yourself happier—just by taking longer steps.

his fingertips." Even though people can control their words, and sometimes their facial expressions, there is often a "leakage" of feelings—perhaps in a gesture, a shift of position, or a tone of voice. Any one of these nonverbal signals may help you to interpret the messages you receive.

Body language is also remarkably *diverse*. Mario Pei, a communications expert, once estimated that humans produce up to 700,000 different physical signs. The face alone is capable of 250,000 different expressions. Other researchers have identified some 5,000 separate hand gestures and 1,000 kinds of postures. Clearly, we send messages by a dizzying array of nonverbal means. These messages are fun to watch and challenging to interpret. And unlike verbal communication, which is intermittent, body language is constant.

Learning to Read Body Language

Recognizing body language is an inexact art, so you must be careful about how you interpret it. A certain movement or facial expression may be quite meaningful, or it may mean nothing at all. As a starting point, the lists below provide common body language terms and their generally accepted meanings.

Positive Body Language Certain physical cues can be quite reliable as indicators of positive feelings. Here are some things you can do, for example, to signal interest in another person during a conversation:

- *Relaxed posture.* Sit comfortably and breathe in a relaxed manner. Avoid abrupt movements.
- *Arms relaxed.* Uncross your arms and hold your hands palms up as a sign of openness.
- *Good eye contact.* Look the other person in the eye, particularly when she or he is speaking. Look away occasionally to avoid staring.
- *Nodding agreement.* When you nod your head at something the other person has said, you indicate that you agree or understand. But don't overdo it. Continuous head bobbing usually means that the listener has tuned out.
- *Smiling at humor.* This signals a warm personal relationship.
- *Leaning closer.* Reducing the distance between you and a partner, particularly when the other person is speaking, indicates interest is up and barriers are down.
- *Using gestures.* Talking with your hands indicates involvement in the conversation and openness to the other person.

For all of these positive behaviors, moderation is the key. When these movements are exaggerated, they can become more negative than positive.

Negative Body Language Most positive gestures are *distal*; that is, they are directed toward others. Most negative gestures, on the other hand, are *proximal*; they are directed toward your own body. Negative body language is somewhat less reliable as a method for reading another person's mood, because actions that are generally considered negative may just be a sign of nervousness. Still, be on the lookout for these behaviors:

- *Body tension.* A wrinkled brow, jerky body motions, or hands clasped in front can all indicate discomfort with the topic or the other person.
- *Arms folded.* This creates a barrier and can indicate resistance to what is being said.
- *Speaking hand to mouth.* Putting your hands near your mouth, scratching your cheek or eyebrow—these are things that say, "Don't listen to me, I'm not sure of what I am saying."
- *Fidgeting.* If you move around a lot, play with things, or drum with your fingers, you send signals of boredom, nervousness, or impatience.
- *Yawning.* This often happens if the other person is talking too much or in too much technical detail.

Using Body Language Effectively We normally think of body language as a reflection of what a person is feeling, and it is. But it is also true that if you change your body language, your feelings will begin to change as well. That's why, when you feel yourself dragging in the middle of the afternoon, a quick walk around the block can rejuvenate you. You also tend to feel better when you put on fresh clothes, or if you just smile.

This principle has two practical applications: (1) You can make yourself look and feel better by using more positive body language. The famous football coach Vince Lombardi used to tell his players before an away game, "You've got to look good getting off the bus." In other words, if you look and act like a winner, you are more likely to be one. (2) Body language is contagious. If person X uses neutral body language, and person Y uses positive body language, person X will gradually begin to mirror Y's behavior. Thus, your positive body language can gradually affect the behavior of those around you.

Negative Body Language

Recalling the Facts

Try this quick quiz to see how well you can interpret nonverbal messages. Match the action in the left column with the message in the right column:

1. What is the difference between active and passive listening?
2. Name and briefly identify four listening styles.

Action	Message
1. Slapping your forehead with the heel of your hand	a. "I'm angry."
	b. "I forgot something."
2. Wrinkling your forehead and frowning	c. "I'm getting impatient."
3. Tapping your fingers on a desk or table	d. "I don't understand."
4. Slamming a book down on a desk or table	e. "I don't like that."
5. Wrinkling your nose	

Thinking Critically

1. Why do actions speak louder than words?
2. To learn more about body language, try a mirroring exercise. Find a partner and stand facing each other. One of you now becomes the mirror image for the other by trying to copy your partner's body movements. Try holding a conversation. After a while reverse roles and repeat the activity. What are each person's characteristic gestures?

Taking Charge

1. To observe body language in action, try an experiment the next time you ride a crowded elevator. When you board the elevator, don't turn around and face the door. Instead, stand facing the other people in the elevator. If you want to create even more tension, grin and stare at everyone. Very likely, the other passengers will glare back, and they may appear to be surprised or upset. The reason? You have broken the (unspoken) rules.

    Discuss with your classmates what you discover. Brainstorm other situations in which breaking the nonverbal rules might affect others.
2. Pair off with a partner and try to communicate the following feelings nonverbally: frustration, tension, joy, anger, hate, and happiness. Think of a few other feelings, and attempt to see whether your partner can guess what emotion you are trying to communicate.

Interpreting Nonverbal Messages

Learning to read body language is complicated by the fact that people often express different and even contradictory messages in their verbal and nonverbal behaviors. Are you nodding your head yes while you're saying no?

A common example of this double message is the experience of hearing someone with a red face and bulging veins yell, "Angry? No, *I'm not angry!*" Like this person, you may sometimes try to put on a false front. You try to keep a straight face, for example, when laughing might hurt someone's feelings, or you try to act calm when you don't want someone to worry about you.

We all try to "massage our message" from time to time. In other words, we attempt to use our bodies to disguise our real feelings. For example, we may pretend not to be hurt even though our hearts are breaking.

We have learned how to "behave" ourselves, how to hide our true feelings. We choose roles and act our parts. But rarely do we turn in a perfect performance. Thus, who we really are and what we really mean often slip out in our behavior—in what we say, the way we say it, and the way our bodies act.

Here are some tips for reading the *true* meaning of nonverbal communication:

- Don't just look, but *observe*.
- Consider the person's normal physical and verbal behavior patterns, and be alert for variations from those norms.
- Remember that one signal alone may mean nothing; what you're looking for are clusters of signals.

Facial Expressions

Because of their visibility, we pay a great deal of attention to other people's faces. Babies, for example, take special interest in the huge faces they see peering over their cribs. Although the face is capable of making hundreds of distinct movements and communicating many emotional states, six emotions seem to cause most expressions: surprise, fear, anger, disgust, happiness, and sadness. Blends of these primary emotions account for nearly all of our facial expressions.

No single area of the face best reveals emotions, but for any given emotion, certain features may be more important. For example, the nose-cheek-mouth area is most important for showing disgust. For fear, the eyes and eyelids are most important. Sadness can be detected or expressed best in the

What nonverbal message are these students sending?

Exactostock/SuperStock

brows and forehead, while happiness can be found in the cheeks and mouth.

If you watch a person's face in slow motion (on film or video), you discover that people change expressions rapidly. Some expressions last only a few hundredths of a second; in fact, they are so fleeting that they are rarely noticed in everyday conversation.

Some of these fleeting expressions reveal a person's true feelings, but they are quickly replaced by deliberate expressions the person feels are more socially appropriate. You can disguise your face more easily than almost any other part of your body. That means that despite our natural tendency to search faces for meaning, they are not necessarily the best place to look.

Tone of Voice

By contrast, **tone of voice** offers a valuable clue to a speaker's feelings. The pitch and *timbre* (distinctive tone) of a person's voice and the pauses and rhythm of a voice can express things above and beyond the words themselves. The psychotherapist Rollo May once asked himself, "What does the voice say when I stop listening to the words?"

The simple word *oh*, for example, says very little as you see it printed here. But in spoken form, *oh* can have many different meanings. According to the way it is spoken, *oh* can mean any of the following:

- "You surprised me."
- "I made a mistake."
- "You're a pain in the neck."
- "You make me so happy."
- "I'm bored."
- "I'm fascinated."
- "I understand."
- "I don't understand."

The rate of speech also tells us something about the speaker's feelings. People tend to talk fast when they are excited or anxious. They also tend to talk fast when they are trying to persuade us or sell us something. On the other hand, people tend to talk more slowly when they are depressed, disgusted, or simply tired.

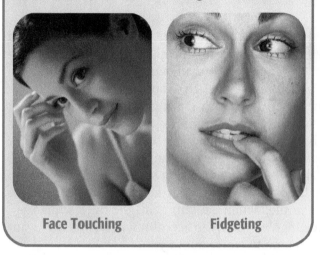

How to Tell If Someone Is Lying

Increased face touching, avoiding eye contact, and fidgeting can indicate that someone is not telling the truth.

Face Touching   **Fidgeting**

John Hull learned to be especially sensitive to tone of voice when he became visually impaired at age 48. "With the people I know very well," he said, "I find that all of the emotion that would normally be expressed in the face is there in the voice: the tiredness, the anxiety, the excitement. My impressions based on the voice seem to be just as accurate as those of sighted people. The capacity of the voice to reveal the self is truly amazing."

How to Tell When Someone Is Lying

According to Desmond Morris, author of *The Naked Ape*, we control some parts of our bodies better than others. The easiest parts to control are those whose actions we are most aware of. Smiles and frowns are easy to control. So facial expressions are a poor test of someone's sincerity.

General body postures, on the other hand, can be very revealing, because we are not fully conscious of them; we don't usually know, for example, whether we are slumping or standing tall. Legs and feet are the parts of the body we are usually least aware of.

Then what can we do to discover a person's true thoughts? Are there specific body messages we can look for? Morris conducted a series of experiments to provide some answers. He asked a group of nurses to lie about a movie they had seen. He then assembled a set of behaviors that seem to persist during moments of deception:

- **Decreased hand activity.** The hand gestures the nurses would normally use were reduced. The reason may be that hand actions, which illustrate what we say, are not entirely under our conscious control. Unconsciously, when you are not being truthful, you may sense that your hands will give you away, so you *suppress* them. You hide them, sit on them, stuff them into pockets, or clasp them together.
- **Increased face touching.** We all touch our faces from time to time when we speak, but the frequency of this simple action rises during moments of stress, such as lying. Hand-to-face favorites include the chin stroke, the lip press, the mouth cover, the nose touch, the cheek rub, the eyebrow scratch, the earlobe pull, and the hair groom.

Why these actions might indicate lying can be explained with the mouth cover. According to Morris, as false words emerge from the speaker's mouth, one part of his brain becomes uncomfortable and sends a message to his hand to "cover up" what the lips are doing. The other part of his brain, however, cannot permit this cover-up to work. The result is a halfhearted motion, with the hand-to-mouth gesture ending up as a slight brush.

How can you tell whether a smile is genuine?

Smiles are much more complicated than many people realize. Paul Ekman, a researcher at the University of California at San Francisco, has identified eighteen distinctive smiles—most of them phony. One of the most common is the "qualifier" smile, which superiors often use when rejecting an idea or criticizing an employee. In such a smile, the corners of the lips are usually tightened, with the bottom lip pushed up slightly. But Ekman says most people can identify the real thing. Look at the upper half of a person's face. Genuine, or "felt," smiles involve the muscles that make the corners of the eyes crinkle with pleasure.

- **Stiff and rigid posture.** "Most people move less when they're lying," says psychologist Albert Mehrabian. "Their movements and body positions become less fluid." However, some people move more when they feel conflicted, as the next point shows.
- **Increased body shifting.** Most of us can remember squirming as children when we were being interrogated by our parents. Our squirms were symptoms of an almost overpowering desire to escape. As adults, we learn to suppress these actions, but they do not disappear entirely. If you know a person well, you may be able to spot times when he or she seems unusually restless. That body language may indicate that the person is uncomfortable about something he or she is saying.

Recalling the Facts

1. Tone of voice is one way that we can communicate feelings. Descibe the different ways that a person can say the word "oh" to convey feelings.
2. Because we all try to disguise our real feelings from time to time, reading body language can be difficult. Describe ways we can use body language to distinguish genuine feelings from false ones.
3. How can you tell a genuine smile from a phony one?
4. What nonverbal message would a person send if she brushed her fingers across her mouth when she was speaking?
5. How does a person use his or her hands to send noverbal messages?

Thinking Critically

Ask a partner to tell you two stories about something that happened to him or her—one true and one false. Your partner should try to make the false story sound reasonable, so that wild exaggerations don't give the story away.

Listen to both stories, carefully observing your partner's body language and tone of voice. Can you guess which story is true? After you have tried to guess, reverse roles and tell two stories to your partner.

Now work with a partner and take turns saying the words "thanks a lot." Keep track of the different feelings you can convey by changing your tone of voice as you say the words.

Taking Charge

Watch a recording of a film or a TV show (a cartoon works well) with the sound off, and try to guess what is being expressed by body language alone. Then play the recording again with the volume up. How well did you do with your guesses? Reverse this procedure, so that you listen but do not look. How much do you feel you lose by relying only on verbal messages?

Try the same activity watching singers perform a song in a televised competition. Turn off the sound as they sing. What does their body language and facial expression tell you about the feelings expressed in the song?

Multicultural Messages

While practiced everywhere, body language is not a universal language. The familiar thumbs-up gesture that means "everything's OK" or "good going," especially when used by a pilot or an astronaut, has other meanings in other places. North Americans recognize the thumbs-up gesture as a sign that you are hitchhiking, but don't use it to get a ride in Nigeria; there it's a rude insult.

Despite the seemingly infinite number of gestures, there are some universal gestures, such as smiling, blushing, or the wide-eyed expression of fear, that are known everywhere and have the same significance in any part of the world.

These gestures are rarely, if ever, misunderstood because they are absolutely universal to nonindustrial peoples and world leaders alike. Other universal gestures or expressions recognized regardless of culture or location might include shrugging your shoulders or crying.

Cultural Differences

Generally, we expect to communicate better face to face than indirectly—say, on the telephone. Nonverbal information—such as one's appearance, tone of voice, facial expression, and body language—provides extra information that enriches understanding. However, when cultural differences are involved, more nonverbal information is not always better.

For one thing, when you do not have good command of a foreign language, you tend to lose some control over your nonverbal expressions. So, English spoken with a foreign accent not only is hard to understand, but it can also lead to a poorly controlled tone of voice or awkward facial expressions. Sometimes it is hard not to judge a person based on such behaviors, and it takes patience to move beyond first impressions.

Most Americans reserve hugs for their families and close friends, but people in other cultures may hug when greeting strangers.

Gestures Around the World

If humans can produce 5,000 different **gestures**, why do we use the same ones over and over? Probably because they are the ones we need for everyday situations: when we greet each other, beckon to one another, and especially when we touch one another.

Nodding your head up and down means yes—unless, of course, you live in Bulgaria or parts of Greece, Turkey, and Iran, where it means just the opposite. Tapping your head with your forefinger can have two meanings. Sometimes it means, "That person is very intelligent!" and sometimes, "That

CHAPTER 4 Nonverbal Communication **83**

person is crazy!" It all depends on the facial expression that goes with the gesture.

All over the world, scratching your head seems to mean, "I am confused." Apparently, everyone gets confused. In an Italian study, psychologists filmed people in telephone booths. One clip shows a man holding the receiver in his left hand and gesturing vigorously with his right. As the conversation seems to agitate him more, he tucks the receiver under his chin to free both hands for gesturing, beating the air with his fists.

This man probably couldn't talk at all if we tied his hands behind his back. Let's take a closer look at what other gestures can mean in different cultures.

Signs of Greeting Some *anthropologists*, scientists who study human cultural development, believe that an outstretched hand as a form of greeting goes far back in history. Citizens of the Roman Empire greeted each other with a hand-and-forearm clasp, mainly to show that neither party was carrying a weapon. The hug or embrace (a form of greeting common in Mediterranean countries) may have had a similar purpose. The hug gave people physical assurance that no weapons were hiding beneath anyone's robe.

Worldwide, many other forms of greeting are used. In the Middle East, citizens can still be seen giving the salaam. To give the salaam, you sweep your right hand upward, first touching the heart, then the forehead, and finally up and outward, perhaps with a slight nod of the head. At the same time you say, *Salaam alaykum*, meaning "Peace be with you."

Many Inuit people greet by slapping their hands on each other's head or shoulders. Some Polynesians welcome strangers by embracing them and then rubbing their backs. Maori people in New Zealand rub noses, and some East Africans spit at each other's feet. Americans traveling to Tibet should be culturally alert. People there are said to greet one another by sticking out their tongues.

Handshakes Handshakes seem to come in three styles: gentle, firm, and Texan. Britain's Prince Charles, who travels widely and must be something of an expert on international greetings, has complained about the finger-crunching grip of Americans, "especially Texans."

Kisses French people like handshakes, but many of them don't stop there. Close friendships require warmer greetings. Men kiss each other, squeeze each other's shoulders, slap backs, punch kidneys, and pinch cheeks. When men greet women or women greet other women, a kiss on each cheek is expected.

Bows The most polite greeting of all is the bow. In many Asian countries—especially Japan, where style and courtesy are highly valued—a bow from the waist is the preferred way to greet someone. A bow indicates respect and humility, and it often reflects social status. To the Japanese, bowing is indispensable, because it allows them to greet one another without invading each other's personal space.

Who bows first? In Japanese society, rank is very important. In business, for example, a mid-level manager in a large company outranks a department head. Therefore, the person of lower rank (in this case, the department head) bows first and lower. Normally, American travelers are not expected to make a full bow to their Japanese companions, but they might make a slight bow to indicate that they respect Japanese customs.

Even being culturally sensitive, however, won't keep you from awkward situations. Many Japanese people, especially those who travel abroad, have adopted Western ways. As a result, you may find yourself bowing in a Japanese person's direction just as she or he reaches out to shake your hand. When cultures collide, we often meet each other somewhere in the middle.

Touching Customs

We live in a world of extremes: some cultures enjoy lots of body contact; others avoid it completely. One psychologist measured this desire to touch by watching how people behave in busy downtown coffee shops. He found that couples in San Juan, Puerto Rico, touched each other about 180 times per hour, while couples in Paris touched about 110 times per hour. The *comparative* numbers for the United States and northern Europe were dramatically different. Couples in Gainesville, Florida, touched each other just twice an hour, and couples in London never touched at all.

Touching is the language of physical *intimacy*. Because of this, touch can be the most powerful of all the communication channels. Brigitte Gerney was trapped for six hours beneath the wreckage of a collapsed construction crane in New York City. Throughout her ordeal, she held the hand of a rescue worker, who stayed by her side as heavy machinery removed the tons of twisted steel from her crushed legs. A stranger's touch gave her hope and the will to live.

Touch appears to affect the sexes differently. Women sometimes react much more favorably to touch than men. In one study, psychologists asked a group of nurses to lightly touch a patient once or twice shortly before the patient underwent surgery. The touching produced a strongly positive reaction—but only among women. It appeared to lower their blood pressure and anxiety levels both before and after surgery.

For men, however, the touching proved to be very upsetting. Both their blood pressure and their anxiety levels rose. The psychologists suspect that because men are taught to be more *stoic*—that is, to hide their feelings and to ignore their fears—the touching rattled them by reminding them that life is fragile.

How do you feel about touching and being touched? Salespeople *think* they know—research shows that it is harder to say no to someone who touches you when making a request—but not everyone is happy about being touched by a stranger. Think about your own comfort level when you find yourself in a crowd. Are you relaxed and loose, or does physical contact make you feel awkward and tense?

Andersen Ross/Blend Images LLC

In Japan a bow from the waist is the preferred greeting.

Gestures Gone Awry

While a kiss on the cheek or a hug in public is acceptable—and even expected—in Hollywood, such gestures are not acceptable in Bollywood (India's film industry, located in Mumbai). In 2007 actor Richard Gere, star of *Chicago* and *Pretty Woman*, learned this lesson the hard way when he kissed Bollywood actress Shilpa Shetty at an AIDS awareness rally in Jaipar, India. His act sparked protests across the country and landed Gere and Shetty in court for violating "public obscenity" laws. Some followers of the Hindu religion felt Gere's gesture not only damaged Shetty's reputation but insulted Indian culture. The high court, however, dismissed the charges.

In 2006 President George W. Bush made a similar cultural blunder when he squeezed the shoulders of German chancellor Angela Merkel at the Group of 8 Summit in Russia. Merkel appeared shocked by the gesture, and the German media called Bush's act a "love attack." Bush has been known to hug or kiss people in public, but these displays of affection are definite "no-nos" in countries where public touching is unacceptable.

In some situations, we can't help touching each other. In a crowded elevator, for instance, people stand shoulder to shoulder and arm to arm, accepting such close contact without complaint. The rule seems to be "Touch only from shoulder to elbow, but nowhere else." Even though many people regard Japan as a "nontouching" society, its crowded cities force people to be jammed into subways and trains. Edward T. Hall, an anthropologist, says the Japanese handle their uneasiness about being packed into public places by avoiding eye contact and drawing within themselves emotionally, thus "touching without feeling."

Watch My Space

Sometimes we speak of "keeping our distance" from someone we dislike or "getting close" to someone we like. Anthropologists say that we all live inside a "bubble" of **personal space**. The bubble represents our personal territory, and we resent it when someone invades our space.

International businesspeople need to be aware of what kinds of touching are acceptable in different parts of the world.

Sometimes you cannot avoid contact at rush hour because you have no personal space.

Americans tend to prefer standing about 24 to 30 inches from one another. This just happens to be an arm's length away. "When two Americans stand facing one another in any normal social or business situation," says George Renwick, an expert on intercultural communication, "one could stretch out his arm and put his thumb in the other person's ear." Asian people tend to stand farther apart when talking. Latin Americans and Middle Easterners, on the other hand, tend to stand much closer, literally toe to toe. They also tend to like touching their partner's arm or elbow when conversing.

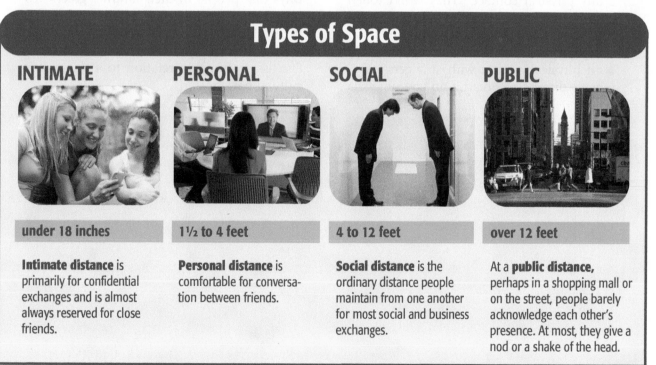

Types of Space

INTIMATE
under 18 inches

Intimate distance is primarily for confidential exchanges and is almost always reserved for close friends.

PERSONAL
1½ to 4 feet

Personal distance is comfortable for conversation between friends.

SOCIAL
4 to 12 feet

Social distance is the ordinary distance people maintain from one another for most social and business exchanges.

PUBLIC
over 12 feet

At a **public distance**, perhaps in a shopping mall or on the street, people barely acknowledge each other's presence. At most, they give a nod or a shake of the head.

SECTION 3 REVIEW

Recalling the Facts

1. Give a few examples of the ways in which greetings differ from one country to another.
2. In what two ways could people interpret the gesture of tapping one's head with the index finger?
3. How does touch affect some men and women differently?
4. In what cultures are people most likely to stand close and touch you while they are talking?
5. What is the difference between public space and private space?

Thinking Critically

1. Touching customs that vary from culture to culture can have unfortunate consequences. In Korea, for example, when merchants make change for a customer, they usually place the money on the counter to avoid any physical contact. "They won't touch my hand," one American customer complained. A Korean merchant explained that in his homeland, people are taught to avoid all physical contact with strangers, especially direct eye contact. Can you suggest a way that Korean merchants could be consistent with their cultural customs but still make foreign customers feel welcome?
2. How important is it to be familiar with the body language customs of other cultures? Do you think it would it be better if all cultures had the same body language? Why or why not?
3. How do you think greetings change when people see each other frequently? Do you greet your parents, whom you see almost every day, the same way that you greet relatives you have not seen for months or years?

Taking Charge

Invite several recent immigrants to class and ask them to discuss the differences they notice in nonverbal communication between the United States and their homelands.

Take a survey among classmates about the ways that people in their families greet each other. How many have relatives who hug them? How many have relatives who kiss them? How many have relatives who bow? Discuss greetings in relation to a classmate's cultural background.

COMMUNICATION *BREAKDOWN*

One Woman's Experiment to Act Like a Man

As mentioned earlier, men and women communicate differently. Deborah Tannen, in her book *You Just Don't Understand: Men and Women in Conversation,* says that the sexes inherently speak in an entirely different manner. This divergent communication translates into body language idiosyncrasies. Journalist Sheila Feeney conducted an experiment a number of years ago to prove this hypothesis. She interviewed experts familiar with the body language differences among men and women and came up with several notable characteristics of the way men use their bodies:

- **Taking up space.** Men are territorial, Feeney found, when they're in group settings. They're more likely to grab the armrest in a car or in a theater, and they simply take up more space in general. In business settings, they tend to act the same way, so women might think about staking out their space at a meeting table or by sweeping their arms out in conversation to mark off territory.

- **Making contact.** Men are more likely than women to touch people in the workplace. Whether it's a pat on the back, a tap on the shoulder or a fist-pump, men make contact more often while women restrict touching to mostly handshakes.

- **Face to face.** When men talk with anyone, research shows they tend to turn to one side. They stand face to face only when they're angry or if they feel the need to be territorial.

- **Staring before talking.** While women look to give approval or seek it out while in public, men more often look directly at the people they're speaking with for longer periods of time. In doing research for her story, Feeney stared at several men on the street to see how they would react. While some of them approached her to talk or smiled, many turned away uncomfortably.

- **Looking away while talking.** Feeney found that men will not make eye contact as often as women when they're engaged in conversation. They'll often look at another object in the room, or at their watch or phone when talking. Women, however, tend to make more contact visually. Feeney said she tried this experiment while in conversation but found it strange to keep looking away all the time.

Question:

What other types of ways do you think men and women use body language? Which types do they use more or less than the opposite sex?

Looking Back

Listed below are the major ideas discussed in this chapter.

- Nonverbal messages are a vital part of face-to-face communication.
- Nonverbal messages frequently overpower verbal messages.
- Although body language is used worldwide, it is not a universal language.
- Some cultures are much more comfortable with touching than others.
- The distance you keep between yourself and others (your "personal space") helps define the kind of communication that is taking place.

- We tend to look for nonverbal messages in other people's faces, but the face is the part of the body that can be most easily controlled and therefore disguised.
- We can learn to spot someone who is lying by studying body language. People who are lying tend to use fewer hand gestures, to touch their faces more often, and to shift position more frequently.
- You should assess your own body language from time to time, especially to see whether it contributes to a professional demeanor.

Speech Vocabulary

Match each vocabulary term on the left with the correct definition on the right.

1. nonverbal message
2. body language
3. gesture
4. tone of voice
5. personal space
6. intimate distance
7. personal distance
8. social distance
9. public distance
10. eye contact

a. all our physical movements
b. the distance for a conversation among friends
c. looking directly at your communication partner
d. any means of communication other than words
e. the distance we keep between ourselves and strangers
f. style or manner of expression
g. the distance for normal business conversations
h. the distance for personal conversations
i. our "personal territory"
j. hand or arm movement

Academic Vocabulary

Use context clues to write the meaning of each vocabulary term. Then use a print or online dictionary to check the accuracy of your definition.

sympathetic
diverse
distal
proximal
timbre

suppress
anthropologist
comparative
intimacy
stoic

To Remember

Answer the following, based on your reading of the chapter.

1. Approximately how many different gestures can human beings produce?
2. The handshake and other forms of greeting go far back in time. What purpose do anthropologists think these gestures originally served?
3. Name two cultures where touching among friends is common and two where it is not.
4. How far apart would two close friends ordinarily stand or sit during a friendly conversation? What about two strangers?
5. What might a tendency to touch his or her face suggest about a speaker?

To Do

1. Challenge your classmates to do short pantomimes of situations. Ask them to nonverbally present an ER room in a hospital, a nursery school, or an amusement park.
2. Try a game of charades with your friends. Act out movie titles or current events to see how well you can communicate without words.
3. Watch a film or video of the great mime Marcel Marceau. What could a mime teach you about using more expressive body language? Try pantomiming the action of throwing a ball. Have the ball change in weight and size. Have it become sticky, muddy, hot, wet, or cold.
4. Bring some home videos to class. After reading the discussion of facial expressions on pages 83–84, watch the available videos, focusing on the facial expressions. When a face is prominently displayed on the screen, stop the video and take turns with your classmates commenting on what you think that particular expression "says." How would you assess your skill at reading expressions? Do some of your classmates seem more skilled than others at interpreting facial expressions?
5. Take turns telling about one of the following, with your hands held behind your back.
   - How to shave
   - How to mix a cake
   - How to serve a tennis ball
   - How to shake a rug
   - How to apply makeup
   - How to pass a football
   - How to use a curling iron

6. When you want to express confidence, you try to look bigger. You stretch yourself up to your full height—head back, chest out, nose up. We call this "walking tall." When you're sad or discouraged, you make yourself look smaller by bending over, tucking your head in, and looking down. Practice trying these different kinds of walks at school. What kinds of reactions does each style elicit?

To Talk About

1. How important is nonverbal communication in everyday life? In school? On the job?
2. How big is your bubble? How much room do you need around yourself to be comfortable? Does that change with different social situations or different people?
3. How do you know when someone is not telling the truth? What clues do you look for? Reread the discussion "How to Tell When Someone Is Lying" on pages 84–85. Which of the different types of body language mentioned do you think are the best indicators that someone might be lying? Do you think reading this information will make you more apt to recognize when someone is lying to you?
4 The Instant Impact on page 80 discusses the distinct way of walking that each individual has. The feature even refers to a person's walk as his or her "second signature." Have you noticed the way that a particular person walks? Do you agree with the idea that everyone has a distinct walk? How would you describe your walk?

To Write About

1. Keep a log of your personal space for one day. Each time you have a conversation, make a note of how close to you the other person stood or sat. Observe how the spatial distance between you and others varies according to the following factors: their status or authority, sex, age, and social or cultural background. Compare your log with those of classmates.

2. Write a description of how to do one of these things:
   • shoot a free throw
   • wash a dog
   Next, write a speech explaining the same process, and plan to use hand gestures and facial expressions to illustrate it. How many words did body language save you? What parts of the explanation became easier?

Related Speech Topics

How to speak body language

You're in my space!

The sure-fire liar detector plan

Read a person like a book

Gestures around the world

Eye contact: Don't forget it!

Smiles: the universal language

Fear, anxiety, and the body

Talking without hands: Can you do it?

Clothes make the man or woman: true or false?

INTERPERSONAL COMMUNICATION

Gossip is the art of saying nothing in a way that leaves practically nothing unsaid.

—Walter Winchell

Learning Objectives

After completing this chapter, you will be able to do the following.

- Understand the value of effective interpersonal communication.
- Understand the importance of assertiveness, courtesy, and tact when dealing with people.
- Implement effective strategies for successful one-to-one communication.
- Use communication to build positive professional and social interpersonal relationships.

Chapter Outline

Following are the main sections in this chapter.

1. Appropriate Tone
2. People Skills

Speech Vocabulary

In this chapter, you will learn the meanings of the speech terms listed below.

interpersonal
  communication
social
  communication
professional
  communication
courtesy
tact
tone
aggressive tone
nonassertive tone
assertive tone
people skills
dialogue

Academic Vocabulary

Expanding your academic vocabulary will help you become a more effective communicator. Listed below are some words appearing in this chapter that you should make part of your vocabulary.

prospective
etiquette
brash
manipulating
criticism
reprimanded

Each year, *Fortune* magazine releases its list of "America's Most Admired Companies." *Fortune* polls more than 13,000 executives to determine what specific factors make a company successful. Two major factors remain constant: (1) successful companies have solid reputations with the public, and (2) they put a high priority on communication. Similarly, if we wish to be admired in our social and professional lives, we need to pay attention to how we associate and communicate with others.

Paying attention to this might be easier said than done. Effective communication takes into consideration the people involved, the nature of the message, and the circumstances. Let's face it: we don't always act and talk the same way with everyone—and we shouldn't. You have words and behaviors that you use when you are with your friends. These words and behaviors might not be suitable, however, if you are talking with your family or if you are with a potential employer. Regardless of the situation, if you don't take the time to *think* before you communicate, your words and actions might lead to serious problems.

Therefore, the purpose of this chapter is to show you the power of **interpersonal communication**, or the art of getting along with and communicating effectively with other people—especially in a one-on-one setting. So, regardless of the situation, let's examine some of the components of an effective communicator when dealing face-to-face with another person.

Introduction

Interpersonal communication is not a concept that is easily handled in one chapter. The authors of this book believe that your ability to deliver different messages to different individuals results from learning a number of skills that are dealt with in various chapters. For example, you must have *confidence* (Chapter 2) if you want to convince your boss that your idea for a new procedure is a good one. In addition, you must exhibit the power of *organization* (Chapter 9) if you want to present your ideas in a logical, systematic order that your friends and classmates can follow. In other words, to be effective at interpersonal communication, you must consider all of the components of a good communicator.

Indeed, getting along with and communicating effectively with another person are complex. However, the big picture of communication would be incomplete if we didn't deal with the specifics of interpersonal communication—particularly when the concept involves certain rules that are *appropriate* in both social and professional situations.

Whether you're playing a game of Monopoly or basketball, you must know the rules. If you don't know what's allowed and what's not, then you have no chance of winning, because you are constantly playing in the dark. **Social communication** is communication in your personal and your community life, while **professional communication** is communication on the job or related to your career. Both types of communication are like board games and sporting contests in one respect: certain rules should be followed. Yes, even though they are often unspoken or unwritten, certain rules or procedures apply if you want to get ahead in your social and professional life. Knowing what to do when is the sign of a person who is smart and who wishes to be in charge of a situation.

Studies indicate that more than 70 percent of our day is spent working and interacting with other people. Thus, remember that appropriate interpersonal

Appropriate and respectful communication will help you get ahead in whatever career you choose.

communication is respectful communication. For example:

- When you speak to a person, make direct eye contact.
- When you meet your *prospective* boss, offer a firm handshake.
- When you bring a friend into your house, introduce her or him to your family.
- When the teacher is ready to begin, end your personal conversation.

Benjamin Franklin's advice about communication is as valuable today as it was centuries ago.

The importance of knowing how to act or behave in a given situation is not new. History notes that our country's first president, George Washington, often referred to a book on *etiquette*, or social appropriateness, to help him in politics and in society. Even one of the greatest American statesmen, Benjamin Franklin, wrote in the 1700s, "Use no hurtful deceit. Think innocently and justly; and, if you speak, speak accordingly." Both Washington and Franklin were showing the value of two key words that, regardless of the time period, are crucial for interpersonal communication success: *courtesy* and *tact*. And what was true then is still true today, in the twenty-first century!

The word **courtesy** refers to the way that you treat people. It means "politeness." When you are courteous, you exhibit respectful consideration for others; in addition, you show good manners. The word **tact** is slightly different in that it refers to the way that you deal with people. To be tactful means to be diplomatic. You try to say or do what best fits the occasion.

In this chapter, we will examine the ways that courtesy and tact work together with the "art of appropriateness." Specifically, we will look closely at how tone, people skills, and respecting differences can contribute to your interpersonal communication skills.

CHAPTER 5 Interpersonal Communication   97

Appropriate Tone

When communicating with other people, it is important that you use the correct **tone**, or the mood that you verbally—and non-verbally—create. In addition to the words that you use, your tone is the attitude that you express to others. Do you have an angry tone? Is your tone positive and upbeat?

You may have heard the expressions "It's not what you say but the way that you say it!" or "Don't use that tone of voice with me!" These expressions probably mean that your tone is rude or discourteous.

Courteous, tactful, respectful communicators are aware of what to do and what not to do when creating the correct communication mood. Let's take a look at three different tones you might use.

Communicating respectfully might benefit you more than using an aggressive tone.

An Aggressive Tone

People tend to think that an **aggressive tone** or communication approach is pushy and *brash*. An aggressive person considers only one point of view: his or hers. This method of communication shows little concern for the feelings of others; it is a my-way-or-the-highway attitude, with little or no room for compromise or meaningful discussion. The aggressive approach wants to win at all costs, even if that means intimidating, *manipulating*, or belittling others in the process.

Analysis: This is not an appropriate interpersonal communication tone to set in either a social or a professional setting. Chances are that in the long run you won't get what you're after. Studies have shown that when you use your words to bully or steamroll others, you discourage their creativity and their enthusiasm. Your friends might not be friends for long! And your colleagues will probably turn away from you— or simply turn you off. So don't come on too strong for too long!

A Nonassertive Tone

You could characterize a **nonassertive tone** or communication approach as one that shows a lack of action and energy. A nonassertive person rarely speaks and often appears disinterested or uninvolved to the point that others don't know how to read him or her. This particular tone communicates to everyone, "I lack self-confidence, don't believe that my ideas are any good, or just don't care about what is going on."

Analysis: This interpersonal communication approach can be particularly inappropriate at work. While some of your friends may take the time to get to know the real you, employers and coworkers might interpret your silence and lack of involvement as boredom or low self-esteem. Others might think that you are simply rude. So get involved. Make your voice heard. Speak up and show others that you can vocally and attitudinally be a vibrant part of what is happening.

An Assertive Tone

What you're after is an assertive tone. The middle ground between aggressive and nonassertive, the **assertive tone** or communication approach is direct yet tactful. Assertive communicators know when to talk, when to keep quiet, and how to give their opinions courteously and respectfully. They create an overall mood of harmony, because they always consider these specifics before acting or speaking:

- Location: Is this the right place to talk?
- Timing: Is this the right time to talk?

- Intensity: What can I do to keep calm and not come off as overbearing?
- Relationships: How well do I know the person to whom I'm about to speak? Also, how does each person's role and responsibility affect this situation?

Analysis: You are sure to be a winner if you use an assertive tone when you deal with people. Whether in social or professional situations, the assertive communicator has a warm, friendly voice; uses respectful words; has a calm, relaxed appearance; sends positive nonverbal signals to others; and makes direct yet nonthreatening eye contact.

Using an assertive tone will help you solve problems and avoid shouting matches, because your communication attitude will set the stage for brains and cool heads to prevail. So be assertive. It's the appropriate thing to do!

INSTANT IMPACT

High-Tech Gossip

Gossip has long been a fact of life in offices, but in today's high-tech world, gossip can spread faster and farther than ever before. According to a recent study, 10 percent of office gossip is now spread through e-mail, Internet blogs, and instant messages. Whether spread through old-fashioned chats in a break room or through e-mail or blogs, gossip not only decreases productivity and reduces a gossiper's chances for promotion, it can also have devastating effects.

For example, in Hooksett, New Hampshire, four employees were fired for gossiping about the personal relationships of two employees. In other cases, copies of e-mails and blog entries have been used as evidence in cases of workplace harassment.

To protect your reputation and your job, follow this age-old advice: If you don't have something nice to say, don't say anything at all.

Using the Telephone Effectively

You just read about the importance of using the correct tone when communicating both verbally and nonverbally. In the next section, you will learn the value of people skills. Let's take a look at how these two topics play a role in using the telephone. Perhaps we can dramatize telephone etiquette by eavesdropping on phone conversations. Imagine that a young man is calling to ask about a job he has seen advertised in the newspaper. This is how the conversations might go:

Operator: Hello, this is Poppa Lock Company. How may I help you?

Kevin: Uh, yeah. I'd like to speak to someone in charge.

Operator: In charge of what?

Kevin: Well, I'm kinda looking for a job.

Operator: That would be Ms. Hansen. Just a moment, please. I'll connect you.

Assistant: Hello, this is Renee Jones.

Kevin: I'm trying to reach Ms. Hansen.

Renee: May I ask in reference to what?

Kevin: Yeah, I'm calling about a job. So, could you put her on?

Renee: What job is that, sir?

Kevin: Well, the one where you drive around and help people who are locked out of their cars.

Renee: Do you mean one of our customer assistants?

Kevin: (a little annoyed) I suppose.

Renee: What are your qualifications for this job?

Kevin: I don't know. I never had a job like this before.

Renee: (clears her throat) Have you graduated from high school yet?

Kevin: Not quite, but can I talk to Ms. Hansen now?

Renee: (coldly) Unfortunately, Ms. Hansen is not available, but if you give me your phone number, I'll have her call you if she wants any more information.

Kevin: 424-6223.

Renee: Thank you. (Hangs up)

After Ms. Hansen reads a summary of this conversation, do you suppose she will call Kevin back? It seems unlikely; Kevin probably lost the chance to get the job because of the mistakes he made. For example, Kevin gave the impression that he really didn't care about the job. Expressions such as "So, could you put her on?" indicate a lack of respect and courtesy.

Some of Kevin's other mistakes—those that might have been overlooked, had his attitude been better—were as follows:

- He didn't give his name to Ms. Hansen's assistant or use the word please. His lack of politeness got the conversation off to a bad start.
- He didn't state his purpose for calling until he was asked.
- He didn't mention that he had seen an ad for the job in the newspaper.
- He failed to mention any qualifications.

(continued)

What could Kevin have said and done during these telephone conversations to help him make a good impression? Certainly, he should have patiently and politely repeated his name and reason for calling to each person he spoke with. He should have answered the question about qualifications by mentioning skills and experience that would show that he could do a good job. For example, he might have said, "I had a good attendance record at school. I know how to keep accurate records, and I know how to follow directions."

Kevin should have avoided using slang, such as "yeah"; use your best English in professional situations. He should also have used the name of the person he wanted to speak with: "May I speak with Ms. Hansen?" rather than "So, could you put her on?" Calling a person by name is polite and makes a good impression. He might have asked for information about the job, such as the hours and the type of work.

Finally, he should have found out if he could have an interview. Unfortunately, Ms. Hansen's assistant cut him off long before he could ask. She probably decided that Kevin was not the kind of person the company wanted to hire.

Tips for Success

Here's what the conversations might have been like if Kevin had handled them better:

Assistant: Hello, this is Renee Jones.

Kevin: Hello, Ms. Jones. My name is Kevin Lee. I'm calling in regard to your ad in Sunday's *Omaha World-Herald* for a customer assistant.

Renee: Just one minute; I'll put you through to Ms. Hansen.

Ms. Hansen: This is Jane Hansen.

Kevin: Ms. Hansen, my name is Kevin Lee. I'm calling in regard to your ad in Sunday's *Omaha World-Herald* for a customer assistant.

Ms. Hansen: Fine, Mr. Lee. What are your qualifications for the job?

Kevin: Well, Ms. Hansen, I'm responsible. In fact, I was a stock clerk in a grocery store last summer. I also got good grades in math, and I have a good attendance record.

Ms. Hansen: Did you graduate from high school?

Kevin: Not yet, Ms. Hansen, but I hope to next June. Can you tell me something about the job? What would I be doing?

Ms. Hansen: You would be on call for people who are locked out of their cars. You drive to the location they give you and then, using one of our special devices, help the customers into their car.

Kevin: That sounds like something I could do.

Ms. Hansen: You sound like someone we might be interested in, Kevin. Why don't you come over to my office for an interview tomorrow at 10:00 A.M.?

Kevin: Certainly. Where should I come for the interview?

Ms. Hansen: My office is Suite 105 in the Agoura Hills Building, at 7th and Maple.

Kevin: (reading his notes) That's Suite 105 in the Agoura Hills Building, 7th and Maple, at 10 o'clock tomorrow morning.

Ms. Hansen: That's right.

Kevin: Thank you, Ms. Hansen. I'll be there. Good-bye.

Notice that Kevin made a good impression on the assistant because he was prepared. That is probably why she put him through immediately to Ms. Hansen.

SECTION 1 REVIEW

Recalling the Facts

1. What is the difference between social communication and professional communication?
2. Approximately how much time per day is spent interacting with other people?
3. What is the difference between courtesy and tact?
4. List the three types of tones discussed, and tell which of them is the most desirable for effective social and professional communication.
5. What are three important points to remember when calling to follow up on a job opportunity?

Thinking Critically

Sports journalist John Feinstein delivered a speech in which he stressed that professional athletes had a "social obligation" to stay in school before they turned pro. Feinstein also said that they needed to be effective speakers.

Do you agree? Explain. What tone of voice would you expect an athlete who is an effective speaker to use?

What is the difference between an aggressive tone of voice and an assertive tone of voice? Give examples of each style.

Which of the three tones of voice would you say that you use most often? How does your tone of voice change when you are in or out of school? Home? Work?

Taking Charge

People tend to react to your words by the way that you speak. Say each of the following statements in different tones. After saying each statement, analyze the way you said it for the effect that it might have.

a. I plan to do my homework right after dinner!
b. Does someone else have an idea to share with the group?
c. Would you go to a movie with me?

People Skills

Before you take the time to know language, you should get to know people. What do they like? What upsets them? What makes them comfortable or uncomfortable? You may have heard the expression "That person has people skills." When you have **people skills**, you exhibit the ability to work well with others because you take the trouble to make them feel at ease. People possessing such skills know and then apply certain polite communication procedures that are appropriate just about anywhere.

How would you rate your people skills? If need be, you can improve.

If you have people skills, friends and coworkers like to be around you. You and your words create a friendly, productive environment. When you and others show such interpersonal communication skills, not only are spirits high, but work gets done. Those with people skills know the value and appropriateness of (1) making introductions, (2) participating effectively in conversations, (3) offering and receiving criticism, and (4) giving clear and accurate directions.

Making Introductions

If you want to help make people feel at ease and a part of the group, then make sure that they know each other. Find out people's names. Take the time to introduce each other. For example, if you are with a friend and others join you, social and business appropriateness demands that you know how to introduce people. Here are a few suggestions:

Handshakes are a common introduction.

- Stop what you are doing.
- Be friendly.
- Address everyone by name: "John, Maria—I would like you to meet my coworker Constance."
- State what you are doing: "She and I have been working on the inventory report that is due on Monday."
- Introduce the other people involved: "Constance, this is John, who works in the Production Department; and this is Maria, who works in Advertising."
- Ask a question or make a comment to get others talking: "John, I think that you and Constance are from the same part of the country. Didn't you say that you were from Texas?"
- Work to make everyone feel included in the conversation.

A firm but relaxed grip expresses "the hand of friendship" in American social and professional situations.

If the relationship or meeting is more formal, the terms *Mr.* or *Ms.* might be used. Also, even though people may think that the practice has fallen out of favor, introducing women or elders first is often a sign of appropriateness and respect—and it can help you and your introduction make a lasting impression.

Another way that you can make a positive impression is through a handshake. Usually you shake hands with another person not when you are introducing others, but when you are being introduced. In job interviews, when you are meeting adults, or on more structured occasions (such as banquets, weddings, or graduation ceremonies), it is a good idea to shake hands with the person you are meeting, particularly if it is the first time that you two have met. When making the handshake, keep these ideas in mind:

- First, make friendly eye contact.
- Next, don't be afraid to extend your hand first.
- Finally, offer a firm but relaxed grip on the other person's hand.

Socially and professionally, the "hand of friendship" is appropriate and is seen as a sign of respect.

Participating Effectively in Conversations

Developing your people skills means knowing how to properly participate in a conversation. Conversation, or **dialogue**, is the oral exchange of thoughts and feelings involving two or more people. You may have heard the saying "It takes two to tango." Well, just as it takes two people to dance the tango, it takes two to talk in a conversation. Avoid falling victim to three conversation killers: talking too much, talking too little, or interrupting.

- **Talking too much.** Nobody likes a motormouth or a know-it-all. Dominating a conversation by talking too much (particularly about yourself!) irritates people and makes them feel left out. It focuses all the attention on you. Instead, let other people talk. Find out what they think. How do they feel about certain subjects? What's new and exciting in their lives? You can't build positive relationships if other people feel that the conversation is one-sided. Respect other people's ideas, and give them the time to express those ideas. Use some interpersonal communication sense by sharing the talk time.

- **Talking too little.** By contrast, talking too little in a conversation can end the conversation quickly. Those long dead spots of silence make everyone uncomfortable. Talking too little can cause others to think that they are uninteresting or boring—or, even worse, that you are bored or not interested in what they have to say. Don't give this impression. If you are going to make people skills inroads, then you must actively participate in the conversation. Be congenial, enjoy people, talk! And don't think that you have to talk a lot. Sometimes the person who talks occasionally but talks at the right time (saying the right things) is the one who is admired and remembered.

- **Interrupting.** The quickest way to break up a conversation is to cut people off when they start to speak or to interrupt them while they are speaking. In the social world, it doesn't take people long to size you up and decide what kind of a person you are. Authors Camille Lavington and Stephanie Losee, in the article "You've Only Got Three Seconds," say that at work, it takes your coworkers about three seconds after meeting you to decide how you are going to fit in. So don't interrupt when other people are talking. Allow others to finish their

thoughts. Not only will doing so help the conversation, it will also help your image—which will be that of a person who understands interpersonal appropriateness.

Offering and Receiving Criticism

The word *criticism* means "an evaluation or a judgment." We usually hear this word used in a negative context, in which someone or something is being corrected or *reprimanded*. Appropriate people skills, however, teach that giving or receiving criticism doesn't have to be a negative, miserable experience. There's a right way and a wrong way to do most things, and the way that we offer and receive criticism is no exception.

Offering Criticism. We should view offering criticism as a way of encouraging someone to improve. Earlier, you read about the assertive, the aggressive, and the nonassertive tones, or the communication attitude or mood that you create. When you are talking to a friend about a problem that has come up between you two, the worst thing you can do is to start condemning the other person. At work, don't criticize a fellow worker to the extent that you break off a relationship. Use an assertive tone, not an aggressive one. Also, don't criticize someone by using the silent treatment. It just causes friction.

Instead, convey a constructive interpersonal communication attitude. Don't hurt people's feelings or make them feel silly. Make people feel as if they belong. Giving criticism should be viewed as a way of encouraging someone to improve. Therefore, use language that shows tact and politeness. Remember, criticism should work to build up, not tear down, a relationship.

Constructive Language	Destructive Language
"I'd like you to . . .	
. . . show more incentive.	"You're lazy!"
. . . pay greater attention to detail."	"You're so careless and sloppy!"
. . . value punctuality more."	"You're late too often!"
. . . work to improve your skills."	"You make far too many mistakes!"

Don't make the person you are criticizing feel as if you are on an emotional rant or are verbally abusing

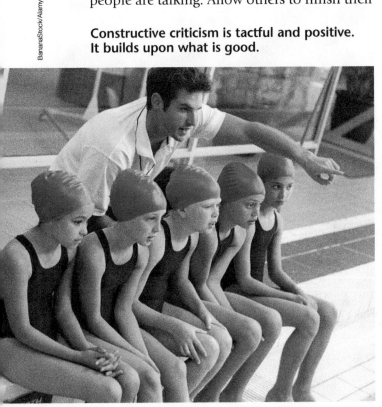

Constructive criticism is tactful and positive. It builds upon what is good.

BananaStock/Alamy

him or her. If you are angry, it might be a good idea to wait to address the problem. Cool off! When you criticize someone, your comments should focus on the quality of the work or the specific behavior—not on the person. Create a communication situation in which everyone can win.

Your language should be friendly, your nonverbal communication congenial, and your overall message informative and instructive. Don't just criticize; offer possible solutions as well. Let the other person know exactly what might be done to correct the problem. Finally, offer good news! You can bet that this positive interpersonal communication approach will be appreciated.

Receiving Criticism. There is also a proper way to respond when receiving criticism. It is often difficult for us to hear that we are doing things wrong or that our work is not up to par. Maybe this difficulty is just part of human nature. But we must remember that sometimes paying close attention to constructive criticism is the way that we learn how to improve, both as friends and workers. Here are some steps to follow:

a. *Maintain your composure.* Don't fly off the handle and become defensive.

b. *Allow others to finish what they have to say.* Let your friend, family member, coworker, or boss say all that he or she wants to say.

c. *Don't interrupt.* Maybe your question or comment will be handled later in the discussion.

d. *Be a good listener.* What you are hearing might be referring to a behavior that really does need to be improved.

e. *Ask questions (courteously).* The answers might help you clear up a point that you were unsure about.

Be a good listener and let others finish what they have to say.

f. *Thank the person for her or his thoughts and observations*, and ask for a follow-up meeting to see if any changes have been noted.

Communication consultants Peter and Susan Glaser believe that the best interpersonal communication occurs when simple language is honestly presented face-to-face. Whether you are giving or receiving criticism, remember that you are intent on *solving* problems, not creating them. Show others that you have both verbal and nonverbal people sense and handle criticism both respectfully and appropriately.

Giving Clear and Accurate Directions

Have you ever been told the wrong directions to someone's house? Have you ever received an assignment or a task to do at home, in school, or at work—but not received all the information? If so, then you know the confusion and irritation that poorly given directions can cause. When directions are unclear, then the people involved are frequently themselves unclear on how to complete a task or get from point A to point B effectively.

But how do you give directions? If you are working with a group of your friends on a class project, does everyone know who is responsible for what at what time? If having people skills means that you work well with others, are a real team player, and promote group harmony, then you realize the importance of giving clear and accurate directions. When the directions are clear, people feel more organized and confident. Why? Because they know where they are going and what is expected of them.

But what is the appropriate way to give directions? Socially and professionally, remember the four ABCs when it comes to pointing people in the right direction:

- *Always Be* Clear.
- *Always Be* Complete.
- *Always Be* Concise.
- *Always Be* Considerate.

Always Be Clear. Use words that leave no room for interpretation or possible confusion. If you are giving someone directions to a location and you say to turn south at the stoplight, you might want to follow up that direction with the word *left*. If you tell someone to read "pages 1 to 4" in the Worker's Manual, do you mean pages 1, 2, 3, *and* 4 or the pages up to but not including 4? Be clear. And to ensure clarity, present your ideas in a logical, well-organized manner.

- Think before you speak.
- Go slowly.
- List your directions in sequential order.
- Use transition words (such as *first of all, next,* and *finally*).
- Stress key words, such as action verbs (such as *turn, copy,* or *print*) and concrete nouns (such as *red light, computer, folder,* or *time sheet*).
- Eliminate unnecessary words and steps.
- Watch for nonverbal signs of confusion.
- Ask for the directions to be repeated back to you when you've finished.

Always Be Complete. Be thorough. Don't stop short with your words and leave out important information. Give the whole story so that your audience isn't guessing. Don't assume that people can fill in the blanks or that they know what you are saying. To ensure that you have been complete, when you are finished giving your directions, restate your point and summarize important information.

Always Be Concise. Shakespeare said, "Brevity is the soul of wit." So be brief with your directions. Get to the point. Use your words convincingly and conversationally, but use them sparingly. Your directions can be better followed if you don't surround them with unnecessary words and irrelevant ideas.

Always Be Considerate. If directions are to be given clearly and totally understood, then they must be given in the proper environment. Consider, for example, the appropriateness of the following:

- Location: Ask yourself, "Is this area too noisy for these directions to be heard?"
- Timing: Think, "Is this the right time to give these directions? It's just about noon; I guess I'll wait until after lunch instead."
- Tone: Think, "I can't be aggressive in the way that I give these directions. I had better relax so that I don't set everyone on edge."

Before you ask someone a question, make a request, or give directions, ask yourself these three questions: "Is this the appropriate place to talk?" "Is this the appropriate time to talk?" and "Is this the appropriate way to talk?" Answering yes to these questions before you speak can help you avoid interpersonal communication breakdowns and show others that your people skills are hard at work.

Building Relationships

At the 1998 Group of 7 Summit, which was held in Denver, the heads of the world's seven leading industrialized nations plus Russia had a very full agenda. The Colorado State International Business Protocol Office issued guidebooks to representatives from all the countries involved, so that no international incident would get in the way of business. Of course, there is no way to predict how every person might react in certain situations. Nevertheless, the guidebooks included the following advice:

- Do not mimic Italians' hand gestures.
- Arrive on time for meetings with Germans.
- Keep your suit jacket on when dining with French associates.
- Be reserved about touching or demonstrating other displays of affection with the British.
- Try to bow at a fifteen-degree angle when meeting Japanese delegates.
- Make eye contact when you shake hands with Americans.

If this man follows the ABC's of giving directions, this mother and her son should be able to find their way.

- Do not shake hands or exchange greetings with the Russians in doorways, as they believe that it may bring bad luck.

The organizers knew that the countries involved had different customs and ways of doing things. These different customs had to be treated with both dignity and respect if the summit was to be successful.

Is the international community really that much different from your own? Knowing the appropriate rules of communication—specifically, interpersonal communication—when dealing with a diverse group of people not only makes you more appealing, it also allows you to be a more effective communicator with all types of audiences.

More than 200 years ago, the writer J. Hector St. John de Crèvecoeur called America the great "melting pot"—a divine mixture of nationalities, customs, and traditions. Today, in a world that is so interconnected, where communications media such as the Internet can transport us to another continent in a matter of seconds, doesn't it make sense that we all should work hard to understand each other and get along?

Realistic Reflections

Hurricane Katrina: Is Anybody Out There?

After the terrorist attacks on September 11, 2001, Congress approved nearly $1 billion for the creation of a communications system that would keep government agencies and emergency workers connected during emergencies. But when Hurricane Katrina struck the Gulf Coast in 2005, Louisiana Senator Robert Barham learned that "we're no better off than we were then."

Katrina was one of the costliest and most destructive hurricanes to hit the United States. The heavy winds and rainfall destroyed hundreds of thousands of homes and buildings in the southeastern states. More than a million people were evacuated, and hundreds of thousands were left unemployed and homeless.

When the levees protecting New Orleans broke and the city began flooding, radio towers were severely damaged, making communication between the police and fire departments nearly impossible. Though some radio towers could have been repaired, technicians weren't allowed to enter the city for three days. Why? State troopers who were surrounding the city to keep people out of the flooded areas weren't able to communicate with other officials, so they didn't know that they should allow the technicians in to repair the towers.

Cell phone and regular phone service were also lost, so the first people on the scene couldn't share important information. The national guard finally had to resort to communicating through messengers. An Internet phone link to allow communication between government agencies was pieced together, but not quickly enough. Federal officials claim they had no idea how dire the situation really was, so help didn't arrive for days.

According to Louisiana Senator Mary Landrieu, the hurricane exposed a "totally failed communication system." Though the Department of Homeland Security has given states millions of dollars to create emergency communication systems, it has not told states what to buy. It has only told states that the systems should be able to communicate with other agencies' systems. When creating public safety communication systems, time is another consideration. According to Adrienne Dimopoulos, a spokeswoman for Motorola, "It takes a long time to design them; it takes a long time to implement them. They're costly."

Yet even with the best equipment, communication breakdowns can't be avoided entirely. Human errors and poor interpersonal skills can be just as costly and devastating. If people aren't on the same page, mistakes will happen. Agencies need to train their staff to know how to use the equipment and how to communicate so messages are understood by everyone.

Question

Miscommunication can occur at any level of government—local, state, or federal. Cite a recent instance of government miscommunication that resulted in the misspending of tax dollars or in public embarrassment for the officials involved.

SECTION 2 REVIEW

Recalling the Facts

1. Behaviors that contribute to getting along with others and communicating appropriately include (1) making _____ , (2) participating effectively in _____, (3) offering and receiving _____, and (4) giving clear and accurate _____.
2. What are three conversation killers?
3. List the four ABCs for giving directions.

Thinking Critically

Willis Johnson is the president of Classic Cinemas, based in Downers Grove, Illinois. Johnson has 13 theaters with 41 screens. He says, "Everyone is entitled to enjoyment of a film without distraction." He adds that even though people can sit at home and talk to their TV sets, it's not appropriate to sit in a theater and "talk to the screen or to each other." Do you agree? What are some other places, events, or occasions in which talking might be considered inappropriate? When is it OK to talk at a public gathering? Give some examples.

Taking Charge

Giving clear and accurate directions takes time and thought. For example, how do you explain to someone how to use a copy machine? How do you fix a copy machine that is jammed? You must explain the process in the correct order and use clear language. Select one of the following and clearly explain the process. Be prepared to speak in small groups or before the class.

   a. yesterday's homework assignment
   b. your school's attendance rules
   c. your school's substance abuse policy
   d. a favorite recipe
   e. changing a tire
   f. a favorite game (chess, Monopoly, or hockey, for example)

If you have another process idea, check with your teacher for approval.

Looking Back

Listed below are the major ideas discussed in this chapter.

- Effective interpersonal communication skills are important, particularly in social and professional settings.
- Smart interpersonal communicators always choose what is appropriate for the occasion and the audience.
- The communication tone that you use will telegraph to others your mood or attitude; avoid being aggressive or nonassertive, but practice your assertiveness.

- Whether you are at work or out in public, it is important to use courtesy and tact. Your verbal and nonverbal communication should be polite and exhibit people diplomacy.
- People skills—such as introducing a friend, shaking hands, making a request, or asking a question—are appropriate means of communication.
- Positive communication can help you not only get along, but also get ahead.

Speech Vocabulary

Match the speech vocabulary term on the left with the correct definition on the right.

1. interpersonal communication
2. social communication
3. professional communication
4. courtesy
5. dialogue

a. conversation
b. politeness
c. language spoken at work
d. communicating constructively with others
e. language spoken with your friends

1. tact
2. tone
3. aggressive tone
4. nonassertive tone
5. assertive tone
6. people skills

a. apathetic, uninvolved mood or attitude
b. being diplomatic
c. pushy or bossy mood or attitude
d. mood or attitude
e. confident yet respectful mood or attitude
f. ability to use words to create a warm, productive environment, so that others like to be around you

Academic Vocabulary

Create a multiple-choice definition question with three options (a, b, and c) for each vocabulary term. Example: *Intensify* means (a) to weaken, (b) to strengthen, or (c) to enlarge.

1. prospective
2. etiquette
3. brash

4. manipulating
5. criticism
6. reprimanded

To Remember

Answer the following based on your reading of the chapter.

1. According to *Fortune* magazine, what two factors determine a company's success?
2. What is the difference between an aggressive tone and an assertive tone?
3. What does it mean to say that a person has people skills?
4. What three things should you keep in mind when you shake hands with another person?
5. When should the terms *Mr.* or *Ms.* be used when making introductions?

6. What are three errors that a person might make when participating in a conversation?
7. What does the word *criticism* mean?
8. What are the four ABCs for giving clear and accurate directions?
9. What kind of information was included in the guidebooks issued at the 1998 Group of 7 Meeting?
10. What is meant by the term *melting pot*?

To Do

1. Find out the number of students or the percentage of different nationalities in your school. How many females are there, and how many males? What is the age range? Break down your findings by class and grade level. Talk to your guidance counselors or to your administrators. Your classroom teacher might be able to assist. Give your findings orally to the class or to a small group.
2. Talk to a business professional about appropriate dress. Ask questions about how particular outfits might be appropriate or inappropriate, depending on the job or the situation. Also find out the following: If you are hired as a high school graduate, what do different professions expect you to know regarding language, behavior, and interpersonal communication skills? Write the responses.

3. Ask a businessperson about the importance of the specific people skills listed in this chapter. Can he or she add any others? Be prepared to report your findings to the class.
4. Work with a group to role-play assertiveness in the following situations:
   - Someone cuts in front of the lunch line.
   - Someone walks into the room and changes the TV channel while you're watching something.
   - A friend who has stayed overnight has pulled almost all of your CDs out of their cases and is about to leave without putting any of them back.

   After role-playing assertiveness in each situation above, discuss the advantages of assertive behavior versus aggressive or nonassertive behavior.

To Talk About

1. We often live in a world of in-your-face interpersonal communication, where being big, bold, and brash seems to be effective. While this approach might work in championship wrestling or on talk shows, this approach does not necessarily work in business. Why not? How can an in-your-face approach prove to be a negative communication tool in your social

dealings as well? How does the entertainment business often differ from the "real world" when it comes to effective communication and convincing or motivating people?

2. Almost everyone would agree that casual talk is the language of the streets. How could this language be inappropriate in certain jobs or professions? Give examples. On what kinds of social occasions would casual talk be appropriate? Which kinds might call for more formal language? List the kinds of occasions and explain how our language might differ depending on where we are and who is in the audience.

3. Work with a group to define *assertive, passive,* and *aggressive communication.* Now come up with examples of the difference between assertive and aggressive communication. Consider the following situations and discuss how an aggressive person, and then an assertive person, would communicate.

- A coworker is not doing his or her fair share of the work.
- A classmate is disrupting class, making it hard for others to concentrate.
- A brother or sister is spending too much time listening to your music in your room.

To Write About

1. Students often argue that education makes no difference when it comes to earning an income. However, a report published by the U.S. Census Bureau said that, on average, college graduates could expect to make $2.1 million over their lifetimes. The average high school graduate who does not attend college can expect to make about $1.2 million over his or her lifetime. What does this say to you about staying in school and trying to improve on your education? How can school help

your abilities to communicate with others effectively? Write your answers.

2. Technical training is often as valuable as a college degree. What are some technical professions or skilled trades that are highly valued in the U.S. market? What type of schooling do you need? Where can you get it? What is the cost? What are the opportunities? Why are strong interpersonal communication skills important in these trades? Do some research and then write your findings.

Related Speech Topics

This chapter has shown that the best speaking occurs when we demonstrate tact, courtesy, and respect. With that in mind, examine these possible speaking topics.

Illegal immigrants contribute significantly to the U.S. economy.

Age should not matter when it comes to hiring or firing.

Having bilingual skills can be an advantage in many professions.

Sexual and emotional harassment can be stopped if different groups get tough and make a stand.

Friends play a greater role in the language that you use than do your parents or other adults.

Regardless of the organization, teamwork is critical for success.

We are often a nation that lacks self-discipline, particularly when it comes to school, work, and personal relationships.

INTERVIEWING

An interview is frequently the course you chart between what you came in knowing and what you're finding out as it's happening.

—Terry Gross, host of Fresh Air, National Public Radio

Learning Objectives

After completing this chapter, you will be able to do the following.

- Use interviews to gather material for your speeches.
- Schedule an interview at a time and place that will increase its chances for success.
- Create open-ended questions to draw out the best possible answers.
- Dress appropriately and present yourself in a professional manner.

Chapter Outline

Following are the main sections in this chapter.

1. Using Interviews to Gather Information
2. Preparing for an Interview
3. Conducting an Ethical Interview
4. Interviewing for a Job or Scholarship

Speech Vocabulary

In this chapter, you will learn the meanings of the speech terms listed below.

interviewer	leading question
subject	portfolio
rapport	puff ball
verbatim	pause
open-ended question	bridge
follow-up question	sparkler
yes-no question	sound bite

Academic Vocabulary

Expanding your academic vocabulary will help you become a more effective communicator. Listed below are some words appearing in this chapter that you should make part of your vocabulary.

pollster	chauffeur
proxy	embalm
vicariously	unobtrusive
grovel	canned

Looking Ahead

Interviewing plays a vital role in how we communicate with each other. In this chapter, you will learn to use interviews to gather firsthand information. This information will add credibility and authenticity to your speeches. It can also provide the "punch," or the personal anecdote that makes your speech memorable.

As you study this chapter, you will learn that interviewing others is a challenging but rewarding exercise. Careful preparation and sound strategy will help you get the most out of every interview. Sometimes it will be your turn to be interviewed. This chapter will show you how to prepare for an interview and how to maximize your chances of success. The chapter will also give you tips for answering tough questions and for handling yourself courteously after an interview.

Introduction

Interviews are among the best ways to find out something new. Most of the informative reports and speeches you give in school are based either on library research or on firsthand interviews. Talking with an expert can often be more helpful than reading an article or a book, and it's almost certain to be more fun. You can spice up any speech with a few well-chosen quotations and stories from a lively interview.

An interview is a conversation controlled but not dominated by one person who asks questions of another person. In other words, an interview is a conversation with a special purpose. That purpose might be to learn what someone thinks or to gather information about a new idea or discovery. It might also be to find out more about someone who has applied for a job or admission to college.

You can learn about something you've always been interested in by interviewing an expert in the field.

Using Interviews to Gather Information

Interview comes from the French word *entrevoir*, which means "to see one another." Interviewing, you might say, is a contact sport—eye contact, that is. A good interview grows out of a personal relationship between people. Don't think of it as Ping-Pong; think of it as a handshake.

Learning good interviewing skills is one of the smartest investments you can make in your future. People in many different careers conduct interviews. A book editor interviews prospective authors; an insurance agent interviews clients about their homes, cars, or other possessions; a teacher interviews students about their academic problems. A financial adviser, a lawyer, and an architect—all these professionals use interviews in their jobs.

We focus this chapter on how to be an **interviewer** (the person who asks the questions), because you will frequently use interviews to gather material for your speeches. We believe that if you can learn how to conduct a good interview, you will also have a better chance of being a good **subject** (the person who answers the questions). When your turn comes to be interviewed—for a job, for instance—you will be better prepared by being a good interviewer yourself.

Consider Your Audience

The number of interviews that take place is staggering. Opinion *pollsters* alone conduct an estimated 20 million interviews each year. Add to that figure the enormous number of interviews for jobs and college admissions. We read about interviews every day—when we check the sports page, for example, to see how an Olympic athlete felt about winning a gold medal—and we watch countless interviews on television. In fact, your ideas about interviewing may have been formed by watching television news shows like *60 Minutes, 20/20,* and *48 Hours Mystery*.

A professional interviewer has one specific purpose: to act as a *proxy* for the audience. We can't all sit down for a chat with Brad Pitt, for instance, or Beyoncé, but we are grateful that someone else can do it for us. Thus, we depend heavily on interviewers to act as our stand-ins.

Interviewers head into locker rooms for postgame reports, climb on board *Air Force One* to interview the president, and travel with troops heading into battle. Talk shows like those hosted by Oprah Winfrey and Larry King give audiences the chance to ask questions of celebrities and guest experts. We listen in on these shows, hoping that the interviewer asks the questions we'd like to ask, so that we can *vicariously* take part in the interview ourselves.

Your task as an interviewer, then, is to keep the interests of your potential audience in mind. Who will ultimately hear the information you are gathering? The teacher? Your classmates? The general public? Try to ask your subject what those people would like to know. The ability to anticipate what

A good interviewer will travel to many different places to ask questions of many different people.

an audience wants to know is part of what has made Barbara Walters one of television's most celebrated interviewer. It's an ability that gives Lesley Stahl and the rest of the *60 Minutes* crew the courage to leap over barriers and smash down doors in pursuit of a good story.

Be Curious

The quality you need most to become a good interviewer is curiosity. Do you want to know about people's thoughts, words, and deeds? The best interviewers bring a passionate curiosity to the job. They have a burning desire to know. They get the answers people want to hear about fascinating characters and about those caught up in interesting events. Great interviewers are brave enough to ask the natural questions, even at the risk of making themselves seem foolish.

While you may be more eager to interview a star basketball player or a world-class model than to interview your algebra teacher, you must always make an effort to generate some curiosity about whomever you choose to interview. Everyone has an interesting story to tell, and you can find it if you ask the right questions. Who would suspect, for instance, that your physical education teacher once shot baskets with Shaquille O'Neal or that your math teacher was in a movie as a child?

American television journalist and talk-show host Katie Couric typifies the passion and curiosity that are qualities of all successful interviewers.

INSTANT IMPACT

"I Won the Jackpot, You Know"

It was a beautiful day in Beverly Hills, but then things went sour. Retired Air Force colonel Barney Oldfield was listening to his favorite radio show when he became annoyed with the phrase *you know.*

Oldfield decided to keep track of the *you knows* for his own amusement. He was stunned when the total reached 117 during the 60-minute broadcast.

"It was an oral abomination," said the 1933 University of Nebraska journalism graduate, who now lives in California.

Oldfield created an annual "You Know" contest, and a recent winner was high school senior Jessica Reinsch, who uttered the phrase *you know* 61 times during a 15-minute radio interview.

"I had been conscious of it, but it didn't ever connect that it was that annoying," she said. "Now I hear it all the time. I catch myself now."

As you prepare for an interview, take special note of the "quickie" words that we all tend to use in everyday speech. Words like "gonna," "yeah," "y'know," "like," and "kinda" are job killers. They can make you sound uneducated and coarse, and possibly cost you a job offer.

A lack of curiosity, on the other hand, leads to lazy thinking. If you're not genuinely interested in what your subject has to say, you may find yourself behaving in the following ways:

- I make up a list of questions and go through them from beginning to end—no matter what the person I'm interviewing wants to talk about.
- I don't listen much to each answer. I just worry about the next question.

- If an answer confuses me or the subject mentions something I haven't heard about, I don't like to admit it. I just go on to the next question.
- I'm so edgy about what the subject thinks of me that I can never get comfortable. All my energy in the interview goes into playing the role.

Having a great interest in the person you're interviewing helps you overcome self-consciousness. It also drives nervousness away and gives you the courage to interview someone you respect or admire.

Keep in mind that most people like to talk about themselves, their work, and their opinions. The slightest hint that you're interested is often all the invitation they need to start talking. Curiosity might make you seem naive at times, but a true desire to know is the only proven way to bring an interview to life. If you have the right attitude, you may hear yourself making these enthusiastic comments during an interview:

- "That's fascinating. Tell me more."
- "I had no idea—whatever made them do that?"
- "How did you feel when that happened?"

SECTION ① REVIEW

Recalling the Facts

1. Curiosity may have killed the cat, but it will help you be a good interviewer. What role does curiosity play in an interview?
2. Provide three short comments you could make during an interview that would encourage your subject to continue talking.

Thinking Critically

Watch an interview program such as *Larry King Now* or *Nightline*. What research do you think was involved in preparing the questions? How did the interviewer react to vague or unsatisfactory answers? Did the interviewer offer any personal information, or "open up," to encourage a subject to talk?

Taking Charge

1. Conduct a "kid in the hall" poll. Think of an interesting, timely question that can be answered quickly (yes or no, agree or disagree). The question could relate to school policies or community issues. A possible question is "Should we limit all elected officials to two terms?" Ask the question of 20 people in your school. Record their responses and report your findings to the class. You might even offer your information to the school newspaper as a "roving reporter."
2. Conduct an opinion survey. Work in a small group to develop a questionnaire on some subject of interest. Write or type a list of eight to ten questions on a single sheet of paper and reproduce enough so that you can hand out 100 copies. Ask if you can pass out the survey in some of your other classes or at lunch. Collect the surveys, tabulate the results, and report the outcome.

Preparing for an Interview

"Bend and *grovel* if you must," suggests John Brady, founder of a communications consulting firm, "but get the interview. This may turn you into a wimplike creature, but do it. You ain't got nothing 'til you've got that person sitting down to give you a couple of hours of his or her time."

Brady overstates the case, but his point is clear: Without a person to talk to, you have no interview. Carefully choosing a person to interview and arranging a time and place suitable for the interview are problems you must solve before you can ask the first question.

Getting an Interview

John Brady is not above taking his own advice. To get an interview with the author Jessica Mitford, he once volunteered to be a *chauffeur*. Mitford was

Interviewing a person can result in learning things that you won't find in any book or on any Web site.

visiting a college near Brady's home, but her schedule was packed. College officials had arranged for a student to drive Mitford from campus to the airport when her visit was over, a distance of about 75 miles. Brady persuaded the student to let him drive Mitford instead. The student didn't mind ("I really don't know what to talk with her about," he said), so Brady picked Mitford up, turned on his tape recorder, and got a terrific interview.

Interview situations aren't usually that difficult, of course. You will probably find that most of the people you want to talk with are agreeable and cooperative. At times, however, it may take some persistence on your part to get them to agree to speak. And then there are those who are just too busy or stubborn. Let them alone and find someone more willing to talk.

Select a Subject Carefully No matter how skillful you are, an interview won't work if you haven't chosen the right person. Suppose you decide to do a speech on dreams. You discover a sleep research lab in town by thumbing through the yellow pages of the phone directory. A few calls later, you have scheduled an interview with the lab's director to discuss the current state of research on dreams. By interviewing that expert, you are sure to learn more and gain better information than you would have by asking a few friends about their dreams.

By the way, it's probably easier than you think to interview public officials. They know speaking about their jobs is one of their most important responsibilities. (Most politicians like the attention, too.) Public officials also have access to up-to-date information, and though you may get put on hold, you generally won't be turned down.

Realistic Reflections

Before you call Mandy Moore for a soul-searching interview, however, you should realize that a casual fan doesn't have much pull in Hollywood. Large organizations with enormous numbers of readers, such as *USA Today*, can get interviews where you cannot. But don't be discouraged; even a high school paper carries some weight. If you are having trouble setting up an interview, volunteer to write a story about your subject for the school paper. The added prestige (and exposure) may persuade your subject to grant you an interview after all.

Choose When and Where The best setting for an interview is a place where you won't be disturbed. You want to have your subject's undivided attention. Many people like to be interviewed where they work—in their offices, for example. That may be convenient for them, but it can create problems for you. The telephone is sure to ring, and coworkers will stop by to chat. Any interruptions during the interview will distract your subject, break the **rapport**—the feeling of trust and cooperation—you have developed with the subject, and stretch out the time the whole interview takes. Getting your subject off somewhere private can do your interview a world of good.

Be sure, too, that you don't cheat yourself on the amount of time you request. Beginners often worry that they will take too much of the subject's time. Consequently, they ask for too little and quit too early. Ask for an hour of your subject's time. You can probably get a good interview in less time than that, but you run the risk of not getting the information you need if you ask for less.

You can always leave an interview early, but it's rude to take more time than you requested. By asking for an hour, you also tell your subject that you have plenty of questions and that you feel he or she has worthwhile answers. If your subject is so busy that only a few moments can be spared, consider interviewing someone else.

Doing Your Homework

Having arranged an interview, you next need to learn all you can about your subject. "You should read every single thing that you can possibly get on

A quiet location where you have your subject's undivided attention is the best place to conduct an interview.

the person you're about to interview," advises long-time talk-show host Phil Donahue. "It keeps you out of trapdoors and keeps you from looking foolish."

The preparation you do for an interview helps you create good questions. If you wanted to interview a new teacher at your school, for example, you could find out beforehand where the teacher previously taught, the teacher's area of expertise, and where he or she went to college. Once you have the basic biographical facts, you will be free to concentrate on more imaginative questions—the kind that produce the most interesting answers.

Make a distinction between a simple question and a foolish one. You can ask the principal about open campus policies in a sensible way, but if you ask how long the lunch period is, you are asking the principal to do your legwork for you; that's a question you can answer for yourself. Nothing will irritate a subject more—especially one who has been interviewed many times—than being asked a question whose answer you could easily have found in many other ways. Asking a subject such questions shows you haven't done your homework. It wastes that person's time and undermines his or her opinion of you.

Dress for Success Students often wonder what they should wear to an interview. Even though you may prefer to dress casually, you should wear whatever you think will bring the best response from the person you are interviewing. Good school clothes (avoid T-shirts and the latest fashion statement) should work well, but an interview with the governor or some other VIP (very important person) is going to require more-formal clothing. Your credibility is at stake.

If the governor is used to people who wear suits, you must wear an outfit that he or she will take seriously. You don't have to overdo it, of course—especially if you're going to conduct your interview while leaning on a tractor tire—but you want your subjects to know that you're serious and that their comments will be treated with respect.

Take What You Need Be sure you take the right equipment with you to an interview. You should always have a small notebook and pen, even if you plan to use a voice recorder or camcorder. The notebook shows your subject that you mean business, and it encourages talking.

Many interviewers use a voice recorder to help them remember an interview. For one thing, using such a device is the only way to be absolutely accurate. With a recorder, you can always be sure of getting information **verbatim** (word-for-word). For another, no matter how good you are at taking notes, you may miss something important. With a recording, you can go back and find what you left out of your notes. In many situations, a portable voice recorder is well worth the bother, especially if the interview is likely to be unusually long.

Given all that a voice recorder can do, you might be surprised to learn that some professional interviewers prefer not to use one. Some interviewers say they carry only a pen and notepad because a voice recorder can make a subject ill at ease. Recordings don't protect you against mistakes, either. "You misquoted me," a subject might say. "I know that was what I said, but it wasn't what I meant."

Collect as much background information about your subject as you can before your interview. Newspapers, libraries, and the Internet are useful resources.

Image Source/Getty Images

Asking Effective Questions

Once you've contacted a subject, arranged a time and place to talk, and done your background research, you're ready for the last step before the interview itself: preparing a list of questions. Your goal is to guide the conversation where you want it to go. You want your subject to relax and to talk freely, but you also have an agenda with questions that need answering. The way you phrase these questions and the order in which you present them will determine, to a great degree, the success of your interview.

It is absolutely critical to prepare a list of questions in advance. Doing so will force you to think through the entire interview and plan the best order for your questions. Ideally, the answer to one question will lead naturally into the next question. "You start a question, and it's like rolling a stone," said the writer Robert Louis Stevenson. "You sit quietly on the top of a hill; and away the stone goes, starting others." Preparing questions ahead of time is also the best way to make sure each minute of your interview counts.

Keep Your Questions Brief Make your questions brief and to the point. Avoid those complicated two- or three-part questions you may have seen television reporters use during press conferences: "Mr. President, can you tell us what you know about plans to export more wheat, and where those shipments will be going, and when they'll start?"

You would be wiser to give your subject one manageable question at a time. Keep your questions simple and direct. If the subject has trouble interpreting your question, rephrase it. Suppose you ask this question: "Did the school board drop its laundry program for athletics in the interest of economy, or was it bowing to community pressure?" If this question is too much for your subject, try this: "Why do athletes have to wash their own towels this year?"

Is this style of dress appropriate for an interview?

Use a Variety of Questions Build your most important questions on the famous five Ws and an H (*who, what, why, when, where,* and *how*). Imagine, for instance, that the parents of one of your classmates have opened a new pet cemetery in your town. You want to give a speech on how people handle the death of a pet, and you decide to interview the parents. By using the five Ws and the H, you develop this list of questions:

- WHO brings their pets to your cemetery? Can you tell me about your customers?
- WHAT kinds of burial or funeral arrangements do they request?
- WHY do people spend so much money on their pets?
- WHEN did you first decide to start a pet cemetery?
- WHERE are other pet cemeteries in our region?
- HOW do you *embalm* a pet?
- HOW do you restore the appearance of pets who have been killed in car accidents?

Open-Ended Questions Strive as much as possible to develop open-ended questions. These are similar to the essay questions on a written test. Instead of asking for a narrow response (such as yes or no, or true or false), this type of question allows the subject to decide how best to answer.

Your goal is to use short questions to produce long answers. For example, instead of asking, "Did you really fall into a vat of chocolate?" ask, "What was it like to fall into a vat of chocolate?" In the following interview, notice how the interviewer uses open-ended questions to draw out the interviewee, who is a member of a classic rock band and is still playing at age 70:

Q: **Congratulations on your latest world tour. What's it like to know that you've been at this thing for more than five decades?**

A: Well, thanks; if nothing else it means that not enough people have gotten sick of us. Yet. Really, I think we all have good genes, and there's been nobody willing to hire us to do anything else for 50-plus years. Plus, we're all lucky we were never bumped off.

You can organize an interview and use the time allotted for it efficiently by preparing a list of questions in advance.

INSTANT IMPACT

Say What?

Good questions elicit good answers—and anticipating the answers is half the fun of interviewing. Do you suppose the person who interviewed the following job applicants was surprised by their answers?

- Elvis Presley: "My last boss and I . . . say, are you going to eat those fries?"
- Lady Godiva: "What do you *mean* this isn't business casual?"
- Macbeth: "Would I go after my boss's job? Do I look like the kind of guy who would knock off his boss for a promotion?"
- Julius Caesar: "My first job involved a lot of office politics and back stabbing. I'd like to get away from that."
- Pandora: "I can bring a lot to your company. I like discovering new things, and I've got a *boxful* of ideas."
- Jesse James: "My experience and skills include leadership, extensive travel, event planning, intimate understanding of firearms, and a knowledge of security measures at numerous banks."

Q: **True, true. But in all honesty, your music seems to span the years and appeal to multiple generations. Why do you think that's happened?**

A: It's rock 'n roll's appeal, really. It has a transcendental quality that has the ability to move you. No matter who you are, no matter when you were born. We're just plugged into that beat, and it never gets old, and we have no intention of quitting.

Open-ended questions leave room for the subject to maneuver. While such questions may cause you to lose some control over the interview, what you gain is worth it. You may hear the subject tell you something that takes your breath away.

Be ready to react and think on your feet, but don't lose control over the interview.

Follow-Up Questions Inexperienced interviewers tend to look for safety in long lists of prepared questions. Of course, as noted, you must plan what to ask. But a long "must ask" list can drain the life from an interview, turning it into a tedious trip from Question A to Question Z. Along the way, you can miss a lot of good conversation in your concern to cover everything on your list.

What's the solution? Prepare your list of questions, but stay flexible; be ready to react to the twists and turns of conversation. Listen for intriguing statements, and when you hear one, ask a **follow-up question**. Such questions help you pursue topics that pop up unexpectedly. One of the best questions is simply "Why?" Chase good ideas, even if it means letting some of your prepared questions slide.

To use follow-up questions well, you must think on your feet. Recall for a moment the interview with the classic rocker. By listening attentively, the interviewer could recognize that the artist's last concert won't be his last, a comment that deserved to be explored at length.

Prepare a list of questions, but remain flexible.

Q: Wait, wait here. Are you saying there will be more tours after this one? Isn't this one dubbed the "Say Goodbye Tour?"

A: Sure it is. And what do you think the next one will be called?

Q: "Say Hello?"

A: "Again." "Say Hello Again!" Seriously, we plan these things out long in advance. We've never actually come out and said, none of us in an interview on the radio, TV or print, that this is our last tour. I can't see it, anyway. We're having too much fun to retire."

Q: So I suppose I walked into a real scoop here today, huh?

A: I suppose you have!

Sometimes people tell you things that are so interesting, unusual or meaningful that they deserve your complete attention, regardless of whatever other question you were poised to ask. Follow your instincts. If someone tells you something of exceptional interest or importance, ditch your old questions and follow this new topic for all it's worth.

Questions to Avoid Some kinds of questions work better in an interview than others. **Yes-no questions**, for example, should be avoided. For one thing, they allow your subject to answer the question without telling you anything. They also give the subject an excuse to stop talking.

Suppose that while interviewing Barbara Walters, you said, "Several years ago you caused a sensation

---

Interview Follow-Up

Dear _____:

We appreciate your willingness to be interviewed for a future newspaper story and would like your responses to the following questions. They will help us evaluate our reporters and improve their skills. Feel free to make any comments you feel are appropriate.

1. **Was the interviewer courteous, prepared, and alert?**
2. **Were the questions thoughtful and to the point?**
3. **Did the interviewer double-check the spelling of names, important facts, and significant quotations?**

Please read the attached story and also answer the following questions:

1. **Does the story seem fair and accurate?**
2. **Do you feel you were misquoted or misrepresented?**
3. **Use camera metaphors for how the writer handles the subject. Where does he or she move in close, where fade back? Where is the story sharp or fuzzy?**
4. **Any other comments, pro or con?**

Thank you. Please return this sheet to the journalism room or put it in Mr. Schaffer's mailbox in the office as soon as possible.

You can use a form like this to follow up the interviews you do and to make sure the interviewees feel like they have been represented fairly.

---

by signing a $5 million contract with ABC. Are you worth that much money?" If Walters answers yes, she will only have told you what you already know—that she accepted the contract. If she says no, you'll think she's just being modest. Either way, you won't have learned anything, and you'll have nothing new to tell anybody else.

But what if you asked the question this way: "Ms. Walters, what do you think of the public reaction to your $5 million contract with ABC?" Now Walters will be free to talk about how she has earned respect in a male-dominated profession. She might tell you

Strong interview questions are even more important in situations where many people will be asking questions.

about how she studied camera work and editing or about the thousands of letters she sent and phone calls she made to set up interviews.

If your questions are superficial and limited, the answers will be, too. Reword your yes-no questions into open-ended ones. In most cases, your reworded questions will lead to replies that are more interesting and useful.

You should also avoid **leading questions**, as they influence the answers. For example, instead of asking, "Was the UFO shaped like a saucer or like a cigar?" say, "What was the UFO shaped like?"

Celebrities or public figures who have been interviewed often will be more likely to respond at length to open-ended questions.

SECTION 2 REVIEW

Recalling the Facts

1. What are three things you should do to prepare for an interview?
2. What are two kinds of questions that you should *avoid* during an interview?
3. Describe three kinds of questions that you should try to use during an interview.
4. Why is a digital or tape recorder an important tool for an interviewer?
5. What is a follow-up question?

Thinking Critically

1. Discuss the places in your school where you could conduct an interview. Which are the best? Which are the worst? Try conducting an interview with a classmate in one of the best places, and then move to the worst and continue the interview. Report back to the class on how the different environments affected your interview.
2. Think of a famous person you would like to interview. Write a list of ten questions you would ask that person if you had the chance. (Don't hesitate to do a little research.)

3. Suppose someone was interviewing you. Make a list of questions that you think a good interviewer should ask you. Then make a list of questions you definitely would not want to be asked.

Taking Charge

Rewrite the following yes-no questions to make them open-ended. (Assume your subject is Will Smith.)

- Did you like working in television?
- Is it important that movies and TV shows have characters who can be good role models for young people?
- Will you work in television in the future? Did you enjoy working in the music business before you worked in television?

Take each of the rewritten questions and write a follow-up question based on what you think Will Smith's answers will be.

Make a list of the things you would do to prepare for an interview with the President of the United States.

Conducting an Ethical Interview

The most important thing you can do while conducting an interview may be obvious, but it's still important: Listen well. (See Chapter 3.) Good listening keeps you attentive and encourages your subject to speak. She or he is much more likely to talk openly if it's clear that you are listening carefully. Maintain a polite but professional distance, neither arguing nor agreeing. A nod from time to time encourages the subject but does not necessarily mean that you agree; it just means that you understand.

Try to remember that each time you do an interview, you influence the future. If you treat your subject fairly and honestly, that person is likely to be cooperative the next time someone asks for an interview. On the other hand, if you bungle the job, the subject may swear off interviews forever.

It's not unusual for someone who has had a bad experience to refuse to talk again; several major league baseball players, for example, have taken this position and refuse to talk to reporters. Give your subjects respectful attention no matter what their ideas may be. The people who march to a different drummer often make the best interviews.

A person is more likely to open up if he or she feels comfortable.

Exactostock/Superstock

Getting Off on the Right Foot

When you arrive for the interview, remind your subject of who you are and why you want the interview. You can say, for example, "I'm gathering information for a speech I'm giving to my class." In any case, the subject needs to know how you plan to use the information that he or she will provide.

Beginning an Interview

The first part of your interview should include several routine, get-acquainted questions that the subject will have no difficulty answering. These nonthreatening, factual questions get the conversational ball rolling. They also give you a chance to show some interest and enthusiasm about the person you're interviewing. Don't be a phony, though; find something that genuinely interests you in what the person is saying.

If possible, use each answer as a springboard for the next question. By carefully drawing on what the person has just said, you can lead him or her smoothly toward the next question. For example, "You say you enjoy rock concerts? Which one was your favorite?" Or, "I'm an oldest child, too, and I always liked being the oldest. How do you feel about it?" Questions like these allow you to "warm up" the subject before you get into the heart of the interview.

Take Quick Notes and Look Up Often If you're gathering information for a speech, you will certainly want to take notes during the interview. Taking notes gives you a record of what was said and helps you to be a better listener. Note taking also gives you a convenient and *unobtrusive* way to check off the questions you wanted to ask as you move along.

Most professional interviewers have developed their own brand of speed writing for taking notes. Some note takers omit vowels and word endings; others use abbreviations. You may already have a

Research a person's background, especially a public figure or celebrity like Fran Drescher, to know which topics might be sensitive to ask about.

few of your own shortcuts. Develop a personal system or study a manual on speed writing. But whatever route you take, remember that what matters most in an interview is the ability to listen, think, and write all at the same time.

Although you do need to take notes, don't let yourself get buried in your notebook. Look up from time to time. It will help your subject know that you're still holding up your half of the conversation. Many beginners have tried to write down every answer in longhand and then panicked when they forgot a word or didn't hear an important phrase because they were too busy writing. The more effort you spend on recording the conversation, the less energy you have to keep up with it. Thus, take quick, brief notes and maintain good eye contact.

Handling Sensitive Questions with Care

Some of your questions are bound to hit a nerve. If you sense that the subject is touchy about a topic but you still think you must ask about it, watch for an opening. Wait until your subject happens to mention the topic, and then gracefully follow up. For instance, you might say, "Really. Now who would accuse you of anything like that? Tell me about it."

If the subject doesn't mention the sensitive topic, wait until the end of the interview to ask about it. That way, you and your subject have had an opportunity to establish some trust. Ask your tough question matter-of-factly, in the same tone of voice as your other questions; don't broadcast that the "bomb" is coming, and try not to react when you hear something big. Subjects will probably freeze up if they think they said something that shocked you.

Be Persistent What should you do if your subject doesn't answer your question? This happens occasionally to every interviewer. The fact that someone talks in response to your question does *not* mean that the question has been answered.

The subject may have misunderstood your question. If that seems to be the case, repeat or rephrase the question. Don't be afraid to ask a question twice. Doing so won't make you look dumb or hard of hearing; most people will probably be impressed that you seem to know what you want.

Of course, sometimes subjects will ignore your question and try to answer a different one—one they would prefer answering. Here you need tact, but you also need determination. Ask the question again if you aren't satisfied with the answer. If you sense that the subject is reluctant to talk about that particular question, try being silent for a moment. Many times, an uncomfortable silence tells the subject that you want to hear more.

In fact, silence is one of the best ways to get another person to talk. Be patient if you think your subject is dredging up some long-lost memory. Remembering can take time. Let your subject break the silence. If you are quiet, the subject will probably realize that you are waiting for what you hope will be the rest of the answer.

Concluding the Interview

When you have finished all your questions, give your subject one last chance to talk. Ask, "Is there something else you would like to tell me?" Usually there is. After that exchange, thank the subject and take your leave. Sending your subject a thank-you message a day or two later adds a classy touch to your interview.

Lars A. Niki

COMMUNICATION *BREAKDOWN*

War of Words

On TV talk shows, the hosts, the guests, and the viewers can be in for big surprises—and not the good kind. In fact, things can get downright ugly.

In 2007, *The View* cohosts Rosie O'Donnell and Elisabeth Hasselbeck had a debate over the war in Iraq that turned personal. The fight between O'Donnell and Hasselbeck had begun the week before, when O'Donnell claimed that nearly 660,000 Iraqi civilians had been killed and then asked, "Who are the terrorists?" O'Donnell was later criticized for her comments and was accused of calling U.S. soldiers terrorists. The following week, O'Donnell accused Hasselbeck of being a coward for not defending her. The debate became so heated that the show's producers split the screen and didn't break for commercials. O'Donnell later wrote on her blog, "a split screen, new heights, or lows, depending on who u ask." Though it turned personal, the debate was really over the question of war and of what people can and can't say about it in a public forum—a question many Americans have asked themselves during times of war.

Interviews can also turn sour. Just ask Matt Lauer, host of the *Today* show. During an interview in 2005 with actor Tom Cruise, Cruise criticized actress Brooke Shields for taking antidepressants and then criticized the psychiatric profession for prescribing medication. Cruise claimed he knew the history of psychiatry and that there was no such thing as a chemical imbalance. Lauer continued the interview and commented that he knew many people who had been helped by taking antidepressants. Lauer's comment prompted Cruise to say Lauer advocated using the medication Ritalin. Cruise later apologized to Shields for his negative comments about antidepressants. The two have since become friends.

Questions

1. If you were a producer of *The View*, how would you have reacted to the debate between O'Donnell and Hasselbeck? Why do you think the producers chose to use a split TV screen and not to break for commercials?

2. Where would you draw a line between appropriate and inappropriate questions and discussions for a talk show? If you were Lauer, how would you have responded to Cruise's statements?

Write up your notes as soon as possible after the interview, while the subject's words are still fresh in your mind. Your notes will make much more sense to you then than they will a few hours later. In fact, if you wait several days to read over your notes, you may find that they no longer make sense at all. Don't hesitate to check a fact if you're in doubt. Was the figure she gave you $1 million or $1 billion? A mistake makes both you and your subject look bad.

Conducting Interviews over the Phone

An interview is probably best done face-to-face, but sometimes doing so just isn't possible. An alternative you may wish to consider is interviewing someone over the telephone. A phone interview forces you to really concentrate on what your subject is saying.

Ingram Publishing

Listen to each answer during a phone interview. Based on the responses, ask new questions that aren't on your prepared list of questions.

class. When you check your notes, you may notice ideas you should have pursued and notes that don't make sense. When you do a phone interview, therefore, keep distractions to a minimum.

Conducting an E-mail Interview

Interviews can also be conducted through e-mail. Simply contact your subject and then e-mail a list of questions for him or her to answer. These questions should be the same types of questions you would ask in a face-to-face interview. Since you're e-mailing the questions, make sure you ask the subject to explain or provide details or examples. The subject will type his or her answers to your questions, and e-mail the responses back to you. If you need additional information, ask the subject if you can send some follow-up questions.

You can also conduct an interview through instant messaging. This interview format resembles a phone conversation, because it allows you to exchange ideas in real time.

Keep in mind, though, that it's easy to let your mind wander when you don't have your subject right in front of you. You may find yourself doodling or thinking about an assignment for another

SECTION 3 REVIEW

Recalling the Facts

1. What is the best way to begin an interview?
2. What question should you use to end an interview?

Thinking Critically

Arrange with your teacher to have a public official visit your class for a group interview. Have each member of the class prepare three questions ahead of time. Then, during the visit, notice whether any questions are repeated. Are class members listening well and creating follow-up questions, or are they simply sticking to the questions they have prepared?

Taking Charge

1. Pair off with a classmate and interview one another. Imagine that your classmate is new to the school and you will soon give a short speech introducing him or her to the rest of the class. Prepare a list of at least ten questions and find out something fascinating.
2. Conduct a practice interview in front of the class, and then ask the class to critique your effort. For a twist, ask your subject (perhaps a teacher or an administrator) to be as obstinate or tight-lipped as possible. How can an interviewer deal with a potentially hostile subject?

Interviewing for a Job or Scholarship

Interviews are certainly vital to your future success. Many colleges are relying less on standardized test scores (the ACT and SAT, for instance) as criteria for admission and giving greater emphasis to personal interviews. Consequently, how well you do in an interview can determine whether you are accepted by the college of your choice.

Sooner or later, too, you will interview for a job. How you conduct yourself in interview situations will be a great test of both your speaking and your listening skills. Remember, though, that the employer must satisfy you too.

Submitting Résumés

Before you can get an interview for a job, you will need to submit a résumé, or a summary of your job experiences and accomplishments. Most likely, this is the first communication you will have with an organization. Some organizations may want you to submit your résumé by e-mail. In this case, you should compose a short, formal e-mail that resembles a cover letter. The e-mail should give some information about yourself and your work history and state why you are interested in the job. You can also attach a formal cover letter along with your résumé. In this case, your e-mail will simply tell the recipient that your cover letter and résumé are attached. Spell-check your e-mail and double-check that you have attached your résumé before you send the e-mail.

Some organizations will ask you to send a hard copy of your résumé in the mail. With your résumé, include a cover letter stating who you are, the reason you are sending a résumé, your background and skills, and your interest in the job. Your cover letter and résumé are the first glimpse an interviewer has of you. Work hard to make them the best they can be so you will get an interview.

Instead of sending a résumé, you may need to fill out an online application and upload your résumé to a Web site. There may be space to compose a short cover letter.

Use Communication Skills to Your Advantage

Remember that prospective employers are not out to embarrass you; they only want to gain an accurate impression of you and your abilities. In particular, they want to know how you communicate with other people. Of course they are interested in your qualifications, but they can find that information on your résumé. Do you fit the organization? Employers say they are always looking for certain traits, no matter what the job: confidence, enthusiasm, and dependability. "Your personality and how you conduct yourself during the interview have the greatest impact on your chances of landing the job," says Guyla Armstrong, assistant professor of business at the University of Nebraska at Kearney.

Remember that during an interview, it's important to be an attentive and active listener.

Make sure to call your interviewer if you are running late for an interview.

The advice that follows is intended to give you an idea of what to expect during an interview. Some people believe that just being themselves is enough, but you may well find yourself in a highly competitive selection process. You need to know how to effectively communicate your skills and experience, as well as how to portray your personality as one that will fit the organization.

INSTANT IMPACT

Are You Missing an Earring?

Susan Bixler, author of *The Professional Image*, recommends that job candidates conduct a 30-second check in front of a mirror prior to any interview. The check provides the reassurance needed to concentrate on people and matters at hand. To perform the check, start at the top of your body and work down. Check your hair, teeth, makeup, and earrings. Straighten your tie; check for stains or unbuttoned buttons. Then check your belt, zipper, socks or stockings, and shoes.

Be Alert and Energetic During the interview, try to show energy and enthusiasm. Sit on the edge of your chair and lean slightly forward. When you make gestures (and it's helpful to do so if they come naturally), get your hands about chest high. Using gestures burns off tension and looks good; it makes you seem animated.

Keep eye contact with your interviewer. Don't become so wrapped up in answering questions that you forget to connect with the interviewer on a personal level.

Pay Attention Pay attention to the interviewer's name, and use the name occasionally in your answers. Doing so helps the interviewer know that you notice people and remember their names. As much as possible, turn the conversation toward things you know. However, remember to be an active listener and show respect for the interviewer.

Professional interview adviser Susan Bixler recommends that if the interviewer doesn't extend his or her hand at the end of the interview, you should wait one moment and then extend your own hand. Doing this shows a high level of confidence and business awareness.

Get There on Time A day or two before the interview, call to confirm the time and place. Ask how long you should allow for the interview and if there's anything you should bring, such as a portfolio. A **portfolio** is a tool for sharing information about yourself and examples of your work with others. In the past, portfolios were compiled in binders. Today, electronic portfolios are a simple and effective way of presenting your ideas. You can include text, pictures, Web pages, digital video, and slide-show presentations in an electronic portfolio. Your portfolio should clearly reflect your background, strengths, and work experience.

Electronic portfolios can be stored on an external hard drive, a CD, a flash drive, or a Web site. You can bring a laptop to the interview so you can show employers your electronic portfolio, or you can send it ahead of time so they can look at it before or after your interview.

Plan to arrive at an interview about fifteen minutes early. If you will be driving to the interview and you are unfamiliar with the route, ask for directions and do a practice drive. You don't know what

David Buffington/Blend Images LLC

traffic problems you'll encounter or if you'll get lost. And if you drive, you'll have to find a parking place. Lastly, go to the interview by yourself. It shows confidence. Many teens want to take along a friend for moral support, but that is not perceived as professional behavior.

Anticipate the Questions

Good interview planning means that you try your best to guess what questions you may be asked and think about how you might answer them. For example, the interviewer will almost certainly ask you to describe yourself. Other questions may be more difficult.

The interviewer may want to know, for example, why you've never held a job for very long. You should guess that a question like this will be coming and have a reasonable answer in mind, such as "I've had many responsibilities at home, looking after my younger brothers and sisters, but they're all in school now."

Most interviews boil down to why you are applying, what kind of person you are, and what you can do. Know the answers to those questions. Here are some other questions you might face:

General
- Why do you want to work for us?
- What are your strengths and weaknesses?
- What would you like to be doing five years from now?

Educational
- What is your grade point average?
- What have been your favorite and least favorite courses?
- Were your extracurricular activities worth the time you put into them?

Job-Related
- Why should I hire you?
- How long do you plan to work here?

Personal
- Tell me something about yourself.
- What accomplishment in your life has made you the proudest?
- What is the last book you read?

Think about how you would answer those questions, so that you don't stumble for words when they do come up. Some students even memorize their answers, but be careful that they don't seem *canned.* You don't want to sound like a robot. Instead, your goal is to be so well prepared you can relax and be yourself.

Make Positive Points

Answering questions may make you feel as if you're playing defense. That's only natural, but you also need to have an offense planned for your interview. Prepare a short list of positive points you wish to make about yourself.

How can you get your positive points across? Be alert for situations in which you can bring them into the conversation. Here are a few possibilities:

1. **Puff balls.** Puff balls are easy questions lobbed in your direction. A typical puff ball might be, "Tell me about yourself." Use a question like this as a springboard to tell the interviewer something you have planned to say.

   But beware: if you haven't practiced ahead of time, such questions may leave you at a loss for words.

2. **Pauses.** Inevitably, you will feel a lull in the conversation. Every interview has some down time. Perhaps the interviewer has looked down at her or his notes, scratched a shoulder, or taken a sip of coffee.

   In any event, a pause gives you another chance to use some initiative. While the interviewer is momentarily distracted, jump in and offer to talk about a subject you know will show your skills and experience to best advantage.

   You might say, "By the way, Mr. Youssefi, may I tell you a little about my work on the Habitat for Humanity project our school did last year?"

3. **Bridges.** A bridge is a transition from one answer to another. Suppose the interviewer asks, "Have you ever been late for work?" Obviously, the interviewer expects a one-word answer—yes or no—but you can give more.

   You first answer the question—"Yes," for example—and then, by cleverly using a bridge, you

If you offer a story about yourself during an interview, be sure that story is true.

turn the original question toward something else you wanted to talk about. "I was late once," you say, "but it was because I stopped to help a child who had fallen off a bike." (Of course, any story you tell about yourself should be true.) This bridge gives you a chance to show how responsible you are—so responsible, in fact, that you realize some things are even more important than being on time.

Positive points aren't effective, however, if they sound like propaganda. So add a **sparkler**—something that makes the point come alive: an analogy, a story, an anecdote, or a quotation. Creating a picture in the interviewer's head helps activate both sides of his or her brain. You might say, "When my government class was doing a unit on Congress, I invited our representative to speak to us. He was in the middle of a reelection campaign, and his visit made the evening news."

You can help make your positive point stand out by being brief. Think of your interview as if it were being televised and keep your answer to the length of a **sound bite**. Sound bites are those short excerpts from interviews that we hear on television and radio broadcasts.

Sound bites last, as a rule, no more than 30 seconds. Plan to answer each question in 30 seconds. If time permits, be ready with a two-minute answer or even a five-minute answer.

Rehearse Tough Questions What questions do you dread being asked in an interview? Common anxiety-inducing questions include "Where do you see yourself in five years?" and "Why should I hire you?" When you think about them, they are all legitimate questions, and each presents you with an opportunity to sell yourself.

- "Where do you see yourself in five years?"

The interviewer probably wants to know if you are ambitious. If you find it hard to look five years down the road, try responding like this: "Five years seems like a long time. I can see myself going to college and studying for a degree in sports management."

- "Why should I hire you?"

Here's where the interviewer finds out how well you understand the organization's needs. How about a response like this: "I think you should hire me because I have the skills you need in this position. My computer courses at school have taught me how to use your software, and my communication skills are strong because of my student government experience."

- "Why do you want to work here?"

This is where the interviewer finds out how much you know about the organization. You want to convey your interest in contributing to its mission. For example: "Some of my older friends have worked here, and they said they liked their jobs and were treated fairly."

If the interviewer asks why you are lacking in a particular area (be it grades, work experience, or participation in extracurricular activities), you need to stay positive. In response to a question about a low GPA, for example, you might say something like this: "I had not yet learned how to say no. I was

Ariel Skelley/Getty Images

on the soccer team and the speech team and in student council. There just weren't enough hours in the day, and my grades began to slip. But I learned my lesson and now know how to prioritize."

Phone Interviews

As an alternative to a face-to-face interview, you may be asked to schedule a phone interview. Some organizations use phone interviews as a screening tool to determine which candidates they want to bring in for a face-to-face interview.

During a phone interview, you will be asked the same types of questions that you would be asked in a face-to-face interview. The preparation for both types of interviews is the same. Compile a list of questions you might be asked, and prepare answers to those questions. Have a copy of your résumé in front of you and a pen and paper ready to take notes. Listen when your interviewers introduce themselves. Write down their names so you can refer to them by name later. Find a quiet location that is free of loud noise. Wait for the interviewer to finish a statement or question before you speak. Take your time answering each question. Pause to think about what you want to say, and speak clearly. Provide short answers, just as you would in a face-to-face interview. Be yourself and smile. Your positive attitude will come across to your interviewers, and they will know that you really want the job.

Scholarship Interviews

Some college scholarships you apply for may require an interview. To prepare for the interview, think about your background, the courses you plan to take, the colleges you have applied to, and the type of job you would like to obtain after you graduate. If you are not sure what your major will be, be prepared to tell interviewers about the areas of study that interest you. Dress for a scholarship interview as you would for a job interview, prepare in the same ways, and thank the interviewers for their time.

After the Interview

Consider every interview a learning experience. As soon as possible after the interview, jot down some notes on how you would like to improve. Replay the highs and the lows. What went well? What could you have done better?

Always follow an interview with a thank-you letter. Begin by thanking the interviewer for taking the time to meet with you. Then restate your interest in the position.

Interview Checklist

As a final check before you go to a job interview, ask yourself these questions:

1. Do I have copies of my résumé?
2. Do I have a list of three references with addresses and telephone numbers?
3. Have I made sure I will be on time?
4. Have I dressed neatly and appropriately?
5. Even if I feel tired, can I remember to sit up and look alert?
6. Can I remember not to criticize others, especially past employers?
7. Can I make good eye contact with the interviewer?
8. Can I remember the interviewer's name and use it during the interview?
9. Can I remember to thank the interviewer at the close of the interview?
10. Have I turned off any electronic devices (beepers, cell phones, etc.)?

You might also keep in touch with the organization. After a week or two, call to find out if the job has been filled. If you accept another offer in the meantime, be sure to notify the interviewer that you're no longer a candidate. You never know when you might be applying to that organization again.

Finally, if you do not get the job, you may want to ask the interviewer for some constructive criticism or recommendations for future interviews.

Sending a thank-you card or letter after an interview reminds y[...] interviewer that you are interested in the job.

SECTION 4 REVIEW

Recalling the Facts

1. Why is it wise to arrive ten to fifteen minutes early for an interview?
2. How can you make a positive point even if you aren't directly asked about it?

Thinking Critically

What are some ways that interviews can be misused? Could a company, for instance, use job interviews to find out what people think of competing companies?

Taking Charge

Ask a counselor to conduct some mock job interviews for you and your classmates, or invite the manager of a local business to class to conduct mock interviews.

CHAPTER ⑥ Review and Enrichment

Looking Back

Listed below are the major ideas discussed in this chapter.

- Interviews play an important role in our efforts to gather information.
- The best place for an interview is a quiet location where you can have your subject's complete attention.
- Learn as much as possible about your subject before interviewing him or her.
- Dress appropriately for an interview. Wear whatever you think will bring the best response from the person you are interviewing.
- You must be on time for an interview, and bring a pen and notebook. Some interviewers also like to use a voice recorder or camcorder.
- It may be best to begin an interview with several get-acquainted questions—ones that will put your subject at ease.

- Questions should be brief and to the point.
- Open-ended questions allow the subject great flexibility in answering. Such questions may lead to new and surprising pieces of information.
- Follow-up questions help you pursue statements that need clarifying.
- Yes-no questions and questions that require a one-word answer should usually be avoided.
- Keep eye contact with your subject. Don't become so wrapped up in note taking that you forget to hold up your end of the conversation.
- Gestures can be useful during a job interview; they can burn off tension, add life to your voice, and help you seem energetic.
- Stress a few positive points about yourself when opportunity permits.

Speech Vocabulary

Match the speech vocabulary term on the left with the correct definition on the right.

1. interviewer
2. subject
3. verbatim
4. portfolio
5. rapport
6. open-ended question
7. follow-up question
8. yes-no question
9. leading question
10. puff ball
11. pause
12. bridge
13. sparkler
14. sound bite

a. a "soft" question
b. a transition from a question to a positive point
c. quoting someone word-for-word
d. a sample of school assignments and other work
e. an excerpt of an interview designed for broadcast
f. supporting material—an anecdote, for example
g. someone who asks questions of another person
h. lull in the conversation
i. a person who is being interviewed
j. a sense of trust between two people
k. question that requires a one-word answer
l. question that leaves room for full, informative answers
m. question that hints at an answer
n. question that follows a train of thought

CHAPTER 6 Review and Enrichment

Academic Vocabulary

Match each term on the left with the correct definition on the right.

1. pollster
2. proxy
3. vicariously
4. grovel
5. chauffeur
6. embalm
7. unobtrusive
8. canned

a. to treat a corpse with preservatives
b. overly rehearsed or memorized
c. to cringe or humble oneself
d. someone who drives a car for someone else
e. not easily noticed
f. one who acts in place of someone else
g. in a way that involves participating through imagination in someone else's experience
h. a person who takes opinion surveys

To Remember

1. What do an interviewer and an interview subject want from an interview?
2. If, as an interviewer, you find yourself overly concerned with your next question or whether your subject likes you, you may lack an important quality. What is it?
3. Why would the principal be a better source of information than a teacher for some interviews? For what kinds of interviews would a teacher or a student be the best source?
4. What are some reasons that a subject's office, though convenient, is not the best place to conduct an interview?
5. Name several sources of information you could use to find out about a person you wish to interview.
6. Why is it important to dress appropriately for an interview?
7. What are some of the reasons that you might want to use a voice recorder or camcorder during an interview?
8. What are the advantages of writing out your questions before conducting an interview?
9. Why should you usually avoid asking yes-no questions during an interview?
10. The best strategy for an interviewer to take is to pretend to agree with everything the subject says. True or false? Why?
11. Name three opportunities that may present themselves during an interview—opportunities for you to talk about your own positive points.

To Do

1. Attend a local press conference. They are called frequently by state and local officials. Prepare a few questions ahead of time. Ask the officials if you may ask questions; if not, compare your questions with those asked by professional reporters. Evaluate the questions asked and the responses given.

2. Check up on yourself. Send a follow-up sheet to a person you have recently interviewed. Ask that person about how he or she thought the interview went. Were you courteous, well-prepared, and alert? Were your questions thoughtful and to the point? Use the evaluation to improve future interviews.

3. Have two students interview the same person. Have one interviewer stay outside while the other interview is going on. Discuss the differences in both questions and responses.

4. Assume you have been assigned to interview the president of your student council. What research would you do to prepare for the interview? What questions would you ask?

5. As you learned in this chapter, curiosity is one of the most important qualities of a successful interviewer. What are you curious about?

6. Make a list of 20 or 30 things that you would like to know. Then, for each question on your list, think of at least two sources of information that could answer it. Find the answers to the two questions that you are most curious about.

To Talk About

1. What problems can be caused by the need to take notes at an interview?

2. What are some ways you might deal with an interview subject who is reluctant to give out any information?

3. When might a phone interview be preferable to a face-to-face interview?

4. Discuss who the best subjects would be to interview for a variety of speeches. Have half the class think of the speeches and the other half think of the subjects. For example, who would be the best subject to interview about the history of homecoming at your school? The first basketball team? The growth of women's athletics?

5. Interview a family member. Doing this would be a good way to begin developing your interviewing skills, because you wouldn't find it threatening. Do not, however, take this interview lightly, just because the subject will be someone close to you. Pick a topic that interests you, and ask probing questions. Try to find out something you don't already know.

To Write About

1. Oral history has become a popular way to learn about the past. Draft a proposal for an oral history of your school, an institution in your community, or a major national event. Such events include the September 2001 terrorist attacks on the United States, Hurricane Katrina, and the California wildfires of 2007. Include possible interview subjects and sample question lists.

2. Compare your note-taking techniques with those of your classmates. Do you use an outline form? If not, do you use a combination of letters, numbers, indentions, underlining, stars, or some other system for separating major points from minor ones? What can you do to improve your system for taking notes?

Related Speech Topics

Barbara Walters
Larry King
TV talk shows
The ethics of sound-bite news reporting

An individual's right to privacy versus the public's right to know
The most interesting person you have ever met

CHAPTER 7
GROUP DISCUSSION

Nothing is interesting if you're not interested.

—Helen MacInness

Learning Objectives

After completing this chapter, you will be able to do the following.

- Explain why cooperative attitudes are necessary for group discussions.
- Describe the major kinds of group discussions.
- Discuss the factors that determine the success of group discussions.
- Identify the steps of the problem-solving process.
- Develop a list of questions you could use to direct a group discussion.

Chapter Outline

Following are the main sections in this chapter.

1. Working Together Makes Sense
2. Group Problem Solving
3. How to Contribute to a Discussion

Speech Vocabulary

In this chapter, you will learn the meanings of the speech terms listed below.

discussion
cooperative
competitive
panel discussion
roundtable
talk show
symposium
town hall meeting
mock trial
cohesion
criteria

brainstorming
constructive conflict
disruptive conflict
moderator
questions of fact
questions of
  interpretation
questions of
  evaluation
consensus
groupthink

Academic Vocabulary

Expanding your academic vocabulary will help you become a more effective communicator. Listed below are some words appearing in this chapter that you should make part of your vocabulary.

sequential
scenario
bombard
status quo
polarizing

apathetic
mediator
monopolize
paraphrase

We are all born into a group—our families—and spend much of our lives interacting with groups. Groups are important, because they tend to have more power than any one person, and their decisions usually carry great weight.

In this chapter, you will learn how to help shape group decisions by participating in discussions. A good group discussion is a spirited exchange of lively thoughts, clever remarks, and interesting stories. You will learn here how to make valuable contributions to discussions as well as how to appreciate different points of view.

Introduction

You know how it goes. José gets an idea and sketches it out on a piece of paper with a few doodles. Then along comes Mary, who says, "Hey, wait a minute—that makes me think of something. . . ." Soon Fred comes over and says, "But look, if we change this or add that, we can probably make your idea better." Before long, a group of people working together has surpassed what any one person could have accomplished working alone.

We do some things better by ourselves—reading, for example, or riding a unicycle—but we do many things better in groups.

Group work helps us learn the skills we need to cooperate in an increasingly interdependent society. A strong group goal can help us overcome our reluctance to ask for help or perhaps to offer help to another student. Group work also helps us overcome some of the misunderstandings we have because of our different racial or ethnic backgrounds. When we have a stake in each other's success, we have a strong motivation to cooperate.

Groups can start with a simple idea and brainstorm together until the result is an exceptional plan.

Photodisc/SuperStock

SECTION 1

Working Together Makes Sense

We all think of ourselves as individuals, but we actually gain much of our identity from student council meeting on where to hold the prom. Group discussions help us learn something about ourselves that's different from what we learn in unplanned and spontaneous conversations. Group discussion has a goal.

We can define **discussion** as a cooperative exchange of information, opinions, and ideas. In practical terms, discussion is one of the best methods we have for solving problems. In a discussion, group members help bring all sides of a problem to the surface for consideration. We tend to talk each other out of biases and preconceived ideas. More important, we are usually willing to support solutions if we have played a part in developing them ourselves.

The Right Attitude for Group Work

An ideal group member is open-minded—someone who can interact with fellow group members in a **cooperative** rather than **competitive** atmosphere. A discussion, for example, is not a debate; you don't have to defend a particular point of view. All discussion is dynamic; people are welcome, even encouraged, to change their minds as they hear other ideas and gain more information.

Discussion does require patience. Compared with conversation, discussion can seem somewhat slow, because every member has a chance to speak, and some people who aren't listening may repeat what's already been said. Many of us complain, too, that meetings waste time. The people who do most of the talking seem to have the least to say. You may sometimes feel you must give in to work with a group. You may not agree with the group's decision, for instance, but you don't want to make everyone upset with you by being difficult.

Just because group discussion isn't perfect, however, doesn't mean it isn't valuable. Like everything else, group discussion works when we make it

work. The best discussions give each of us a chance to be heard and, more important, a chance to make good decisions.

In many ways, discussion is the basis of our democratic system. We face conflict every day—rubbing shoulders with each other—but we can find ways to resolve our differences. Through sharing information, ideas, and feelings in discussion, we can find solutions that help all of us become wiser and more understanding people.

If you prefer just to let things happen and go with the flow, you will not do well at discussion. Discussion is purposeful talk by people who are committed to working together. A discussion is

Group members should be open-minded and cooperative.

Peopleimages/Getty Images

Businesses Find Teamwork Productive

Schools are becoming more cooperative, and so are U.S. businesses. Many companies have already discovered that teamwork raises morale and productivity. Consider these success stories:

- At a General Mills cereal plant in California, teams of workers schedule, operate, and maintain machinery so effectively that the factory runs without any managers during the night shift.
- A team of Federal Express clerks spotted and eventually solved a billing problem that was costing the company more than $2 million a year.
- Teams of workers in Sheboygan, Wisconsin, helped Johnsonville Foods decide to go ahead with a major expansion. The workers convinced top executives that they could produce more sausage if allowed to streamline the process. Since then, production has gone up 50 percent.

These teams have proven that groups can be more effective than the old boss-worker arrangement at getting the job done.

truly effective only when each member takes his or her share of the responsibility. Too often, discussions are held back by people who avoid that responsibility. Whenever one group member decides to let others do the work, that person weakens the discussion. All members must be committed to listening, to thinking, and to reasoning with one another.

Discussion Formats

Group discussions take many forms. You may be most familiar with classroom discussions that focus on interpreting literature or analyzing historical events. You may also be familiar with group or club meetings that use parliamentary procedure. (See Chapter 20 for a description of its rules.) There are, however, other kinds of discussions, including the panel discussion, the symposium, the town hall meeting, the mock trial, and the mock press conference. Let's take a closer look at each.

Panel Discussion The **panel discussion** is a relatively informal discussion that takes place before an audience. Panel members, often three or four in number, sit facing the audience. Most of the time, panelists talk directly to each other, but each may make a short introductory speech to the audience.

Panel discussions help audiences become better informed on public issues. A school might set up a panel discussion on teen smoking, for example, and use teenagers, parents, a school counselor, and a representative from the local cancer society as panel members.

In a **talk show** format, a host or cohosts lead a discussion on a particular topic, interview guests who have knowledge on the topic, and may allow

Panelists talk directly to each other at panel discussion.

Many town hall meetings allow people from the community to ask city officials questions.

CDC/Cade Martin

the audience to ask questions. There are many different shows that you can watch on TV to help you get an idea of how to organize your own talk show. *The View, Larry King Now and Live with Kelly and Michael.* The format you choose depends on your topic. Some talk show hosts spend most of their time interviewing celebrities, while others deal with important local and global issues and speak with experts on those issues.

A special kind of panel discussion called a **roundtable** is commonly used in business and industry. As the name suggests, a small group of participants, usually three to eight, talks about a topic of common concern while sitting around a table. If a number of accidents have occurred in a manufacturing plant, for example, the company supervisors might be asked to discuss their suggestions for new safety procedures.

Symposium A more formal kind of discussion is the **symposium.** The usual purpose of a symposium is to present opposing points of view. During a symposium, invited experts deliver short speeches on a particular subject.

A discussion leader usually introduces each speaker and may give a brief statement at the end of each presentation to link together the entire discussion. Each speaker stands and faces the audience,

and after all the speeches have been heard, the audience may ask questions or make comments.

Town Hall Meeting Another kind of discussion is the **town hall meeting,** which dates back to early New England. In those days, colonists would assemble in a large hall to discuss their problems. After the discussion a vote would usually be taken to settle the issue. Today, technology enables people all over the country to take part in town hall meetings on television or via the Internet.

Mock Trial A **mock trial** is just what it sounds like—an imitation of a court trial. It includes a prosecution team that presents a case, a defense team, witnesses, a judge, and a jury. As an extracurricular program, mock trials give students a chance to compete against each other. This format helps them learn important skills in the areas of speaking, listening, critical thinking, and questioning.

In speech or history class, one of your assignments may be to participate in a mock trial in which a historical figure is tried. You'll take on the roles of the historical figures, prosecution, defense, witnesses, judge, and jury.

Mock Press Conference A similar type of discussion could imitate a press conference for a public figure in history. In a literature class, for

Circle discussions allow all participants to be face-to-face.

example, you might hold a mock press conference for a historic author who is coming out with a new book or short story. You might choose Edgar Allan Poe at the time his story "The Tell-Tale Heart" was first published. A few students could introduce him and the story, and then another student could take the role of Poe to answer questions asked by students playing reporters.

Factors for Success

Some discussions work better than others. We can improve a discussion's chances for success by paying attention to two physical factors: the size of the group and how group members are seated. We should also consider one psychological factor: group cohesion.

Group Size Face-to-face communication helps make a group a group. Clearly, the size of a group affects how comfortable people are in sharing their ideas.

Some researchers say five to seven members is the best size for a group, because people participate best in small, informal settings. Even the least talkative person, research has shown, will talk in a small group. Groups of four or fewer are probably too small, because they lack the diversity needed to give the discussion some spark.

As a group gets bigger, of course, each person has fewer opportunities to speak. Thus, many large groups delegate most of the work to small groups called committees.

Seating Arrangements The way people are seated in a discussion can have a good deal to do with its success or failure. If someone in the group takes a central position—at the head of a U-shaped group of chairs, for example, or in front of a row of desks—talk appears to flow through him or her. That person then dominates the discussion.

On the other hand, if the group sits in a circle, all participants can easily look at one another, and talk tends to flow from member to member or from a member to the entire group without being channeled through one person.

Class discussions sometimes fail to come to life because of their unfortunate physical arrangements. If the teacher stands at the front of the classroom and all comments are directed toward him or her, there is little student-to-student interaction.

Studies show that people who participate in groups with circular seating feel more satisfied with their contributions, more pleased with the group's work, and more confident that they have done well

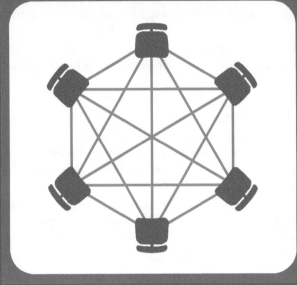

Lines of Interaction in a Circular Seating Arrangement

in solving problems than people who participate in leader-oriented groups. People in groups also need breathing space. Studies of rats, monkeys, and humans show that close confinement produces high levels of stress.

Cramped quarters seem to increase conflict and aggression. If the members of your group don't know each other well, have them sit several feet apart. As they get to know each other, they will probably move closer together.

Cohesion The success of a group discussion also depends on an intangible quality called **cohesion**. When members have respect for each other, share some of the same values, and look to each other for support, they may be called cohesive.

Generally, cohesive groups are those in which people are pulling in the same direction. In contrast, members in a noncohesive group seem to care less about what the group does and more about their own personal goals.

If belonging to the group is important, members will become more cohesive. Belonging to groups matters to many people because it gives them a chance to socialize and feel a sense of purpose. When a group has a good track record—when it has a history of solving problems, for example—its members will more likely remain loyal. On the other hand, if a group fails to meet its objectives, members may lose interest in belonging and show little enthusiasm for finding new members. Thus, success in group discussions often leads to more success, because it helps build cohesion.

SECTION 1 REVIEW

Recalling the Facts

1. How is a discussion different from a conversation?
2. Explain the differences between a panel discussion, a symposium, and a town hall meeting.

Thinking Critically

Imagine the school board is planning to adopt a school dress code. How would you organize a discussion in your school on the topic? Whom would you invite to participate? What are some of the issues that should be addressed?

Taking Charge

1. Conduct a self-critique by asking yourself these questions: How well do I participate in discussions? How often do I speak? Do I see myself as a regular or occasional contributor? Is there something I can do that isn't being done well by anyone else in the group?
2. Watch a televised discussion (a news program like *Face the Nation* or *Meet the Press* would work well) and analyze it in terms of the size of the group, the seating arrangement, and what the group accomplished or failed to accomplish. How did the knowledge of the topic shown by each member seem to influence the discussion?

Group Problem Solving

We form groups to do a variety of tasks. Sometimes the purpose of the group is to gather information (you might join a study group, for example, to help you pass a chemistry exam) and sometimes to make decisions (should our Spirit Week theme be *Tarzan* or *Buffy the Vampire Slayer*?). But groups are never so important as when they are formed to solve problems.

Stick to the Pattern

Unlike conversations, which flow from topic to topic on a whim, discussions generally follow a logical, *sequential* pattern. This allows everyone to know what progress is being made. By relying on an established pattern, groups can complete their work more quickly and with less wasted effort.

Many discussion groups follow a pattern developed by an American educator and philosopher named John Dewey. Dewey said that discussion members need to cultivate what he called the "vital habits of democracy." Members need to "follow an argument, grasp the point of view of another, expand the boundaries of understanding, and debate the alternative purposes that might be pursued."

The following six steps are an update of Dewey's system. If you stick to them in problem-solving discussions, you should have a good chance for success.

1. Define the Problem The first step in solving a problem is to make sure you understand it. This step may require the group to consider how the problem came about and why it needs to be solved. The group should also establish what problems it does not want to consider. In other words, a group tries to limit its objective so that it can focus on finding a specific solution to a specific problem.

To see how this step might work in real life, consider the following scenario. The story is based on an incident that really happened (the names and places have been changed).

A recent pep rally at Centerville High School has everyone upset. The principal interrupted the rally during one of the skits because he found it offensive and in poor taste. He has suspended the nine students who were involved and has threatened to ban all pep rallies for the rest of the school year.

Now a group of student leaders, including members of the student council, the captains of the athletic teams, the editors of the newspaper and the yearbook, and several cheerleaders, has gotten together to see what can be done. Let's listen in on their discussion:

> "I think the principal is completely out of bounds on this one," says Fred Jones, captain of the football team.
>
> "I do, too," replies Nancy Beeler, a cheerleader. "But let's face it. We aren't going to make him change his mind about the suspensions. Those students and their parents are going to have to fight that decision."
>
> "Nancy's right," comments Bobby Vasquez, student council president. "But maybe we can do something about his ban on pep rallies. I think

Defining the problem is the first step in solving it.

StockByte/SuperStock

we can make a big enough stink that he'll let us have some more pep rallies, especially if we can prove that responsible people will be in charge."

These students have identified their problem—a possible ban on pep rallies—and have begun to define that problem by limiting it. The students are upset with the principal for suspending nine of their classmates, but they're not going to let that issue sidetrack them from their real goal—namely, to get pep rallies reinstated for the rest of the year.

By the way, this is a good place to remind you that listening is an important part of problem solving. If each person listens to and understands everyone else, you will be able to reach a solution more quickly. Strategies such as asking questions, summarizing, paraphrasing, and making insightful observations will help you define the problem and thus bring you closer to a solution.

2. Establish Criteria for a Workable Solution
After defining the problem, the group should decide on **criteria,** or a set of standards, that its solution must meet. By establishing these standards at the beginning of a discussion, much unnecessary arguing can be avoided. It would do no good, for example, if a new club planned a fund-raising dance and then found out the school calendar was already full. If the group had first determined that open dates were available, its members could then have discussed the kind of dance they wished to have.

The students in our pep rally group have agreed, after considerable debate, on the following criteria:

1. Pep rallies should continue to be part of the regular school schedule.
2. The pep rallies will continue to be planned and organized by students, but the students must have faculty supervision.

3. No students should be suspended or otherwise disciplined for participating in pep rallies, provided the faculty sponsor has been involved in planning the skits.
4. The pep rallies will not use vulgar jokes or offensive language, although school officials should recognize that rallies are meant to be fun.

The students have everything they want in this list: a guarantee that rallies will be run and organized by students and a promise that the administration will not punish students who participate in pep rallies. But they also believe that the list contains a few things important to the principal: faculty supervision and a promise to keep the rallies free of the kinds of jokes that caused the problem in the first place.

Once the group has established its criteria for an acceptable solution, it can get more specific about what exactly must be done. In our example, the students know they want at least a minimum number of rallies, with a maximum of student input. They know, in other words, what a possible solution might look like.

3. Analyze the Problem
The next step in a discussion is to analyze the problem. The object is to break the problem down into small pieces for closer inspection. Some groups call this fact-finding.

When a doctor analyzes a patient's illness, for example, he or she begins with a thorough examination. The doctor takes an inventory of the patient's current condition (pulse, blood pressure, temperature, and so on) and examines the patient's medical history, looking for clues as to the cause of the patient's illness. Similarly, groups gather as much information as they can to throw light on a particular problem.

Our pep rally students spent some time talking about other school problems that might have caused the principal to be so sensitive:

"Hey, do you remember that swimsuit issue in the school paper last month?" says Bobby.

"I sure do," responds Tammy Swanson, the newspaper editor. "The principal was really upset with us—at least that's what our advisor said."

"And he wasn't too happy about all the publicity we've had lately about teen mothers," comments Marisa Ruiz, another cheerleader. "I know he got quite a few phone calls from angry parents."

"I guess maybe he has good reason to be a little touchy right now," says Bobby.

"That might be right," replies Nancy, "but I still think he overreacted. Maybe we can change his mind if we can prove to him that we have a responsible plan."

We tend to forget that problems don't happen overnight. Most usually have long histories. Learning the background of a problem can often help us gain insights into why people react to the problem the way they do. It never hurts to see the situation from another person's point of view.

By establishing your criteria for a workable solution, you can reduce group conflict.

4. Suggest Possible Solutions The fourth step in the problem-solving process is to propose as many solutions as possible. One of the best ways to create solutions is called **brainstorming**. In brainstorming, a group tries to *bombard* the problem with fresh ideas. Every idea is welcome; none is laughed at or rejected.

Group members offer their ideas as quickly as possible, not bothering to decide whether the solutions are practical. "Everyone is creative," says James Ferry, president of an idea development company in Boston. "It's just a matter of making them believe it." The theory behind brainstorming is that the more ideas a group can produce, the more likely it will be to find one that works.

John Dewey's System for Discussion (Updated)

1. Define the problem.
2. Establish criteria for a workable solution.
3. Analyze the problem.
4. Suggest possible solutions.
5. Evaluate each solution and select the best one.
6. Suggest ways for testing or carrying out the solution.

Alice Salmon, editor of the school yearbook in our pep rally case, shows her creative thinking when she suggests that pep rallies should be scheduled at the beginning of each athletic season rather than once a month, as they have been in the past.

"I think one pep rally for each sports season is enough," she says. "That way, we can have a more positive purpose. We can focus on wishing our teams well instead of focusing on the opponent. I hate those rallies where all we do is chant, 'Kill the Bulldogs,' or, 'Throttle the Meadowlarks.'"

Another student, Miguel Fuentes of the cross-country team, reminds everyone that good rallies take lots of effort.

"Alice has a point. Plus, It's hard work to make a good skit," he says. "We've got to make sure the principal understands that."

"I have an idea," offers Tina McIntire of the volleyball team. "If the principal won't let us have any more pep rallies, let's boycott all the games. Let's all stay away from the football field this Friday night."

You probably brainstorm every day. Brainstorming allows everyone's creativity a chance to shine.

Once the group has generated a large number of ideas (including some like Tina's, which will be rejected in the end), it may discover that the obvious solution is not the best. Too often, a group reaches this phase only to have someone say, "Well, the solution seems pretty obvious," or, "I guess we're pretty much in agreement." Comments like these undermine discussion, because they stop any further thinking.

No solution should be accepted until several have been proposed, examined, and compared. Accepting a solution without considering the alternatives is like playing the lottery: It gives the group only one chance, and a feeble one at that.

5. Evaluate Each Solution and Select the Best One The next step is to consider your options. If two or three solutions seem equally good, the group members should turn back to their criteria and make a careful comparison. Does each solution meet the standards they agreed on in the second step of this process? If not, that solution should be changed or eliminated. The best solution is the one that most clearly fits the criteria.

In the case of our pep rally students, they have decided to support Alice's idea about one pep rally per season:

"I really like Alice's idea," says Marisa. "I think it will show the principal that we're acting in good faith if we're willing to give up some of the pep rallies we've had in the past."

"I agree," says Tammy, "but if the principal is going to buy our idea, we've got to convince him our rallies will be in good taste."

"Let's not go overboard here," comments Bobby. "I want to remind him that pep rallies are supposed to be fun. Can't we be outrageous without being offensive? He was a teenager once—where's his sense of humor?"

"How about this," offers Fred. "Let's take Alice's idea, urge the principal to trust the faculty sponsor, and keep Plan B as a backup."

"Plan B? What's Plan B?" asks Tammy.

"If the principal won't let us schedule pep rallies during the regular school day," says Fred, "maybe he'll let us have them before or after school."

6. Suggest Ways for Testing or Carrying Out the Solution Discussing how to carry out a solution is the final step in the problem-solving process. Group members must make sure that their solution is practical. If possible, the group might give its idea a brief test. That's what our pep rally students decided to do:

> "How about this?" says Alice. "Let's take our idea to the pep club sponsor and several of the coaches first. They might have some suggestions for us."
>
> "Why not?" says Miguel. "And if they like the idea, they might tell the principal they're supporting us."
>
> "Sounds good to me," responds Tammy. "I'd like to have all the backing I can get when we take this to the principal."

Once you have evaluated a solution, you should also test it in some way.

Managing Conflict

A good discussion will inevitably cause conflict. "Where all men think alike," said the columnist Walter Lippmann, "no one thinks very much." Differences of opinion—over ideas and issues—are the very heart of discussion. Problems that appear simple at first appear more complex as you discover what other group members have to say about them.

Discussion can cause disagreements between members over facts, interpretations, and solutions. And such conflict will surely produce stress. We all find it difficult, for instance, not to take attacks on our ideas personally. Yet, only when we entertain conflicting ideas can we understand how complex most problems really are. Conflict, when effectively and sensitively managed, can be extremely valuable in our efforts to reach the best solution.

Conflict as a Positive Force As Mark Twain said, "A difference of opinion is what makes a good horse race." Discussion is not worth the trouble unless it addresses a genuine problem and people have real differences about how to solve the problem. Peter Drucker, a well-known management consultant, says that disagreements are valuable because they provide alternative ways of looking at a problem. Alternatives,

he says, are necessary if a group is going to do more than simply approve the first idea that comes along.

Constructive conflict develops when members use their differences to discover the best ideas and not to score points against one another. Group members should especially seek out ideas that are contrary to the prevailing opinions. Find a few off-the-wall ideas—solutions that seem far-fetched at first. By analyzing these ideas, the group will become less committed to the *status quo* and more willing to try something new.

Disruptive Conflict Some conflict, however, can be disruptive. **Disruptive conflict** can destroy a group by *polarizing* the members (dividing them into competing sides that refuse to compromise) and by turning the discussion into a debate, in which personal victory is more important than a successful group decision. If getting your way is more important to you than helping the group, you have lost that cooperative attitude so essential to good discussion. If the captain of the football team in the pep rally example had insisted on having a rally before each home game, his stubbornness might have made it impossible for the group to go ahead with its plan.

COMMUNICATION *BREAKTHROUGH*

Going Live: Giving Group Presentations

More and more often these days, teachers are asking students to work in small groups. The benefits to you are terrific:

- The task is distributed among all the members of the group.
- Groups generate more ideas than any one person.
- There's less pressure; the spotlight shifts from member to member.

On the other hand, group work can have a few drawbacks. For example, one person can get stuck doing all the work. Sometimes members argue with each other and avoid working at all. And the logistics of a presentation can be tricky (one person might want to use PowerPoint, another might have posters to show, and so on). Still, for most of us, group work offers an exciting and stimulating way to tackle a problem.

As your group begins to work, pay close attention to group dynamics. Beware of struggles for leadership. When a group meets, the first person who talks often becomes the leader, but that may not be the best thing. Carefully consider the various roles available in a group presentation and choose the best person for each role.

For example, you might want to organize your presentation so that one member gives the introduction and conclusion. This person also introduces the other members and gives a brief preview of what they'll be doing. Each of the other members gives a main point. In a ten-minute presentation, for example, each main point deserves about two to three minutes.

It's vital to practice your presentation. For one thing, your teacher probably has given you a time limit. As you practice, time yourselves to see if you're within the guidelines; if you're asked to give a ten-minute presentation, don't quit after five minutes or persist for twenty minutes. Be sure to balance the time allotted to each person. Remember: rehearse, rehearse, rehearse.

When it's time to give your group presentation, present a solid front. Arrange your chairs so that all group members are sitting together. As each person's turn comes, stand up to gain the audience's attention.

If you're planning to use visual aids, be sure to have a backup plan. Be prepared, in other words, for things to go wrong. It's also not a bad idea to have someone outside your group run the computer if you're doing a PowerPoint presentation. Doing that frees the group members to focus on making eye contact with the audience.

You might also be wise to allow a little time at the end of your presentation for questions and answers. These can be fielded by the presentation director (the student who opened and closed the program), who directs each question to the group member best able to answer it.

Tip: Dave Whitt, speech coach at Nebraska Wesleyan University, urges groups to plan their transitions. Well-planned transitions give the presentation a seamless quality and make it appear much more integrated than simply a series of individual presentations.

Almost every group has a few people who become nuisances—people who seem to fight the discussion process every step of the way. Often, these people can learn to be productive; they're simply acting like nuisances temporarily, because they are bored or distracted. The health of the group, however, depends on dealing with them head-on. Look for the following behaviors in your next meeting and take steps to turn these negatives into positives.

Nitpickers want everything spelled out and will quibble until they get what they want. "If it weren't for me," such people seem to be thinking, "this group would be in trouble." Nitpickers need to have a say but not get their way. Be sure these group members get opportunities to speak, but insist that they keep their comments brief.

Eager beavers want to offer a solution whether or not they have given it any thought. In their eagerness, they may distract the group's attention from ideas that have been more carefully considered. If the group can help funnel their enthusiasm, eager beavers can turn into valuable members.

Fence-sitters don't dare take a position until they're sure what the "key people" will say. If the group can make it clear, however, that their opinions really matter, they may slowly gather courage and begin to say what they think, not what they think they should say.

Wisecrackers are the group clowns, people who seek attention in any way possible. Wisecrackers tend to appear in groups whose members are bored and looking for a diversion. In a more serious group, members quickly become impatient with such antics. If you find a wisecracker or two in your group, pick up the pace of the discussion; your group may have too much time on its hands.

Superior beings look down their noses at the whole business. Perhaps they didn't want to be part of the group in the first place. The group's best course with these members is to make them feel needed. The group must show it values their opinions, regardless of how superior and indifferent these people appear.

Dominators don't know when to quit talking. Once aware that they're preventing others from contributing, however, they can become top members. Making such persons recorders or evaluators (members who must be quiet during the meeting) is one way to help them become more aware of who's talking and who isn't during the discussion. Once they know this, they may be more receptive to other people's ideas.

Some group members may prevent others from contributing.

Recalling the Facts

1. List the six steps of John Dewey's system for discussion.
2. Explain the difference between constructive conflict and disruptive conflict. Give an example of each.

Thinking Critically

John Dewey claimed that his system for organizing a discussion would help develop the essential skills needed for a democratic society. In what ways does his system promote democracy? Are there any elements of his system that could be considered undemocratic? If so, explain.

Taking Charge

1. Observe a discussion from start to finish (you might watch a city council, school board, or legislative meeting). Can you state a problem or issue the group attempted to resolve? How many of the members actually took part in the discussion? Did the discussion follow the steps outlined in Dewey's problem-solving process? When the group got off course, did any members try to steer the discussion back to the main point? If possible, speak with one of the participants after the discussion and compare your impressions with his or hers.
2. Learn to deal with annoying group members. Plan a topic of discussion for a group and label six cards ahead of time with the words *nitpicker, eager beaver, fence-sitter, wisecracker, superior being,* and *dominator*. Secretly give one card to each of six persons in the group. Ask each person with a card to play the assigned role as well as possible (refer to the chapter text for a description of each role). As the discussion develops, observe how other students react to the six cardholders. Notice what kind of leadership develops and what kinds of frustrations occur. After the discussion, ask the students what they thought each cardholder was doing.

SECTION 3

How to Contribute to a Discussion

Groups need participation from every member because people are more likely to support decisions that they play a role in shaping. On the other hand, group members become *apathetic* or even hostile toward ideas that are handed to them from on high.

During World War II, government officials tried to convince people to use less popular meats, such as kidneys and sweetbreads, as a conservation measure. A follow-up study showed that while only 3 percent of those who heard lectures on the subject used these meats, 32 percent (ten times as many) of those who discussed the idea in group meetings were persuaded to do so.

Contributing as a Participant

We can't all be leaders—at least not all of the time. But everyone in a discussion has an important role to play. Indeed, the group can only be as effective as its weakest member. Remember, the objective of a group is to blend the knowledge, information, and reasoning of every member into a decision that represents the group's best collective thinking.

As a member of a group discussion, you have a number of responsibilities. Some of them involve the way you present what you have to say:

1. Be clear and simple. Reinforce what you say with looks and gestures.
2. Encourage members to react to your ideas. Questions like "Was I clear?" "What do you think about what I just said?" and "Do you have any questions?" indicate that you want feedback.
3. Be interesting. Although most of us dislike performing, it doesn't cost much to speak with vitality and enthusiasm.
4. Offer reasons for what you say. Make sure you take into account what other people are think-

ing. "The fool tells me his reasons," Aristotle said; "the wise man persuades me with my own."
5. Think before speaking, but don't think so long about what you want to say that an opportunity slips by. When your comment matters, seize the moment.

Active Listening Everyone who participates in a discussion must also be an active listener. That means that even if you don't have anything to say at a particular time, you aren't free to loaf. You need to examine ideas as they are presented and figure out whether you understand them. Then, when it's your turn to contribute, you can make a meaningful comment.

Expressions and gestures help to reinforce your ideas and keep the interest of your listeners.

As you listen to what others say, try to be impartial. Free yourself from preconceived ideas. Don't be like the people who say, "My mind is made up. Don't confuse me with facts." Such people come to a discussion unwilling to accept any opinions different from their own. If left unchallenged, such people can wreck the whole discussion.

Most important, be attentive and courteous. If you find yourself asking people to repeat themselves or to go back over ground they have already covered, you are slowing the process down and making the meeting dull for everyone. Avoid making silly or irrelevant comments. Contributions to the discussion are meaningful only when they connect with what has just been said.

Preparing for Discussion

It's a fact of life that you often come to a discussion with your head full of other thoughts and interests. You probably have not reviewed your notes or even tried to decide what you think about the issues that will come up in the meeting. But taking a little time to prepare can pay big dividends, both for you and for the group.

Preparation is largely a matter of looking ahead. Considering ahead of time what questions and objections might be raised about your position will help you cope with the give-and-take of the discussion process.

It's also a good idea to know how you work under pressure. Some people love the hubbub of discussion and enjoy each conflict that arises. Others find arguments and clashes over ideas very stressful. Understanding who you are will help you define your role in a group. Try experimenting with varying degrees of participation to find your comfort level.

No matter what, always keep in mind that you have skills and talents to offer the group. You may take good notes or be able to make a joke at a tense moment. Try to find out what the group needs from you. Be aware, though, that if you start out as a silent member, people will expect you to be silent the next time. They may try to encourage you to talk at first, but if you don't respond, they may come to ignore you. So don't wait till the second meeting to make a contribution; take the plunge right away.

Contributing as a Leader

Although some groups can function well for a while without a leader, there are clearly times when every group needs one. A certain nudge of guidance seems to be necessary for a group to function smoothly.

For that reason, it may be unwise for a group to wait for a leader to emerge naturally. Instead, the group should designate a leader, at least for a particular meeting or a particular goal. With a designated leader, the members of the group know who is responsible for settling disputes and maintaining an atmosphere in which everyone's comments are welcome and appreciated. Without such a person, groups can break into cliques, become chaotic, or just waste time.

Leadership may change hands as the attitudes of the group or the areas of discussion change. Members may want the leadership of one person on one topic and turn for leadership to someone else at another time. The group decides not only whom it will follow but also how much authority it will give to the leader and how long it will accept that person's leadership. Fortunately, any interested member can learn to be an effective leader.

What a Leader Should Know

Any group member should be willing and prepared to become a leader if asked. We can summarize a discussion leader's responsibilities this way:

1. A good leader should know how to run a meeting.
2. A good leader should know the people in the group.
3. A good leader should know the issues the group will discuss.

A discussion leader should pay greatest attention to matters of procedure. She or he should know how to run a meeting, partly because of experience and partly because of a solid understanding of parliamentary procedure (see Chapter 20). This knowledge allows the leader to remain impartial. He or she becomes a neutral *mediator* to whom participants in a discussion can turn when disagreements threaten to get out of control.

A shrewd leader should know the people in the group. That way, she or he can plan to calm down those who talk too much and encourage those who talk too little. The leader should know whom can be relied on to speak and who needs to be prodded.

A leader should also have a full grasp of the issues the group will discuss. Knowing the issues does not mean knowing more than anyone else. In fact, a competent leader may know very little about details. The leader must, nonetheless, understand the problem and the most productive way to analyze it.

Getting a Meeting Started The leader of a group is first and foremost a **moderator.** A moderator must get the discussion started, keep it moving, and bring it to a close. Getting a discussion started can be a major challenge, especially for an inexperienced leader.

Most groups need to be led into useful discussion. Imagine a situation in which your leader, after giving an introduction (which might be a brief welcome and a reminder of why the meeting has been called), simply says, "Well, who wants to begin?" This tactic is almost certain to fail. Groups need greater direction, especially in the beginning.

A useful method for starting a discussion is to pose a question. This opening question should be directed to the group as a whole and not to any one individual. It would be unwise to put someone on the spot this early in the discussion.

Most discussion questions can be grouped into three categories: fact, interpretation, and evaluation. **Questions of fact** ask group members to recall information that touches on the business at hand. **Questions of interpretation** ask them to give their opinions on what the information means. **Questions of evaluation** ask members to agree or disagree with possible solutions and to make value judgments.

A leader should use interpretive questions at the beginning of a discussion and, if possible, write them out ahead of time. Suppose you are preparing to lead a group discussion. The best interpretive questions are those that you have no ready answers for but that you believe can be answered. Prepare a question for the group and then ask yourself whether the group has enough information to deal effectively with the question. If not, throw that question out and find another.

Good interpretive questions are questions you care about—ones that really matter. You can never be sure, of course, that everyone in the group will share your enthusiasm for a particular question, but if you are eager to get an answer, chances are that others will be, too. If you don't care, why should anyone else?

Let's Stop Wasteful Meetings

Many companies waste time and reduce productivity by holding ineffective meetings. This conclusion was underscored in a story in the *Wall Street Journal*, which reported that CEOs throughout the country felt that meetings accounted for the largest share of unproductive time on the job.

A study by the Wharton Center for Applied Research found that managers spend from 10 to 23 hours a week in meetings. The study also concluded that nearly one-third of those meetings could have been handled better through face-to-face talks, by phone, by memo, or by e-mail.

Here are some suggestions to make your meetings effective:

- Before deciding to hold a meeting, ask yourself whether the meeting is *really* necessary—or could whatever needs to be done be handled some other way?

- If your group holds regularly scheduled meetings, ask yourself whether you could skip one from time to time when nothing urgent is pending.

- Make sure that the people who are needed to make decisions attend the meeting. Don't invite those who aren't needed; you'll only waste their time.

- Develop an agenda and distribute it a day or so before the meeting. Insist that people come prepared to discuss the items on the agenda. Putting your goals in writing will help sharpen your focus.

- Don't pass out material at the beginning of a meeting. People will read it instead of listening to you.

- Start and end every meeting on time.

- Be sure that everyone knows who's responsible for doing what as a result of the meeting. Put the assignments in writing promptly to help prevent misunderstandings.

We can summarize the qualities of good interpretive questions like this:

1. They contain doubt.
2. They can be answered.
3. They are likely to interest the group.

Think back for a moment to the students who were worried about their pep rallies being canceled. During their discussion, they asked several interpretive questions: "What will students think about having fewer pep rallies?" "How will the principal react to our idea about faculty supervision?" "How important are pep rallies, anyway?" They also asked at least one question of fact: "Have we ever had problems with pep rallies before?" And they asked one evaluative question: "Is this plan good for our school?"

Keep the Discussion Going Once underway, a well-informed group will usually move along without much prodding from the leader. Good leaders strive for balanced participation.

Usually, groups have at least one person who talks too much and one who talks too little.

Leaders should make sure that everyone participates and that no one *monopolizes* the group's time. If several speakers try to speak at once, preference should be given to the one who has spoken least. Sometimes real diplomacy is needed to keep the discussion from becoming one-sided. Leaders must rely on tact and good humor to see that everyone talks but that no one talks too much.

Leaders must be especially careful with members who are reluctant to speak. For example, leaders should resist the temptation to ask a timid person a direct question. This tactic can backfire, because if the person is taken by surprise, he or she will be even less likely to speak thereafter. It may be safe, however, to ask for a comment on an idea already being considered, as in "Sean, what do you think of Samantha's idea?"

Leaders should occasionally *paraphrase* what someone has said. They may sometimes need to repeat in their own words what a member has said, especially if the person has been talking for a long time. Leaders should also provide occasional summaries of what the group has accomplished so far. Summaries help the group avoid repetition and spotlight areas of agreement or disagreement. Both paraphrases and summaries help everyone know where the group is in the discussion.

Set an Example A leader can increase group members' desire to participate by recognizing and praising (when appropriate) their contributions.

Like an orchestra conductor, a good leader directs the discussion toward harmony.

Make eye contact with group members. It gives important nonverbal support.

Leaders give such recognition with statements like "That's an important point; thank you for bringing it to our attention" as well as nonverbal support like good eye contact and head nodding. Carefully timed praise also encourages group loyalty.

Finally, leaders should avoid sending negative nonverbal signals. For example, a leader shouldn't yawn when someone else is talking. Nothing will turn a group off more quickly than an inattentive leader.

Consensus rarely happens without hard work.

Handling Meeting Distractions and Disruptions

Occasionally, a group member's behavior may sidetrack or disrupt a meeting discussion. It may be behavior that monopolizes, or dominates, the discussion. Or, it may be behavior that distracts the group from the meeting's purpose. Either way, a good leader should establish standards, identify problems before they escalate, and take action. The leader should keep the group focused on the meeting's purpose and the main topic.

Close the Discussion

At some point, the leader will move to end the discussion. A leader should be alert for signs that the group is ready to quit, or at least ready to be done with the question at hand. The group may begin to repeat itself, to take up minor points, or to wander away from the question. Such behaviors mean that the group members have probably gone as far as they can with the question. The leader must also be aware of any time limits (the bell is about to ring, for instance) that mean the discussion must stop. In either case, it is time to settle the question.

The ideal conclusion of a group discussion is reaching a **consensus**. Consensus means a *nearly* unanimous agreement among the group's members about a particular solution. It happens most often when members unselfishly seek common ground. But it doesn't happen all the time, and it rarely happens without a great deal of effort.

As desirable as consensus is, you should guard against giving up an argument or a position too easily just to go along with the group. In its most extreme form, this desire to go along with the group causes people to abandon their personal beliefs. People sometimes call this very human desire to get along **groupthink**, because it's an instance of letting a group do our thinking for us.

If you let your friends talk you into doing something although you have serious misgivings, you have become a victim of groupthink. Thinking for yourself within a group can be tough, but no group can profit when its members give up their individuality.

OJO Images Ltd/Alamy

SECTION 3 REVIEW

Recalling the Facts

1. Name at least three of the responsibilities each person accepts by joining a group discussion.
2. What are the three most important things a group leader should know?

Thinking Critically

What should a group do if no one wishes to be the leader? What are some possible methods for choosing a group leader no matter how reluctant he or she might be?

Taking Charge

1. Make a list of interpretive questions for a discussion on one of the following topics:
   - What qualities should a good presidential candidate possess?
   - Is year-round school a good idea?
   - Should term limits be imposed on all elected officials?

   Once you have selected a topic and written a list of interpretive questions, write five factual questions and three evaluative questions for the discussion.
2. Find a newspaper article that explains how two groups disagree on an issue. Analyze each group's position to see how it would respond to these questions:
   - How does our side see the problem?
   - What solution can we suggest?
   - What are the advantages of our solution?
   - What are the disadvantages of our solution?

   Can you suggest a way these two groups could resolve their differences and settle on a compromise solution? Must one group give in, or can both groups find middle ground?

Looking Back

Listed below are the major ideas discussed in this chapter.

- Participants exchange information, discuss ideas, and solve problems in a group discussion.
- Group discussion is valuable because people usually support decisions that they help make.
- Public forms of discussion include the panel discussion, the symposium, the town hall meeting, and the mock trial.
- The ideal group size is five to seven people.
- Many groups use a standard problem-solving process based on John Dewey's six steps.
- Differences of opinion within a group should be encouraged as a way of exploring alternatives.
- Disruptive conflict can occur when group members put greater importance on getting their way than on supporting a group decision.

- Good discussion participants use active listening skills and wait for the right moment to speak.
- A leader can help a group function smoothly and effectively.
- A group leader can begin a discussion by asking an interpretive question, which requires members to provide evidence and reasoning to support their opinions.
- The leader can also help the group by occasionally summarizing what the group has done and paraphrasing what members have said.
- Groups must strive for consensus but beware of groupthink, when members allow beliefs to be overcome by the pressure to conform.

Speech Vocabulary

Match the speech term on the left with the correct definition on the right.

1. discussion
2. cooperative
3. competitive
4. panel discussion
5. talk show
6. roundtable
7. symposium
8. town hall meeting
9. mock trial
10. cohesion
11. criteria
12. constructive conflict
13. disruptive conflict
14. moderator
15. question of fact
16. question of interpretation
17. question of evaluation
18. consensus
19. groupthink
20. brainstorming

a. difference of opinion that leads to creative alternatives
b. set of standards for evaluation
c. creative process for coming up with ideas
d. cooperative exchange
e. helpful and unselfish
f. informal discussion before an audience
g. discussion format in which a few experts give short speeches
h. general agreement
i. social glue that holds a group together
j. tendency to conform to group opinion
k. discussion format in which a small group talks about a concern
l. discussion format involving an entire community
m. disagreement that prevents a group from making a decision
n. question about opinions
o. question about value judgments
p. question about information
q. impartial person who organizes a discussion
r. discussion format in which guests are interviewed
s. discussion format that imitates a trial
t. involving rivalry

Academic Vocabulary

Complete one of the two following sentence frames for each of the vocabulary terms: (1) The opposite of *sequential* is _____. Or, (2) A synonym of *sequential* is _____.

1. sequential
2. scenario
3. bombard
4. status quo
5. polarizing
6. apathetic
7. mediator
8. monopolize
9. paraphrase

To Remember

Answer the following based on your reading of the chapter.

1. Give three reasons why discussion is one of the best methods for solving problems.
2. Why is a group of five more likely to have a successful discussion than a group of three or a group of twelve?
3. What are the six steps of the problem-solving process?
4. What is brainstorming?
5. What are the major duties of a group discussion leader?
6. Explain the difference between questions of fact, questions of interpretation, and questions of evaluation.
7. Why should a leader occasionally summarize what the group has done?
8. What is a consensus?
9. How can you prepare for a discussion?

To Do

1. Make a participation diagram of the next discussion you attend. On a sheet of paper, arrange a group of circles to represent the group members and where they are seated. Put each person's initials in his or her circle. Next, draw lines to connect each circle with every other circle.

   Each time someone says something to someone else, put a slash mark through the line connecting the two people's circles. If an individual makes a comment to the entire group and not to anyone in particular, place a mark inside that person's circle. At the end of the discussion, analyze the group's interaction. Who spoke the most? The least? To whom were most of the comments directed?

2. Form two groups of five students each. The remainder of the class will form one large group. Have each group discuss the same question— perhaps, "Should school lunches be catered by fast-food chains like McDonald's and Burger King?" Have an observer in each group report back to the entire class on how many people participated and how much each said. Are there noticeable differences between the participation levels in the larger and smaller groups? Were the decisions the same in each group?

To Talk About

1. What would you do if the following occurred in a group discussion?
   - One person who obviously has not done any research on the topic criticizes many valid remarks made by other members.
   - Two members sit and whisper while other members talk about the topic.
   - One member insists on dominating the discussion. The fact that this person has many notes shows that he or she has done plenty of research.
   - The discussion leader shows signs of being hopelessly disorganized. The group is drifting and beginning to repeat itself.
2. Why is equal participation from all members a good goal for group discussion?
3. How important is achieving consensus in a group discussion?
4. How can you tell whether conflict in a group discussion is creative and constructive or self-centered and disruptive?

To Write About

1. Write a letter to a leader in your community. Ask that person for a definition of leadership and a few examples of how good leadership has made a difference. Share the reply with your classmates.

2. Suppose your class wanted to plan a school assembly to help inform students about the dangers of driving while intoxicated. Would it be better to have a panel discussion, symposium, roundtable, or town hall meeting? Explain your answer in a one-page paper.

Related Speech Topics

The claim that groups make better decisions than individuals do
Things my parents taught me
Things I wish my parents had taught me
Leadership styles of famous people
A friend as being someone you can talk to

Making decisions for dinner
How to choose a leader
How to be a good group leader
How to be a good group member

UNIT
3
Preparation and Process

UNIT CONTENTS

RESEARCHING YOUR PRESENTATION

If truth is beauty, then why don't more people get their hair done at the library?

—Lily Tomlin

Learning Objectives

After completing this chapter, you will be able to do the following.

- Discuss the impact of the information age on your future.
- Develop a plan that will help you focus your research efforts.
- Identify four shortcuts that will reduce the time you spend researching.
- Use library resources to find material for your speeches.
- Distinguish between plagiarism and intellectual honesty.

Speech Vocabulary

In this chapter, you will learn the meanings of the speech terms listed below.

audience analysis
interlibrary loan
database
online search engine
catalog
table of contents
index
periodical
periodical index
almanac
atlas
plagiarism
paraphrasing

Chapter Outline

Following are the main sections in this chapter.

1. Your Research Plan
2. Using the Library
3. Using What You've Found

Academic Vocabulary

Expanding your academic vocabulary will help you become a more effective communicator. Listed below are some words appearing in this chapter that you should make part of your vocabulary.

prerequisite
entrepreneur
alienate
compendium
attribution

How can you find your way out of the library wilderness? Shortcuts can help you use your research time effectively as you acquire the necessary information to prepare a successful speech. Furthermore, library access to the Internet enables you to gather a wealth of information. Note taking is essential to any research effort, but how do you decide what to write down? What is plagiarism, and how can you avoid intellectual dishonesty? These questions and others arise as you research any topic for a presentation. Developing the ability to find the answers to such questions is a *prerequisite* for anyone who wants to succeed in this information age. This chapter is one step in your journey toward that goal.

Introduction

We live in the information age. More than 150,000 books are published each year in the United States. By the year 2000, the store of available knowledge and information was doubling every five years. The current amount of information in cyberspace is almost beyond estimate. Furthermore, the potential for additional growth on the World Wide Web is mind-boggling. The author Richard Saul Wurman points out that "a weekday edition of the *New York Times* contains more information than the average person was likely to come across in a lifetime in seventeenth-century England." It is not surprising, then, that the enormous amount of available information can seem overwhelming to the student researcher who needs evidence for a speech.

At the same time, students are becoming increasingly aware that information skills are essential to success in the world today. Whether you're a college student studying the latest advances in organ transplants or a young *entrepreneur* starting an auto repair shop, you need to know how to find the right answers. This crucial concern was addressed by the members of the U.S. National Commission on Libraries and Information Science: "A basic objective of education is for each student to learn how to identify needed information, locate and organize it, and present it in a clear and persuasive manner."

Clearly, researching materials to support each of your assigned speeches challenges you to become a

One of your biggest research assignments will be to investigate a college or university you want to attend. You can learn more by talking to recruiters.

more effective problem solver. As a problem solver, you will soon experience the thrill of the hunt and the joy of finding that juicy—but effectively hidden, until now—bit of information. The trick, of course, is to have a plan.

Your Research Plan

Let's assume you have just chosen a speech topic. Chances are that you know something about the topic. Fortunately, one of the best ways to begin organizing your thoughts is to assess what you already know. You will soon realize, though, that with most topics you need assistance. Successful speeches require supporting information. Supporting information requires specific research. Specific research provides sources to quote—people who know more about a given topic than you. The ancient Greeks referred to this process of accumulating information as building a "storehouse of knowledge."

Have you ever been stopped at a shopping mall or in front of a store to answer a researcher's questions?

Playing the Research Game

Before you start accumulating information, you should have carefully thought out a plan. If you are like most beginning researchers, though, you don't yet know how to plan—how to play the research game. Although you can gather supporting materials through such methods as interviewing or surveying, most of the research game is played in the library. Entering a library, though, you may feel as if you are trapped inside some gigantic alien pinball machine—the flippers frozen, the tilt beyond your control. Thus, the time you spend "playing library" is largely wasted.

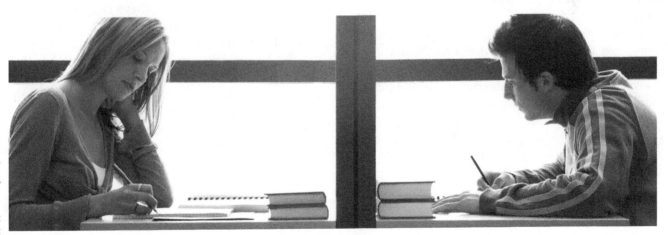

Successful speeches require research.

(t) enis izgi/Getty Images; (b) UpperCut Images/SuperStock

Gathering Information

So how do you avoid wasting time? Speakers disagree as to the best method. Some begin with a rough outline of their speech and then find evidence to support the subpoints. Others do some preliminary research and then create an outline that incorporates the facts they have gathered. In choosing one of these approaches, perhaps the most important factor is how much you know about the topic before you begin. If you are speaking on the topic of reducing unemployment and you are not well-informed about economic theory, then you should probably do some reading before making any decisions about how to organize your speech. If, on the other hand, you are speaking on the topic of how active a role the student council should play in your school, you might want to start by jotting down a rough outline of your views on the topic.

To save more time, consider finding an expert to give focus to your research. A phone call to a government official, a college professor, or an author can save you hours of wading through books and articles that are not relevant to your search. Experts can suggest the best sources on a particular topic, and they can often provide quotable statements to work into your speech. You can even become your own expert by undertaking opinion polls on controversial topics or by conducting a series of interviews with representatives on both sides of a specific issue.

As you gather information for your speech, remember to adapt your findings to the audience that will hear your presentation. For example, a speech before your classmates during second period may require less formality than a commencement address before members of the community. In any speaking situation, keep in mind that the audience may not have the same interests as you do. Skateboarding, for example, may occupy your every waking thought but be of little consequence to most members of your audience. Therefore, you have to plan your speech, no matter what the topic, by first considering the needs and expectations of those people who will be listening to you. This process, **audience analysis**, involves asking yourself the following questions:

- What do my listeners already know about my topic?
- How do I capture their interest?
- How formal should my language be?
- What should I avoid saying that might *alienate* audience members?
- What can I say to change the minds of people who might disagree with my positions?

You should make it clear that you care about your audience and that you want to share the information in your speech with them.

Analyzing and Evaluating

Besides analyzing your audience, you will need to analyze the sources of information that you find. Not all sources are created equal, and you will need to determine whether the material you find is reliable and whether it will contribute to your speech.

So how do you go about determining whether your information is reliable and useful? First, look at who wrote and published the material. Did you find the information in *National Geographic* or the *National Enquirer*? Does the book jacket list the author's credentials, and if so, what are they? Does the author cite other sources to support his or her point of view? Do book reviews call the source reliable? Do you find similar information in multiple sources? Is the information presented clearly, consistently, and coherently? Answers to these questions will help you evaluate the reliability of your sources.

After you have evaluated the sources you have gathered, you will need to analyze the information for how well it fits your topic. As we have already noted, you will need to fit your speech to your audience. People who don't know much about a particular topic will tune out very technical details. People who know a lot about the topic will tune out basic information. Be sure that the information you have gathered targets your audience appropriately.

You will also need to synthesize the information you have found in multiple sources. Your information will be coming from a variety of places, and in order to come up with a coherent presentation, you will need to draw conclusions from the many reliable sources you have gathered. Be sure to focus on the common threads running through the sources to support your main points. You may even discover that you need to adjust your topic as a result of the research you have done.

SECTION 1 REVIEW

Recalling the Facts

How do you avoid wasting time when preparing a presentation?

Thinking Critically

World War III is about to take place. You are responsible for selecting and saving three books that you think would have a major impact on future generations. One must be a children's book, one a book that significantly affected your life, and one a reference book. You have three minutes to explain why these three books would be an important contribution.

Taking Charge

Choose a topic for a speech, a project, or even self-improvement, and head to the library. Find at least four sources of information for your topic and evaluate how helpful they will be. Which ones will give you information that best fits your audience or your plan? How reliable are these sources? Rank them from most to least helpful.

Using the Library

"You know what scares me," the author Stephen King once said, "are people who don't use the library." King was suggesting that research is a crucial step in writing—whether you're preparing a speech, an essay, or a report. You can significantly increase your credibility as a speaker by quoting authoritative sources. For example, a medical doctor knows more about the causes of sports injuries than you, so quoting a doctor will make your speech about sports injuries more convincing.

You need to supplement your personal knowledge with solid research. Unfortunately, the amount of information available in libraries and online can make it difficult to know where to begin and how to conduct a successful search for supporting material. Do not be intimidated by the library. Once you learn how to get at information, you'll become an efficient and productive researcher.

How do you get the most out of a library? To help you use the library, this section gives useful tips and explains how to find all the sources of information you'll need.

Four Shortcuts

You can use your research time effectively by employing four shortcuts:

1. **Ask Questions** Whether you use your school library or another library nearby, make certain to take advantage of a reference librarian's knowledge. Reference librarians can answer your questions and help you locate sources, which can save you hours of frustration.
2. **Call Ahead** A public library's reference department can usually answer your questions over the phone. They may even find facts for you. Suppose you're researching the Supreme Court's most recent ruling on capital punishment. First call the library and ask some basic questions about recent cases and where you can find information about them.
3. **Use the Library System** Most libraries have Web sites that list all the books within their library system. So, rather than going to your library only to find it doesn't have the book you need, you can check to see if it's available before you go. If it's not, your library can probably get it through interlibrary loan. **Interlibrary loan** is a cooperative system through which libraries lend specific books to one another on order. You can often request an interlibrary loan online. Or you can call the library and have the book you need ordered for you.

The library is a complete resource for researching any topic, on your own or with a group.

4. **Print from Home** Most of the Web sites you can access at the library to search for articles can also be accessed right from your home—a fact that can save you a lot of time and frustration. Such sites not only allow you to search for journal and magazine articles, but they also allow you to print them. These capabilities not only can save you a trip to the library, but can also give you access to library materials 24 hours a day.

Each of these Web sites acts as a gateway to a **database**—a collection of related information and articles gathered from hundreds of publications. **Online** services provide rapid access to different computer databases containing information on many topics, and they are the best place to search for articles. Some databases, such as the Literature Resource Center, are specific to one topic. The Literature Resource Center contains biographies and articles about authors. So, if you're giving a speech about Nathaniel Hawthorne, you can use the database to find information about his life and his work. Other databases are more general and can be used to search for articles about many topics. Infotrac Junior is a database created specifically for

Librarians can help you find resources in a reference section or any other areas in a library.

INSTANT IMPACT

Americans Still Check It Out

Even in today's high-tech world, Americans continue to use and value the library. In fact, according to "The 2014 State of America's Libraries" report conducted for the American Library Association, 96 percent of Americans say public libraries are still important because they hold links to research and access to materials. A like number found them valuable because they promote literacy. Meanwhile, the study found that more than 90 percent of public schools had a library although funding them has become a challenge.

Although many people use libraries to check out books and use the Internet, libraries have a lot more to offer. Library users can check out CDs, DVDs, and software. They also can participate in book clubs, reading circles for children, and cultural programs, such as movie showings and lectures.

The library study found that school librarians must be able to teach children about the latest technologies, spur creativity and imagination, and create safe spaces for students to grow both socially and emotionally.

students that offers full-text articles from atlases, dictionaries, magazines, and newspapers. Students can use the database at home, at the library, or at school. If your library subscribes to such databases, you can usually access them for free. If your library doesn't, you can access them by using the Internet, but you may have to register and pay a fee to use them. Remember, when you're searching a database, use specific keywords that best describe the information you're looking for. For example, if you're researching a speech on pollution and simply type in the keyword *pollution*, you'll probably end up with thousands of entries. You can narrow your search by typing keywords for specific topics you want to cover, such as *effects of pollution, air pollution, water pollution, reducing pollution,* or even a keyword referring to pollution in your area.

Unweaving the Tangled Web

According to *Wall Street Journal* columnist Jared Sandberg, "One of the Internet's strengths is its ability to help consumers find the right needle in a digital haystack of data." In order to find that needle in a haystack, you first need to know how to use the Internet.

For certain, this can be a daunting task. All of the world's information is online, and with the proliferation of smart phones, tablets, and other mobile devices, we can access that data nearly anytime from anywhere. Over the past decade, cloud computing has allowed us to access remote servers linked together to put the power of a supercomputer at our fingertips. We've seen this change the dynamics of certain industries, such as transportation (how Uber has challenged taxis), health care (linking physicians and their patients remotely), and information technology (data storage).

When you use the Internet, virtually any topic imaginable is at your fingertips. But because there's so much information available, finding what you need isn't always easy. Professor John Allen Paulos described the Internet as "the world's largest library. It's just that all the books are on the floor." Search engines can help you find those "books." A **search engine** is a site that allows you to search for information based on keywords, names of persons, or titles of works. There are several search engines, and the most popular is Google.

Nearly everyone has "Googled" some fact or bit of information. But not everyone knows how to use Google, or other search engines, to their highest utility. Here are a few tips on how to use Google to help you in your search for information:

• Don't post questions: Rather, Google works better with keywords.

• Use search term "operators" to help you drill down through vague information to unearth what will truly help you.

• Define the site by using the word "site," then the location you choose. For instance: "site:loc. gov" for the Library of Congress Web site.

Finding exactly what you're looking for on the Web isn't always easy. A search engine, such as Google, can help you complete your research.

• Use quotation marks for specificity: If you want to search for an exact phrase, surround it with quotes: "Washington Monument."
• Use a tilde for related terms: ~granite
• Use a minus sign to exclude items: -Lincoln Memorial
• Use ellipses to define a time period: 2011…2014
• Use stars, or asterisks, (*) to find common terms.
• Use "filetype" to search for certain types of files: "filetype:jpg"

It's also important to note that some engines, such as Google, list sites by popularity; the site at the top has the most hits. Just because it's listed first doesn't mean it's the site you need. Read the site description, and pay attention to the Web address. Many sites whose address includes *.com* or *.net* are commercial sites that may be selling products or informing readers about products. Other . com and .net sites belong to individuals. If you're doing research, it may be more helpful to stick to news sites or research sites, such as *.org*, *.gov*, or *.edu* sites.

Evaluating Web Sites

Global media executive Rupert Murdoch once said, "There is so much media now, with the Internet and people, and [it's] so easy and so cheap to start a newspaper or start a magazine; there's just millions of voices, and people want to be heard." On the Internet, anyone can publish anything about any topic. Thus, the question has become, Who is providing the information?

The key to that question is what kind of information. Not just any information, but the best data that can be accessed in the short period of time that you have to conduct your research. The best information is complete, accurate, unbiased, and corroborated by reliable sources.

For many decades of news gathering, for instance, the only way to get this information was to go to the source—either through in-person interviews, phone conversations, or trekking to the local courthouse, police station, business, or other location of record and either speaking with people or looking things up. That method still has value, but the Internet has revolutionized the way that reporters gather material for their stories. A recent survey by Arketi Group showed that 91 percent of journalists say they use the Internet to search for news sources and story ideas. The simple task of finding out where a business is headquartered, for instance, used to at least require a phone call to the local office and perhaps hours of waiting for someone to call you back. Now, a dizzying array of data can be yours with a few clicks of the keyboard.

Even more than in the past, reporters and researchers must be careful to validate sources and verify facts if they use computers to search. The very existence of a robust Internet and powerful digital tools has made it easy for them to complicate even the simplest facts with various types of data. However, because there is so much information available, finding what you need isn't always easy. The keys are where you're searching and being as specific as you can when you enter keywords into the search engine.

Many people use social media, Wikipedia, and a search engine such as Google as sources of information. Google, indeed, is a verb as well as a noun. That's fine, as long as you are certain that the information is accurate. For instance, if you want to find out where Honda Accords are made, you might search with Google. You'll find a link to Wikipedia that states they're made in Marysville, Ohio. There also may be a recent news article that corroborates that information as well as a retail automobile site that has a short story about Honda's manufacturing locations. You then double-check the Honda of America Manufacturing Web site and find that it's true. Honda makes Accords in Marysville, Ohio. That's good information.

But simply because information is online does not mean that it's accurate. Take the case of Gabrielle Giffords, the congresswoman who was shot outside an Arizona shopping center in 2011 but survived. Soon after the incident occurred, NPR circulated a tweet stating that Giffords had died. Other news outlets repeated this erroneous information, some on their own and others attributing it to NPR. Shortly thereafter, CNN tweeted that Rep. Giffords' press secretary said she was in surgery but "law enforcement sources say she has died." Reuters then tweeted: "FLASH: Congresswoman Giffords still alive…" Other news sources followed suit. Most of the next hour was dedicated to backtracking and exposing the original mistake instead of advancing the story. When covering breaking news, think about what you need to do to get the story right instead of only getting it first.

When conducting online searches, you'll invariably be directed to one or another Web site for the information. Web sites have varying degrees of reliability, so get into the habit of asking the following questions:

- *Who can edit the site*? One of the most popular is Wikipedia, which is open to editing by anyone. The reliability factor of a Wikipedia entry increases in proportion with the number of editors, so be careful.

- *Is it a personal site*? That might induce you to ratchet down your trust level.

- *Has it been a long time since the site was updated, or is the site sloppily designed*? If so, question the source even more than usual and double-check your information with live sources as much as possible.

- *Who owns the site?* This is truly important as it points to bias. For instance, you might look up information on public employment and run across a site that purports to conduct unbiased studies on public worker salaries. But if you look closely you'll see inflammatory language, one-sided blogs or other negative prose on the site. This is a clue that you should find out who owns the site and perhaps discount the statistics presented.

- *Are statistical methodologies clearly explained?* There are a lot of sites out there purporting to providing the "truth" and using statistics to back them up. Remember the old adage: "There are lies, damned lies, and statistics."

Despite the drawbacks of many Web sites, the Internet provides rich resources of information to people looking for it. Here's a look at some of the more-popular online research sources and what they offer.

- **Twitter:** Many reporters are now tweeting their stories in pieces or at least providing updates on what they're doing throughout the day. So Twitter can be a terrific resource for people researching any number of topics. Just type in a keyword or two along with the hashtag (#) and see what comes up.

- **Facebook:** This social sharing site can be useful if you're trying to contact a person or business but don't have the phone number or e-mail address. However, be wary when using material that you find online. It's very easy to copy and publish photos or comments that Facebook members post. Your school should have a policy on the usage of Facebook posts. While the argument can be made that every comment made on Facebook is public, many comments clearly are made to a targeted group of followers. One good solution would be to contact the source and request an interview rather than simply repeating posts without permission.

- **Google:** Many people use this search engine as a jumping off point for their research. You can find a wealth of information by entering search terms in this powerful tool. Google has sections on news, images, maps, videos, and more. Searches yield links to news stories, company Web sites, blogs, and many other informational resources. Google's tools allow you to limit your search to specific time periods and reading levels.

- **YouTube:** Videos posted on this site owned by Google are astounding in their number and variety.

- **IRE Resource Center:** This is a huge research library that contains more than 25,000 investigative stories and offers thousands of tips culled from national conferences that

A library's catalog, which is accessible by computer, tells which materials are available and where to find them.

A library's reference area is a great place to come up with possible topics for an upcoming speech.

journalists attend. IRE also has story packs that help reporters think analytically about their beats, which can be useful for any type of research you're doing.

- **Corporate Web sites:** Business Web sites have come a long way—some say too far, as content tends to get buried under the weight of product promotion. A recent study by Webtrends indicated that almost seven out of every 10 Fortune 100 Web sites have recorded average declines in traffic of 23 percent. And nearly all traffic is generated by just 10 percent of content. Still, when you're searching for the basics about a company, go to the Web site and click on "About." The friendliest Web sites for journalists also have "Newsroom" or "Media" links that offer contacts. When in doubt about a fact, statistic or trend, send the media contact an e-mail.
- **General research sites:** There's so much information on the Internet that it's hard to know where to begin. Some of the following more trustworthy sources include government-sponsored sites such as the U.S. Census Bureau and the National Center for Educational Statistics, as well as media outlets, social media sites, and public records databases. You also should become familiar with county records offices, prison registries, and your local secretary of state's office, which has a lot of helpful information about businesses.
- **My Virtual Reference Desk:** This site links to dictionaries, encyclopedias, and other reference materials useful for research.
- **LibrarySpot:** This site links to more than 300 libraries. They include the Library of Congress, which is the largest library in the world. It offers resources for students and an "Ask a Librarian" option.
- **Ask.com:** Type in a question, and this search engine will take you to one or more Web sites that may have the answer.

Using a Library's Catalog to Find Books

In the old days, a library's catalog—a list of the library's books and other materials—was printed on cards stored in small drawers. Today the catalog is electronic, and it's much easier to use. The catalog is organized much like an Internet search engine—you type in words, and the computer searches for matches. The catalog is organized in three ways: by author, title, and subject. If you know which author you are looking for, you can type in the author's name (usually last name first). All the books or articles written by this author will appear. If you are searching for a particular book, you can search by the book's title. When you don't have specific books in mind, or when you need to find several sources on a subject, you can search by the subject. Remember to be as specific as you can when you do a keyword search. And you may need to try several combinations of words or different words to find the information you need.

Once you find the information on the books you need, print it out or jot down the title, author, and call number. When you find the books on the shelves, look over the books nearby. Books are grouped by subject matter, so you might discover other material that can help you in your research.

Finding Information in Books

When you find a book you think you need, the first places you should look at are the table of contents and the index. These two features can help you quickly locate the specific information you're looking for. **The table of contents** outlines the general plan of the work. It may include the page number on which each chapter begins, a summary of each chapter, and a breakdown of each chapter into its major sections. For example, in the book *The New Rules of College Admissions: Ten Former Admissions Officers Reveal What It Takes to Get into College Today*, the table of contents provides this information:

Chapter 2—Standardized Tests	36
Chapter 3—College Selection	58
Chapter 4—The Application	84
Chapter 5—The Application Theme	107
Chapter 6—Essays and Personal Statements	124

If you're preparing a speech on standardized tests, the table of contents makes it clear that you should turn to page 36. However, if you are preparing a speech on the importance of your grade

point average when applying for college, then the table of contents isn't very helpful.

The index, on the other hand, informs you that grade point averages are discussed on several pages, and the importance of them is discussed on pages 3 and 4. The **index** (from a Latin word meaning "one who points out") tells exactly where to find particular information. The key to using an index effectively is to look up the right term. In our example, you would need to look under the acronym *GPA*, not under *grade point average*.

Finding Periodicals

As discussed earlier, computerized databases are the best way to find articles in **periodicals** (newspapers and magazines). You can search databases online or on your library's Web site. For instance, the database NewsBank (www.newsbank.com) gives you access to millions of newspaper articles and contains information on virtually every newsworthy issue in the United States.

Newspapers and magazines also have their own Web sites. For example, you can read the current edition of the *New York Times* every day at www.nytimes.com, or you can search its database for past articles on any topic. (In fact, you can get the current edition e-mailed to you every day). If you're looking for more-specific information, such as facts about baseball, you might want to check out the Web sites of magazines likely to cover your topic, such as the *Sports Illustrated* site or that of other sporting magazines.

If you're not sure which magazine might have the information you need, you can use a **periodical index**. The listings in a periodical index are usually arranged by subject and author. One of the best-known indexes is the *Reader's Guide to Periodical Literature*. The *Reader's Guide* is an index to hundreds of newspapers and magazines. Abstracts, or summaries, of the articles will help you quickly determine if the articles will be useful. Many articles include links to other Web sites for additional information.

Other Sources of Information

Libraries contain other sources of information, such as almanacs, atlases, biographies, encyclopedias, quotation collections, government publications, and news sources.

Almanacs An **almanac** is an annual publication that provides statistics and general facts. *The World Almanac and Book of Facts,* one of the most popular almanacs, describes itself as a *"compendium* of universal knowledge." This knowledge includes everything from offbeat stories about the world's dumbest robbers to the records of your favorite college and professional sports teams. You will find an almanac useful for learning the order in which the events of a particular year happened, as well as for discovering facts about countries and their governments. *The Facts on File Yearbook* and the *Information Please Almanac* are also available in most libraries.

Atlases Maps and other geographical information are collected in **atlases.** *Rand McNally Goode's World Atlas,* for example, may give you geographical information for your speeches. In addition to maps of climate, rainfall, and time zones, the atlas contains tables and indexes concerning water resources, demographics, income, education, life expectancy, population change, labor structure, and westward expansion. A special feature is the pronunciation index. When using an atlas, be sure to check the date of publication. Atlases can quickly become outdated when country borders shift or nations change names.

Biographies If your speech topic involves a well-known individual, you should consult a biographical reference work. *Biography Index,* published since 1949, is a quarterly cumulative index to biographical material in both books and magazines.

Unfortunately, few biographical collections bother to verify facts. Generally, the people who are written about fill out questionnaires. Sometimes they lie. Consider the case of one man who managed to get a fictitious biography of his dog into *Who's Who in America.*

Unlike *Who's Who,* the magazine *Current Biography* details both positive and negative information about each person it covers. *Current Biography,* issued monthly and then published annually as a combined volume, contains well-documented biographical articles about leaders in all fields of human accomplishment.

The multivolume *Dictionary of American Biography* (DAB) is known for its scholarly articles and objectivity. Though it is a bit more difficult to read, its thoroughness and reliability make it worth checking.

Encyclopedias Most encyclopedias are available online to registered users. In coverage and style, the *Encyclopaedia Britannica* (www.britannica.com) is said to be the most scholarly. Oxford Reference Online (www.oxfordreference.com) gives users access to all of Oxford University Press's dictionaries and encyclopedias (170 titles). The search function finds all related articles on the topic, including biographies, maps, quotations, and time lines, as well as dictionary, thesaurus, and encyclopedia entries.

Specialized encyclopedias can help you research some speech topics. For a speech on genetic

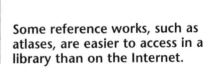

Some reference works, such as atlases, are easier to access in a library than on the Internet.

engineering, for example, you might want to use the *McGraw-Hill Encyclopedia of Science and Technology* (www.accessscience.com). The *International Encyclopedia of Social Sciences* covers topics in fields such as anthropology, history, political science, and sociology.

Quotation Collections Books of quotations are important tools for speakers. You can add colorful phrases, clear examples, and humorous insights to almost any speech by using well-chosen quotations. *Bartlett's Familiar Quotations* (www.bartleby.com) is probably the most familiar collection and the most widely available. You may want to turn to *Peter's Quotations*, though, for more-recent quotations. If you were preparing a speech on the topic of work satisfaction, you might use the following quotations from the *Oxford Dictionary of Modern Quotations* to suggest that we all approach work differently:

> One machine can do the work of 50 ordinary men. No machine can do the work of one extraordinary man. (Elbert Hubbard)

The Internet has made researching information easier, but it can sometimes make it more difficult to obtain reliable knowledge and information.

> I do most of my work sitting down; that's where I shine. (Robert Benchley)

Government Publications The U.S. government is the largest publisher in the world, churning out tens of thousands of books and pamphlets each year. According to researcher Robert I. Borkman, these publications cover topics on nearly all forms of human endeavor—from "starting a business to finding a mortgage to getting rid of acne."

There are more federal government agency databases than you would care to count. However, you can connect to more than 100 of them by linking up with FedWorld (www.fedworld.ntis.gov). FedWorld has a link to USA Search, which allows you to search 30 million government Web sites.

News Sources You should try to read your local newspaper every day. You can also subscribe online or in print to other newspapers, such as the *Christian Science Monitor* and the *New York Times* (the *New York Times* will send the daily paper directly to your e-mail account). Newspapers from around the world can be located online at the Refdesk (www.refdesk.com.com) Web site. You can listen to National Public Radio online or on the way to school in the morning. CNN, MSNBC, Fox, and other television news channels constantly vie for your attention on TV and on the Internet. In short, the world is at your fingertips today.

Another valuable resource is *Facts on File*, a weekly world news digest with a cumulative index. *Editorials on File*, a similar publication, collects and indexes editorials from major newspapers around the world. If you've ever wondered what the *Sydney Telegraph* (Australia) has to say about a topic, you'll be able to find it via these sources.

Recalling the Facts

1. What is a database? Why would a database be helpful in writing a report about a famous person?
2. What is a search engine? Briefly explain how to use a search engine.
3. How do library catalogs list information?
4. How can a table of contents and an index help you find information in a book?
5. What is the *Reader's Guide to Periodical Literature*? When would you use it?

Thinking Critically

Why is it important to evaluate Web sites? Which criteria do you think are most helpful for evaluating a Web site? Explain your answer.

In what ways has the Internet made researching information easier for students? In what ways has it made research more difficult?

How can plagiarism become a problem for someone using information from the Internet for a paper?

Taking Charge

Now that you know how to use search engines and evaluate Web sites, choose a topic, such as "school uniforms" or "music censorship," and do an Internet search on it. Review several sites, and find three that you think would be credible and useful in preparing a speech on your topic. Explain how you evaluated the sites to determine their credibility and usefulness.

Work with a partner to develop a plan for a presentation on graffiti. List what you know about the topic. List what you want to know about the topic. Have one person research information on the Web. Have another research information in the library without using the Web. Compare the information you get and how long it takes to get the information.

Using What You've Found

O nce you've located books or articles on your speech topic, how do you use them effectively? Which information do you include? What about quotations from your sources? This section discusses taking notes and quoting material. Finally, it describes how one student successfully carried out a research plan.

Taking Notes

Whenever you investigate a written source of information or interview an expert, you should take notes. A rule of thumb is to record more notes than you think you will need, because a return trip to the library is inefficient. Still, you shouldn't record everything. Select information that is the most important, supports your point or argument, and will interest your audience.

Your notes should be organized so that you can easily incorporate them into your speeches. You may find it useful to write your notes on index cards. If you place only one item of information on

Take specific notes while you complete your research.

each card, then you can rearrange the cards until you're satisfied that you have the subtopics arranged in a logical order.

Each note card should have a general heading at the top and a complete source citation at the bottom. Use quotation marks if you are copying the text verbatim.

Quoting Material: Avoid Heavy Lifting

Plagiarism is copying or imitating the language, ideas, or thoughts of another person and passing them off as your original work. In discussing plagiarism, it is important to draw some distinctions.

Commitment to Liberty:

"Let every nation know, whether it wishes us well or ill, that we shall pay any price, bear any burden, meet any hardship, support any friend, oppose any foe, in order to assure the survival and success of liberty."

John F. Kennedy from his inaugural address, delivered Friday, January 20, 1961.

AmmentorpDK/Getty Images

Material considered "common knowledge" is traditionally (by agreement among scholars) handled differently from material protected by copyright. That means you do not need to quote a source if you are reciting a fact that is available from many sources (for example, that George Washington was the first president of the United States).

The general rule is this: If you're in doubt, cannot say it in any other way, or do not want to misinterpret a fact, name and quote your source. As Mark Twain advised, "When in doubt, tell the truth." If you give credit, then you are not plagiarizing. Also, avoid Web sites that offer to write your papers or speeches for you. And never simply copy and paste information into your speeches and call it your own; to do so is plagiarism.

Paraphrasing another's unique ideas is not an acceptable way of avoiding *attribution*. **Paraphrasing,** or simply rewording the original passage, is still taking someone else's ideas. Excessive paraphrasing made then Senator Joseph Biden of Delaware one of the most famous political plagiarists of our time. On September 12, 1987, the *New York Times* reported that Biden, then a presidential candidate, had "borrowed" crucial passages of a campaign speech he gave in Iowa from a speech that Neil Kinnock, a Labour party leader, had delivered during his election campaign in Britain.

While it is common for politicians to borrow from other sources, Biden exceeded the limits of fair use. For example, Kinnock's speech inquired "Why am I the first Kinnock in a thousand generations to be able to get to university?" While Biden's stated the following without crediting Kinnock "Why is it that Joe Biden is the first in his family ever to go to a university?"

Biden went on to lift more of Kinnock's speech, questioning their ancestor's literacy, their work ethic, and their being constrained by lack of a platform upon which to stand.

Biden eventually withdrew from the presidential race. He announced his candidacy for president again in 2007, and the plagiarism controversy was usually only mentioned in passing in most articles about him.

Unfortunately, Biden wasn't the first politician to plagiarize, and he probably won't be the last. In fact,

the Internet has made plagiarism even easier and more tempting than ever. Today, you can find copies of thousands of speeches and papers, and copying and pasting has led to the end of many people's careers.

Consider the following cases. In 2004, Mark Latham, a member of the Australian Labor Party, plagiarized President Bill Clinton's 1997 State of the Union address. Critics claimed that "Latham's ideas are essentially generated by Internet search engines." He

Senator Joseph Biden, shown here in 2012, withdrew from the 1988 presidential race after it was discovered he had plagiarized a British politician's speech. In 2007, he declared his intention to run for president again.

CHAPTER 8 Researching Your Presentation   187

The subjects you discuss with friends at lunch could provide speech topics.

resigned the following year. In 2005, Nevada congressman Jim Gibbons plagiarized a speech—15 of the 21 paragraphs—he gave at a fundraising event in Elko, Nevada. That same year, New Mexico congressman Steve Pearce was accused of plagiarizing speeches and newspaper columns. His speechwriter resigned, saying he was the one guilty of plagiarism.

Plagiarism isn't just a problem in politics. Principals, deans, teachers, musicians, authors, movie directors, screenwriters, researchers, and students have all been found guilty of plagiarizing.

New technologies for checking plagiarism help teachers and organizations analyze writings to identify the source of plagiarized content.

Students find themselves tempted to plagiarize for many reasons; low self-esteem and the pressure to get good grades are often cited. If you feel that you must have that A or that your own ideas are of little worth, plagiarism is not the answer. The consequences of stealing another's work are high. Some students have failed courses, and others have been expelled from school. People have lost their jobs.

Putting Your Research Together

Ideas for your speeches can come from almost anywhere, but your research should follow a plan. A typical research plan might include the following steps:

Putting Your Research Together

- Incorporating Real Life
- Surfing the Web
- Reading Books
- Finding Reviews
- Poring over Periodicals
- Checking Out Columnists
- Finding Quotations
- Interviewing Sources
- Creating Structure
- Following the Rule of Three

Recalling the Facts

1. What is plagiarism?
2. How many ideas should you record on a single note card?

Thinking Critically

Most politicians have ghostwriters (people who write for others using the other people's names). Imagine a future in which politicians were required to offer sound ideas instead of sound bites (brief statements made to catch the public's interest or attention). Would different candidates be elected to office? Why or why not?

Taking Charge

Choose a topic for a speech that you would like to present. After coming up with at least five steps you would take in researching this topic, share your ideas with the rest of the class.

CHAPTER 8 Review and Enrichment

Looking Back

Listed below are the major ideas discussed in this chapter.

- Before you start accumulating information, you should have a research plan.
- Thorough research will increase your credibility as a speaker.
- Consulting with a reference librarian can save you valuable time.
- A database stores related information.
- The library's catalog lets you know what books and other materials the library has and where to find them.
- The Internet is a communication tool, but it is not a remedy for all a researcher's difficulties.

- The table of contents outlines the general plan of a book.
- The index helps you locate particular information in a book.
- The best-known periodical index is the *Reader's Guide to Periodical Literature*.
- Notes should be organized so that you can easily incorporate them into your speeches.
- When taking notes, you should place only one item of information on each note card.
- Plagiarism is intellectually dishonest.

Speech Vocabulary

Match the speech term on the left with the definition on the right.

1. database
2. online
3. index
4. table of contents
5. interlibrary loan
6. paraphrasing
7. plagiarism

a. service based on a cooperative system among libraries
b. accessible via the Internet
c. a collection of related information
d. restating in your own words
e. using another person's ideas as your own
f. the general plan of a work
g. from the Latin for "one who points out"

Academic Vocabulary

Use context clues to write the meaning of each vocabulary term. Then use a print or an online dictionary to check the accuracy of your definition.

prerequisite
entrepreneur
alienate

compendium
attribution

To Remember

Answer the following questions based on your reading of the chapter.

1. The ancient Greeks referred to the process of accumulating information as building a _____.
2. A _____ librarian may be able to help you begin researching a speech topic.
3. The database _____ can give you access to millions of newspaper articles.
4. _____ is a Latin word meaning "one who points out."
5. _____ is copying or imitating the language, ideas, or thoughts of another and passing them off as your own.

To Do

1. With the help of a reference librarian, find articles that discuss plagiarism. Discuss your findings in class.
2. Ask a librarian to help you devise a scavenger hunt in the reference section. The hunt should acquaint you with some of the most important reference works, including a dictionary of word and phrase origins.

To Talk About

1. What is wrong with excessive paraphrasing if you give credit to the original source?
2. To support their positions on controversial issues, politicians often quote opinion polls. What issues in your school would lend themselves to opinion polling?

To Write About

1. Write an essay about plagiarism. A possible topic: Why intellectual honesty matters.
2. Write an essay in which you examine censorship as it affects what books are on the shelves of a school library.
3. According to author Richard Saul Wurman, "Information anxiety is produced by the ever-widening gap between what we understand and what we think we should understand. It is the black hole between data and knowledge." Write a creative essay or a play describing a typical day in the life of someone terrified by the information explosion.

Related Speech Topics

Ghostwriting: the invisible touch
To quote or not to quote: that is the question
Information skills: a survival course
The school librarian: a friend in deed

Censorship: how far is too far?
Information anxiety
The Internet: How valid is the information?

CHAPTER 9

Organizing Your Speech

Corbis/SuperStock

To me, things are organized when all of the piles of clothes in my room are stacked to the same height!

—Lucille Ball

Learning Objectives

After completing this chapter, you will be able to do the following.

- Use effective strategies to organize and to outline presentations.
- Use effective verbal strategies in presentations.
- Apply effective organization to aspects of your life.
- Develop appropriate introductions and conclusions for your speeches that will give positive first and final impressions.
- Develop a meaningful body for your speech that shows clarity and logical progression.
- Identify and use the various patterns of organization for speeches.

Chapter Outline

Following are the main sections in this chapter.

1. The Introduction
2. The Body
3. The Conclusion

Speech Vocabulary

In this chapter, you will learn the meanings of the speech terms listed below.

organization
introduction
rhetorical question
quotation
narrative
link
thesis statement
preview statement
body
outline
purpose statement
subordination

main heading
supporting materials
transition
chronological pattern
climactic pattern
spatial pattern
cause-effect pattern
problem-solution
  pattern

Academic Vocabulary

Expanding your academic vocabulary will help you become a more effective communicator. Listed below are some words appearing in this chapter that you should make part of your vocabulary.

equilibrium
vested
gigantic
fiasco
illustration
jeopardy

enhanced
haphazardly
intensification
analogy
indented
inhibition

You don't have to read reams of paper to realize what it means not to be organized. Homework doesn't get finished, phone calls don't get made, jobs don't get accomplished, invitations don't get sent out, the car doesn't get washed, and the alarm clock doesn't go off in the morning. Whether at the library or at work, without proper organization, you waste much time and energy in your frantic rush to find what you are after or to meet deadlines.

In addition to sacrificing time and energy, you might also lose out educationally if you lack organizational skills. A study done at UCLA's Higher Education Research Institute found that more than 30 percent of all students who entered a four-year college or university had to take special courses designed to strengthen their study and organizational skills.

Organization offers you a sense of balance and personal *equilibrium*. Organization helps you take the loose ends of your life, put them in order, and, in the process, keep sane! When eighteenth-century British statesman and orator Edmund Burke said, "Good order is the foundation of all good things," he was implying that through structure and organization, both individuals and societies have the potential to progress.

Thus, in this chapter, you will learn about organization and about how directed planning can often be beneficial in your personal life, your work life, and your speaking. In addition, you will work with the three parts of the speech—the introduction, the body, and the conclusion—and examine their components. You will learn about outlining and then examine five types of organizational patterns that can help you develop your thoughts. You will also recognize how important it is for the introduction, the body, and the conclusion to work together for maximum speaking effectiveness.

Introduction

In ancient Babylonia (2700–538 B.C.), a home builder had to "bet his life"—literally—that each house he built would hold up. According to the Babylonians' Code of Hammurabi, if a builder made a house that collapsed and caused the death of the house's owner, the builder would also be put to death. Needless to say, the builder had a profoundly *vested* interest in constructing a house that was guaranteed to be strong and reliable.

The consequences of a poorly presented speech aren't nearly so dramatic or life threatening. The "death of an idea," however, might result if a speech fails to communicate because it hasn't been built with care. One way that you as an effective speaker can provide this care is to present your message with clear organization.

Do the following statements sound familiar?

- "How could I forget to do that?"
- "We should have done this step first!"
- "I have no idea how I'm going to get this job done!"

If so, there is a good chance that you need a lesson in effective organization. Effective organization is a systematic plan that makes sense and helps you to get things done. Generally speaking, **organization** is the logical grouping and ordering of "like" parts. This systematic grouping and logical arrangement allow you to keep a handle on what is happening.

SECTION 1

The Introduction

Thomas Boyden, an executive for Shell Oil, says that when he was interviewing top collegiate applicants for prospective management positions, he would give each applicant approximately 15 minutes. During that 15-minute evaluation, he would observe three different things: (1) the confidence and congeniality that the applicant showed at first, (2) the sense of logic, organization, and self-discipline that the applicant could exhibit under fire during the interview, and (3) the poise that the applicant showed when leaving the interview. In other words, the interview would be divided into three distinct parts, and each part was important in making the whole interview a success.

What is true in the business world is also true in the oral communication world. Just like Boyden's interview, your speech should be organized into three distinct parts that, when presented effectively, can make a positive impression. We now examine these three parts, starting here with the introduction.

A secondary teacher once said that he was confident that his students would always give speeches that had an introduction, a body, and a conclusion—but not necessarily in that order! It is your job to make sure that your speeches are organized so that you put things in the correct order. That means you should begin with a well-thought-out introduction.

Whatever you are doing, isn't it important to get off to a good start? Doing so often supplies you with the momentum and confidence that you need to complete your task. Many speakers say that, psychologically, the toughest part of a speech is the beginning, or the **introduction**. It is during your introduction that you find out whether your audience accepts you. Consequently, a good introduction can make or break your speech because it sets the tone—at least in your head—for the remainder of the speech.

What is an introduction, and what is it supposed to do? See if you can determine the function of an introduction by reading the following example.

Does your room look like this? Does this show whether you are organized?

(Remember this introduction. We will refer to it later in the chapter.)

(1) Have you ever heard the saying "Let a smile be your umbrella"? What about the observation "Laugh and the world laughs with you"? Both of these sayings deal with how a positive attitude and a sense of humor can make a bad situation a little bit better for both you and the people around you. (2) However, did you know that your ability to laugh can mean a great deal more than a pleasant smile or momentary delight? As a matter of fact, laughter can be very beneficial in many ways. (3) Consequently, I would like to discuss the various areas in your life where laughter can play a significantly positive role. (4) Let's take a look at how laughter can help you on the job, with your friends and family, and with your health.

Do you see how the interesting information in the beginning (1) might encourage an audience to listen? Next, do you see how a clear connection is made

COMMUNICATION *BREAKDOWN*

The Battle of the Crater

General Ambrose Everett Burnside

One of the most famous battles of the U.S. Civil War took place at Petersburg, Virginia, in 1864. Under the leadership of General Ambrose Everett Burnside, federal forces had undertaken the monumental engineering task of burrowing below the enemy and forming a shaft 500 feet long that stretched under the Confederate lines. The shaft was then filled with four tons of dynamite. When the dynamite was ignited, the explosion blew more than 250 rebel soldiers high into the air and created a *gigantic* hole that measured over 150 feet long, 50 feet wide, and 30 feet deep! The blast was so powerful that both sides stood in awe at its effect, but it didn't take long for the Southern troops, shocked and stunned, to hurry for cover.

The problem for the North was that no clear plan had been developed for a follow-through. General Burnside, as historians tell it, was so shaken by the sight of the blast that he stood at the back of his troops and drank rum. He gave no verbal command. As a result, the Battle of the Crater turned into a *fiasco*.

Acting mainly on instinct, Northern soldiers charged *into* the crater, not to the left or the right of it. No ladders were taken in the unorganized attack, and the men reached the end of the crater only to find that they were trapped. Realizing the plight of the North, the Southern troops regrouped and picked off the federal soldiers one-by-one.

Civil War experts agree that the absence of effective organization and leadership by the North not only prevented a glorious victory at Petersburg but also cost hundreds of Northern soldiers their lives! To this day, the crater remains in Petersburg, Virginia, as a monument to the soldiers who fought and died there.

Questions
1. What should Northern leaders have done prior to setting off the explosion?
2. Who do you feel was specifically at fault for this tragedy?

---

between the introductory material and the speech topic (2)? Also, do you see exactly what the speech will be about (3)? Finally, do you see a clear statement of the areas that the speech will discuss (4)?

Basically, an introduction does four things:

1. It gets the attention of the audience.
2. It provides a clear link from your attention-getter to your speech topic, or thesis statement.
3. It gives your specific thesis statement.
4. It presents a preview of the major areas that you will discuss.

Attention-Getters

The first words that you say to an audience must make them want to listen to you. You must grab your audience's attention. You have probably heard that telling a joke is a good way to start a speech. No one will deny that humor is refreshing and that everyone likes to laugh. You must ask yourself, however, what type of humor works for you. Is a humorous opening appropriate for your speech topic? What happens if nobody laughs? A humorous approach can backfire.

While it is true that a light, funny attention-getter can be a tremendous boost to your confidence, you do not have to use humor or a funny story to get off to a solid start. Examine your personality and then realistically answer the following questions: What works for you, and what do you feel comfortable presenting? With these matters in mind, let's examine five types of attention-getters that can help you to get your speech off to a smooth start.

1.   Asking Questions One of the best methods of gaining an audience's attention is to get audience members directly involved in what you are saying. Immediately asking them a question or a series of questions not only fires up their curiosity about your topic, it also makes them active participants in your speech.

If you were doing a speech called "The Power of Word Building," you might begin by asking your audience this:

> How many of you know the meaning of the word *verisimilitude*? Do you know what *veracity* means? What about the word *verity*? Well, all three of these words have something to do with the word *truth*, and I wouldn't be telling you the truth if I didn't confess that I had to look these words up in a dictionary. However, building vocabulary is a challenge that each of us should accept if . . .

How about these questions for a speech on shifting blame:

> Have you ever heard someone say, "The devil made me do it"? Have you ever heard the expression "Don't blame me. It's not my fault"? If you answered yes to one or both of these questions, then you would probably agree with me that many people in today's society find it easy to make excuses and blame someone or something else for their problems. I would like to talk about . . .

Do you see how questions can provide the attention-getting spark you want to begin your speech? You might ask audience members to respond to your questions by actually raising their hands or speaking out loud. But beware! While this technique can sometimes promote spirited audience involvement, it can also lead to chaos and loss of concentration if the responses to your questions

don't turn out as you expected. Are you prepared to handle such a situation? Is it worth the risk?

Often, it is best to use rhetorical questions. **Rhetorical questions**, like the ones given in the examples, don't really demand a spoken response. Instead, they ask the members of your audience to answer silently in their heads. Rhetorical questions are "safe" questions, because they often answer themselves: "Do any of you like to get your feelings hurt?" "Do any of us in this room want our friends or families to join the thousands who die each year because of people who drink and drive?" Such questions don't demand a response, but they do challenge your audience to think. This type of mental stimulation offers you the potential for immediate attention-getting success.

2.   Making References Like asking questions, making references can allow you to work well with your audience. You might refer to people in the audience, your physical surroundings, other speakers who are on the program, or the significance of the occasion. This approach allows you to be comfortable, congenial, and conversational with your audience by including it in your opening remarks. Audiences like to be included, and including them provides a type of speaker-audience unity that says, "You and I are in this speech together!" For instance, you might say this:

> I see that John and Ina are in the audience. When we first started this class project over two months ago, they were the ones who provided the leadership and enthusiasm that the rest of us

Introductory Attention-Getters			
?	?	?	Questions
			References
!	!	!	Startling statements
			Stories
"		"	Quotations

needed then. The word *leadership* is exactly what I wish to talk about tonight because . . .

Or you might say this:

For some reason, every time that we are in this auditorium, the air-conditioning is out. Maybe we should all bring our own fans next time. However, the temperature might not be the only thing that is sticky tonight. My topic, "Why AIDS Needs to Be Talked About in Schools," could also make some people warm and uncomfortable. I have confidence, nevertheless, that if we work together . . .

As usual, of course, you must use good taste and common sense. For example, it might be risky to make a casual reference to someone in the audience whom you barely know. Making references should get you off to a positive start with your listeners, not put your speech in *jeopardy*. In general, though, audiences appreciate a speaker who shows that he or she is aware of and in tune with what is happening.

3. Making a Startling Statement

Sometimes your best attention-getter is one that jolts your audience into paying attention.

One student spoke to a high school audience about the problems associated with violence in society. While she spoke, she comfortably moved her right hand as if she were keeping the beat to a song that only she could hear. Her first words were these:

I love music. I love dancing. I love how men and women, young and old, rich or poor, can move and smile and laugh and keep the rhythm to their favorite songs. However, today I'm not here to talk about music—because, ironically, every time that my hand comes down to "keep the beat," a young child is physically or sexually abused in this country. And the violence is real . . .

Picture yourself in this audience. Wouldn't you be immediately drawn in by the speaker and the tremendous power of her message?

You may also choose to use startling statistics to grab the attention of the audience. While conducting your research, notice any data or studies that might surprise the listeners and make them even more interested in the topic. For example, if your research indicated that one in ten families will be the victims of a drunk-driving accident, or that one in five people will be the victim of a violent crime, you may be able to shock your audience into the reality of these social problems. Use the numbers to quantify the extent of the issue in our lives and to grab the audience's attention.

As impressive as this technique might appear, it has its drawbacks. Too many speakers have tried to startle their audiences, only to find that their attention-getters offended people instead. Don't be foolish. An audience will forgive an honest mistake, but it will rarely forgive bad taste! Yes, the startling statement can work for you, but you must use sound judgment and take the time to know your audience.

4. Giving a Quotation

You deliver a **quotation** each time you repeat the exact words that someone else has used. Giving a quotation is a popular attention-getter. For one thing, quotations can add a degree of style and sophistication to speech presentations. For another, quotations are abundant and fairly easy to find, so you can surely find one that fits your needs.

Choose quotations that are clear and appropriate for your speech topic and select authors who

Your audience may enjoy answering questions in your speech. If you use questions, however, you need to be ready for any answer.

(c) Image Source/Alamy

are reliable. Although some famous people need no introduction, it is a good practice while delivering your attention-getter to give your audience some idea of who your author is and what he or she did that was noteworthy. Why is this a good practice? Audiences are likely to be impressed if the sources that you are quoting are impressive.

Here's how one student started his speech on "What Has Happened to Friendship?"

> "First in war—first in peace—and first in the hearts of his countrymen." These are the words that began Revolutionary War general Henry Lee's famous funeral oration for George Washington. The quotation shows us a man of conscience and a man who cared for his fellow man. However, do we care for our fellow man today the same as Washington did in his day? I would like to take a look at . . .

The quotation immediately gives the speech an academic and historical flavor. Henry Lee's words say to the audience, "Take this speech seriously and give it your attention, please!" Another student, speaking on "Americans—Why Are We So Gullible?" began with a similar historical quotation:

> "You can fool all of the people some of the time and you can fool some of the people all of the time, but you can't fool *all* of the people *all* of the time." Abraham Lincoln, the author of this quotation, might have added the words *"except* in America," because Americans are often easy prey for those wishing to make a fast buck. Let's examine why Americans are so gullible and take a look . . .

Don't think that your quotation must be serious or must have been delivered by someone who lived centuries ago. On the contrary, some of the most effective quotations are lighter and have been given by people who are alive right now. Take the time to search through your resources so that you can find the quotation that will be the perfect attention-getter for your speech.

5. Telling a Story One of the most popular attention-getters is the **narrative**—the telling of a story. Everyone loves a story, especially one that is told well. Illustrations and personal accounts can quickly give you an "in" with your audience because these stories give your personality a chance to work

and are so much in demand. Americans are storytellers (and story *listeners*) at heart.

Keep in mind that your story should be short and to the point. Don't get so caught up in your account that you lose sight of your speech's purpose. The best stories are those that hold the interest of the audience yet lead clearly into your speech topic.

Have you had an experience that you would call special? Have you gone through some heart-stopping ordeal that you would like to share? Such experiences can make good stories. Here is an example:

> A few weeks ago, my mom and dad had gone out for the evening, and I was alone at home. About 2 A.M. I heard noise by a downstairs window. Even though I hoped that the sounds would go away, they didn't. As a matter of fact, they got louder. It sounded as if someone were struggling to reach the latch of the window. I was petrified, but somehow I managed to go downstairs. Slowly, I moved the curtain to see what was outside. You can imagine my fear when I saw two eyes looking right back at me! It was a *raccoon*. The good news is that, in this instance, I was able to deal with my *fear*. The bad news is that I almost collapsed in the process. What does fear mean and how can we . . .

Stories can be insightful, and they can also be fun for you to deliver and for your audience to hear. And stories don't have to be personal. They can be interesting accounts about other people, places, events, and so on. Any story can be an effective attention-getter if it sets the mood that you are after and creates an effective picture in the minds of your listeners that relates to your speech thesis.

Let's move on to the next aspect of the introduction, the link.

The Link

Probably the section of the introduction that students most often overlook when preparing their speeches is the **link**. It serves two purposes. First, the link is the statement that comes between the attention-getter and the thesis statement and logically connects the two. It does you little good to have a clever attention-getter if the audience sees no relation between it and the focus of your speech. Second, the link should develop a bridge between the audience and the topic. Here, your objective is to connect with audience members so that they are motivated to listen to your topic. Much as with the attention-getter, you are continuing to draw in the audience members by helping them to understand the value of the topic. Helping the audience in this way will probably make them feel that listening is worthwhile. The motivation for listening may stem from showing your audience how your speech and they have common ground—how your speech is relevant to their lives. You can also motivate them by showing them how your topic has real significance, or why it might be "a big deal" in their lives.

Read the following introduction, which could be prepared and delivered by a high school student. Pay particular attention to the role of the link sentences (italicized). The link to the topic is labeled A. The link to the audience is labeled B.

When preparing a speech, keep in mind that everyone loves hearing a story.

> "Ladies and gentlemen, boys and girls, especially boys, I'd like to introduce you to Katie, the perfect girl. She has perfect proportions, perfect skin, a perfect face, and the perfect silhouette. She looks like a model, because she is one—a model of perfection. Best thing of all, she can be found every day at your local supermarket."

> Katie, and a bevy of gorgeous girls just like her, grace the cover of magazines designed to appeal to us, teenagers. But while Katie is beautiful, she doesn't actually exist. That's because her body has been extensively edited with computers. In other words, she's unreal. **(A)** *My speech today will concern airbrushed images in popular media, images that are digitally altered to create the perfect person.* **(B)** *According to a Change.org petition to Seventeen Magazine, which resulted in the magazine banning photo enhancement of its models,* "Those 'pretty women' that we see in magazines are fake."

The problem with this phenomenon is that they create an unattainable goal for us girls, and boys, too, to reach. Therefore, I would like to examine ways that we can change this type of thinking.

The author opens with an attention-grabbing device: that the perfect girl can be found by anyone at the local supermarket. Then, in order to clearly explain her attention-getter, the author explains her point. She then logically links this point about the way photos are altered with the Change.org petition that resulted in a magazine banning such practices. This is important because it shows the students in the audience that their efforts can have results. She then commented about the result of this type of image manipulation—that it creates unrealistic goals for young men and women to reach.

Even though the link can be more than one sentence long, one sentence usually can do the job.

The impact of both your attention-getter and your speech thesis is enhanced when your link statement connects as it should. In addition, you stand a better chance of connecting with your audience.

The Thesis Statement

The third part of the introduction is the sentence that will tell your audience exactly what you will be speaking about. This sentence, which we will discuss further in Chapter 13, "Speeches to Inform," is called the **thesis statement.**

If you have a catchy attention-getter and a smooth link to a thesis statement that is vague, your speech may be unclear. The reason that you wanted to get the audience's attention is that you had something worthwhile to say. That something is your thesis statement, or the focus of what your speech is going to address. Your audience must never wonder, "What exactly is this speech about?" A brief, to-the-point thesis statement can help you avoid such a problem.

One way to make sure your audience knows that you are introducing your thesis is to say as much. Don't permit your audience to take an organizational detour. Saying something like "This leads me to my thesis, which is . . . " can be a smart way to make sure that both you and your audience are following the same communication road map.

Generally, a thesis should both clarify the overall goal of your speech (to inform, to persuade, or to entertain) and state your specific topic. Be sure to let your audience know the particular focus of your topic.

For example, if you are going to inform the audience, use words in the thesis such as

> Today, I will *inform* you about . . .

> My goal is to *explain* . . .

> With this information, I hope you will better *understand* . . .

What do you think about the values portrayed in the type of teen magazine these girls are reading?

If the goal is to persuade, use words or phrases such as

> I want to *persuade* you that . . .

> My goal is to *convince* you that . . .

> I believe that each of you *should* . . .

In addition to stating the goal of your speech, the thesis should clarify the angle or slant of your topic. Simply to say you are going to talk about "music" is too vague. Tell the audience the specific focus of your topic. Perhaps you want to inform the audience specifically about the different types of summer music programs offered by your community. Or perhaps you want to convince students that joining the school's marching band has distinct benefits. Both speeches would deal with music, but their goals and slants would be different. Your audience deserves to know the exact point of your speech. Making your thesis clear and specific will also help you to keep your speech focused and your information on target.

The Preview Statement

If you have gone to the movies or watched television, you have no doubt seen previews of upcoming films or television episodes. These brief sets of "snapshots" usually focus on the high points of what you would see in the complete production. Similarly, speeches include previews in the form of preview statements.

The **preview statement** is usually one sentence at the end of the introduction that gives the audience an overview of the major areas that will be discussed in the body of the speech. If you were giving a speech on the negative effects of drinking alcohol, your preview might mention the physical, mental, and societal effects of drinking. A speech on success stories in the Olympics might include a preview statement on physical and mental preparation.

Of course, the major areas mentioned in your preview statement will be repeated later in the body of your speech, with specific examples added for support. Often, the examples and evidence you have collected will determine what your areas of discussion will be and, thus, what your preview statement should include. Although not all speeches have a preview statement, it is often wise to provide one for your audience. Audience members can't catch everything the first time. They might miss your main points when said within the body of your speech. A preview statement tells your audience where your speech will be heading and, as a result, makes the body of your speech easier for your listeners to follow.

Speakers often use gestures to emphasize the key statements of their speeches.

Recalling the Facts

1. What is the name for the part of the introduction that students most often overlook when preparing their speeches?
2. You want your audience to listen to you because you have something worthwhile to say. What do you call that something, or the statement in the introduction that expresses the focus of your speech?
3. What is the introduction's last part, which gives the audience snapshots of the areas that you will cover in your speech?
4. There are various types of attention-getters that you could use in your introduction. One very popular type is the narrative. What does the word *narrative* mean?

Thinking Critically

Nineteenth-century British writer Edward Bulwer-Lytton once said, "Every great person exhibits the talent of organization—whether it be in a poem, a philosophical system, a policy, or a strategy." In other words, being organized is an attribute shared by most successful people. Analyze and evaluate how organization can be important when you are (a) trying to get a job, (b) on the job, (c) having a party, or (d) trying to solve a problem that you have with a friend.

Taking Charge

Select one of the attention-getting devices from the chapter and use it to introduce a classmate to the rest of the class. Be sure to explain your attention-getter, link it to the fact that you are introducing someone, introduce the person, and then mention two of the person's interests. Have some fun, but stay focused on your objective—providing an introduction that will make your classmate glad you are the one doing the introduction. Write what you will say before speaking.

The Body

The **body** of the speech is the heart, the brain, even the nerve center of the entire presentation. It is the place where you exhibit in an organized manner your powers of persuasion and reasoning. Audiences need to be convinced. They need to be informed. They need to be shown. After your audience hears your introduction and knows your speech thesis, you need to show or prove your point. You do this in the body of the speech.

Your outline is like a map for your speech.

Let's take a look at two important ways to make the body of your speech clear and convincing: outlining and using organizational patterns.

Outlining Your Speech

Have you ever taken a trip that involved driving a long distance? If so, someone in your family probably used a map to study various routes and then mark the selected route for the drive.

An **outline** is the speaker's map. It is the way that you give form and direction to your organization. An outline allows you to know not only where you are going but also where you are and where you have been. An outline keeps you on course.

The author Victor Hugo is credited with stating, "No army can withstand the strength of an idea whose time has come." However, few will support an idea that they can't understand. Similarly, few people can follow a speech that appears to be *haphazardly* thrown together or that is difficult to comprehend because of poor organization.

You have probably heard the story about the driver who is miserably lost. Miles off the main highway, the driver stops to ask a farmer for directions, only to be told, "Sorry, I know where you're goin', but you can't get there from here." It should comfort you to know that by following your outline, you can always "get there from here" because you have stayed on your planned speaking course.

How do you actually make an outline? Even though you will outline your entire speech, most of your outlining will deal with the body. Therefore, let's use the body of the speech to examine outlining. First, look at the components of a speaking outline:

Purpose Statement
  I. Main heading (roman numeral)
    A. Supporting material (capital letter)
      1. Detail (arabic numeral)

Now let's examine in simple language exactly how a speaking outline works. You will usually begin by establishing the central idea of your speech, or the purpose statement.

Purpose Statement The **purpose statement** is closely associated with the thesis given at the end of your introduction. It is placed near the top of your paper (without numerals or letters) and states both the topic and the specific purpose of your speech. Here are some examples:

> The purpose of this speech is to inform the audience about the pros and cons of midyear high school graduation for seniors.
> The purpose of this speech is to explain to the audience the steps that a person must go through to become certified in lifesaving.
> The purpose of this speech is to persuade the group that immediate action must be taken if we wish to save our local environment.

In your actual speech, you might not say your purpose statement exactly as you have written it. You will probably reword your ideas when you formulate your thesis. However, the purpose statement needs to be written out at the top of your outline to serve as a primary reminder of what your speech is going to be about.

Outlining follows the process of **subordination**, or ranking in terms of importance. Your purpose statement, written at the top of the page, is the most important part of your speech. Everything else spoken—whether in the introduction, the body, or the conclusion—will fall under its direction.

Main Headings After you have determined your purpose statement, you need to decide what your main headings will be. **Main headings** are the major divisions, areas, or arguments of your purpose statement. They represent the main ideas that you wish to analyze. Main headings are indicated by the use of roman numerals. Suppose your purpose statement is this:

> The purpose of this speech is to show my audience the serious harms related to smoking.

The main headings in the body of your speech might read as follows:

INSTANT IMPACT

Must Followers Have Focus?

We live in a world where it is desirable to be in charge. Many people who wish to be in charge realize the value of effective organization and seek out what organizational experts say. They don't have to look far. The bookshelves are loaded with books and pamphlets on such topics as *Management and the Mind* and *Organization and the Power Person*. However, a valuable bit of information about followers was released from the Carnegie Mellon Graduate School of Industrial Administration.

According to the Carnegie Mellon report, two of the most important traits of a good follower are self-management and a sense of focus. The report stated that for any group to function cohesively and efficiently, followers must have a sense of organization regarding how they manage their time, how they prioritize issues, and how they zero in on what matters. Without skilled followers, the study said, society could become filled with robots—people who are easily manipulated. The study concluded that great leaders are often the result of great followers who see, adhere to, and carry out a definite plan of action.

What's the point? Whether you are in the spotlight or on the sidelines, it takes everyone to make a solution work.

> I. Smoking can lead to significant *health problems for the smoker.*
> II. Smoking can even affect the *health of others* near the smoker.
> III. Smoking can contribute to *economic problems.*

Notice by what is italicized that each main heading is a clear division of exactly what is going to be addressed in the speech.

Supporting Materials The supporting materials you gather provide *intensification* and reinforcement for the main headings. They are listed under the main headings; each main heading has its own supporting statements. Supporting materials make up the "Now I would like to get more specific" sections of the speech. In these sections, you present the examples, personal stories, and pertinent observations that all audiences need to hear if they are going to believe you.

Remember that your supporting materials must be logically narrower and more specific than your main headings. Furthermore, if your organization is accurate, your supporting materials not only will support each main heading but will also link back to support the purpose statement. Keep in mind that while the main headings logically divide and prove the purpose statement, the supporting materials extend what has been suggested by the main headings.

Supporting materials are identified in your outline by capital letters. They don't have to be written out in great detail. Most of the time, a key word or phrase should be enough to jog your memory and allow your speaking talents and your preparation to take over. An outline is not supposed to be a substitute for memory. Ultimately, it is up to you, based on your familiarity with your material, to remember what you want to say.

Here are examples of supporting materials you might use in the previously mentioned speech on the harms of smoking:

> The purpose of this speech is to show my audience the serious harms related to smoking.
> I. Smoking can lead to significant health problems for the smoker.
>   A. Lung disease often results.
>   B. Thousands die each year.
>   C. Members of my family are among the victims.

Details Many speakers go one step deeper into the outline and give details. Details narrow the outline even further, providing information that breaks down the supporting materials to pinpoint accuracy. When you get to the detail part of your outline, you will almost always be able to include exact names, dates, events, numbers, or personal accounts that will impress your listeners and solidify your point. Note how details, which are indicated by arabic numerals in the outline, can give real impact to the working outline on the harms of smoking:

> The purpose of this speech is to show my audience the serious harms related to smoking.
>
> I. Smoking can lead to significant health problems for the smoker.
>   A. Lung disease often results.
>   1. Men are at 40 percent greater risk than women.
>   2. Smoking causes over 60 percent of all lung problems.
>   B. Thousands die each year.
>   1. 390,000 die annually.
>   2. Over 100,000 are under the age of 50.
>   3. 20 percent are teenagers.

Another way to add depth to your outline—and eventually to your speech—is to include illustrations and analogies. An *illustration* is an example that clarifies your point or adds a human note to your speech. In the speech on smoking, you might include a personal illustration from your family, as follows:

> C. Members of my family are among the victims.
>   1. My grandfather died from lung disease caused by smoking.
>   2. My father has to take oxygen twice a week.

An *analogy* is a comparison that uses something familiar to explain or describe something less familiar. Using an analogy can help you make or empha-

Illustration:

My grandfather died from lung disease caused by smoking.

size a point in an interesting way. For example, if you wanted to make an analogy about the dangers of smoking, you might say this:

Given the dangers of smoking that we know today, beginning smoking now is like boarding the *Titanic* after it hit the iceberg.

Details, illustrations, and analogies can give life to your speech. They can add dimensions of personality, humanness, and intellectual stimulation to the coldest of topics. As a result, they will help draw your audience members in and make them feel a part of your speech, which is one of your goals.

It is possible to go still further and subdivide the details of your outline, but this isn't generally a good idea. Remember, not only do you have to keep track of where you are in your speech, but so does your audience.

And your audience doesn't have a script of your speech handy. Make things meaningful, but keep your organization simple and easy to follow. You'll be happier with the results.

Proper Outlining Form As you write your speech outline, you'll want to follow some standard guidelines. For example, notice how the various parts of the outline (the purpose statement, the main headings, the supporting materials, and the details) are *indented* differently. The indentions indicate the subordination of ideas. Also notice the period after each roman numeral, letter, and arabic numeral.

It is important to remember that each part of an outline should contain at least two items. First, you must have at least two main headings. You can have more than two, and usually you will, but you *must* have at least two. After that, you need not have further subordinate parts, but at each outline level, if you have one part, you must have at least one more. Thus, if you have an A, you should at least have a B. If you have a 1, you should have a 2, and so on. The reason for this rule is that you can't divide anything into one part.

At times, you might perceive the indenting, roman numerals, letters, and arabic numerals as busywork. Keep in mind, however, that outlining means order, order means effective organization, and effective organization means you'll be in charge. What the bones are to the body, the outline is to the speech. If you take the time to think of a significant purpose statement, group your ideas logically into main headings, and create valid supporting materials and details, you will be on your way to building a speech that will be ordered, structurally sound, and—unlike some homes in ancient Babylonia—certain not to crumble.

Do you remember the sample introduction given earlier in the chapter? The thesis was, "I would like to discuss the various areas in your life where laughter can play a significantly positive role." The first main heading might deal with how laughter can help on the job. Let's hear how this main idea might sound if used to begin the body of the speech. This speech is outlined in its entirety on page 221.

Analogy:

Given the dangers of smoking that we know today, beginning smoking now is like boarding the *Titanic* after it hit the iceberg.

First of all, laughter can help you on the job. Did you know that a sense of humor can help make you a more productive worker? For instance, the pamphlet *Smart Management Skills* states that employees and bosses who will take the time to laugh at their shortcomings are more likely to turn out more work of higher quality. The reason? The pamphlet explains that giving in to your funny bone relieves stress and allows you to see the occupational big picture better. The consequence, says author John C. Smith, is that "you actually work faster and more accurately if you will laugh and not take yourself too seriously." Next, laughter can help you cut down on absenteeism from work. A study done at Walker University showed that workers who frequently told jokes and laughed with fellow workers missed 20 percent fewer days a year than workers who were serious most of the time. One worker even added, "The laughing and having a good time makes me want to come to work. I don't like to miss."

Do you see the main heading? Can you pick out the supporting materials? What about the details?

Next, look for the words and phrases that signal where the discussion is going. These expressions—such as *first of all, for instance,* and *next*—are termed **transitions.** They will appear throughout your speech, but they are especially helpful in the body of the speech. At a minimum, be sure to have a clear transition at the beginning of the body of your speech and between the end of each main point and the beginning of the next. Also, use a transition to indicate that you are moving to the conclusion of the speech so that the audience is prepared for the ending. These are the road signs for the speech. Transitions allow both you and your audience to know exactly where you are in your speech and how all of the parts of your outline fit together.

See the table for some transitions that you might use.

Organizational Patterns

Let's now take a look at ways that you can organize the body of your speech. Think once again of the trip that you might take in the family car. You could probably use a number of routes to reach your destination. After looking at the various options, you would probably choose the one that best satisfied your desires in terms of time, scenery, road conditions, points of interest, and the like. You need to make this same type of study when deciding how to organize the body of your speech.

Just as there are often several roads that lead to a specific location, there are several organizational patterns from which you can choose. Let's take a look at the five patterns of organization that speech teachers from across the country say they find most

Proper outlining ensures that your whole speech will be strong.

appropriate for student speeches. As you are reading, keep in mind that these organizational patterns can sometimes be combined for greater effect.

1. Chronological Pattern The **chronological pattern** of organization puts things in a time sequence, or in the order in which they happened. Chronological order is an excellent choice if you want your audience to see the parts of your speech building into a complete picture from beginning to end. Here are examples:

The Role of the Political Cartoon in Shaping Public Views

   I.   Colonial times
   II. Revolutionary days
   III. Later developments

The Evolution of Batman as a Heroic Figure

   I.   Initial comic book portrayal
   II. 1950s comic book portrayal and 1960s TV portrayal
   III. 1980s, 1990s, and 2000s movie portrayal

Sample Speech Outline

Purpose statement: The purpose of this speech is to inform the audience of the positive role that laughter can play in their lives.

Introduction

I. Have you ever heard the sayings "Let a smile be your umbrella" and "Laugh and the world laughs with you"?
  A. Both of these sayings show how a positive attitude and laughter can work to your advantage.
  B. Laughter can do more than provide a pleasant smile.
II. I would like to discuss the various areas in your life where laughter can play a significantly positive role.
  A. Laughter can help you on the job.
  B. Laughter can help you with family and friends.
  C. Laughter can help your health.

Body

I. Laughter can help you on the job.
  A. Laughter can make you a more productive worker.
    1. Mention pamphlet on employees and bosses.
    2. Giving in to your funny bone relieves stress and lets you see the occupational big picture.
  B. Laughter helps you cut down on absenteeism.
    1. Walker University study gives the 20 percent fewer days missed statistic.
    2. Worker who laughs wants to come to work.
II. Laughter can help you with family and friends.
  A. Family problems can be handled better.
    1. Northwestern University reports that most family disputes can be "defused" by a well-timed joke or a laugh that the family is involved in together.
    2. Trust often results from taking the time to laugh with one another.
  B. People are often drawn to laughter and a sense of humor.
    1. Friends believe that your ability to laugh with them is a sign that you accept them.
    2. Psychological study: people are attracted to those who laugh heartily, because they see those laughers as potential leaders.
III. Laughter can also benefit your health.
  A. Laughter can help people with serious illnesses.
    1. My aunt who had cancer found that watching cartoons and laughing gave her a positive attitude about her condition.
    2. Terminally ill patients in Chicago lived two to four years longer when they laughed often.
  B. Laughter can help with common ailments.
    1. Doctors state that the energy it takes to laugh is actually a form of exercise that helps the body fight aches and pains.
    2. They add that laughing keeps the throat and vocal cords loose and active and helps ward off serious sore throats and colds.

Conclusion

I. Thus, laughter can make you a better worker, a more sensitive family member and friend, and a healthier person.
  A. It takes no special talent.
  B. It costs nothing.
II. So "Let a smile be your umbrella" is certainly good advice.

2. Climactic Pattern You will often want to save your most important point for last. In the **climactic pattern** of organization, you organize your main headings in order of importance. This type of organization can give your speech dramatic impact, because it allows the speech to build in significance:

Types of Crime in America

I. Shoplifting
II. White-collar crime
III. Violent crime

You can also use a chronological pattern of organization that advances in a climactic manner:

The death of John F. Kennedy Jr., his wife, and her sister

I. Plane dives into sea off Martha's Vineyard.
II. Millions mourn.
III. Conclusion: crash probably caused by inexperience.

3. Spatial Pattern When you use the **spatial pattern** of organization, you divide your topic on the basis of space relationships. This arrangement lets your audience picture how the body of your speech fits together:

Introducing the Modern School

I. Library is the central hub.
II. Classrooms radiate from library.
III. Offices are extensions.

The World of Drugs

I. North American involvement
II. Central American involvement
III. Asian involvement

4. Cause–Effect Pattern In the **cause-effect pattern** of organization, you say to your listeners, "Because of *that, this* happened." In other words, the one area (the cause) leads directly to the other

Relationship Intended Between Parts of Your Speech	Possible Transitional Words and Phrases
To add ideas	beyond that, in addition, besides, likewise, moreover, also, futhermore, next, finally
To illustrate or demonstrate	for example, in other words, even though, for instance, that is, to illustrate, specifically, as proof, a case in point
To yield a point	granted, of course, since this is so, although true
To show contrast	conversely, however, nevertheless, on the contrary, on the other hand, while this may be true
To emphasize a point	above all, indeed, more important, in fact, surely, without a doubt
To compare	at the same time, in the same way, likewise, similarly
To show order	first, second, in the second place, finally in conclusion, last, next
To repeat or restate	in other words, that is to say, in short, in any case
To summarize	for these reasons, in conclusion, all in all, overall
To show relationships in space	close by, nearby, next to, in front of, behind
To show relationships in time	before, afterward, formerly, later, meanwhile, next, presently, previously, subsequently, ultimately, soon after

area (the effect). Often, the main headings in a cause-effect outline will be the words *cause* and *effect*, and the supporting materials will supply an analysis. Here are examples:

Anorexia

I. Causes
    A. Media influences
    B. Low self-esteem
II. Effects
    A. Physical problems
    B. Emotional problems

Child Abuse

I. Major causes
    A. Cycle of violence
    B. Drug and alcohol abuse
II. Major effects
    A. Physical harm
    B. Mental harm
    C. Social harm

5. Problem-Solution Pattern The **problem-solution pattern** of organization does exactly what its name suggests: It presents a problem and then discusses how to solve it. Like the cause-effect pattern, this pattern is logical and it gives you an opportunity to show insightful analysis that is easy for your audience to follow:

Getting Serious About Recycling

I. Problems
    A. Lack of knowledge
    B. Economics
    C. Lack of incentive
II. Solutions
    A. Education in schools and the media
    B. Government encouragement
    C. Personal commitment

Keep in mind that not all speeches must include profound solutions. Sometimes the best solutions are those that are simple, practical, and easy to understand. Solutions and action steps usually fall into three categories: policy, attitudinal, and awareness.

Policy Solutions A *policy solution* asks your audience to write the president or a congressperson, to start a petition drive for signatures in favor of a local candidate, or to rally as a group for a local march to the capital. Policy solutions usually demand some

---

INSTANT IMPACT

Advice from a Former First Lady

Barbara Bush, wife of former President George H. W. Bush, spoke to the graduates of Pepperdine University and told them that family life and contributing to one's community are important measures of success. Speaking to more than 500 graduates, Mrs. Bush said, "If you had invited the CEO of General Electric, he would have discussed business. If you had invited the head of the American Red Cross, she would have discussed how to help others in distress. But you invited a mother of five to speak, so I'm going to talk to you about your own families."

She went on to add that the graduates would probably never regret missing a certain test or a specific meeting. She noted, however, that they would most certainly miss the times in their lives that they hadn't spent with their husbands, wives, children, or community. The answer, she suggested, was for them to organize their lives so that the important things came first.

---

form of physical action on your audience's part. In addition, policy solutions actively challenge an existing institution or problem.

Attitudinal Solutions An *attitudinal solution* deals more with attitudes, opinions, and moods. It asks your audience to change or strengthen their mental state regarding an issue. An attitudinal solution might ask your listeners to become more open-minded about people or to change their perspective about what the word *success* really means.

Awareness Solutions An *awareness solution* reminds your audience to be conscious of what they have heard and possibly to implement it in their own lives. The awareness solution is especially appropriate for

In a speech, you could provide solutions to raise awareness about recycling programs in your area.

informative speeches or demonstration speeches, in which the speaker is not offering the solution to a problem. The awareness solution can remind the audience that a wealth of information has been shared—that, for instance, "cross-country skiing can be fun if you will just try to apply the steps that we've looked at today."

Of course, the type of solution you use depends on the type of speech you are delivering. You do have some choices, though. If your speech deals with the problems of the inner city, you can suggest that audience members write to their state representatives to find out what assistance plans for the inner city are in the works—a policy solution. Or you can challenge audience members to examine their sense of justice and urge them to open their hearts to the less fortunate—an attitudinal solution. Audiences want to hear something that is within the realm of possibility.

Beverly Hubbs, a one-time guidance counselor and spokesperson for the Positive Life Program at a large Midwestern high school, tells both students and parents that many different roads lead to feelings of personal success: "All people aren't the same. There is usually a right answer out there for all of us if we will take the time to hunt."

This is good advice for you to follow as you organize your speech. Different topics call for different organizations. You have been presented with five organizational patterns that are tried and true. Combine your content with your originality and choose wisely. Remember, the body of your speech is the majority of your speaking "trip." Organize your speech so that your audience enjoys the journey. Let's now move to the final part of the speech, the conclusion.

SECTION ② REVIEW

Recalling the Facts

1. An _____ is the speaker's map. It is the way that you give form and direction to your speech's organization.
2. The major divisions or areas in the body of a speech are called _____.
3. What is the name of the organizational pattern that puts things in a time sequence?
4. The attitudinal solution is part of which organizational pattern?

Thinking Critically

1. Look at the chapter quotation on page 205. Analyze and evaluate it. Do you agree with it? How does it apply to organization and speech writing? If you don't take the time to outline a speech, will it be like the clothes piled around the room—not quite organized?
2. Outlining and organizing are critical when explaining something to someone. For example, analyze what would happen if a teacher tried to explain a lesson without a plan. At work, what if your boss tried to explain your job to you but didn't use any verbal organization? Why, do you think, is the body the most important part of an explanation?

Taking Charge

1. Pick a topic for a potential speech. Choose two main headings and decide on two levels of supporting materials for each heading. Then arrange your headings in correct outline form. Your outline should take the following form (be sure to make indentions):

   Topic
     I.
       A.
         1.
2. Using the speech topic you just picked, choose three details, illustrations, or analogies to reinforce your point. Add those details to the outline you developed.

How to Win Friends and Influence People

It has been called "calculatedly corny and cunningly folksy," but the Dale Carnegie course on public speaking and public relations has influenced millions of graduates from all walks of life. The main word that the Carnegie course stresses is *positivism*—looking at what can go right rather than what can go wrong in a person's life and career. Author of the book *How to Win Friends and Influence People,* Dale Carnegie started to advise individuals and businesses on public speaking in 1912. Since that time, more than 75 countries have adopted the principles of the course. In the United States, more than 150,000 students enroll each year.

Much of the Carnegie course's success has been achieved by attracting businesses that pay for their employees to take the fourteen-session course, which costs around $1,000 per student. Carnegie administrators say that 400 of the Fortune 500 companies—the most prestigious companies in the nation—send people to take the course.

The course tries to stamp out the *inhibitions* and insecurities that people have about themselves. It is organized around the following principles:

1. Become genuinely interested in other people.
2. Smile!
3. Remember that people want to be called by name.
4. Be a good listener.
5. Talk in terms of the other person's interest.
6. Make the other person feel important—and do it sincerely.

With converts from around the globe, the Dale Carnegie approach to feeling good about yourself, about your future, and about other people has been a speech communication breakthrough. It allows people to work with real issues and come up with real answers. Millions of people can't be wrong.

Questions

1. Why do you think the Dale Carnegie course on public speaking is still popular after all these years?
2. How could the six principles listed above help you to "win friends and influence people"?
3. Which of the six is the most important to you?

The Conclusion

It has been said that if you want to deliver a good speech to your audience, you should "tell 'em what you're gonna tell 'em, tell 'em, and then tell 'em what you told 'em." This statement not only is amusing but also contains a great deal of truth. What is the lesson? First, your speech needs an introduction that previews for your audience your specific purpose in speaking. Next, your speech needs a body that proves your point. Finally, your speech needs a conclusion in which you wrap up what you have to say in a neat communication package.

Read the following conclusion for the speech on the positive role that laughter can play. Parts of the speech were used as examples earlier in the chapter. As in the sample introduction, pay attention to the numbers:

(1) In conclusion, you have seen how laughter can make you a more productive and effective worker, a more sensitive friend and family member, and even a healthier person. I think that after hearing that laughter can actually help us overcome serious illness and can help terminally ill patients live two to four years longer, we should all start to smile. So let's establish and maintain a laughing attitude. We can all do it—and it costs nothing. (2) Therefore, the words that you heard at the beginning of this speech, "Let a smile be your umbrella," might be sound advice. Go ahead and laugh. Hopefully, the world will laugh with you!

The conclusion effectively summarizes the major points of the speech and restates the thesis (1). It also offers a final clincher section, or a final impression (2). Let's examine the role of each.

The Summary The first part of your conclusion is usually the summary. (You might go back and see how the word *summarize* was used in Chapter 3, "Listening.") The summary should remind your audience of the main headings, or major areas of analysis, that you covered in your speech. Your summary might even include a particularly memorable or hard-hitting detail. (However, the summary should not become so repetitive that it leaves your audience thinking, "Wait a minute! Didn't you tell me all that already?") In addition, repeat your speech thesis in the summary. This approach guarantees that your audience will remember the point you were trying to make.

Use the conclusion to call attention to the most important aspects of your speech and offer a final impression.

©Dave and Les Jacobs/Blend Images LLC

Remember that a summary is a quick wrap-up. Get to the point and then move on.

The Final Clincher or Final Impression

Just as it is important to make a good first impression, it is important to make a solid final impression. Your final statement ends your speech, clinches your argument, and makes a memorable final impression. While some speakers may hold that you should always "leave 'em laughin'," this isn't necessarily true. The tone and nature of your speech should determine your final clincher.

If you go back to the types of attention-getters discussed earlier, you will see methods that can be effective for your final lines as well. For instance, asking a question, making a startling statement, giving a quotation, telling a story, or making references can work for you at the end of your speech as well as at the beginning. You might also consider ending the speech the same way that you started it. In other words, if you begin your speech with a quiz, you might end your speech by answering the questions for your audience in a creative, insightful manner. Did you begin with a quotation? Why not end with a quotation that makes a similar point or one that accentuates what your speech has promoted? Just keep these points in mind about the words that you choose to end your speech:

- They must fit the mood of your speech.
- They must make sense.
- They should bring some finality to your speech so that your audience realizes that you have finished.

SECTION 3 REVIEW

Recalling the Facts

1. What is the name for what is usually the first part of the conclusion?
2. In addition to quickly repeating your main headings, reminding the audience of your _____ is a smart idea.
3. What is the name for the part of the conclusion that challenges, inspires, or motivates your audience?

Thinking Critically

Like good teachers, good business managers always conclude a meeting with a quick wrap-up of what has happened or been discussed. They have found that not providing a solid summary can lead to communication problems. One executive even believed that her final words to a group might be her most important. Evaluate this belief. Do you agree? Regardless of your opinion, analyze what communication problems might result if the executive did not give the group some type of conclusion or quick, accurate summary.

Taking Charge

Pretend that you are being given one opportunity to convince your teacher that you deserve an A in the class. Give your reasons, supply evidence, and then end with a quick summary. Tell a story or give a personal example that would be an entertaining final clincher or final impression. Your teacher will ask you either to outline your conclusion or to write it out word for word. Be creative. Be logical. Have fun.

Looking Back

Listed below are the major ideas discussed in this chapter.

- Organization is the plan that you develop to get things done. Organization brings order and direction to the task at hand.
- The introduction is the beginning of your speech and usually consists of four parts: the attention-getter, the link, the thesis statement, and the preview statement.
- The body of your speech is the meat of your presentation and must be organized so that the audience can clearly follow what you are saying.
- Subordinating ideas—ordering them by importance—allows you to outline your speech effectively.
- The thesis statement is the most critical sentence in your speech, because everything else in the speech revolves around it.
- Main headings (indicated by roman numerals) are the major divisions of your purpose statement or thesis.
- Supporting materials (indicated by capital letters) divide the main headings into more-specific categories and present more-detailed information.
- Details (indicated by arabic numerals) are divisions of the supporting materials; they include specific names, dates, and statistics.
- Transitions are the links that take you from area to area throughout your presentation and keep the audience informed as to where you are in your speech.
- Different patterns can be used to organize the body of a speech; the pattern to use is the one that will work best with the thesis.
- The conclusion is the final part of the speech, and it consists of the summary and the final clincher or final impression.

Speech Vocabulary

organization
introduction
rhetorical question
quotation
narrative
link
thesis statement
preview statement
body
outline
purpose statement
subordination
main heading
supporting materials
transition
chronological pattern

climactic pattern
spatial pattern
cause-effect pattern
problem-solution pattern

1. For each new speech term, find and then write the definition given in the text. List the page number on which each word is introduced. Now write an original sentence showing each vocabulary word in action.
2. Make flash cards. On one side of each card, print a new speech term. On the other side, write the definition. Keep track of the words that give you problems and eliminate the words that you can handle. This will prepare you for a vocabulary exam.

CHAPTER 9 Review and Enrichment

Academic Vocabulary

equilibrium	jeopardy
vested	enhanced
gigantic	haphazardly
fiasco	intensification
illustration	analogy
inhibition	indented

1. Use the dictionary to define the academic vocabulary terms. Dictate each of the words to a classmate to work on the spelling. Next, read the definitions out loud, and have the classmate tell you the word that matches each definition. Try mixing up the words.

2. Write an original sentence using each general vocabulary word. After you are finished, write a short essay, titled "What Might Happen If I Don't Organize My Life," using at least five of the words. Make your story make sense!

To Remember

Answer the following questions based on your reading of the chapter.

1. What type of question does not really ask for a response from the audience?

2. The part of the introduction that combines your introduction with your speech topic is called the _____.

3. The _____ states exactly what your speech is going to do and reminds you what you must accomplish with your audience.

4. The organizational pattern that saves your most important point for last is called the _____ pattern.

5. The words or short phrases that link ideas together are called _____.

6. Name the three types of solutions: _____, _____, and _____.

7. Quotations, stories, and questions are all types of _____ that can be used in the introduction.

8. The organizational pattern that uses space as a factor is called what?

To Do

1. Using the school extracurricular activities "Sports," "Music," "Academics," and "Other" as topics, find all the information that you can and outline your findings. For "Sports," what are the teams? What are their records? Who are the key players? An outline for "Sports" might begin like this:
   - I. Baseball
       - A. 2014 record: 18–3
       - B. Strengths
           - 1. Hitting
           - 2. Bench strength
   - II. Basketball

2. Organize *tomorrow*. Begin with the hour that you get out of bed. Keep a running record of at least two or three objectives that you would like to accomplish during each hour up to the time that you go to bed. For school, you can list what you would like to accomplish in each class. For leisure time at home, be specific about how you want to spend it. Give honest, constructive answers that might actually improve your overall sense of personal organization.

To Talk About

1. A person speaking about stress management said to her audience, "In this life, where grabbing for the gusto may mean one more demand on an already overflowing life calendar, it's important to decide what's really important." She was referring to the ability to prioritize, or rank things in their order of importance. How do you think that prioritizing could help cut down on stress in your life?
2. Why is it important to use details when you are trying to defend a particular position? Why isn't your opinion enough? What would be the value of organization if you were trying to convince someone to do something?
3. Which types of introductions and final appeal techniques do you find most impressive? Give your reasoning. Which types do you find least desirable? Why?
4. Do some problem-solution brainstorming. What are some school problems? What are a few possible solutions? What are some societal problems? Solutions? Be practical! Also, for each of the following, discuss how a cause-effect relationship could exist: drugs and crime, alcohol and suicide, preparation and success, trust and friendship, education and employment opportunities.

To Write About

1. The report *Voices from the Classroom* (conducted by Sylvan Learning Centers) is based on a survey of nearly 1,500 eleventh and twelfth graders from 20 different high schools around the country. Believe it or not, nine out of ten students said that it is important for parents to help students with homework and to set definite study rules and guidelines! The students said that parents need to start this procedure when children are young. Write an organized paper giving reasons why you agree or disagree with this finding.
2. Write a one-page paper detailing the plan that you would have if you could map out your future. Before you write, make an outline. Be sure to include main headings, supporting materials, and details. What about transitions? Think through your reasoning and create a credible plan. Be sure to include your specific job choice.

Related Speech Topics

People should earn equal pay for equal work.
The school day should be shorter.
Only juniors and seniors should be able to attend the school prom.
Volunteer work should be a requirement for high school graduation.
Students should have to pay if they wish to be involved in extracurricular activities.

Competition has serious drawbacks.
A politician convicted of a crime should be removed from office immediately.
A student's self-discipline in class should be a significant factor in the student's grade for that class.

CHAPTER 10
LOGIC AND REASONING

"Contrariwise," continued Tweedledee, *"if it was so, it might be; and if it were so, it would be; but as it isn't, it ain't. That's logic."*

—Lewis Carroll, ***Through the Looking-Glass***

Learning Objectives

After completing this chapter, you will be able to do the following.

- Distinguish among several different types of reasoning and recognize faulty or misleading types.
- Better adapt your use of logic to a specific audience.
- Analyze your own logic to determine if your conclusions are valid.

Chapter Outline

Following are the main sections in this chapter.

1. Evaluating Ideas: Methods of Reasoning
2. Fallacies
3. The Ethics of Audience Adaptation

Speech Vocabulary

In this chapter, you will learn the meanings of the speech terms listed below.

evidence
reasoning
logic
induction
case study
sign
analogy
deduction
premise
syllogism
fallacy

hasty generalization
false premise
circumstantial
  evidence
causality
correlated
false analogy
ignoring the question
begging the question

Academic Vocabulary

Expanding your academic vocabulary will help you become a more effective communicator. Listed below are some words appearing in this chapter that you should make part of your vocabulary.

integrate
systematic
internship
segregation
degraded
incorrigible

manipulate
distortion
rigorous
rebuffed
rife
expedient

Although sound reasoning is an essential component of communication, speakers often spew forth illogical statements that show little understanding of a speaker's responsibility to the audience and to the truth. In this chapter, you will learn the fundamental rules of logical reasoning and how to apply these rules effectively in your speaking. You will also explore how to *integrate* evidence into a speech and how to recognize the faulty logic that is often used. In short, you will take an important step toward becoming more logical and therefore more effective as a communicator.

Introduction

If you want to be an effective speaker, you should support your ideas with sufficient evidence and valid reasoning. **Evidence** is anything that establishes a fact or gives us reasons to believe something. **Reasoning** is the process of thinking and drawing conclusions about that evidence. You apply reasoning in choosing and developing arguments. **Logic**, the science of reasoning, uses a system of rules to help you think correctly during the process.

As you construct arguments, remember that an argument is not the same thing as a fully developed, persuasive speech. You should use several arguments to make a complete presentation. Think of writing your speech as if you were building a bridge. Each argument becomes a girder that holds up your bridge. One weak or misplaced girder and the entire bridge may come crashing down.

Supporting your ideas with evidence, reasoning, and logic is like building a bridge in which each part works together to support the other parts.

Eyecon Images/Alamy

Evaluating Ideas: Methods of Reasoning

To become more logical, you must learn about the types of reasoning. Understanding them can make your thinking clearer and more *systematic*.

Inductive Reasoning

Mathematicians have a technique for proving a theorem: they use certain specific cases to help prove a general truth. This process is called inductive reasoning, or **induction.** Induction isn't used only by mathematicians, though. Anyone who argues from specific instances to a generalization is using inductive reasoning.

Suppose that you are preparing a speech about the importance of learning to read. You want to determine whether students who begin reading at a younger age earn better grades in school than students who begin later. You find five studies that link early reading with better performance in history but poorer performance in science. Based on inductive reasoning, you can conclude that starting to read at a younger age does not necessarily mean earning better grades.

As another example, think about the local politician who argues in favor of year-round school because students in countries that have such a system score better on international math, science, and geography tests than U.S. students. This politician is reasoning inductively.

A special type of inductive reasoning is the **case study.** A case study allows you to analyze a "typical" example in great detail so that you can draw general conclusions. For example, to learn more about the life of a journalist, you might undertake a month-long *internship* with a local newspaper and then apply your observations in a speech on the field of journalism as a whole.

Suppose you want to argue in your speech that journalists work long hours. You could record the daily schedules of four different journalists whom you meet during your internship. If you find that these four journalists work long shifts, you might argue that it is likely that all journalists work long hours. In making this argument, you are using inductive reasoning.

If a reporter saw this basketball player make two spectacular dunks and concluded that he was the "next Michael Jordan," the reporter would be using what kind of reasoning?

Purestock/SuperStock

Navajo Code Talkers

During World War II the United States Marines found that enemy forces were intercepting their transmitted messages. Even when they converted conversations to code, the encryptions were frequently broken.

In 1942 Philip Johnston, a Los Angeles engineer, came upon the idea of creating a special code that he reasoned would work because it was based on a language, Navajo, that was only spoken and was very complex. But how would the plan be carried out? The only way was to employ native Navajos to make the transmissions. Hence, the Navajo Code Talkers were born.

But Lt. Col. James E. Jones, a Marines signal officer, had his doubts. How would native Navajos be able to communicate war-related information when they had no words for certain terms in their language? The solution was simple: They would substitute words. So "battleship" became "whale," and "hummingbird" was used to signify "fighter plane."

By the end of the war, 420 Navajos had contributed their talents to defeating the enemy. Because none of them was captured, the system worked perfectly and the experiment was a success.

Consider these examples from the Navajo code:

A	wol-la-chee	ant
B	shush	bear
C	mosai	cat

Reasoning by Sign A special type of inductive reasoning is reasoning by **sign**. It involves drawing conclusions about a given situation based on physical evidence. Perhaps the most familiar example of reasoning by sign is the work of Sherlock Holmes, the fictional sleuth. Holmes seems capable of solving the most complicated mysteries by simply studying the dust balls under the sofa. Reasoning by sign can be persuasive. For example, in Sir Arthur Conan Doyle's novel *The Hound of the Baskervilles*, Holmes explains to his associate Dr. Watson that it is "elementary" to determine the breed of a dog by observing the dog's teeth marks on a stick:

> "Being a heavy stick, the dog held it tightly by the middle, and the marks of his teeth are plainly visible. The dog's jaw, as shown in the space between these marks, is too broad in my opinion for a terrier and not broad enough for a mastiff. It may have been—yes, by Jove, it is a curly-haired spaniel."

Fictional sleuth Sherlock Holmes often drew conclusions about a given situation based on physical evidence, or signs, to solve mysteries.

COMMUNICATION *BREAKTHROUGH*

Thurgood Marshall

Separate but Unequal

In 1951 Oliver Brown, an African American railroad worker from Topeka, Kansas, sued the city of Topeka for preventing his daughter from attending a local all-white school. Eight-year-old Linda Brown was forced to ride a bus for five miles when there was a school only four blocks from her home. The case, which went all the way to the Supreme Court (*Brown v. Board of Education*), challenged the constitutionality of an 1896 ruling, *Plessy v. Ferguson.* In *Plessy,* the court had decided that *segregation* was permissible as long as blacks and whites had access to "separate but equal" facilities. But Thurgood Marshall and his team of lawyers presented evidence demonstrating that "separate but equal" was a logical impossibility. There could be no such thing as "separate but equal" facilities when society was arranged unequally.

In a 9–0 landmark decision, the Supreme Court ruled that segregated facilities *degraded* minorities and prevented them from having equal educational opportunities. As Chief Justice Earl Warren wrote, "Separate educational facilities are inherently unequal." *Plessy* was overturned. Although the *Brown* decision applied only to education, it inspired minorities to seek rights in other fields, and it became a turning point in the civil rights movement. Marshall would later become a Supreme Court justice. He served as a justice from 1967 to 1991.

Questions

1. Do you believe that minorities have equal educational opportunities today? Why or why not?

2. What can be done to improve educational opportunities for everyone?

Reasoning by Analogy Another common method of inductive reasoning is the use of **analogy**. An analogy is an illustration in which the characteristics of a familiar object or event are used to explain or describe the characteristics of a less familiar object or event. Analogies are used by the creators of standardized tests to measure intelligence. For example, "Hand is to person as (a) tree is to sky, (b) dirty is to laundry, (c) foot is to powder, (d) paw is to dog." The point of such exercises is not to make you blind from filling in thousands of tiny bubbles with No. 2 pencils but to see if you can pick out similarities.

When you reason by analogy, you demonstrate similarities as you develop an argument. Suppose that a particular food is found to cause cancer in white rats. You might then reason by analogy that there may be some risk to humans as well. Because no two sets of conditions are exactly alike, though, the perfect analogy doesn't exist. (White rats rarely guzzle soda as they gorge themselves on tortilla

What Did You See?

To reach a verdict, juries often depend on witnesses who reason by sign. This method of reasoning is not foolproof, though. Take the case of rabbi and Jewish Defense League head Meir Kahane, who was shot to death in a crowded hall in a New York City hotel on November 5, 1990. The prosecution called 51 witnesses to support its charge of murder.

"Many witnesses," reported the *Washington Post*, "testified that they were standing only a few feet away when they heard the shots and turned to see El Sayyid Nosair cradling a .357 revolver and crouching near Kahane." One witness saw Nosair pointing the gun at Kahane. Furthermore, as Nosair attempted to escape, he shot two people.

The prosecution thought the case against Nosair was a slam dunk, but the jurors disagreed and returned a verdict of "not guilty." Why? According to the jurors, there wasn't enough real evidence, such as fingerprints or bullet trajectories showing that Nosair fired the weapon that killed Kahane. Although 51 witnesses said they saw Nosair with a gun, no one actually saw him shoot Kahane. While the witnesses reasoned that seeing Nosair with a gun was a sign that he killed Kahane, the jurors couldn't be sure. The judge denounced the verdict as "devoid of common sense and logic" and "against the overwhelming weight of evidence."

Jurors are right, however, not to rely on eyewitness accounts alone. Studies show that nearly 50 percent of eyewitness accounts are wrong and have accounted for the conviction of hundreds of people for crimes they didn't commit. According to experts, a witness's memory often can't be trusted and many factors—such as race, the presence of a weapon, and trauma—can lead to inaccurate identifications. While reasoning by sign may seem logical, it's certainly not proof of anything.

Even with physical evidence such as fingerprints and what observers may think is an obvious outcome, a jury may reach a verdict that some find surprising.

chips.) Therefore, you should not rely entirely on an analogy to prove your position in any speech; rather, you should always supplement your arguments with other forms of proof.

Deductive Reasoning

A counterpart to inductive reasoning is deductive reasoning, or **deduction**. Inductive reasoning moves from specific instances to a generalization; deductive reasoning moves from generalizations, or **premises**, to a specific instance. Premises are the statements on which reasoning is based.

Consider this simple example of deductive reasoning. It consists of two premises and a conclusion, and it is called a **syllogism**:

1. All students go to school.
2. You are a student.
3. Therefore, you go to school.

Deductive reasoning is not always this straightforward. For example, let's look at the role of justices on the U.S. Supreme Court. Their task is to apply a set of widely accepted principles (premises)—the Constitution—to specific cases. However, it is often difficult to tell whether the principles actually apply. Therefore, the justices must reason from the general principles to the specific cases to decide if the cases are valid.

Suppose that you are preparing a speech in which you plan to argue that flag burning should be allowed. By using deductive reasoning, you can develop an argument based on the First Amendment to the U.S. Constitution. The First Amendment is a general principle that is supposed to protect free expression, but does burning the flag count as "expression"? If it does, then you could invoke the First Amendment and, by deduction, conclude that flag burning is legal, as follows:

1. The First Amendment says to allow all types of expression.
2. Flag burning is a type of expression.
3. Therefore, flag burning should be allowed.

Of course, the premise that flag burning is a form of expression must be true if listeners are to accept the argument in your speech.

SECTION 1 REVIEW

Recalling the Facts

1. What is the difference between inductive and deductive reasoning?
2. Why is there no such thing as a perfect analogy?

Thinking Critically

The phone book has been described as the ultimate example of unbiased writing—no opinions involved, just a list. Often, our biases interfere with our ability to present logical speeches. How can we balance the need for truth with our desire to persuade people to agree with our opinions?

Taking Charge

Now it's your turn. Using three of the forms of reasoning discussed in this chapter, develop three arguments for a topic of your choosing. For example, if you were trying to persuade your audience that they should all attend college, you might offer these arguments:

Inductive reasoning—You interviewed ten people who graduated from college, and they all agreed that a college education was a good idea for them.

Deductive reasoning—College-educated people get better-paying jobs than people without that education. You want a better-paying job. Therefore, you should get a college education.

Reasoning by sign—The last time you visited a college campus, you saw a group of students having fun at a dormitory party. If you attend college, you will have fun at parties, too.

Fallacies

The arguments just presented to support college attendance for everyone are not without their flaws. In this section, we examine common forms of flawed arguments, or fallacies. **Fallacies** are errors in reasoning or mistaken beliefs. They are the don'ts of logic. Because fallacies weaken your credibility as a speaker, it is important to learn to understand, recognize, and avoid them. Common fallacies include hasty generalizations, false premises, circumstantial evidence, mistaken causality, misuse of numbers, false analogy, ignoring the question, and begging the question.

Hasty Generalization

A **hasty generalization** is a faulty argument that occurs because the sample chosen is too small or is in some way not representative. Therefore, any conclusion based on this information is flawed. For example, you flip through three television channels with your remote control, and all you see are commercials. Your conclusion that the only thing on television is commercials is a hasty generalization—wrong but, unfortunately, not by much. Or suppose that you are an alien from another planet who saw only Antarctica on your first visit to Earth. You might conclude that the only inhabitants of this planet are fish and penguins and the only landscapes are glaciers. Your sample size is large—there are plenty of glaciers, fish, and penguins in Antarctica—but your conclusion is still wrong, because the sample is not representative of the whole.

False Premise

A **false premise** is an error in deduction. For example, parents like to tell their children, "All teenagers are irresponsible. You are a teenager. Therefore, you are not responsible enough to leave the house tonight." Now study the example to find the premise based on a hasty generalization.

Although it may be true that you are an *incorrigible* slacker, the premise that all teenagers are irresponsible is false. Of course, if you choose to argue the fine points of logic with your parents, they might choose to restrict your opportunity to watch all of those commercials on television.

Circumstantial Evidence

People like to draw conclusions based on **circumstantial evidence**—the evidence at hand. If

Protestors illegally blocked the entrance to the capitol. If you conclude that all protestors are radicals who take the law into their own hands, what type of fallacy would you be using?

Glow Images

they rely too much on circumstantial evidence, though, they commit an error in reasoning by sign. For example, it might seem perfectly logical to assume that the person holding the smoking gun at the scene of a murder was the one who committed the crime—but is it logical? What if it turned out that the person holding the smoking gun was trying to defend the person who got murdered, while the actual murderer ran away? The point is that circumstantial evidence only suggests a conclusion; it does not prove it.

Mistaken Causality

To say two events are causally related is to claim that one event brings about the other. For example, one billiard ball strikes another and causes the second ball to bounce off a cushion at an angle. There is a causal relationship, because the first ball caused the action of the second ball. To say that two events are **correlated**, however, is to claim only that the two events are related in some way. The relationship may not be causal. For example, a bus passes a church every day at twelve o'clock, and the clock in the church rings twelve times. This would be an example of a mistaken **causality**, because the bus doesn't make the bell ring; the two events just happen at the same time.

One of the most common errors in causal reasoning is to assume that one event causes another simply because it happens before the other. This error usually goes by a Latin name: *post hoc, ergo propter hoc* ("after this, therefore, because of this"). Suppose you pass a major math test after going out to the movies the night before. If you then count on the cinema instead of careful preparation each time you face an exam, you are guilty of a *post hoc* fallacy.

Playing with Numbers

Many speakers *manipulate* statistics to misrepresent facts. They numb you with numbers in an attempt to persuade you to agree with their cause. Statistics, however, are subject to built-in biases, insufficient samples, and other forms of *distortion*. A

A church bell ringing when someone pulls a rope connected to the bell is an example of causal relationship.

classic example of playing with numbers comes from Mark Twain. In *Life on the Mississippi*, Twain, writing in 1874, observed that the lower part of the Mississippi River had been shortened 242 miles during the past 176 years—a little more than a mile and a third each year. Twain concluded, "Any calm person who is not blind or idiotic can see that in the Old Oolitic Silurian Period, just a million years ago next November, the Lower Mississippi River was upward of one million three hundred thousand miles long. . . . And by the same token any person can see that seven hundred and forty-two years from now the Lower Mississippi will be only a mile and three-quarters long."

Although Twain admitted he couldn't afford to tell the whole truth because he had a family to support, not everyone is so honest. You should watch out for speakers who spout statistics to sound impressive. Be especially wary of politicians who use statistics to predict the future. Darrell Huff, in his book *How to Lie with Statistics*, points out that "the future trend represents no more than an educated guess."

False Analogy

As mentioned, no two sets of conditions are exactly alike, so no analogies are perfect. A **false analogy** compares two things that are not really comparable.

Analogies are often misapplied. Suppose you are arguing that students ought to be able to use notes and textbooks during examinations. After all, lawyers don't have to memorize every law, and physicians don't have to remember entire medical journal articles by heart. Rather, in a courtroom or a hospital, they are allowed to look up facts as needed. Similarly, students should be able to use their notes and textbooks during an examination. At first, this argument seems plausible. Isn't the purpose of education to prepare students for the "real world"?

The analogy is flawed, however, because the situations are not really the same. The purpose of

Mark Twain manipulated numbers for comic effect in *Life on the Mississippi.*

a trial or an operation is not to test whether the lawyer or doctor has learned law or medicine, whereas the purpose of a test in school is to see how much students have learned. The situations are fundamentally different.

Ignoring the Question

Speakers often attempt to divert the attention of the audience from the matter at hand. When they do so, they are **ignoring the question**. They may focus on personal attacks or appeal to popular prejudice. Political speeches by politicians from both major parties are *rife* with this strategy. In a presidential campaign in the late 1980s, some campaigners linked Massachusetts governor Michael Dukakis with the early parole in his state of a convicted murderer, Willie Horton. The perception that Dukakis was soft on crime—a conclusion not supported by the facts—could not be shaken, and he lost the election.

The success of mudslinging (as personal attacks are sometimes called in politics) in recent campaigns makes this strategy a significant threat to the democratic process. As a speaker, you have the responsibility not to mislead. Avoid emotional appeals that resort to the passion of the moment rather than reinforcing the truth. As the political leader and diplomat Adlai Stevenson once said, "He who slings mud generally loses ground."

Begging the Question

When your argument assumes that whatever you are trying to prove is true, you are **begging the question**. Circular reasoning is a common form of this fallacy. A circular argument assumes that a premise is true, draws a conclusion from the unsupported premise, and then uses this conclusion to prove the premise: "Students will devote more time to studying if they have more study halls. We should decrease the number of classes a student takes and increase the number of study halls if we want students to study more."

A word or phrase may beg the question, as when your grandmother asks, "How do you like my delicious apple pie?"

Good Miles per Galleon

"Columbus's calculations were illogical," wrote Samuel Eliot Morison, "but his mind never followed rules of logic. He knew he could make it, and had to put the mileage low in order to attract support." To the everlasting glory of Spain, Ferdinand and Isabella had perhaps less *rigorous* mathematicians than those of the princes who had *rebuffed* Columbus. The strength of his convictions aside, it is still a lucky thing that in the midst of his 10,000-mile journey, America got in the way.

Will students devote more time to studying if they have more study halls?

Recalling the Facts

1. What type of fallacy occurs when you rely on a sample that is too small or is not representative of the whole?
2. Explain mistaken causality.

Thinking Critically

In attempting to give their client the best possible defense, how far should attorneys go in trying to persuade a jury? Can they justify omitting facts that might damage their client's case, even though that information might better serve the truth?

Taking Charge

To ensure that you recognize the fallacies discussed in this chapter, create three of your own. For example, if you were writing a speech as a candidate for president of the student council, you might include these fallacious statements:

- In a recent survey, 100 percent of the students polled preferred me for the presidency (playing with numbers—you asked only four friends).
- Whenever my opponent speaks at a pep rally, we lose the next game. Therefore, if we want to win, he should be forbidden from speaking (causality—an example of the *post hoc* fallacy).
- Furthermore, my opponent shouldn't be allowed to run for office because he himself is a loser, a zero, a nothing (ignoring the question—this strategy involves attacking your opponent before he has had a chance to speak).

Now it's your turn. Create three fallacies for one of the following situations:

a. Trying to persuade a teacher that you should have to attend class only when you want to
b. Discussing with your parents the need for you to have a car of your own
c. Asking your boss for a raise

The Ethics of Audience Adaptation

Logic and reasoning are often sacrificed when a speaker tells an audience only what it wants to hear. To vary your convictions and beliefs simply to please your audience may be *expedient*, but it is unethical. Of course, that depends on "what the definition of is, is." As you probably know, President Bill Clinton learned many painful lessons about expediency. Clinton was not, however, the first leader to play fast and loose with logic. Take the politician who promises no new taxes and then, after being elected, raises taxes by calling those increases "revenue enhancements."

Ronald Reagan pledged during his 1980 presidential campaign that any tax increase would have to come over his dead body. Later as president, Reagan approved House Bill 4961, the Tax Equality and Fiscal Responsibility Act of 1982. This law generated $99 billion in tax revenues, and somehow the president survived. Republican leaders referred to the legislation not as a tax bill but as a "reform bill," because they knew what voters wanted to hear.

As a citizen in a democracy, you have an obligation to be highly skilled in the use of logical reasoning. You must recognize half-truths and untruths so that those who misuse the power of speech can't use speech against you. Furthermore, you have the responsibility to communicate what you know to be the truth.

An ethical speaker should try to give the audience the information that it needs most. If audience members are prejudiced against certain people, the ethical speaker should try to be the objective voice of reason. A speaker who believes in equal rights for everyone must challenge any practice that is discriminatory.

The best leaders do not just say whatever is most expedient; they say what they truly believe.

Furthermore, you should never present false evidence. Never appeal to the emotions of your listeners at the expense of logical reasoning. Never pretend to be an authority on a subject if you are not. In short, the responsible speaker must always be ethical. The ancient Roman historian Sallust made the role of the responsible speaker clear: "Prefer to *be* rather than to *seem* good."

An ethical speaker should always take the high road and never pass along false information.

SECTION 3 REVIEW

Recalling the Facts

1. Why is political expediency unethical?
2. Why is logic important to a citizen in a democracy?

Thinking Critically

1. Political speechwriter Peggy Noonan argues that it's not the flowery words or flourishes that matter but the logic behind your case. She contends that logic "shows respect for the brains of the listeners." Do you think politicians show this respect? Explain.
2. Politicians often come to mind when the topic is ethical speaking. However, ethical speaking is also an issue in other areas of our daily lives. Make a list of topics, such as advertisements, in which ethical speaking plays an important role.

Taking Charge

Now it's your turn. How is it important to use "cool" language with your friends? Why? How important is it to be "logical"? Why? Incorporating your knowledge of contemporary attitudes, construct your own examples of fallacies.

Looking Back

Listed below are the major ideas discussed in this chapter.

- Speakers should support their ideas with valid evidence and correct reasoning.
- Reasoning is the process of thinking and drawing conclusions about evidence.
- Inductive reasoning uses specific cases to prove a general truth.
- Reasoning by sign is drawing conclusions based on physical evidence.
- An analogy attempts to describe a fact or set of data in terms of its similarity to another fact or set of data.

- Deductive reasoning moves from generalizations, or premises, to a specific instance.
- Common fallacies include the hasty generalization, the false premise, circumstantial evidence, confusing causality with being correlated, playing with numbers, the false analogy, ignoring the question, and begging the question.
- Logic and reasoning are often sacrificed when a speaker says to an audience only what it wants to hear.

Speech Vocabulary

Using the speech terms listed below, fill in the blanks of the sentences in this exercise.

induction
deduction
case study
sign
causality
correlated

circumstantial evidence
begging the question
hasty generalization
false analogy
ignoring the question

1. The federal government has recently declared that it wants to learn more about how states spend their budgets. It is planning to conduct a _____ of Arkansas's budget plans over the past five years.

2. You study drunk-driving laws in 20 states and conclude that harsher penalties for driving while intoxicated could benefit every state in the nation. This process is an example of reasoning by _____. However, 20 states might not be a large enough sample to justify changing the laws in all states. The conclusion, if false, might turn out to be a _____.

3. "My client's presence at the scene of the crime does not mean that she is guilty," argued the attorney. "Her presence is merely _____."

4. "Ninety-five percent of serial killers have milk in their refrigerators. Therefore, milk has a 95 percent chance of causing one to become a serial killer." This flawed reasoning is an example of two things that are _____ but that do not have _____.

5. If a highway patrol officer observes a car weaving from lane to lane and deduces that the driver of the swerving car may be drunk, he is reasoning by _____.

6. When you reason from general premises to specific cases, you are using the process of _____.

7. If the authors of this book asked you, "How do you like this great quiz so far?" they would be _____.

Academic Vocabulary

Choose two pairs from the following word list and describe how they are alike or different.

integrate   degraded   rigorous
systematic   incorrigible   rebuffed
internship   manipulate   rife
segregation   distortion   expedient

To Remember

Answer the following based on your reading of the chapter.

1. What is the difference between inductive and deductive reasoning?
2. A case study allows you to examine a _____ example in great detail in order to draw more general conclusions.
3. Sherlock Holmes was known for his ability to examine physical evidence and reason by _____.
4. Because no two sets of conditions are alike, the perfect _____ doesn't exist.
5. The fallacy of _____ often occurs when you rely on a sample that is too small or is not representative of the whole.
6. Assuming that one event causes another because it happens before the other is committing an error in reasoning known as the _____ fallacy.
7. When Mark Twain predicted that the Mississippi River would someday be only a mile and three-quarters long, he was guilty of _____.
8. Circular reasoning is a common form of the fallacy known as _____.
9. A _____ compares two things that are not really comparable.
10. Speakers who attempt to divert the attention of the audience from the matter at hand are guilty of _____.

To Do

1. Attend a public discussion or political rally on a current hot issue (or watch a speech on television). List the fallacies you hear. Try to decide whether the speaker is advancing the truth or a personal cause.
2. Pick a topic that a friend and you disagree about. Construct arguments for both sides that are free from fallacious reasoning.
3. Research the use of logic and reasoning in TV or radio advertising. Discuss with your classmates how advertising claims violate the principles of logic.

To Talk About

1. You learned earlier that we live in an information age. Do you think that the abundance of information has helped us become more logical, or do you think that all of the facts and figures have made it increasingly easy to "play with numbers"?

2. Why is it important for a citizen in a democracy to understand the process of reasoning?
3. What careers rely heavily on the use of logic and reasoning?
4. Work in a small group to gather information and obtain evidence about the relationship between city services and crime rates. Groups should present their conclusions using deductive reasoning.

5. Conduct a brief poll of fellow students. Ask at least five students (one at a time) if they would like shorter class periods. (It's likely that all five students will say yes.) From these results, what does inductive reasoning suggest?
6. Work with a group to gather several newspaper articles on the same topic. Use inductive reasoning to develop a group opinion about the content of the articles.

To Write About

1. In the 1960s, Mr. Spock was a character on the original version of the television program *Star Trek*. Spock had an unemotional, logical way of doing things. Create a fictional character that is the evil twin of Spock. Every statement made by this character should be illogical. Write a brief monologue in which this flawed reasoning is evident.
2. Write an essay about a school rule that you believe is wrong. Try to provide a logical alternative to this rule.
3. Construct an imaginary conversation between two friends in which one person is always logical and the other is not.
4. Work with a partner to examine an editorial page from your local newspaper. Apply inductive reasoning to determine whether the conclusions are correct. Then describe in a brief

written summary what editing changes you would make to the editorials.
5. Create a list of your own examples of hasty generalizations. Remember that most stereotypes are really examples of this fallacy (for example, claiming that all football players are dumb). What other hasty generalizations can you list?
6. Write a step-by-step process you follow at work or at home when doing chores. Beside each step, write an explanation of the reasoning behind the step. (For example, if you pile dishes on the left side of a double sink before rinsing them, explain that you do this because the garbage disposal is in the left basin.)

Related Speech Topics

Aristotle and logos
Mudslinging in politics
Sound bites: does logic bite the dust?
Mother does not always know best
Doublespeak
The reasoning of our Founding Fathers
The logic of humor
Advertising claims
Hasty generalizations I have known

The fallacies in hate speech
The logic of analogies
Business ethics
Statistics you can trust
Causal relationships
Correlated relationships
Reasoning by deduction
Reasoning by induction
Signs I should have recognized

EFFECTIVE LANGUAGE

I know that you believe that you understand what you think I said, but I'm not sure that you realize that what you heard is not what I meant.

—Richard Milhous Nixon

Learning Objectives

After completing this chapter, you will be able to do the following.

- Show how the spoken word differs from the written word.
- Know the value of language that creates word pictures.
- Explain why using effective oral language is important in professional and social settings.
- Use effective strategies in presentations.
- Understand how using sound devices in language can create musical effects.
- Recognize language that can prevent effective communication.
- Evaluate language effectiveness of speeches.

Chapter Outline

Following are the main sections in this chapter.

1. The Spoken Word Versus the Written Word
2. Creating Word Pictures: Figures of Speech
3. Making Music with Words: Sound Devices
4. Language to Avoid

Speech Vocabulary

In this chapter, you will learn the meanings of the speech terms listed below.

concrete word	hyperbole
abstract word	understatement
denotation	euphemism
connotation	personification
imagery	repetition
metaphor	alliteration
simile	assonance
allusion	consonance
antithesis	parallelism
oxymoron	jargon
irony	slang

Academic Vocabulary

Expanding your academic vocabulary will help you become a more effective communicator. Listed below are some words appearing in this chapter that you should make part of your vocabulary.

tangible	pervasiveness
conscience	cadence
picturesque	emancipation
crystallize	demeaning
exaggerate	braille
compression	

Mark Twain told us that the difference between the right word and the almost right word is the difference between lightning and the lightning bug. Indeed, there is a world of difference between the word or phrase that will say exactly what you mean and the word or phrase that is simply "in the ballpark." Consider these automobile accident reports that people filed with their insurance companies:

- I pulled away from the side of the road, glanced at my mother-in-law, and headed over the embankment.
- An invisible car came out of nowhere, struck my vehicle, and vanished.
- I was on my way to the doctor with rear-end trouble when my universal joint gave way, causing me to have an accident.

Even though you might laugh at these reports, they prove a significant point: selecting the wrong word or using unclear phrasing causes confusion. It is important to pick the right words.

Barack Obama

No one is exempt from this requirement. It is especially important for political candidates! For example, in the 2008 presidential campaign, then Democratic candidate Senator Barack Obama was widely praised for the quality of his speeches. In one speech to Democratic voters in Iowa, Obama explained why he was running for the presidency:

"I am not in this race . . . because I believe it's somehow owed to me. I never expected to be here, I always knew this journey was improbable. I've never been on a journey that wasn't. . . . I am running in this race because of what Dr. King called 'the fierce urgency of now' . . . Because I will never forget that the only reason that I'm standing here today is because somebody, somewhere stood up for me when it was risky . . . And because that somebody stood up, a few more stood up. And then a few thousand stood up. And then a few million stood up. And standing up . . . they somehow managed to change the world."

Soon after that speech, Obama won the Iowa Caucus, an important early contest for the presidential nomination.

However, even the best communicators can make mistakes if they are not careful. In this chapter, you will learn that effective oral communication depends, in part, on accuracy and economy of language. You will examine the figures of speech used to create the language of effective imagery. In addition, you will be introduced to the sound devices that help to produce the "music" heard in language. Finally, you will be warned about specific types of language that should be avoided because they can create communication barriers between you and your audience.

Introduction

Imagine that you are in the circus. As an acrobat you perform high above the ground without a net, and the path you must follow from point A to point B is merely a tightrope. Your steps must be measured and exact. One false step and your career, as well as your life, could be over. You know that your movement must be absolutely precise. Simply being close to the tightrope would likely result in your becoming just a memory in the circus world.

What do you do? You touch, you feel, and you don't move until you know that the next step is exactly right.

This chapter isn't about the circus world, but it is about exactness—the exactness of language. Like the tightrope walker, you must painstakingly search—only this time it is for the most effective words and phrases to communicate your ideas. In the job world as well as in social settings, using effective language when you speak can make a sensational impression on your audience.

Earlier chapters compared building a successful speech to building a well-constructed house. We can extend that comparison by saying the successful builder of a speech knows that effective language, along with an effective delivery, is what covers the planks of confidence that were discussed in Chapter 2. Your listeners can't see your words, but they can certainly hear them. And language that is appropriate, informative, and colorful will establish a communication "open house" that is sure to draw an audience, whether it be at work or with friends.

We now take a look at areas of effective delivery that can help you brighten up your house of oral communication.

How successful a speaker is in communicating ideas will depend to a large extent on his or her ability to choose exactly the right words.

The Spoken Word Versus the Written Word

You probably have a favorite author. If not, you will someday. Perhaps there is a good book that you like to read over again, an editorial that says exactly what you believe, or a song that contains words that you never grow tired of reexamining. One of the fantastic things about the written word is that you can experience it as often as you like.

The written word has a distinct advantage over the spoken word: It offers language that you are given time to consider, and with time often comes understanding. Think about how often you didn't understand a reading assignment in school until you had gone over the assignment a second, a third, or even a fourth time.

Studies show, however, that 90 percent of all communication is not written but spoken. Indeed, the word *language* comes from the Latin word *lingua*, which means "tongue." Spoken language must be different from written language if it is to communicate effectively. The audience must "get it" the first time. With the spoken word, you rarely have a second chance to make an impact on your audience.

What must speakers keep in mind regarding language if they want to make the right impression? Good speakers know the value of two key concepts: accuracy and economy.

Accuracy of Language

The average person has a vocabulary of approximately 10,000 words. You might use a certain part of your vocabulary only with your friends, and another, rather different part only with your parents or other adults. Why? Because you realize that certain language is appropriate in some situations but not in others. Despite this realization, however, we may use words that confuse our listeners because those words don't accurately communicate what we think we are saying. We may be speaking about one thing while our audience is hearing something totally different.

Whether talking with your friends during lunchtime or with your teachers in school, your language needs to be accurate.

Design Pics/Kelly Redinger

If you want to be an effective speaker, regardless of the situation—with your friends at the mall, with your teachers, with colleagues at work—then you need to understand the importance of language accuracy. Accuracy means using words that say exactly what you mean. How can you develop accuracy in your verbal expression? Let's start by taking a look at concrete words as opposed to abstract ones.

Concrete and Abstract Words Concrete words name things we can perceive through sight, hearing, touch, taste, or smell. Abstract words, on the other hand, don't deal with the senses but are names for qualities, attributes, concepts, and the like. Words such as *baseball, car,* and *radio* are concrete words. They name things we can see and hear and touch. Compare this list with the words *recreation, transportation,* and *media.* These words are much more general. As a result, they are open to personal interpretation.

Look at a few lines of a song that you've probably heard several times:

Take me out to the ball game,
Take me out with the crowd.
Buy me some peanuts and Cracker Jack,
I don't care if I never get back.

Can you identify the concrete words that are used to help create the atmosphere of a baseball game? Can you almost taste the peanuts and Cracker Jack? These *tangible* objects are being used to communicate a message. It is often highly effective to use concrete words that say clearly what we want our audience to hear. In contrast, using abstract words without clearly defining them means taking the risk of not communicating accurately with the audience. When you use abstract words incorrectly, your language is not working for you. It might even be undermining your intent. Sometimes the most effective language is created when the speaker uses concrete and abstract words together, clearly and accurately.

Denotation and Connotation Closely associated with the terms concrete and *abstract* are the terms *denotation* and *connotation*. **Denotation** refers to the basic meaning of a word, which can easily be found in the dictionary. **Connotation** refers to the meaning of a word that goes beyond the dictionary definition; it is whatever meaning we associate with the word.

What about the word *mother? Mother* can be defined as "a woman who bears a child," but many of us would also associate *mother* with ideas such as love, friendship, and family. Suppose you were going to speak on the idea that women should have the same opportunities as men in the job market. It would probably be unwise to say, "I think that women can make excellent contributions to any job and should be paid the same as men. Women shouldn't be limited to simply being mothers!" Because of connotations associated with the word *mother,* this statement might imply to some people in your audience that you see mothers as relatively low in status, that you are antifamily, or that you think raising children is easy.

Use words that clearly denote a certain meaning. Think through the different connotations that a word might have before you use it in your speech. For example, the words *rebel, loner, eccentric,* and *mediocre* might mean one thing to you but something entirely different to your audience.

Abstract words may have many different connotations. Consider the words *success, failure, family, patriotism,* and *justice.* How might these words be interpreted differently by different people? For example, is success in your eyes the same as it might be in someone else's?

Don't think that you must always avoid abstract words because of this difficulty. Abstract words can be powerful. They can inspire us and appeal to our emotions. We must, however, use them with care.

Economy of Language

Just as you must be accurate in the words that you select for your speech, you must also be economical in the number of words that you use. Keep in mind that the members of your audience, contrary to what they must do when reading the written word, must remember all that you say. *Economy* means "careful or thrifty use." Thus, economy of language suggests carefully managing the quantity of words you use to communicate verbally.

The essay "Civil Disobedience" by Henry David Thoreau was originally delivered as a lecture in 1848 under the title "Resistance to Civil Government." It dealt with the role of individual *conscience* versus the role of state authority. Here is a portion of that speech:

> Must the citizen ever for a moment, or in the least degree, resign his conscience to the legislator? Why has every man a conscience, then? I think that we should be men first, and subjects afterward. If I devote myself to other pursuits and contemplations, I must first see, at least, that I do not pursue them sitting upon another man's shoulders. I must get off him first, that he may pursue his contemplations too. . . . There will never be a really free and enlightened State, until the State comes to recognize the individual as a higher power.

This material given as a speech had little impact. It wasn't until later, as an essay, that it gained prominence. Can you see why it would be difficult to digest as a speech?

This speech offers a great deal of intellectual content to absorb at one time. In addition, notice the number of words that it takes for Thoreau to say what he thinks. As an essay to be read at one's leisure, "Civil Disobedience" is a masterpiece because readers can take the time to study the words and ideas in print. As a speech, it would probably be difficult to listen to. Why? If spoken language becomes long and involved, the listener can get lost.

How can we prevent this? Thoreau himself offers us sound advice when he states in his masterpiece Walden, *"Simplify, simplify."* Apply his advice to both your spoken words and the organization of your ideas if you wish the audience to march to your drumbeat.

How? First of all, pay attention to the number of words that it takes for you to say something. For instance, see how each of these statements might be shortened:

Original Statement: At the beginning of the day, before I have my breakfast, I always work to keep my blood circulating and my body fit.

Shortened Statement: I like to exercise first thing in the morning.

Original Statement: Because of the way you look and because we have always had so much fun together, you and I might not find it a bad thing to talk and do stuff together.

Shortened Statement: I'd like to spend some time with you.

Original Statement: The way that my math teacher evaluates me in school shows that there are areas in which I can do a lot better.

Shortened Statement: I'm failing algebra.

Notice how words can get in the way and clutter up your message. This clutter can confuse your audience. Remember to avoid unnecessary prepositional phrases ("In the beginning of the story, at the top of the page"). Avoid using too many clauses run together in one sentence ("The main character, who is in his mid-twenties, knows that the sister who is hiding in the closet is innocent, because she wasn't at the scene of the crime that had taken place earlier"). Avoid repeating the same idea with different wording ("The main character was an excellent student, had received A's on her report card, and had always done very well in school").

One effective way to be simple and direct is to use rhetorical questions. As discussed in Chapter 9, rhetorical questions are questions that you ask the audience but that you don't really intend the audience to answer out loud. "What do all of these statistics mean?" and "Where is the solution to this problem?" are rhetorical questions. Each could allow you to express with one question what it might have taken you two or three sentences to express otherwise.

The Irish poet and playwright William Butler Yeats once said, "Think like a wise man, but communicate in the language of the people." If you give priority to accuracy and economy when choosing your language, then you might achieve with your spoken words the spirit of what Yeats is saying. Let's look at how figures of speech can make your language memorable.

SECTION ① REVIEW

Recalling the Facts

1. Research has shown that each person has an average vocabulary of how many words?
2. Words that we can understand through the senses are called _____ words, while words that express qualities and attributes are called _____ words.
3. Two terms used in this section are *denotation* and *connotation*. Which one refers to the dictionary definition of a word?
4. This section talked about the economy of language. Henry David Thoreau's *Walden* reinforced this point by stressing the word "_____" when it came to keeping one's life in order.

Thinking Critically

At the beginning of this chapter, you saw a statement by Richard M. Nixon. Here is a statement by another president of the United States, Dwight D. Eisenhower: "How can we appraise a proposal if the terms hurled at our ears can mean anything or nothing? . . . If our attitudes are muddled, our language is often to blame." What was Eisenhower saying? He was speaking specifically about the language of government. Can you think of any examples in which governmental language seems to take on different meanings? Can you find any instances in which governmental language is muddled and confusing? What about the language of sports? The language used in your home? The language used in certain professions?

Taking Charge

This section discussed abstract words and gave specific examples. Write your own definitions (don't use the dictionary) for the abstract words *honesty*, *patriotism*, and *friendship*. Talk with a classmate to see what your definitions have in common. What are the differences? Be ready to discuss your findings in class.

Creating Word Pictures: Figures of Speech

You have probably heard stories about how ancient royalty—without the advantages of the printing press, a modern postal service, the telephone, or the Internet—used messengers to communicate from kingdom to kingdom. (You have probably also heard that some of these messengers were put to death for being bearers of ill tidings.) The messengers, similar to the deliverers of singing telegrams today, would often sing the words of the messages, using rhyme and colorful, descriptive language. Using picturesque language, presented musically, undoubtedly made the message easier to remember. It also made a sound pleasing to the ears of listeners. Spoken language is most effective when it creates music for the ear and pictures for the imagination.

Language that creates pictures in our minds and excites our senses is called **imagery**. Figures of speech are specific types of imagery. Here we describe figures of speech in terms of three categories: comparison, contrast, and exaggeration. Understanding figures of speech and then using them effectively will help make your speeches vivid.

Comparison Imagery

Which statement in each pair has more impact?

> Education is important.
> Education is the key that unlocks many of life's opportunities.

> You have to work hard to make a marriage work.
> Marriage is like a plant: If you care for it and give it time and attention, it will grow and prosper.

> You are not always nice to me.
> Why must you act as if you're Napoleon when we're together?

The second example in each pair is more dynamic; it presents a more exact picture. The first example in each pair isn't necessarily wrong; it is simply not as lively.

The second example in each pair uses comparison imagery. Comparison involves showing similarities. As mentioned, imagery refers to word pictures. Consequently, to use comparison *imagery* means to show similarities by using picturesque language. Let's look at the three most common forms of comparison imagery: metaphor, simile, and allusion.

Metaphor and Simile A **metaphor** is a figure of speech that compares two unlike things by saying that one thing is the other thing. A **simile** is like a metaphor, except that it uses a term such as *like* or *as* to make the comparison.

For example, if you were talking to your classmates on the value of a high school education and employment, you could say,

> A high school diploma can be important in determining the job choices you will have.

Or, you could say,

> A high school diploma can be a key to unlocking occupational doors.

The second example uses a metaphor. It compares a diploma to a key that can open doors to a successful future. The comparison shows that even though diplomas and keys are basically different, they are similar, because each is of definite worth. Do you see how a metaphor can help to liven up your language?

If you wanted to stress that our government is spending large amounts of money each day, you could say,

> Every day, our government spends extremely large sums of money.

Alternatively, you could say,

> Every day, our government spends money as fast as McDonald's sells hamburgers!

The second sentence is a simile, indicating that Washington is like the fast-food industry when it comes to handing out billions of dollars (rather than millions of hamburgers) each day.

If you used the fast-food simile throughout your speech, you would be creating an analogy, which was discussed in Chapter 10. An analogy, which can also take the form of a story, is the extended use of a metaphor or a simile.

Allusion Another way to create an effective word picture is through the use of allusion. An allusion is an indirect reference to a well-known person, place, thing, or idea. Unlike other kinds of reference, an allusion does not specifically identify whom or what it is referring to.

Earlier, a reference was made to Napoleon, showing how someone was comparing a friend to a dictator, implying that the friend was acting very bossy. Obviously not a comparison to be taken literally, the Napoleon reference made the point that one person was not happy with the other's "I'm in

A diploma could be called the "key to success." Can you think of other metaphors that emphasize the value of education?

INSTANT IMPACT

A Meaningful Metaphor

R obert W. Goodman was the father of Andrew Goodman, one of three civil rights workers who were murdered in 1964 in Mississippi. In response to his son's death, Goodman said, "Our grief, though personal, belongs to the nation. The values that our son expressed in his simple action of going to Mississippi are still the bonds that bind this nation together—its Constitution, its law, its Bill of Rights."

charge" attitude. Had the reference been to "the Little Corporal" instead of to Napoleon, it would have been an allusion—an indirect, and yet potentially more telling, reference. (Napoleon was called this partly because of his small stature.)

Be sure, however, that your audience knows what the allusion means. The most effective allusions tend to be those that can be recognized by just about everyone. They do little good if they leave your audience wondering what you are talking about.

Use good judgment. Effective language involves creative comparisons that stick with your audience. If the comparisons don't stick, the language hasn't been effective.

Contrast Imagery

Near the conclusion of John F. Kennedy's 1961 inaugural address are the famous words "Ask not what your country can do for you; ask what you can do for your country." Kennedy contrasts the ideas of "country" and "you." *Contrast imagery* is the general term used to describe language that sets up opposition for effect. Contrast imagery often takes the form of antithesis, oxymoron, and irony.

Figure of Speech	What it Does
Metaphor	Compares two usually unrelated things, without using *like* or *as*.
Simile	Compares two usually unrelated things, using *like* or *as*.
Allusion	Refers to a well-known person, place, thing, or idea.
Antithesis	Balances or contrasts a term against its opposite.
Oxymoron	Places opposite terms side by side.
Irony	Implies the opposite of what seems to be said on the surface.
Hyperbole	Makes more of something.
Understatement	Makes less of something.
Personification	Gives human characteristics to nonhuman things.

Antithesis One type of imagery, **antithesis**, is the specific balancing or contrasting of one term with its opposite. Look at these pairs of words: *hot-cold, young-old, dry-wet, up-down, small-large, success-failure, love-hate, leader-follower, temporary-permanent.* These are a few examples of antithesis. A fair question right now would be, "How can I use antithesis in my speech to make the impression I want?"

Speaking to encourage citizens to volunteer at a soup kitchen, you could begin by saying, "It doesn't matter whether you are young or old, experienced or inexperienced, rich or poor; you can make a difference in this organization." Whether you are attempting to inform, persuade, or motivate your audience, this use of opposites in language can be effective.

Oxymoron Another type of contrast imagery places terms that contradict each other side by side. The result is called an **oxymoron**. The oxymoron forms a contrast image that often jolts listeners and demands that they think and pay attention. Note the following examples:

She is the *momentary love-of-my-life.*

My parents want me to have such *boring fun.*

Because I always fall gracefully, friends say I'm *athletically clumsy.*

Parents of teenagers often exhibit *smiling insecurity.*

Why must our society have so many instances of *selective equality?*

An oxymoron can create not only a quick, clever image for your audience to envision but also some impressive intellectual pictures that you can proudly display.

In his epic poem the *Iliad* (which was based on stories passed down orally from generation to generation), the ancient Greek poet Homer used an oxymoron in the phrase "the delicate feasting of dogs." The obvious contrasting of the words *delicate* and *feasting* (since dogs do not feast delicately)

Using antithesis can help you make the impression you want to encourage people to volunteer for community service.

Steve Debenport/Getty Images

formed the image Homer wanted. He was able to *crystallize* a scene and a message by carefully selecting two words.

Irony Another type of contrast imagery, **irony** is a figure of speech using words that imply something different from, and often the opposite of, what they seem to say on the surface. When you use irony, you say one thing but mean something entirely different.

Here is a story that shows how irony can be used in "picture making." You wake up Monday morning to find that your alarm clock hasn't gone off and that you are going to be late for school. Because you are in a hurry, you pour orange juice on your cereal instead of milk. The bowl tips, spilling its contents onto your Spanish homework. Your mother lets you off at the front door of the school, and you notice that you have two different-colored socks on. As you rush into the building, a friend in the hallway says hello to you and asks how your morning is going. Your response: "Fine! Great! I'm having a *tremendous* morning."

What you really mean is, "This is a terrible morning. I wish I had stayed in bed!" It's obvious here that your words don't say what you really mean.

Here's another example. A television news commentator was talking about a man who sued a rock group, claiming that the intense volume of the group's music at a concert he attended damaged his hearing. Said the news commentator, "Yes, you certainly wouldn't go to a rock concert thinking that there was going to be loud music, now, would you?"

Did he actually mean those words? Of course not. What he was saying to his television audience was, "How in the world could someone go to a rock concert and not expect loud music? Loud music and rock concerts go together."

Of course, the speaker's delivery and body language helped to show everyone watching that he didn't mean what he was saying. The creative power of contrast allowed his real message to come through to his audience. Irony is most effective when your words and your delivery work together.

Exaggeration Imagery

Our third and final category of figures of speech is exaggeration imagery. To *exaggerate* means to make something seem greater than it actually is.

What figure of speech would this man be using if he said, "How lucky I am that my car broke down; now I don't have to wash it this afternoon"?

This image is an example of what figure of speech?
Francis Bacon—a seventeenth-century English philosopher, essayist, and statesman—once said that the only people who should be forgiven for exaggeration are those in love. In addition to those in love, Bacon might have included those in public speaking. While exaggeration in some situations—when giving testimony in a courtroom, for example—might not be wise, exaggeration imagery in front of an audience can do wonders to accentuate the words we speak. Two types of exaggeration imagery are hyperbole and understatement.

Hyperbole Mark Twain gave us Tom Sawyer. William Shakespeare gave us Falstaff. Both of these authors gave us likable literary characters who exaggerate the truth. Tom Sawyer makes too much of adventure, and Falstaff makes too much of himself. Both humorously overstate their accomplishments. This overstatement is called **hyperbole**, and for speakers it is a method of emphasizing something by saying more than is true.

Have you ever heard statements like these?

I called you a million times last night, and the line was always busy!

I have *worked my fingers to the bone* cleaning this house!

Mom, *I don't have a single thread of clothing* to wear to school!

I laughed my head off!

No one actually called a million times, had bare bones for fingers, was totally without clothes, or had his or her head come off. Hyperbole is a form of imagery that blows a picture out of proportion and stretches the audience's imagination.

It can also add a refreshing touch of humor. For example, a basketball team had lost 17 consecutive games before it finally won one. In its next game, it won again on a last-second shot. The student announcer, who was broadcasting from his school radio station, chanted wildly over the air, "The *streak* is still alive! The *streak* is still alive!"

Exaggeration imagery can intensify your message tremendously. You should not, however, exaggerate to the point that no one trusts what you have to say. Use exaggeration to enhance your speech, but be sure to convey your central message in unambiguous language.

Understatement Whereas hyperbole makes *more* of something, understatement makes *less* of something. Even though understatement doesn't exaggerate, it can logically be included in this section because it is the opposite of hyperbole. Understatement uses language that draws the listener in, because it cleverly distorts in its own way and makes us see an absurdity more clearly. Here are examples of understatement:

Families out of work and without a paycheck can experience some economic *discomfort*.

The winner of the basketball Slam Dunk competition can jump *a little*.

Clearly, a family without a paycheck could experience major financial problems, not mere discomfort; and a Slam Dunk champion could probably soar, not just jump a little.

Understatement doesn't always have the shock power of hyperbole, but it can work as an effective language tool. For instance, a student who was giving a speech on the problems of modern technology offered as an example the radar gun that state troopers use to catch speeders. Trying to show that the devices aren't always accurate and that, consequently, motorists can be unfairly victimized, he produced evidence showing that a radar gun once mistakenly clocked a tree going more than 30 miles an hour!

He followed this example by saying, "Now isn't it obvious that the radar gun might show a slight difference in what it registers as your speed and the speed that you're actually traveling?" The words *slight difference* were obviously understating what he actually meant (the difference between zero and 30 miles per hour is more than slight). Nevertheless, they created the impact that he was after. The image was powerfully made through reverse exaggeration, or understatement.

Personification

Personification is giving human characteristics to nonhuman things. Walt Disney, the cartoonist and moviemaker, thrilled millions of people by making animals and other parts of nature act like humans. People of all ages are fascinated when teapots can talk, when sea creatures can fall in love, or when jungle animals can dance and sing. All of a sudden, these things seem like human beings.

"Wayne Gretsky was a fairly good hockey player" is an example of what figure of speech?

Personification communicates a message through language and pictures that people can easily understand. It can be as effective in speaking as it is in animation, for it allows listeners to visualize in human terms. Look at these examples:

The *eyes* of profit can be deceiving.

Don't allow dishonesty to *sneak up* on you!

Crime can *dress up* in many disguises when you are at work.

Profit doesn't have eyes, dishonesty can't physically sneak up, and crime can't dress up. Each example takes something abstract (profit, dishonesty, crime) and gives it a human dimension for emphasis.

Using exaggeration imagery and personification can add color and style to your speaking presentations. Try it. Hyperbole, understatement, and personification can mean the world to your speech content—and to your speaking confidence!

Cartoonists use personification by giving nonhuman things human traits to help us identify with the characters.

Euphemism

A euphemism is mild or indirect term or expression substituted for another that may seem offensive or suggest something unpleasant. Euphemisms can be used in a benign manner, such as when a doctor substitutes the term passed away for died to spare the feelings of family members when a patient has died. But euphemisms may also be used deliberately to downplay or conceal the truth. Such euphemisms are called doublespeak. Some examples might include a business using "downsizing" for mass firings to boost profits, parents telling their children that an ill or aged family pet has gone to live on a farm in the country rather than telling them it was euthanized by a veterinarian, or the military using "collateral damage" for "civilian casualties".

SECTION ② REVIEW

Recalling the Facts

1. When you say one thing but mean something entirely different, you are using _____.

2. Using opposites such as hot and cold and success and failure is known as _____.

3. An indirect reference to a well-known person, place, thing, or event to create a mental picture is termed an _____.

4. Using word opposites side by side ("In the workplace, friendly hostility does little to promote a positive work environment") is called _____.

Thinking Critically

The Indian leader Jawaharlal Nehru once said, "A language is something infinitely greater than grammar and philology [literary scholarship]. It is the poetic testament of the genius of a race and culture, and the living embodiment of the thoughts and fancies that have molded them." Consider what this quotation means. What does Nehru mean by "poetic testament"? Is language greater when it comes from the head? From the heart? From both? Evaluate Nehru's statement and then explain your response.

Taking Charge

You have two tasks:

a. Create your own metaphor or simile for the following: your report card, music, pizza, and money. (Example of a simile: My best friend, Thuy, is like a compass. She always gives me a sense of the direction my life is going in.)

b. Make a list of at least three television or radio advertisements for products or services that use imagery as a sales tactic. Be ready to say what specific figure of speech (such as simile or antithesis) is being used in each and why the advertisement is or is not effective.

The Gettysburg Address

Abraham Lincoln

The Gettysburg Address was delivered by President Abraham Lincoln on November 19, 1863, in Gettysburg, Pennsylvania. It was delivered on the field where, four months earlier, one of the bloodiest battles of the Civil War had been fought. Lincoln gave the speech to dedicate the site as a graveyard and memorial for the soldiers who had died in the battle.

Although it received little attention at the time, the speech is now acknowledged to be a masterpiece of *compression.* Its brevity (the speech lasted less than three minutes) contrasted greatly with the two-hour speech of the accomplished orator Edward Everett, who had spoken earlier that day.

The Gettysburg Address was a communication breakthrough because it eloquently put into words the belief that, even for a country torn by civil strife, there was hope for the survival of democracy and the nation.

Four score and seven years ago our fathers brought forth on this continent, a new nation, conceived in Liberty, and dedicated to the proposition that all men are created equal.

Now we are engaged in a great civil war; testing whether that nation, or any nation so conceived and so dedicated, can long endure. We are met on a great battlefield of that war. We have come to dedicate a portion of that field, as a final resting place for those who here gave their lives that the nation might live. It is altogether fitting and proper that we should do this.

But, in a larger sense, we can not dedicate—we can not consecrate—we can not hallow—this ground. The brave men, living and dead, who struggled here, have consecrated it, far above our poor power to add or detract. The world will little note, nor long remember what we say here, but it can never forget what they did here. It is for us the living, rather, to be dedicated here to the unfinished work which they who fought here have thus far so nobly advanced. It is rather for us to be here dedicated to the great task remaining before us—that from these honored dead we take increased devotion to that cause for which they gave the last full measure of devotion—that we here highly resolve that these dead shall not have died in vain—that this nation, under God, shall have a new birth of freedom—and that government of the people, by the people, and for the people, shall not perish from the earth.

Later in this chapter, we will examine the Gettysburg Address further.

Question
What words and phrases make Lincoln's address so poignant and memorable?

Making Music with Words: Sound Devices

SECTION 3

We have discussed the importance of figures of speech and have shown how language can come alive when speakers use imagery to excite the imagination of the audience. Now, what about the *sound* of the language when spoken?

The music of words can combine with the imagery of words to make communication even more effective. Maybe this is why more than 20 million greeting cards are sold every day in the United States. Greeting cards tend to be written in language that speaks in pictures and sounds pleasing to the ear. Most of us are attracted to language like this.

The twentieth-century English playwright Christopher Fry once said, "The pleasure and excitement of words is that they are living and generating things." Much of the living and generating that Fry spoke of results from well-chosen sound devices, which we can cleverly incorporate into our speaking. Most of the music of language comes from some form of repetition, the act or process of repeating. We can use **repetition** to make music with words by repeating individual sounds and by repeating words or groups of words.

Repeating Individual Sounds

We can repeat individual sounds in three ways: through alliteration, assonance, and consonance.

Alliteration Say each of the following sentences out loud:

A *c*orporation must *c*are about the *c*onsumer.
*P*arents *p*rovide their children with the *p*ower to succeed.

Winter winds whip through a windy city as walkers wear their wraps.

(c) Ingram Publishing / AGE Fotostock

The *will* to *win* is the combination of a *work* ethic plus the *willingness* to dedicate yourself to a *worthwhile* cause.

As you can see, in each sentence, a sound is noticeably repeated—in the first sentence, the *c* sound; in the second sentence, the *p* sound; and in the third sentence, the *w* sound. All of these sentences exhibit the sound device known as alliteration. **Alliteration** is the repetition of the initial sound of two or more words that are close together.

All you have to do to see the *pervasiveness* of alliteration is to watch television or to read the tabloids at the supermarket checkout counter. Weather forecasters might say, "Yes, folks, the winter winds whipped through the Windy City today," stressing the first *w* sound in the words *winter, winds, whipped,* and *windy* to make their forecast stand out and make people take notice. Similarly, a tabloid headline might read, "My Mother Married a Martian."

Do you see why alliteration works? It gives special significance to the specific language you choose to speak. In the following passage, the American patriot Benjamin Franklin used alliteration as a key sound device to enhance the impact of his statements regarding the newly drafted Constitution of 1787. Read this speech out loud so that you can better hear the language at work.

> Mr. President,
> I doubt . . . whether any other convention . . . may be able to make a better constitution; for, you assemble a number of men, [with] all their prejudices, their passions, their errors of opinion. . . . From such an assembly can a perfect production be expected? It therefore astonishes me, Sir, to find this system approaching so near to perfection as it does.

He went on to say,

> Thus I consent, Sir, to this Constitution, because I expect no better, and because I am not sure that it is not the best.

The repetition of initial *m, p,* and *b* sounds in nearby words draws attention to Franklin's statements. Can you hear the musical effect that alliteration produces when you read the words aloud?

Assonance Read Franklin's speech again. What about the words *may, able,* and *make* at the beginning of the speech? Notice the long *a* sound in each word. The repetition of vowel sounds is known as assonance. The vowel sounds can occur anywhere in the words. Thus, the sentence "We believe that peace means a chance for all of the oppressed people of the world," plays on the long *e* sound in five words for effect.

Consonance In the preceding sentence, examine the words *peace, oppressed,* and *people.* Notice that the *p* sound is repeated not only at the beginning of *peace* and *people* but also near the middle of *oppressed* and *people.* The sound device used here is known as **consonance.** Whereas assonance involves repeating vowel sounds, consonance involves repeating consonant sounds anywhere in words.

Let's look at other examples of the ways to repeat individual sounds, so that all three will be clear:

- I love to leap in the air and to land in the lake. (*l* sound, alliteration)
- I love to hike high in the mountains and see the sunrise. (long *i* sound, assonance)
- In dealing with hardships at work, I depend on my friends and family for direction. (*d* sound, consonance)

Rereading Franklin's speech should show you that all three of these devices can be used simultaneously. Point out places in the speech where alliteration, assonance, and consonance work together to give the message its music and make the language memorable.

Repeating Words or Groups of Words: Parallel Structure

A student in a high school speech class was talking about his enthusiasm for automobiles: "If you want to be knowledgeable about a car engine, you have to work, work, work!" He later mentioned that he worked on cars "before school in my garage, during school in automotive class, and after school at a friend's house." He finally said, "Treat your car with respect. Your car will take care of you only when you take care of your car."

Whether he knew it or not, the student was using parallel structure to help convey his message. Using parallel structure, also known as **parallelism**, means using the same grammatical form to express ideas that should be treated equally because they are logically related. Often, parallelism involves repeating words or phrases.

Look at what the student speaker said. Notice how he repeated the word *work* three times for emphasis. He also repeated the word *school* in three successive phrases that are grammatically and logically related. He concluded by stating, *"Your car will only take care of you when you take care of your car."* Notice how the two parts of the sentence use the same form and almost the same words. Parallel structure reinforces an idea or a series of ideas. It also creates a musical effect that can help a speaker get the message across to the audience forcefully.

Let's go back to the Gettysburg Address (Communication Breakthrough, page 270) and analyze it for three specific instances in which Abraham Lincoln brilliantly implemented the technique of parallel structure:

1. At the beginning of the third paragraph, Lincoln declares, "But, in a larger sense, *we can not dedicate—we can not consecrate—we can not hallow—*

Using alliteration, assonance, consonance, or parallelism can help keep your speeches fresh and lively.

this ground." Music, in the form of a driving cadence, results from the repetition of the word arrangement introduced by "we can not."

2. Two sentences later, Lincoln states, *"The world will little note . . . what we say here,* but *it can never forget what they did here."* Even though only a few of the words are repeated, the structure of the two parts of this sentence is the same.

3. Lincoln concludes by declaring "that this nation, under God, shall have a new birth of freedom—and that government *of the people, by the people,* and *for the people,* shall not perish from the earth." The parallel structure of the three prepositional phrases offers a climactic ending to one of the most monumental speeches in American history. In addition, "this nation . . . shall have a new birth of freedom" and "that government . . . shall not perish from the earth" are strikingly similar in construction.

Lincoln's Address at the Dedication of the Gettysburg National Cemetery, November 19, 1863.

Lincoln used parallelism in his monumental three-minute Gettysburg speech.

We conclude this section by examining how another speaker of Lincoln's time, Frederick Douglass, used parallel structure. Douglass was born enslaved in Maryland around 1817 and became a prominent voice in the antislavery movement. A well-educated man, Douglass saw that *emancipation* was a necessary step in the struggle of blacks for independence. During the Civil War, he helped organize regiments of African American soldiers for the Union army, and later he held numerous government positions. Note that Douglass delivered the following speech, "What the Black Man Wants," at the annual meeting of the Massachusetts Anti-Slavery Society in 1865—two years after Lincoln's Gettysburg Address. (Be sure to read the speech out loud.)

Everybody has asked the question . . . "What shall we do with the Negro?" I have had but one answer from the beginning. Do nothing with us! Your doing with us has already played mischief with us. Do nothing with us! If the apples will not remain on the tree of their own strength, if they are worm-eaten at the core, if they are early

Library of Congress Prints and Photographs Division [LC-DIG-ppmsca-19926]

CHAPTER II Effective Language **257**

ripe and disposed to fall, let them fall! I am not for tying or fastening them on the tree in any way, except by nature's plan, and if they will not stay there, let them fall. And if the Negro can not stand on his own legs, let him fall also. All I ask is, give him a chance to stand on his own legs! Let him alone! If you see him on his way to school, let him alone—don't disturb him. If you see him going to the dinner table at a hotel, let him go! If you see him going to the ballot-box, let him

Frederick Douglass

alone—don't disturb him! . . . Let him fall if he can not stand alone! If you will only untie his hands, and give him a chance, I think he will live.

By now, it should be clear that your speaking effectiveness is often only as good as your language effectiveness. But part of language effectiveness involves avoiding certain language pitfalls that can cause both you and your audience to take a communication tumble.

SECTION 3 REVIEW

Recalling the Facts

Match each of the numbered examples with the letter choices:

(a) parallel structure (b) alliteration (c) assonance (d) consonance

1. The *boss* was *busy* buying merchandise for the display.
2. The product was successful, the workers were confident, and the management was happy. (Analyze the sentence in its entirety.)
3. *Applying* for the *perfect* job takes exceptional planning.
4. A complete speech will encourage your audience to believe your message.

Thinking Critically

Reread the speeches by Lincoln and Douglass. Both speeches seem to deal with aspects of (a) life, (b) death, and (c) hope. Analyze each speech and then provide examples of where

each topic (a, b, and c) is addressed. Evaluate how each speaker seems to deal with these three topics a little differently. Point out examples.

Taking Charge

In newspaper and magazine headlines, find two examples of effective sound devices (alliteration, assonance, consonance, or parallel structure). Next, apply what you have learned. Find an ordinary headline and rewrite it, creating your own headline. You might want to write a serious headline and then create a humorous one.

National Archive photo no. 558769/FL–FL-22

Language to Avoid

The quotation spoken by President Nixon on the first page of this chapter is an excellent example of how not to communicate. Even though eventually you may be able to figure out what the quotation means, who wants to wait? Besides, audiences don't have time to stop and figure out a confusing statement when a speech is being delivered. The next idea is on its way.

You have already seen one potential communication problem, euphemisms, in Section 2. Euphemisms can cloud clear communication by offering language that is puzzling and distorted. Unfortunately, the losers are usually the listeners.

Here, we take a look at three other kinds of language you should avoid in your speaking: jargon, sexist language, and shocking or obscene language.

Avoid Jargon

Jargon usually refers to the specialized vocabulary of people in the same line of work, such as doctors or computer programmers. Because only a relatively small group of people understand what the language means, it is often unintelligible to most of the general public. In this sense, it is similar to **slang**—nonstandard words that may also be associated with certain groups, such as teenagers. Like euphemisms, jargon is often heard in government circles, but it can pop up in any discussion.

Suppose you are giving an oral presentation about your job at a computer company and your audience is unaware of certain technical terms. How effective would the communication be if you used the following terms, devised in high-tech circles?

Green washing—Making an unsubstantiated or misleading claim about the environmental benefits of a product or service (as in "In an attempt to convince consumers of its commitment to the environment, the company greenwashed all its packaging, labeling the product as energy-efficient.")

Heisenbug—An unpredictable software bug that disappears or alters its behavior when you try to detect and study it (as in "While attempting to debug a program, John humorously blamed the phases of the moon for code modification caused by a Heisenbug.")

yottabyte—A multiple of the unit byte that is equal to one septillion bytes, or a quadrillion gigabytes (e.g., a unit of measurement that is a number larger than any human can comprehend)

You can see how jargon can be colorfully expressive, yet it is language to avoid when speaking in certain formal professional contexts.

Avoid Sexist Language

Sexist language is language that unfairly groups women—and some would argue, men too—into stereotyped categories. Such stereotyping can be

Every occupation has its jargon. Computer technologists need to carefully monitor their language if giving an address to a general audience.

CHAPTER II Effective Language **259**

Which sexist stereotypes does this photograph put to rest?

demeaning. Schools, textbooks, speakers, and even dictionaries now recognize the importance of fair play regarding the language used for men and women.

Society has traditionally associated girl babies with pink blankets and boy babies with blue blankets, girls with dolls and boys with trucks. Similarly, society has tended to stereotype males as tough, take-charge, dominant leaders and females as weak, passive, subservient followers. Is this fair? Your spoken language must show that you believe that both sexes possess and can demonstrate equal abilities and talents and that gender has no relevance to a person's worth.

Look at these pairs of words: *mankind-humankind, fatherland-homeland, spokesman-spokesperson, congressman-representative, man-hours–working hours, and manmade-synthetic.* Do you see how the second word in each pair avoids the sexist connotation that the first word presents?

Don't think that sexist language applies only to women. How fair is it, for example, to use the term *housewives* when nowadays it is not uncommon for men to stay at home and contribute to household duties? Why not use the term *homemaker,* instead, in your speech? Remember, be vigilant to avoid any language that unfairly stereotypes men and women. Always keep in mind that the words you speak should promote the idea that all people have dignity.

Avoid Shocking or Obscene Language

Speakers often try to appeal to their audiences by speaking casually or by using street language. Street language, however, can be shocking to an audience not expecting it. Use good judgment. While shocking language might draw your audience's attention, it might also quickly turn off most people.

Obscene language is any language that offends by going against common standards of decency. Since what is considered obscene may vary from place to place, speakers must avoid any possibility that their words might be construed as indecent. Recently a canoeist battling a rough river swore loudly and repeatedly about his troubles and was later convicted of using obscene language within earshot of children.

While a startling fact or statistic can work to your communication advantage, using an off-color story or a derogatory term will not. A student once started his speech by walking to the front and saying, "Hello, morons!" To him, this was clever. Granted, some of the students in the audience laughed (perhaps out of shock), but many seemed offended by his introduction and tuned out what he said next.

If you find yourself about to include shocking or obscene language in a speech, ask yourself the following questions: Is a curse word worth the price? Is vulgarity ever worth the sacrifice of effective verbal communication? The answer to each question is no. Your audience deserves better.

Consider the story of Helen Keller, which attests to the power of language. Keller was born in Alabama in 1880. She was diagnosed at 18 months of age with being unable to see, hear, or speak. Doctors early on said that she was mentally handicapped and that she would never be able to function like other human beings. However, when Keller was eight years old, Anne Sullivan, from the Perkins Institution and Massachusetts School for the Blind, began working with her. The two were to be close companions for nearly half a century.

Helen Keller learned from Sullivan what words meant. Sullivan spelled into the palm of Keller's hand the names of such familiar things as a doll and a puppy. At first slowly, but later rapidly, Keller learned the names of objects. Within a few years, she was reading and writing *braille* fluently.

When she was ten, Keller pleaded to be taught how to speak. Sullivan discovered that Keller could learn by placing her fingers on the larynx of her teacher's throat and sensing the vibrations.

The story is told of how Keller was once asked which she would choose if she had the choice—seeing or hearing. She said that she would choose hearing. If she could hear the language used effectively, she said, the speaker could create for her all the things that her eyes could not see. In other words, spoken language would allow her to "see" in her imagination, and she would have the best of both worlds.

Helen Keller, as a girl, and her teacher Anne Sullivan

SECTION 4 REVIEW

Recalling the Facts

1. What is the term for a specialized vocabulary understood by only a special few?

2. One of the most moving stories in American culture is that of Helen Keller. She once said that if she had a choice, she would choose being able to hear over being able to see. What was her reason? (Give the exact words from the page.)

3. Teenagers are often said to have a language of their own. These nonstandard words are called _____, and should be avoided when speaking to a varied audience.

Thinking Critically

In Australia teenagers have a language of their own. The statement "She was given *the elbow* by her boyfriend," for example, means that she was "dumped" by him. When do you think that it is appropriate to use slang? When is using slang a bad idea? Can slang ever be a problem for your audience—for example, for a group of professional people? What can you do to make sure that it isn't a problem for *you?*

Taking Charge

Interview a friend, a parent or relative, a teacher, or a community member whose job has a specialized vocabulary. Have the person name and then define for you at least five terms that could be categorized as jargon. Finally, ask the person to explain how jargon can sometimes be beneficial at the workplace. Write down the responses and be prepared to offer a short speech about them to the class.

CHAPTER ⑪ Review and Enrichment

Looking Back

Listed below are the major ideas discussed in this chapter.

- Choosing the correct words is like walking a tightrope: it must be done with care.
- The spoken word must communicate immediately with the audience, while the written word offers the reader the luxury of time.
- Accuracy of language and economy of language are two qualities that help create a positive speaking impression.
- Concrete words name things that you can perceive through your senses. Abstract words deal with intangible concepts.
- Denotation is the dictionary definition of a word; connotation goes much further, involving all of the meanings that a word might suggest.
- Using figures of speech, or word pictures, can make your speaking come alive.

- Comparison imagery stresses similarities and includes metaphors, similes, and allusions.
- Contrast imagery takes the form of antithesis, oxymoron, and irony.
- Exaggeration imagery includes hyperbole and understatement.
- In addition to imagery, sound devices—the "music" found in words—are also important.
- Most of the "music" of speech is a result of the repetition of sounds and the repetition of the same or similar words or groups of words.
- Certain language should be avoided: jargon, sexist language, and shocking language, which might be viewed as obscene or vulgar.

Speech Vocabulary

concrete word
abstract word
denotation
connotation
imagery
metaphor
simile
allusion
antithesis
oxymoron
irony

hyperbole
understatement
euphemism
personification
repetition
alliteration
assonance
consonance
parallelism
jargon
slang

1. For each word in the speech vocabulary list, give the definition found in the chapter. Prepare a quiz by listing any ten vocabulary words and numbering them from 1 to 10.

Read these to another student and have him or her spell them. Mix up the definitions, write them on the same paper as the word list, and letter them from a to j. Have the student write the letter of the correct definition beside each vocabulary word.

2. Make up ten sentences using a total of at least ten different vocabulary words from the speech vocabulary list. Divide your sentences into the following groups: two sentences with alliteration, two with assonance, two with consonance, two with personification, and two with hyperbole. Have fun making up your sentences, but be sure that they make sense. Be prepared to read your sentences out loud to the rest of the class.

Academic Vocabulary

tangible	exaggerate	emancipation
conscience	compression	demeaning
picturesque	pervasiveness	braille
crystallize	cadence	

Use context clues to write the meaning of each vocabulary word. Then use a print or an online dictionary to check the accuracy of your definition.

To Remember

Answer the following questions based on your reading of the chapter.

1. The term _____ differs from the term *denotation* in that it refers to the meaning of a word that goes beyond the dictionary definition.

2. A metaphor compares two unlike things by saying one thing is the other thing, while a _____ makes a comparison that uses a term such as *like* or *as*.

3. Hyperbole exaggerates for effect, saying more than what is true, while its opposite, _____, makes less of something to get a desired response.

4. The repetition of the sound at the beginning of two or more words that are close together is called _____.

5. A question that doesn't really call for a spoken response from the audience is a _____ question.

6. Language that unfairly stereotypes males or females is called _____.

7. Referring indirectly to something or someone well known to make a creative comparison is called making an _____.

8. Giving human characteristics to nonhuman things is called _____.

To Do

1. Go to a library and find a speech. You can find speeches in books or in periodicals such as *Vital Speeches*. Analyze your speech by listing the concrete words and the abstract words, the imagery, and the key sound devices used. What is effective to you, and what is unclear or lacks impact? Be specific. In addition, be sure that you can give a complete explanation of your entire speech.

2. Find someone in your school or community who is familiar with sign language or the world of the hearing impaired. Interview the person and discover how the language works.

3. Think of a pleasant experience that you have had. Using a voice recorder, close your eyes and record your memories. Use vivid imagery and descriptive phrasing. Next, play back the recording. Did your language work for you? If not, repeat the task—this time choosing a different experience.

4. Keep a notebook listing the jargon that you hear around school, at your job, at a parent's workplace, and so on. Include definitions of the terms. Over time, does the jargon seem to change? Why?

To Talk About

1. In Oregon, a newspaper notified readers that it would no longer print news about or recognize any sports teams that have mascots it considered degrading to American Indians. Thus, it would no longer mention team names like the Braves and the Redskins. What is your opinion about this issue? What about a professional women's basketball team called the Missies or the Babes? Are such names sexist? Why or why not? Where should we draw the line between offensive and inoffensive language? Give logical answers and give evidence whenever possible.

2. Find a copy of Benjamin Franklin's "The Way to Wealth." Notice how this collection of maxims (sayings) not only teaches lessons but also communicates through effective language. Give your favorite maxims from the work and explain what images or sound devices they use.

3. Are commercials fair in their language? One television advertisement spoke of the need for romance and the personal touch in viewers' lives. It invited people to dial a phone number. When people called, however, a recording talked to them. When is the advertiser at fault in such situations? When are we at fault? What language should we especially look out for?

To Write About

1. Forming oxymorons can be fun and challenging. (An example is quiet war.) Write five of your own. Then, create euphemisms for these jobs: dog catcher, window washer, custodian, elementary school teacher, dance chaperone, and person who cuts lawns. (For example, a short person might be called "vertically challenged.") Have fun, but see that your euphemisms make sense.

2. Write an introduction for a friend in class as if you were going to introduce him or her to your friends at work. Fill your introduction with job jargon. Now rewrite the introduction and replace all of the jargon with standard language. Be prepared to read your introductions out loud.

3. Write a description of how your day has gone so far. Use the following devices: personification, parallel structure, and simile or metaphor. Describe not only what has happened around you but also what has happened inside you.

4. Write about a favorite song of yours. Why are the words to the song important to you? What do they mean? What are your favorite images in the song? What pictures does the song bring to mind? Be specific and give examples.

Related Speech Topics

What goes on in my first-hour class
A day at my job
The best thing about a school dance
"Rush hour" at my house before school
Why I enjoy the beach
If I had only 24 hours to live, I'd . . .
The excitement of a sports event

The day I had to perform for an audience
My first day driving
Equal opportunity in the professional world
Slang
Euphemisms
Sexism
Racism

EFFECTIVE DELIVERY

As a vessel is known by the sound, whether it be cracked or not, so men are proved, by their speeches, whether they be wise or foolish.

—Demosthenes, ancient Greek orator and statesman

Learning Objectives

After completing this chapter, you will be able to do the following.

- Explain the components of an effective delivery.
- Understand what delivery means and how it applies to oral communication.
- Identify types of nonverbal communication and their effects.
- Use appropriate delivery techniques to gain command of your information.
- Use effective verbal and nonverbal strategies in speech presentations.
- Evaluate the effectiveness of your own and others' presentations.

Chapter Outline

Following are the main sections in this chapter.

1. Types of Delivery
2. Using Your Voice
3. Using Your Body
4. Using Your Face

Speech Vocabulary

In this chapter, you will learn the meanings of the speech terms listed below.

delivery
manuscript method
memorized method
extemporaneous
  method
impromptu method
vocalized pause
power source
vocal process
phonation
oral cavity
rate
pace

pitch
monotone
stress
inflection
volume
articulation
pronunciation
platform movement
proxemics
posture

Academic Vocabulary

Expanding your academic vocabulary will help you become a more effective communicator. Listed below are some words appearing in this chapter that you should make part of your vocabulary.

regurgitating
methodically
syllable

alienated
superficial

The U.S. Postal Service has a very simple advertising slogan: "We deliver for you." This statement is saying that you can count on the post office and mail carriers to get your mail to you in a timely fashion. Similarly, as a good speaker, you must "deliver" your spoken words so that your audience gets the message. Your words are the "mail," so they must be delivered accurately and effectively.

Your speech delivery is made up of two elements: verbal and nonverbal communication. Both are vital to making the right impression, because the audience not only hears what you have to say but also sees how you say it (through body language). Do not underestimate your delivery. A book titled *Emotional Contagion* says, to put it simply, that moods and language patterns are contagious. Studies reveal that if your words are delivered in a slow, boring manner, your audience will give off a bored response. On the other hand, a congenial, uplifting speaker can light up a group. If our words and emotions can potentially influence the moods and communication of others, shouldn't our vocal messages be constructive and helpful?

This chapter will help you understand and apply specific delivery skills. First, you will learn that your delivery is the actual "selling" of your verbal message. Next, you will look at various methods that you can select to deliver your speech. Finally, you will analyze the specific components of delivery—your voice, your body, and your face—and see how your speech can be a "special delivery" when these three work in harmony.

Introduction

Once, while talking to a group of college students, the great jazz musician Miles Davis was asked, "What specific musical philosophy do you give credit for making your trumpet style what it is?" Davis looked calmly at the student and said, "The only way that I ever started to get any type of 'style' was when I picked up my trumpet and blew!"

Similarly, you have no real speaking style until you actually speak. The manner in which you speak is called your **delivery**. When we discuss delivery, we're not talking about what you say but about how you say it. Your delivery is your style of presentation—your personalized means of giving life and significance to your words. If we put this in a mathematical format, it might look like this:

Messages + Communication = Delivery

Miles Davis on the trumpet at the Three Deuces, New York, N.Y., 1947.

William P. Gottlieb/Ira and Leonore S. Gershwin Fund Collection, Music Division, Library of Congress

All good speakers know the value of delivery. The first two chapters of this book discussed how a speaker begins to build a good speech by

- constructing a solid foundation made up of values, and
- attaching the planks of confidence.

But regardless of how solid the foundation of a house might be, few people will buy the house if the outside is in poor condition. Appearance, of course, is an important selling point, and most houses are spruced up and painted before being put on the market. Delivery is the "outside" selling point of a speech.

Well-written words that are poorly delivered will likely have little impact on an audience. Poorly written words delivered with great style will also probably fail to affect the audience. However, well-written words delivered with purpose and conviction will prove to be convincing.

Real estate agents have a term to describe something certain people do when they try to sell their homes. It's called dynamizing. This means that the owners will take time and special care to enhance the appearance of their homes to make a dynamic first impression. You need to give this same care and effort to dynamizing your speech delivery. Let's start by examining the different types of delivery you might choose. Like Miles Davis, let's now "pick up the trumpet and start to blow."

Just as you would work hard to get your house ready to sell, you must also work to dynamize and sell your speech.

Types of Delivery

A number of singers can deliver the same piece of music, yet each singer will probably sound different from the others when the notes come out of his or her mouth. The style of Willie Nelson, for example, doesn't sound the same as the style of Aretha Franklin or Elton John. Different people have different approaches based on what sound works and what sound doesn't work for them. The same is true for speakers.

What works for you? What method of delivery will be effective, depending on your audience, the speaking occasion, and your specific speech purpose? To help you answer this question, let's examine the pros and cons of the following four types of delivery:

- *manuscript* method
- *memorized* method
- *extemporaneous* method
- *impromptu* method

The manuscript method—reading from prepared notes—is often used for political addresses.

The Manuscript Method

First is the **manuscript method.** In this method of delivery, you write out your material word for word and then deliver your speech from a lectern, or a stand used to hold your papers. You primarily read your material. The manuscript method is often used when speaking to very large groups. Political figures often use the manuscript method of delivery (via an unseen teleprompter and a set of monitors) because they want to be absolutely sure of their words and the phrasing of their ideas. Business leaders speaking at their annual stockholders meeting usually hold a manuscript because they want to present financial data (and the company's spin on them) accurately for their investors. Sports figures often use the manuscript method to give a prepared statement about retiring.

A good thing about the manuscript method is that when you use it, you are unlikely to make an error in the content of your speech. The words are right on the paper in front of you. Also, most likely, you will have had ample time to plan exactly what you want to say. Often, the manuscript method is an excellent way for new speakers to practice getting up in front of people. The manuscript functions as a security blanket, allowing speakers to be more comfortable with their audience.

Potential problems arise with this method, however. You might lose touch with your audience because you are concentrating on your paper. While you are looking at your speech, you can't be looking at the people in the room. Remember, if the members of your audience do not feel that you are involved with them, they will very quickly turn you off, and you will lose credibility as a speaker. People don't believe someone who won't look at them. In short, the manuscript method has real advantages, but be sure not to allow the words on your paper to take priority over the eyes of your audience.

"Special Delivery" Tip: When your speech is written out word for word, make sure that your writing is easy to read, that your words are large enough, and that you have key words highlighted or underlined. Typing or printing your words is a smart choice. Be sure the actual manuscript appears professional to the audience. Writing should be on only one side of the paper, and the paper should never be wrinkled or torn.

The Memorized Method

The second method of delivery is the **memorized method.** In this method of delivery, you commit every word of your speech to memory. You use no notes and have no papers to place on the lectern.

The memorized method has many of the same advantages as the manuscript method. You know each word of your speech by heart. Each idea has been thoroughly examined beforehand and each word carefully put into place. You can even have a good idea of where appropriate gestures, facial expressions, and movement will fit.

Here, too, difficulties present themselves, however. Even though it might seem that memorizing your speech would make you more relaxed and confident in your delivery, that is not always the case. As a matter of fact, you might become even more tense the second you realize that you have forgotten a word in your speech.

How many times have you seen someone responsible for introducing a speaker memorize the material and then forget his or her place? Have you ever seen students running for student government, class office, or offices in school clubs who have memorized their speeches, only to go absolutely blank the first time their eyes met the eyes of the audience?

The main problem with the memorized method, especially with beginners, is that you usually end up spending so much time thinking of the words in your head that you forget to share your message vibrantly. Like the manuscript method, the memorized method of delivery puts the words in charge! Remember, you must be in charge. Audiences don't want to see a robot in front of them simply *regurgitating* words from a memorized speech. Audiences want to listen to people who will talk to them per-

Has the speaker lost touch with the audience?

son to person, openly and honestly. As with the manuscript method of delivery, then, be careful. Always give your utmost attention to the eyes of your audience.

"Special Delivery" Tip: Memorize in small sections. Practice your memorization out loud. The more times you say the words, the more likely you will be to deliver them as planned. The most important parts of your speech to memorize are the first lines and the final lines. This way, you can be confident about the beginning and the ending of your speech. Finally, always have a "safety valve" in case you forget where you are. This could be a relevant personal story, a reference to someone in the audience, or a series of important statistics that relate to your topic. By buying time you, might remember where you were in the speech and then continue.

The Extemporaneous Method

The third method of delivery, and perhaps the best, is the **extemporaneous method.** With the extemporaneous method, you don't write out your speech word for word, nor do you commit the words to memory. You may use an outline to keep your carefully prepared ideas in order, but you are free to choose on the spot the words that you will use to voice those ideas. You have some verbal latitude.

A three-by-five or four-by-six notecard is often used for the extemporaneous speech. For example, you might want to jot down each of the major transitions (discussed in detail in Chapter 9), or words or phrases that make your speech flow from one section to another (*in the first place, next, last*, and so on). You could include key words related to major divisions of the speech to make sure that your main points are clear (for example, "The economy is my next area of concern"). But you are also free to think on your feet.

The greatest advantage of the extemporaneous method is that you can be natural; you can be yourself. You can look at your audience and know where you are going in your speech and how your audience is reacting to what you're saying. The extemporaneous form of delivery allows you to pay attention to audience feedback and, if needed, to do some immediate adjusting.

Another good thing about the extemporaneous method of delivery is that your body is allowed to become a part of the communication process.

It is no secret that the extemporaneous style is the most believable. This is because it allows you to be you. It lets you and your audience connect logically and emotionally. There is some danger that when

Impromptu speaking with friends can occur every day.

you use the extemporaneous method you may flub your fluency or forget something you wanted to say. In the long run, though, this is the method of delivery that can dynamize an audience.

"Special Delivery" Tip: Get control of your notecards! Chapter 2 offered some sound advice: even though notes can give you a sense of security, they are not supposed to be a substitute for memory. Don't have too many notecards. No more than a few should do the trick in most instances. Put down key words and phrases in the form of an outline. The outline highlights the key points and will be easy for your eyes to follow. Finally, practice with the actual notecards before the presentation so that you are comfortable holding them.

The Impromptu Method

Finally, consider the **impromptu method**. *Impromptu* means "not rehearsed." This method of delivery involves speaking spontaneously, or off the cuff, usually for a relatively short time. With the impromptu method, you have little time for preparation. The impromptu method calls for a quick mind and instant audience analysis.

The impromptu method of delivery, like the extemporaneous type, allows you to be yourself. You don't have time to be phony with your audience or to appear artificial or contrived. Many of the good points that characterize the extemporaneous method of delivery also apply to impromptu speaking.

An effective impromptu speaker can come across as witty and intelligent. The impromptu method can be impressive if you have the talent, organizational skills, and confidence to pull it off.

As you might expect, the impromptu method of delivery has drawbacks as well. With no notes, you might lose your train of thought and appear disorganized. Or you might be at a loss for the right word and come across as lacking an adequate vocabulary. Probably the greatest problem with impromptu speaking is the potential for "dead space," an interval in which you don't know what to say. This is where **vocalized pauses**, such as *and uh, you know, like*, and *uh*, are often used as filler. If used too often, vocalized pauses can become extremely distracting to an audience because they prevent a fluent presentation of your ideas. Usually,

Impromptu speaking is a necessity in everyday life.every day.

when we lose our fluency, we also lose our confidence. It's no wonder that impromptu speaking is the most frightening of all of the delivery options.

In spite of its drawbacks, impromptu speaking is probably the method of delivery you will most often be called on to use in your life. Don't run from it. At home, at school, at community functions, on the job, or with friends, impromptu speaking is a necessity. Think about it. Have you ever been asked to give your reasoning for an answer in class or to state your opinion on an issue? Have you ever been asked to say how you feel? To explain why you think your idea might work? To describe a problem that you perceive? To solve a community concern?

You can do it! Think in simple terms, prepare a list of organizational words that you can frequently use; be clear; and be brief. Remember the value of reading and being informed. You must recognize that the impromptu method of delivery is a real-world necessity. If you practice it, you can master it.

"Special Delivery" Tip: Don't get caught off guard. Using the impromptu method of delivery can show that you have both the brain and the word power to communicate instantly. Whether in a social or a business situation, you will probably have an idea of what's coming. Be prepared.

Know who is in attendance.
Know the mood of your audience.
Know what makes your audience laugh.
Do your homework.

Show your audience that you are a thinker and that your words express both emotional and intellectual conviction.

Comparing Delivery Methods

So which method of delivery is best? You would be wise to incorporate aspects of all four methods in your speaking. There will be times when you will want to read a section of your material to your audience, as when you have a list of facts or a long quotation that you don't want to misquote. Also, you may find that memorizing your introduction and your conclusion will boost your confidence and help you establish rapport with your listeners. In addition, having a working outline that allows you to extemporaneously speak on your feet is a good way to gain credibility with your audience. Finally, the impromptu method of delivery makes you seem believable and up-to-the-minute, because you are responding without preparation, on the spot—much as a broadcast news reporter does at the scene of a major unfolding event.

Whichever method of delivery you use, remember that you are showing your audience how you choose to say your words. Say them with thought, say them with feeling, and, most of all, say them well.

Next, take a look at how you can use your voice to make your delivery come alive.

Recalling the Facts

1. Of the four delivery methods, which one allows almost no time for preparation? Which one is read from a script?
2. Which delivery method uses notecards but is not intended to be read?
3. When using notecards, what are two pitfalls that you should avoid?
4. Give an instance in which the memorized method of delivery might be appropriate.

Thinking Critically

1. It has been said that the ultimate compliment in speaking is when the audience believes you. In other words, regardless of the delivery type, you are effective if your listeners feel that you are being honest and fair. With this in mind, do you think that a person who uses notecards when speaking is more or less believable, or does it depend on the speaking situation? Explain what you mean. How can using notecards sometimes add to a speaker's credibility? Give a speaking circumstance in which notes might not be a smart choice.

2. Take an informal poll in your classroom to identify the brightest, most intelligent living Americans. Make a list of the top vote getters. Discuss the backgrounds of these people with your teacher. What has each person contributed to American society? What do these people seem to have in common? Do you see any major differences? Did any entertainers, sports figures, or Nobel Prize winners make the list? Why or why not? Be specific.

Taking Charge

Practice three of the four methods of delivery using the student speech by Joseph Wycoff at the end of this chapter. First, find a paragraph that you enjoy and deliver it to a classmate or to the class by reading from a script. Next, try to commit that same paragraph (or most of it) to memory and deliver it. Finally, using a three-by-five or four-by-six notecard, deliver that same paragraph and look down at your notecard only when you need to be reminded of key words or phrases. Which method was the most effective for you? Why? Be ready to discuss your answers with the class.

Using Your Voice

It doesn't matter whether you are a weightlifter, a sports car driver, or a scientist; you need a power source. A **power source** is the energy that makes things go. The power source for the weightlifter is muscle; for the driver, the engine; for the scientist, brain power. For speakers, the power source is the entire **vocal process.**

The power source used to produce the voice is also used to help us breathe, chew, and swallow. However, in the vocal process, it is specifically our breathing system that provides the power for voice production, or **phonation.** The breathing system consists of the lungs, the rib cage, and all of the associated muscles. Let's examine how all of this works.

First, think about your lungs. From the lungs, we get the air necessary to produce sound. However, the lungs have no muscles; they are just two sacks, like balloons, waiting to be filled with air. We fill them when we breathe in. The muscles of the chest can help in this filling process, but the real power source for breathing is the diaphragm.

This diagram shows the main components of the human respiratory system.

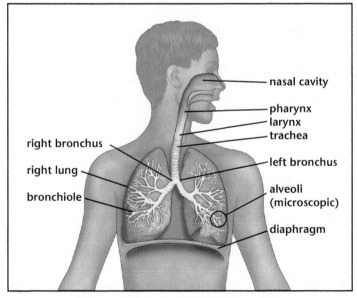

nasal cavity
pharynx
larynx
trachea
right bronchus
left bronchus
right lung
bronchiole
alveoli (microscopic)
diaphragm

The diaphragm is a muscle that separates the chest from the abdominal area. It reaches from the front of the ribs to the spine. Breathing from the diaphragm, not from just the chest, produces a resonant voice—one that is full, rich, easily heard, and pleasant to hear.

Bette Ambrosio, a former speech teacher at Highland Park High School in Dallas, devised a method of teaching diaphragmatic breathing. First, she had her students lie on the floor and put both of their hands on the diaphragm area, fingertips touching. If the students were breathing correctly, the fingertips would part at each breath. "If the fingertips don't," she said, "students are chest breathers. Chest breathers are short of breath and weak in volume." Put her exercise to good use and breathe correctly—from your diaphragm.

Where does the air go after it leaves the lungs? From each lung, it travels through a tube called a bronchus. The bronchi meet and form the trachea, or windpipe. The windpipe leads upward to the larynx (pronounced *lar-inks*), also known as the voice box. The larynx is the voice-producing organ; it contains the vocal cords. From the larynx, air moves on to the pharynx, or **oral cavity**—the area in the back of the mouth and nose. The pharynx is connected to the outside air.

This overall power system performs two major functions for the speaker:

- It delivers the air needed to speak.
- It regulates the amount of air specifically needed to speak.

While it is true that the product of your power source is only air, it is also only air that goes into a tire. Just as a tire without air doesn't roll well, a voice without a sufficient amount of air doesn't communicate well. You must pump up your lungs to give your words a smoother ride.

Specific features of voice must also be taken into account. These are rate, pitch, stress, volume, articulation, and pronunciation.

Rate

The speed at which we speak is the **rate** or the **pace**. The average rate of speaking is approximately 120 to 180 words per minute. Sometimes people speak too quickly, and sometimes they speak too slowly. If you have a problem with rate, it will usually be that you are speaking too fast. People often speak faster than they realize. Furthermore, when people are in any way frightened (as when they have stage fright), they tend to speed up their speech.

When speakers talk too rapidly, audiences don't have time to understand fully what is being said. The words are difficult to understand, and the meaning is unclear. Of course, it is possible to speak too slowly, but this is better than speaking too fast. Your audience can adjust to a rate that is very deliberate but will have difficulty trying to digest a ton of information in a hurry.

Another problem with speaking very fast is that you run out of breath. This makes you swallow at awkward times, start to sweat, or think that you are going to pass out. Thus, a fast pace makes everything go wrong.

How can you avoid speaking too fast? Try pacing yourself—take a deep breath (as basketball players do at the free throw line), give each word its due, and speak deliberately and with feeling. Your audience will not only understand your message better, but they will also have the time to actually feel as you do. With a slower rate, you can think on your feet. In addition, you can read audience feedback and tell how you are doing. Think about watching your favorite video while fast-forwarding the entire time. You might see and hear the whole video, but you won't be able to enjoy it fully because you won't be able to understand the words. Don't play your speech at the wrong speed.

History can teach us a lesson. Demosthenes, who gave us the quotation on this chapter's opening page spread, is credited by scholars as being the greatest ancient Greek orator. His teachings represent the highest achievement in Greek rhetoric. Legend has it that as a small child, he stammered or had a speech defect. To overcome this problem, he placed pebbles in his mouth and stood beside the sea, shouting into the wind, so that he would be forced to speak slowly and deliberately. This method made him slow down his

The ancient Greek orator Demosthenes is said to have overcome his speech difficulties by shouting into the wind.

rate of speech. This slower rate allowed him to pronounce words accurately and enunciate distinctly.

We have emphasized one point about rate: Speak slowly enough to be understood. It is also important to vary your rate somewhat, as you will see in the next section.

Pitch

Your **pitch** is the vocal notes that you hit while speaking—the highs and lows of your voice. Think of a musical scale played on the piano. At one end is a low note, and at the other end is a high note. Of course, many other notes occur in between.

You can't easily sell a house whose exterior is dull and lifeless; likewise, you can't sell a speech

© Pixtal/age Fotostock

delivered in a very narrow vocal range; you will bore everyone to death. In other words, you must avoid **monotone.** You speak in a monotone when you deliver all of your words *methodically,* at almost the same rate and pitch.

Rate and pitch work together. If you vary your speed of speaking and the notes that your voice hits, then you will be on your way to using your voice well for an effective delivery. Imagine rate and pitch as the bouncing of a ball inside a circle. While the ball is bouncing around all over the circle, your rate and pitch are showing variety and are working well together. However, if the ball is bouncing in just one spot, you are in trouble. You are hitting a very small vocal range at the same speed. You are in "the dead zone," and what is dying is your speech (and maybe your listeners' attention as well!).

How many times have you complained about a teacher who always spoke the same way at the same speed? You probably said something like "That teacher just about puts me to sleep every time she lectures! Why can't she liven things up a little?" The same is true for you.

Of course, you can't liven things up by simply hitting different notes at random. You can, however, use pitch to **stress,** or emphasize, the most important word or words in a sentence, thus making the audience aware that some of your words are more important than others. Altering your vocal tone or your pitch is called voice **inflection,** and it is often used to help create emphasis.

Repeat the following sentence, each time stressing a different word for a different effect.

- *I* think that you are the best.
- I *think* that you are the best.
- I think that *you* are the best.
- I think that you *are* the best.
- I think that you are *the* best.
- I think that you are the *best.*

Consider how emphasizing a different word each time changes the meaning of the sentence. Now repeat the sentence as a

question. Do you see the impact that your voice can have? Changing the inflection of a word or a specific phrase can help you communicate your information effectively.

In addition to stressing words by varying rate and pitch, you can stress them by varying volume, which is the next area of analysis.

Volume

It does little good for you to have an outstanding speech if no one can hear you. On the other hand, people don't want to hear your words shouted at them. You must learn to control your speaking volume. **Volume** is the loudness or softness of your voice.

Picture yourself in these situations:

- seated next to a friend at a rock concert
- seated next to a friend before the morning announcements at school
- seated next to a friend in the library
- seated in a small conference room for an employees' meeting

What would your volume be in each situation?

Would a rock concert be a good place to try out your most outstanding speech on a friend next to you?

INSTANT IMPACT

A Kingly Voice?

Charlemagne (742–814) was a king who ruled a large area of Western Europe during the Middle Ages. He was considered one of the greatest warriors of his time. He stood nearly six feet five inches tall and weighed nearly 300 pounds. Charlemagne had particularly strong legs and powerful arms. It was said that he was among the finest hunters and riders in his court and that he could kill a man with a single blow of his fist. However, he was often the object of ridicule (behind his back, of course) because he spoke in a high and squeaky voice. His contemporaries compared his voice to that of a twelve-year-old child.

These examples might be obvious, but you will need to vary your volume for other situations as well. For instance, the volume you use at the family dinner table will be quite different from the volume you use to give a speech in English class. The volume for a roundtable discussion in science class greatly differs from the volume for addressing a crowded room at a community function. Your volume is adequate when everyone in the room can comfortably hear you.

This means that you have to be alert to physical problems that might arise. What do you do if you are speaking in a small room and the air conditioner is blasting? What if the windows are open and the sound of automobiles and machinery outside is loud and distracting?

Of course, you could walk over and turn off the air conditioner or shut the windows. But this might be unwise if the weather is hot and muggy. Your audience might revolt. Thus, it is wise to be ready to speak over any problem by adjusting your volume level. If the audience is saying to themselves while you are speaking, "Turn it up, please!" they will probably tune you out soon. Don't let this happen. Give your words a chance to be heard.

How can you accomplish this? By practicing taking deep breaths and using the power source described earlier, you can have adequate volume in any speaking situation. Breathe from your diaphragm, open your mouth, and drop your lower jaw. Allow the amount of air moving naturally through the oral cavity to produce the volume you desire. Inhale deeply through your nose and slowly exhale through your mouth as you form your words.

Articulation and Pronunciation

In the hit musical *My Fair Lady*, Professor Henry Higgins worked to turn the uneducated flower peddler Eliza Doolittle into a woman of refinement. He tried to rid her of her working-class accent by having her repeat such classic lines as "The *rain* in *Spain* falls mainly on the plain." She was to speak slowly, clearly, and distinctly, making sure to pronounce the long a sound in the words rain and Spain. Higgins was working with the way Eliza used her voice. Specifically, he was working with her articulation and pronunciation.

Articulation, or enunciation, refers to the crispness, the distinctness, with which we say the *syllables* in a word. The jaw, the lips, and the tongue are known as the main articulators.

Do you say your words clearly, or do you sometimes have the "mushmouth syndrome," in which syllables in words are run together or omitted entirely? Most of us are aware that the word *probably* has three syllables, for example, but we often leave out the middle syllable and say *probly*. Can you think of similar examples?

Middle *t* sounds (as in *water, matter,* and *better*) are particularly troublesome. You might have a tendency to articulate a *d* sound instead of the *t*. Another problem is the *ing* sound at the end of words (as in *coming* and *going*). Don't drop the final *g* sound in *swimming* so that the word becomes *swimmin'*.

Poor articulation is most evident in the way people say entire sentences. Have you ever heard these?

"Whataya gonna d'night?"	(What are you going to do tonight?)
"Didja see'm doot?"	(Did you see him do it?)
"Doya wanna talk ter ona-phone?"	(Do you want to talk to her on the phone?)

The most common articulation problems occur when people speak too fast, fail to open their mouths when they speak, or fail to use their tongues adequately to produce specific sounds. To avoid these problems, don't be lazy with your voice.

The actor James Earl Jones, the original voice of Darth Vader in the *Star Wars* movies, has a deep, booming voice and superb articulation. You can clearly hear every syllable of every word he says in his plays and movies. Did you know that as a child he stammered so badly that he was forced to write notes to his friends and teachers if he wanted to communicate?

How did he overcome this speaking problem? He went through speech therapy. He also joined his high school speech and debate team. In other words, he was aware of his speaking problems and actively worked to overcome them. Follow Jones's example and practice to make your enunciation the best that it can be. It will show your audience that you are

Use the dictionary to help you improve your pronunciation.

serious not only about your verbal message but also about your individual words and sentences—their crispness, their clarity, their sharpness.

Pronunciation refers to saying the sounds of a word properly and stressing the correct syllable or syllables. Nothing can destroy a good speech more quickly than a mispronounced word. It shows the audience that you haven't done your homework in preparation for your speech. Two excellent ways to

Preparing for your speech can help you articulate, or say your words clearly.

COMMUNICATION *BREAKDOWN*

Family Talk

Who is your hero? What makes you happiest? If you're like most teens, it's not a celebrity or the latest tech gadget. According to a 2007 study done by MTV and the Associated Press, the top answer wasn't money or things. Nearly 75 percent of the respondents said their relationship with their parents made them happiest. Most teens said their parents were their heroes.

Even more shocking to some people might be the findings of a study done by the National Center on Addiction and Substance Abuse at Columbia University. The study showed that family members are eating together more frequently: 59 percent of teens ate with their families at least five times a week in 2007, compared with 47 percent in 1998. The study also showed that teens who frequently ate with their parents were less likely to use drugs, tobacco, or alcohol. In fact, teens who ate with their families fewer than three times a week were 3.5 times likelier to have used drugs and 2.5 times likelier to have smoked. Teens who ate with their families also tended to earn better grades than teens who didn't.

Why is eating together important? It comes down to communication. What better time is there to communicate than during or right after dinner? Studies have shown that the more parents communicate with their teenage children, the more likely the teenagers will be to make responsible decisions and have the confidence to make those decisions.

It's not always easy for parents to talk to their teens—or for teens to talk to their parents. Communication breaks down for several reasons. Teens think their parents don't know anything and don't understand them. Parents sometimes feel uncomfortable discussing certain topics with teens. To keep lines of communication open, parents and teens need to remember to stay calm and listen. And having a bite to eat together can't hurt.

Questions

1. Why is parent-teen communication important? How do you think parents and teens can communicate about difficult topics?

2. How does frequently eating meals together tend to affect family members?

---

improve your pronunciation are to use the dictionary whenever in doubt and to listen to how educated people around you are speaking.

Be especially careful about your pronunciation of the following kinds of names and terms. Make sure that you have learned how to pronounce business associates' names, the names of countries, and the names of special groups before you speak. Also be careful in pronouncing foreign names and scientific terms. Rightly or wrongly, people will tend to associate how smart you are with how you articulate and pronounce your words. Make the correct impression on the job by polishing not only your shoes but also your voice skills.

Recalling the Facts

1. In the vocal process, our breathing system provides the power for voice production, or _____.

2. In the hit musical *My Fair Lady*, Professor Higgins wants Eliza Doolittle to speak slowly, clearly, and distinctly. Specifically, they work on her _____ and her _____.

3. Altering your vocal tone, or your pitch, is called voice _____, and it is often used for emphasis.

4. When you deliver all of your words methodically at almost the same rate and pitch, you are speaking in a _____.

Thinking Critically

1. You have read about the value of delivery in oral communication. There is no question that the method of delivering your words is of paramount importance if you wish to influence or inspire your audience. With this is mind, consider the following words from Zhuangzi, a Chinese philosopher of the third century B.C.: "Great wisdom is generous, petty wisdom is contentious. Great speech is impassioned, small speech cantankerous." What do you think that Zhuangzi meant by this statement?

2. Name the television personality or celebrity whose delivery you believe is best at selling a product. Name the person in your school or community whose delivery you believe is best at selling an idea. In your opinion, what makes these people the best at delivering a message?

Taking Charge

As a class and then in small groups, say the following tongue twisters out loud. With each, start slowly and repeat, trying to pick up speed. If you are slurring, you need to stop and go back to a more controllable rate. You—and your mouth—must be in charge.

a. Pat's pop shop
b. Chrysanthemum/geranium
c. Aluminum/linoleum
d. Unique New York
e. Red leather/yellow leather
f. Toy boat
g. Sister Susie's sewing shirts for soldiers.

Now, try these tougher ones:

h. Peter Piper picked a peck of pickled peppers. If Peter Piper picked a peck of pickled peppers, where's the peck of pickled peppers Peter Piper picked?

i. Theophilus Thistle the thistle sifter sifted a sieve of unsifted thistles. If Theophilus Thistle the thistle sifter sifted a sieve of unsifted thistles, where is the sieve of unsifted thistles that Theophilus Thistle the thistle sifter sifted?

j. Betty Botter bought some butter. "But," she said, "this butter's bitter. If I put it in my batter, it will make my batter bitter. But a bit of better butter will but make my batter better." So, she bought a bit of butter, better than the bitter butter, that made her bitter batter better. So, 'twas better that Betty Botter bought a bit of better butter.

Using Your Body

In the novel *The Scarlet Letter*, by Nathaniel Hawthorne, many of the seventeenth-century Puritan characters show one face to the public but are very different on the inside. While this two-sidedness might be an excellent literary device for character and thematic analysis, using it in your speaking isn't smart. Your body, like your voice, must be a positive extension of your message. You can't allow your speech to say one thing while your body is saying something entirely different.

You have already read about the impact of non-verbal communication. Such communication does not actually deliver your words, but it does deliver your attitude about those words.

You read about body language in other chapters, specifically Chapter 4. When you deliver a speech, many things you do with your body—whether standing with one leg bent, tilting your head back, slouching, lowering your chin, keeping your arms in extremely close to your body, leaning toward your audience, scratching your head, standing with your entire body rigid, or standing relaxed with your hands comfortably at your side—convey non-

verbal messages to your audience. If you are speaking on the value of a product that you are selling, but your body telegraphs to the audience that you are bored or uneasy, who in the world will want to buy your product?

Your body language, then, is a key contributor to nonverbal communication. So is your face; we will deal with that later in the chapter. Let's now take a look at two other aspects of body language—platform movement and gestures—and consider their effects. Both are important in promoting an effective delivery.

Platform Movement

A good speaker is similar to a good dancer in that both must have a sense of rhythm. In the speaker, all body movement should have a natural rhythmic flow that goes along with the words being spoken. This rhythm should be apparent in the speaker's platform movement.

Very simply, **platform movement** means walking in a purposeful manner from one spot to

COMMUNICATING THROUGH BODY LANGUAGE

While delivering a speech, what you do with your body conveys a nonverbal message to the audience.

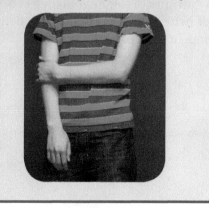

Hearing Your Favorite Book

Today, people spend more time commuting to work or jetting off to business meetings than ever before. Who has time to read anymore, right? The audio publishing industry has taken literature to a whole new level—the high-tech level. Now people can download their favorite books to an audio player or computer or buy the CD version and sit back and listen.

Before the mid-1980s, the audiobook business was nonexistent, but in 2006, annual sales reached $871 million. "What we find," said Leslie Nadell of Random House Audio Publishing, "is that once people have listened to one audiobook, they become instant converts." Nearly 25 percent of Americans listen to audiobooks. And young listeners are some of the biggest customers.

Though literary purists might be bothered by audiobooks' abridgement of some texts (many audio-books are now unabridged), authors have praised audiobooks, and listeners are impressed by the convincing voice characterizations and the vibrant, exciting delivery that many narrators give. Many of the best narrators are the authors themselves, but many famous actors have narrated books as well, and some audiobooks feature a full cast.

The audiobook market has become so large that the Audio Publishers Association (APA) now awards Audies—the audio publishing industry's equivalent of Oscars—in 31 categories to recognize excellence in the audiobook field. At the 2007 awards ceremony, APA president Michele Lee Cobb explained: "Each year, the bar continues to be raised, and each year the industry grows as a result." In 2007, the APA named Inspired by . . . The Bible Experience: New Testament as Audiobook of the Year. This audiobook features a full cast of actors, including Angela Bassett, Cuba Gooding Jr., Samuel L. Jackson, Blair Underwood, and Denzel Washington.

Questions
1. Some people might argue that an audiobook diminishes the role of the reader's imagination. What advantages can audiobooks offer?
2. In what instances might audiobooks be a practical asset?

Platform movement is effective when going from one section of a speech to another, when changing emotional appeal, or when it feels natural.

Movement should accentuate your speaking. It should make sense to your audience. Not only does platform movement show your audience that you are literally moving from one part of your speech to another, but it also gives the audience a break from staring at you in one spot the entire time. It provides a type of eye relief. This makes you seem a little more dynamic and exciting if you do it correctly.

"But how do I move, and when are the right times to move?" you may ask. Three situations allow for effective platform movement.

First, it is logical to move when you are going from one section of your speech to another. For instance, after you have delivered your introduction, you might want to move a bit, to set up and draw attention to your thesis or topic sentence. In addition, many speakers like to use movements between their main points and again before their conclusion. These movements add variety and emphasize specific sections of a speech. Always begin your speech by "squaring up"—centering yourself with your audience, not necessarily with the room. You should also end your speech near the middle of your audience. This lends a sense of cohesion, courtesy, and completeness to your speech.

Second, movement is often effective when you are changing your emotional appeal. Suppose you are describing the problems that teenagers face in society today. You might be speaking at a fairly even rate and emotional level. However, when you start listing the startling statistics related to teenage suicide, your emotional level might rise. You might start speaking more quickly and becoming more emotionally intense. At this point, a platform movement might be logical to show that your body is involved in what you are communicating. Similarly, if you were speaking on the problems of stereotyping teenagers, and then began to report on the great things that teenagers have done for others,

another while speaking. Obviously, it need not involve a real platform. While you may at times be onstage (introducing a guest speaker for a meeting or an awards program, for example), you will usually stand at the front of your classroom or some other room when you deliver your speech.

Before discussing what you should do regarding platform movement, let's take a look at what you shouldn't do:

- Don't pace back and forth as if you are a duck in a shooting gallery.
- Don't wander, or take strolls from spot to spot with no purpose.
- Don't avoid movement because you are afraid you will look silly.

such as working with disabled children and supporting community projects, a change in emotional level and movement might be appropriate. When your emotions are in action, often so are your feet! Allow your movement to help set the speaking mood you want.

Finally, platform movement is often appropriate when it just feels right to you. Don't let rules always direct what you do in speaking. Sometimes it is appropriate simply to allow yourself to be yourself. After you have practiced your speech, trust your communication instincts.

You might have an urge to move while delivering an example or while giving your conclusion. Go ahead and give it a try. Once you've finished speaking, your audience (and your teacher) will let you know if your movement was distracting or ill timed, and then you can make adjustments for the next time you speak.

Platform movement should be done so naturally that your audience isn't even aware of it. You should not have to be told how to move or at what speed. You simply move while delivering your speech as you would move anywhere else. When you are walking in the hallway at school, no one has to tell your legs and feet what to do. You move instinctively. Let your legs and the rest of your body work together so that your movement is believable, parallels the tone of your speech, and, most of all, is you.

Nevertheless, there are a few specific points to remember about how to move.

- Always move in a comfortable, relaxed manner by leading with the leg that corresponds to the direction you are moving. If you are walking to the right, for example, move the right leg first. There are two good reasons to do this. First, it keeps your body open to the audience. If you are crossing your legs over as you move, you might turn almost sideways and present a profile to your audience. When this happens, your audience members lose part of your face and potentially some of your words. They might not hear what you are delivering to the walls. Second, it keeps you from tripping over your own feet.

INSTANT IMPACT

"Delivery" Has Its Day in Court

Creators of a play about the rock legend Janis Joplin once won a key court ruling. Heirs of the blues/rock-and-roll singer, who died in 1970, had sued the authors of a play titled *Janis,* claiming that they, as the heirs, had exclusive rights to Joplin's performance style. The heirs claimed that they owned the rights to her "voice, delivery, mannerisms, appearance, dress, and actions (gestures included) accompanying her performance."

The judge disagreed, saying that even though Janis Joplin's style was indeed unique, people have too many similarities in delivery for one person to claim them exclusively. If the heirs' position were upheld, the judge asked, how could comedians or satirists ever imitate a celebrity without facing a possible lawsuit?

- Move toward your audience. When you are moving in your speech, your walking should be directed toward some portion of the audience or even a specific listener. You should be moving as if to say, "Here's a point that I particularly want you to hear." In other words, you are moving because you are sharing your words with your listeners. Vary the direction of your movement. This is a good way to make sure that no portion of your audience feels neglected or ignored.

Of course, you shouldn't make the angle of your movement too extreme, and you shouldn't move so close to an audience member that he or she might feel uncomfortable. Be aware of **proxemics**, or how much physical space you leave between you and your audience. Use your common sense in determining your distance from the audience. Know the speaking area, and always make sure that you can comfortably move back to the center of the room, leaving an appropriate amount of space between you and your audience.

- Know exactly the number of steps that you are going to take. You can usually be comfortable with taking one step forward (toward your audience) or with using a three-step or a five-step method.

The three-step method is fairly easy to master. You simply take your first step (moving the correct leg, of course), cross over with the second step, and then move the first leg forward so that you are once again standing firmly on both feet. This method is especially appropriate for moving in small speaking areas, but it is recommended in any setting because it is easy to control. Control is what you are after.

The five-step method works exactly the same way as the three-step method except that, obviously, you take two more steps. This method can be used in large speaking areas. The danger with the five-step method is that you might forget what you are doing and start to roam around the front of the room.

Even though an experienced speaker might not need to plan exactly how many steps to take (that is, three steps or five steps), a beginner should. So keep your movement centralized and be sure to avoid situations in which you might lose control of your movements and walk right out the door (as tempting as that might be).

Gestures

Even though they are nonverbal, gestures definitely communicate. Gestures, as explained in Chapter 4, are actions in which the body or parts of the body move to express an idea or emotion. We might think of **posture** as referring to the position of the body when it is still (as when your teacher

tells you, "Stand up straight. Stop slouching. Don't lean on that desk. Get your hands out of your pockets."). Gestures, however, refer to the body in motion.

Let's take a look at how gestures specifically relate to delivery. Like platform movement, gestures should be natural and fit what you are saying. They should not be contrived or artificial. Body gestures are usually associated with the arms, the hands, the shoulders, and the head. Like a good jazz band, a good corporation, or a smoothly running engine, gestures work best when all of the parts work together. A good speaker does not allow an individual part of the body to work in isolation.

If you want to know how to gesture effectively, then watch people (especially professional communicators, such as talk show hosts) when they talk. Watch what the shoulders do when the hands are in motion. Notice how the head can accentuate a point.

Probably the single greatest problem that you might have will involve this question: What do I do with my hands?

Eighteenth-century American clergyman John Witherspoon once said, "Never rise to speak till you have something to say; and when you have said it, cease." In other words, he was advising all speakers not to overdo it with their words. This same principle can be applied to gestures. Make your gestures clear, but don't overdo them. There is nothing wrong with having your arms and hands comfortably at your sides, at your "base." This relays to your audience that you are relaxed and in control.

If you are using notecards, you may hold them with one hand or with both hands. Either way, your notes should be comfortably held at your waist, and they should not be a distraction.

Even though some instructors permit students not using notes to put their hands behind them or fold their hands in front of them, it is best to start practicing as soon as possible bringing your hands back to your sides.

When you do gesture with your hands, bring your gestures up and out. Remember, again, that

Does this man seem like he is using a gesture to help him make a point?

these gestures aren't supposed to be the center of attention or sell popcorn. They are supposed to supplement your content.

Here are three tips that can help you become more comfortable with your hands.

1. Learn the Gesture Zone It is important that you develop a sense of control with your hands. Too often, our hands will take off, almost as if they have minds of their own, and do things that we aren't aware of. One method that will help you control your hands is to learn your gesture zone.

The gesture zone is an imaginary box in front of you, similar to a television screen. To find your gesture zone, start by placing your arms in front of you with your palms up and your elbows fairly close to your

body. Your arms should be near waist level. Now draw the *bottom* of the gesture zone by moving your hands together. Repeat this to get a feel for how your hands can move near your waist and be effective.

Next, put your hands back in the original position—arms in front of you with both palms facing up (don't let your arms be too far apart). Turn your hands so that your palms are at right angles to the floor (parallel to your body). Move your hands up and down, but be sure never to go higher than your shoulder area. (From the audience's point of view, if you gestured higher than the shoulder area, your face would be partially covered by your gestures, and this should never happen—because many listeners watch your lip movements to help them "hear" your words.) You are now drawing the *sides* of the gesture zone.

Finally, after you have found the sides of your gesture zone, draw in the *top* by repeating the procedure you used to find the bottom—only, now turn your palms down so that they are facing the floor.

Now, draw the entire gesture zone. Do it again. Notice how your box ranges from your waist to just below your shoulders. Practice gesturing inside of this imaginary control zone. Certain gestures will call for you to gesture outside of the zone, but don't get fancy until you know what you are doing. Pay particular attention to gestures that are too sweeping or wide. The idea is to keep the audience focused on your face.

2. Learn to "Lift and Lay" Your Hands
Gestures can be a distraction if you don't work at doing them correctly. Three common errors in gesturing are the following:

- the "flyaway" gesture, in which your hands simply shoot out from your sides like missiles and appear directionless
- the "judo-chop" gesture, in which you appear to mercilessly and repeatedly hatchet your message into the minds of your audience
- the "penguin-wave" gesture, in which you have your hands down at your side and then attempt to gesture by simply flicking your wrists or fingers as a penguin might flick its wings while walking on land.

In contrast, when you "lift and lay," you lift your arms and hands so that they move comfortably up and out, and then you lay your hands at the end of a gesture as if you were laying them on a ledge or a table. Of course, laying your hands on an actual ledge or table also takes place in the gesture zone. In a sense, you are using this gesture to lay your ideas on the table to be considered. Just as you can give finality to your gesture, you can give emphasis to your words. Even though the distance traveled isn't great, this technique gives a sense of control and finality to your gesture.

3. Practice the "String" Idea As mentioned, taking the time to watch and analyze people while they are speaking is a good idea. It teaches you about what happens during both verbal and nonverbal communication. It also teaches you what makes sense and what doesn't. For instance, have you ever seen anyone gesture without moving a portion of his or her upper body—the shoulders, the neck, or the head? Unless you watched this happen in a science fiction movie, the answer is probably no.

When you speak informally, you don't think about your body. However, you *should* think about it. If you are upset about a test score and throw your hands up in despair, what do you do with your shoulders? Your head? Do they move also? If you are questioning a group about its position on a controversial issue, and you use your hand and fingers emphatically to make your point, what do you do with your head? Does it move? Of course.

What does all this have to do with the "string" idea? Imagine that you have a long piece of string. Hold one end with one hand and the other end with the other hand. Now, tie the two ends together. Place the string around your neck. Pretend to place one arm (or both) through the loop, as if it were a sling. What happens when you extend that arm? Doesn't the string force your head to move too? It is as though your body is connected by a series of strings (or rubber bands) that react to one another.

What is the point of this exercise? The "string" idea is simply a good way to remind yourself to keep the upper portion of your body actively involved when gesturing.

Use only gestures that help illustrate or bring attention to a point you are trying to make.

After practicing gestures a while, you will begin to do some things that are more natural for you. At first, though, paying attention to the gesture zone, the "lift and lay," and the "string" idea—will give you a good start on gesturing properly and making your hands believable.

You may feel uncomfortable practicing gestures. Remember, though, that it makes little sense to spend a great deal of time writing speeches but hardly any time working at the exercises needed to deliver your speeches well. All good musicians and all great athletes pay their dues by doing drills. The drill work may be monotonous, but in the long run, the basics are invaluable. Performing nonverbal gesture drills is a good way to give precision to your body movement.

Recalling the Facts

1. The term given for walking from one spot to another is _____ _____.

2. You can control your hands when you are gesturing by being aware of the _____ _____.

3. You should involve your entire body when you gesture. The "_____" exercise is a method of showing you how your head and shoulders should be an active extension of arm gestures.

Thinking Critically

Nineteenth-century Irish politician Daniel O'Connell said, "A good speech is a good thing, but the *verdict* is the thing." This means that the audience has to determine whether you have delivered or not. Analyze or evaluate three people, famous or not, whom you consider to have delivered in some fashion. They might have developed an idea, performed an amazing feat, or excelled during a time of crisis. Explain what they did, how they did it (the steps involved), and the impact that their delivery had.

Taking Charge

List at least five types of hand and arm gestures that people use and the emotions or attitudes that go along with them. Create a sentence to go with each emotion or attitude and gesture. Be prepared to demonstrate.

Using Your Face

Probably the most important nonverbal element in an effective delivery is your face. Studies have shown that more than the words spoken or even the body language, the face determines whether a speaker is believed or not. The expressions on your face while you talk can show your listeners how you feel about them, how you feel about your material, and how you feel about yourself as a speaker.

Many people think that a genuine smile is a person's best sales tool.

You have already read about the role of nonverbal communication; however, this text can't emphasize enough the importance of your unspoken attitude. Quite frankly, if your face doesn't "sell it," your audience doesn't "buy it." If you are speaking on the value of teamwork at your workplace but you convey to fellow employees that they are beneath you in intelligence—not by your words but by your facial gestures—how can you expect them to ardently support your position? You will only have *alienated* them.

If you are speaking about drug abuse or about how street people are being victimized, but your face wears an expression that says you are uninterested, bored, or disgusted, what will your audience think about your attitude toward your subject? What if you are discussing a serious topic and a broad smile appears on your face? Why are you smiling? Your face just doesn't match the mood or tone of the speech.

One of the most common errors in speaking is to present a well-thought-out speech, only to have its impact ruined by an absolutely petrified facial expression. If you seem frightened, you lose credibility. If you appear to lack confidence in yourself, your audience will lack confidence in both you and what you are saying.

A picture is worth a thousand words, and your face while you are speaking is that picture. What part of the face is the most important?

The Eyes

"The eyes are the windows to the soul." This famous saying is vital for the good speaker to understand. It is through your eyes that the people in your audience will primarily judge you: your overall honesty, your conviction about your message, and your genuine concern for them.

Digital Vision/Alamy

An effective delivery depends on your ability to look at the people in your audience and make meaningful eye contact with them. Forget about the myths you might have heard about looking at the tops of heads or imagining your audience sitting in their seats dressed in just their underwear. These are simply foolish shortcuts intended to make you seem to have eye contact when you are actually avoiding your audience's eyes.

Are you nervous? Are you a little intimidated by the speaking assignment? If the answer is "Yes, I definitely am!" then you do not need the *superficial* quick fix of pretending to have good eye contact. You need to face the problem and learn the value of eyes.

Keep these eye strategies in mind:

This audience is clearly interested in the speaker's message.

- Look at each person for a number of seconds before moving on to a different person in the audience. This is referred to as sustained eye contact. Deliver a sentence or two, ensuring that you are not making the audience member nervous or paranoid. You don't want to have a stare-down contest or stand too close. Your intent is to make the people in your audience realize that you are interested in each of them. Remember, you are not looking at each person simply because you think that you're supposed to do so. You are offering sustained eye contact because you care about what each member of your audience thinks. Think of your speech as a gold mine and share its wealth with your audience through eye contact.
- Don't forget to make eye contact with people at the far sides of the audience. Some speakers forget about the people at the extremes of the room, the far left and the far right, both in the front and in the back of the room. Beware of having tunnel vision and speaking only to those seated immediately in front of you or to those directly in the center of the room. It only makes sense that the more people you

look at, the more people you have the potential to influence. Look to the corners.
- Make eye contact with people, not things. Your goal is to make a positive impression on your audience. Consequently, you shouldn't talk to the back wall, the parking lot outside, the window, or empty desks. Of course, you can look up or off once in a while if you are in thought. For the most part, though, your eyes should go to the eyes of your audience. Remember, if you avoid eye contact, you probably won't be trusted. Don't negate all of your hard work by delivering some of your best material to the floor. Give people priority!

Audience Feedback

One of the best reasons for you to have good eye contact with the members of your audience is that it allows you to see how they are reacting to what you are saying. You can read the feedback. Are people fidgeting in their chairs? Do they appear irritated? Are they smiling and nodding their heads? Are they leaning toward you or leaning away from you and avoiding eye contact? Do they look confused?

Hero/Corbis/Glow Images

Dynamizing Your Overall Delivery

You have now read about some of the components that make up an effective delivery. Primarily, you have looked at the importance of your voice, your body, and your face. All must work together if you wish to dynamize your verbal message.

If you pay attention to the best speakers, you will notice that the parts of the body and the voice often go together, creating a satisfying blend of all of the individual elements. Notice that when good speakers start to speak, their movement, their gestures, and their words work together harmoniously. Such speakers may make it all look smooth and easy, but it's not. Getting there is a consequence of paying attention to and practicing the parts that make up the whole.

If you are saying, "But I simply can't deliver a speech, and I can't get any better," remember this story: It has been said that you can't make a silk purse out of a sow's ear. In other words, you can't make something beautiful from something supposedly ugly. Did you know that a scientist did? He purchased a sow's ear from the stockyards and ground it down to a gelatinous state. He then devised a method to produce a form of thread from this matter. With the thread, he created two beautiful, elegant purses. One of them is currently on display at the Smithsonian Institution in Washington, D.C. He did it to prove that nothing is impossible if people put their minds to the task.

Apply this lesson to your speech delivery. Whether you are working at music, athletics, academics—or speaking—don't ever give up. The great ones never do.

You should adjust your delivery based on how people react to you.

You need to pay attention to feedback so that you can make necessary adjustments. For instance, you might see that some people in the back of the room are straining to hear you. This should direct you to move closer to them or to raise your volume level. You might notice that some people are wrinkling their brows as if they don't totally understand your point. Stop and explain. Audience feedback is your communication effectiveness yardstick. Take the time to look at your audience and see how you are measuring up.

Recalling the Facts

1. Define the term *sustained eye contact.*
2. List three eye-contact strategies (as given in the section) that can help you communicate nonverbally with your audience.
3. Define *audience feedback.* Why does a good speaker always have to be aware of audience feedback?

Thinking Critically

Studies have shown that a speaker's body language and facial expressions often have more impact than a speaker's words. In other words, delivery is more important than content. If this is true, evaluate whether this finding speaks well of the American public. What does it say about our heroes? Our political elections? When you are interviewing for a job, do you think that the results of the studies still hold true? Consider what jobs or occupations might value your speaking content more than your delivery.

Taking Charge

Read the selection that follows as if you were a news commentator seated behind a desk. Even though the selection was not delivered as a speech, it allows for a variety of facial expressions. Discover how you would deliver the speech. Remember the value of variety.

This selection is from *The American Crisis* by the American revolutionary Thomas Paine.

Paine's first pamphlet, *Common Sense*, appeared in January 1776, at a time when most American colonists were hoping that the colonies' conflict with Britain could be resolved. However, Paine argued for the necessity of a break from Britain and the need for "an open and determined Declaration for Independence." By the end of that year, he had written these words:

These are the times that try men's souls: The summer soldier and the sunshine patriot will, in this crisis, shrink from the service of their country; but he that stands it now, deserves the love and thanks of man and woman. Tyranny, like hell, is not easily conquered; yet we have this consolation with us, that the harder the conflict, the more glorious the triumph. What we obtain too cheap, we esteem too lightly. . . . It would be strange indeed, if so celestial an article as FREEDOM should not be highly rated. Britain, with an army to enforce her tyranny, has declared that she has a right not only to TAX but "to BIND us in ALL CASES WHATSOEVER," and if being bound in that manner is not slavery, then there is not such a thing as slavery upon earth. . . . If there must be trouble, let it be in my day, that my child may have peace!

When you delivered the selection, were you using facial expressions properly? What did you notice that your eyes were doing at different points? Your eyebrows? Your mouth? Your neck and shoulders? Be prepared to read the selection to another student, a group, or the entire class.

Looking Back

Listed below are the major ideas discussed in this chapter.

- Your speaking delivery is the way you "sell" your words—the verbal and nonverbal manner in which you present your material.
- There are four methods of delivery: manuscript, memorized, extemporaneous, and impromptu.
- The extemporaneous method is the most often recommended.
- The voice is the instrument that carries your words, and your diaphragm is the main power source for effective speaking.
- The air that you need for speaking provides you with the power needed for adequate speaking volume, or the loudness or softness of your voice.
- Simply having the air to speak isn't enough. You must speak at a comfortable rate, or speed, with a pleasant pitch range, or range of notes.
- Good speakers vary their pitch and rate often to avoid speaking in a monotone.
- Good speakers also know when to use emphasis. Emphasis is the stress that you give certain words that you wish to accentuate.
- You must also be sure not to slur your words. You must articulate clearly.
- It is essential that you know how to pronounce all the words that you are going to use.
- Another key element in developing an effective delivery is the use of your body. Even though using your body is nonverbal, it definitely communicates a message to your audience.

- Platform movement involves actually taking steps while speaking. The number of steps depends on the size of the room, the size of the audience, and your emotional intent at the time of your movement.
- You should always keep in mind the distance between you and your audience. This knowledge can keep you from making audience members feel uncomfortable.
- Hand gestures concern speakers the most. "What do I do with my hands while speaking?" is a common question.
- Hand and arm gestures should usually be kept in your gesture zone. This is an area the size of a small television screen that extends from your waist to your upper chest.
- Facial expression may be the most important part of your oral communication. When you nonverbally involve your face in your delivery, audience members can see how you really feel about your material.
- The eyes are crucial for an effective delivery. You must sustain eye contact with each audience member long enough to make him or her feel a part of your speech.
- Effective eye contact also makes your audience trust you and what you say.
- The best speakers use all aspects of the voice, the body, and the face.

Speech Vocabulary

1. Divide the top list on page 316 into two fairly even sections. For each word in one list, write the definition as given in the chapter. Use the dictionary or the glossary for additional information. Also write an original sentence using the word correctly.

2. For the second list, provide the definition as given in the chapter. Then, instead of writing individual sentences, write a story or a series of paragraphs using the words. The topic of your story is up to you. Make sure it makes sense.

delivery	vocalized pause	pace	articulation
manuscript method	power source	pitch	pronunciation
memorized method	vocal process	monotone	platform movement
extemporaneous method	phonation	stress	proxemics
impromptu method	oral cavity	inflection	posture
	rate	volume	

Academic Vocabulary

Use context clues to determine the meaning of each academic vocabulary word and then use a print or online dictionary to check the accuracy of your definition.

regurgitating
methodically

syllable
alienated

superficial

To Remember

Answer the following questions based on your reading of the chapter.

1. The speed at which you speak is known as your speaking _____.
2. The highs and lows your voice hits while you speak are known as your speaking _____.
3. Elected officials often use the _____ method of delivery to make sure that they don't miscommunicate their content.
4. The method of speaking that is referred to as "not rehearsed" is _____.
5. What specific parts of the body are used in the gesture zone?

6. When you look at someone in the audience while you are speaking, it is a good idea to use _____ eye contact.
7. When you actually take steps in a speech presentation, you are using _____ movement.
8. The crispness and distinctness of your words show that you have good _____.
9. Proxemics involves a sense of how much _____ there is between you and your audience.

Match the number on the left with a letter on the right.

1. Method of delivery that combines the use of notes with the ability to use words and ideas.
2. Not using emphasis or varying pitch and rate.
3. Medieval king with a high-pitched voice.
4. Wrote *The American Crisis*.
5. Loudness or softness of the voice.

a. Charlemagne
b. extemporaneous
c. impromptu
d. rate
e. monotone

f. articulation
g. volume
h. Paine
i. O'Connell
j. pitch

To Do

1. Write a paragraph on a topic about which you feel strongly. Now give it orally. Make a voice chart or graph. Plot on the chart or graph where your voice moves. Does your pitch go up? Does it go down? Are you using all of your pitch range? If not, you are not totally delivering your message to your audience. A voice or tape recorder is an excellent aid for this exercise.

2. Make an educational video of students walking and talking at school. Take note of how their voices and body movements work together as they talk to each other. Pay attention to their nonverbal communication. What did you learn? List your top five observations.

To Talk About

1. How does the spoken message differ from the written message? What are the advantages and disadvantages of each? What is the advantage that verbal emphasis gives to the speaker? What about eye contact? Is it possible for your words to be saying one thing while your eyes are saying something else? Talk about instances when this might be the case.

2. You have probably heard the phrase "the thrill of victory and the agony of defeat," first popularized on a television sports program. Defeat often occurs because some athlete didn't "deliver" under pressure. In athletics or any other endeavor, why do some people often allow pressure to get to them and keep them from delivering their best efforts? What might be on their mind? How does this specifically relate to delivering a speech? What's your constructive advice?

3. Why, do you think, does a good speaker with an excellent delivery have an advantage with the public over a brilliant thinker who has trouble speaking? Give examples of this phenomenon from the news, your school, history, or your community. Does this advantage always exist?

4. The poet Robert Frost once said, "Half the world is composed of people who have something to say and can't, and the other half who have nothing to say, and keep on saying it." What does this quotation mean? How does it fit politicians? Media figures? Businesses? Educators? Other students? Parents? You?

To Write About

1. Research has shown that a jury, in deciding how believable someone's testimony is, will value nonverbal communication more than verbal communication. Why might this be true? Give three ways in which your body can show others that you are not telling the whole truth. In what situations might you do these things?

2. When you effectively deliver, you get the job done. Select one character from literature who, despite the odds, delivered and achieved his or her objective. What individual elements helped him or her succeed?

3. Why is impromptu speaking so valuable? Describe two situations in which you might be able to use your impromptu ability. How would your voice, your body, and your face have to work with your words? Write at least one paragraph on this topic.

Related Speech Topics

Cooperative education or team teaching
The United Nations
Adoption or foster children
Day care for working mothers
Any championship sports team
A well-known orchestra

The human brain: networking
The Japanese educational system
The Olympics
The Special Olympics
Improving your job skills: going back to school

UNIT
4
Presentations

CHAPTER 13
SPEECHES TO INFORM

Obviously, a man's judgment cannot be better than the information on which he has based it.

—Arthur Hays Sulzberger

Learning Objectives

After completing this chapter, you will be able to do the following.

- Identify the major types of informative speeches.
- Find a good subject for an informative speech, narrow that subject to a manageable topic, and compose a sharply focused thesis.
- Develop interesting material for your speech through the use of anecdotes, quotations, and definitions.
- Integrate audio and visual aids into your speech.
- Give a multimedia presentation using appropriate technology and proven strategies.

Chapter Outline

Following are the main sections in this chapter.

1. Speeches That Instruct, Inform, and Clarify
2. Turning a Subject into a Speech
3. Audio and Visual Aids
4. Creating Multimedia Presentations

Speech Vocabulary

In this chapter, you will learn the meanings of the speech terms listed below.

public lecture
status report
briefing
fireside chat
chalk talk
advance organizer
cultural literacy
narrowing
thesis
anecdote
quotation

definition
map
diagram
graph
handout
overhead projector
model
cutaway
multimedia presentation
download
scanner

Academic Vocabulary

Expanding your academic vocabulary will help you become a more effective communicator. Listed below are some words appearing in this chapter that you should make part of your vocabulary.

concise
concrete
distinction
ambiguous
intuition
demographics
trivia

senile
etymology
infographic
fever chart
pie chart
bar graph
spontaneity

Providing information, a task we perform hundreds of times each day, is one of the most common and important forms of communication. Yet the techniques for providing information efficiently, gracefully, and in a way that will interest the listener are not well known. In this chapter, you will discover how to better understand your audience's wants and needs, how to find a subject listeners will want to learn about, and how to narrow that subject so that you can make meaningful and well-informed comments about it. You will also discover methods for illustrating your information, both verbally (through examples, descriptions, and definitions) and visually (through photographs, slides, maps, and diagrams). While any informative speech you give must be accurate, you never escape the responsibility of being interesting.

Introduction

A lot of talking goes on in the world, and a large part of it is done to give instructions, provide facts, or clarify ideas. You give someone directions to study hall and you tell classmates what went on when they missed a day of school. You explain how to do something, what something is, how it works, or how it is used. In short, you provide information to others every day in a hundred different ways.

The complexity of this task may range from giving simple directions (such as the route to the library) to explaining a complicated process (such as photosynthesis). It may be as basic as merely announcing facts (the plans for the next school dance) or as complex as giving an oral report based on research (the causes of war in the Middle East). In each instance, however, your emphasis is on statements of fact. Your goal is to make the listener understand.

Deep down, we are all curious. It's this curiosity that makes informative speeches favorites with audiences. Telling people something new is great fun. What's more, you will learn that being knowledgeable about a subject gives you confidence when you speak. Many students find that giving informative speeches is closer to "real life" than any other speech assignment.

You can use your knowledge about chemistry or any other subject to make lively, informative speeches.

Speeches That Instruct, Inform, and Clarify

We frequently give casual informative speeches to strangers needing directions, classmates making up missed assignments, and so on. In addition, we sometimes find ourselves in more-formal situations, in which we must provide information. Before long, your teacher will probably ask you to give an informative speech to the class. The assignment may ask you to describe an object (such as the brain), to explain a process (such as how to use a digital camera), or clarify a concept (such as the idea of nonviolent resistance).

Types of Informative Speeches

In the world outside your school, speakers find a variety of opportunities for giving the following types of informative talks:

1. The **public lecture.** As a result of a person's special interest or expertise, he or she may be invited to give a public lecture to a community group or club. If you take a trip to a national student council convention, for example, you may be invited to give an account of your trip to the local Kiwanis Club; and the Garden Club might be interested in your research on the super tomato.

2. The **status report.** Every business and social group must keep up-to-date on its various projects. Periodically, the group will ask a knowledgeable person to give a status report indicating what has been accomplished so far and what plans exist for the future. Suppose you are a committee chair for a volunteer organization that works with senior citizens. If your committee is planning a senior prom, you may be asked to give a status report on prom plans to the group as a whole.

3. The **briefing.** The briefing is a very common informative speech used to tell members of a group about changes in policy or procedure. You may need to tell the members of your swim team about how to order team T-shirts, or perhaps you may want to tell the yearbook staff about a new layout plan.

4. The **fireside chat.** Named for a famous series of radio broadcasts given by President Franklin D. Roosevelt, fireside chats usually feature a group leader addressing the concerns, worries, and issues of the moment. Your principal may schedule fireside chats with parents to review school goals and policies.

5. The **chalk talk.** The speaker giving a chalk talk relies on a visual aid (such as a chalkboard). We can easily imagine a coach showing the team how to arrange its defense or a director outlining plans to present a stage play by using this technique.

President Franklin D. Roosevelt kept the nation informed with his fireside chats.

Media Bakery

Many informative speeches are followed by a question-and-answer period, which gives the audience a chance to participate.

The Six Cs of Informative Speaking

As an informative speaker, you want to shed light on a subject by sharing facts that you have learned through experience, observation, listening, and reading. You can explain, for example, how to bake a cake or describe the drugs being used to fight AIDS or discuss how rock musicians rehearse for a stage show. As you do so, you introduce new facts, show old facts in a new way, and clear up misunderstandings. Your main responsibility is to be accurate, but you must also strive to be clear. The response you want from your listeners is basically, "I understand what you said."

More specifically, we can break down the goals of informative speaking into six Cs, the better to remember them. Ask yourself the following questions as you prepare a speech:

1. Is my speech so *clear* that everyone will understand?
2. Is my speech so *concise* that no one's time will be wasted?
3. Is my speech *complete*?
4. Am I confident that my information is absolutely *correct*?
5. Have I provided *concrete* examples so that the audience can see my point?
6. Can I *connect* my speech with what I know about my audience?

Let's take a closer look at each of these goals to explore just how they can best be accomplished.

1. Be Clear Surprising as it may seem, being clear is neither easy nor simple (try explaining how to design a Web page to someone). How can you be sure your listeners will understand what you mean?

Many speakers make a special effort at the beginning of a speech to help listeners by defining a few important words and phrases. These definitions can be as short as a single word or, in a few special cases, as long as the entire speech. This might be the case, for example, in a speech entitled "The AIDS Virus."

The purpose of a definition is to create some common ground between speaker and listener. In particular, plan to explain any technical terms that may be new to your audience. But keep these terms to a minimum; you can baffle listeners with too many terms that make them scratch their heads.

Another part of being clear is making distinctions. We make *distinctions* by saying what something is and, especially, what it is not. Negative definitions clear your listeners' path of obstacles. You could make a distinction, for example, between the space shuttle's liquid fuel engines, which can be turned off, and its solid fuel booster rockets, which can't. Anticipate situations in which your listeners might find your remarks *ambiguous*. Ask yourself as you prepare a speech, "Could this point be taken more than one way?"

You can make distinctions by comparing and contrasting. A comparison explains how two things are similar. A contrast explains the differences. If you wrote a speech about the movies based on Stephen King's books, for example, you might compare them with horror films of the past, such as *The Phantom of the Opera* and *Dracula*. You might contrast them with science fiction films like *Alien* or *Star Wars*. Be sure, however, that what you use for a comparison is familiar to your listeners. If you compare Stephen

Creating a common ground between you and the listener can help keep you from getting wrapped up in your own points of view.

King to Jules Verne, many high school students will probably follow your comparison. But if you compare King to H. P. Lovecraft, a less well-known author, your audience may be lost.

Ultimately, the value of being clear must be balanced with other, competing values—the value of being concise, for example. If you spend too much time and effort striving for clarity, you may lose your listeners' interest. Audiences often find long explanations boring. Further, if you are too obvious, you lose the element of surprise. A good speaker learns to balance a variety of desirable qualities without emphasizing one at the expense of another.

You may find that visual aids such as a flip chart will help you be concise and organized.

2. Be Concise Many government officials these days seem to work for the Department of Redundancy Department. Too often, official proclamations seem to take 50 words to do the work of 10. Expressions like "Please repeat that again" or "These two are both alike" say the same thing twice. Be conscious of your own language use. Notice whether you say things like "These pens are identically the same" or "She arrived at 8 A.M. this morning." We are all guilty of being too wordy from time to time, but it's a habit that can be broken.

The secret of being concise is to make each word count, and the best way to do that is to use precise and specific language (see Chapter 11 for further details). Using precise language means choosing the word that best fits your meaning. For example, don't say *tree* if you mean *oak*, and don't say *temporarily reassigned* if you mean *fired*. To become more precise, you may need to enlarge your vocabulary. Take advantage whenever possible of lessons designed to increase your word power.

3. Be Complete No speech can be complete in the sense of covering all the possible material. You can, however, create a sense of completion in the

minds of the audience by raising certain expectations and then satisfying them. For instance, tell the audience you have three major points. When you say "first," they know you are beginning, and when you say "third," they know you've reached the end. They won't expect a fourth or fifth point even though they realize you haven't covered the subject as thoroughly as possible.

Statements that tell the audience what to expect are called **advance organizers**. If you say to your audience, "I'm now going to present the three reasons that local officials have tried to censor rap music," the audience is set to listen for three different chunks of information. If you introduce each reason with a reinforcing statement, such as "Now let's take a look at the first reason," the audience is reminded of the structure of your speech. When audience members perceive that your speech has a plan and can begin to recognize pieces of that plan, they will feel satisfied when you finish speaking.

Working from a plan forces you to put your information in order. Clearly, some information is more important than other information. If you fail to distinguish major points from minor ones, the listener must try to remember everything and hope

Surgeon General's Report on Smoking

Few government reports have had the drama or impact of the one that was delivered on January 11, 1964, in the auditorium of the Old State Department Building in Washington, D.C.

On that Saturday morning, a day carefully chosen to make headlines in all the big Sunday newspapers, Surgeon General Luther Terry told the nation that "cigarette smoking is a health hazard of sufficient importance . . . to warrant appropriate remedial action." In other words, it was time to do something about smoking.

Although the basic facts about smoking and health had been known for some time, the federal government kept shying away from the issue. Not until 1962 did President Kennedy decide that the government should study the problem. Kennedy asked Terry, the nation's chief health officer, to select an expert committee that would decide, simply, whether smoking was harmful.

Terry and ten people chosen from leading universities worked like prairie dogs, burrowing into stacks of research five stories underground in the basement of the National Library of Medicine at Bethesda, Maryland. After fourteen months of study, the committee issued a 150,000-word report that made the following points:

- Cigarette smoking "contributes substantially to mortality"—that is, smoking can kill you.

- Cigarette smokers have a death rate almost eleven times higher than nonsmokers. The sharpest risk from smoking is lung cancer.

- Quitting smoking is helpful.

As a result of Terry's report, the major TV networks decided to reexamine their advertising policies. Within a few years, smoking ads disappeared from the nation's television screens. Later, the government required cigarette makers to carry warning messages on their ads and packages. The number of smokers in the United States began to decline. But it would have been very difficult to change attitudes without the surgeon general's dramatic announcement.

Questions
1. How effective have efforts been to educate students on the dangers of smoking?
2. Can public speakers help change people's behavior?

Musician Sean John Combs

to sort things out later. Since no one can do this, a great deal of the information will be forgotten.

This is one of the reasons that many students have trouble taking notes. They assume that everything a teacher says is equally important. As a result, their notes look like a hodgepodge of large concepts and tiny details. In contrast, when your listeners have a sense of your speech's overall pattern, that pattern helps them to separate more-important ideas from less important ones. As a result, not only do they remember more, but they also remember what you believe is most important.

4. Be Correct There is no substitute for being accurate. Checking and double-checking the accuracy of the information you present goes right to the heart of your credibility. One of the best ways to convince an audience that your information deserves attention is to tell where you found it. As in any communication, when you use ideas that are not your own, you should indicate the source of your material. Writers can do this with footnotes, but speakers need a more subtle technique.

Normally, you identify your sources briefly at the end of the information itself. For example, you might say, "The verdict in the subway shooting trial was an outrage to justice, according to an editorial writer in this morning's paper." For variety, you can occasionally put the identification first: "In an article in the February 27 issue of *U.S. News and World Report*, we read that cheating on standardized tests is widespread."

You don't need to use all the information that would appear in a bibliographical citation. In fact, it would be a poor idea to do so. Usually, the name of an author or the name of a magazine, newspaper, television show, or movie is sufficient. An inquisitive listener can catch you after the speech to obtain a complete rundown of your sources.

5. Be Concrete Another valuable technique for making an informative speech effective is to be concrete. Focus on the immediate and the actual. Instead of talking in abstractions, talk in terms of people, places, and things. Individual cases are far more interesting than generalities.

Don't talk about candy if you can talk about gourmet jelly beans. Plan your speech on baseball around a particular person, perhaps "Shoeless Joe" Jackson. Focus your speech on musicians by concentrating on one, like Sean Combs.

A concrete example helps listeners get a mental picture of what you mean. Suppose that you have decided to make a general point like this: "Most accidents happen at home." So far, so good, but at this point the audience has only a vague idea of what you mean. The careful speaker immediately

"Shoeless Joe" Jackson

supports every general statement with an example: "Kerry Shea, a fourteen-year-old, said she 'just lost control' of her toothbrush and swallowed it. 'I was brushing the back of my tongue,' she added, 'because I saw on TV that it helps to get a lot of sugar that way, when the toothbrush slipped and I swallowed it.'"

Concrete examples contain physical details. If you were doing a speech on teen crime and needed a concrete example, you could use the case of the New York City transit system. Kids there were caught stealing subway tokens by sucking them out of turnstile slots. According to one official, some kids were making $50 to $100 a day. This example has great details—subway tokens, turnstiles, and teens performing weird physical stunts.

Being Brief

"Brevity," Shakespeare told us, "is the soul of wit." Unfortunately, we don't always take his statement to heart. Audiences appreciate speakers who get to the point quickly. Don't be like the speaker who told his listeners, "I've been asked to speak for 30 minutes. I don't have enough material to fill that time, so I'll talk for 10 minutes and make it seem like 30."

One of the most popular informative speeches given regularly is the president's inaugural address. On a January day following each election, the nation's leader outlines a vision for the future. The shortest inaugural address in history was the first: George Washington spoke just a few minutes, and his speech was a bare 135 words. The longest address was a fatal one. William Henry Harrison delivered a two-hour, 9,000-word speech in 1841, straight into the teeth of a freezing wind. Harrison came down with a cold the following day and died a month later of pneumonia. Take the hint.

Connect with your audience by imagining how they may feel about your topic.

Sometimes you may find that a series of short examples works best to support your main point. At other times, a long storylike example may be what you need. In any event, you should never let a general statement stand alone without a supporting example.

6. Connect The last C, connect, requires you to analyze the people who will be in your audience. This may be difficult because most of us tend to see the world from a single point of view—our own. Without ever meaning to, we become prisoners of our own perspective; we have little awareness of what another person is thinking or feeling. With a little extra effort, however, we can learn to imagine how the world looks to someone else. The more we can predict how an audience will interpret what we say, the better we will be able to communicate.

If you are speaking to classmates, you already have a number of insights into their backgrounds and attitudes. Think how you would react if you heard your speech for the first time—would it strike you as interesting, informative, and up-to-date? Or dull and old hat? Your own *intuition* can help guide you as you prepare a speech for a group of peers.

You can probably make a good guess, for example, about what your classmates know and don't know. Such guesses will help you avoid the mistake of delivering a speech on how to water-ski to a classroom full of experts on the subject. If the audience knows quite a bit about your subject, find a way to highlight some less well-known aspect of it.

Of course, you sometimes need to prepare a speech for a general audience—an audience of parents, community members, or other adults—that you don't know well. You can probably learn some things about the audience by asking the person who invited you to speak. But for the most part, you must depend on educated guesses to predict what kinds of people are in the audience and what they have in common.

You can make some assumptions about an audience by studying their *demographics*—that is, their social, economic, and cultural characteristics. Will the members of the audience, for example, tend to come from the same neighborhood, be about the same age, or have similar political opinions? You may wish to consider the following checklist when you think about the audience you will be facing:

1. How many people will be present? What will be the average age of the audience? Will the audience be mostly male, female, or evenly mixed?

2. What are their interests, attitudes, and beliefs?
3. What do they know about the subject?
4. What is their attitude toward it?

Generally speaking, you may assume that adult audiences have what is called cultural literacy. **Cultural literacy** is the ability to recognize and understand information that an average adult can be expected to know. The average listener should know that Columbus sailed in 1492 and that Columbus is the capital of Ohio, for example, but not that *Goodbye, Columbus* is a book by Philip Roth. You won't need to explain a reference to the Supreme Court or the Supremes, but you will have to explain the term *supremacist*.

Simply put, sensitivity to the audience is one of the keys to successful communication. While you can't choose your audience, you can choose a speech to fit a particular audience. Knowledge of the audience can help you fine-tune your speech as you make changes, both large and small, to suit a specific group of listeners. For more information on audience analysis, see Chapter 14.

SECTION 1 REVIEW

Recalling the Facts

List five kinds of occasions where you might give an informative speech.

Thinking Critically

1. Explain how your approach would change if you were to give a speech on the effects of cigarette smoking to five different audiences: classmates, parents, people between the ages of 20 and 25, retired people, and elementary school children.
2. Using the same five audiences as above, suggest three topics best suited to each.
3. The critic and educator Neil Postman wrote a book about how we all need to develop a better sense of what is garbage.

He meant that we need to be alert to what we hear. Some of the information we hear is misleading, based on weak evidence, or is just plain wrong. What are some of the ways we can improve our ability to sort out useful and accurate information from all the rest?

Taking Charge

Develop a survey to measure attitudes toward a variety of possible speech subjects (such as the media, government, and the entertainment industry), and give the survey to several classes in your school. Tabulate and analyze the results. Discuss what these results tell you about potential listeners.

SECTION 2

Turning a Subject into a Speech

Almost without exception, students' biggest gripe about giving speeches is "I don't know what to talk about." Finding an interesting and appropriate subject is always a challenge, but never more so than with an informative speech.

Find a Subject

Knowledge is the stuff from which new ideas are made. But knowledge alone won't write your speech. Anyone can compile a list of facts, but it takes an alert mind to connect those facts.

Suppose you decide to do some research for a speech on national holidays. You gather a number of facts, but they seem to have nothing to do with each other. Now think of those facts as dots in a dot-to-dot puzzle. Unfortunately, no one has numbered the dots. You have to do that for yourself. "Discovery," noted the Nobel Prize–winning biochemist Albert Szent-Györgyi, "consists of looking at the same thing as everyone else and thinking something different." Thinking differently is part of finding good speech topics. Where, then, can we look for topics, assuming we have the right attitude?

Personal Experience You already have a lifetime of experiences, and they can be a major source of information. No matter what the subject, firsthand knowledge contributes unique and original information. Even if your own knowledge is incomplete, it provides a good starting point for further research.

You are almost certainly an expert on something—whether it's changing the points and plugs on a car or baking chocolate chip cookies. Think small. Find an area of interest where you have considerable experience—something you collect, for example. Anything you do often and do well is a likely subject for an informative speech because you can speak from experience. That gives you instant credibility.

Observations Another place to look for speech subjects is your immediate environment. Whenever you find a scrap of unusual information, file it. You might read, for example, that a newspaper carrier delivering the *Los Angeles Times* heaved a copy of the Sunday paper toward the front lawn of a Hollywood mansion. The paper hit a pet dog dozing on the porch and killed it. A subsequent report by the newspaper industry noted that at an average of 2.3 pounds per day, the *Times* is the heaviest newspaper in the world. Such an item could make a nice lead-in for a speech on the mass media and its ability to overwhelm us.

Your personal experiences can be the basis for creative speeches.

You might also take the opportunity to be a participant observer. We all attend meetings, sports events, and public performances. What you see and hear during these events may prove to be just what you need for an interesting speech.

Surveys Thanks to our consumer-driven economy, we have become survey-happy. Almost everyone, it seems, wants your opinion. Were you happy with the mechanic who changed your oil? Have you tried the new cereal with nuts, raisins, and tree bark? All these surveys provide new sources of information and new ideas for speech topics.

According to a poll sponsored by the Corporation for Public Broadcasting, for example, we now have a good idea of what teens have on their minds. America's school-aged kids, we learn, are more worried about pollution than about getting into college. Listen to the subjects that come up again and again in your conversations. Be alert to news events, trends in movies and television, prominent personalities, and interesting ideas that crop up in your classes. Browse chat rooms on the Internet to read what subjects are hot. Clever speeches grow from the smallest of insights; sometimes a little-known scientific fact or discovery will lead to a fascinating speech.

The Internet When you need a subject for a speech, search the Internet. You can start by reading blogs posted on networking sites. Such sites provide many ideas that may spark your interest in a particular topic or help you look at a subject in a new way.

In addition to the blogs you will find on networking sites, you can find blogs written by television and movie actors, athletes, and musicians. Searching through these may provide you with a subject for your speech.

Open your e-mail. If you subscribe to any e-mail newsletters, your subject may be right in front of you. Read the ideas presented in the newsletter. Could you work any of them into a speech? A newsletter about your favorite sport might highlight a new product being marketed to athletes and describe the benefits it will provide. You could develop this information into a speech about training and the positives and negatives of different types of equipment that can be used.

Visual aids can demonstrate the value of the information you find in surveys.

Other Media Sources In addition to the Internet, various other media outlets are great places to get subject ideas. Turn on the television. Browse various talk shows. Listen to the viewpoints of the hosts and those being interviewed. Do any of their opinions trigger an idea for a subject? You may have listened to a mother talk about losing her child to an act of school violence. Afterward, you research the subject of increasing the level of security at your school. This becomes the basis for your upcoming speech. Newspaper editorials and magazine articles can also be great search tools when looking for a subject for your speech.

Narrow Your Subject

Finding a subject is only half the battle in creating an effective informative speech. A subject is a broad area of knowledge, such as romantic literature, astronomy, or soccer. A topic is one particular aspect of a subject. Once you have chosen a general area, you must cut your subject down to size, **narrowing** it to manageable proportions. You can't expect to cover every aspect of your subject in a ten-minute speech, so you have to make some choices about what to include.

Suppose that you decided to speak about America's westward expansion. You could whittle that enormous subject down by confining it within certain

Hero Images/Getty Images

boundaries. You could start by limiting your subject geographically, to a certain area of the West—say, California. Then you could limit your subject to a particular time—perhaps 1849, when the gold rush took place.

The following guidelines may help you narrow your subject down to manageable size:

1. Limit your subject in time. A speech on the high cost of presidential elections could be limited to just one month of a campaign.
2. Limit your subject in space. In a speech on recycling efforts, avoid state or national statistics and concentrate on efforts in your own community.
3. Limit your subject in extent. Instead of describing all the elements of a well-balanced diet, tackle just one. Speak about how eating fiber affects health, for example.
4. Limit your subject by using the principle of divide and conquer. Just when you think you have a manageable topic, try dividing it in half. Let's say you have narrowed your original idea—the world's most famous fictional detectives—to the career of Sherlock Holmes. Now narrow that topic down again: focus only on Holmes's uncanny sense of smell.

Limiting your subject is helpful in several ways. First, it forces you to say more about less; second, it helps you focus your research; and third, it helps you decide what belongs in your speech and what does not. Every speaker can find many tempting pieces of material—funny stories, clever quotes, odd bits of history—but choosing what to keep is critical, especially when your speech may be limited to five minutes or less. Sometimes even the most interesting material must be left out to keep your speech focused and on track.

The California gold rush could be a starting point that leads your speech to Sutter's Mill.

State Your Thesis

Once you have a manageable topic—the California gold rush, say—you've made great progress, but you're not out of the woods. The next step in turning an idea into a speech requires that you make a positive statement about your topic—a statement often called a **thesis** or a statement of purpose.

In your research on the California gold rush, for example, you learn that the employee of a pioneer named John Sutter discovered large nuggets of gold near Sutter's Mill. As news of the discovery spread, thousands of adventurers rushed to the area to stake their claims. These "forty-niners" helped boost California's population from about 15,000 to more than 100,000 in less than a year, and their free spending turned San Francisco into a flourishing city.

This research leads you to develop a thesis for your speech: "The California gold rush sparked the development of the city of San Francisco." Now you've got something you can hang your hat on. A thesis should take the form of a declarative sentence with a subject and a verb, and it should convey in clear language the most important message

Historicus, Inc.

of your speech. Remember that the more you sweat working out a sensible thesis, the less you'll have to sweat once you begin to speak. Here are some possible topics and thesis statements:

Topics	Theses
Movies as sources of teenage slang	The slang teenagers use often comes from the latest popular movies.
Cancer-preventing diets	Eating five servings of fruits and vegetables each day can dramatically reduce your chances of getting cancer.
How Beethoven's hearing loss affected his work	Beethoven's hearing loss may actually have helped him compose music.

Support Your Thesis

Once you have a topic and a thesis, you can turn to the matter of developing your support. Let's assume that you have already completed your research. The problem now is how to use material that you have uncovered to support your thesis. Let's look first at the kinds of material your research has turned up and then at how you can use that material to bring your speech to life.

Facts "Just the facts, ma'am," says Sergeant Joe Friday, a police officer on the old television show *Dragnet*, and that's the attitude many of your listeners may take. Information consists of a network of facts—those small statements about people, events, and other phenomena that make games like Trivial Pursuit possible.

William Shakespeare, for example, had been dead seven years before his plays were published. That statement is a fact; you can look it up. At his death, Shakespeare left just one thing to his wife:

INSTANT IMPACT

High-Tech Storage

In 1993, Congress designated a 100-acre site in Fort Meade, Maryland, for the creation of new storage facilities for the Library of Congress. The first facility was completed in 2002, and three more were to be completed by 2008.

The Library had several very specific requirements for the facilities. First, the location had to be close to Washington, D.C., so items could be easily sent to and received from storage. Second, the climate in some rooms had to remain at 50 degrees Fahrenheit and 30 percent relative humidity. According to Steven J. Herman, chief of the Collections Access, Loan and Management Division, "These conditions extend the lifetime of a paper product by six times, from about 40 years on Capitol Hill to 240 years at Fort Meade." The temperature in other rooms had to be even colder to preserve microfilm and photographs. The third requirement was using sodium vapor lighting to eliminate ultraviolet rays that can harm paper.

According to Herman, more than 2 million books have been transferred to the first two storage units. Units three and four will eventually house more than 10 million manuscripts; 2.3 million prints, drawings, and photographs; 2.1 million music sheets; 340,000 maps; 1.1 million items of American folklore; 6.5 million negatives, transparencies, and color prints; and nearly 500,000 reels of microfilm.

How do they find one book among millions? Before a book is stored, it is given a barcode, which links to a barcode on a box, which links to a barcode on the shelf where the box is. All of this is entered into a database. When librarians need to find a book, they simply put the barcode into the database, and the database tells them exactly where it is.

his second-best bed—a decision that has intrigued historians ever since. Neither of these statements may throw much light on Shakespeare's life or career, but they are both facts because they can be verified. Their accuracy can be determined by anyone with access to the right documents.

All facts are true; *actual facts, real facts,* and *true facts* are redundant phrases. If a thing is not true, it is not a fact. Facts are the basic building blocks of a speech—they support everything you say. Without them, an informative speech is just a house of cards, ready to topple at the slightest breeze. But some facts are more important than others. The fact that the juice of one lemon, if diluted thinly enough, could cover the state of Oregon is both true and meaningless. The world is full of facts. The challenge is to make facts count for more than mere *trivia*.

Facts should be used to support ideas. Suppose you wish to prepare a speech on the life of Marie Curie, one of the world's greatest scientists. The thesis of your speech is that Curie overcame many disadvantages and achieved success at great personal sacrifice. To convince the audience that your thesis is sound, you present the following facts:

- As a young student at the University of Paris, Curie lived on 60 cents a day.
- She could afford to buy only two sacks of coal for the winter and spent many nights shivering under towels, pillowcases, extra clothing, and any other scraps she could find.
- The scientific community doubted her discovery of a new chemical element, radium, and challenged her to prove her claim.
- After four years of struggle, she and her husband produced one decigram of radium (about half the size of a small pea) by boiling down and refining eight tons of ore.
- Despite an opportunity to patent a radiation treatment for cancer, Curie refused to accept any money for her discovery. "It would be contrary to the scientific spirit," she said.

Taken together, these facts help convince the audience that you know what you're talking about.

Statistics are a special kind of fact—a fact expressed in numbers—and they can be particularly difficult for listeners to grasp. "It is now proved beyond doubt," noted the author Fletcher Knebel, "that

smoking is one of the leading causes of statistics." If you use numbers, round off or approximate wherever possible. Avoid saying "two hundred and ninety-six point five," for example, if you can accomplish your purpose by saying "about three hundred."

Everyone Loves a Story Although facts are the backbone of an informative speech, they are not the only kind of material you can use. Another way to convey information, and one of the most appealing, is the **anecdote**. An anecdote is simply a brief story that illustrates a point. Although people often think of anecdotes as humorous, they can also be sad or touching.

Anecdotes can be easily located in a variety of resources, including *The Little, Brown Book of Anecdotes* (edited by Clifton Fadiman). In this volume, you will find stories like this:

- Johnny Carson, longtime host of television's *Tonight Show*, was once asked by a reporter what he would like his epitaph to be. "I'll be right back" was Carson's reply.

Polish physicist and chemist Marie Curie was a pioneer in the field of radioactivity.

When using anecdotes, be sure not to distract listeners from your main point.

Purestock/Getty Images

Anecdotes spice up a speech. People love to hear stories because stories dramatize ideas and situations. Stories are also far more memorable than any other way of conveying information. Carefully chosen, one or two anecdotes can give your speech the pizzazz it needs, but use caution. Keep in mind that anecdotes can also distract listeners from your main point and entertain more than they inform.

Quotable Quotes Another form of information that you can use to develop your speech is the **quotation**—a selection of someone else's words repeated exactly, usually with acknowledgment of the source. Again, resources are relatively easy to find. *Bartlett's Familiar Quotations* is undoubtedly the most famous, and *The Yale Book of Quotations* is widely considered to be the most reader-friendly

and reliable. Other, more lighthearted books include *Morrow's International Dictionary of Contemporary Quotations*, where you can find gems like these:

- "The first problem for all of us, men and women, is not to learn, but to unlearn." (Gloria Steinem, feminist)
- "Awopbopaloobopalopbamboom!" (Little Richard, rock star)
- "I love Mickey Mouse more than any woman I've ever known." (Walt Disney, animator)

You can also search the Internet to find a wealth of interesting and unusual quotations. You might try Web sites where you can search for quotations by subject, keyword, or author name. Other sites are organized by themes such as vegetarianism or animal rights.

Quotations can be used more freely than anecdotes, because they tend to be much briefer. They also help add credibility to your speech. "Wow," your listeners may think, "Abraham Lincoln agrees with this speaker!" Quotations do have their drawbacks. If you quote someone unfamiliar to your listeners, they may become confused. Quotations can also be overused. You may find that the speech is no longer yours but belongs instead to all those you are quoting. Used wisely, though, quotations tend to make audiences think you are both well-read and believable.

Definitions A fourth kind of information to use in developing your speech is the **definition**. Sometimes simply defining a term is the best way to get an audience headed in the right direction. You might wish to use a familiar word in a special way. "I am using the word *dog* not in the sense of a pet," you might explain, "but in the sense of a 'hip buddy'—as in 'What's up, dog?'"

You might also wish to trace the history of a word for your listeners. This tactic might help them understand why your choice of a particular word is apropos. Etymological information (*etymology* means "the history of a word") can sometimes help correct mistaken ideas. The term *ten-gallon hat*, for example, comes from a mistranslation of the Spanish term *sombrero galon*, which is a hat with braid decoration.

Descriptions The final form of information we will discuss here is descriptions—images that stimulate the audience's imagination. Suppose you want to tell an audience about the difference between an alligator and a crocodile. You could explain their physical features, of course, but why not try a fresh twist? Consider this "personalized" description:

> Alligators have rounded snouts and crocodiles have pointed ones, though if your leg is caught in either, you probably won't appreciate the difference. If the jaws are completely closed around your leg, you might look on either side of the snout to see whether a lower tooth is jutting outside the upper lip. If it is, the creature is a croc.

Descriptions can help you emphasize certain aspects of your topic. They can bring to life an interesting character or create a vivid impression of a particular place. Practice writing descriptions and then try including them in your speeches.

SECTION 2 REVIEW

Recalling the Facts

1. How can personal experience be used as a source to find a subject to speak about?
2. List four ways to narrow your subject.

Thinking Critically

Narrow the following subjects into speech topics. Then write a reasonable thesis for each.
- rain forest
- indoor sports
- heroes and heroines
- scientific discoveries
- household chores

Taking Charge

1. Find an anecdote related to a famous person of your choice.
2. Take a technical topic, such as how a cell phone works, and define five terms related to that topic.
3. Develop a thesis on a topic of interest to you. How would you develop a line of argument to support your thesis? What supporting materials would you use? Outline your topic, your argument, and at least three details—such as facts, stories, quotes, definitions, or descriptions—that support your argument.

Audio and Visual Aids

"You can't really appreciate the thrilling beauty of these South American aardvarks unless you can see and hear them in their natural surroundings." Surprisingly, the speaker of these words is stuck in a classroom in Billings, Montana, nowhere near the Amazon rain forest. Is there a way this speaker can bring his audience nearer the topic? "Luckily," the speaker continues, "I have brought with me some slides I took in Brazil, and I've also brought some on-the-spot recordings of the noises the aardvarks make."

When you can't bring the real thing to your audience (in other words, nearly all the time), you can arrange the next best thing. In the aardvark example, the speaker brought both pictures and sounds to the audience. Such material is referred to as visual and audio aids. Visual aids include anything the audience can see, such as photographs, cartoons, color slides, video clips, posters, transparencies, or drawings. Audio aids include anything the audience can hear, such as music, sound effects, or recorded conversations.

Visual aids, especially, can help a speaker make a point, because vision is most people's dominant sense. Research indicates that people pay 25 times as much attention to visual information as they do to audio information. Remember, however, that no matter how powerful or striking visual aids may be, they are meant to enhance, not replace, a well-constructed speech.

Two-Dimensional Visual Aids

Illustrations that can be represented on a flat surface are called two-dimensional aids. They include charts, diagrams, maps, drawings, and photographs. You can display such visuals on a classroom chalkboard or whiteboard (either drawn there or held up with tape) or on a flip chart (a large pad of paper mounted on an easel). You can project the visuals on a screen or hold them up by hand for the audience to see. If you can show the visuals without having to hold them, you will be free to use a pointer to describe particular features.

Photographs, Drawings, and Cartoons If a picture is worth a thousand words, then using one in your speech can mean a big savings. Furthermore, with a photo you can make people see things that you can't easily explain. Make sure that you mount photographs on heavy construction paper or art board so that they are easy to handle. Photos should be at least 8½ by 10 inches (preferably larger) so that the audience can see them easily.

Drawings are popular visual aids because they are easy to prepare. If you can use a compass and a straightedge, you can draw well enough for most speeches. Cartoons, a special kind of drawing, use humor or satire to make a point. The editorial page of a newspaper can be a good place to get ideas for your own cartoons.

Graphic Representations Maps, diagrams, and graphs are among the many other two-dimensional visual aids that speakers, particularly in the business world, use with success. Maps are certainly

How can audio and visual aids help a speaker make a point?

the best way to show a geographical relationship. If you want to show the route of the Appalachian Trail from Georgia to Maine, a map is a necessity.

Diagrams are useful when you want to explain a process. If you want to show how an internal combustion engine works, a diagram might save you time and help your audience achieve a better understanding. You might want to use a desktop publishing program to create infographics. An *infographic* (short for *information graphic*) turns numbers into pictures. An infographic can be as simple as a pizza divided into slices (to illustrate proportions of favorite pizza toppings) or as complicated as a diagram of the human eye (to show how laser surgery works). What all infographics have in common is the ability to communicate a message at a single glance.

Designers usually choose one of three main types of infographics: *fever chart, pie chart,* or *bar graph.* A fever chart resembles the pattern you might find if you recorded the varying temperatures of someone with a fever by plotting points and connecting the dots. A fever chart works well to illustrate financial information or how things have changed over time. A pie chart looks like a circle with individual wedges, each representing a different component. You can make pie charts from drawings or photos. Used to make comparisons, a bar graph consists of parallel bars whose lengths represent different quantities.

No matter what your topic, each infographic must contain certain essential elements. George Rorick, former director of the Knight-Ridder Graphics Network, says that the following five items should appear in every infographic:

1. *Headline.* The headline is usually an easy-to-read label.
2. *Body.* The body of an infographic consists of the raw data or numbers.
3. *Credits.* The person or persons who created the graphic should be identified.
4. *Explainer.* A short sentence should explain what the infographic is about and why it might be important.
5. *Source.* Where did the information come from?

Most modern projection units can display whatever is shown on a computer screen.

Whatever type of infographic you choose, be sure to make it interesting. Adding a cartoon, character, or drawing to your infographic is the final touch that will make it memorable.

Handouts Handouts include any flyers, brochures, or information sheets that you prepare ahead of time and duplicate so that each member of the audience can have a copy. On the plus side, handouts can look professional, and people can take them home after your speech. On the negative side, they can create distractions. It takes time and trouble to distribute handouts, and your audience may study them instead of making eye contact with you. Experienced speakers usually distribute handouts at the end of a speech to avoid interrupting the speech itself.

Projections

Speakers can use a variety of tools to project a visual aid. These tools include an overhead projector, slides, and video.

Overhead Projector An **overhead projector** is a simple device that projects and magnifies material from a transparent sheet of plastic. One advantage of using an overhead is that you can prepare transparencies ahead of time and then lay them on the overhead for viewing. Be sure you know how to use the overhead before your speech, paying special attention to how to straighten and focus the image. Try to avoid reading a transparency to your audience. Instead, point out the highlights.

Slide Shows In the past, people used color film slides to illustrate informative speeches, because slides had a size and vividness unmatched by almost any other visual. The modern equivalent of slides are digital photos that can be presented in "slide shows." Slide shows can be created and incorporated into speeches by using software such as PowerPoint. Great care should be taken to use only photos that illustrate the points you are trying to make.

As valuable as they are, slide shows have been overused and can easily lull an audience to sleep.

Because they have to be used in a darkened room, the slides themselves can become the focal point of your speech.

Video It might be helpful to create your own movie to illustrate a speech. A speech on the fundamentals of pole-vaulting, for example, could be improved with clips of someone actually vaulting.

Digital video cameras allow you to capture and edit video clips easily by using digital editing software. After shooting the footage, upload the video to a computer hard drive. Using the editing software, you can put the clips together in any order you like, add audio clips or voiceovers, and add titles and headings.

To incorporate your video into a speech, all you have to do is project your video from a computer onto a large screen by using a projector and video cable. Your audience will clearly see the video and text and hear any audio you added to the video.

Instead of projecting your video onto a screen, you can copy it on a DVD. If you are using a DVD as part of your speech, make sure you know how to work the DVD player so it does not disrupt the flow of your speech.

You might also wish to use material that you have recorded from national or local television programs. Pay close attention to copyright laws to be sure that you do not make illegal use of anything. Often, copyright owners permit limited educational use of their programs. Copyright laws do change from time to time, and your teacher will have current information to help you.

Three-Dimensional Visual Aids

Sometimes an actual object—something with height, width, and depth—can make a greater impression than a picture or projection. If you were to give a speech on porcelain dolls, showing the audience actual dolls would have much greater appeal than simply using pictures or slides. In some cases, especially with smaller groups, it may even be possible to let the audience handle the objects. If you decide, however, to pass an object among the members of the

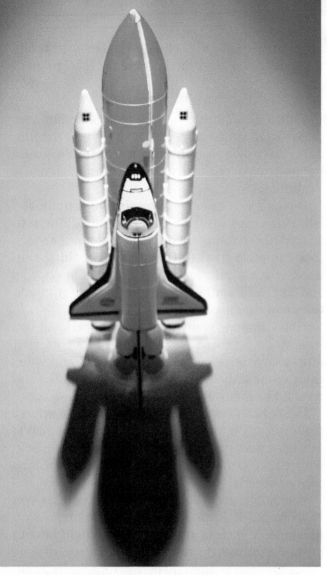

A model can help you demonstrate specific points you want to make in a speech.

Cutaways A **cutaway** is essentially a model sliced in two. Your model of the space shuttle, for example, might have a removable side panel that would allow the audience to look inside, to examine the flight deck or the crew's quarters. Both models and cutaways need to follow the same rules we have discussed for other visual aids. Make sure they are large enough to be seen and clearly relevant to the point you're making. In addition, be sure to practice handling the objects so that you won't drop or fumble them at a crucial moment.

As an alternative to models or cutaways, you might want to download images or videos from the Internet. During your speech, use these images or videos in place of actual cutaways.

Sound Recordings

Sound recordings are also useful for presenting a speech. For example, in a speech that illustrates how poetry is similar to music, you might want to share a song. You can cue a CD to a particular song before your presentation so it is ready when you need it. CDs can be played in a CD player or on a computer. Digital audio players can also be connected to speakers to allow your audience to hear music or sound clips you have downloaded.

Downloading digital recordings from the Internet is another option when using sound to enhance a presentation. Many Web sites allow you to purchase music. Other sites may offer short sound clips you can download for free as long as you cite them as your source.

Guidelines for Using Aids

Now that we have discussed a variety of audio and visual aids, we want to give you a few guidelines for their use. Whatever visual image you use must be large enough for the audience to see. The larger the audience, the larger the visual aid must be. For an audience of classmates, you can probably use images that fit on a sheet of 8½-by-11-inch paper. Even for an audience the size of a normal

audience, be aware that you will lose the attention of each listener in turn as he or she examines the object.

Models Occasionally, an object is too large to bring to a speech. You would have a tough time, for example, wheeling in the space shuttle *Atlantis* for a talk on space research. But you could use a scale **model**. A plastic model of the space shuttle, scaled down to perhaps one-twentieth of the actual size, would enable you to show the features of the vehicle in an informative way.

Be sure your visual aids are large enough for everyone to see easily.

class, however, the larger the image is, the more likely it is to be meaningful.

You should master the mechanics of any equipment you plan to use. Take time to become familiar with devices like overhead projectors, DVD and CD players, digital audio players, and computer projectors. Set up any equipment early so that you are not adjusting it while delivering your speech. Make sure you have markers available if you're using an overhead or a whiteboard. Have any handouts you need available and have a plan for distributing them quickly and efficiently.

Remember, too, that the visual aid is *not* the audience. Rookies tend to speak to the aid as if it could hear. If you need to look at the visual aid, get plenty of practice so that you are thoroughly familiar with the procedure you're going to use.

The following summarizes our advice for the use of audio and visual aids:

- Be sure the aid is large enough to be seen or loud enough to be heard.
- Be sure the aid contributes to the idea being presented. If you can get along without it, don't use it.
- Don't stand in front of the aid.
- Talk to your listeners, not to the visual aid.
- Keep any visual aid out of sight until you are ready to use it, and then put it away again when you have finished.
- Don't overdo a good thing. A long succession of slides or charts can become boring or can take away an element of *spontaneity* from a speech.
- Remember Murphy's Law: If something can go wrong, it will. Have a backup plan in case your equipment fails.
- Practice, practice, practice.

Finally, remember that visual and audio aids are only means to an end. If these aids overwhelm the speech or draw undue attention away from you as the speaker, you would be wise not to use them. Don't forget that you yourself are a visual aid. Consider whether the clothing you plan to wear will contribute to or detract from your message. Can you give a serious speech in a clown costume or a humorous speech in your best clothes?

SECTION 3 REVIEW

Recalling the Facts

1. How much more likely are people to pay attention to a speech using visual aids than to a speech using audio aids?
2. What are some examples of two-dimensional visual aids?
3. What is an infographic?
4. When is the best time during a speech to distribute handouts to the audience?
5. What is one negative aspect to using a slide show during a speech?

Thinking Critically

1. How can high school speakers enhance their credibility when speaking to an adult audience? How can an adult speaker hold the interest of a high school audience?
2. Why is it important to have a trusted source for information presented on a chart or graph?
3. Why is it important for speakers to avoid looking at their visual aids when speaking?
4. In what ways is the person giving a speech a visual aid?

Taking Charge

1. Find an online almanac and choose an information "nugget"—a small group of facts that can be developed into an infographic. Use a desktop publishing program to express your nugget in the form of a fever chart, pie chart, or bar graph.
2. Using the Internet, research your favorite movie. Create three overhead transparencies or PowerPoint slides for a speech on that movie. Show your slides to a classmate and ask for feedback. On the basis of your classmate's feedback, revise the slides for your speech.
3. Research a speech topic that would benefit from using a three-dimensional visual aid or aids, such as the development of the modern football helmet or changing and tuning the strings of a guitar.

Creating Multimedia Presentations

By some measures, cell phones and e-mail represent great advances in communication, but by other measures, they're still rather basic. The new frontier in communication technology probably lies in multimedia presentations.

What a Multimedia Presentation Includes

A **multimedia presentation** is a speech supplemented with special computer software. This software enables the speaker to combine several kinds of visual and/or audio aids (including charts and graphs, slides and photographs, even animations, video clips, and sound) into one presentation.

Multimedia presentations can include charts and graphs as well as sound and video.

Popular presentation software includes PowerPoint, Astound, and HyperStudio.

Depending on the resources available at your school, you may be able to give multimedia presentations in your classes. Such presentations provide good training for speeches you may give outside the classroom—especially in business settings, where multimedia resources are used every day.

Although each multimedia presentation program operates a bit differently from the others, all allow you to use a wide range of material. Suppose that you are talking about the Lewis and Clark expedition and you want to show your audience a painting of Lewis and Clark's guide Sacagawea.

If the image can be found on the Internet, you can **download** (transfer data from one computer's memory to the memory of another, usually smaller, computer) it directly to your computer. Remember to see whether the image is in the public domain, and thus available at no charge, or is protected by copyright. If the image is from a book or magazine, you can transfer it to disk with a **scanner.** Once the digitized image is in your computer, you can then manipulate it to suit your own purposes.

Suppose you want to explain how special effects are used in movies such as *Star Wars*. You can download video clips from the movies, including sound, for presentation in your speech. You can also program your photographs, slides, animations, and other visuals to appear automatically at preset times—leaving you free to concentrate on connecting with your audience.

During the speech, you use a computer to control the order, content, and timing of your presentation. The computer is usually hooked up to a television monitor, a large-screen video projector, or an LCD (liquid crystal display) panel. Some systems have a wireless mouse or remote control that lets you move through your presentation without distracting your audience.

Advantages of Using Computer Presentation Programs In a multimedia presentation, you coordinate various media (music, text, illustrations, and so on) to enhance your message. The advantage of using a combination of media is that you can appeal to more than one of your audience's senses. Some of us are visual learners; others need to hear; some need a hands-on approach. No matter what their learning styles may be, your audience will be more stimulated with a multimedia presentation, and therefore more interested in what you have to say.

Computer presentation programs offer a number of important advantages. The slide program you create, for example, serves as an outline for both you and your audience. Rather than looking at your notes, you can glance at the screen along with the audience to check your place in the script. These presentation programs also give your materials a professional appearance. Many programs allow you to choose a design and various templates for your presentation. These allow you to organize your ideas and keep the theme (background patterns and colors) consistent from one slide or screen to the next.

In addition, computer presentation programs offer a number of special features. They allow you to make quick insertions of new data (in tables or charts, for instance). They also allow you to change presentations easily—unlike more-permanent media, such as flip charts.

A high school group working on a science project might use multimedia to improve the effectiveness of its presentation. To make the idea of a black hole more vivid, the group might use a clip from a movie such as *A Brief History of Time.* In addition, they might use some futuristic background music to help establish a mood of mystery and awe as they explain their topic. Often, video and audio clips can be linked to buttons you insert on your slide screen. These can easily be played during your presentation.

Even churches, synagogues, and mosques are getting into the act. Several presentation companies are now working with religious groups to make worship services multimedia experiences. For example, some groups are projecting the words for hymns on a wall. Others present missionary reports or news of congregational interest—such as births, baptisms, weddings, bar and bat mitzvah celebrations, and anniversaries—in a multimedia format. Religious leaders can even press a button to project a key sermon point on a screen as they speak.

Often, you will visit a Web site that includes multimedia presentations on several of its pages. You, too, can link a presentation to your own Web site so visitors can view your presentation even if you aren't in front of them.

Effective Graphics

Choosing the right type of graphic or visual aid can make presentations interesting and can help you present complex information clearly.

Consider these graphics and applications:

- **Table**—for organizing a lot of words, ideas, or numbers.
- **Bar graph**—for showing differences in size or quantity.
- **Pie chart**—for showing the various parts of a whole.
- **Photograph**—for instances when words aren't adequate.
- **Diagram or flowchart**—for explaining a complicated procedure.
- **Map**—for showing a particular location essential to your message.
- **List**—for itemizing your main points to help your audience remember them.
- **Video**—for illustrating your topic clearly.
- **Animation**—for enlivening your presentation.

Possible Disadvantages Today's high-tech audiences not only want to hear your ideas, they expect to be entertained at the same time. But because modern audiences are information saturated, it takes powerful tools to get your message across. Computer programs enable you to turn important words and phrases into animated action statements that fly across the screen. But multimedia presentations do have potential drawbacks—not the least of which is the cost of the equipment required to show them. Another disadvantage is that it takes a good deal of time to learn how to use the software, to design graphs and charts, to edit sound and video clips (a few hours would not be unusual for a 30-second clip), and to organize and rehearse a presentation. If you plan to give a multimedia presentation, be sure to give yourself plenty of time to make sure it comes off just right.

Preparing a Presentation Multimedia presentations certainly take time to prepare, but the results may be worth the effort. A group of researchers at 3M found that speakers who used audiovisual aids were generally more convincing than those who only spoke. Audiences described the multimedia presentations as clearer, more professional, and more interesting.

Perhaps most telling of all, the study revealed that those who saw the multimedia presentations needed 24 percent less meeting time later to finish their business. The underlying conclusion of this study—that multimedia can significantly enhance our persuasiveness—takes on new meaning in an era when virtually every presenter has access to communications technology.

Keep these guidelines in mind as you prepare a multimedia presentation:

- *Know what you are presenting.* Have a good research base; knowing the material well can give you confidence.
- *Know your audience.* Find out who they are, as well as their level of interest, knowledge, and experience. Anticipate their questions and build the answers into your presentation.
- *Use an outline.* Prepare your script in advance (with an opening, a body, and a closing). Break down the major topic into supporting

Working on multimedia presentations may give you experience with video and sound equipment that you could use in a career.

topics. An outline presented on a slide orients the audience and helps keep you on track.

- *Develop a format.* The most effective presentations use a format that is consistent from slide to slide. Typeface, type alignment, type size, and graphic elements should all figure into an overall plan. Once you have established the format, all you need to do is change the text from one slide to the next, allowing plenty of room for charts, illustrations, video, sound, and animation.
- *Make it easy to read.* Limit each slide to a maximum of seven lines of text. The more you ask the audience to read, the less attentive they'll be to what you're saying. Use large type and set off each of your points with a bullet or number. Make sure you review the text carefully to catch typographical, punctuation, and spelling errors.
- *Rehearse.* This is a step that's easy to overlook, so discipline yourself to set up the presentation and go through it as if an audience were there.
- *Arrive early.* On presentation day, come early and test everything. Check the room setup to make sure that everyone can see the screen.

Aaron Roeth Photography

Strategies for Success Presentations may seem as if they run themselves, but it's not quite that simple. You need to think just as much about your people skills as you do about your technical skills. No matter how many high-tech special effects you use, they will be wasted if you can't relate to your audience. Here are a few strategic ideas to consider as you develop your presentation:

- Analyze how the size and seating arrangement of the room may affect your presentation.
- Get off to a good start and end with a big finish.
- Connect with your audience. Relate to their needs and draw them into your message.

- Use humor, anecdotes, and personal stories to highlight points you want to drive home.
- Never go in without a backup plan. What will you do if the computer program fails to start up? Always carry a backup disk of your presentation just in case. Take a printout of your script as well.
- Be prepared to give your speech even if all the multimedia equipment fails. The speech may not be as dazzling as the presentation you had planned, but it will be much better than no speech at all.

SECTION 4 REVIEW

Recalling the Facts

1. What are some advantages of using a multimedia presentation?
2. Why is displaying your outline during a speech a good idea?

Thinking Critically

1. Discuss with your classmates how you might use a multimedia presentation in each of these situations:
   - You've been chosen to deliver some disappointing news at the company meeting, and you expect to encounter some hostility from the crowd.
   - Your last presentation was dry and not very memorable. You're wondering what you can do to improve on it in your next presentation—a report on intramural participation.
   - You've just begun speaking when a member of the audience asks you a loaded question that catches you off guard.

2. What kind of graphic would you use to illustrate each of the following?
   - The per-person rate for one night at five hotels in town is $107, $172, $62, $97, and $67.
   - Tourism has increased steadily over the last ten years.
   - Some hotels are in the downtown area, while several others are in nearby suburbs.
   - A view of one of the hotel rooms.
   - Where the hotel swimming pool and restaurant are in relation to the lobby.

Taking Charge

Create ten imaginary slides you might use in a multimedia presentation about your school that you plan to give to foreign exchange students.

Looking Back

Listed below are the major ideas discussed in this chapter.

- Much of our daily communication is designed to give instructions, provide facts, or clarify ideas.
- Speakers who hope to inform should be sure to be clear, concise, complete, and correct. They should also use concrete examples and connect with listeners.
- One reason we sometimes have difficulty imagining what our listeners are thinking is that most of us are wrapped up in our own points of view.
- Asking some basic questions about your listeners can help you prepare an effective speech.
- Finding subjects to speak on can come from surveys, newspaper articles, conversations, the Internet, and other classes.
- Create a manageable topic by limiting the subject in time, space, and scope.
- A clearly focused thesis will help you decide what material belongs in your speech.
- Develop your speech through the use of appropriate facts, anecdotes, quotations, definitions, and descriptions.
- Audio and visual aids can reinforce your message and enhance your presentation.
- Visual aids must be large enough to be seen and significant enough to be worthwhile.
- Audio and visual aids are valuable if used confidently but can detract from your speech if presented in a distracting way.
- Presentations that include visual aids are more likely to be remembered.
- A multimedia presentation can include video clips and animated text.
- A speaker should always be prepared to deliver a speech without any visual aids, in the event that the equipment fails.

Speech Vocabulary

Fill in each blank with the correct word from the list below. No word can be used more than once. Not all words will be used.

briefing
advance organizer
narrowing
quotation
handout
cutaway
public lecture
fireside chat

definition
thesis
diagram
overhead projector
status report
chalk talk
cultural literacy
anecdote

graph
model
map
multimedia presentation
download
scanner

1. You would be wise to depend on what you know of history, science, and literature—your _____ _____—when you suspect someone has made a mistake.
2. Three useful visual aids include a _____, which tells you where places are; a _____, which shows you how something works; and a _____, which shows relationships among numbers.
3. An _____ can show an audience cartoons, drawings, and other materials on a screen without darkening the room.
4. After choosing a subject, you can limit it by _____ and then condense your major point into a _____.

5. To bring appealing material to your speech, you can use a brief story—called an _____—or the exact words of another person—a _____.

6. Some of your teachers may be fond of giving a _____, while a sports coach is more likely to give a _____.

7. The president's press secretary gives reporters a _____. The president may give a more personal talk called a _____.

8. Organizations often hear a _____ from one of their committees.

9. A statement such as "I will first describe the best breeds for show animals and then look at poodles in particular" helps preview a speech and is called an _____.

10. A small-scale version of the Globe Theater is called a _____. If part of it can be removed so people can see inside, that portion is referred to as a _____.

11. One kind of visual aid that can be distributed to the audience is called a _____.

12. To prepare a _____, the speaker first decided to _____ an image from the Internet and use a _____ to digitize a picture from her photo album.

Academic Vocabulary

Use context clues within the chapter and a dictionary to determine the definitions. Match each of the terms on the left with its definition on the right.

1. concise
2. concrete
3. distinction
4. ambiguous
5. intuition
6. demographics
7. trivia
8. senile
9. etymology
10. infographic
11. spontaneity

a. a difference, something unlike another
b. brief, to the point
c. capable of having two or more meanings
d. characteristics of human populations
e. exhibiting a diminished capacity (especially to think or remember) due to old age
f. a visual representation of facts
g. impulsive, unpredictable behavior
h. insignificant information
i. real, perceptible
j. special insight or a "sixth sense"
k. the origin and development of a word

To Remember

Answer the following questions based on the information in the chapter.

1. What are some ways in which we provide information every day to others?
2. Name the five major kinds of informative speeches.
3. What are some of the ways a speaker can support general statements?
4. Define the term *cultural literacy.*
5. What are some of the questions you might use to learn more about your audience?
6. List several good methods for finding a subject for a speech.
7. How can a potential subject be narrowed to a manageable topic?
8. What are the characteristics of a thesis?
9. What can a speaker do if the audience's attention appears to wander?
10. What should you keep in mind if you decide to use a visual aid during your speech?

11. Why shouldn't you fill your allotted speech time with visuals?

12. In what three ways can multimedia visual aids enhance an oral presentation?

13. When creating a multimedia slide, how much text is enough and how much is too much?

To Do

1. Attend a school or public meeting, as held by the city council, the school board, or a club. As you listen, sort out the comments people make according to what is genuine information and what is simply opinion. Determine a rough ratio of information to opinion and report back to your class.

2. Practice giving a presentation by telling classmates how to get to various locations around town. Give clear directions and use visual aids if possible. Then your classmates can analyze your presentation and suggest any changes.

3. Write to a government agency or your congressional representative for information on a subject of interest.

4. Choose a topic for a speech. (Consult the list at the bottom of the page if you need ideas.) Decide what your thesis will be and then outline an argument to support your thesis. Be sure to include at least two supporting details to bolster each main heading in your outline.

5. Use a computer program to create a graph or chart, or download a visual aid from the Internet to reinforce the thesis you chose in Exercise 4.

To Talk About

1. Consider whether the explosion of new information over the past few years has been a blessing or a curse. Are high school students, for example, better informed than their peers of 10 or 20 years ago?

2. What techniques might a speaker use to keep audience interest at a high level?

3. To what extent would a rock concert qualify as a multimedia presentation? How is a concert like and unlike a business presentation?

To Write About

1. Write a letter to the editor of your local newspaper regarding the public image of high school students. Teenagers perform much of the volunteer work and convenience labor that keep a community going, but they often face negative stereotypes. Use facts, quotations, and anecdotes to support your position.

2. Gather a group of five anecdotes and five quotations to use in a speech about the "typical" day of a high school student.

Related Speech Topics

Contemporary musicians, writers, or artists
The future of cable television
New medical frontiers
Tanning: healthy glow or risky choice?
Tattoos: bizarre fashion statements or
    something more?

How safe is bungee jumping?
What is a laser beam?
The causes of smog
Jazz: America's music
What makes a good driver?
The Peace Corps

CHAPTER 14

SPEECHES TO PERSUADE

Character is the most effective means of persuasion.

—Aristotle

Learning Objectives

After completing this chapter, you will be able to do the following.

- Recognize the specific features of the persuasive speech.
- Apply what you have learned about effective persuasive speaking to both your dealings with others and your own life.
- Analyze the type of audience to whom you are speaking.
- Adapt your persuasive approach to match the makeup of your audience.
- Understand and implement logical, emotional, and personal appeals.

Chapter Outline

Following are the main sections in this chapter.

1. What Is Persuasive Speaking?
2. Analyzing Your Audience
3. Appealing to Your Audience

Speech Vocabulary

In this chapter, you will learn the meanings of the speech terms listed below.

persuasive speaking
supportive audience
uncommitted
  audience
unbiased
indifferent audience
captive audience
opposed audience
compromise
disclaimer
logos
proof
pathos
ethos
goodwill
integrity
reputation
sincerity
competency
credentials
composure

Academic Vocabulary

Expanding your academic vocabulary will help you become a more effective communicator. Listed below are some words appearing in this chapter that you should make part of your vocabulary.

temperament
cognizant
burgeoning
analytical
palatable
assert
instinctively

In this chapter, you will learn about persuasive speaking. You'll learn effective techniques to enable you to convince others to "buy" what you are "selling," whether it be a product, a belief, an attitude, or an idea. Next, you will analyze the various types of audiences that you might have to persuade and the specific methods of persuasive speaking most likely to be effective for each of these audiences. Finally, you will see how the understanding and implementation of Aristotle's three appeals can add both depth and impact to your persuasive speaking.

Introduction

Would you like to talk to your parents about having some friends over for a party this weekend? Would you like to have a later curfew? Would you like to convince your science teacher that it would be a good idea to work in groups for the next major project? Would you like to make a little more money per hour when you babysit for the neighbors? If you answered yes to any of these questions, then you had better know how to speak persuasively.

Attempting to teach her students about the persuasive speech and about how it differs from the other types of speeches, a teacher gave the following explanation to her class: "Remember, if you show us how to put a car engine together, that's a demonstration speech. If you explain to us how the car engine works, that's an informative speech. If you then convince us to buy the car, that's a persuasive speech!"

Parents and children use persuasive speech with each other every day.

Tetra Images/Getty Images

What Is Persuasive Speaking?

A persuasive speech asks your audience to "buy" something that you are "selling." It can be a product, but it can also be a belief, an attitude, or an idea. While the informative speech primarily supplies important information to increase understanding, the persuasive speech goes one step further and asks the audience to *do* something based on the information presented.

Whether you are speaking in a court of law, trying to influence a public policy, or simply trying to persuade your friends to see a particular movie, **persuasive speaking** demands that you effectively (1) induce your audience to believe as you do and (2) influence your audience to act as you've proposed.

Consider the following situations:

- You wish to convince your parents that you should be able to attend a local concert.
- You want to convince your teacher that more time is needed to complete a class project.
- You wish to show your friends that drinking and driving is not an intelligent way to have a good time.

In each of these situations, you would need to be a persuasive speaker. First of all, you would have to awaken a belief in your listeners that what you are proposing is a good idea. Next, you would have to show them that you have a well-thought-out plan of

action available. Finally, you should be able to convince your audience that your plan of action is realistic and the right thing to do. People act and react on the basis of what they want, how they think, and how they feel. Consequently, it is your job to push the right buttons, whether logical or emotional, so that your audience agrees with what you are promoting.

Scholars say that the greatest ancient Roman orator was Marcus Tullius Cicero. In his work *On Oratory*, Cicero wrote that the skilled speaker is a person of learning and insight. The most important insight that a speaker must have is knowledge of his or her audience. As a skilled persuasive speaker, your first task is to evaluate accurately and perceptively

Persuasive speaking skills come into play whenever you try to influence your friends to do something.

Design Pics/Darren Greenwood

how your audience feels about you and your message. This evaluation, called *audience analysis*, is an invaluable element in persuasive speaking. You have to realize that giving a canned speech—a planned speech that you deliver the same way to every group—is not always going to work. Each audience is unique. You must be ready to make adjustments so that your spoken words are appropriate and get or keep the audience on your side. Next, we'll look at the different types of audiences that you might have to persuade.

Daniel Webster is considered to have been one of the United States' finest orators.

SECTION 1 REVIEW

Recalling the Facts

1. Persuasive speaking demands that you are effective at doing what two things?
2. Why is audience analysis important?

Thinking Critically

It has been said that the most difficult audience you will ever have to persuade is yourself. Why might this statement be true? Do you see yourself as a threatening audience? Why?

Taking Charge

Think of specific instances in school, in your community, at a job, or with your friends that would require you to take a persuasive approach. Then make two lists. In the first, write products that you might have to persuade people to buy. In the second, write ideas that you might have to promote. Be ready to discuss your lists with other students.

Analyzing Your Audience

Suppose that a sign in your high school locker room says this:

Get Ready to Play!

Below the sign is a photo of your team's next opponent. Beneath the photo are key statistics about the opposing team, information on each of that team's members, and an analysis sheet that predicts what the individual opposing players and their team will do in specific game situations. Studying the picture and statistics for several days will help prepare your team for the upcoming game.

Just as good athletes must be aware of the strengths and weaknesses of their opponents, good persuasive speakers must be aware of the attitudes and beliefs of their audiences. These speakers might post a sign that says this:

Get Ready to Speak!

As Chapter 2 told you, your audience should never be perceived as the enemy. However, your audience deserves to be well scouted, or analyzed. You cannot prepare the most effective, persuasive speech if you have not taken the time to get to know the people who will be listening to you. How old are they? What is their economic status? Will most of them be male or female? What about their political or religious views? How many will be attending? How many are in favor of your position? Against it?

Suppose you were speaking to each of these groups:

- a parent group (about chaperoning a school dance)
- a group of community business owners (about sponsoring a school moneymaking project)
- your neighborhood (about an extensive local cleanup campaign)
- your teachers (on the need for them to teach an extra class each day)

Wouldn't the mood or *temperament* of your audience be different in each situation? Wouldn't the mood vary depending on what you were asking the group to "buy"? Most likely, moods would range from very positive to very negative. You owe it to your audience to be *cognizant* of the speaking climate and to present your message accordingly.

A football coach has to tailor his remarks to the mood of the team. How would you categorize a team that has been losing?

Hero/Corbis/Glow Images

Authorities generally agree that most audiences can be classified into one of four categories: supportive, uncommitted, indifferent, or opposed. Often, your audience will be a mixture of these four types. Regardless of the type of audience you are addressing, *your main purpose is to gain the most supporters possible.* Use all of the tools at your disposal. An effective introduction and conclusion, convincing arguments, congeniality, a sharp appearance, and a sense of humor can help you persuade your audience.

Audiences can be supportive (above), uncommitted, or indifferent (left).

The Supportive Audience

Every speaker would like to have a supportive audience. The **supportive audience** is friendly; its members like you and what you have to say. This is the easiest audience to address, because the members are ready to support and promote your ideas. Laughter, hugs, and handshakes come easily with this group. A political candidate asking his staff for its continued efforts after a big win would be addressing a supportive audience. A school team asking the student body at a pep rally for continued support would probably be met with enthusiastic cheers. Your main objective with listeners in this type of audience is to reinforce what they already accept. You want to strengthen your ties with them.

Generally, the supportive audience doesn't need a great deal of information. Sometimes, though, the supportive audience has "bought" you as a person but doesn't know much about what you are "selling." In such a case, take time to present your material thoroughly. For instance, students might strongly support you for a class office because you are well known, well liked, and well respected. If,

however, you propose a new homeroom concept as part of your platform, you had better be ready to offer persuasive, well-thought-out details to support your idea. If you don't, your audience might begin looking for another candidate.

The supportive audience is a speaker's dream. Don't take these listeners for granted, though. Your key to persuasive success is to keep them enthused about you and your objectives.

The Uncommitted Audience

You have a good chance of persuading the **uncommitted audience** because it is neutral. This type of audience isn't for you or against you; its members simply need information to make up their minds. The prevalent attitude among the members of the uncommitted audience is usually, "OK, let's hear what you have to say. Convince me!" It is then your job to be convincing.

When you are interviewing for a job, employers will usually be impartial. They aren't taking sides; they want the best person for the job, whoever it might be. Similarly, a scholarship committee or a representative from a college you wish to attend will most likely be **unbiased**—free from favor toward one side or another. These interviewers want the best applicants to be rewarded and accepted; they have no reason to favor one student over another. With these audiences, you have the task of selling yourself, your talents, and your potential. Specific information—such as your past working experience, your current grade point average, your participation in extracurricular activities, and your community involvement—might provide the substance needed to bring your listeners over to your side.

Examples of uncommitted audiences can be found every day in courts of law. It's the defense lawyer's job to persuade the jury that the defendant is not guilty. The jury is, of course, supposed to remain uncommitted until all of the evidence is in and fairly weighed. Only then can a rational, just decision be reached. Similarly, you face a type of jury every time you speak in front of an uncommitted audience. You can often win your case if you present your position clearly and persuasively and support it with solid information.

The Indifferent Audience

With the **indifferent audience**, your job as a persuasive speaker gets a little tougher. This type of audience is difficult to adapt to because its members are apathetic toward you. While they aren't opposed to you, they can appear openly bored. Part of the problem is that the indifferent audience is often a **captive audience**—an audience that is being forced to attend. Often, the listeners don't believe that what you are saying is relevant to their personal situations.

Your job might be to jar the members of such an audience into paying attention to what you have to say, by offering a different approach. It is also your job to show them how your message applies to their lives. Information is important, but information alone is not enough.

For instance, a teacher was working with a group of students whose academic performance was less than noteworthy. The students kept telling him that their main objective was to get out of school, get a job, make some money, and buy a car. He couldn't persuade them to improve academically until he tried a new approach. The teacher brought in three business owners from the community who told the students what it took to get hired in the

INSTANT IMPACT

Eustressing Out

More and more corporations are being persuaded that they need more laughter in the workplace. Humor consultants have convinced employers that fun and games can be healing for their employees. For example, Gary Krane, author of *Simple Fun for Busy People*, suggests that employees spend five minutes of each workday "cackling like chickens, or meowing like kittens, or pairing off into thumb-hat wrestling matches, using those office coffee sugar packets." Krane also recommends having a secret handshake for your office, and bringing in a boom box to lift morale by playing Afro-Haitian music or a few polkas.

Syndicated columnist John Leo says that these humor advisers have evolved their own technical terms, including "eustress" (good stress), "psychoneuroimmunology," "humor quotients," and the peril of "TS" (terminal seriousness).

Like all *burgeoning* fields, Leo points out, the humor biz has also evolved trends and a number of statistics.

Loretta Laroche, a stress management and humor consultant who has appeared on PBS TV, once said that healthy people laugh some 100 to 400 times a day. Leo did the math on what this would mean. Yukking it up at this recommended peak capacity for 17 minutes a day would be awesome—24 times an hour, 384 times a day, 2,688 times a week, 139,776 times a year. Are you laughing *with* these humor consultants or *at* them?

current job market. The teacher also had a car salesperson come to the class. The salesperson went through an itemized analysis of how much money per week each student would have to make to buy a car and to pay for gas, insurance, and repairs. The students then understood that without basic academic skills, they couldn't get a job that would pay enough for them to buy what they were after. Things now made more sense to them. They saw a reason to try.

This particular approach won't work in every situation. You must put work to find an approach that will get the attention of the apathetic audience. Be dynamic in your approach, and show your listeners that what you are selling is important to them and directly affect their personal well-being.

The Opposed Audience

Be ready to handle a potential confrontation with the **opposed audience**. The members are hostile to you, to what you are promoting, or to both. Unlike the supportive audience, this type of audience feels no warmth for you and is in no way sympathetic to your feelings or your cause.

With the opposed audience, your objective should simply be to get a fair hearing. Try your best to determine specifically what your audience is hostile about: You? Your cause? A specific statement that you made?

When you have determined the reason for the hostility, work with the audience to put out that specific fire. It is often wise when addressing a hostile audience to show that you are willing to **compromise**, or make some concessions of your own. Let these listeners know that you see merit in some of their arguments and that you know you aren't perfect.

A student government representative was to address the student body of a rival school. When she was introduced, many of the students booed. However, her first words were these:

I'm not surprised at your reaction. May I share with you that I am currently scared to death!

Even though we might be adversaries on the basketball court, could we be friends at this assembly and meet each other halfway? Could we forget our differences and work together today? I respect so many things about your school. Today, I trust that we can talk with each other about how our respective schools operate. I also trust that one of you will catch me if I faint!

The audience laughed; the students were courteous throughout the remainder of the speech. The speaker had endeared herself to her audience through her personality and her sense of fair play.

Another way to gain favor with the hostile audience is to use a disclaimer. A **disclaimer** tells listeners what you are *not* saying or lets them know that you don't consider yourself an expert. This reduces the tendency the audience might have to overgeneralize your views. For example, if speaking to school officials about needing a skateboard area, you could say this:

Now I'm *not* saying that every time students have a concern the school should bow down and passively agree. I'm also *not* saying that I am the person who has all of the answers. However, I would appreciate it if you would listen . . .

You stand your best chance of getting a fair hearing from hostile listeners if you can do the following:

- Convince them that you know how they feel and you believe that their position has worth.
- Avoid needless confrontation.
- Create a situation in which there are no winners and losers.

You have now read about the four types of audiences that you might face in a persuasive speaking situation. You have also read advice on how to adapt to each. However, analyzing your audience is only the first part of your speaking task. Next we'll look at how to be an appealing persuasive speaker.

Recalling the Facts

1. Briefly describe the four different types of audiences.
2. No matter what type of audience you face, what is your primary purpose?
3. What tools beside the speech itself can help you win supporters in an audience?
4. How can a willingness to compromise help persuade an opposed audience?

Thinking Critically

1. List one real-life example in which you might have to adapt to (1) a supportive audience, (2) an uncommitted audience, (3) an indifferent audience, and (4) an opposed audience. Remember, an audience might be as small as one person. Now analyze the differences between audiences in real life.
2. How would you change the introduction to a speech if you suddenly discovered you were scheduled to speak to an opposed audience instead of a supportive audience?
3. What is the difference between an uncommitted audience and an indifferent audience?

Taking Charge

1. Choose a topic for a speech. Imagine that you will be giving this speech to two audiences, one supportive and one opposed. How will your style and tone change for the two audiences? Write a draft of the speech for each audience, paying attention to the level of detail you need for each and the organization that will best present your point of view.
2. Suppose you wanted to speak to the Board of Education in your town about the problem of students smoking cigarettes on school grounds. It is against school rules, but you feel the principal and teachers are not enforcing the rules. You want to persuade the board to make the administrators enforce the no-smoking rules. However, the principal and other administrators are among the people in the audience at the meeting. What can you do to prepare a speech that will persuade the board but not anger the principal and other teachers?

Appealing to Your Audience

The saying "love is blind" means that a couple in love tend to overlook each other's faults or weaknesses. The saying also suggests that people are attracted to others for a variety of reasons. Some of the reasons can be logically explained, and some can't. Often, we can't articulate why we are drawn to certain individuals or things—that is, why they appeal to us.

What exactly does the word *appeal* mean? Let's scrutinize it. *Appeal* has two different meanings. It can mean "an urgent request." It can also refer to what is attractive or interesting about someone or something. Everyone finds certain people, books, movies, automobiles, or music personally appealing. What about persuasive speakers? Must they too have appeal?

If your job is to convince others, it makes sense that you must present an appealing image and message. A persuasive speaker without appeal is like a race car driver without a car; both lack the vehicle needed to bring about success. How can you develop appeal as a speaker? How can you arouse a favorable response when addressing your audience?

In Chapter 1, you read about Aristotle and the art of persuasion. Aristotle, in his work *Rhetoric*, stated that the persuasive powers of speakers depend on their reasoning, the emotions that they can stir in their audience, and their character. In other words, speakers' success depends on their logical appeal, emotional appeal, and personal appeal. Each of these forms of appeal deserves a closer look.

Logical Appeal

Someone once said that each person's mind has its own logic but the mind seldom lets others in on that logic. As a persuasive speaker, you must definitely let others in on how your thoughts connect. Nothing can turn off listeners more quickly than a

speech that has them scratching their heads in bewilderment.

With a logical appeal, you appeal to the intellect of your audience by offering a clearly defined speech that contains solid reasoning and valid evidence. The logical appeal is also known by the Greek word **logos**. It satisfies the *analytical* side of your audience and says to your listeners, "I want this to make sense to you!" and "Do you see how all of this logically fits together?" You can promote your logical appeal by being organized and by offering proof to your audience.

Be Organized One way to enhance your logical appeal is by presenting a well-organized speech (the topic of Chapter 9). A student speaker was talking to a women's club about America's preoccupation with entertainment:

Persuasive speakers can often be successful by appealing to their audiences' sense of logic.

The way to the top these days lies with "putting on a show." However, in our quest for "ultimate entertainment," we've forgotten to look beyond the sizzle to see if what lies behind is truly worth supporting. As we examine this situation, three major areas seem apparent: (1) the entertainment industry, (2) our political system, and (3) education. Let's look at these areas individually …

Not only is the beginning of this speech well organized, but it is also easy to understand. It tells the audience specifically what the speaker's thesis is and what her three major areas of analysis will be.

A commentator on a television station was alarmed at the number of young adults who, because of financial hardships, were being forced to return home and live with their parents. The commentator said that more than 50 percent of all adults age 18 to 24 were living with their parents. She then gave three reasons why this might be occurring:

- lack of jobs
- layoffs
- problems paying back student loans for college

Her reasons were clearly stated and logically *palatable* to the audience. However, you can't merely *assert* that what you are saying is true. Audiences need proof.

Offer Proof Providing proof is another means of appealing to logic. As you read in Chapter 10, **proof** is specific evidence; proof is what establishes the truth of something. Furthermore, it is part of the supporting materials and details discussed in Chapter 9.

Suppose you are discussing art with a group of friends. Someone says that too much of what is considered art today is nothing but trash. That person objects to the National Endowment for the Arts giving "all of its money" to art that is considered obscene.

You could object by saying, "Oh, yeah, what do you know?" or "I suppose you could do better!" Neither response would persuade your friend to come over to your way of thinking, though. If instead you told him that even though some of what he says might have merit, he should consider that over the past 25 years, nearly 100,000 grants have been

A speech about our dependence on fossil fuels and their effect on the environment will probably have some elements of emotional appeal.

awarded by the NEA. Of those 100,000 grants, fewer than 20 have been considered controversial.

Do you see how these facts provide proof? Providing proof shows your listeners that you have intelligence, and intelligence is appealing.

Working to improve your logical appeal is a smart thing to do. However, logic by itself isn't always enough. You can also appeal to others emotionally.

Emotional Appeal

What do the following topics have in common?

- the homeless
- cruelty to animals
- nuclear power
- abused children
- senior citizens
- sex education in schools
- gun control
- victims of crime

Of course, it would be easy to find volumes of information on each topic and present numerous facts. However, all of these topics cause many people to react *instinctively* in an emotional manner and let their feelings show. As Aristotle reminds us, emotional appeal is a major consideration in persuasive speaking. Indeed, it often has a stronger impact on an audience than logic or reason. People would like to think that they make decisions based on reason. The truth, however, is that people tend to rely on their feelings at least as much as on their reasoning. They know that the car that gets 35 miles per gallon is the smart buy, but they may go with a sportier model with the sunroof instead.

If it is true that logical appeal aims for the brain, then emotional appeal aims for the heart. Emotional appeal, or **pathos,** involves appealing to people's feelings of love, anger, disgust, fear, compassion, patriotism, or the like. Notice, for example, the

intensity of William B. Travis as he tried to light a fire under the people of Texas and the United States while he was defending the Alamo against Mexican forces in 1836:

> Fellow citizens and compatriots: I am besieged by a thousand or more of the Mexicans under Santa Anna. I have sustained a continual bombardment and cannonade for 24 hours and have not lost a man. The enemy has demanded a surrender at discretion; otherwise the garrison are to be put to the sword if the fort is taken. I have answered the demand with a cannon shot, and our flag still waves proudly from the walls. *I shall never surrender nor retreat.* I call on you in the name of liberty, or patriotism, and everything dear to the American character, to come to our aid with all dispatch.

His words got the attention of the entire Texas territory and the United States, and even though the siege turned into a massacre, the phrase "Remember the Alamo!" became a battle cry in the struggle for Texan independence from Mexico. The words hit an emotional nerve and inspired people's patriotic spirit. Would logic have worked as well? Probably not.

The twentieth-century British prime minister Winston Churchill once said that "the human story does not always unfold like a mathematical calculation on the principle that two and two make four. Sometimes in life they make five or minus three." He was saying that life is not always logical. Often,

Teresa is annoyed by Andrew's lack of patience.

McGraw-Hill Education

Why was the phrase "Remember the Alamo" an appeal to people's emotions and not to their sense of logic?

it is the emotional, intangible world of our feelings that charts the real course of life.

All people have the potential for laughter, remorse, hopes, and dreams, and your ability to move them depends on stirring their emotions. Few people enjoy listening to uninterrupted evidence, long lists of facts, and cold, sterile statistics. They may enjoy listening, though, if that evidence is presented in a manner that excites or moves them. Read how one high school student used evidence to persuade her audience, but primarily emotional appeal, to persuade her audience of her view on one aspect of the Department of Defense's failure to follow documented procedures.

What could be more significant than thousands of human lives? Evidently the Defense Department shirked its responsibility and accepted aircraft from Lockheed Martin's Marietta plant with defective engines and other "non-conforming" parts and planes that were improperly serviced. Did you know that a recent independent report by the inspector general's office for the Defense Department said Lockheed used an increasing number of substandard parts and services that don't meet government specifications? Some problems included aircraft whose engines had known design defects or whose wiring systems did not match diagrams that the company had provided. Other problems

stemmed from the fact that the government gave Lockheed the authority to classify defects and assess whether they should be accepted, used "as-is," or repaired.

How could the government fail to verify that the aircraft conform to government specifications? Is carelessness and failure to follow documented procedures worth sacrificing lives?

Do you see her evidence? More importantly, do you feel her message? Do you see why her audience would probably be shocked and alarmed by this portion of her speech? She was saying to her audience, "Let's take action and demand that our government value people more than cutting corners!" She used evidence to help set the emotional tone that she was after.

Your tone refers to your vocal quality, but it also reflects your overall manner of nonverbal expression. Your attitude about your words as you deliver them contributes to your tone. The tone could be angry, considerate, hopeful, or optimistic, for example. The tone with which you deliver your words can have astounding impact. In 1938, Orson Welles's radio adaptation of H. G. Wells's novel *The*

Orson Welles shocked listeners across the United States with one radio program.

(t) Jill Stephenson/Alamy; (b) Ingram Publishing

Three Appeals in Persuasive Speech

Logical Appeal

The speaker offers an organized, clearly defined speech containing solid reasoning and valid evidence.

Emotional Appeal

The speaker's words arouse feelings in the audience, like anger, disgust, and compassion.

Personal Appeal

The speaker wins the audience's trust through honesty, competency, and credibility.

War of the Worlds caused a nationwide panic by dramatizing a supposed invasion from Mars and presenting it in the form of a newscast. His tone of urgency seemed so real that many listeners believed him and thought that space creatures had landed.

Even though the emotional appeal is aimed at stirring the emotions of your audience, keep in mind that your audience's reaction is often based on your emotional telegraphing. Telegraphing, which was mentioned in Chapter 12, means leading the way and showing your audience the emotion you wish them to feel by feeling it yourself. How is an audience supposed to feel sympathy or outrage if you aren't supplying an emotional example for them?

Let's examine a real-life story. It involves one woman's fight to have a stoplight erected at a busy intersection. The town board of her Midwestern community was initially opposed to supplying money for the stoplight. At a meeting of the board, town "experts" provided numerous facts and figures to show that the stoplight was not needed. Even though they agreed that cars traveled at high rates of speed through the area and that accidents had occurred, they also argued that few of the accidents were serious and that there had been only one fatality over a two-year period.

Then the woman spoke. She provided facts about the number of speeding tickets issued at the intersection by the police each month and about the number of people from a nearby subdivision who had to cross the intersection each day to get to a local shopping mall. Then she concluded her presentation by holding up a picture of a small child about eight years old. In a compassionate speech, she told her listeners that the child in the picture was that one traffic fatality. The woman was not the child's mother, but a friend of the family. She said that she didn't want the members of the board or any other members of the audience to experience the pain of losing a child. A stoplight, she pleaded, could help prevent that pain from becoming a reality.

The town board voted unanimously to erect the stoplight. Her emotional involvement set the tone for her persuasive message and helped turn the town board around. She turned foes into friends, partly by using a logical appeal, but even more by establishing a strong emotional bond between her and her audience. She cared about the stoplight, yes, but she also showed others that she cared about them and their welfare. Showing the audience that you have their interests in mind is a key component of Aristotle's final appeal, the personal appeal.

Personal Appeal

A famous Hollywood producer once said that he didn't know exactly what talent was but he knew it when he saw it. Personal appeal is much like talent in that people know when someone has it, and they know when someone doesn't have it. If you have personal appeal, or **ethos,** your listeners will tend to buy what you are selling, because they sense your credibility—your believability. Donald Queener, a nationally recognized speech and debate educator who has coached scores of interpretation and oratory champions, says that of all the appeals, personal appeal is the most desirable and the most effective because it can be immediate. It can work with an audience instantaneously.

If you have personal appeal, your listeners trust you. You come across as having their best interests at heart, and your **goodwill** proves that you care about them and about worthwhile issues. Even though being well liked is important for the effective speaker, congeniality is not what Aristotle was stressing in his use of the term *personal appeal*. Each day, the news is full of stories about smiling, friendly swindlers who dupe unsuspecting victims. Instead, Aristotle focused on two essential elements, which he believed formed the backbone of personal appeal: honesty and competency.

Honesty People are attracted to honesty. If you are honest, you tell the truth and exhibit personal **integrity,** or a strong sense of right and wrong. Your audience believes what you have to say because your **reputation**—how you are known by others—proves that you are a person of your word and therefore someone to be taken seriously. Honesty has appeal for two reasons. It shows others that you will be an example of what you say—that you will practice what you preach. It also reveals that you are a person of **sincerity,** of genuineness, and that you mean what you say and speak from your heart.

Don't think that appealing to an audience through honesty is limited to interpersonal communication or large audiences. Sometimes you can be your own audience. Chapter 1 used the term *intrapersonal communication* for these situations. Intrapersonal communication involves the talks that you have with yourself. Often, you can persuade yourself to take a particular course of action based on your own honesty and your personal character. You might make a crucial decision based on believing that honesty is the best policy, and you'll feel good about your decision. In other words, honesty can direct your decision making and actually encourage you to appeal to yourself.

A group of more than 400 actors, writers, and agents known as Young Artists United wanted to change the world. Using the motto "It's Cool to Care," they spoke at high schools on the dangers of drug and alcohol abuse. They also spent time painting orphanages and funding teen runaway centers. The actor Michael J. Fox said that he got involved in the group because he wanted to give something back to a world that had given him so much. When Fox spoke at one Los Angeles school, a student responded this way:

> I really listened to what this guy said today, and it made me think about what I'm doing with my life. I hear that he does this kind of stuff for kids all the time. He acts as if he really cares, you know, really wants the best for us

In the example above, Michael J. Fox, representing many others who feel the same way, used his personal appeal—his reputation and his honesty—to appeal to students to do what's right. He told them, "If you don't do drugs, continue to stay away from them," and "If you are involved with drugs, take action and change the course of your life before it is too late!" This is a good example for all of us to follow. Clearly, honesty can do more than make us appealing speakers; it can also help us contribute to changing people's lives.

Aristotle, on the left, believed that honesty and competency link a speaker with the audience.

Your competency in the lab could allow you to speak comfortably on scientific topics.

Competency The second essential element of Aristotle's personal appeal is competency. **Competency** means "capability." If you are a competent person, you can get the job done. You probably have a solid work ethic, and you value being prepared.

People known to be competent often have impressive **credentials,** or qualifications. These might include an extensive education, a number of outstanding achievements, or a long list of successes in a particular field. Indeed, many people equate competency with hard work and expertise in a particular field. They are impressed by the person who can offer a clear, focused stance on a topic because of such expertise. Special expertise enables such a person to speak with confidence and composure.

A somewhat different kind of expertise is the knack of dealing with people. Have you ever heard someone called a "people person"—someone who naturally gets along with everyone? If you are a people person, you stand an excellent chance of convincing your listeners to agree with you, because you too present your message with confidence and composure.

Speaking with **composure**—speaking in a calm, controlled manner—telegraphs to your audience that you feel in charge of the situation. The competent speaker adheres to the saying, "Never let 'em see you sweat!" After all, few listeners will be willing to count on a person who rattles easily or chokes when the pressure is on. Remember, if your listeners don't believe that they can count on you, then they probably won't be persuaded by you, either.

Providing clear examples for Aristotle's concept of personal appeal is difficult, because much of the persuasive power of this appeal comes from a form of internal energy that doesn't translate well to the printed page. However, one example might illustrate this quality. Read out loud the words of Thomas Jefferson, delivered on March 4, 1801, at the first presidential inaugural address in Washington, D.C. Notice the tone that he establishes and how he attempts to persuade the people of a young nation to aid and support him during his presidency:

> I shall often go wrong through defect of judgment. When right, I shall often be thought wrong by those whose positions will not command a view of the whole ground. I ask your indulgence for my own errors, which will never be intentional…
> Relying, then, on the patronage of your good will, I advance with obedience to the work.

Jefferson's words exemplify how honesty and competency can work hand in hand to produce a feeling of confidence. "We're all in this together," he seems to say. "We can work as a team to achieve success."

You might be saying, "This isn't the era of Aristotle, and the year 1801 was a long time ago. How do I actually apply all of this to my own life and to today's world?" Maybe the following example will help.

United Approach

A group of students from Apple Valley High School in Minnesota—under the direction of award-winning speech coach, debate coach, and teacher Pamela Cady—was asked this question: "If you had just gotten your driver's license, what would you say to your parents to persuade them to allow you to drive the family's brand-new car?"

At first, the students responded with short, one-sentence answers, including, "I'd cry, stomp my feet, and scream, 'Please!'" However, after they had studied this chapter, they compiled a much more thorough list, utilizing all three of Aristotle's forms of appeal. What do you think of these persuasive ideas?

The following represent logical appeals:

- "Wouldn't my driving be more convenient than your having to drive me everywhere?"
- "I could help you with the errands!"
- "There would be less chaos at home, with people rushing to drive everyone everywhere."
- "I could learn how to follow directions."
- "I have done well in Driver's Education. The school and state believe that I am a good driver."
- "I have checked it out, and the insurance would not go up much."
- "The new car would be less likely to have engine problems."
- "I'll pay for my own gas and insurance, plus I will keep the car clean."
- "I'll be sure to call you when I get where I am going."

The following represent emotional appeals:

- "When you were a kid, didn't you want to be given some responsibility, too?"
- "Will you consider my driving if I only ask on special occasions? You know how special some things can be, don't you?"
- "If I'm driving, you don't have to worry about my being in a car where the driver has been drinking."
- "I would feel so proud for others to see me in our new car!"
- "If I thought you didn't trust me, I would never ask."
- "How would you feel if you were always having to bum a ride with other people?"
- "I would love the responsibility!"
- "I know that you worry about me, so out of respect for you, I would be extra careful."
- "I would love you guys so much!"
- "This would really enhance my self-esteem."
- "Think what this could do for our communication. We would talk more and understand each other better!"

The following represent personal appeals:

- "I promise to always tell you the truth about where I am going."
- "I don't feel that it is right that my friends always have to drive."
- "Since my sister was allowed to drive a nice car when she first got her license, I think that this would be the fair thing to do, don't you?"
- "Please don't judge me before I have had a chance to prove to you that I can handle this."

If you want someone to buy you a car, you should use all three forms of appeal—logical, emotional, and personal.

COMMUNICATION *BREAKTHROUGH*

The Kennedy-Nixon Debate of 1960

The following account shows how a communication breakdown and a communication breakdown occurred simultaneously during one of the most famous debates in American history.

On September 26, 1960, technology brought to the U.S. public the first of four televised debates between the Republican presidential nominee, Richard M. Nixon, and the Democratic presidential nominee, John F. Kennedy. Nixon and Kennedy would come together, face to face, to be evaluated by more than 70 million viewers. Each candidate was trying to persuade the nation that he was the person to lead the country. Before the first debate, Nixon was the front-runner in the polls; Kennedy was a distant second. However, after the first debate, Kennedy made a significant breakthrough by means of an amazing appeal— an almost immediate bond that he formed with television viewers. Nixon lost ground.

John F. Kennedy came to Chicago, the site of the first debate, organized and prepared. He was aware of pertinent information regarding domestic policy and was ready to discuss it. When Kennedy arrived at the studio before the airing of the live debate, he was wearing a dark gray suit and a white shirt. However, he noticed that the lights shining on the white shirt caused a glare. Consequently, he had a staff member dash back to his hotel room and get a blue shirt.

Nixon, on the other hand, had been ill; thus, his complexion was pasty, and he had dark circles under his eyes. Arriving with just a little time to spare, he wasn't aware of how his light-colored suit and his white shirt faded into the background when hit by the studio lights. To make matters worse, even though Nixon wore makeup to cover his five o'clock shadow, it didn't prevent the camera from picking up the sweat as it ran down his face.

What was the result? Kennedy came across as having more appeal. Even though Richard M. Nixon was a skilled debater and handled himself admirably in addressing the issues (radio listeners called it a draw), he failed to persuade the voters who watched that he was the more capable presidential candidate. He had lost the "impact of images" battle. When Kennedy spoke, he was calm, controlled, and energetic; he spoke to America as a man with a vision. When Nixon spoke, he appeared tense, almost frightened; and instead of speaking to America, he spoke to Kennedy. Nixon was in the midst of a communication breakdown. He appeared to lack the power and the imagination of his political counterpart.

As one observer said, "Every time that the two men were close together for the nation to see, Kennedy would win a little and Nixon would lose a little." The outcome: Kennedy defeated Nixon for the presidency in one of the closest elections in U.S. history.

Questions

1. Which form of appeal do you think Kennedy used most effectively?
2. Where do you think Nixon made his mistake(s)?

- "I would like to show you that I can be as disciplined with a car as I have been with my life."
- "I give you my word that I will be a good and responsible driver."

Some of the statements could fit into more than one category, couldn't they? The sophomore students, after discussing their ideas, decided that using a united approach—using two or three of the forms of appeal—would give them a better chance for success than a one-dimensional approach. One student noted that her mother and father would require different approaches. She decided that her mother would need to be approached with logic, while her father would probably relate better to the emotional argument. Does this sound familiar? As you can see, you can persuade more effectively when you intelligently use Aristotle's three forms of appeal.

Persuasive speaking is not easy to explain. So many human factors go into what makes a person convincing that it is difficult to offer a real-world prescription for success. Often, you will have to develop the ability to read your audience and to use in the same persuasive speech all that this chapter has presented. This won't be an easy task.

However, don't believe that good persuasive speakers are simply born with talent—that either you have it or you don't. There is a step you can take that will help you become the convincing speaker you wish to be. What is that step?

As the saying goes, the world is made up of three groups: those who watch things happen, those who make things happen, and those who wonder, "What just happened?" Be a person who makes things happen. Join the movers and shakers of the oral communication world. Work to understand what persuasive speaking is, who your audience is, and how Aristotle's forms of appeal can work to your advantage. Then you will have an excellent opportunity to convince others to accept your ideas, motivate others to act, and, yes—as the teacher explained at the beginning of the chapter—persuade someone to buy the car!

SECTION 3 REVIEW

Recalling the Facts

1. According to Aristotle, what are the three forms of appeal? Briefly explain.
2. Which two elements form the backbone of personal appeal? Why?

Thinking Critically

Here is your dilemma: You are running for a class office against a very popular student. You are not the best-looking person in your class, but you are a hard worker, and you care about excellence. One of your biggest obstacles is that you are brand-new to the school, having only been there for one month. At your previous school, you made good grades and were well liked and respected by students and the faculty. Prepare an extensive list—like the sophomores' list of arguments for driving the family car—giving all the logical, emotional, and personal arguments that you could use to appeal to the student body to vote for you.

Taking Charge

Keep a journal for at least one day. In it, write about all the times that you had to use persuasive speaking that day. You might have asked someone out on a date. You might have pleaded with your younger brother or sister to do one of your chores at home. Keep close track of when persuasive speaking is a part of your communication life, regardless of how small that part is. Next, note which form or forms of appeal—logical, emotional, or personal—seemed to work best for you and explain why you think so.

Looking Back

Listed below are the major ideas discussed in this chapter.

- Persuasive speaking involves your ability to convince your audience to believe as you do.
- Persuasive speaking means that you are trying to "sell" a product, an idea, or an attitude.
- To become an effective persuasive speaker, you must keep in mind that people react on the basis of what they want, how they think, and how they feel.
- Audience analysis occurs before you speak and is your estimation of how your audience feels about you and your verbal message.
- Audiences are often divided into these types: supportive, uncommitted, indifferent, and opposed.
- The supportive audience likes you and what you are saying.
- The uncommitted audience hasn't made up its mind about you or your message.
- The indifferent audience can take you or leave you; you need to persuade this group that what you are saying has relevance and practical application.
- The opposed audience doesn't like you or what you have to say.

- Audiences are often combinations of these four categories. You must make adjustments to deal with each type.
- For the persuasive speaker, the word *appeal* refers to what makes someone attractive or interesting to an audience.
- Persuasive powers depend on logical appeal, emotional appeal, and personal appeal.
- Logical appeal (logos) attracts an audience with an analytical, reason-based approach.
- Emotional appeal (pathos) hits the heart of the audience and stirs feelings of love, anger, compassion, patriotism, togetherness, or the like.
- Personal appeal (ethos) links the speaker with the audience because of the speaker's honesty and competency.
- The best persuasive speaking often results from combining the various forms of appeal appropriately for a given audience.

Speech Vocabulary

1. For each speech vocabulary word, find the definition as given in the text, along with the page number where you found the definition. Write an original sentence for each word to show the word in action. Select the five speech vocabulary words that are most important to you. Explain why you made these choices and how these words can assist you as a persuasive speaker.

2. Prepare a quiz on a sheet of paper. On the left side, list fifteen of the speech vocabulary words (number them 1–15). Leave out a few letters from each word. For example, you might write *per___si_e s_eaki_g* for *persuasive speaking*. The person taking your quiz must fill in the missing letters to spell each word. Next, on the right side of your paper, list (in mixed order) the

definitions for your 15 words and letter them from *a* through *o*. The person taking the quiz must place the letter of the correct definition beside each speech vocabulary word. Prepare an answer key ahead of time.

persuasive speaking	proof
supportive audience	pathos
uncommitted audience	ethos
unbiased	goodwill
indifferent audience	integrity
captive audience	reputation
opposed audience	sincerity
compromise	competency
disclaimer	credentials
logos	composure

Academic Vocabulary

1. Use the dictionary to define each of the academic vocabulary words. Dictate each word to a classmate to work on the spelling. Next, read the definition of each general vocabulary word out loud, and have your classmate tell you the word that matches the definition.
2. Write an original one-page story titled "The Day I Made My First Sale." Decide what you are selling. Are you going to sell a product? Are you going to try to convince someone that your idea is a good one? Use and underline at least five of the general vocabulary words in your story.

temperament	palatable
cognizant	assert
burgeoning	instinctively
analytical	

To Remember

Answer the following based on your reading of the chapter.

1. In a persuasive speech, what are some of the things you might be selling?
2. What are the characteristics of a skilled speaker according to the ancient Roman orator Cicero?
3. A jury is an example of what kind of audience?
4. If an audience opposes your ideas, what might you do?
5. Why is proof so important in persuasion?

To Do

1. Go to the library and find additional material about the Kennedy-Nixon debates. What are some specific things that were said in the first debate? In the other three debates? Prepare a report detailing your findings. You may be able to find recordings of the debates. If you can, listen to the persuasive techniques. List the pros and cons of the persuasive speaking of each. Identify and list the persuasive strategies that each speaker uses.
2. Interview someone in sales and find out how he or she "reads" an audience and how he or she deals with an opposed audience. Finally, find out what the salesperson thinks about the three forms of appeal—logical, emotional, and personal. Which works best for the salesperson? Do the three often work together? Get detailed answers and examples.
3. Make a chart describing the appeals used in at least six commercials that you see on television (you might also include radio advertisements or billboards). In one column, list the name of the product or service being advertised. In the second column, name the type of appeal (or combination of appeals) being used: logical, emotional, or personal. Finally, give a quotation (exact words) from the advertisement that proves your point. At the bottom, state which appeal you think is the most persuasive and why.

To Talk About

1. The writer Johann Goethe said, "He who wishes to exert a useful influence must be careful to insult nothing." What do you think he meant? Should Goethe's advice always be followed? Can you think of an exception?

2. A national survey of more than 270,000 high school students was conducted. The survey concluded that student boredom results from (1) unvarying routine in the school day, (2) uninspiring subject matter, (3) unimaginative teaching, and (4) failure to make a connection between what students are expected to learn and real life. Which of these four would you put first? Explain. Are the teachers the only ones to blame? How can students, parents, the community, teachers, and school administrators all use aspects of persuasive speaking to help remedy the negative perceptions? Remember to consider intrapersonal as well as interpersonal communication skills.

To Write About

1. One important ingredient of personal appeal is reputation, or how you are known to others and what they think of you. Why could your reputation significantly affect your persuasiveness? Write a one-page paper on how a positive reputation could enhance your persuasiveness.

2. In speaking, you compromise by finding a workable middle ground that is acceptable to both you and your audience. Write three reasons why compromising is a wise idea for those trying to persuade others. Give specifics to show when compromising could help you to persuade your parents and your friends. Finally, when is compromising the wrong thing to do?

Related Speech Topics

Persuade your audience of the following:

Dogs are better pets than cats (or change pets).

Year-round school is a bad (or good) idea.

A school dress code is a good (or bad) idea.

Students should have a voice (or no voice) in how their school is run.

Classroom tests are helpful (or not helpful).

Discipline is needed (or not needed) in your life.

The group is more important than the individual in a society (or vice versa).

Reputation is more important than accomplishments or awards (or vice versa).

Now go to the library or get on the Internet and do some research on one or more of the following topics:

Nuclear weapons

The homeless

Scientific experimentation on animals

Capital punishment

The prison system

Smoking

Drunk drivers

Instant replay in sports

Women's rights

Censorship

CHAPTER 15

EXTEMPORANEOUS AND IMPROMPTU SPEAKING

Extemp is life.

—Austan Goolsbee, Professor of Economics, University of Chicago

Learning Objectives

After completing this chapter, you will be able to do the following.

- Define both extemporaneous speaking and impromptu speaking.
- Describe the differences between extemporaneous speaking and impromptu speaking.
- Deliver an extemporaneous speech.
- Deliver an impromptu speech.

Chapter Outline

Following are the main sections in this chapter.

1. Extemporaneous Speaking
2. Impromptu Speaking

Speech Vocabulary

In this chapter, you will learn the meanings of the speech terms listed below.

impromptu
extemporaneous
conversational
  quality
foreshadowing
justification

compelling insight
topic-specific
label
analysis
zinger

Academic Vocabulary

Expanding your academic vocabulary will help you become a more effective communicator. Listed below are some words appearing in this chapter that you should make part of your vocabulary.

faltering
fiasco
prescriptive

qualms
erudite
insinuated

Introduction

Have you ever found yourself chuckling as you listened to a friend mumble and stumble through an oral presentation in class? You really didn't want to hurt your friend's feelings by laughing, but in the immortal words of Homer Simpson, it was funny because it wasn't happening to you.

But wait. What happened when your turn came to speak? How did you do? The situation probably wasn't so funny after all when *you* had to get up in front of the class.

In this chapter, you will learn more about taking your turn with the two most common forms of speaking: extemporaneous and impromptu.

Mastering these two common forms of speech will help you feel more comfortable thinking and speaking on your feet. You will learn how to organize your thoughts and prepare your speeches. Furthermore, you will be better able to say what you mean.

Practicing and preparing for a speech are both excellent ways to avoid embarrassing yourself in front of an audience.

Extemporaneous Speaking

Although some people believe that extemporaneous speaking is the same as impromptu speaking, there are differences. An **impromptu** speech is generally defined as talking with little or no preparation. Speaking with minimal preparation is sometimes described as talking off-the-cuff. An **extemporaneous** speech, by contrast, is a presentation that is carefully prepared and practiced in advance. When delivering a speech extemporaneously, you rely on notes or on an outline. Your notes should contain key words or phrases to remind you of the important ideas. Using an outline has two advantages: (1) it will jog your memory and remind you of where you are in the speech, and (2) it allows you to adjust the length of your speech because you can add or drop information as you adapt to an audience's reaction.

Furthermore, you can make last-minute notes on your outline if you become aware of the needs of a particular audience. This flexibility allows you to use essentially the same speech for different audiences. Additionally, an outline can save preparation time and provide better organization than is possible in an impromptu speech. Finally, you will have more control over your thoughts and your use of language.

Developing a Natural Style

The key to effective extemporaneous speaking is to develop a co nversational quality. When you speak with a **conversational quality,** you sound spontaneous to the audience. You don't want to sound over-rehearsed, as if you are reciting from rote memory. Sounding as if you are reciting rather than sounding conversational makes you seem mechanical or stiff. Worst of all, mechanical recitation becomes boring. You need, instead, to develop a conversational style of speaking. And you need to establish the strong eye contact that can only come from not being tied to your notes. In short, to look natural you must practice looking as if you haven't

been practicing. After all, the most accomplished actors never appear to be acting. They seem natural, spontaneous, real. And so should you.

Preparing for Competition

Now that you know the basics of extemporaneous speaking, you may want to take your act on the road. Many students polish their skills by participating in interscholastic competition. Your teacher can explain how you can become involved in these contests. Not only will you learn, but you will have a lot of fun as well.

"Extemp," as it is known, requires that you analyze a current topic and prepare a speech on that topic within 30 minutes. Usually you must then deliver your speech in less than seven minutes. Generally, you draw three topics from an envelope

Political campaigners must be ready to speak extemporaneously on almost any subject.

McGraw-Hill Education

and choose one for your speech. Topics, ordinarily in question form, include such issues as these:

- How can we fight teen drug abuse?
- What is the future of the Middle East?
- Should the U.S. government provide a national health care system?

Once you have selected a topic, you refer to files of collected newspaper and magazine articles that you have brought to the tournament. During your speech, you quote from articles to help support your answer to the question. The challenge is to organize your thoughts and present them in a clear and meaningful way in only 5 to 7 minutes. Some tournaments allow you to use one note card; others do not. Judges evaluate how well you answer the question you have chosen. What follows on the next three pages is a sample extemporaneous speech by Jeremy Mallory on the topic "Should Prozac Be Banned?" Prozac's introduction to the U.S. market in the 1980s caused some controversy because of its possible side effects and because some people thought it could be prescribed as a way to "fix" someone's personality. This is a transcript of the speech Mallory delivered to win first place in the final round of the Catholic Forensic League Grand National Tournament. Study this example to learn one way you can organize a contest speech. Remember, though, that the opinions expressed are those of the speaker; the speech is not intended to be an endorsement for Prozac or any other drug.

Extemporaneous Contests

Extemp speech contests require competitors to think quickly and organize and present their thoughts in a clear and meaningful way. Use the following tips to improve your extemp speech skills and ability.

- Use old speeches, or pick a topic out of the newspaper, to practice before a competition. Focus on **foreshadowing** during one practice. Then, work on the wording of the **justification** in another. Finally, work on having a strong delivery and using gestures to help engage the audience.
- Select a topic that you like. Draw from experiences and information that you are knowledgeable about and that you want to share with others.
- Quickly organize your thoughts into an outline. Focus on a limited and specific purpose, and be succinct and to the point.
- Be creative. Avoid using the same introduction over and over. Keep the speech interesting and relevant for the audience and topic.
- Choose a *prescriptive* topic that requires you to prescribe, or set down, specific policy suggestions. It may be more challenging, but speaking on a prescriptive topic is more likely to impress a judge.

Analysis	Speech

Analysis

An introduction with a **compelling insight** tells listeners something they don't know and something they are likely to find interesting. Please note how the discussion of risk introduces the idea of evaluating the risks of Prozac later. When you directly connect your introduction to the remainder of the speech, the introduction is **topic-specific.**

The justification step explains the importance of the topic you are discussing. You need to justify for the audience why they should care. Furthermore, you should make a smooth transition from the introduction to the statement of the question to be answered.

Make certain that you state the question exactly. It is your responsibility to answer this question accurately and completely.

The answer to the question is the equivalent of the thesis in an essay. As you remember, the thesis is the central idea or message in either an essay or a speech. You answer the question immediately so that your arguments will follow directly from that answer.

This is the foreshadowing step. Foreshadowing simply means that you are providing a map to the rest of the speech. This listing of what is to come in the body of the speech is sometimes called partitioning, forecasting, signposting, or mapping.

At this point, you need to return to the first issue that you foreshadowed. Avoid saying tired phrases like "Now let's go back to the first issue." You also indicate how many subpoints will be discussed under this issue.

Speech

In an article entitled "Boo! You're Dead!" several Harvard professors tried to figure out what it would take to raise your chance of death by one-millionth: smoking 1.4 cigarettes, drinking a half liter of wine, staying in a coal mine for three hours, spending six minutes in a canoe, drinking Miami tap water for one year, or staying in New York for two days.

Some amount of risk accompanies anything we do, but that doesn't stop us from trying to avoid the big ones. We try to weigh the benefits against the risks to see if that two-day stint in New York City is really worth it. Recently, a drug called Prozac hit the market, then hit the magazine stands on the cover of *Newsweek*, a feat rarely accomplished by a pharmaceutical. People were excited because it was billed as one of the likely cures for depression. Others dismissed it as a modern snake oil. Still others found dangerous side effects.

Now we need to figure out whether Prozac is a miracle drug or medical disaster, and ask ourselves the question: "Should Prozac be banned?"

The answer to that question is that Prozac should not be banned.

On one hand, the risks are small, and on the other hand, the possible benefits outweigh the risks.

So what do Prozac's critics think the drug can do to you? What risks do you take by using the drug? Most critics agree on three potential harms.

Continued on following page

Analysis	Speech

Analysis

"Schizophrenia" is the **label** for the first subpoint under the first major issue. The label is the brief explanation of what you are about to discuss. Labels should be short and memorable.

The information from the *New York Times* is evidence that supports your argument. The "talking to the walls" comment is an inside joke about the way that students prepare for competition.

This is the second subpoint under the first major issue. Note that following the label "does not help everyone," the speaker offers more evidence. The discussion of how "no drug works for everyone" is **analysis**. Analysis is a detailed examination of the information at hand.

The third subpoint begins here. Again, the speaker provides a label, analysis, and evidence to support his thesis.

This is a summary statement that refers to the entire first major issue.

The transition into the second major issue mentions what went before and foreshadows what is coming next.

Speech

The first potential harm is schizophrenia. Studies documented in the *New York Times* show that 12 out of 1,000 patients using Prozac develop schizophrenia. Given the number of people talking to the walls in the prep room for this event, this seems like a small risk indeed.

The second potential harm is that Prozac does not help everyone. Some who take Prozac may expect the drug to work and have their hopes dashed when it doesn't, which may worsen their depression. But, as the *Christian Science Monitor* points out, "no drug is a panacea except chicken soup, of course." No drug works for everyone. And the easiest cure for high expectations is to lower them—then people won't be disappointed if Prozac fails for them.

The third, and perhaps the most frightening, potential harm is addiction. Whether or not the drug works, people might come to depend on Prozac for their happiness, and since the pills are relatively expensive, that could be a costly prospect. The *Wall Street Journal* argues, however, that any drug can become addictive. The *Wall Street Journal* explains that true addiction, actual physical need, is fairly rare and that physicians can stop prescribing Prozac for patients who merely have a psychological need for it.

The risks, then, all things considered, are really quite low.

But what about the benefits? Even a small risk is not worth taking if no benefit can come from it. I'm sure none of us would cross the street in New York unless there was some very good reason to do so. In the case of Prozac, there are two important benefits.

Analysis	**Speech**

Here is the beginning of the first subpoint of the second major issue. Again, you will find a label, analysis, and evidence.

The second subpoint also features a label, analysis, and evidence. Since this is the last subpoint, it should be your strongest argument. Save the best for last.

Quoting Shakespeare in this context shows the speaker's ability to make connections. Hamlet's observation about the nature of perception could be applied to many topics. General Hamlet, for example, might argue that it is difficult to win a war without people's perception that the conflict is justified. Professor Hamlet might argue that people must think that teacher pay raises are necessary for those raises to happen.

This transition leads into the conclusion of the speech. Avoid saying "In conclusion" or other such obvious statements. If you say "final analysis," it implies that you actually had analysis earlier. Be sure to restate the question and your answer. Also, summarize the major issues briefly as the speaker does.

This is the zinger. A **zinger** is a concluding statement that is a powerful reminder of the rightness of your position. The audience will remember best what you say last.

The first, and most obvious, is that it can cure depression. The *Washington Post* estimates that about 20 percent of the people who take Prozac are cured of their depression. For somebody suffering from this incapacitating mental disorder, this is a significant benefit worth considering.

The second major benefit is the so-called placebo effect. Even if the drug has no actual physiological effect, the *New York Times* reports a high number of people who pull out of depression anyway. Some cases of depression, especially those caused by a lack of confidence, can cure themselves if the people believe they should be cured.

Doctor Hamlet would agree: "There is nothing either good or bad but thinking makes it so." The *Times* even notes cases of people who were actually taking sugar pills and who were cured, literally, by the name of the drug. This may not say much for the honesty of Prozac's manufacturers, but if the depression is lifted, even if it be the name that lifts it, Prozac has proven its benefits to outweigh the risks.

So in final analysis, Prozac should not be banned. The small risks of harm are outweighed by the significant potential benefits. Whether or not you want to subject yourself to this particular risk, like that six-minute canoe trip, it must be your decision. You must weigh the risk of harm against each potential benefit each time.

If you do not, you may come to understand the words of philosopher Bertrand Russell all too well: "Some people would die sooner than think. In fact, they do."

SECTION 1 REVIEW

Recalling the Facts

1. What is the difference between extemporaneous speaking and impromptu speaking?
2. How much time do you have to prepare a speech in an extemporaneous competition?
3. How much time do you have to give you speech in an extemporaneous competition?
4. What is a prescriptive topic in an extemporaneous speech?
5. Why do you want to develop a conversational style of delivery?

Thinking Critically

1. Many speakers begin their presentations with a joke. Why might an introduction with a compelling insight be a safer strategy than a humorous introduction?
2. Why would a political candidate have to be a good extemporaneous speaker at a debate with other candidates?

3. Is a basketball coach who speaks to her players at halftime to get them excited about the second half of the game giving an extemporaneous speech or an impromptu speech?

Taking Charge

1. Find the text of a speech from a source such as *Vital Speeches*. Outline a brief section of the speech. Working from this outline, deliver the ideas extemporaneously in your own words. Ad-lib as much as possible. Record your best practice speeches for review and critique.
2. Suppose you are at a extemporaneous competition. You are given the topic: Should the United States have a national service requirement for all high school graduates? Briefly explain how you would prepare for the speech. Where would you look for information? What kind of introduction would you use? Would humor be appropriate for a speech on this subject?

Impromptu Speaking

Although you may frequently be asked—often to your surprise and dismay—to speak impromptu on almost any occasion, you have actually been preparing for such situations all of your life. You may not be as prepared as you would like, but you have a lifetime of experience from which to draw. The effective speaker selects appropriate supporting materials from memory, organizes them into an easy-to-follow pattern, and delivers them confidently. In other words, you learn how to think on your feet.

Keep It Simple

Since impromptu speeches are generally brief, simplicity is essential. You should establish a single point of view, choose one or two clear examples or illustrations, and conclude with a short summary and restatement of your main idea. If you have more than a few minutes for your impromptu presentation, you should divide the body of your speech into two or three issues and develop each one with supporting materials. Like all speeches, your impromptu presentation should have a definite beginning, middle, and end.

A typical organizational pattern for a brief impromptu speech might include the following:

1. Statement of the main point of your presentation. A short introduction to the main idea can be effective if you have the time (and an idea).
2. Support of the main idea with appropriate reasons, examples, illustrations, statistics, and testimony. Ordinarily, you should rely on your first thoughts, because if you struggle to generate more information, you may forget your initial ideas.
3. Conclusion with a summary and a restatement of the main idea. Be brief; needless repetition is boring and reduces your credibility as a speaker.

If you are called on in a business meeting and have nothing to say, the worst thing you can do is to apologize. Rather than admitting you're unprepared, take a deep breath, and say something like "I will look into this issue and get back to you."

Business and civic meetings will test your ability to organize impromptu speeches properly.

PhotoAlto/SuperStock

Nelson Mandela would be an ideal choice for a people/places/events impromptu presentation.

Generally there are three types of impromptu topics: (1) *words*, such as *orange, love, greed*, and *happiness*; (2) *quotations*, such as "The only thing we have to fear is fear itself," or "A bird in the hand is worth two in the bush"; (3) *people/places/events*, such as Nelson Mandela or the Vietnam Veterans Memorial or Hurricane Katrina.

Remember, though, that the key is to practice. Only through practice can you begin to feel comfortable with the pressure of such limited time to prepare. Also, through practice you will become more skilled at connecting what you know to the precise wording of the topic. Of course, increasing what you know by reading more and discussing more would be advisable as well.

To help you with your first competitive impromptu speech, here is a student example on the topic of elephants. Study the comments that accompany the speech on the following pages to learn one effective way that you can organize an impromptu speech.

Don't Panic

Similarly, the worst mistake you can make in an impromptu speech is to panic. Panic usually results in uneasy silence or unnecessary rambling. As a prospective impromptu speaker, you should minimize your concerns by reading widely and by being a good observer and listener. Remember, too, that your audience is aware that you're speaking off-the-cuff and will adjust its expectations accordingly. Most audience members will respond positively if they sense you're trying to incorporate your knowledge into a clear and meaningful presentation.

Getting Ready to Compete

As with extemporaneous speaking, you can polish your impromptu skills through competition. The rules for impromptu speaking, though, vary greatly from contest to contest. The National Forensic League, for example, allows each student five minutes for preparation and then another five minutes to present the speech. At the college level, the American Forensic Association allows a total of seven minutes for both preparation and speaking; the speaker may choose how to divide those minutes.

INSTANT IMPACT

Be a Cabbage

A speaker at a club luncheon gave a tremendous talk and received a standing ovation. The president of the club was so impressed that he said to the speaker, "Everyone here is so enthused. Won't you please say a few more words, since we have ten minutes left of our regular time?"

The request challenged the speaker to draw on all of her impromptu skills. How would you have responded to this difficult situation? This speaker thought for a moment and said, "Once there was a little baby cabbage who said to his mother, 'Mommy, I'm worried about something. As I sit in this row of cabbages and grow and grow day after day, how will I know when to stop growing?' 'The rule to follow,' said the Momma cabbage, 'is to quit when you're a head.'"

Good advice for all of us.

DoD photo by R. D. Ward.

Analysis	Speech

Because you have limited time to come up with an introduction, you must search your memory for appropriate stories, examples, or illustrations. Your first thought should be to brainstorm everything you can think of that has some connection to elephants or whatever the topic happens to be. This brainstorming will not only generate an idea for an introduction but can also give you supporting material for the rest of the speech.

This transition connects the opening illustration with the thesis, or main idea of the speech.

This thesis statement is made more memorable because of the play on the word "mammoth."

Here the speaker explains what she will discuss in the rest of the speech. This is the "tell 'em what you're gonna tell 'em" step.

The first issue starts with a joke, but note that the speaker then turns to serious concerns. Raising the possibility of extinction gives importance to discussing this particular topic.

There is a story about six visually impaired men touching an elephant. One man feels the tail and says, "Oh, it's a rope." One comes in contact with a leg and thinks it's a tree. Another man grasps the ear and speculates that it's a fan or a leaf. Still another man walks along the side of the elephant and concludes that it's a mountain. But none of these men realizes that it's an elephant.

Although this story illustrates how we must see the whole of anything in order to understand it, it is also true that most of us, in fact, do not recognize the whole importance of the elephant.

I believe that we should not overlook the "mammoth" relevance of these pachyderms.

Let us consider their importance in two areas: the elephants themselves, and what the elephants can teach us about ourselves.

Each elephant makes a significant sacrifice for our benefit. Did you know that every time you munch a peanut butter sandwich, you are grabbing goobers out of the mouths of baby elephants?

On a more serious note, many people have boycotted the use of ivory in products. These people have expressed the concern that elephants are hunted down and destroyed just for their tusks. Furthermore, they have expressed the fear that elephants may become extinct someday as a result of people's greed.

Continued on following page

Analysis	Speech

Analysis

Here the speaker moves to the second issue. She begins discussing this issue by referring to a familiar children's story. If you can, you too should try to incorporate supporting material that has universal appeal.

This second lesson that we can learn from elephants simply adds further support to the argument. It also reminds the audience that one can learn interesting things by listening in class.

This brief conclusion refers back to the thesis and then ends with a strong last thought. You want the audience to "never forget" you either.

Speech

The selfish slaughter is even more depressing when we consider what elephants can teach us about ourselves. In one of Dr. Seuss's best-loved stories, Horton the elephant promises, "I meant what I said and I said what I meant, an elephant's faithful one-hundred percent." This faith, this commitment, is an important lesson for all of us.

But perhaps the elephant is most familiar to us as the symbol of the Republican Party. We learned in history class that the elephant as a symbol for Republicans came from the imagination of nineteenth-century cartoonist Thomas Nast. Let us not forget that teacher told us that the elephant was chosen because it is clever but not easily controlled—just like so many of us!

So we should be clever enough to remember these powerful pachyderms, for as we all know, the elephant never forgets.

SECTION 2 REVIEW

Recalling the Facts

Name the three elements in a typical impromptu speech's organizational pattern.

Thinking Critically

In *Silent Messages*, Albert Mehrabian argues that a speaker's facial and body language accounts for more than 50 percent of a listener's emotional response. About 40 percent of the response is triggered by nonverbal vocal qualities. The words themselves account for only 10 percent or less of the response. Why do you think that words matter so little?

Taking Charge

Everyone in class is to write three to five impromptu topics—each topic on a separate slip of paper. The slips are then collected, and each student draws three topics. Choose one topic on which to give an impromptu speech. Give yourself a minute to gather your thoughts. Deliver your speech in approximately two minutes.

Evaluate each student's speech to determine if it used the three elements of an impromptu speech outlined in this section.

Looking Back

Listed below are the major ideas discussed in this chapter.

- An impromptu speech is generally delivered off-the-cuff, while an extemporaneous speech is prepared and practiced in advance.
- The key to effective extemporaneous delivery is to develop a conversational quality.
- Extemporaneous speaking contests require that you analyze a current event topic and then prepare a speech on that topic within 30 minutes.
- An impromptu speech should establish a single point of view, choose one or two examples or illustrations, and conclude with a short summary and restatement of your main idea.
- The worst mistake you can make in an impromptu speech is to panic.

Speech Vocabulary

Using the following list, make flash cards. On one side of each card, print each new speech term. On the other side, write the definition. Keep track of the words that give you problems and eliminate the words you can handle.

impromptu	justification	analysis
extemporaneous	compelling insight	zinger
conversational quality	topic-specific	
foreshadowing	label	

Academic Vocabulary

Create a multiple-choice definition question with three options (a, b, and c) for each of the academic vocabulary words. Example: *Intensify* means (a) to weaken, (b) to strengthen, or (c) to enlarge.

faltering	prescriptive	erudite
fiasco	qualms	insinuated

To Remember

Answer the following based on your reading of the chapter.

1. What is the purpose of the justification step in an extemporaneous speech?
2. What makes a zinger important?
3. What are the advantages of a speech outline?
4. A typical impromptu speech would follow what organizational pattern?

To Do

1. Prepare an outline for your next speech. Read your outline aloud to see whether it works when spoken. Are the main points clear? Is it interesting? Is it persuasive? Is it too long? Revise your speech as needed.
2. Watch *Headline News* on CNN. After two minutes, turn off the television set. Repeat what you heard, combining the wording of the professional announcer with your own. Repeating this exercise every day will increase your working vocabulary, build your fluency, and enhance your knowledge of current affairs.

To Talk About

1. You can learn a great deal from the mistakes of others. Have the class discuss instances where they observed problems in someone's presentations. How do you apply what you have observed?
2. Discuss some of the benefits of participating in extemporaneous speaking competitions. Consider the advantage of being able to organize your thoughts quickly during a timed essay exam. What other skills might you gain from extemporaneous speaking?

To Write About

1. Pick a current event in which you are interested. Now write an essay about this topic, in the form that you have always used for English class. Next write an essay on the same topic, using the form of the model extemporaneous speech in this chapter. Which is the better essay? Why?

2. Pick an impromptu topic from the list of Related Speech Topics below. Write out an impromptu speech, trying to follow the form of the model impromptu speech in this chapter. Take only a few minutes to prepare and then begin writing. Could you think of enough examples and illustrations?

Related Speech Topics

Extemporaneous
How should Congress reform welfare?
Is there a cure for health care?
What are the long-term effects of Internet shopping?
What is ahead for the stock market?

Impromptu
Scandals
Censorship
War
Work
Astrology

CHAPTER 16
ORAL INTERPRETATION

©Hill Street Studios/Blend Images LLC

Above all, the art of reading aloud should be cultivated.

—Alfred North Whitehead

Learning Objectives

After completing this chapter, you will be able to do the following.

- Define oral interpretation.
- Choose material to read aloud.
- Analyze the meaning and feeling of a selection.
- Practice the oral delivery of a selection.
- Discuss the elements of Readers Theater.

Chapter Outline

Following are the main sections in this chapter.

1. What Is Oral Interpretation?
2. Choosing Your Material
3. Interpreting Your Material
4. Presenting Your Material

Speech Vocabulary

In this chapter, you will learn the meanings of the speech terms listed below.

oral interpretation	interior monologue
rhapsode	omniscient
anthology	rhythm
theme	meter
mood	rhyme
persona	auditory
first person	scene setting
third person	offstage focus
second person	aural
dramatic monologue	

Academic Vocabulary

Expanding your academic vocabulary will help you become a more effective communicator. Listed below are some words appearing in this chapter that you should make part of your vocabulary.

enhanced	paraphernalia
mimic	apoplectic
minstrel	nectar
recitation	motif
spellbound	

In this chapter, you will learn about the remarkable history of oral interpretation and how the long tradition of sharing literature orally continues today. You will discover that this experience of sharing can benefit you and others. As you become a better oral interpreter, your understanding of literature will be *enhanced* because you will become a more careful reader. Careful reading will lead you to new insights about the meaning of the literature as well as make you more sensitive to the beauty of language. The audience, too, will share in this intellectual and emotional experience, for you will not only entertain audience members with your performance, you will bring literature alive for them.

Introduction

When Dr. Seuss died, an entire nation mourned. Appearing on the television program *Saturday Night Live,* the Reverend Jesse Jackson read from Dr. Seuss's beloved story *Green Eggs and Ham.* It was a fitting tribute. Millions of children, after all, have grown up in a world peopled by Hunches in Bunches and Brown Bar-ba-Loots. In fact, your first experience with oral interpretation might have been when one of your parents interpreted Dr. Seuss for you: "I do not like green eggs and ham. I do not like them, Sam-I-am."

Whether you realize it or not, oral interpretation is still an important part of your life. When you read aloud in class from an essay you've written, you're interpreting your words for your classmates. When you listen to the news on radio or television, the reporters are practicing the art of oral interpretation for you. Storytelling, a form of oral interpretation, has become an important tool for persuasion in the boardrooms of the United States. Moreover, oral interpretation can be great fun. In a memorable episode of the television show *The Simpsons,* Marge (the mother) experiences a flashback to her high school days and her participation on the speech team. In one scene, Marge, an academic standout, performs her interpretation of the play *Butterflies Are Free* and wins the heart of the classic bad boy Homer (the father).

Dr. Seuss stories, read aloud to you as a child, might have been one of your first experiences with oral interpretation.

SECTION 1

What Is Oral Interpretation?

I f you can accurately *mimic* the voice of your favorite celebrity or cartoon character, you are gifted in the skill of impression. You should not, however, confuse this ability with the art of oral interpretation. In oral interpretation, you do not impersonate a familiar voice—be it Eddie Murphy's or Bugs Bunny's. Rather, you try to create an appropriate and original voice to give life to words on a page. After analyzing the meaning and feeling behind those words, you use your voice and body to share the words with others. **Oral interpretation**, then, is the art of communicating works of literature by reading aloud well.

The history of oral interpretation as a distinct art—apart from public speaking and theater—is difficult to trace. The formal study of oral interpretation as a separate activity didn't begin in the United States until early in the nineteenth century. In 1806, Harvard College offered courses that included "the interpretive approach to literary materials."

However, oral interpretation is one of the oldest of human social activities. Until writing was developed to aid memory, people needed to communicate ideas orally. Literature was passed down from generation to generation in oral form. Professional storytellers made their living by traveling through the countryside and entertaining people. Recently,

Many people enjoy having someone read to them. You can entertain your friends by interpreting your favorite literary passages.

storytelling has experienced a rebirth in the United States. The business world now realizes that storytelling can be an effective tool to persuade a potential client of the quality of a product, or to convince employees of the need for a policy change.

How can businesses use storytelling?

Being Prepared

Speakers who can interpret words with passion and power can inspire people to change the world. Nelson Mandela mastered this art of oral interpretation. Born the son of a Tembu tribal chieftain in 1918 in South Africa, he renounced his right to succeed his father and, instead, chose a political career. He became a lawyer and an honorable member of the African National Congress (ANC). In 1962 he was arrested by the South African security police for his bold opposition to the white government and its apartheid policies of racial, political, and economic discrimination against the nonwhite majority. In 1964, more charges were brought against Mandela, including high treason, sabotage, and conspiracy. On the foggy morning of April 20, 1964, while standing on a crowded dock, he delivered his famous "I am prepared to die" speech:" with: On the foggy morning of April 20, 1964, Mandela, who had dedicated his life to the struggle of the African people to fight against white and black domination, delivered his famous "I am prepared to die" speech:

I have cherished the ideal of a democratic and free society in opportunities. It is an ideal which I hope to live for and to achieve. But if needs be, it is an ideal for which I am prepared to die.

His words inspired many that day to continue to fight for freedom. One such man was Alan Paton—famous for his impassioned speeches and writings that brought notice to the suffering of blacks under apartheid. So, like Nelson Mandela and Alan Paton, remember that nothing you write or say will ever be as passionate or powerful as the truth.

Poetry readings offer exposure to oral interpretations.

Even though oral traditions have been with us as long as human interaction, historians point to ancient Greece as the birthplace of the art of oral interpretation. Wandering *minstrels* known as **rhapsodes** would assemble to read their works in public competition. The *recitations* were often accompanied by music from a lyre or other primitive instrument.

Poetry recitations were also popular in ancient Rome. It is said that the emperor Nero would allow no one to leave a recitation contest in which he was competing until he himself had finished reading. Paul Hunsinger, a professor of speech, characterized Nero as a "ruthless contestant," who paid five thousand young men to applaud him at one competition. After losing to the poet Lucan, Nero ordered forbade Lucan's poetry from ever being read in public again. Nero went so far as to destroy the statues and busts of other poetry reciters.

Recitation contests continued throughout the Middle Ages among minstrels, who competed for prizes provided by the nobility. In Margaret Bahn's book *A History of Oral Interpretation*, you can learn about Anglo-Saxon, Celtic, and Norse oral literatures. Any study of oral traditions should also include a review of the literary works of India, China, Africa, and the Middle East.

NASA/Bill Ingalls

Reading aloud has played an important role in the cultural history of our country as well. Before radio, television, and personal computers, many families would read aloud in the evenings. Young children, *spellbound* by the great works of literature, would spend hours in shared adventure. Much as musicians give concerts today, oral interpreters around the turn of the twentieth century would go on tour. These tours brought entertainment and culture to even the most remote regions of our country.

Today, as writers attempt to reach a wider audience, performance poetry has gained popularity, sometimes in the form of poetry slams in coffeehouses or bookstores. Larry Goodell, a poet and practitioner of the art, explores the creative possibilities of oral interpretation. Costumed in an old robe and makeup, Goodell dances and chants. He has been known to read poem fragments written on cardboard dog biscuits as a musician accompanies him on an electronic saxophone. Although few poets perform oral interpretation with such *paraphernalia*, most writers now recognize the need for students to hear the range and diversity of contemporary works—works that enrich and expand our enjoyment of literature and each other.

Homer was a skilled Greek poet whose works, including the Iliad and the Odyssey, provided models in persuasive speaking and writing that were emulated throughout the ancient and medieval Greek worlds.

SECTION 1 REVIEW

Recalling the Facts

1. Why is impersonating a familiar voice not interpretation?
2. How might businesses use the art of storytelling?

Thinking Critically

At current rates, some 90 percent of the world's languages will vanish during this century. As these languages face extinction, what can be done to preserve the stories and memories that will be lost in the disappearing words?

Taking Charge

Performance poets like Larry Goodell are dedicated to "oral poetry." These artists use things other than the words—such as costumes, props, and music—to help the audience appreciate the power and magic of language. Goodell explains: "Things I make extend from the words, sometimes cradle them like a mouth cradles the words you say, before they are said."

Now it's your turn. Choose a short poem to read. As you interpret the poem for the class, incorporate things that will extend the meaning of the words. You could, for example, perform dribbling tricks with a basketball as you interpret John Updike's poem "Ex-Basketball Player."

Choosing Your Material

When you are assigned to give an oral interpretation in class, you have a problem: where to look for material to perform. Although you have a seemingly unlimited range of material available to you, how do you find it? Many interpreters have found **anthologies** to be useful, because such books include a wide selection of literary works in a single volume. In some anthologies, literary works are arranged by subject matter, such as love, war, or nature. Anthologies may include poems and different types of prose, such as short stories, essays, and humorous pieces. If you are interested in contemporary music, you could turn to the anthology *The Poetry of Rock,* edited by Richard Goldstein.

Another way to find material for oral interpretation is to ask your teachers to provide suggestions. They have a wealth of reading experience that they can share. Your school librarians also can recommend literature that they believe might be suitable for reading aloud.

In addition to these resources, you can use the Internet to search for material to interpret. When searching the Internet, use specific keywords. For example, you will get many thousands of hits if you simply enter the word *love* in the search field. However, the phrase *teenage love and heartbreak* in quotation marks will bring up fewer sites. The more hits you get, the more time you will have to spend sorting through them to determine which sites have the material you need. Narrowing your search will provide the most useful links.

Your most important consideration, though, should be your own tastes in literature. You are more likely to devote time and energy to the performance of material that you care about.

Think back over the poems and stories you have read. Which ones moved you the most? Which ones made you stop and think? Chances are that the selections you remember as favorites will be good choices for your first oral interpretation.

As you select material to read aloud, you will also want to consider the quality of the literature. Why? Because literature that has worth gives you, the reader, something to interpret. True, a grocery list is writing that matters, but how many different interpretations can you give to a gallon of milk and a loaf of bread? If, however, you read Henry David Thoreau's observation that "the mass of men lead lives of quiet desperation," then you have layers of meaning to interpret. What did Thoreau mean by "quiet desperation"? How does that desperation affect people's lives? As a reader, Thoreau gives you a lot to think about and interpret.

Look for writings that are valued both for their beauty and for their permanence or universal interest. You can learn a lot from literature, because it offers insights into life—inner truths that teach lasting lessons. In choosing material, you should also consider the occasion and the desires of your audience. If you have three minutes to share a work of literature in class, you may want to avoid long, complex stories or poems. Your material should suit the occasion and meet the audience's expectations.

Consider the works of Henry David Thoreau for oral interpretation.

CHOOSING MATERIAL FOR ORAL INTERPRETATION

Ralph Waldo Emerson

Robert Frost

William Shakespeare

When selecting material for an oral interpretation, you should consider your personal tastes in literature and the occasion for the interpretation. The writers shown here will appeal to different speakers and be appropriate for different occasions.

George Bernard Shaw

Emily Dickinson

Zora Neale Hurston

SECTION 2 REVIEW

Recalling the Facts

1. Name three things you should consider in selecting material for an interpretative reading.
2. What is the name for books that collect a variety of literary works in one volume?

Thinking Critically

Some 57 percent of U.S. children age three to five are read to by a family member every day of the week. What might be done to bring reading oral interpretation into the lives of the other children?

Taking Charge

Make a list of five selections that you might use for an oral interpretation in class. Remember to consider these four factors: your personal tastes, the quality of the literature, the occasion, and the desires of the audience.

Interpreting Your Material

To interpret a selection well, you must first understand it. You reach this understanding by considering both the meaning and the feeling of the selection. Once you have determined the meaning and feeling of a particular work, you must adapt your interpretation to the requirements of the form: prose, poetry, or drama.

Meaning

The meaning of any selection includes all the ideas that are communicated by the work. You analyze those ideas as a means to an end—the performance. An important part of the analysis is to make sure you know what each word means (and how each word relates to every other word) so that you can share that understanding with the audience. For example, if you are reading a passage from Harper Lee's novel *To Kill a Mockingbird* and you don't know that the word *apoplectic* can describe a person in a fit of rage, then you may not correctly understand how to interpret that passage.

You must, of course, determine the denotation— the dictionary definition or explicit meaning—of words like *apoplectic*. You should also determine the connotation, or the range of meanings associated with a word that go beyond its dictionary definition. Connotations are especially important to an interpreter. If you were to ask your classmates to define *love*, you would have as many different definitions as you have classmates. The same is true for poets writing about love: some will say love is affection; some, an affliction.

To make sure you understand the meaning of a selection, try paraphrasing it. If you can put the ideas of the work into your own words, then you are off to a good start in understanding what the author is trying to say. These "author messages" or central ideas in a literary work are the **themes** that you must make clear in your interpretation. In *To Kill a Mockingbird*, for example, an important theme is that one shouldn't judge people simply by what they look like or what other people say about them. Knowing the theme helps you to make choices in interpreting the denotative and the connotative meanings of all the words.

Feeling

After you have analyzed the connotative meanings of the words in your selection, you will begin to understand not only the themes of the work but also the feelings the author is trying to arouse. The overall feeling or atmosphere in a piece of writing is often referred to as the **mood.**

Just as your mood changes throughout the day, so can the mood of a work of literature. Dylan Thomas was a master at using words and literary techniques like repetition, rhythm, and alliteration to express feelings, moods, and musical effects.

Knowing the theme will help you interpret the meaning of your material.

Locate and read the Dylan Thimas poem "Do not go gentle into that good night."

What is the general mood of the Thomas poem? If you knew that Thomas was angry that his father had given up the will to live, do you think it would make a difference in your interpretation? Do you think Thomas admired the "wild men" described in the poem? If you do, then you must use your voice to show the mood changing from anger to admiration and back to anger.

Interpreting Prose

When you tell a personal story, you are the narrator of the events that you relate. In interpreting a work of prose, however, you need to analyze the form of the written narration to determine who is the narrator. The form of the narration tells you who is telling the story, to whom that person is telling the story, what relationship that person has to the events described, and how much knowledge that person has of those events.

Once you have determined who is the fictional speaker (the **persona**), you use your imagination to fill in the details—such as vocal characteristics and facial expressions—necessary to re-create that speaker, that "voice," in the mind of listeners.

The outlook from which the events in a novel or short story are related, called the point of view, varies from story to story and within stories. Many authors write in the **first person**, using *I* to identify the narrator. Others prefer the **third person**, describing characters as *he, she,* or *it.* Occasionally, you will find a work written in the **second person**, in which the author addresses *you* (for example, this sentence and this textbook). Let's look at each of these points of view more closely.

First-Person Narrations In a first-person narration—a story whose narrator is *I*—the author may be using a variety of approaches. One popular form of first-person narration is the **dramatic monologue**. A dramatic monologue presents a single character speaking. Although you may associate this approach with the theater, authors of prose use

Author Langston Hughes' writing could provide you with excellent material for interpreting prose.

the technique when they want you to overhear somebody speaking aloud to another person. Another form of first-person narration is the **interior monologue**. Here, the author has the narrator speaking to himself or herself. We hear the narrator's thoughts. Consider this passage from *The Adventures of Huckleberry Finn*, by Mark Twain:

Well, I got a good going over in the morning from old Miss Watson on account of my clothes; but the widow she didn't scold, but only cleaned off the grease and clay, and looked so sorry that I thought I would behave awhile if I could. Then Miss Watson she took me in the closet and prayed, but nothing come of it. She told me to pray every day, and whatever I asked for I would get it. But it warn't so. I tried it. Once I got a fish-line, but no hooks. It warn't any good to me without hooks.

Read the selection again and ask yourself these questions: What does the narrator look like? How is he dressed? Where does he live? What kind of accent does he have? How old is he? How does the narrator feel about Miss Watson? Answering these kinds of questions will help you decide how to portray this narrator in your interpretation.

Third-Person Narrations In a third-person narration, the narrator is not *I*—the person to whom the story is happening—but an observer of the action. Third person can allow the narrator to tell the story through the eyes of more than one character. Typically, the narrator is all-knowing—or **omniscient**—and moves freely into and out of the minds of various characters. As an example, consider this passage from Flannery O'Connor's short story "A Good Man Is Hard to Find":

> The grandmother didn't want to go to Florida. She wanted to visit some of her connections in east Tennessee and she was seizing at every chance to change Bailey's mind. "Now look here, Bailey," she said, "see here, read this."

Read this selection again, asking yourself the same kinds of questions that you answered for the Twain passage. Note that a significant difference exists between the Twain and O'Connor stories. As you interpret the Twain story, you must portray one character: the "I." In the O'Connor story, however, you have two characters: the author's omniscient narrator's "voice" and the grandmother's "voice." The challenge for you as an interpreter is to create two unique voices for these characters. The grandmother must talk the way this specific grandmother would talk. Furthermore, the narrator must sound different from the grandmother.

Interpreting Poetry

As you interpret prose or poetry, some scholars think you should be sensitive to the author's intent. They say that determining the author's intent is crucial, because you must always respect the integrity of the words in the work. Others place less importance on the author's intent and stress that you should instead thoroughly study the text itself. Understanding how some common features of poems work can help you determine how to orally interpret the poems. These features include rhythm, meter, rhyme, and imagery.

Rhythm In the English language, **rhythm** is the natural back-and-forth or rise-and-fall movement between stressed and unstressed syllables. It is pres-ent in prose and even in everyday speech, but it is most strongly marked and patterned in poetry. The effect of rhythm on meaning should be your primary concern when reciting a poem. Listeners can concentrate on a given idea for only a brief time. Therefore, you must pace your recitation to allow listeners to relax occasionally and reflect on what you have read.

A poet may use pauses within a line to vary a poem's rhythm, thus adding interest and emphasizing certain words. Walt Whitman was a master of rhythm, creating those "sounds of silence." Note the breaks created by his use of commas in his famous poem, "O Captain! My Captain!"

> O CAPTAIN! my Captain! our fearful trip is done;
> The ship has weather'd every rack, the prize we sought is won;
> The port is near, the bells I hear, the people all exulting,
> While follow eyes the steady keel, the vessel grim and daring:
> > But O heart! heart! heart!
> > O the bleeding drops of red,
> > > Where on the deck my Captain lies,
> > > Fallen cold and dead.

Read the passage again as if there were no commas in lines 2, 3, and 4. Do not pause at all as you read these lines. Do you hear how the poem's rhythm has been flattened out? As an oral interpreter, you must always be aware of the rhythm of any literature that you perform.

Meter When you hear the word *meter*, you probably think of a unit of measurement. Meter, in poetry, is also a way of measuring. Instead of measuring length, width, or capacity, though, **meter** measures more or less regularly repeating units of rhythm in a line of poetry. Specifically, meter measures the number of stressed syllables or of stressed and unstressed syllables in the words that make up the line.

You place stress on particular syllables, based on your knowledge of proper pronunciation and on your interpretation of a poem. You can look up proper pronunciation in any dictionary, but your understanding of the poem is up to you. You should never sacrifice meaning as you vocalize the meter, but you should also never lose sight of the basic rhythmic pattern provided by the poet. As an interpreter, you must balance these two factors: meaning and pattern.

The choices you make about meter do make a difference. By noting how a poet varied the rhythm within the meter of a poem and then conveying that to your listeners, you can heighten their attention to what is going on in the poem musically and you can reinforce the poem's meaning.

Rhyme In a poem, **rhyme** is usually the repetition in different words of the last stressed vowel, and of any sounds following it, at the end of lines. Rhyme may also occur within lines. This repetition tends to please the ear; literary scholar M. H. Abrams described the effect as the "delight given by the expected but variable end chime." You, as an oral interpreter, must be careful not to spoil this "delight" for your listeners by falling into a singsongy or predictable pattern of delivery. To ensure that the rhyme scheme and meter don't overwhelm meaning, experienced interpreters pause where punctuation and sense require—which isn't always at the end of lines.

Let's consider how to balance meaning and pattern by examining a poem by Emily Dickinson. The poem describes how those who lose at something

understand better what it means to win than those who win. Perhaps you know this truth already.

> Success is counted sweetest
> By those who ne'er succeed.
> To comprehend a nectar
> Requires sorest need.
>
> Not one of all the purple Host
> Who took the Flag today
> Can tell the definition
> So clear of Victory
>
> As he defeated—dying—
> On whose forbidden ear
> The distant strains of triumph
> Burst agonized and clear!

Note how Dickinson rhymes the second and fourth lines in each stanza—for example, *succeed* and *need* in the first stanza. One way that you might avoid a mechanical or singsongy delivery of the first stanza would be to give special emphasis to *ne'er* and the last syllable of comprehend. In addition, you might try pausing briefly after requires rather than *nectar*. A final suggestion: When you read the word *need*, lower your pitch slightly and say the word quietly. By doing so, you will deemphasize the rhyme and also suggest the mood of the poem.

If you study the second stanza, you will find an imperfect rhyme of the second and fourth lines: *today*

Analyze your narration selection to determine the point of view.

and *victory*. We think of Dickinson as a modern poet, and one of the reasons is her willingness to subordinate rhyme to meaning. As an oral interpreter, you have to be willing to make the same artistic choice.

Imagery As you may recall from Chapter 11, the word *imagery* refers to language that creates mental pictures. These pictures in the mind of the oral interpreter will differ from those in the mind of each listener. An image sparks in each person an association with some real-life experience that is unique to that person. For example, the image of a bicycle in a poem may remind you of your first trip to the grocery store alone. The person sitting next to you may think, instead, of crashing into a neighbor's new car. This recalling of what we have experienced can give poetry (or prose) emotional power.

As an oral interpreter, you should pay special attention to a poet's use of imagery. In the poem "Birches," Robert Frost juxtaposes the pressures of modern life with the beauty of nature. In reading the opening lines of this work aloud, you must use your voice creatively to suggest the meaning and feeling of the poet's themes of youth and nature.

When I see birches bend to left and right
Across the lines of straighter darker trees,
I like to think some boy's been swinging them.
But swinging doesn't bend them down to stay
As ice-storms do. Often you must have seen them
Loaded with ice a sunny winter morning
After a rain. They click upon themselves
As the breeze rises, and turn many-colored
As the stir cracks and crazes their enamel.

Strong rhythm and rhyme can make a poem a good candidate to interpret orally.

Soon the sun's warmth makes them shed crystal shells
Shattering and avalanching on the snow-crust—
Such heaps of broken glass to sweep away
You'd think the inner dome of heaven had fallen.

Interpreting Drama

When a play is performed onstage, the actors attempt to become the characters they portray. The goal of the actors is to make the performance seem as close to real life as possible. In contrast, the reader in traditional oral interpretation of drama tries only to suggest characters. For example, a reader, at a dramatic moment in a script, might have tears welling up in his eyes. An actor portraying the same character at that moment might go beyond the mere suggestion of an emotional climax; she might have tears streaming down her face.

In contemporary speech competitions, "Humorous Interpretation" and "Dramatic Interpretation" are events in which participants recite material they have memorized. Such participants are often described as "acting from the waist up." This description arises from many participants' practice of pretending to be the characters in their material. Their performances may include extensive use of gestures and actual movement around the room. By taking on the techniques of acting, these participants may no longer be presenting a traditional oral interpretation, but they are creating a powerful union of the two arts.

"Duo Interpretation" has become a popular event at many speech tournaments. This event lets two interpreters work as a team, allowing each performer the chance to respond to the genuine emotions and rhythms of another. Rules vary. For example, some tournaments require scripts; others do not.

Regardless of your approach, as an interpreter of drama, you need to help your listeners create a mental image of each character you portray. You must provide the visual and **auditory** (hearing) clues that will stimulate the imagination of each audience member.

Humorous interpretation and dramatic interpretation involve participants "acting from the waist up.

Working with a partner allows you to react to each other's emotions and gestures in a reading.

Recalling the Facts

1. What is the difference between the theme and the tone of a work?
2. Why is imagery important to oral interpretation?

Thinking Critically

Modern speechwriters have argued that the quality of modern speeches has declined because we no longer learn the rhythm of public utterances from Shakespeare and the Bible. If this assessment is accurate, then what should be done to improve oratory today?

Taking Charge

Many oral interpreters read two or more selections built around a single theme. This program of reading provides an opportunity to show how different authors approach the same theme. You will find an example of a student's programmed reading at the end of this chapter. The student chose selections that celebrated the many sounds of poetry that cause the listener to want to "speak like rain" (her theme).

Now it's your turn. After deciding on a subject—death, friendship, patriotism, or the like—find two to five short poems and formulate a theme that shows the relationships among them.

Presenting Your Material

Choosing and analyzing material for oral interpretation is only part of your preparation. Next, you have to prepare and practice for the actual performance. Unlocking the mystery of effective presentation involves introducing material, cutting material, developing material, and practicing material.

Introducing Your Material

You will need to prepare an introduction for your interpretation. The principles you learned in earlier chapters about writing a good speech introduction still apply here. But you should note the following distinctions.

First, you are responsible for giving your listeners the information they need to understand your material. Characters need to be identified, relationships explained, and important plot points outlined. You don't want to spoil the story by giving away the ending, but you don't want to confuse your listeners either.

A second requirement for an effective introduction is to establish a mood that is consistent with the mood of the material itself. For example, if you were reading from *Romeo and Juliet,* a Shakespearean tragedy, you probably wouldn't begin by cracking jokes. A humorous introduction, however, might be appropriate for *Romeo and Juliet* if you were going to perform only the scenes with speeches by Juliet's nosy nurse, who provides comic relief in the play.

Finally, keep your introduction brief. If you are allowed five minutes for your entire performance, you shouldn't spend most of that time explaining what you're going to do. Most introductions can be kept to around a minute (or less). Remember, you need only include the information necessary for the audience to share the meaning and feeling of your selection. (For an example, see the student speech at the end of the chapter.)

Cutting Your Material

You may need to cut, or condense, your material. This may be necessary for several reasons: You may have too much material for the time allowed, certain parts of your selection may be inappropriate, or a particular episode may lessen the overall effect you are seeking. If you are working with a lengthy short story or a novel, you will probably need to choose a climactic scene and present only that scene. In that case, when writing the introduction, plan on telling the audience what they need to know to understand the scene. Other guidelines that may prove useful include the following:

- Always cut in, not out. In other words, build your selection by including your favorite lines and the lines that you feel are the most

"ROMEO & JULIET."

What type of introduction is appropriate for the scene depicted on this poster for Romeo and Juliet?

important to understanding the selection. If you tried to cut *Gone with the Wind* down to a five-minute presentation by taking out, one by one, the lines you didn't need, you would quickly lose interest in the project (and your youth). Instead, pick your favorite scene and highlight the lines you most want to keep (in priority order), as well as the lines needed to make sense of the story. As soon as you've highlighted a total of four minutes' worth of lines, stop! Save the extra minute for your introduction.

- Eliminate dialogue tags, the parts of written dialogue that tell us who is speaking. Consider the following example:

  "May I have another chocolate bar?" Jane asked.

  "But you have already had three this morning," Elizabeth replied.

  "Jane asked" and "Elizabeth replied" are dialogue tags. Such tags can usually be cut. However, if they are needed to make clear who is speaking or if this is the first time a character has spoken in the material you are using, the tags should not be cut.

- In drama, eliminate stage directions *(Elena rises, crosses left)* as well as lines that suggest physical action. For example, suppose that in your selection Larry asks Melvin why he is tap-dancing. You have to eliminate that line so that your listeners don't expect you to tap-dance. (Alternatively, you could suggest the movements in some limited way or start taking tap-dancing lessons.)

- Eliminate minor characters that might confuse your listeners.

- Cut references to events that you do not have time to fully explain.

Eye contact is necessary for effective oral interpretation.

Developing Your Material

In developing your material for performance, you need to work on certain skills that will improve your effectiveness as an oral interpreter. These delivery skills include eye contact, character placement, characterization, word color, and showmanship.

Eye Contact You have already learned about the importance of eye contact. In oral interpretation, how much eye contact is enough? How often should you look up from the script, and when? These questions are a source of great controversy among the teachers of oral interpretation. Some say that a 50-50 balance is appropriate. Others argue for maintaining eye contact with the audience as much as 90 percent of the time. Regardless of your position on this issue, you need to remember two factors: (1) You must look at the script often enough to remind the audience that you are sharing a work of literature; (2) you must not be tied to the script, or the audience will soon tire of staring at the top of your head.

Effective interpreters often use a technique known as **scene setting.** They use their eyes to focus the scene that they are describing on an imaginary stage in front of them. This helps the audience members to see that same scene in their imagination. When not scene setting, these interpreters look into the eyes of individual audience members or at the script.

Character Placement If you are portraying various characters, then you must "place" them by looking at a different location for each one. By directing your focus to different locations, you can create the illusion that a number of characters are speaking to each other. Readings of drama require this skill, but prose, too, can necessitate character placement. In prose readings, most interpreters place the narrator directly in front of them, with the rest of the "voices" distributed to the left and to the right. In drama, the most important characters are placed closest to the center, with the minor characters farther to the sides.

Take care not to place characters too far apart. If the characters are widely separated, the time it will take for you to rotate your head to the proper position will cause you to pause too long between speakers. The effect of these long pauses is similar to what happens in plays when actors do not pick up their lines: the performance drags. It is also important to be consistent in your character placement, or the audience may become confused as to who is speaking.

Characterization Look around your classroom. No two of your classmates sound or act the same. Similarly, each character you portray in a selection must be distinct. Each should be characterized by a unique voice, facial expression, and body position.

To create distinctions in voice, some interpreters experiment with a variety of pitch patterns. Some vary the pacing, making the characters speak at different speeds. Others try to re-create dialect, the pronunciation that is used in a particular geographical area. Whether or not you use dialect should depend on your ability to make it sound convincing. An annoying or distracting characterization damages the integrity of the selection and makes for a disappointing performance.

Let each characterization reflect the unique qualities of the "voice" for whom you are speaking.

You should also avoid using a stereotypical voice that lessens the believability of a character. Stereotypical voices usually turn into nothing more than caricatures, comic exaggerations that lack uniqueness. Not everyone from the South talks with a drawl, and not every football lineman plays without a helmet.

Along with vocal distinctions, you should respond with your face and the rest of your body to each word spoken by a character. If a character is happy, the audience should not only hear that happiness in the warmth of your voice but see it in a smiling face and relaxed body as well. Each character and each moment in the script require subtle changes in facial expression and posture. The audience must see you suggest the individual traits of each character in the selection to get caught up in the illusion that the character is a real person.

Word Color You must give each word in your selection its due. Your responsibility is to change written symbols into sound symbols by "coloring" them with your voice. You would not, for example, say "I want to kiss you" and "Please pass the butter" in the same way. You must suggest the denotative and connotative meanings with vocal variety. But how? Experienced oral interpreters use, in combination or alone, some of the following techniques: pauses of varying lengths before key words, changes in pitch, holding vowels, hitting consonants, manipulating tempo, and unusual or unexpected emphasis.

To see how these techniques can make a significant difference in an oral interpretation, experiment with them on any literary work included in this chapter. You can change the entire meaning of a particular work by varying your voice in these ways.

Showmanship The sense of professionalism that you must have when performing is called showmanship. From the moment you leave your seat until you return to it, you should make clear that you enjoy sharing literature with an audience. If you mumble misgivings under your breath or seem hesitant at any point, the experience of your listeners will be lessened. Care about your material. Care about the people in your audience. Show them.

Word color and showmanship can help you give a convincing interpretation.

Practicing Your Material

You need to practice your material by reading it aloud. Silent rehearsal does not allow you to experiment with a variety of vocal approaches. Furthermore, you should try to practice the material exactly as you plan to present it. In the early stages, however, you might want to break the performance down by practicing a few lines at a time. By polishing shorter sections, you won't fall into the trap of simply running through the material to get the practice session over. Memorized material should never sound as if you are merely reciting the words from rote memory. You must make the material seem fresh, as if you were performing it for the first time. You must seem to be thinking as the character you are portraying. This quality is necessary for a believable reading.

Try recording your practice and listening to it several times to check word color, articulation, pronunciation, pacing, and use of pauses and emphasis. It is important that you have absolutely crisp, clear vocalization. Some oral interpreters find it helpful to mark scripts to remind themselves of when to pause and which words to emphasize. Whether you mark your script or not, you should spend the time necessary to become completely familiar with your material. In other words, by the time of your recitation, you should be able to look down at your script because you choose to, not because you have to. Avoid looking down while saying words: The up-and-down movement of your head should come between words so as not to create motion that will distract from giving each word its full worth.

In using a script, be careful not to wave it around as you gesture. The script should remain still at all times. Furthermore, do not hold it too low. If you hold it too low, you will have the tendency to drop your head too far as you struggle to see the words on the page. A final suggestion: Rather than reading from a book, most oral interpreters photocopy, type, or print out their material. They cut and paste the sections they are going to read and place them in a binder.

Readers Theater

Group reading of literature offers participants the opportunity to create a theater of the mind. In group

These students are participating in a theater performance. Do they appear to be enhancing the story?

reading, most of the action takes place in the imagination of the audience. Typically, the readers suggest movement rather than actually moving as actors do. Group reading sometimes takes the form of Readers Theater. Although definitions vary, Readers Theater generally involves two or more oral interpreters sharing a reading with an audience.

The sharing in Readers Theater includes vocal and physical suggestion as well as elements of staging. Staging is usually minimal, but scenery, lighting, costuming, and makeup have been used successfully in some productions. Staging choices should depend on whether they will clarify the meaning of the literature. They should always enhance the literature.

Other common characteristics of Readers Theater include the following:

- A narrator who introduces the different portions of the program and provides transitions between them
- **Offstage focus**—a technique by which the readers use scripts and envision the scene out in the audience

Remember, the primary concern in Readers Theater is intensifying the **aural** appeal of the performance—that is, the performance's appeal to the sense of hearing.

Recalling the Facts

1. Explain the five guidelines for cutting material.
2. Why is showmanship important?
3. What is offstage focus?

Thinking Critically

A "duo interp" team from Florida performed an excerpt from the recorded conversations of Clinton White House intern Monica Lewinsky and her confidante Linda Tripp. The team consisted of two boys parodying these women in highly unflattering ways. Are there limits to how real people should be portrayed? What are those limits?

Taking Charge

Successful oral interpreters introduce a selection to create an environment that will help the audience understand the selection. This introduction not only should suit the selection and the audience but also should demonstrate the imagination of the interpreter.

Choose a short poem and write an imaginative introduction for it. Share both your introduction and the poem in a performance for the class.

Learning Objectives

Listed below are the major ideas discussed in this chapter.

- The oral tradition is as old as human interaction.
- Ancient Greece is considered the birthplace of the art of oral interpretation.
- When selecting material to read aloud, you should consider the quality of the literature, the occasion, and the desires of the audience.
- To interpret a literary selection, you must analyze it for meaning and feeling.
- As an interpreter of narrative prose, you must analyze selections to determine the point of view.
- In interpreting poetry, you must show sensitivity to the meter, rhythm, rhyme, and imagery in the work.
- When interpreting drama, you must help listeners create a mental image of the characters you are suggesting.

- Your introduction to a recitation should give listeners the information they need to understand your selection.
- You may need to cut your selection when you have too much material, when certain sections are inappropriate, or when a particular section lessens the overall effect.
- Effective recitation requires mastery of these techniques: eye contact, character placement, characterization, word color, and showmanship.
- Recording your practice sessions can help you evaluate your progress as you prepare for a performance.
- Readers Theater offers participants the opportunity to create a theater of the mind.

Speech Vocabulary

Match the speech term on the left with the appropriate description on the right.

1. rhapsode
2. persona
3. anthology
4. mood
5. rhythm
6. meter
7. aural
8. scene setting
9. omniscient

a. fictional speaker
b. measurement of rhythm
c. a wandering minstrel
d. all-knowing
e. creating an imaginary scene
f. a book that includes a variety of literary works
g. related to hearing
h. rise-and-fall movement of stressed and unstressed syllables
i. a literary work's overall feeling or atmosphere

CHAPTER 16 Review and Enrichment

Academic Vocabulary

Use context clues to write the meaning of each academic vocabulary word. Then use a print or online dictionary to check the accuracy of your definition.

enhanced
mimic
minstrel
recitation
spellbound

paraphernalia
faltering
apoplectic
nectar
motif

To Remember

Answer the following based on your reading of the chapter.

1. Impersonating a familiar voice is not interpretation but _____.
2. Poetry reading was popular during the _____ Age in ancient Rome.
3. Name three things you should consider in selecting material for oral interpretation.
4. The _____ is the emotional atmosphere that predominates in a selection.
5. A story in which the narrator uses *I* is written in _____ person.
6. When an author moves freely into and out of the minds of characters, the story is probably written in _____ person.
7. Rhyme is usually the repetition of the last _____, and of any sounds following it, at the end of lines.
8. When readers use their eyes to place what they are describing on an imaginary stage, they are using a technique known as _____.
9. _____ refers to the sense of professionalism you have when performing.
10. Name three guidelines that you should use in cutting, or condensing, material.

To Do

1. Young children are a responsive audience who give immediate and honest feedback. Arrange to visit an elementary school to read to children. After reading an appropriate selection, ask the children to critique your effort.

2. Record yourself reading a brief poem aloud. Evaluate your interpretation for word color, pacing, articulation, pronunciation, and use of pauses and emphasis.

To Talk About

1. When a news anchor reads a story about the damage caused by an earthquake, is that oral interpretation? Why or why not?
2. What is suitable material for oral interpretation? The list of ingredients on a cereal box? The telephone book? Instruction manuals? Explain.
3. If you were going to read a Dr. Seuss book to children, which one would you choose? Why?

To Write About

Answer the following based on your reading of the chapter.

1. Write a poem consisting of nonsense words that suggest meaning by the sounds they produce.
2. Write a one-page essay discussing why parents should be skilled at oral interpretation.
3. Choose a country in which you are interested. Research and write a brief description of the oral tradition in that nation.

Related Speech Topics

Professional storytellers
Learning dialects
Norse oral literature
Celtic oral literature

African oral literature
The history of Readers Theater
Your favorite poet

CHAPTER 17
SPEECHES FOR SPECIAL OCCASIONS

I am the most spontaneous speaker in the world because every word, every gesture, and every retort has been carefully rehearsed.

—George Bernard Shaw

Learning Objectives

After completing this chapter, you will be able to do the following.

- Define the specific purposes of several special-occasion speeches.
- Discuss the characteristics of these speeches.
- Describe popular kinds of contest speeches.

Chapter Outline

Following are the main sections in this chapter.

1. Courtesy Speeches
2. Ceremonial Speeches
3. Contest Speeches

Speech Vocabulary

In this chapter, you will learn the meanings of the speech terms listed below.

speech of
  presentation
speech of acceptance
after-dinner speech
commencement
  address
commemorative
  speech
testimonial speech
eulogy
original oratory
dramatic
  interpretation
humorous
  interpretation

Academic Vocabulary

Expanding your academic vocabulary will help you become a more effective communicator. Listed below are some words appearing in this chapter that you should make part of your vocabulary.

reiterate
eloquent
procession
miffed
transformation
hoke
dignitary
converse
evoking
suffice
combustion
refrain

Although the primary purpose of most special-occasion speeches is not to inform or persuade, they do require the same fundamentals of public speaking, the same analyzing of purpose. In this chapter, you will learn to present three general types of special-occasion speeches: courtesy, ceremonial, and contest speeches.

Introduction

When *Sesame Street's* Kermit the Frog won an honorary degree from Southampton College, Samantha Chie, a marine biology major, said, "Now we have a sock talking at our commencement. It's kind of upsetting." Clearly, Chie was not impressed by Kermit's "doctorate of amphibious letters."

Although you may never upset people as a commencement speaker, you will be called upon someday to speak at a public or business gathering. Special-occasion speeches are part of our everyday lives. These speeches are special because they focus on particular situations: an address given at a school assembly, a testimonial speech offered at an awards banquet, a eulogy spoken by a friend at a funeral. What follows will help you learn how not to upset people.

Commencement addresses are one type of special-occasion speech.

Courtesy Speeches

You present a courtesy speech to fulfill certain social customs. If you need to say thank you, for example, you may find yourself preparing a speech of acceptance. Typical courtesy speeches include introduction, presentation, acceptance, and after-dinner speeches.

Introductions

If you have had the uncomfortable experience of being the new kid in school, then you know the need for successful introductions. Waiting to make friends can be one of the loneliest periods in a person's life. You find yourself wondering if you will be accepted. You worry about what people think of you, what they might be saying.

Although more formal than making friends in a new school, speeches of introduction matter in the same way, because they break down the barriers between people. Introductory speeches serve two functions: to make the audience want to hear the speaker and to make the speaker want to address the audience. You need to achieve these goals in only a minute or two.

Mark Twain was a brilliant satirist.

Because most speeches of introduction are brief, they must be well planned. You should plan to do some or all of the following in your speech:

- Refer to the occasion that has brought the audience together.
- Name the speaker (mention the name again at the end of the introduction).
- Build enthusiasm by relating information about the qualifications of the speaker.
- Share information about the subject to heighten interest, if the speaker wishes you to.
- Explain why this speaker is to give this talk to this audience at this time.
- Conclude by welcoming the speaker to the microphone or the podium.

Successful writers of introductions are usually fans of Mark Twain. Why? Twain understood one factor that contributes to a memorable speech: humor. If you can combine humor with a meaningful message, then your chances for writing an effective introduction are greatly increased. Consider the following excerpt from one of Twain's many humorous speeches of introduction.

> I see I am advertised to introduce the speaker of the evening. . . . As a pure citizen, I respect him; as a personal friend for years, I have the warmest regard for him; as a neighbor whose vegetable garden adjoins mine, why—why, I watch him. That's nothing; we all do that with any neighbor.
>
> General Hawley keeps his promises not only in private but in public. . . . He is broad-souled, generous, noble, liberal, alive to his moral and religious responsibilities. Whenever the contribution box was passed, I never knew him to take out a cent. He is a square, true, honest man in politics, and I must say he occupies a mighty lonesome position. . . . He is an American of Americans. Would we had more such men! So broad, so bountiful is his character that he never turned a tramp empty handed from his door, but always gave him a letter of introduction to me. . . .

Pure, honest, incorruptible, that is Joe Hawley. Such a man in politics is like a bottle of perfumery in a glue factory—it may modify the stench if it doesn't destroy it. And now, in speaking thus highly of the speaker of the evening, I haven't said any more of him than I would say of myself. Ladies and Gentlemen, this is General Hawley.

Twain's introduction takes a few satirical swipes at General Hawley, which is fine, but you must be careful not to embarrass the person you are introducing. Hawley was a public figure and a personal friend; therefore, Twain could take certain liberties in this particular case. Good judgment is always a must.

Here are a few reminders for making a successful introductory speech: Check the pronunciation of all words, including the speaker's name; verify the accuracy of all biographical and other information; analyze the audience's expectations.

Speeches of Presentation

When a person is publicly presented with a gift or an award, a **speech of presentation** is needed. The presentation speech is usually brief. Of course, the length depends on the formality of the occasion. Typically, when you give a speech of presentation, you are speaking on behalf of some group, and you should reflect the shared feelings of that group. You can focus those feelings by choosing words that give deeper meaning to the circumstances that surround this special occasion. For example, the audience's expectations at a retirement party vary significantly from those at the annual Motion Picture Academy Awards (Oscar) ceremony. Certain guidelines, however, generally apply.

1. State the person's name early in the presentation (unless building suspense is appropriate).
2. Explain the award's significance as a symbol of the group's esteem.
3. Explain how the person was selected for the award.
4. Highlight what makes this person unique. Use anecdotal information and a brief list of achievements.
5. Hand the award to the recipient.

A presentation speech should be brief.

Does this girl look like she could be the "most valuable player" described in the text?

Here is an example of a typical speech of presentation. The speech was given by a student to honor her teammate who was about to receive the most valuable player award on their high school golf team.

No one is more deserving of most valuable player recognition than Alysen. True, she is only a sophomore, but she led the team as if she were our most experienced golfer. If you've ever played a round of golf with her, you know what I mean by "led." In any foursome, she always seemed to be ten paces in front of everyone else, and you felt like you had to run to keep up.

And this year, no one was able to keep up with her or with her success. As a district medalist and a top ten finisher in the state championship, Alysen capped what was a remarkable year in competition. But speaking on behalf of her teammates, we are most proud of Alysen for the character she demonstrated both in victory and defeat. We voted her this honor because of that character. If she made a birdie or if she missed a three-foot putt, there was always a smile for everyone, a joy in the simple playing of the game.

As Will Rogers once observed, "It is great to be great, but it is greater to be human." So this Most Valuable Player award is presented to Alysen—a great human being.

Speeches of Acceptance

Jack Benny was a comedian and an actor in radio, television, and movies. Once, when accepting an award, he ad-libbed, "I don't deserve this, but then, I have arthritis and I don't deserve that either." Even though recipients of awards or gifts usually have some advance notice, a **speech of acceptance** is most often, at least in part, impromptu (impromptu speaking was discussed in Chapters 12 and 15). Even if you are able to prepare your acceptance speech, part of it will need to be impromptu because you will need to tailor your remarks to what was said by the presenter. The remarks that you make serve a double purpose: to thank the people who are presenting the award or gift and to give credit to people who helped you earn this recognition. The formality of the situation should guide you in preparation, but generally you should consider the following:

An award acceptance speech is usually impromptu—and should be brief, sincere, and direct.

© Atlo Foto Agency/Alamy Images; (b) McGraw-Hill Education/Jill Braaten

1. Be brief, sincere, and direct.
2. Thank the group for the award.
3. Discuss the importance of the award to you.
4. Thank others who helped you win the award. Minimize your worth, and praise the contributions of your supporters.
5. *Reiterate* your appreciation.

If you have ever been a member of a team that lost the big game, then you can appreciate politician Adlai Stevenson's famous concession speech—a speech in which he accepts not an award but defeat. In that speech, he compares himself to a boy who has stubbed his toe in the dark—"too old to cry, but it hurts too much to laugh."

Stevenson was one of the most *eloquent* politicians of the twentieth century. Consider this excerpt from his speech accepting the nomination as Democratic candidate for president on July 26, 1952.

> I accept your nomination—and your program.
>
> I should have preferred to hear those words uttered by a stronger, a wiser, a better man than myself. But after listening to the president's [Harry Truman's] speech, I feel even better about myself. . . .
>
> None of you, my friends, can wholly appreciate what is in my heart. I can only hope that you understand my words. They will be few. . . .
>
> And, my friends, even more important than winning the election is governing the nation. That is the test of a political party—the acid, final test. When the tumult and the shouting die, when the bands are gone and the lights are dimmed, there is the stark reality of responsibility in an hour of history haunted with those gaunt, grim specters of strife, dissension, and ruthless, inscrutable, and hostile power abroad. . . .
>
> Let's face it. Let's talk sense to the American people. Let's tell them the truth, that there are no gains without pains, that we are on the eve of great decisions, not easy decisions, like resistance when you're attacked, but a long, patient, costly struggle which alone can assure triumph over the great enemies of man—war, poverty, and tyranny—and the assaults upon human dignity which are the most grievous consequences of each.

After-Dinner Speeches

As hard as it may be to swallow at the time, many banquets or meals are followed by someone presenting what is known as an **after-dinner speech**. The traditional after-dinner speech is expected to be entertaining. Remember, though, that you can be entertaining without being funny.

The key is to enjoy yourself, and then the audience is more likely to enjoy your presentation. On these occasions, most audiences want a message of some sort presented in a lighter, if not humorous, way. Be likable. Share your message in a relaxed and uncritical manner, and adapt to the mood of the audience. If the audience is not responding to your humorous stories, then you should shift the focus of your speech away from jokes to avoid bombing.

The casual style that you need requires careful preparation. You should organize your presentation around a theme. All of your supporting material—illustrations, statistics, examples, narrations, anecdotes—should relate to that theme.

After-dinner speeches are generally expected to be entertaining, but you still need to focus on your message.

The following excerpts are from a Nebraska student's state championship after-dinner speech. Note how all of the supporting material reinforces his theme of "too many intellectuals."

A dim chamber.
Velvety dust creeping across the floor.
The scent of dead books.
Blue haze falls from the pipes as a dreary voice flows from a shadow in the corner. Seven enchanted bibliophiles cluster around a worn, scarred table, performing the ancient rites. These members of the Duluth Directory on Deductive Discussion carry the illness

Another scene. The depths of a dirty, empty library hold the bodiless mind of one Aristotle P. Chaucer, Jr. Pen choked by hand, it struggles across the paper, attempting to write that crucial document for which so many wait. The Fred Friendly Fan Club Constitution is in the hand of one afflicted by that same disease.

Still another scene. A hand attached to some distant brain guides a stub of chalk on an enormous gray slate. Chalk dust settles to the floor as the long-sought formula for the chemical composition of armadillo saliva is revealed. The same malaise affects this being.

Yes, a plague creeps through our society. While some euphemistically refer to the illness as knowledge, we now recognize it for what it really is: the cancerous growth of intellectualism.

While the illness receives very little attention—the telethon never made it on the air— millions of Americans are afflicted with this awful disease. It is entirely possible that someone in this room is an intellectual.

I perceive your sudden nervousness as you wonder if the person next to you is a carrier. Don't worry. While it is true that "a little knowledge is a dangerous thing," small doses encountered by most people present an insignificant health hazard—our lack of logical thinking provides natural immunity. . . .

When we realize, however, how firmly entrenched in our society intellectualism is, we begin asking ourselves more and more: "Gee whiz, what can we do?" Well, the first step in halting the spread of intellectualism is the realization that you—yes, you—may suffer from some latent form of this syndrome.

INSTANT IMPACT

A Robotic Listener

Boring! You've probably heard plenty of speeches in which speakers utter a *procession* of statements in a flat tone of voice. There is a term for such speakers: robotic. But that term has always *miffed* Dr. Cynthia Breazeal. It gives her robot a bad name.

Dr. Breazeal directs the Robotic Life Group at the Massachusetts Institute of Technology. She is most well-known for Kismet, a robot she developed in the late 1990s. Kismet is a humanoid robot with ears, eyes, eyebrows, and lips. The fifteen computers that operate Kismet's "brain" allow the robot to hear different tones of voice such as greeting, praise, warning, and comfort. When Kismet hears a certain tone, its face undergoes a *transformation:* eyebrows move, eyes widen, ears wiggle, lips wrinkle. Then Kismet responds in a voice that sounds like a small child. It can only make sounds, but its tone of voice expresses surprise, anger, fear, and joy. That's more than you can say for many human speakers.

Breazeal is now working to create actual speaking robots. She points out that the talking robots most people are familiar with are *hoked*-up inventions of science fiction. But she believes that someday Kismet will actually make a speech.

"I want to build a creature, not a robot," she says.

SECTION ① REVIEW

Recalling the Facts

1. What are the guidelines for a speech of presentation?
2. How should you organize an after-dinner speech?

Thinking Critically

Imagine that you are creating Kismet's first public speech. Make a list of five sentences that are frequently used in speeches. Then describe the tone of voice and facial expressions that Kismet should use when speaking the lines.

Taking Charge

Now try your hand at preparing a courtesy speech. Write and deliver a brief speech of introduction for one of the following:

1. a friend running for the student council
2. a teacher recognized for excellence in the classroom
3. a college financial officer addressing the senior class about scholarship opportunities

Ceremonial Speeches

The addresses known as ceremonial speeches are usually part of a formal activity. They often help the audience tie the past, present, and future together. The most common types of ceremonial speeches are commencement addresses and commemorative speeches, which include testimonials and eulogies.

Commencement Addresses

Some high schools select a member or members of each graduating class to present a valedictory, or farewell, speech. Another common practice is to invite a *dignitary* to address the graduating class. In either case, the speaker is giving a **commencement address,** or graduation speech. A commencement address should both acknowledge the importance of the ceremony and honor the graduates. The challenge for the speaker is to keep the attention of restless students and relatives who are already looking past the ceremony and toward the future. Therefore, most commencement addresses pay respect to the past but focus on the future of the graduates. If you are chosen to speak at a graduation ceremony, you should choose examples and illustrations that celebrate the collective experiences of the audience members. Humor, if appropriate, can ease the tension and make the ceremony more enjoyable for everyone. Successful commencement speakers are positive and uplifting.

The graduation speech excerpts that follow come from a graduation speech delivered by United States Secretary of State John F. Kerry at Boston College on May 19, 2014.

> It's a great honor to be with you. You all might remember from English class that the great American novelist Thomas Wolfe wrote that you can't go home again. Or maybe you know that quote because it's the same thing that your parents are telling you now.
>
> Well, Wolfe had obviously never been to Boston College. It is nice to be off an airplane, but my friends, it is great to be home. I am really happy to be here.
>
> I know that many of you stayed up all night so you could see your last sunrise at BC. Some of you thought it would never come, graduation that is. I've got news for you: Some of your parents and professors didn't think so either.
>
> Now, I notice a lot of you are wearing shades. It won't work, folks. I'll still hear you snoring.
>
> I was on the campus of one of your rivals yesterday in New Haven. And while I let them know that they could be proud of their title in men's hockey last year, I also had to put it in perspective: Yale is still four titles behind BC.
>
> There are many things actually that Yale and Boston College have in common, but one is probably the most powerful: mutual dislike of Harvard. Although to be fair, hundreds of schools don't like Harvard very much.

Vice President Dick Cheney delivers a commencement address at the U.S. Naval Academy.

CHAPTER 17 Speeches for Special Occasions **403**

As Secretary of State, I track many factions and rivalries around the world. BC versus Notre Dame is at the top of my list. Of course, there's also Alec Baldwin versus the NYPD. Beyoncé's sister versus Jay Z. And then there's the rivalry: Red Sox and Yankees. We absolutely loved the last ten years: Yankees – one World Series, and Red Sox – three. That's my kind of rivalry, folks.

Commemorative Speeches

You have heard the expression, "a picture is worth a thousand words." Some commemorative speakers in our country's history demonstrate that the *converse* is true: the right words are worth a thousand pictures. A **commemorative speech** is an inspiring address that recalls heroic events or people. John F. Kennedy's inaugural address, Douglas MacArthur's "Old Soldiers Never Die," and Ronald Reagan's speech following the *Challenger* space shuttle disaster are commemorative speeches that succeeded in capturing the collective imagination, in inspiring people to reaffirm ideals, in taking snapshots of history.

Another example is President Franklin D. Roosevelt's first inaugural address, delivered on March 4, 1933. That address contains one of the most memorable lines in speechmaking history: "The only thing we have to fear is fear itself." According to speechwriter and columnist William Safire, that phrase was added at the last moment to avoid the negativity in an earlier draft: "This is no occasion for soft speaking or for the raising of false

General Douglas MacArthur's "Old Soldiers Never Die" is a classic commemorative speech.

hopes." The lesson for you is that careful revision can strengthen not only a commemorative speech but any writing that you do. Let's look more closely at Roosevelt's revised draft in the following excerpt:

This is preeminently the time to speak the truth, the whole truth, frankly and boldly. Nor need we shrink from honestly facing conditions in our country today. This great nation will endure as it has endured, will revive and will prosper.

So, first of all, let me assert my firm belief, that the only thing we have to fear is fear itself—nameless, unreasoning, unjustified terror which paralyzes needed efforts to convert retreat into advance.

Roosevelt's inaugural address recalls a special event. Other commemorative speeches are given to honor individuals: the testimonial speech and the eulogy.

Testimonials You have witnessed countless testimonials by simply watching television ads. When a well-known and respected athlete hawks a particular brand of athletic shoes or you are told that "nine out of ten doctors agree," the advertisers are hoping that the prestige of their spokespersons will persuade you to purchase their product.

Cashing in on the name and prestige of someone else, though, is not the only form of testimonial. A **testimonial speech** is an address of praise or celebration honoring a living person. The purpose of these presentations is to pay tribute to a special person—to generate appreciation, admiration, or respect. These speeches are often given at celebrity roasts or as toasts at retirement dinners or wedding celebrations. You may hear a testimonial speech at a farewell banquet for a favorite teacher. The length of these speeches varies, but generally they last no more than a few minutes.

How can you make your testimonial speech successful? First, research carefully the person honored. If you can offer insights into what makes the person so deserving, your speech will be more successful. Language choice is crucial; the level of formality should fit the occasion. The tone of your speech should be warm and caring. A creative approach with appropriate humor that makes this special event memorable is desirable. Remember, audience members are there to pay tribute as well. Honor their feelings by *evoking* a strong sense of celebration.

A toast at a retirement party or wedding celebration is an example of what type of speech?

During a heartfelt speech delivered on June 07, 2011, at a State Dinner in the White House Rose Garden, President Obama paid tribute to German Chancellor Angela Merkel and presented her with the Presidential Medal of Freedom.

> Good evening. Guten abend. Michelle and I are honored to welcome you as we host Chancellor Merkel, Professor Sauer, and the German delegation for the first official visit and State Dinner for a European leader during my presidency.
>
> Angela, you and the German people have always shown me such warmth during my visits to Germany. I think of your gracious hospitality in Dresden. I think back to when I was a candidate and had that small rally in Berlin's Tiergarten. So we thought we'd reciprocate with a little dinner in our Rose Garden.
>
> Now, it's customary at these dinners to celebrate the values that bind nations. Tonight, we want to do something different. We want to pay tribute to an extraordinary leader who embodies these values and who's inspired millions around the world—including me—and that's my friend, Chancellor Merkel.
>
> More than five decades ago—in 1957—the first German chancellor ever to address our Congress, Konrad Adenauer, spoke of his people's "will of freedom" and of the millions of his countrymen

INSTANT IMPACT

More than Fourscore and Seven Years Ago . . .

On the afternoon of November 19, 1863, Abraham Lincoln delivered his Gettysburg Address. This famous commemorative speech consisted of only ten sentences and lasted less than three minutes. In the years since Lincoln's brief remarks, millions of American students have committed these cherished words to memory. At the time of the speech, though, news coverage of it varied from praise to condemnation.

- *Chicago Times*—"Mr. Lincoln did most foully traduce [slander] the motives of the men who were slain at Gettysburg."
- *Chicago Tribune*—"The dedicatory remarks of President Lincoln will live among the annals of man."
- *London Times*—"The ceremony was rendered ludicrous by some of the sallies [lively remarks] of that poor President Lincoln. . . . Anything more dull and commonplace it would not be easy to produce."

forced to live behind an Iron Curtain. And one of those millions, in a small East German town, was a young girl named Angela.

> She remembers when the Wall went up and how everyone in her church was crying. Told by the communists that she couldn't pursue her love of languages, she excelled as a physicist. Asked to spy for the secret police, she refused. And the night the Wall came down, she crossed over, like so many others, and finally experienced what she calls the "incredible gift of freedom."
>
> Tonight, we honor Angela Merkel not for being denied her freedom, or even for attaining her freedom, but for what she achieved when she gained her freedom. Determined to finally have her say, she entered politics -- rising to become the first East German to lead a united Germany, the first woman chancellor in German history, and an

eloquent voice for human rights and dignity around the world.

The Presidential Medal of Freedom is the highest honor a President can bestow on a civilian. Most honorees are Americans; only a few others have received it, among them Pope John Paul II, Nelson Mandela, and Helmut Kohl. So please join me in welcoming Chancellor Merkel for the presentation of the next Medal of Freedom.

Eulogies A **eulogy** is generally thought of as a speech given to praise or honor someone who has died. The speaker, therefore, should try to relate to the audience the significant meaning in that person's life. Because eulogies are usually delivered at funerals or memorial services, the speaker must respect the religious beliefs of members of the family as well as the deceased.

In preparing a eulogy, you should decide whether you want to choose a biographical or a topical approach. As you attempt to chronicle a person's entire life, you will discover that the biographical speech often contains so many details that you lose the significance of the moment. In the topical approach, however, you can focus on personal qualities or specific achievements from which the audience can gain inspiration or understanding.

Although the tone of a eulogy is almost always solemn and the language sincere, you can be creative in your choices. You must, however, select details with great sensitivity and care. The following two examples pay tribute to the deceased in different and unusual ways.

One ninth-grade student eulogized her grandmother in a speech that reminds us that we all have "unfinished business":

> Dear Grandma,
> I'm not quite sure why I'm writing this letter. I know you don't have a P.O. box up there. I just want a chance to tell you how much I miss, need, love, and thank you.
> Unfinished business. We each have our own unfinished business. My math homework was due

President William J. Clinton
Eulogy for Bombing Victims
Oklahoma City, Oklahoma
April 23, 1995

My fellow Americans:

Today our nation is joined with you in grief. We mourn with you. We share your hope against hope that others have survived. We thank all who have worked so heroically to save lives and solve this crime. We pledge to do all we can to help you heal the injured, to rebuild this city, and to bring to justice those who did this evil deed.

This excerpt shows that President Bill Clinton carefully chose details to include in his eulogy for the bombing victims in Oklahoma City in 1995.

Tuesday, and I'm only on problem 3; I can't spend the night at Jenny's because I haven't finished vacuuming the den; and I won't receive my allowance until all the leaves are raked and bagged. Oh, we all have our own incomplete chores, but I'm referring to another kind of unfinished business—the kind between my grandmother and me.

So often, loved ones are taken away, and inevitably we grieve, but too many times our lasting sorrow overwhelms us because we fail to tell others how much we love them in the living years. I deeply regret not telling my grandmother her importance in my life. If only, if only I'd said goodbye, eye to eye, heart to heart. If only we all told our loved ones how much we need, love, and thank them before it's too late. If only we finished our business.

Grandma, I need you. I need the crumpled Kleenex always waiting in your pocket to wipe away my tears, and I need your bedtime fairy tales that taught me morals and made me smile. But most of all I need your good advice.

Today, in our independent society, we seldom feel the need to verbally accept others' spiritual gifts. Psychiatrist and author Gerald G. Jampolsky

National Archives and Records Administration (595142)

writes, "Giving means that all of one's love is extended with no expectations." If only we would accept that gift of extended love and then express our appreciation.

I love your comforting arms that swallow my troubles with every hug. I love your shiny white locks. With every curl lies a bit of wisdom. I love your presence.

Playwright Thornton Wilder states, "There is a land of the living and a land of the dead, and the bridge is love, the only survival, the only meaning." If only we could communicate our love in the land of the living, it could form the bridge to the land of the dead.

Grandma, I thank you for your lessons in life: you taught me to plant pansies and make apple pies, but you also taught me through love that all things are possible.

Thanks that are so often felt but so seldom expressed. It doesn't go without saying. In the book of Job, chapter 1, verse 21, we learn, "The Lord giveth and the Lord taketh away." So before he takes what he's given, let us tell those special individuals what they've given to us. Let us finish our business.

SECTION 2 REVIEW

Recalling the Facts

1. What is the purpose of a testimonial speech?
2. What two things should a commencement address do?

Thinking Critically

Should eulogies be given only for persons who are praiseworthy? Does every human being have some essential worth? Explain your answer.

Taking Charge

Now it's your turn. Prepare a brief eulogy to honor someone who recently died. You might choose to write about someone you knew, a celebrity, or another public figure. For inspiration and ideas, refer to the examples that you just read.

Contest Speeches

Each year, thousands of students participate in interscholastic speech competitions. A tournament hosted by a high school or college takes place somewhere in the United States almost every weekend of the school year. If you would like to benefit from this valuable activity, you should discuss the opportunities available at your school with your speech teacher.

The rules that govern speech contests vary from state to state and from one national speech organization (such as the Catholic Forensic League and the National Forensic League) to another. With a few exceptions, speech events all into two categories: public speaking and interpretation. Popular events include original oratory, extemporaneous speaking, and dramatic and humorous interpretation.

Original Oratory

The speech contest event in which you write on a topic of your own choosing is known as **original oratory.** Most states require that you memorize your speech and limit it to ten minutes in length. The key to oratory is to remember that it is a persuasive speech. To be convincing, therefore, you should pick a topic you feel strongly about. Typical topics include everything from the importance of community to neglect of senior citizens.

Oratory demands careful and complete preparation. Successful orators live with their speeches for weeks or months. Painstaking revision and updating of the material are therefore necessary to keep it fresh.

In preparing a speech, use the organizational principles outlined in Chapter 9, and choose language for grace and precision. Keep in mind that the rules often limit the number of quoted words you can have in your speech. The National Forensic League, for example, allows no more than 150. You have the responsibility to cite the sources from which

you obtained ideas. A rehash of a *Time* or *Sierra* magazine article is insufficient and, if extensively paraphrased, unethical. Furthermore, do not expect your speech coach to write your oration for you. The event is called original oratory for a reason.

Extemporaneous Speaking

As you will recall from your study of Chapter 15, in competitive extemporaneous speaking, participants pick one topic from a choice of three and then prepare a five- to seven-minute speech on that topic. The topic choices are based on current issues and are usually presented in question form. Usually the topic choices come in two divisions: national and international. For example, a contestant might be asked to choose from the following national topics:

- Do politicians have a right to privacy?
- How can we win the war on drugs?
- How can we better provide for senior citizens in our nation?

Contestants are allowed 30 minutes to prepare their speeches. They are allowed access only to the

Interscholastic speech contests generally have two categories: public speaking and interpretation.

Steve Debenport/Getty Images

408 **UNIT 4** Presentations

documents or background information that they have brought to the contest. In some tournaments—especially those that are held early in the competing schedule—extemporaneous speakers may bring a single note card to guide them through the speech. The judge's evaluation of your speech is based on several factors—the most important being how well you answer the question or discuss the topic.

Dramatic and Humorous Interpretation

Competitive interpretation events allow you to choose the material you want to perform. Do you have a favorite role in a play that your theater department is not going to produce? Have you ever wanted to be more than one of the characters in a play? **Dramatic interpretation** and **humorous interpretation**—sometimes separate categories and sometimes combined—give you the opportunity to share your acting talents. To paraphrase Whoopi Goldberg, you are the show.

The fine line between acting and interpretation is discussed in Chapter 16. *Suffice* it to say that in the memorized interpretation events, competitors are generally "acting from the waist up," while in the scripted events, competitors are expected to suggest rather than become a character.

If you like performing scenes with a partner, then duo interpretation may be the event for you. This event allows for the support of a teammate plus—depending on the rules in your state—the fun of using many of the concepts, such as advanced blocking techniques, you may have learned in theater class.

The rules for interpretation events vary greatly from state to state. For example, some states permit extensive movement, and some do not; some permit singing, and some do not. In addition, each judge seems to have a different philosophy about what is preferable and what is acceptable.

How, then, do you know what to do? The skills you need to become an "interper" are treated at length in Chapter 16. In general, study the rules for each tournament carefully, and try to make artistic decisions that honor the integrity of your selection. Do not rewrite Shakespeare because you can't

TYPES OF SPEECHES FOR SPECIAL OCCASIONS

Courtesy speeches, including introductions, presentation and acceptance speeches, and after-dinner speeches.

Ceremonial speeches, including commencement addresses, commemorative speeches, and eulogies.

Contest speeches, including original oratories, extemporaneous speeches, and dramatic and humorous interpretations.

Impromptu speeches.

understand *whence* and *whilst* and *woo*. If you perform "The Belle of Amherst," do not give Emily Dickinson a southern accent. Do not scream or cry as a way to win favor from the judge when it is clear that the character you are playing would not.

Give much thought to the kind of material that is suitable for you. Try to choose a selection that fits your personality and stretches you as a performer but is not beyond your grasp. For example, a male who cannot play female characters should avoid portraying Joan of Arc. Some selections require a number of characters; see that you can make them all unique and believable. Character differentiation that is mechanical or distracting is undesirable. In tournament competition, your goal is to make your performance so affecting, so real, that the judge forgets it is a contest entry.

Other Contests

If you are seeking scholarships for higher education, some clubs and organizations sponsor speech contests for cash prizes—in many cases, for thousands of dollars. The contests offered vary from community to community but include the following:

1. The American Legion Oratorical Contest. You must write, memorize, and deliver an eight- to ten-minute oration on some aspect of the United States Constitution. The contest also requires that you speak extemporaneously for three to five minutes on one of four of the Constitution's articles or amendments.
2. The Veterans of Foreign Wars Voice of Democracy Contest. You must write and record a three- to five-minute speech on a theme that changes yearly. You enter the recording in the competition, and it is evaluated for content and delivery.
3. The Optimist Club Oratorical Contest. You write and deliver a four- to five-minute speech on a yearly theme. The competition is for students under age 16, giving younger students an excellent opportunity to compete. The text of a winning oration is included in this chapter.

But What If You Don't Win?

Most students who compete in speech soon tire of hearing this familiar *refrain* at every award ceremony: "There are no losers today. You are all winners simply by participating." Since speech contests are competitive, it is only natural that you will want to win. Unfortunately, the ranking of contestants is a subjective undertaking. Judges will disagree. One

INSTANT IMPACT

The Speech Collector

"Curse of a Malignant Tongue," "Not Just a Farmer," and "Before the Diet of Worms" are just a few of the many world-famous orations and speeches included in Roberta Sutton's *Speech Index,* an index to collections of speeches. Other speech indexes provide more recent works. These references include responses to toasts, responses to speeches of blame, speeches concerning commencement, and speeches concerning *combustion*—usually not at the same time. The original date and place of presentations are given, along with the title of the anthology in which the presentations appear.

judge may compliment you on your creative approach to a topic; another may say that same approach is overused.

If you are to find satisfaction in speech competition, then you should set your own standards. Strive for excellence as you define it, and settle for no less. Certainly, you need to adapt to the audience—your judges—but not if that means compromising your integrity. Ultimately, your success in any competitive activity depends on the goals you have for yourself. Satisfy your own high standards of performance, and the reward will always be there. If the only goal you have is to win, you have already lost.

Recalling the Facts

1. What is the key to writing an original oratory?
2. What is the difference between original oratory and extemporaneous speaking?
3. What is dramatic interpretation?
4. In which category of popular contest speech events do you have to memorize the speech you give?
5. Name three speech contests that give monetary awards to the winners.

Thinking Critically

1. Most students write original oratories on topics of their choosing, because they feel strongly about the topic. Some students are given topics by their coaches. Do you think speakers should try to persuade an audience about topics they themselves don't care about? Explain your answer.
2. If you were a judge at a dramatic interpretation competition, what would you look for in a winning interpretation? Make a list of four things you would look for in a winner.

Taking Charge

1. A popular speech event at some tournaments is original prose and poetry. In this event, student competitors write and perform their own literary efforts. Now it's your turn. Write a poem or a short piece of prose (two to three minutes long) and perform it for the class. Include a brief introduction to help the audience understand and enjoy your performance.
2. Choose one character from TV, movies, or another source that you would like to interpret. Locate a clip or a script that features the character. Prepare a list of what you would do to present an interpretation of that character. Would you change your voice? What clothes would you wear? What props would you use?
3. Choose one of the speaking competitions listed in the section to research. Decide whether you would enter the competition and list the reasons why.

Looking Back

Listed below are the major ideas discussed in this chapter.

- Introductory speeches serve two functions: to make the audience want to hear the speaker and to make the speaker want to address the audience.
- Introductory speeches refer to the occasion, name the speaker, build enthusiasm, share information, and explain why this speaker is giving this talk to this audience at this time.
- Presentation speeches should reflect the feelings of the group. These speeches usually state the name of the person receiving the award, explain the award's significance, describe how the recipient was selected, and highlight what makes this person unique.
- Speeches of acceptance are usually brief and impromptu but generally thank the group for the recognition, discuss the importance of the award, and thank supporters.

- The traditional after-dinner speech is entertaining; any humor used in it relates to a specific theme.
- Commencement speeches should both acknowledge the importance of the ceremony and honor the graduates.
- Commemorative speeches recall special events or pay tribute to individuals.
- A testimonial speech honors a living person; a eulogy honors the dead.
- An original oratory is a persuasive speech the contestant writes on a topic of his or her own choosing.
- In competitive extemporaneous speaking, the speaker draws a topic on a current event and prepares a speech within 30 minutes.
- Dramatic and humorous interpretation are contest events for students who want to perform works of literature.

Speech Vocabulary

In each of the following sentences, fill in the blank with the missing term.

speech of presentation
speech of acceptance
after-dinner speech
commencement address
commemorative speech
testimonial speech
eulogy
original oratory
dramatic interpretation
humorous interpretation

1. Audiences expect an _____ to present a message in a light, if not humorous, way.
2. A _____ acknowledges the importance of the ceremony and honors the graduates.
3. Testimonials and eulogies are two types of _____.
4. When a star athlete hawks a particular brand of tennis shoe, that is a form of _____.
5. A _____ is generally thought of as a speech given to praise or honor someone who has died.
6. An _____ is a speech you write on a topic of your own choosing.

7. In the memorized _____ event, the competitors are usually "acting from the waist up."

8. If a classmate was to be publicly presented with a gift, you would prepare a _____ for the occasion.

Academic Vocabulary

Choose two pairs from the following word list and describe how the words are alike or different.

reiterate	dignitary	miffed	hoke	evoking	suffice
eloquent	procession	transformation	converse	combustion	refrain

To Remember

Answer the following based on your reading of the chapter.

1. List five guidelines to follow in a speech of introduction.
2. Speeches of acceptance serve a double purpose: to _____ and to _____.
3. In his concession speech, _____ compared himself to a boy who has stubbed his toe in the dark: "too old to cry, but it hurts too much to laugh."
4. Ronald Reagan's speech following the *Challenger* space shuttle disaster in 1986 is considered an inspiring example of a _____ speech.
5. Kareem Abdul-Jabbar's tribute to Earvin Johnson is a form of the _____ speech.

6. If you wanted to find a particular oration in a collection of speeches, to which reference work in the library would you turn?
7. List five guidelines that you might follow in a speech of presentation.
8. _____ is a contest speech event that requires you to draw a topic and prepare a speech within 30 minutes.
9. In the scripted interpretation events, competitors are expected to _____ rather than "become" the characters.
10. List five guidelines to follow in a speech of acceptance.

To Do

1. Question your parents about their past. Choose one incident from the discussion and prepare a short speech on the topic "A Turning Point."
2. Attend a speech tournament. After watching a few rounds of competition, be prepared to discuss the differences between what the speech competitors did and what you do in class.

3. Experienced speakers know that libraries contain reference works that are collections of humorous anecdotes. These anecdotes can be used to spice up an occasional speech. To learn how to use these valuable resources, find three humorous anecdotes on a general topic of your choosing—fashion, sports, education, health, or the like.

To Talk About

1. Some schools—perhaps yours—select students to speak at the graduation ceremony. How should these speakers be chosen? Based on their grades? Talent? Popularity? Who should select these speakers? Administrators? Teachers? Committees of teachers and students?

2. Most audiences expect after-dinner speeches to be entertaining. What are some topics you would find worthwhile and enjoyable? Why?

3. Lanny Naegelin, former coordinator for five high school speech and theater programs in San Antonio, Texas, believed that students involved in competitive sports received more public recognition than students involved in speech activities. If that was the case, was it fair? What can be done to educate the community about the value of speech?

4. Judging speech tournaments involves subjective evaluation. For example, a judge must choose one humorous interpretation over another. This process is analogous to deciding who is the funnier of two popular comedians. How can we judge artistic endeavors more fairly?

5. Your best friend has been invited to be the after-dinner speaker at a banquet honoring a basketball coach whose team had a losing record. What advice might you give your friend?

To Write About

1. You are invited to be a guest speaker at a banquet honoring students who have volunteered their time for community service. Write a speech of introduction for yourself.

2. Imagine that you have been asked to speak at your twenty-year high school class reunion. Write a brief speech in which you look back on how the world has changed.

3. Write an introduction for one of your classmates that could be used during the next series of assigned speeches in your class.

Related Speech Topics

Pay tribute to a personal hero.
Present an award or a gift.
Accept an award or a gift.
Introduce someone famous to the class.
Speak at a celebrity roast.
Give a toast that butters up.

The special-occasion speeches of one of the following:
  Ronald Reagan
  John F. Kennedy
  Martin Luther King Jr.
  Mark Twain
  Madeleine Albright
  Cesar Chávez
  Sally Ride

UNIT

5

Problem Solving and Conflict Management

UNIT CONTENTS

SUPPORTING YOUR VIEWS

There is no polish without friction.

—Frederick Douglass

Learning Objectives

After completing this chapter, you will be able to do the following.

- List the five common strategies for resolving conflicts.
- Practice the four techniques for negotiation.
- Give examples of the ways in which people participate in informal debate.
- Define basic debate terms.
- Prepare for and participate in an informal debate.

Chapter Outline

Following are the main sections in this chapter.

1. The Art of Negotiation
2. Informal Debate
3. The Advantages of Debate
4. Debate Terminology
5. The Debate Process

Speech Vocabulary

In this chapter, you will learn the meanings of the speech terms listed below.

negotiation
debate
I-message
avoidance
accommodation
competition
compromise
collaboration
integrity
informal debate
proposition
resolution

affirmative
negative
status quo
burden of proof
argument
case
brief
constructive
refute
rebuttal
format
flowsheet

Academic Vocabulary

Expanding your academic vocabulary will help you become a more effective communicator. Listed below are some words appearing in this chapter that you should make part of your vocabulary.

barter
alienate
equitable
innuendo

intimidation
vouchers
deficit

In this chapter, you are going to learn about another kind of communication: debate. You'll learn what debate is, its different forms, and its special terminology. You'll also learn how studying and practicing debate can help you achieve your goals. But first, you will learn some important principles of negotiation. Both debate and negotiation will be invaluable as you support your views throughout your life.

Introduction

We do not live in a perfect world. You will not always agree with everyone you meet in life. You can probably think of plenty of examples: the bully who won't leave you alone, the parent who won't let you stay out late enough, the boss who won't give you a raise, and on and on.

Each of these situations creates a problem for you. Often you will be able to reach a solution through negotiation. **Negotiation**, at its best, is a cooperative relationship in which both sides want to reach an agreement. Sometimes, though, negotiation is less than cooperative. Therefore, you need a more formal method of solving problems. **Debate**, from a Latin word meaning "to battle," is an important method of solving problems in a democracy.

In fact, the founders of the United States were highly skilled debaters. By the 1650s, most colonial colleges required debate as a means of training young scholars. For example, when Thomas Jefferson was a student at the College of William and Mary, he participated in debates. Jefferson was taught by George Wythe, the same debate coach who tutored such famous orators as Henry Clay and John Marshall. At the time, debate was considered to be the best way to develop the character and skills required of citizens in our young nation.

George Wythe instructed both Thomas Jefferson (left) and Henry Clay (above) in the art of debate.

The challenge of learning to negotiate and to debate awaits you in this chapter. True, hard work lies ahead, but the rewards are significant. You will improve your ability to research and develop arguments, to organize your thoughts, and to speak extemporaneously. Moreover, you will be able to support your views.

The Art of Negotiation

Y ou may think negotiation is not very important to you. But just wait until you find yourself haggling over the price of your first car. You'd better believe that the used-car salesperson trying to sell you the latest lemon on the lot knows how to negotiate. You should know what he or she knows, if only to protect yourself. But saving a buck is not the only reason to learn the principles of negotiation.

Why Negotiate?

Negotiation is not always about money. Certainly, learning negotiation skills can help you get pay raises, sell your home for more, even *barter* to borrow your neighbor's lawn mower. More important, though, is the opportunity to improve your personal relationships. You, too, can win friends and influence people.

Suppose your best friend wants to borrow money from you. The amount he wants to borrow is more than you can afford, and your friend gets angry when you refuse to help him. Suppose your father insists that you wash the car every Saturday, but your older brother has no chores. Suppose your curfew is an hour earlier than for any of your friends. Clearly, for each of these situations, you need to develop ways to resolve a conflict. Conflict expert Dr. Kenneth Thomas has developed strategies for resolving conflicts, as outlined in the chart on page 458. It explains the strengths and weaknesses of various options for dealing with conflict.

Techniques of Negotiation

There is more to negotiation than getting your own way. You might want to avoid the strategy, recommended by Scott Adams's comic strip character Dilbert, of making the final suggestion in any meeting. This maneuver involves waiting until the allotted meeting time is almost up, when "patience is thin and bladders are full." At this point, Dilbert says, offer your suggestion. Explain that your suggestion is based on all of the good thoughts that have been presented at the meeting, "no matter how ridiculous they might be."

Perhaps more useful than Dilbert's Final Suggestion Maneuver are these four techniques for effective negotiation:

1. Be Positive
Negative words can close the door to negotiations. These words turn people off to your message. These words limit, because they suggest

Negotiating can sometimes lower prices during a big purchase.

©Ariel Skelley/Blend Images LLC

refusal and denial. Think, for example, how much you dislike it when someone tells you "no."

2. Use Three-Part Messages
Most of us rely heavily on **I-messages**, statements that emphasize what we want. Such messages can *alienate* people, and therefore can be counterproductive in negotiation. For example, saying, "Stop talking so I can get a

Strategies for Conflict Resolution

The following are a few general strategies for resolving conflict.

 Don't ignore the conflict or deny that a problem exists. By clearly identifying and articulating what the issue is, you can focus on resolving the problem through open discussion and negotiation.

 Acknowledge the views and expectations of each person. By recognizing and accepting that your may opinions differ, you can work together to resolve the problem.

3 Communicate views and possible solutions without accommodating, or minimizing, your position or outshining the competition. The goal is to find a mutually satisfactory solution to resolve the conflict.

4 Don't make trade-offs in order to meet in the middle. Compromising to arrive at satisfactory outcomes, may reduce conflict without actually resolving it.

5 Collaboration is the key to resolving conflict. Working together to satisfy the concerns of all parties builds consensus that leads to conflict resolution.

word in edgewise!" will not bring you closer to a satisfactory resolution. If you were to attend a business seminar on negotiation, you would learn that two-part messages are more effective: "When you keep talking, it hurts my feelings." Even better, though, is the three-part message advocated by Dr. Thomas Gordon, a leader in effectiveness training.

Using this pattern, a teacher might say: "When you don't do your homework, I feel disappointed, because you don't learn what you need to know." The three-part message is an important tool in negotiation because both sides are forced to clarify the key issues.

①	②	③
When you X	I feel Y	because Z

3. Be Prepared

Aristotle once observed that "the way to achieve success is first to have a definite, clear, practical ideal." Today, Aristotle might have said that you need an "ideal deal." In other words, you have to define what it is you want. You shouldn't ask the boss for a pay raise without having an amount in mind. Therefore, you must have the reasons for a raise carefully researched and documented. Do your homework. Know the facts before you open your mouth. Talking off the top of your head rarely impresses anyone.

It is wise to have alternatives in mind. You may not get exactly what you want in any negotiation. Be able to justify your best alternative. Suppose you make a case for being paid $10 each time you wash the car. If your father says you have to continue washing the car and he still refuses to pay you, you might want to offer an alternative. Perhaps your older sister could wash the car every other week. If not profitable, at least you could suggest that it's *equitable* (fair).

Finally, you should know as much as possible about the position of the other party. Try to understand the "why" of his or her position. Perhaps your parents won't extend your

I-messages seldom lead to satisfactory resolutions. In fact, they can alienate others.

Whether negotiating with your siblings or others, be prepared to state your position.

curfew because your grades are low. Or maybe it's because they don't trust your friends. Without knowing the "why," you will find it difficult to prepare satisfactory responses to their concerns.

4. **Tell the Truth**

Your reputation is built on your integrity. To have **integrity** means that you are true to yourself. You should never sacrifice your values or standards to achieve your negotiation goals. You gain the respect of others by doing what is right. Never make promises you can't keep. Never put others in a position that forces them to compromise their integrity. Peter Scotese, the retired CEO of Spring Industries, once said that "Integrity is not a 90 percent thing, not a 95 percent thing; either you have it or you don't."

SECTION ① REVIEW

Recalling the Facts

1. Name the three parts of the three-part message.
2. What does *integrity* mean?
3. What are some strategies for resolving conflict?

Thinking Critically

Suppose that your school administration has decided to require all students to wear uniforms. It will let the students choose the type of uniform. In this section, you learned that it is easier to work with people than to work against them. And yet not all high school students get along with or even like each other. What are some things you could do to convince people who dislike each other to collaborate?

Taking Charge

1. Attend the next meeting of the student council or any other school organization. Which of the five approaches to negotiation did you see employed? How did the approaches used affect what was accomplished?
2. To learn how three-part messages can affect your message, write a brief speech trying to persuade the audience to take action on a particular issue. For example, ask them to donate blood. Incorporate a three-part message to clarify the key issues.

Informal Debate

We have defined *debate* as a battle of ideas. When people disagree and each person puts forward an idea he or she thinks is superior, a debate is going on. Negotiation is a kind of informal debate. **Informal debate** is any debate conducted without specific rules. It's an unstructured, open-ended discussion of opposing ideas.

Before we begin our study of formal debate, let's take a quick look at some different types of informal debate. You may be surprised at how much you already know about debate and at how many debates in which you have already participated.

Personal Debate

You could say that people debate themselves all the time. This is the intrapersonal communication discussed in Chapter 1. When you have a personal problem, you consider alternatives as you try to solve the problem. Maybe you can't decide whether to go out for the basketball team or the marching band. You like both, but the schedules conflict. There's no way you can do both. In such a case, you might make a list of the pros and cons of both options. You might sit in your room and think to yourself, "If I went out for basketball,

I'd get to hang out with all my hoop buddies, but I'd also have to put in a lot of hours of hard work— all that running every night. But if I joined the band, . . ." In cases like these, your mind is a battleground for opposing ideas. In other words, a silent debate is going on inside your head. Eventually, one side's ideas will overpower the other's, and there will be a winner. You engage in this kind of internal debate several times a week as you solve life's everyday problems.

Disagreements and Arguments

You probably don't need to be told what an argument is. Very few people go through life without getting into at least an occasional argument. Of course, there are all kinds of arguments—friendly ones, heated ones, serious ones, or amusing ones. All of these arguments are, in a sense, debates. They are battles between opposing ideas.

In a personal debate, you might be debating whether to study or hang out with you friends.

(bl) © Robert Daly/age fotostock; (br) Design Pics / Don Hammond

Your brother claims it's your turn to mow the yard, but you say it's his turn. You give your reasons and try to show your mother why his reasons don't make sense. He does the same. In this case, there is a clash of ideas and a parent acts as a judge to determine whose reasons are better. Your skills as a debater may determine whether you lounge coolly in front of the computer surfing the Internet or strain and sweat behind the lawn mower. Later those same skills might help you persuade a boss to accept your proposal for a new project.

Group Discussion

Often, members of a group disagree about a course of action. In these cases, an informal debate occurs. Here's an example. It's a hot summer day, and you and several friends have decided to go swimming. The problem is that some of your friends want to go to the community pool, but some of them want to go to the lake outside of town.

How do you solve the problem? If only one person has a car and a driver's license and that person is bigger and stronger than everyone else and always likes to get his or her way, the problem is solved. If, however, everyone has an equal say, the group will probably solve the problem by listening to the reasons different people give for going to the lake or the pool:

- The pool is closer.
- The lake is prettier.
- The pool water is cleaner.
- The lake water doesn't have chlorine in it.
- There will be more boys (or girls) at the pool.
- They've got a great water slide at the lake.

This battle of ideas goes on for a while, and during the conversation more people begin to favor either the pool or the lake. The reasons for picking one solution tend to outweigh those for picking the other. Some members of the group argue more persuasively than others. Eventually, several people swing over to one side, and the problem is solved. The group as a whole has acted like a jury in deciding the outcome of this informal debate.

Developing your debate skills could help you present your side of an issue the next time you and your parents disagree.

Organizations and Meetings

You probably belong to at least one organization that has meetings from time to time: your school class, Girl Scouts, a church committee, the athletic letter–winner club, Future Farmers of America, or the yearbook committee. Your meetings may be very informal, perhaps not much different from a discussion among a group of friends. In a larger organization, your meetings might be conducted according to the rules of parliamentary procedure (see Chapter 20). In either case, informal debate will occur as you and the other organization members discuss ways to solve problems.

Let's say that your sophomore class needs to raise a great deal of money to finance next year's prom. You've got several ongoing projects to raise money, but you're looking for one big project for your sophomore year. One person has suggested an elaborate series of car washes every weekend over a six-month period, while another has recommended "selling" members of the class to local businesses. The businesses would then contribute money to your class based on the students' work. Both ideas would require a lot of volunteer time from class members, so it's not practical to do both. One idea must be chosen. A debate begins.

If you have a strong opinion as to which method would be more fun and interesting—and, of course, would raise more money—you may participate in the debate by giving reasons for or against one of the alternatives. Even if you don't express an opinion in front of the group, you will probably participate in the debate as a judge, since the class will finally vote. Whether you speak or not, you will be participating in an informal debate.

A car wash is one common fund-raiser you might vote for or against at a school meeting.

SECTION ② REVIEW

Recalling the Facts

1. Debate is a battle between _____.
2. When you debate without specific rules, the process is described as _____.

Thinking Critically

Working in pairs, observe each of your school's clubs and other organizations. Contact the officers of each group to find out when it will have its next meeting and whether it would be all right for members of your class to attend as observers. The observers should report back to the class how much and what types of debate took place in the meetings. Discuss and evaluate what advantages might result from using formal debate procedures and skills.

Taking Charge

1. Make a list of the ideas you've debated with yourself over the past several days. Compare your list with your classmates' lists. If any ideas appear on more than one list, discuss whether the debates led to the same conclusion.
2. Role-play an argument between siblings. First, brainstorm as a class to generate a list of common topics over which siblings disagree. Then role-play the situations, which could involve two to four siblings. Evaluate each situation to see if there were winners. If so, discuss which arguments or tactics proved most effective for the winners.

The Advantages of Debate

There are many ways in which you can benefit from studying and practicing debate. Becoming an accomplished debater will help you now and in the future. Here are just a few of the advantages of becoming a better debater and a better evaluator of debates.

Career

In many of the careers you might pursue after leaving school, you will encounter situations in which you may or may not be chosen to move up to a position of higher responsibility and pay. In those careers, your success will often depend on your ability to persuade people. Most of the workplace situations in which you'll need to impress and persuade other people will involve some degree of debating skill. Managers and coworkers will challenge your opinions the way a debater is challenged. You'll have to think quickly and improvise rather than rely solely on prepared remarks. You can begin developing all of these skills as a debater.

by presenting the arguments for and against each alternative clearly and logically, and by helping the class evaluate those issues fairly.

In debate, you learn to narrow the issues so that they can be analyzed one at a time. You also learn how to present logical, well-supported arguments and how to find and point out errors in other arguments. All of these skills help everyone move closer to the truth and to the best solution for a problem. In so doing, you help everyone involved.

As a Voter

As you learn about debate, you will become a more and more effective evaluator of arguments. You will become a more analytical listener. If you listen to two political candidates debate, you'll be better able to tell which is more prepared, more logical, and quicker thinking—all qualities that would help that person perform her or his duties successfully if elected. You will also become more knowledgeable about the candidates and thus be

Helping Others

We all feel good when we can help other people. Think back to the class meeting example you read about earlier, when the class was deciding how to raise money for the prom. In that situation, the person who understands debate will be able to assist everyone in the class. How? By helping the class members focus on the key issues,

Managers and coworkers help each other by examining and analyzing issues at work..

International Debate

In 1992 Tim Averill planned to take his championship high school debate team from Manchester, Massachusetts, to London to celebrate the team's twentieth anniversary. But while he was organizing the trip, his London contacts kept suggesting that Manchester represent the United States in the World School Debating Championships. Averill finally accepted the invitation, and Manchester joined twelve other countries to face off in London.

Some topics were sent to the debaters several months before the competition, and the remainder of the topics were announced with one and a half hour's notice and prepared by the teams with no assistance from their coaches. The team from Manchester was assigned the following topics:

- This House believes that nuclear energy is worth the risk.
- This House believes that today's heroes are hollow.
- This House would abolish all monarchies.

Manchester was also assigned the following topics, for which they had 90 minutes to prepare:

- Resolved: that this House welcomes the fall of Communism.
- Resolved: that this House would close down Hollywood.
- Resolved: that this House believes that the war against discrimination has been fought badly.

Would you close down Hollywood?

In international debating competitions, "the emphasis is upon 'public persuasion,'" said Averill, "and the careful use of a relatively small amount of evidence." Each team is encouraged to have an advocacy position, but it is the ethos of the individual speakers that determines the outcome; humor and wit are required and rewarded. Unlike policy debates in the United States, international debates focus more on the speakers' own knowledge than on documentation.

The first World School Championship was held in 1988 in Australia, and six countries participated. Today, teams from around the world compete in the championship. The event is about more than debating; it's about learning. According to Averill, "We had the opportunity to get to know students from all over the world, to share ideas and opinions, and to assess our educational system by comparison." In 2008, the United States hosted the event for the second time.

Questions
1. Do you think the ethos of individual debaters should determine the outcome of debates? Why or why not?
2. What arguments might you have presented on the resolution to "close down Hollywood"?

able to make a more informed choice for the candidate you felt had the right ideas. As Thomas Jefferson argued, an informed electorate is necessary for a democracy to work.

As a Citizen

What are some of the "hot topics" at your school or in your community right now? Do you have strong feelings about any of these issues? If so, wouldn't you enjoy standing up at a school board meeting or a city council meeting and clearly and logically pointing out to everyone there why your solution was preferable to the other solutions being offered? If challenged or attacked, wouldn't you gain satisfaction from being able to respond to the challenge with several well-supported counterattacks? Even more important than your personal satisfaction would be the community service that would result from your informal debate efforts. When you feel strongly about an issue, you can help the members of your community by helping them choose the best solution to their problem.

How might learning debate strategies help you to become a more informed voter?

See It Again

In March 1954, Edward R. Murrow, a prominent broadcast journalist, used his television series *See It Now* to debate Joseph McCarthy, the Wisconsin senator and Communist hunter. Pointing out contradictions in McCarthy's statements and challenging his "facts," Murrow invited McCarthy to respond.

On April 6, McCarthy responded on *See It Now* that Murrow was "the leader and the cleverest of the jackal pack which is always found at the throat of anyone who dares to expose individual Communists and traitors." Throughout the broadcast, McCarthy used the very tactics—*innuendo, intimidation,* and falsehood—that Murrow had accused him of using. This second broadcast defined the characters of the two debaters. Wanting to be precise, Murrow read from a prepared text, while McCarthy made personal attacks on Murrow. McCarthy resorted to exaggeration; Murrow documented claims carefully.

Kathleen Hall Jamieson and David S. Birdsell, in *Presidential Debates,* conclude that "Had McCarthy not engaged Murrow in debate before a common audience, and in the process confirmed the charges he was attempting to dispatch, the damage to McCarthy's credibility would have been less severe."

By the end of 1954, McCarthy was condemned by other members of the Senate. His public support eroded, and McCarthy died in 1957 from health problems.

Recalling the Facts

1. Describe the ways that debate can help you in a career.
2. How can debating skills help you assist other people at your school?
3. How can understanding debate help you as a voter?
4. Explain how learning about debate will make you a better citizen.

Thinking Critically

1. Do you believe that debate can change the minds of people? Select a recent presidential campaign and research the debates between the candidates. If possible, obtain a transcript or a video of one of the actual debates. Re-create that debate for the class. Have class members vote for a candidate before the debate, and have them vote again after the debate. If opinions shifted, to what do you attribute those changes?

2. What do you think are the key skills that a good debater needs?
3. Why is it be important for a person who wants to be a good debater to keep up with current events?

Taking Charge

1. Attend a school debate competition. Afterward, give a brief speech on "What Excites Me About Debate" or "What Frightens Me About Debate."
2. Choose a debate topic about which you have strong feelings. It could be a social issue that affects the entire country or an issue that is important in your school. Write down all of the arguments you would make to get people to agree with your views. Then write down all of the arguments that a person who disagrees with you might make.

SECTION 4

Debate Terminology

Part of what confuses many students as they begin to learn about debate is the terminology. Debate has a language all its own. Many of the terms are not used anywhere except in debate, which means you might never have seen them before. So you may need to learn many new words in a hurry. It's like trying to read Shakespeare for the first time, or learning chemistry. Of course, the terminology offered here is just an introduction to the world of debate. If you want to learn more, consider participating in interscholastic debate. Talk to the school sponsor for more information.

Once you learn the meanings of the new terms, you can proceed to the more fun and exciting parts of debate. Let's take some time to study the terminology of debate so that we can then move on to actual debating.

Proposition

One of the most important debate terms is **proposition**. It is the statement of the point to be debated. It states a fact, a belief, or a recommendation to do something. Another way of explaining proposition is to say that it's a formal way of stating an opinion. Here are some examples:

- The minimum age for drinking alcohol should be raised to 25. (a proposition of policy)
- Christopher Columbus discovered America. (a proposition of fact)
- Honesty is more important than friendship. (a proposition of value)

Debaters are very careful about the way they word their propositions. The reason for their concern is that each word in a proposition can have a major influence on what happens during a debate. You will learn more about good and bad wording for propositions later in this chapter.

Resolution

Resolved is a formal word used to introduce a proposition. It doesn't affect the meaning of the proposition; it just introduces it formally. It does imply that careful thought went into stating the proposition in those exact words.

A proposition that begins with the word *resolved* is often called a resolution. A **resolution** is a formal statement of opinion. Here are some examples of resolutions. Note that they include the same

In a debate, you might resolve that the federal government should establish a policy to increase renewable energy use.

propositions used in the previous examples. The propositions have not changed in meaning; they are just more formally stated.

- Resolved: that the minimum age for drinking alcohol should be raised to 25.
- Resolved: that Christopher Columbus discovered America.
- Resolved: that honesty is more important than friendship.

Affirmative and Negative

Affirmative and *negative* are two words that you probably already know. **Affirmative** means "yes, or true"; **negative** means "no, or false."

These terms are important in formal debate because every proposition is worded so that you must either agree or disagree with it. You say either "Yes, that is true" or "No, that is false." During a formal debate, one side, called the affirmative side, tries to prove that the statement is true. The other side, called the negative side, tries to prove that it's false. For example, in a debate of the proposition that the minimum drinking age should be raised to

25, the affirmative side would argue that, yes, it should be raised. The negative side would argue that, no, it should not be raised.

Status Quo

Status quo may sound more complicated than it really is. It is a Latin phrase that simply means "state in which"—that is, the way things are now, the existing conditions. The opposite of status quo is change. If every year for the last ten years your school has had a total enrollment of about 1,200 students, then an enrollment of 1,200 is the status quo. If next year the enrollment suddenly jumped to 2,000, that would be a change from the status quo. In formal debate, the negative side usually defends the status quo, arguing that there's no need to change—that whatever exists now is what should continue to exist.

Burden of Proof

Burden of proof is a term used both in formal debate and in law to refer to the duty or responsibility to prove something. In a criminal trial, for example, the prosecution has the burden of proof. It's the prosecuting attorney's job to prove that the accused person is guilty.

There is no burden of proof on the defense attorney. The defense attorney doesn't have to prove that the accused person is innocent. According to the U.S. system of law, the accused person is "innocent until proven guilty."

In formal debate, the burden of proof is on the debater arguing for the affirmative. He or she must prove that there is a problem with the status quo, so it should change. Just as the jury assumes the accused to be innocent until proven guilty, the debate judge assumes the status quo to be the best solution until it is proven otherwise.

© Corbis Premium RF / Alamy

Lawyers must be skilled debaters.

Argument

You know what an argument is; you've probably had your share. In debate, the word *argument* has a meaning a little different from the one you're used to. Debaters use the word **argument** to refer to a reason for favoring their side of a proposition. The argument also includes the facts that support that reason. Each debater goes into a debate with several arguments that he or she will try to use to win the debate.

Evidence

You also know the word *evidence*. As Chapter 10 pointed out, it refers to information that helps prove something. Fingerprints and eyewitness accounts are evidence in trials. Facts, statements, reports, and quotations from experts are examples of evidence used in debates. Each side tries to find as much evidence as possible to prove its side of a proposition.

Case

If you've watched courtroom dramas on television, you've probably heard the lawyers talk about "winning the case" or how they have "a great case." These lawyers are using the word **case** much as formal debaters use it—to mean "the total group of arguments." A case is a combination of all the debater's ideas and evidence, organized to be as convincing as possible. Knowing that lawyers carry their written arguments in a brief*case* may help you remember the meaning of this debate term.

Brief

Briefcase may also help you remember another term. Again, like lawyers, debaters talk about their briefs. A brief is what you might expect: something less than total, something that's not complete. In debate, a **brief** is an outline of both the affirmative and the negative cases. Debaters use a brief as a guide and summary before and during a debate. The brief allows them to see all the relevant issues of the debate at a glance.

Constructive

The word *constructive* has a special meaning in formal debate. You can see in this adjective a clue to its meaning: the verb *construct*, which means "to build something." In debate, **constructive** describes specific speeches that debaters make to build an argument for one side or the other. When debaters give constructive speeches, they are building or presenting their arguments.

Refute

To **refute** something means to show that it is wrong—to prove that something someone said is false. If someone said that your grandmother wears

You could select photos to help you reinforce an argument.

no shoes other than army boots, you could refute this by producing a photo of your grandmother in her house slippers. If your teacher said you hadn't handed in your homework, but then you found it in her or his stack of homework papers, you would be refuting the statement.

An important part of formal debate is refuting your opponent's arguments. You do this by offering evidence to show why your opponent's statements are false. When you refute an argument, you are offering a refutation.

Rebuttal

A **rebuttal** is a speech that contradicts an earlier statement. The rebuttal tries to show that the earlier statement is wrong or false. Its meaning is similar to that of *refutation*. In formal debate, however, there is an important difference: refutation is the act of attacking your opponent's argument; rebuttal is the act of countering your opponent's attacks on your arguments so that you can rebuild your argument. Consider this example:

- You present an argument in your constructive speech: "People age 25 are more mature than people age 21, so there would be fewer accidents if we raised the drinking age from 21 to 25."
- Your opponent refutes your argument: "There is no evidence to support the claim that 25-year-olds are more mature than 21-year-olds."
- You rebut your opponent's refutation: "In a study conducted by the psychology department at Harvard, 25-year-olds were shown to score significantly higher on maturation scales than 21-year-olds."

SECTION 4 REVIEW

Recalling the Facts

1. What is the opposite of status quo?
2. What do you call an outline of both the affirmative and the negative cases?

Thinking Critically

Debaters take great care in defining the terms in a debate. Suppose you were debating the proposition "Resolved: that honesty is more important than friendship." Does it make a difference how each debater defines *friendship*? Why or why not?

Taking Charge

Write ten propositions dealing with issues you'd like to see debated. Following each proposition, tell whom you would like to see debate it. For example, you might want to see a national high school debate champion and your mother debate the proposition "Resolved: that adults will no longer be allowed to limit the time their children spend watching television." Be sure to begin each proposition with the word *resolved*. Make sure that each proposition is a yes-or-no statement.

Ingram Publishing

The Debate Process

Let's now look briefly at how a debate works. We'll outline the basic process so that you'll have enough knowledge to conduct a debate in your classroom. Remember that if you want to participate in interscholastic competition, you should talk to the debate sponsor in your school. The sponsor will explain the two types of formal debate practiced in high school contests—Lincoln-Douglas debate and policy debate.

Getting Started

Of course, every debate begins with a topic. You need a problem, and you need a proposed solution to that problem (the proposition). While there are countless problems that could be debated, people often pick the more controversial issues. These are the topics about which many people on both sides of the issue feel strongly. Here are some broad issues that could serve as topics for debate:

- Changing the minimum driving age to 18 years old
- Uniforms in public schools
- *Vouchers* for public education
- The federal *deficit*
- Health-care legislation

Working with a friend may help you get started on your first debate.

- Penalties for driving while intoxicated
- Public employees' right to strike
- Censorship of rock music
- Term limits for legislators

It's not enough, however, to pick an issue. You can't just choose one of the issues above and say, "Let's debate." To make the issue debatable, you must write a proposition in its proper yes-or-no form. Furthermore, the proposition must focus on one part of the issue, and it must be clearly worded so that there's no confusion about what's being debated.

The careful wording of a proposition is a key difference between debate and the heated discussions people sometimes get into. In those discussions, the arguments usually aren't clearly focused on one definite part of an issue. Instead, everybody offers his or her own propositions, and people rarely take the time to define terms. That is why little progress is made in clarifying the issues or solving the problems in such discussions.

Here are some examples of poorly worded propositions:

- Resolved: that uniforms are bad.

The language is vague (what does "bad" mean?), and it is not clear what is being proposed.

- Resolved: that the federal deficit should be reduced by raising taxes and cutting military spending.

This states two different propositions, and you can't debate two at once.

- Resolved: that the penalties for drunk driving are necessary.

This proposes no change, and the proposition must clearly state a change from the status quo.

As soon as you have your proposition, you are ready to divide into teams. You need a team for the affirmative, a team for the negative, and a judge. It's up to the affirmative team to prove the proposition.

The negative team defends the status quo and tries to discredit the proposition.

Formats

Several different formats are used for formal debate. **Format** refers to the procedure that will be employed to conduct a particular debate. The format specifies the order in which the debaters will speak and the amount of time allowed for each speech. The main purpose of establishing a format is to give both sides an equal opportunity to make their cases. Since the affirmative side is proposing change (arguing for the proposition), it speaks first and usually speaks last as well. For a classroom debate, you can devise whatever format you like, as long as the rules are clear ahead of time and fair to both sides.

Public Forum Debate

The most popular formats for formal debate are policy, Lincoln-Douglas (see chapter 19), and public forum. Rich Edwards, a professor of communication studies at Baylor University, cites three reasons for the rapid growth of public forum debate:

1. The topics are ripped from the headlines and change monthly.
2. The media focus on these headline topics helps lessen the need for complicated argument theory and debate jargon.
3. No special training is needed to judge such a debate.

This format works particularly well for classroom debates, because you can complete an entire round in 35 minutes. See the following time allocation for speeches:

Public Forum Debate Timing Schedule

First Speaker, Team A = 4 Minutes
First Speaker, Team B = 4 Minutes
Crossfire = 3 Minutes

Second Speaker, Team A = 4 Minutes
Second Speaker, Team B = 4 Minutes
Crossfire = 3 Minutes

Summary: First Speaker, Team A = 2 Minutes
Summary: First Speaker, Team B = 2 Minutes
Grand Crossfire = 3 Minutes
Final Focus: Second Speaker, Team A = 1 Minute
Final Focus: Second Speaker, Team B = 1 Minute
Prep Time (per team) = 2 Minutes

For an explanation of speaker duties and for tips on how to execute effective cross-examination techniques (for crossfire), consult the following Web sites or talk to your school's debate coach.

www.nflonline.org (National Forensic League)
www.nfhs.com (National Federation of High Schools)

To get you started, here are three sample public forum topics:

- Resolved: use of a cell phone should be prohibited while operating a motor vehicle.
- Resolved: all young adults in every nation should be required to perform at least one year of national service.
- Resolved: the United States Constitution should be amended to establish a mandatory retirement age for Supreme Court justices.

Strategy

Following are a few general suggestions for preparing and arguing your case. Basically, you want to gather as much evidence as possible to support your case and to refute your opponent's case.

- *Work hard.* Many debates are won or lost before they begin. Everyone on the team must work to gather evidence.
- *Anticipate.* In your research, you'll come across evidence that will support your opponent's arguments. Don't overlook this information. Use it to anticipate your opponent's arguments and then plan how you will respond.
- *Build a sound case.* Pick the three or four strongest reasons for your side of the proposition and support those reasons as best you can with strong evidence. Organize your case logically (refer to Chapter 10).
- *Listen.* Listen closely to what your opponent says. You want to find weaknesses in your opponent's evidence and arguments. Remember to listen to what the evidence actually says, not what your opponent claims it says. For example, your opponent may make an illogical assumption based on his or her evidence. The

Take careful notes while listening to the opposition in a debate.

fact that 10,000 seventeen-year-olds were killed in car accidents doesn't by itself prove that the driving age should be raised to eighteen.

- *Take notes.* As the debate goes on, take careful notes to keep track of both your statements and your opponent's. Formal debaters call their notes a **flow-sheet.**
- *Speak clearly and logically.* Organize your thoughts before you speak, so that you are sure to make your points. It's important not to get too excited or rushed in your effort to refute your opponent's arguments.

SECTION 5 REVIEW

Recalling the Facts

1. What is the key difference between a formal debate and a heated discussion?
2. Give two examples of poorly worded propositions and explain why they create problems.

Thinking Critically

Students who participate in policy debate competitions learn that if the judge believes that the debate is a tie, he or she will vote for the negative team. Does this practice seem fair to you? Why or why not?

Taking Charge

1. As a class, pick the two or three most interesting topics from the list on page 473 and debate them in class.
2. As you prepare for the debates, keep in mind that the best debaters anticipate arguments from the opposing team. Take time to think of opposing arguments and how you would respond to them.

Looking Back

Listed below are the major ideas discussed in this chapter.

- Negotiation can be a cooperative relationship.
- The five common strategies for conflict resolution are avoidance, accommodation, competition, compromise, and collaboration.
- Four techniques for effective negotiation are be positive, use three-part messages, be prepared, and tell the truth.
- Debate is a method used to solve problems.
- You can help your career, help others, and help as a voter and citizen by becoming a better debater and a better evaluator of debates.
- Debatable issues must be stated in proper form to allow for a successful debate. A proposition must be worded so that it can be answered yes or no; it must focus on one part of an issue; it must be clearly worded; and it must not favor one side or the other.
- Several different formats are used to structure debates. The affirmative side usually speaks first and last.
- To be successful at debate, you must work hard, anticipate your opponent's arguments, build a strong case, listen closely to your opponent's arguments, take notes, and speak clearly and logically.

Speech Vocabulary

Match the speech term on the left with the definition on the right.

1. argument
2. status quo
3. case
4. proposition
5. negative
6. refute
7. debate
8. negotiation
9. affirmative
10. rebuttal

a. existing conditions
b. problem-solving method that involves a battle of ideas
c. yes
d. statement of a point to be debated
e. total group of arguments
f. reason for favoring a particular side of a proposition
g. show how something is wrong
h. speech countering your opponent's attacks on your arguments
i. way of reaching a cooperative relationship
j. no

Academic Vocabulary

Create a multiple choice definition question with three options (a, b, and c) for each of the academic vocabulary words. Example: Intensify means (a) to weaken, (b) to strengthen, (c) to enlarge.

barter
alienate
equitable
innuendo

intimidation
voucher
deficit

To Remember

Answer the following based on your reading of the chapter.

1. What is the difference between negotiation and debate?
2. Name four broad areas in which learning about debate can be helpful.
3. What word is used to introduce a formal debate's proposition?
4. What are the two sides in a formal debate called?
5. Find a word that means the opposite of status quo.
6. Is the negative side in a debate more like the prosecution or the defense in a court trial?
7. Does a debater's case include his or her evidence, or does the evidence include the case?
8. Which comes first—a constructive speech or a rebuttal speech?
9. How many parts of an issue can be included in a properly worded debate proposition?
10. What is the main purpose of establishing a debate format?

To Do

1. If your television receives cable broadcasts of either local or national political proceedings (for example, on C-SPAN), record a debate. Bring the recording to your class. After watching it, analyze the strengths and weaknesses of the debaters involved.
2. Debates usually deal with the most serious, emotionally charged issues. Brainstorm with the class to create a list of the most trivial, unimportant issues possible. Then choose three or four of the least important issues to debate. Divide the class into two sides for each of the issues, and debate the propositions.
3. Survey the school population to find out what issues in your school and community concern students. Pick the three or four issues that most concern students, and schedule debates for each issue periodically throughout the school year. Assign different members of the class to alternating sides of the various issues, and then stage the debates at a scheduled school assembly. Have the student body vote for the winner in each debate. You may want to experiment with various formats. For example, in some debates, members of the student body could ask specific questions of each debate team.

To Talk About

1. Some people seem to enjoy arguments and have a flair for arguing. Are you one of those people? If so, why do you enjoy arguments? If you are not one of those people, why do you dislike arguments?
2. Have you ever held back in an informal debate during a meeting, even though you felt you had something important to say? Why did you hold back? What effect do you think your comments would have had on the discussion and its results?
3. Recall debates you have seen on television or at debate contests. Which speeches or qualities of the debaters impressed you the most?
4. When you are arguing with friends, do you usually get your way? If so, what strategies do you use to convince your friends? If you often lose arguments with friends, what strategies have you observed being used by the friend or friends who usually win?

To Write About

1. Write a short story two to four pages long. Write it in the third person, and have the main character be someone at a meeting. This character has something to say but is afraid to speak up. What happens?
2. Opportunities for argument present themselves constantly. As a rule, most of us either respond to an issue and debate it, as long as the other person is willing, or shy away from the confrontation. Write an essay explaining which course of action you believe to be better. If you think that the decision to debate an issue depends on the issue and its importance, give specific examples of issues that are worth debating and issues that aren't.
3. Over the next few days, note debates that you have with yourself. Pick one of them and write the arguments that each side of you is presenting. Using two different names for yourself, write the debate as a back-and-forth discussion.

Related Speech Topics

The following list contains several potential topics for debates.

The minimum voting age should be lowered from 18 to 12.

Potential voters should be required to pass, with a score of 70 or above, a test covering the prominent issues in a given election year.

Failure to vote in an election should result in a 5 percent increase in a qualified voter's personal income tax for the 4 years till the next election.

Loyalty to parents is more important than loyalty to peers.

The experience gained from a part-time job is more valuable than the money earned in that job.

LINCOLN-DOUGLAS DEBATE

It is better to debate a question without settling it than to settle a question without debating it.

—Joseph Joubert

Learning Objectives

After completing this chapter, you will be able to do the following.

- Discuss what values are, what importance values have, and how questions of value are different from other questions.
- Analyze questions in terms of value judgments.
- Write cases that argue for and against value propositions.
- Debate a complete round in the Lincoln-Douglas format, using your organizational, cross-examination, and rebuttal skills.

Chapter Outline

Following are the main sections in this chapter.

1. A Question of Values
2. Preparing for Battle: Writing Cases
3. Structuring Your Speeches

Speech Vocabulary

In this chapter, you will learn the meanings of the speech terms listed below.

Lincoln-Douglas debate
factual proposition
policy proposition
value proposition
value
ought
signposting
value premise
value criteria
first affirmative constructive (1AC)

first negative constructive (1NC)
cross-examination
first affirmative rebuttal (1AR)
negative rebuttal (NR)
second affirmative rebuttal (2AR)
prep time

Academic Vocabulary

Expanding your academic vocabulary will help you become a more effective communicator. Listed below are some words appearing in this chapter that you should make part of your vocabulary.

renowned
sanctity
covert
affluent

surrogacy
evasive
dire

In this chapter, you are going to learn about a particular kind of formal debate—Lincoln-Douglas debate. If formal debate is new to you, you may at first get the impression that formal debaters speak a foreign language. The unfamiliar vocabulary and new concepts may seem very challenging.

Do not be discouraged. Learning formal debate is like learning any activity. If you make a serious effort and are persistent, you will soon master the rules of Lincoln-Douglas. And the effort will be well worth it, since Lincoln-Douglas debate is an attempt to resolve value conflicts—a process that lies at the heart of our democratic process. This means that as you study this chapter, you will be developing skills that will make you a more effective citizen.

Introduction

Should police officers be allowed to stop and search your car randomly as a part of the effort to win the war on drugs? Should high school administrators be able to censor student newspapers? Is it fair for the government to tax the poor to fund new public highways? Politicians too often try to answer these difficult questions with snappy sound bites, like "Just say no" and "Read my lips." Most people would agree, though, that questions such as these require thorough discussion and much thought.

Indeed, these questions can lead to even more-difficult underlying questions:

- Should we value privacy more than we value stopping crime?
- Should students' rights be different from those of their parents?
- Does each citizen have special obligations to every other citizen?

While these broad questions may seem abstract and confusing, they are important questions—questions that need to be answered clearly and intelligently.

How does one even begin to tackle such complex questions? One way is to learn about and then participate in **Lincoln-Douglas debate** (or L-D for short). L-D is a competitive type of formal debate practiced at high schools across the nation. Even if you never compete in a tournament, though, understanding the process of Lincoln-Douglas debate is of

Abraham Lincoln won the famed Lincoln-Douglas debates with intellect, strategy, and speaking ability.

great value. It teaches you to argue logically and persuasively about ethical issues. It also helps you learn to persuade others when confronted with issues that involve ethical decision making. You will learn to analyze and to speak about questions of public policy and personal moral choice by attempting to resolve ethical dilemmas. Such ethical dilemmas occur when choices have to be made between alternatives that are equally desirable or undesirable.

In the previous chapter, you learned about propositions. The first section of this chapter discusses the specific kind of proposition used in Lincoln-Douglas debates.

The Lincoln-Douglas Debates

In 1857 the black enslaved man Dred Scott sued his master for his freedom on the basis of his five-year stay in the free territories of Illinois and Wisconsin. The Supreme Court denied Scott a trial. It ruled that Scott was a slave, not a citizen. As a slave, he was less than a person—mere property. Therefore, said the Court, enslaved people could be taken to any state, free or not, and still could not sue for their freedom. Furthermore, the Court proclaimed that no state could rightly force slaveholders to give up their slaves, because to do so would deprive citizens of their property. The *Dred Scott* decision deeply divided the nation and once again thrust the slavery issue into the forefront of political debate.

One year later, Abraham Lincoln, Republican nominee for senator from Illinois, challenged Democratic nominee Stephen Douglas to a series of debates. After *Dred Scott,* the focus of the debates was fated to be the slavery issue. Lincoln depicted Douglas as proslavery and a defender of the *Dred Scott* decision. Lincoln opposed slavery, although he was forced to adopt the conservative position that he would not force the states to surrender their rights.

Many initially thought that Lincoln, with his unsightly mole, high-pitched voice, lanky stature, baggy clothes, and unshined shoes, had virtually no chance against the polished, confident "Little Giant" Douglas. With his *renowned* oratorical skills, Douglas was considered the foremost debater of his day. Yet Lincoln managed to trap Douglas in a dilemma: He asked Douglas, what if the citizens in a state voted to free the enslaved people in the state? After all, it was Douglas who supported the right of the states to choose.

Douglas was forced to admit that if the citizens wanted to, they could free the enslaved people, regardless of the *Dred Scott* decision. In making this admission, Douglas split his party, many of whose members were counting on him to defend slavery to the last. More importantly, Lincoln won a clear moral victory even though Douglas had won the senatorial seat.

The Lincoln-Douglas debate competitions of today take more than their name from these historical confrontations. Although the formats of the historical debates and today's debates are significantly different, intellect, strategy, and speaking ability remain crucial to the success of the debater. Furthermore, the competitors, like Lincoln before them, try to convince the people judging them that they have won a clear moral victory.

Questions
1. Given Lincoln's unsightly appearance, do you think that the outcome of his debates with Douglas would have been different had television coverage been possible at that time in history?
2. How important is it that a victory be moral?

A Question of Values

You may have found yourself debating with friends about who is the best rock music performer. Most performers, as you know, are popular only for a short time. In a poll of 600 musicians and songwriters, the Beatles were selected as the greatest rock performers of the twentieth century. Not everyone agrees with that choice, of course. Over 700,000 fans make the pilgrimage to Graceland—the home of Elvis Presley—each year. Many of these fans are teenagers. So, Elvis or the Beatles? How are such questions decided in formal debate? In other words, what kind of proposition do such questions involve?

Debate Propositions: Which Type?

At the end of the Beatles' song "Strawberry Fields Forever," does John Lennon say, "I buried Paul," or does he say, "cranberry sauce"? This question is a factual proposition. **Factual propositions** can be debated in terms of truth or falsehood. To determine whether Lennon says, "I buried Paul," you need only play back a recording of this song until you arrive at a conclusion.

Contrast the "I buried Paul" versus "cranberry sauce" question with the following proposition: "Should the United States government conduct scientific studies to determine whether Elvis is alive?" This type of proposition, a **policy proposition**, focuses on the desirability of a particular course of action. To evaluate the action, we could create a plan to find Elvis and then debate the advantages and disadvantages of the proposed plan. By weighing the advantages and disadvantages as well as the workability of our plan, we could answer the question.[1]

The **value proposition**, however, cannot be answered by knowing the facts or by predicting the effects of a plan. Value propositions—such as "Is listening to the Beatles better than listening to Elvis?"—are the basis for Lincoln-Douglas debate. A value proposition to be debated is generally called a resolution. (Recall from Chapter 18 that in formal debate, propositions are stated as resolutions.) Typically, such resolutions involve philosophical judgments and thus are more difficult to answer than questions of fact or policy. Why? Because there is no right or wrong answer. For example, to answer the Beatles-Elvis question, you must somehow compare the worth of listening to the Liverpool lads with the worth of kicking back with the King. How do you decide which has greater "worth"? The answer is, by applying values.

What Are Values?

What is a value? A **value** is simply a standard we apply to judge something right or wrong, good or bad. You have a set of values. You may value the loyalty of a friend or the privacy of being left alone in your room. As the novelist James Michener explained, "Values are the emotional rules by which a nation governs itself. Values summarize the accumulated folk wisdom by which a society organizes and disciplines itself. And values are the precious reminders that individuals obey to bring order and meaning into their lives."

---

1. *Policy propositions are also used in another type of competitive debate: policy debate. In a policy debate, a team of two debaters affirm and a team of two debaters negate a question of social policy. The question of social policy is the resolution. During the 2000–2001 school year, for example, most policy debate students researched and debated the resolution that the United States federal government* should significantly increase protection of privacy in one or more of the following areas: employment, medical records, consumer information, search and seizure. The complexities of policy debate would require another book to explain. If you would like to participate in this worthwhile form of competitive debate, talk to your teacher about the opportunities available at your school.

Value propositions such as "Is listening to rock music better than listening to country music?" form the basis for Lincoln-Douglas debate.

These standards are of different types. They may be moral values: Is something just or unjust, fair or unfair? They may be aesthetic values: Is something beautiful or ugly, artistic or inartistic? They may be political values: Is something democratic or tyrannical, helpful to freedom or harmful to it? To resolve the Beatles-Elvis question, you might apply the value of musical importance. In that case, you would make a choice based on the standard of who played a more important role in the history of rock. If you applied a different value—say, an aesthetic one based on the quality of lyrics—you might come to a different conclusion.

The choices we make as a society reflect the values that we as individuals hold most dear. Consider the question of whether the death penalty ought to be legal. If you believe the *sanctity* of human life is the highest value, then, by that standard, you would oppose the death penalty. Suppose you are debating the question of whether the government ought to place restrictions on certain types of handguns. If you wished to uphold the value of public safety, you might answer yes, handguns should be restricted to protect the general public. If, on the other hand, you wished to uphold the value of personal freedom, you might answer no, handguns should not be restricted, because any limitation would make people less free.

The Rules of the Game: Value Analysis

So you know what values are, and you know that Lincoln-Douglas debate is concerned with questions of value. The responsibility of the L-D debater is to find the values within a resolution, to apply those values, and then to prove or disprove the resolution. Consider, for example, the resolution that the United States ought to value global concerns above its own national concerns. In order to learn how to find values in such statements, you must first understand more about the nature of values. Furthermore, analyzing and applying values involves certain rules. You need to know some of these rules.

Perhaps the best way to understand how value analysis works is to imagine that you wake up one morning and you rule the world. You can do virtually anything you want (within the laws of nature—in your fantasy, you still can't fly, nor can you leap tall buildings in a single bound). Given your great power, you may decide to allow abortion on demand, or you may decide to make abortion illegal. You may choose to force students to perform community service. Maybe not. It's your choice. Whatever you think is right. But before you make your decisions, you have much thinking to do: Why should you prefer one question to another? What is important to you? In short, the ultimate question you must ask yourself is "How *ought* things to be?"

Ought refers to your idea of the ideal. When you are discussing what "ought" to be, you are describing how you think things should be, regardless of how they actually are now. Although some debaters use the terms *should* and *ought* interchangeably, there is a difference. *Should* simply suggests doing what is appropriate or fitting. *Ought* refers to a moral obligation based on a sense of duty. Furthermore, how things ought to be and how things actually are involve two different issues. Many people make the mistake of assuming that things are supposed to be the way they are.

As you learned in Chapter 10, on logic and reasoning, it is an error in reasoning to state that just because something is, it also ought to be. To understand why, consider the following examples: There is homelessness. Does that mean there ought to be homelessness? People are suffering. Does that mean people ought to suffer? People ought not to starve to death in the wealthiest nation in the world, but they do. People ought not to steal, but they do. Lincoln-Douglas debate explores the world of *ought*, not the world of *is*. L-D leaves the world of *is* to economists, scientists, and historians.

Facts and Values: Establishing Valid Arguments

Our explanation of what ought to be may seem to imply that facts have no place in Lincoln-Douglas debate. Not true. Facts and other forms of evidence are a crucial part of debate, just as they are crucial in any discussion. For example, if you were debating whether limitations on fire-

arms sales are justified, you would want to provide statistics indicating the number of deaths caused by handguns each year.

Facts alone cannot establish the validity of a value statement, but facts combined with the right values can. If your best friend is drowning, for example, the fact that you can swim does not necessarily mean you ought to save her. Suppose you agree, though, that all people who can help others in trouble ought to do so (a value judgment). You then point out that you can swim and that your friend is drowning. You have proven that you ought to help your friend. Of course, if it can be shown that both of you would drown in the attempt, then that value judgment can be challenged.

Now suppose you are arguing that the government ought not to legalize drugs. You may list various harmful effects of drug abuse: antisocial behavior, increased crime rates, financial cost to society, and so on. These harmful effects, by themselves, do not prove that drugs should be illegal. You must also make the value judgment that allowing people to harm themselves is wrong. When you make this judgment, the argument is complete: (1) Harming oneself and others is wrong; (2) drugs harm people in numerous ways; (3) therefore, the government ought not to legalize drugs.

Values Commonly Used in Lincoln-Douglas Debate

Democracy

Equality of Opportunity

Justice

Liberty

(bl) Widstock/Alamy

Some Values Commonly Used in Lincoln–Douglas Debate

Some of the values most commonly used in Lincoln-Douglas debate include the following:

1. Liberty. People and governments ought to act so that each individual has the greatest possible freedom (without harming others). *Possible applications:* arguing for free speech, against compulsory national service, for legalizing drugs.

2. Equality of opportunity. Government policies should give all citizens fair access to jobs and services. *Possible applications:* arguing for affirmative action programs to remedy past discrimination, against dividing high schools into vocational and college preparatory programs.

3. Democracy. The people ought to have the maximum possible role in determining questions of right and wrong. Major policy decisions should be put to public debate or vote. *Possible applications:* arguing in favor of making sensitive government information available to the public, against allowing the government to take *covert* actions.

4. Justice. This is usually seen as a value that protects other values, such as liberty and fairness. Plato's classic definition of justice is "giving equal amounts to equals and unequal amounts to unequals." What may be given includes wealth, political privilege, and punishment.

Possible applications: arguing that the *affluent* nations of the world ought to feed the poor nations or that the right to a fair trial justifies limiting press coverage.

Knowledge of these values—liberty, equality of opportunity, democracy, and justice—will help you to analyze most L-D debate resolutions. Many other values are argued over in L-D debate, however.

Remember, a value is a concept, not a particular document or court ruling. Some debaters, for example, try to use the United States Constitution as a value. The Constitution as a document is not, in itself, a value. It does, however, express values, including freedom of speech, the right to a fair trial, and individual liberty.

The Lincoln Memorial in Washington, D.C.

Recalling the Facts

1. What are the three types of debate propositions? How do they differ?
2. Name some of the values most commonly used in Lincoln-Douglas debate.

Thinking Critically

As a class, agree on a topic that is important and controversial in your school. Try to determine what values are at stake in the conflict. If students are not allowed to leave campus during school hours, for example, two values in conflict might be freedom and safety. How can such values—freedom and safety—be compared in making decisions? Do you think the potential for lawsuits is an important factor in most school decisions?

Taking Charge

Ethical issues are debated and discussed by people in all walks of life. Interview someone, and report on the moral complexities that arise for that person in the workplace. Possible interviewees include the following:

- A local politician or judge. Judges sometimes must make decisions that conform to the law but that conflict with their personal beliefs. Politicians often pass laws that sacrifice some people's interests. How do they justify these compromises?

- A reporter. Journalists often have their "journalistic integrity" challenged in cases where they have to decide what to print and what to withhold. What are some of the guidelines they use in making these judgments?

- A teacher. Should a teacher reward a student with a passing grade for exceptional effort even though the student's test scores earn a failing mark? How can a teacher fairly measure and reward areas of student performance, such as class participation, which depend largely on the teacher's personal judgment?

Preparing for Battle: Writing Cases

Armed with your knowledge of values, you are ready to learn how to write cases. Remember from the previous chapter that your case is your total group of arguments—your basic position on the resolution. It is made up of all the arguments that you choose to present. Most L-D debaters use a format that includes four steps: (1) introduction, (2) definitions and analysis of the resolution, (3) establishing the values, and (4) arguments.

A general rule about writing cases: You should always tell the judge and your opponent when you are moving from section to section in your case. For example:

- "First, we should examine the key terms in the resolution" (give your definitions).
- "Now, I will present my value for the round" (give your value).
- "At this point, I will offer criteria" (give your criteria).
- "Next, I will present the first argument" (state the argument).

This technique of telling people when you are moving from section to section of your case is called **signposting**.

The Introduction

In the introduction, you always state your position in the debate—whether you are arguing the negative or the affirmative. Start with a compelling statement to support your position. Many debaters choose to begin their speeches with a quotation. The quotation should lead smoothly into the specific resolution and should support your side. Suppose that you're on the affirmative side, and the resolution is that paid *surrogacy* ought to be legal. You are arguing that the government should allow contracts for surrogate mothers—women who are paid to have babies for others. You might begin like this:

> In *Maher v. Roe*, the Supreme Court ruled, "the right of procreation without state interference has long been recognized as one of the basic civil rights of man, . . . fundamental to the very existence and survival of the race." Because I agree with the Court's ruling that couples must be allowed to establish families without government interference, I affirm the resolution: that paid surrogacy ought to be legal.

If you represent the negative side, on the other hand, you might begin this way:

> The journalist Ellen Goodman recently wrote in the *Boston Globe:* "It is fair to ask about the moral limits of commerce. . . . We impose limits on our medical commerce . . . we cannot sell a kidney. We should not be able to sell a pregnancy." Because I agree with Ms. Goodman that it is morally unacceptable to place pregnancy on the market, I negate the resolution and stand resolved that paid surrogacy ought not to be legal.

The first step in preparing your case could be to consult your debate coach.

Of course, picking an appropriate quotation is not the only way to begin your debate case. Try experimenting with the various methods of introducing speeches that were discussed earlier in the book.

Definitions and Analysis of the Resolution

You will need to offer definitions for key terms in the resolution. Otherwise, there is no common ground for debate. Take, for example, the resolution that honesty is more important than loyalty. What do *honesty* and *loyalty* mean? Since different people have different meanings for these terms, it's important to agree on meanings.

In defining such terms, you should try to be reasonable—not too broad or too restrictive. A definition that is too broad is vague and gives us no starting place for discussion. "Honesty is being faithful" is an example of a too-broad definition. In contrast, definitions can be too restrictive: "Honesty is telling the truth when your mother asks where you were last Saturday night." Such restrictive definitions limit the discussion too much.

Some debaters may try to "define you out of the round" by presenting completely unreasonable interpretations—for example, "Honesty is telling the truth specifically to hurt someone's feelings" and "Loyalty is performing noble acts to demonstrate faithfulness." These unreasonable definitions make fair debate impossible. Skilled debaters point out unfair interpretations to the judge.

In addition to defining key terms, you will need to analyze other aspects of the resolution. Look again at the sample resolution that honesty is more important than loyalty. If you are observant, you noticed that the resolution does not contain the word *ought*. The resolution says *is*. Does this particular wording mean the resolution is one of fact, not values? No. All Lincoln-Douglas debate resolutions are propositions of value. What the resolution really asks is, "Ought loyalty to be valued above honesty?"

Furthermore, in order for the debate to be meaningful, there must be a conflict. That is, you must come down on one side or the other. It is pointless to agree that you can be both honest and loyal, so neither loyalty nor honesty is more important. If you do not discuss times when you had to choose between honesty and loyalty, then why debate at all? Consider this conflict scenario: You are in a grocery store with your best friend. Your friend shoplifts a candy bar but is seen by the store manager. You friend flees as you are detained by the security guard. The guard knows you are innocent but insists that you name the shoplifter. Honesty or loyalty—which is more important?

Clearly, conflict is necessary for debate. The conflict must be real, however. If you can watch *60 Minutes* on Sunday and also go to a movie on Saturday, you do not have to decide which entertainment choice should be more highly valued. But if the movie and the TV show are at the same time on the same day, you have a conflict.

Establishing Values

An important step in developing your case is to establish a value premise. The **value premise** establishes a standard by which one can evaluate whether a resolution is true. A value premise provides a starting point for an argument by summarizing the value you are using as the basis for the argument. In giving the value premise, you are asking the judge to accept it as the standard for deciding the debate. In other words, you are telling the judge that whichever speaker better upholds your value premise should win the debate.

Consider the following example. You are debating the resolution that limitations on the right to bear arms in the United States are justified. If you are on the affirmative side, you want to choose a value that will support the resolution, so you select the value "public safety." By using this as your value premise, you are saying to the judge, in effect, that the decision in the debate should be based on which position—yours or your opponent's—better protects or preserves public safety. You will argue that limiting handguns (the affirmative position) would better uphold public safety and that you should therefore win.

Suppose that you are on the negative side of the resolution that searching through student property to maintain discipline in school is justified. As the negative speaker, you are arguing that random searches through students' property by teachers and other school officials are not justified. Therefore, you might want to choose the value of privacy as your value premise and assert that the side whose arguments allow for greater privacy should win. You will argue that the affirmative speaker favors violating privacy by permitting searches through student property. You, the negative speaker, support a position that better upholds privacy and, by that standard, should win.

Both the negative and affirmative speakers may state value criteria. **Value criteria** provide further standards for evaluating whether the value premise has been realized. If a student upholds the value premise of justice, the student may argue that the value criterion should be based on which position better preserves and protects justice. Preservation and protection of justice become, then, the value criteria (standards of judgment) for deciding who wins.

Arguments

After offering definitions, a value premise, and value criteria, you're ready to present your arguments—the reasons for favoring your side of the resolution. Here are two important points to remember.

1. Always Make Your Arguments Refer Back to Your Value Premise Your value premise is the core of your case. Consider again the resolution that limitations on the right to bear arms in the United States are justified. You are the affirmative speaker and have presented the value premise of public safety. Each of your arguments, then, must mention public safety. For example, in your first argument, you might give statistics indicating that unlimited handgun sales present a high risk to human life. Then you could state that the risk to human life also risks public safety. Therefore, you would conclude, limitations are justified. We could represent the reasoning as follows: (1) Public safety is the most important value. (2) Guns threaten public safety. (3) Limitations on guns are justified to protect public safety.

Suppose, though, that you are debating a resolution that burning the American flag is morally acceptable. As the affirmative speaker, you present the value premise of free speech and state that all political speech is morally acceptable. Your first argument asserts that flag burning is a type of political speech. Because political speech must be protected, flag burning is morally acceptable. In other words: (1) Free speech is the most important value, so all political

(c) Photodisc/PunchStock

This woman speaks in support of public education. She is stating her value criteria.

speech should be protected. (2) Flag burning is a type of political speech. (3) Flag burning is morally acceptable, since it upholds free speech.

2. Always Relate Your Evidence to Your Value Premise Remember that evidence only supports your case if you relate it to your value premise. Suppose you're debating the resolution that protection of the environment ought to be valued above the development of natural resources. The affirmative speaker may present evidence that proves the environment is being destroyed in various ways. This evidence, however, does not help the affirmative case unless the affirmative speaker has also presented a value premise that suggests that the environment ought to be protected.

One type of evidence that L-D debaters commonly use is quotations from famous philosophers. Make certain when you use such quotations that they actually apply to your arguments and aren't just thrown in to impress the judge. Consider the "flag burning is morally acceptable" resolution. It would be appropriate to use the following quotation from former Supreme Court Justice William Brennan: "We do not venerate the flag by prohibiting its desecration, for in so doing, we dilute the freedom that this cherished emblem represents." If, on the other hand, you quote the French philosopher Descartes's saying "I think, therefore, I am," you are not thinking, and you are not debating the specific resolution.

Debate Skills

A good round of debate will include two features: clash and crystallization.

Clash. Clashing means making your arguments directly conflict with your opponent's. Although clashing may be something you try to avoid in your day-to-day communication, it is a desirable goal in L-D debate. Debate rounds without clash are sometimes described as being like two ships passing in the night.

These attorneys are doing research before presenting their arguments in court.

Keep your speeches organized and clear.

You clash with your opponent's arguments by refuting them—by showing how they are flawed. To refute is not merely to repeat what you have said in earlier speeches.

In refuting your opponent's arguments, you should address them in order. You might, for example, say: "In John's first argument, he claims that all political speech should be protected. I have two responses. First, some types of political speech clearly ought not to receive protection. John, you cannot express your dissatisfaction with the president by bombing the White House. Second, . . ."

Note that in giving your refutation, you follow a pattern:

1. You briefly state your opponent's argument.
2. You say how many responses you have.
3. You make the responses, numbering each one as you go.

This pattern will help keep your speeches organized and clear.

Let's look at some common techniques of refutation: counterexamples, analogies, and contradictions.

Counterexamples. Suppose that your opponent offers an example to support a general principle. Suppose further that you are debating whether homeless people who beg are invading pedestrians' privacy. Your opponent points out that some beggars are alcoholics just trying to support their addiction. You could respond with the counterexample of families forced to beg in order to survive on the streets.

Analogies. Analogies can be useful in refuting arguments that are not supported by evidence. Suppose you're the negative speaker debating the resolution that the United States ought to value global concerns above its own national concerns. Your opponent makes the following points: (1) The United States is a world leader with the capability of helping other nations. (2) All leaders capable of helping others in need ought to. (3) Therefore, the United States should value global concerns above its own national concerns. You can attempt to refute this argument with an analogy: Just because you are the best student in your biology class does not mean that you have a study session at your house every night to bring up the grades of the other students. This analogy exposes the fallacious assumption in the argument of the affirmative speaker.

Consider another example. Suppose you are the affirmative speaker, and you're defending global concerns. The negative speaker states the following: (1) The United States must take care of national concerns before addressing global concerns. As the philosopher Hans Morganthau once wrote, A foreign policy guided by universal moral principles, by definition relegating the national interest to the background, is under contemporary conditions, a policy of national suicide, actual or potential.

The negative speaker's reasoning is flawed, because valuing something "before" something else is not the same as valuing it "above" that other thing. You can illustrate the flaw to the judge by analogy. Cocoa beans may come before chocolate, but that doesn't make them more valuable than chocolate. Algebra comes before calculus, but that doesn't make algebra more valuable than calculus. You may ride the bus before you go to school, but that doesn't mean you value the bus more than school. Analogies can be a concise and compelling strategy in debate—as long as they apply to the argument.

Contradictions. Sometimes, speakers present values that contradict their arguments. Suppose that you are debating a resolution that communities in the United States ought to have the right to suppress pornography. If the affirmative speaker defends free speech, you should point out to the judge that

Model United Nations

Have you ever wondered what it would be like to serve in the United Nations? What if you were a delegate representing Denmark? Or Madagascar?

Competitive debate takes many forms, and one popular debate activity for students is sponsored by the Model United Nations Association. This international curriculum belongs to a long tradition of international education through simulation. Model United Nations at the college level traces its beginnings to a national Model League of Nations. In 1974, the sponsors of the National Collegiate Model United Nations decided to develop a program for high school students.

The first National High School Model United Nations conference, held in the spring of 1975, was an immediate success. The difficulties of administering two national conferences, one right after the other, prompted the sponsors to create the International Model United Nations Association to supervise the high school conference.

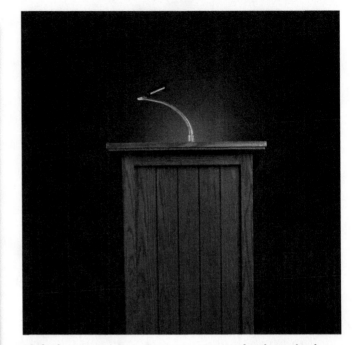

Link the most important arguments back to the key issues of the debate.

Numerous issues will be introduced in any debate. It is your responsibility to focus on the key issues that the judge should weigh in reaching a decision. When you crystallize, you tell the judge the major issues that have been presented and why your value is superior. Finally, you give impact to the process of crystallization by explaining to the judge why you are winning each of the key issues.

suppressing pornography will make speech less free—a contradictory position taken by the affirmative.

Crystallization. Crystallizing means choosing the most important arguments and linking them back to the values presented in the round.

Recalling the Facts

1. In writing cases, most L-D debaters use a format that includes four steps. What are they?
2. What is a value premise? Explain the purpose of the value premise in judging a round of competition.

Thinking Critically

Lincoln-Douglas debate tournaments require that you debate on both the affirmative side and the negative side of a topic. You may have very strong feelings about issues such as abortion and capital punishment. Are there any topics concerning which you would find it impossible to argue for the side that disagreed with your beliefs? Do you think it's valuable to understand all sides of an issue? Why or why not?

Taking Charge

Think of one compelling argument you could use to affirm the following Lincoln-Douglas debate topics. Then think of one argument that you would use to counter that argument for the negative side. Now find one piece of evidence to support each of your arguments.

- Resolved: that no war is ever morally justified.
- Resolved: that speech training is more beneficial than participation in sports.
- Resolved: that domestic assistance programs should be valued more than international assistance programs.

Structuring Your Speeches

Because Lincoln-Douglas debate is practiced nationwide, the National Forensic League has endorsed a special format for all L-D debaters to use:

1. First affirmative constructive (1AC): six minutes
2. Negative cross-examines affirmative: three minutes
3. First negative constructive (1NC): seven minutes
4. Affirmative cross-examines negative: three minutes
5. First affirmative rebuttal (1AR): four minutes
6. Negative rebuttal (NR): six minutes
7. Second affirmative rebuttal (2AR): three minutes

All of these speeches, taken together, make up one round of Lincoln-Douglas debate. Note that for both the affirmative and the negative, the total speaking time is thirteen minutes (with three minutes apiece for cross-examination). Each debater is usually given three minutes of total preparation time to be used throughout the debate.

Let's look at each part of this format in detail to see how each is structured.

The Constructives

Recall from Chapter 18 that constructives are the speeches that put forward your arguments. In L-D debate, the affirmative and the negative speakers have one chance each to present constructives.

First Affirmative Constructive (1AC): Six Minutes The first affirmative constructive (1AC) is the one speech that is prepared entirely before the round. If you are taking the affirmative position,

A legislator introducing a bill will be able to make a strong case using the principles of Lincoln-Douglas debate.

you begin the debate by reading your affirmative case, and then you wait to be cross-examined by your opponent.

The elements of the 1AC were described earlier, when we discussed writing cases: the introduction, definitions, value premise, value criteria, and arguments. In addition, you should include a brief conclusion that summarizes your position. In terms of time allocation, your introduction should be about one-half minute long; your definitions, value premise, and value criteria, about one minute; your arguments, about four minutes; and your conclusion, about one-half minute.

A cross-examination period follows each of the constructives. The same strategies apply to both, so we will consider them together later.

First Negative Constructive (1NC): Seven Minutes In the **first negative constructive (1NC)**, most speakers also begin with their prepared constructive presentation (lasting three to four minutes). The remainder of the speech is devoted to refuting the affirmative constructive. The negative constructive speech, then, should do two sets of things: First, it should include an introduction; a value premise and possibly value criteria; counterdefinitions, if necessary; and the negative arguments. Second, it should clash with and refute the affirmative value and arguments.

Suppose that you and Karen are debating the resolution that communities in the United States ought to be able to decide whether flag burning will be legal. Karen is on the affirmative side, and she chooses to defend the value of democracy. In the following exchange, you gamble with a why question:

> **You:** Karen, you offer us the value of democracy.
> **Karen:** Right.
> **You:** What is the justification for democracy—why is democracy better than tyranny?
> **Karen:** Er . . . because we ought to always allow the majority to decide what is right and wrong.
> **You:** Hmmm . . . the majority, eh? Aren't there certain issues that the majority ought not to be able to decide?
> **Karen:** Er . . . no, I don't think so.

> **You:** What if the majority in this country decided that all people born in 1970 will be executed tomorrow? Would that be OK?
> **Karen:** No, I don't think so . . . (Karen has just contradicted herself).

In this exchange, you have established that some things ought to be outside the influence of majority opinion. All you have to do now is show that flag burning is one of those things.

Responding to Questions

During **cross-examination**, which follows each speaker's constructive, the speaker who has just spoken is questioned. Let's consider some guidelines for responding to questions during cross-examination:

- Never let them see you sweat.
- Respond to each question thoughtfully and confidently. If you appear *evasive*, then the judge may wonder what else you are trying to hide.
- Know your case thoroughly and plan responses to anticipated questions.
- Stick to the question asked; don't offer long, rambling explanations.
- Prepare carefully. Preparation will help you avoid falling into cross-examination traps.

The Rebuttals

As you learned in Chapter 18, rebuttal is the act of countering your opponent's attacks on your arguments so that you can rebuild your arguments. The rebuttal speeches come after the constructives. Before learning about the specific strategies for each rebuttal, you should know some of the general principles:

1. The purpose of a rebuttal speech is to bring the round into focus so that you can defeat your opponent's arguments. You "sign the ballot for the judge" by giving the judge clear and specific reasons to vote for you.
2. You may extend (provide new responses to) arguments introduced in the constructives,

but you should not initiate whole new arguments. Bringing up new arguments in rebuttals is described by some as "sliming." *Sliming* is a term that is also used to describe other debate tactics considered questionable or unethical—for example, distorting your opponent's position or asserting that an argument was dropped when in fact it was not.

3. When you run short on time and still have several arguments to answer, then you must attempt to find a common fault in the arguments. This technique of attacking the common flaw is known as grouping. For example, you and Farzana are debating the resolution that communities in the United States ought to have the right to suppress pornography. You are the affirmative speaker, and in the first rebuttal, you find yourself with only 30 seconds to respond to two more arguments. The arguments are that pornography is a legitimate form of political speech and that communities ought not to have the right to censor political speech. All is not lost, because you can refute both these arguments by proving that pornography is not a form of political speech (much evidence exists to support this position). Here's how you might structure the few remaining seconds of your time:

Farzana has two more arguments. First, she says that pornography is a form of political speech. Second, she says that communities ought to have the right to censor political speech. Realize, however, that both of these arguments assume that pornography is political speech. This assumption is incorrect, because . . .

4. Point out dropped arguments to the judge. Dropped arguments are simply arguments that a debater failed to respond to. The significance of any argument dropped by your opponent should be explained and weighed in the context of the resolution.

5. Fallacious assumptions and glaring contradictions should be highlighted at the beginning of the rebuttal to provide a showcase for these potentially devastating attacks.

6. Most debaters begin their rebuttals by refuting their opponent's analysis, and then they return to their own case. If you end the speech with your own arguments, you focus the judge's attention on the resolution from your perspective. In short, you place the round in your ballpark—a technique known as "ballparking."

7. You should always crystallize, as described earlier. You may be winning some arguments and losing some arguments—clarify why the ones you are winning outweigh the others. Tell the judge why the arguments that you are winning matter in the round. Explain to the judge what is important and what isn't. Finally, link the crucial arguments back to your value. After all, the value is the standard you provided for deciding the round.

First Affirmative Rebuttal (1AR): Four Minutes The **first affirmative rebuttal (1AR)** is generally considered to be the most challenging speech in L-D. You have only four minutes to answer the seven minutes of negative constructive. Beginning debaters, victimized by poor time allocation, often lose rounds because they unwisely drop arguments. To avoid such *dire* consequences, consider this approach:

1. Spend from 30 to 45 seconds highlighting the value clash. Emphasize why your value position is superior.

2. Use approximately one and a half minutes to refute the negative argumentation. Group arguments when necessary, but at least mention each position advanced by your opponent. Clash with any unreasonable counterdefinitions (definitions different from yours) that might undermine your entire case.

3. Use the remaining time to reestablish the strength of your case. Highlight any arguments dropped by your opponent. Incorporate damaging admissions from cross-examination. Extend your original positions with evidence, when appropriate (to respond to challenges for additional support). Link all of your arguments back to your value, and sign the ballot for the judge.

Negative Rebuttal (NR): Six Minutes The **negative rebuttal (NR)** is the negative speaker's last chance to speak. You will have no opportunity to respond to the final affirmative rebuttal, so you must "shut down" the arguments that you anticipate will be raised in that rebuttal. Shutting down arguments means preempting responses that the affirmative debater could offer that could sway the judge to vote for the resolution. You should emphasize the arguments that you think can win the round for you and minimize the arguments that you believe have the potential to defeat you.

The first part of the NR (about four to four-and-a-half minutes) is structured like the 1AR: you begin with the value clash, refute the affirmative case, and return to defending your own case. The last one-and-a-half to two minutes, though, should be spent crystallizing your arguments. Pick what you think are the two or three most important issues in the round, and state why you are winning them. This crystallization will force the affirmative speaker to address the issues of your choosing and to appear to be somewhat on the defensive. Do not get sidetracked by trivial technicalities or dropped arguments that have no significance. Select, instead, the issues that stake out fundamental disagreements.

Second Affirmative Rebuttal (2AR): Three Minutes Although your time is limited for the **second affirmative rebuttal (2AR)**, you no lon-

ger need to be so concerned with coverage. You can focus on three or four issues of crucial importance (one should always be the value clash). You can avoid getting ballparked by the negative if you emphasize the value clash first and then examine the negative crystallization from the perspective of the affirmative case. Link all arguments to the value clash, and conclude by signing the ballot for the judge.

Prepare and know your case thoroughly to avoid falling into a trap during cross-examination.

Something of Value

"I fell off the stage, ripped my skirt, and cut my hand," remembers Mary Ambrose, the first national champion in high school Lincoln-Douglas debate competition. Ambrose took her tumble in June of 1980, immediately following the final round of the National Forensic League tournament in Huntsville, Alabama.

The topic in that first national competition focused on whether social security financing mechanisms should be preserved. Ambrose believes she won the final round because her argumentation was more "values-centered." She offered "self-sufficiency of the system" as her value position. Her opponent presented no competing value, Ambrose recalls.

Eventually Ambrose became a lawyer and a teacher. Ambrose credits her Lincoln-Douglas debate experience for giving her the ability to argue in front of a jury. "I learned that there has to be a theme and persuasiveness, not just the presenting of evidence," Ambrose says. "Lincoln-Douglas gave me added sophistication and it taught me that you need a kernel value."

Using Prep Time

In most rounds, you will be given three minutes of preparation time, or **prep time.** Affirmative speakers try to allocate two minutes before the 1AR and one minute before the 2AR. More time is needed before the 1AR because of the difficulty of organizing responses to the negative constructive.

Most negative speakers split their prep time, using half before the 1NC and half before the NR. You should try to avoid using prep time before cross-examination. Instead, prepare some questions ahead, and generate additional ones during your opponent's constructive.

Gaining debate experience could lead to a career in law.

Political Pinocchios

The purpose of debate is to determine the truth. But how can we tell if politicians engaging in televised debates are being honest? Technology offers a new way to determine who is lying and who isn't.

A recently developed computer system can detect the little movements that a person's facial muscles make when the person is displaying emotion. Smiling makes crow's feet form around the eyes, for example, while frowning involves movements in forehead muscles. The system imposes a grid over a baseline black-and-white photograph of the subject's face when it is free from all expression. Any change in expression, even one that is very small or very fast, is recognized as a departure from baseline.

By analyzing a person's facial expressions, we can often tell how that person truly feels, because facial expressions are hard to fake, even for experienced liars. Suppose a candidate is angered by a certain statement but wishes not to show that anger. According to a leading researcher, no matter how fast the candidate covers an angry frown with a smile, the computer system will detect the changing expression.

What about the lie detector, or polygraph? Isn't it just as effective? We might have trouble convincing politicians to agree to be hooked up to polygraphs during TV debates. But even if we could, we might not want to rely too heavily on the results.

Polygraphs use sensors to record changes in a person's respiration, heart rate, blood pressure, and skin conductance (how much sweat is being produced). The general idea is that a person who is lying will experience emotional stress. Emotional stress will produce certain bodily responses, such as increased heart rate and sweating.

This principle doesn't always hold up. Experienced liars may feel no emotional stress when they lie. Clever liars may be able to manipulate the test in various ways (for example, by taking a tranquilizer before testing). In either case, these persons' bodily responses may indicate that they are not lying even though they are. Also, people who are not lying may be experiencing a great deal of emotional stress during the test. They may be upset because they have been wrongfully accused. The bodily responses of these people may suggest that they are lying even though they aren't.

The new computer system for detecting facial expressions may be harder to fool than the polygraph. As suggested earlier, the muscle movements involved in facial expressions are very difficult to control. Although a flash of anger or embarrassment may pass so quickly that the human eye cannot detect it, the computer will pick it up. So perhaps we can finally tell if those politicians are being honest—or just playing Pinocchio.

Questions
1. How might political campaigns change if the voters always knew when a candidate was lying?
2. Can you think of times when a politician should mislead voters?

Recalling the Facts

1. What is the format for Lincoln-Douglas debate?
2. What should you try to achieve during the rebuttal speeches? What are some strategies you might use?

Thinking Critically

Note that the affirmative speaker has three speeches, while the negative speaker has only two. Although both sides have the same amount of time to speak, the affirmative speaker has the advantage of presenting his or her side both first and last. Why, do you think, was this format chosen? Can you think of a format that would be fairer to both sides?

Taking Charge

The national debate topic for high school students in 1931 was, "Resolved: that chain stores are detrimental to the best interests of the public." That topic might generate some heated debate even today. According to the *Utne Reader*, when 34,300 mall shoppers across the country were interviewed, 75 percent said that they weren't shopping for a specific item. Shopping, it seems, has become a national pastime.

After reviewing the guidelines for wording a debate resolution in Chapter 18, write your own. Try to choose a topic area in which you are interested, such as minimum educational standards, required community service, or student rights.

Note that the wording of the debate resolution from 1931 is better suited to Lincoln-Douglas competition than to policy debate today. The question of what is "detrimental" calls for a value judgment rather than a change in policy.

Looking Back

Listed below are the major ideas discussed in this chapter.

- Debate propositions are of three kinds: factual, policy, and value.
- A value is something we apply to judge something right or wrong, good or bad.
- *Ought* refers to your idea of the ideal.
- Commonly used values in L-D debate include liberty, equality of opportunity, democracy, and justice.
- Common techniques of refutation are counterexamples, analogies, and contradictions.
- Most L-D debaters write first affirmative constructive speeches that have four parts: (1) introduction, (2) definitions and analysis, (3) establishing of values, and (4) arguments.
- The negative constructive should (1) present a value premise, counterdefinitions (if necessary), and the negative arguments, and (2) clash with and refute the affirmative value and arguments.
- The purpose of rebuttals in L-D is to place the round into focus by crystallizing the most important issues and by providing a comparison of the two value positions.

Speech Vocabulary

Match the speech vocabulary term on the left with the correct definition on the right.

1. ought
2. 2AR
3. NR
4. value
5. value premise
6. policy proposition
7. 1NC
8. 1AC
9. cross-examination
10. factual proposition
11. signposting
12. value criteria

a. First speech in a debate round
b. Period for asking and answering questions
c. Final affirmative speech
d. Refers to your idea of the ideal
e. Standard we apply to judge something right or wrong
f. Statement that is either true or false
g. Focuses on the desirability of some course of action
h. Standard in L-D to evaluate whether the resolution is true
i. First time the affirmative constructive is refuted
j. Final negative speech in L-D
k. Additional standards for evaluation values
l. Tells people when you are moving from one section to another

Academic Vocabulary

Use context clues to write the meaning of each academic vocabulary word. Then, use a print or online dictionary to check the accuracy of your definition.

renowned   covert   surrogacy   dire
sanctity   affluent   evasive

To Remember

1. The _____ is considered the most difficult speech in Lincoln-Douglas debate.
2. "Resolved: that the United States government should conduct scientific research to determine whether Elvis still lives" is an example of a _____ proposition.
3. Bringing up new arguments in a rebuttal is commonly referred to as _____.
4. Your _____ is the value that you will be defending in the round.
5. In the original Lincoln-Douglas debates, _____ represented the side of states' rights.
6. If you are running out of time in a speech, you can _____ your opponent's arguments and answer them all at once.
7. Lincoln-Douglas debates consider propositions of _____.
8. The side that supports the resolution is called the _____, while the side that opposes it is called the _____.

To Do

1. Browsing in the current periodicals section of the library, find five magazine articles relevant to the resolution you're debating. Find five more relevant articles by using a print or online version of *Reader's Guide to Periodical Literature*.
2. Using the subject guide to *Books in Print*, find five books published in the last two years relevant to your debate resolution. Talk to your librarian about obtaining one or two of them on interlibrary loan if your library does not own the books, or try to find them in a university library.
3. Research the original Lincoln-Douglas debates in the library. Examine the arguments and strategies used by both sides. Do you think Lincoln or Douglas was more persuasive?

To Talk About

1. What benefits come from studying and debating both sides of an issue, even when you may strongly disagree with one side? Does it compromise your personal sense of ethics to uphold a point of view with which you disagree?
2. Attend a local debate tournament. Discuss how what you observed differs from the fundamentals you learned in this chapter.
3. Four values were mentioned in this chapter: liberty, equality of opportunity, democracy, and justice. What are some other values that you could defend in a Lincoln-Douglas debate?

To Write About

1. Some people advocate a two-track system for education, in which some students receive preparation for college and some students receive vocational training. Those who support the two-track system argue that it increases the quality of American education. Opponents object that a two-track system is unfair and deprives many qualified students of the chance for a college education. Write either an affirmative or a negative case for the resolution that a two-track system of education is justified.

2. Write an essay describing the benefits you might receive from debate. Can it help you in real life? In other classes? Will it help you in the future? How?

3. Although we know today that slavery is morally wrong, there was a time in this country when slavery was acceptable to most people. Write a brief essay about another value that has changed over time.

Related Speech Topics

The following list contains several potential topics for debates.

Competition versus cooperation: Which ought we to value more?

Ought we to allow mandatory prayer in public schools?

Flag burning: Is it morally acceptable?

Should schools teach values, or is that the role of parents?

The values of Martin Luther King Jr.

Political debates

Congressional debate

National security versus the people's right to know: Ought the government to keep sensitive information away from the public?

CHAPTER 20
PARLIAMENTARY PROCEDURE

The job of a citizen is to keep his mouth open.

—Günter Grass

Learning Objectives

After completing this chapter, you will be able to do the following.

- Explain how parliamentary procedure supports the democratic process.
- Organize the first meeting of a new club.
- Participate in a group meeting by making, seconding, and amending motions.
- Lead a meeting in the role of the presiding officer.
- List the most commonly used motions in ranked order.

Chapter Outline

Following are the main sections in this chapter.

1. Learning the Rules
2. Getting Down to Business
3. A Member's Responsibilities
4. The Order of Precedence

Speech Vocabulary

In this chapter, you will learn the meanings of the speech terms listed below.

parliamentary
  procedure
chair
house
bylaws
orders of the day
old business
new business
adjourn
minutes

quorum
executive session
main motion
reconsider
order of precedence
subsidiary motion
privileged motion
incidental motion
table a motion
call for the question
amend

Academic Vocabulary

Expanding your academic vocabulary will help you become a more effective communicator. Listed below are some words appearing in this chapter that you should make part of your vocabulary.

parliament
innumerable
clique
railroad
painstakingly

agenda
restate
germane
preamble
suspend

The best meetings are often noisy, exciting affairs with people bouncing ideas off one another. But beneath the noise and commotion is an orderly system, a system of rules that ensures the right of each person to be heard.

This system, called parliamentary procedure, empowers the members of the meeting to take action through a majority vote. By learning the system and especially by frequently practicing it, you will become a more effective participant in meetings and hence a better citizen.

Introduction

Each player takes the colored token nearest to him on the board, and uses it throughout the game. The player having the red token, Miss Scarlet, rolls the die and moves first.

The description above, in case you haven't guessed, is taken from the rules of the board game Clue. In that game, players try to discover the identity of a murderer. To do so, however, they must follow a strict set of rules. A player could cheat, of course, by ignoring one of the rules (for instance, sneaking a peek at another player's clue cards), but by so doing, that player would defeat the purpose of the rules—namely, to give each player an even chance to win.

We play many games throughout our lives. Some are more serious than others, but in each we agree to play by the rules. Our ability to play well often depends on whether we understand the rules and how well we can use them to our advantage.

Just as rules allow for smooth-running board games, parliamentary procedure allows for smooth-running meetings.

Democracy is much more than a game, of course, but it, too, has its rules. Our ability to act as effective citizens in a democracy depends to a great extent on our knowing the rules and learning how to play by them. Let's look more closely at why we need rules in a democracy. Then we'll begin to examine the rules themselves.

KidStock/Getty Images

Learning the Rules

The rules of parliamentary procedure used in many contemporary legislative bodies have evolved from the model created by the British parliament hundreds of years ago.

W e use several different sets of rules in our democracy. The Constitution, for example, is the basis of our legal system, and the Bill of Rights defines our individual freedoms. When we meet in groups, however, we follow a system of rules called **parliamentary procedure.** We use these rules whether we are meeting with the student council, a school club, or any other organization. These rules also apply to the meetings of all our governing bodies, from the town council to the U.S. Congress.

The rules of parliamentary procedure provide the fair and balanced system we need to work together. The rules are called parliamentary because they follow ideas originally developed by the British *parliament.* In fact, these rules have been shaped by more than 500 years of human history. Over the centuries, people have written and rewritten the rules as they have learned how to improve them. As a result, the rules have come to reflect the experience and wisdom of hundreds of organizations and *innumerable* individuals.

The British rules of government were brought to North America by the early colonists and used at the first New England town meetings. When Thomas Jefferson became president of the United States in 1801, he published the first American book on parliamentary procedure. "I have begun a sketch," Jefferson wrote, "which those who come after will successfully correct and fill up, till a code of rules shall be formed." Jefferson's book became the basis for the rules adopted by Congress and was the foremost authority on American parliamentary procedure for many years.

Robert and His Rules

As time passed, it became necessary to adapt Jefferson's rules to meet the needs of day-to-day life. General Henry Robert, an army engineer, took on the task after a frustrating personal experience. Robert belonged to many church and civic groups and was asked once, quite without warning, to lead a meeting. "My embarrassment was supreme," Robert later recalled. "I plunged in, trusting to

Even foreign ministers follow *Robert's Rules of Order*. The "rules" are used internationally.

Providence that the assembly would behave itself, but with the plunge went the determination that I would never attend another meeting until I knew something of parliamentary law."

Robert studied the rules of the British parliament and the U.S. Congress. Eventually he blended the best of both into *Robert's Rules of Order*, a handbook that he published in 1876. Robert hoped to create a system of etiquette that could guide people through their meetings. He wanted to show group members how to resist overbearing leaders and ruthless *cliques*. He also wanted to give group members the know-how they needed to combat people seeking to railroad their way to power. (*Railroad* means to push something through in great haste.)

Robert's book was an instant hit and has remained popular ever since. In 1970 a team of experts brought out an updated version, *Robert's Rules of Order Newly Revised* (updated again in 1981, 1990, and 2000), which serves today as the parliamentary handbook for most organizations. Thus, Robert's famous book

has become our foremost guide to democratic action. Thoughtful study and a few days of practice will help you master the democratic procedures he so *painstakingly* described.

"The careful reading and use of *Robert's Rules* can help guarantee orderliness and fair play in the conduct of a variety of our everyday activities," said Floyd Riddick, former parliamentarian of the U.S. Senate.

As you begin to learn parliamentary procedure, you may feel intimidated by the complexity of the system. That feeling will soon disappear, though, with a little patience and perhaps a handy reference or crib sheet nearby. Learning parliamentary procedure is important because it gives us a chance to put democracy into practice.

Failure to learn these rules will lead to the frustration of attending meetings where you don't understand what is going on. Worse, it may lead to your suffering defeat because your opponents know more than you about parliamentary procedure.

Fundamental Principles of Parliamentary Procedure

A good place to start learning the rules of parliamentary procedure is with a few basic principles. These principles will enable you to reason out the answers to most parliamentary questions. The principles may seem simple and familiar, but you should be careful not to underestimate their importance. The basic principles of parliamentary procedure are as follows.

1. Do One Thing at a Time The principle "one thing at a time" emphasizes the importance of order. Group members may consider, for example, only one motion at a time. By keeping everyone's attention focused on just one thing, the group leader can keep a meeting on track. This makes it more likely that difficult issues will be resolved in a reasonable amount of time.

2. The Majority Decides A primary purpose of parliamentary procedure is to see that the wishes of the majority are carried out. *Majority* simply means "more than half of the votes cast." (This is also called a simple majority.)

When you join a group, you agree to accept what the majority decides. Until the vote on a question is taken, every member has the right to speak for or against a proposal and to persuade others to share that opinion. Once the votes are in, however, the decision of the majority becomes everyone's decision.

3. The Rights of the Minority Are Protected Truly democratic organizations arrange to protect the members in the minority—that is, on the side with less than half the votes. These members are entitled to the same consideration and respect as those who are in the majority. You may be in the majority today but in the minority tomorrow. That means that everyone has a stake in protecting these rights.

One way that parliamentary procedure protects minority rights is the two-thirds vote. Several motions, including any that limit the right to speak or debate, require a two-thirds vote to pass. Thus, a simple majority of members cannot close off discussion if others still wish to be heard.

4. Conduct a Full and Free Discussion All members of the group have the right to express their opinion fully and freely without interruption, provided they stay within the rules. Members also have the right to know the meaning of the question under discussion and what its effect will be. Members can always request information on any motion that they do not understand so that they can vote intelligently.

"I . . . Looked Down into My Open Grave"

Andrew Johnson

In a lonely grave lies the man who saved a president, the man who performed what one historian has called "the most heroic act in American history." Yet he is a man whose name few people remember: Edmund G. Ross.

In 1866, when Ross became a U.S. senator from Kansas, President Andrew Johnson and Congress were locked in a ferocious battle over how the South should be treated after the Civil War. The president vetoed bill after bill because he thought that Congress wanted to treat the former Confederate states too harshly. Johnson himself was a Southerner. Finally, in complete frustration, many members of Congress decided to get the president out of office. So the House of Representatives voted to impeach (bring charges of official misconduct against) Johnson. If two-thirds of the Senate would vote to convict him, he would be forced to leave.

Senators who opposed the president had reason to hope that Ross would join their side; Ross had a long history of opposing slavery. At the age of 28, he had helped rescue a fugitive slave. Later, he had quit his newspaper job to enlist in the Union Army.

On March 5, 1868, the impeachment trial began. Observers soon realized that matters of law were not important to the senators: they wanted Johnson out; any reason would do. As the trial neared its conclusion, it became clear that only one more vote would be needed to remove Johnson. The one senator who had not yet announced how he would vote was Edmund Ross. Most people were sure Ross would vote to impeach. "I did not think," said Senator Sumner of Massachusetts, "that a Kansas man could quibble against his country." Yet Ross remained silent about his intentions and insisted that Johnson should have a fair trial.

As a result of his silence, Ross was pestered, spied on, and subjected to every kind of pressure, including threats of violence. He seemed to be the target of every eye, his name seemed to be on every tongue, and his intentions seemed to be the leading topic in every newspaper.

At last the fateful day arrived. Ross described it this way: "The galleries were packed. Tickets of admission were at an enormous premium." Every senator was in his seat, including one who was desperately ill and had to be carried in. When it came time for Ross to vote, the Senate chamber fell silent.

"How say you?" said the Chief Justice. "Is Andrew Johnson guilty or not?"

"I almost literally looked down into my open grave," Ross said later. "Friendships, position, fortune, everything that makes life desirable to an ambitious man were about to be swept away by the breath of my mouth, perhaps forever."

Ross spoke so quietly that he was asked to repeat his answer. And then, in a voice that everyone could hear, he said, "Not guilty." The president was saved.

Question

Why does removal from office by impeachment require a two-thirds vote rather than a simple majority vote?

Parliamentary principles grant equal rights to both supporters and opponents of proposals.

5. Act with Fairness and Good Faith Trickery, delaying tactics, and railroading can destroy the fairness of any meeting. Members can ethically use parliamentary principles to support or defeat a proposal. When they use these principles to intimidate opponents or deny the rights of others, their tactics are destructive and contrary to the spirit of fair play.

These five principles show that parliamentary procedure is founded on common sense, which makes them easy to learn and remember. After a little practice, you will feel at home with the vocabulary, patterns, and rhythm of parliamentary procedure. Before long, you will feel confident in presenting and defending your ideas in a group. As you gain knowledge of parliamentary procedure, you will help the groups you belong to become more effective, and you will also take a big step toward assuming a leadership position yourself.

SECTION 1 REVIEW

Recalling the Facts

1. Briefly describe the roles Thomas Jefferson and Henry Robert played in the development of parliamentary procedure in the United States.
2. What are the five basic principles of parliamentary procedure?

Thinking Critically

1. Discuss some of the sets of rules that govern our lives. Examples you might discuss are the rules your parents have established at home, school rules, local and state laws, and perhaps some unstated rules, like the ones that define what is socially acceptable in a given group or setting. Consider how these rules have come into being, how they can be changed, and how they are enforced.

2. Explain the importance of principles 2 and 3, listed on page 513, in the U.S. democratic system. Think of (or research) recent legal cases that demonstrate these two principles.

Taking Charge

1. Invite a representative of a local governing body—such as the town council, the state legislature, or a county board—to visit your class and talk about how parliamentary procedure works. Ask the speaker how the meetings of his or her governing body would be different if they weren't conducted according to parliamentary procedure.
2. List every school and community group you can think of that conducts its meetings according to parliamentary procedure. Can you think of groups that don't? Why don't they?

Getting Down to Business

Let us suppose that you and a group of friends have decided to start a new school club. It seems that all of you are upset about having to dissect a fetal pig in biology class, and you wish to start an animal rights group. As far as you know, the school has never had such a club before. For the purpose of our discussion here, we won't worry about how to get the school to officially recognize your club. We'll focus our attention strictly on how you organize a new club and hold a meeting.

Your first step is to arrange a time and place for the meeting. Let's say that several people who share your interest in animal rights agree to meet after school on Tuesday in a science classroom. On that Tuesday, you call the meeting to order (acting as the unofficial group leader). This is a signal to the people present that from this moment forward, they should conduct themselves according to the rules of parliamentary procedure.

When the gavel comes down, the meeting begins.

You next announce the first order of business—in other words, the first item on the meeting's *agenda*. This task is to elect a president and a secretary. In our case, your three best friends—the only other people attending this meeting—elect you president.

Now that you are legitimately the person in charge of the meeting (called the **chair** in parliamentary procedure), the group can really get down to business. The group, by the way, is referred to as the **house** during its meetings. You will probably start by discussing the purpose and goals of your group, but you will also want to agree on a few special rules called **bylaws**. A rule that sets a time and place for regular meetings is one kind of bylaw.

What Officers Do

An important part of any group's bylaws is a description of the officers the group needs. Let's take a look at these positions and their responsibilities.

The President As the new Animal Rights Club president, what are you supposed to do? In the simplest sense, you conduct the meetings. Your responsibility is to see that the group handles its business fairly and efficiently. Specifically, you must balance two competing claims: the right of the majority to prevail and the right of the minority to be heard. As Thomas Jefferson, the author of the Declaration of Independence, once said, "Let us hear both sides of the question."

Your first task is to call the meeting to order, which basically means that members stop talking among themselves and give you their full attention. Tap the gavel (no chair should be without one) to signal that the meeting is going to begin, and then state in your firmest voice: "The regular meeting of the Animal Rights Club is now open." Having accomplished that, you work your way, step by step, through an agenda—a list, prepared ahead of time, of topics and items of business to be discussed.

As chair, one of the most important tasks is to keep members focused.

The correct parliamentary name for the agenda is **orders of the day**. In most organizations, the orders of the day begin with the reading and approval of the minutes of the preceding meeting, followed by officer reports, committee reports, unfinished business (sometimes called **old business**), **new business** (subjects brought up for the first time), and announcements. The final action of the group is to **adjourn**—in other words, close the meeting.

One of your most difficult jobs as chair will be to keep the members' minds on the business before them. Discussions have a tendency to get out of hand: one stray comment can lead to another, and soon the group is talking about last night's party instead of a committee report. As chair, you must make sure the discussion stays focused.

- **Insist on a motion.** One way you can keep people focused is to ban any discussion unless there is a motion before the group. Members can't actually take any action until a motion has been made. Therefore, discussion without a motion before the house is pointless.

  After a member has made a motion, another member must second the motion (in other words, endorse what the first member said). To assist the maker of the motion, the chair should *restate* it before debate is allowed. Restating the motion helps clarify it for the members and it also transfers ownership: the motion now belongs to the group, not to the maker.

- **Open the floor for discussion.** As chair, you, and only you, decide who "gets the floor." Normally, you call on the person who made

the motion to speak first, though you need not do so. After that person has spoken (and under the rules, no one may speak for more than ten minutes at a time), you call on others who wish to speak.

If possible, choose a speaker in favor of the motion, then one opposed, then one in favor, and so on. You should let everyone who wishes to speak do so before you allow anyone to speak a second time. Ordinarily, no one may speak more than twice on any particular motion.

- **Call the question.** After you feel the discussion is over, say, "Are you ready for the question?" This asks the members if they are ready to vote. If no one objects, you put the question to a vote. If someone does object, discussion continues unless two-thirds of the members vote to close debate.

  To conduct a vote, you say, "The question is on the adoption of the motion to donate $25 to the animal shelter. All those in favor of the motion say aye." Those members who are in favor will now say aye. After you have heard the response, you say, "Those opposed say no." Next, you announce the result with the words, "The ayes have it; the motion is carried" or "The motion is defeated."

  If anyone doubts whether you have correctly interpreted the voice vote, that person may call for a "division of the house." In that case, another vote will be taken. The second time a vote is taken, the chair normally asks members to raise their hands to vote and counts the votes. Then, if a division of the house is called again, the chair may call for a standing vote. Those in favor stand up—the better to be counted—and then those opposed stand up. If the majority wishes, a secret, written ballot may be used.

- **Make rulings.** As chair, you have a number of other, more technical duties. You are required, for example, to determine whether something is *germane*, or pertinent, to the discussion. For example, on a motion to meet with the school's science teachers to discuss their dissection policies, one member begins to speak about how her little brother once put his pet hamster in the microwave. Another member objects, saying that the fate of the hamster is not germane to the motion at hand. You rule that the hamster anecdote is indeed out of order and ask the hamster owner's big sister to confine her remarks to the subject before the group. Anyone bringing up a topic that is not germane may be ruled "out of order" by the presiding officer.

Wait for recognition from the chair before speaking.

The Vice President Ideally, the vice president (and all the other officers) should have poise, a clear, strong voice, and a thorough understanding of parliamentary rules. The vice president's most important responsibility is to take the place of the president when he or she must be absent. Occasionally, the vice president may be assigned additional, special duties.

The Treasurer The treasurer acts as the group's banker. He or she collects and spends money on the group's behalf. Normally, the treasurer gives a report on the group's financial status at each meeting, as well as an annual written report.

The Secretary The secretary keeps written records of the organization's activities. These records, called **minutes**, become the official history of the organization. Members can refer to the minutes of past meetings to find out what they have said about a particular issue before. At the beginning of each meeting, the secretary reads the minutes of the previous meeting to check their accuracy and to remind the group of what it did at the last meeting.

The secretary's minutes should include the following:

1. The date, place, and time of the meeting.
2. The names of the officers and guests present and, if the group is small, of the members.
3. Whether the minutes of the previous meeting were read and approved.
4. A summary of officer and committee reports.
5. All main motions, including the name of the member who made each motion.
6. Major points of discussion and whether main motions were passed or defeated.
7. Announcements and the time of adjournment.

The secretary is also responsible for keeping a roll of all members and for calling the roll when requested. From time to time, the president may

The treasurer must keep track of all accounts.

ask the secretary to read a motion back to the group, especially when the motion has been changed or reworded.

Additional Officers in Large Organizations Large organizations may need additional officers. These officers might include a corresponding secretary, who has the job of writing letters on the organization's behalf; a sergeant-at-arms, who helps maintain order and acts as a door-keeper; and a parliamentarian. The parliamentarian assists the chair by referring to the relevant section of the bylaws or *Robert's Rules* to settle an argument. The chair may ask the parliamentarian for her or his opinion, but only the chair can actually rule on what the group should do.

Quorum and Executive Session

You can play video games by yourself, but you can't hold a meeting alone. No meeting can officially take place without a **quorum** (kwor´ um), which is the minimum number of members who must be present for the group's decisions to take effect. Normally, a quorum comprises a majority of the members. Congress, for example, can make no law unless a majority of its members are present. Although a majority works well as a quorum for most groups, some very large organizations have set their quorum at one-fourth of the membership, one-tenth, or even less if low attendance is common.

Quorum refers only to the number of members present, not the number who are voting. Suppose that an organization has 50 members and its bylaws state that one-half of the membership must be present to constitute a quorum. If 30 members show up for a meeting, a quorum has been reached. Suppose, however, that only 20 of those attending actually vote. The results will still be official.

If there are not enough members present to make a quorum, the group can do nothing more than adjourn. If, during the course of a meeting, the chair notices that a quorum has been lost (members have begun leaving, say, to watch the Super Bowl on television), the chair should stop the meeting.

Minutes record past motions, major points of discussion, and official rulings so that groups may refer back to them for information and guidance.

On some occasions, a group may wish to close its meeting to outsiders. Imagine that a reporter from the school paper is attending an Animal Rights Club meeting when an extremely personal matter comes up. At this point, a member can request that the group go into executive session. An **executive session** is a special kind of meeting or a special portion of a meeting that is open only to members.

Such sessions are called to discuss the conduct and possible discipline of group members. In our case, for example, the group has learned that one of its members recently shot a deer on a hunting trip. Members are honor-bound not to divulge to outsiders what has been discussed during executive session.

Groups can decide issues only if a quorum is present at the time of voting.

SECTION ② REVIEW

Recalling the Facts

1. What are the major responsibilities of a chair before, during, and after a meeting?
2. What are some ways groups can get bogged down in meetings? How can a good presiding officer rescue a meeting from total collapse at such points?

Thinking Critically

1. Have a class discussion on the qualities of a good committee chair or class officer. Who do you feel are the best elected officers—at school and on the local, state, national, and international levels. Why? What leadership qualities does each officer possess? What mistakes might an elected officer make to alienate his or her followers?

2. Practice analyzing a set of minutes. Obtain the minutes of a recent meeting from a school or local organization and analyze what happened during the meeting. Can you determine what decisions the group made and what actions the group took? Discuss with classmates what the most important decision of the meeting was and why.

Taking Charge

Pretend for a day that your class schedule is really a series of meetings. Observe what each teacher does to call the class to order. Discuss with classmates which techniques seem most effective. What is the cost of wasting time at the beginning of a class?

A Member's Responsibilities

Like officers of organizations, members have responsibilities. Even if you are not an officer, you should, for example, attend the meetings with reasonable regularity. During a meeting, you should pay attention to the business at hand and to the speaker who holds the floor. You should not talk, move about, or stand unless you want to be recognized by the chair.

Feel free to express your opinion while a question is being discussed. But once the question is settled, support the outcome. Withhold any criticism you might have of either the action or the members who supported it. This is one of the most important principles of parliamentary procedure—one that allows us to live in an atmosphere of mutual respect and regard no matter how much we may disagree with one another.

We can summarize the responsibilities of a member like this:

1. Arrive promptly at meetings.
2. Address the chair as Ms. President, Madam President, or Mr. President.
3. Wait to be recognized by the chair before speaking.
4. When you are recognized, stand, speak clearly, and then sit down.
5. Make a motion by saying, "I move that . . ." Do not say, "I make a motion."
6. Address all remarks to the chair. Make no personal comments toward another member.
7. Ask questions if you don't understand the question on the floor.
8. Call for a vote if you feel debate has gone far enough.
9. Call out, "Division" if you doubt the result of the vote as announced by the chair.
10. Respect the right of the majority to decide.

One of the most important things a member can do is to make a motion. Most games begin with a throw of the dice, a flick of the spinner, or a card

After you are recognized, address your remarks to the chair, not the group.

drawn from the deck. In parliamentary procedure, the real action begins when someone makes a motion.

Any member has the right to present a motion. To do so, he or she rises, addresses the chair, and waits for recognition. The chair recognizes a member by calling the member's name. That member now has the floor and is thus entitled to speak.

The Main Motion

Motions that ask the group to take action are called **main motions.** (Several other kinds of motions will be discussed later.) Main motions should be stated in a positive form if possible, because most of us find positive statements (such

Curfew in Paradise

A curfew bill created by a group of Honolulu high school students was signed into state law by Governor John Waihee of Hawaii. Although the original bill, drafted by students at Kaimuki High School, was altered by state legislators, its goal of keeping teenagers off the city's streets late at night remained intact when it was signed. The curfew prohibited anyone under age sixteen from being in public areas between 10 P.M. and 4 A.M. unless accompanied by an adult.

The law recommended that violators of the curfew and their parents or guardians participate in family counseling or community service.

"As far as we know," said a spokesperson for the Hawaii Department of Education, "this is the first time Hawaiian students have submitted and lobbied [for] a bill in the state government." The Hawaii Supreme Court later ruled that the curfew law was unconstitutional.

as "let's do this") easier to grasp than negative ones ("let's not do that").

If a member happens to offer a motion in the negative, the chair can suggest changing it. Suppose a member of the Animal Rights Club says, "I move that we don't eat meat at school." Club members may be confused about exactly what the motion means. The chair might ask the person who made the motion to rephrase it like this: "I move that we boycott meals in the cafeteria until the school agrees to provide a vegetarian alternative."

Anyone who proposes a long or complicated motion should prepare a written copy ahead of time and give it to the secretary. (By the way, the chair can request that all motions be submitted in writing.)

Members of the Animal Rights Club might make the following main motions:

- "I move that we ask the school board to ban fur; leather belts, shoes, and watchbands; and any other types of clothing made from animals from the school building."
- "I move that the student council make an annual donation to the local Humane Society."
- "I move that we change our school mascot from the Tigers to the Silicon Chips."

Generally, four things can happen to a main motion. It can be passed, postponed, sent to a committee for study, or defeated. Remember that if a motion is defeated, it cannot be brought up again at the same meeting. Parliamentary procedure stresses the principle that a motion may have only one hearing per meeting, but it does allow one exception. A member may move to **reconsider** a main motion that has already been passed or defeated. Only a member who voted on the winning side may move to reconsider.

Resolutions Special occasions sometimes call for a special kind of main motion called a resolution. A resolution traditionally begins with a *preamble*—an explanation of why the motion should be passed. The preamble includes a list of reasons, each in a paragraph beginning with *Whereas*. Following the preamble, the main motion is stated, usually with this formula: *Now therefore be it resolved,* or simply, *Resolved, that . . .* A complete resolution might look something like this:

WHEREAS Mr. Bob Olson has served our school well as a sensitive counselor, and

WHEREAS his concern for animals has led to his decision to turn his own home into a shelter for stray cats and dogs, and

WHEREAS Mr. Olson has worked as a volunteer for a week at the Humane Society,

NOW THEREFORE BE IT RESOLVED that the Animal Rights Club does hereby congratulate Mr. Olson on his contributions to a better life for small animals and, in recognition thereof, awards Mr. Olson the club's Good Citizen of the Year Award.

Like main motions, resolutions can be passed or defeated.

Seconding a Motion After someone has made a motion, another member must second the motion (this can be done without being recognized by the chair). A motion is seconded to show that more than one person favors the proposal. The major purpose of requiring a second is to prevent groups from wasting time on something that only one person wants to talk about.

If a motion is not seconded immediately, the chair says, "Is the motion seconded?" or "Is there a second?" If no one seconds the motion, the motion is dead. Some routine motions, such as approving the minutes, are frequently put to a vote without a second. (If any member objects to the lack of a second, however, the chair must call for one.) In addition, a few special kinds of motions do not need a second. We will discuss these motions later.

If you intend to present a long or complicated proposal, prepare a written copy ahead of time.

Debate and Discussion

"Democracy is that form of government," wrote James Dale Davidson, former executive director of the National Taxpayers Union, "where everybody gets what the majority deserves." Finding out what the majority deserves—or at least what it wants—is why we have debate. But no matter how freewheeling the debate may be, it must follow certain rules: Speakers are limited to ten minutes at a time, their comments must be germane, they must address their remarks to the chair, and they must always keep their remarks courteous.

If you wish to be successful in debate, you must be well informed, sure of your convictions, and fearless in the face of opposition. At the same time, successful debate depends to some extent on good manners. In debating a motion, you should avoid making comments about someone else's personality and should never question another person's motives. If you feel that another speaker is mistaken, do not call him or her a liar. Instead, simply say, "I think the last speaker was misinformed." Also avoid mentioning another member's name, though you can refer to "the last person who spoke."

A parliamentary discussion should help members reach a better understanding of the proposal before them. If the discussion is carried on in the proper spirit, members will leave their differences at the meeting, thus preventing grudges that would keep the members from remaining friends.

SECTION 3 REVIEW

Recalling the Facts

1. What is one of the most important things a group member can do?
2. What four things can happen to a main motion?

Thinking Critically

Parliamentary procedure stresses the idea that a motion should only be considered once during a meeting. There is, however, one exception. What is that exception and why is it permitted in the rules?

Taking Charge

1. Write motions that could be presented at meetings for each of the following groups: an athletic booster club, a snow-skiing club, an international club, and student council. Try to create three motions for each group.

2. Write short arguments for and against each of the following motions:
   • "I move that we oppose the city's new curfew law, which requires all teenagers to be off the street by 10 P.M. each night."
   • "I move that we support the school board's decision to ban any clothing, like bandannas or pro football jackets, that might show membership in a gang."

3. Find out what constitutes a quorum for several of the governing bodies in your community. Do your school clubs have official quorums? Why or why not?

The Order of Precedence

Parliamentary procedure becomes complicated at times, because people are complicated. Our thinking process is not as simple as yes, no, and maybe. We may feel that we don't have enough information to make a sound decision, that the room is too hot or too cold, or that the meeting has been going on too long and we need a break. Parliamentary procedure makes room for these concerns and many others through a system of minor motions, all of which are governed by the order of precedence.

Some Motions Have Higher Rank than Others

In a large, formal meeting in which people are experienced in parliamentary procedure, the action can seem furious. "Motions seem to dart in and out like bees around a beehive," as one expert puts it. Before one motion can be settled, another takes its place before the house, and then another and another. Sessions of the U.S. Congress, shown on C-SPAN, offer ample illustration of such activity.

All this commotion may be confusing at first, but once the chair sorts things out, this much is clear: Parliamentary procedure requires that some kinds of motions be considered before others.

The concept that underlies the relationship of motions to each other is called the **order of precedence.** You might think of it as a ranking system, with the most important motion at the top (where it has priority over all the others) and the least important at the bottom. (See the chart on page 527 for a detailed description.) When a motion of greater priority is raised, it moves any other business to the back burner. This motion may then be resolved or may itself be pushed out of the way by an even higher-ranking motion.

The order of precedence enables the chair to determine precisely what issue should be discussed. It also tells the chair when a particular motion is out of order and must therefore be ignored for the

Try to attend a session of your state legislature, where you will see parliamentary procedure used to its full extent.

Architect of the Capitol

Parliamentary procedure allows no heated argument, even when a question is referred to a committee.

time being, and in what order votes should be taken on pending motions. Any motion before the house that has not been settled is said to be "pending."

Let's see how the order of precedence actually works. Suppose someone says, "I move that we stage a demonstration in front of Pets R Us to protest the sale of endangered species of parrots." The motion is seconded and debate begins. Before long, someone makes a motion to amend the main motion: "I move that we amend the motion by striking 'Pets R Us' and inserting 'all three pet stores in town.'" The motion to amend is in order at this point because it ranks higher than the main motion. Before the motion to amend is seconded, however, someone else gains the floor and says, "I move that we refer this question to a committee. I don't know if any parrots are really endangered or not." The motion to refer ranks higher than the motion to amend. Thus, this latest motion is now in order and must be considered before the other two.

Handling parliamentary motions is a little like making a stack of blocks. As you work your way up (by making motions), you place one block on top of another. As you work your way down (by voting), the top block is taken off first. When a group does not observe the order of precedence and tries to pull the bottom block out first, the whole structure collapses.

Three Kinds of Minor Motions

Motions other than main motions can be divided into three categories: subsidiary, privileged, and incidental. Each type of motion plays its own role in bringing problems to a reasonable, democratic solution.

- **Subsidiary motions** help to settle the main motion. Sometimes called a parliamentary "tool kit," they give members the means to tinker with main motions until they are in just the right form.
- **Privileged motions** deal with problems aside from the main motion that need urgent attention. You might move, for example, to take a short recess until "the fire goes out and the smoke has cleared." This motion has higher status than a subsidiary motion because what it calls for is of immediate importance.
- **Incidental motions** deal more with the process than with the actual content of any motion. An example of an incidental motion is a request for a roll call vote. Each type of minor motion includes several specific subtypes, as described in the following sections.

Subsidiary Motions While a main motion is pending, members may wish to change it, postpone it, or set it aside. The motion to amend the main motion is a subsidiary motion. Other subsidiary motions include limiting, extending, or cutting off debate.

Let's take a closer look at each of the seven subsidiary motions.

To table a question The purpose of the motion to table a question is to set the topic aside temporarily so that the house can turn to something else. (The term "lay on the table" grew out of

E. Audras / PhotoAlto

an old parliamentary custom of laying a written motion on the clerk's table.)

Suppose a particular subject is being discussed. You want to speak on the subject but must leave the meeting for a few minutes. In such situations, you may say, "I move to lay the question on the table," or simply, "I move to **table the motion**." If you are successful, the issue will be set aside. The idea is not to kill a motion but to delay its discussion. Whenever you are ready to get back to the motion, you can move to "take the motion off the table."

To call for the question When people continue to discuss a subject beyond your patience or endurance, you may **call for the question**. That simply means you move to stop discussion and vote. The chair then calls for a second and, on receiving it, takes a vote on whether or not to close the discussion. Note that members vote on the motion to call for the question before voting on the main motion. In less formal groups, members may call out, "Question!" and the chair, if it seems there is no objection, may simply go to a vote on the motion itself.

To modify debate If time is short, you may wish to limit debate on a particular subject. Although normal procedure permits each person to speak twice for ten minutes each time, you may decide it would be better to limit each person to one five-minute comment. If so, you "move that debate be limited." If, on the other hand, the issue needs more discussion than usual, you may move to extend debate.

To postpone definitely When it seems best to delay the discussion of a question (perhaps because a member who has vital information on the subject is not present), you should use the motion to postpone definitely. In doing so, you must specify the particular date or time the motion will be reconsidered. If, for example, you believe a motion should receive further study, you might say, "I move to postpone until the next meeting." If you think another issue should be decided first, you might say, "I move we postpone considering dues until we have first taken action on our budget."

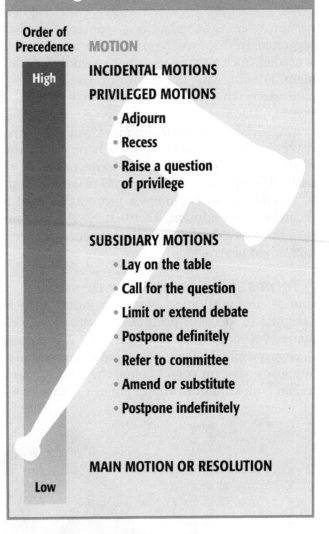

Ranking of Motions

Order of Precedence — MOTION

High

INCIDENTAL MOTIONS

PRIVILEGED MOTIONS
- **Adjourn**
- **Recess**
- **Raise a question of privilege**

SUBSIDIARY MOTIONS
- **Lay on the table**
- **Call for the question**
- **Limit or extend debate**
- **Postpone definitely**
- **Refer to committee**
- **Amend or substitute**
- **Postpone indefinitely**

MAIN MOTION OR RESOLUTION

Low

To refer to a committee Sometimes it may be necessary to send a motion to a committee for fine-tuning. A committee is a small, representative group of members—usually no more than twelve—who give careful attention to a particular topic.

To amend A main motion sometimes needs a few changes before it will be acceptable to a majority of the members. In such cases, you may wish to **amend** the main motion. An amendment to a motion can be made in one of three ways:

1. by inserting, or adding, words
2. by striking words (that is, removing them)
3. by striking some words and inserting others

In simplest terms, the amending process is chiefly a way of editing the original motion.

Sometimes the person who made the original motion agrees to accept a change someone else has suggested. In that case, no vote on the amendment is needed. Such a change is called a friendly amendment. Friendly amendments can often save time, particularly when they reflect only small changes.

Amendments themselves can be amended. During debate on an amendment, you may discover that no one is completely happy with the wording even though everyone seems to favor the basic idea expressed. If so, you may make a motion to amend the amendment, a procedure called a secondary amendment. Fortunately, there is no such thing as a third-degree amendment—or meetings might never end.

To postpone indefinitely Despite how it sounds, the motion to postpone indefinitely is designed to kill, not postpone. Normally, opponents of a motion try to defeat it by a vote, but once in a while they prefer to avoid voting entirely. Suppose a motion comes before the school board to ban junk food from school premises. After some discussion, the board members realize that banning junk food might hurt the speech team. (The team sells candy bars to help pay for trips to tournaments.) Still, the board does not want to vote in favor of junk food. So the members decide to postpone the motion indefinitely. In this way, they can kill the motion without ever actually voting on it.

Privileged Motions Privileged motions have to do with mistakes or problems that must be corrected immediately. Because of their urgency, they are given high priority. Privileged motions include requests to stop the meeting or to set a meeting time for another day. Let's take a closer look at some of the most commonly used privileged motions.

Adjourn Adjourn is the term to use for ending a meeting. A member may move that the meeting be adjourned. More often, the chair just announces that, if there are no objections, the meeting is adjourned. When all the business before the house has been completed, the chair typically says, "Since there is no further business, the meeting is adjourned."

Recess A recess is just a short intermission. Most organizations use a recess to give members a break, usually lasting no more than a few minutes. Following a recess, members take up business where they left off.

Raise a question of privilege A motion to raise a question of privilege is an urgent request touching on the welfare of the group as a whole. You may ask, for example, that the group help you catch the gerbil you let loose by mistake. Or you could request, through the same procedure, that the house go into executive session to discuss a sensitive personal matter.

Incidental Motions The final category of minor motions is a broad group called incidental motions. Like privileged motions, these motions usually apply to something other than the business at hand. Since they arise only

A motion to ban text messaging from school can be killed if the motion is postponed indefinitely.

Motion	Requires Second	Debatable	Amendable	Vote Required
Incidental Motions				
Appeal decision of the chair	Yes	Yes	No	Majority
Point of information	No	No	No	None
Point of order	No	No	No	None
Suspend the rules	Yes	No	No	Two-thirds
Privileged Motions				
Adjourn	Yes	No	No	Majority
Recess	Yes	No	Yes	Majority
Raise a question of privilege	Yes	No	No	Majority
Subsidiary Motions				
Lay on the table	Yes	No	No	Majority
Call for the question	Yes	No	No	Two-thirds
Limit or extend debate	Yes	No	Yes	Two-thirds
Postpone definitely	Yes	Yes	Yes	Majority
Refer to committee	Yes	Yes	Yes	Majority
Amend the amendment	Yes	Yes	No	Majority
Amend	Yes	Yes	Yes	Majority
Postpone indefinitely	Yes	Yes	No	Majority
Main Motions				
Main motion or resolution	Yes	Yes	Yes	Majority
Reconsider	Yes	Yes	No	Majority
Take from table	Yes	No	No	Majority

incidentally—that is, from time to time—and must be decided as soon as they are raised, they have the highest priority of any motion.

Appeal the decision of the chair If you disagree with the chair's decision, you may appeal and ask that the house decide the question instead. The purpose of this appeal is to protect members against unjust rulings or technical errors. You should not hesitate to appeal if you disagree with the chair's ruling, but you should use good judgment, too. Unjustified or excessive appeals may damage the chair's credibility and thereby weaken the whole organization.

Point of information A point of information is usually a request for a simple explanation. For example, you might rise and say, "Point of information. Is there enough money in our account to cover the cost of the dance?"

A Filibuster Stalls the Civil Rights Act

Your parents may think you talk a long time on the phone, but no matter how long-winded you are, you probably can't hold a candle to a United States senator in the middle of a filibuster.

The filibuster has been used as a parliamentary tactic since Roman times, but it is probably most often associated with the U.S. Senate. A filibuster is simply an attempt to delay a meeting for so long that members in the majority will give up whatever motion they wish to pass. Sometimes a tiny minority of members may try a filibuster to block the passage of a motion they have no hope of defeating in a vote. The tactic is especially effective at the end of a congressional session, when senators are pressed for time to pass other major bills.

Filibusters can be quite amusing. Some senators have been known to read from the telephone directory just to waste time. Others have resorted to reading the *World Almanac,* baseball statistics, and Aesop's fables.

In 2005, lawmakers debated whether filibusters should be allowed to be used in Congress.

Senator Strom Thurmond of South Carolina established the one-man endurance record of 24 hours and 18 minutes when filibustering against the 1957 Civil Rights Act, but he had the benefit of friendly interruptions, such as frequent quorum calls. Senator Wayne Morse of Oregon spoke alone and without interruption for 22 hours and 26 minutes, fighting an oil bill in 1953.

Filibusters can be used to stop a group from taking action, even when the majority view is clear. The most notorious filibuster was organized by Russell Long of Louisiana, who led 18 Southern senators in a battle against the Civil Rights Act of 1964. Each of the senators spoke about 4 hours at a time and was interrupted by lengthy questions from sympathetic colleagues. Only after 74 days of this delay were enough senators willing to vote for cloture (a move to end debate, requiring a three-fifths vote) and finally pass the bill.

The major argument for the filibuster centers on the protection it offers for minority rights. Senator Everett Dirksen of Illinois called it "the only weapon which the minority has to protect itself." On the other hand, parliamentary procedure must also ensure majority rights. Massachusetts Senator Henry Cabot Lodge summarized this view by saying to "vote without debating is perilous, but to debate and never vote is imbecilic."

Questions

1. At one time the Senate had no limit on debate. Should governmental bodies set limits on debate and, if so, what should those limits be?

2. Can you find information on filibusters in your state legislature?

Point of order The purpose of a point of order is to enforce the rules. A member can even interrupt another speaker to make a point of order. The chair, for example, may have given the floor to the wrong person. You could rise and say, "Point of order. This speaker has already been given two opportunities to speak." Once a point of order has been raised, the chair must make an immediate ruling.

Suspend the rules A group can *suspend* any of its rules if they get in the way of the group's progress. For example, the Animal Rights Club may have a rule that says all meetings must adjourn by 4:30. If a discussion is still going strong at 4:25, you may move to suspend the rule about adjournment to allow the discussion to continue past 4:30.

Providing information in advance, so all members can examine it before voting, may avoid excessive "point of information" requests at group meetings.

SECTION (4) REVIEW

Recalling the Facts

1. Explain how to apply the order of precedence during a meeting.
2. Briefly explain how incidental motions, privileged motions, and subsidiary motions differ from each other.

Thinking Critically

1. Discuss the ranking of motions. What are some reasons why one motion might be ranked above another? Why is the main motion the lowest-ranking motion? Why is a motion to adjourn the highest-ranking motion?
2. Can small, informal groups adapt the rules of parliamentary procedure to keep their meetings from becoming too techni-cal? What modifications of the basic rules could they use? What shortcuts could they take? What rules should never be altered, no matter how small the group?

Taking Charge

Practice the rules of parliamentary procedure by holding a mock meeting in class to debate the morality of animal rights. Name a chairperson, and appoint someone to be the parliamentarian. The specific issue you might debate could be a ban on all medical research on animals that results in their death. After the meeting, ask the parliamentarian to evaluate how well the students conducted the meeting. Did they consistently follow parliamentary procedure?

Looking Back

Listed below are the major ideas discussed in this chapter.

- The rules we use to make group decisions are called parliamentary procedure.
- The goal of parliamentary procedure is to help people conduct their business in an orderly and effective way. The rules are designed to make sure that the will of the majority prevails but also that the minority has an opportunity to speak and be heard.
- The system we call parliamentary procedure evolved from the rules of the British parliament. An American, Henry Robert, developed a version that ordinary groups could use in their meetings. This version is contained in a guidebook called *Robert's Rules of Order Newly Revised*.
- The basic principles of parliamentary procedure are based on common sense. They include the following: do one thing at a time, the majority decides, the minority must be protected, conduct a full and free discussion, and act with fairness and good faith.
- The chair, or presiding officer, runs each meeting. He or she decides who gets to speak and keeps the group on task. The chair also makes rulings from time to time.

- Typically, small organizations have a vice president, a treasurer, and a secretary in addition to a president. Large organizations may have several officers besides these.
- Groups must have a quorum to conduct business. If a group wishes to close its meeting to outsiders, it may go into executive session.
- Members ask their groups to take action or make decisions through main motions. A main motion must be seconded by another member. It can be passed, postponed, sent to committee for study, or defeated.
- Members use subsidiary motions to fine-tune main motions. They use privileged motions to interrupt current business for something of great urgency, and they use incidental motions to make requests concerning the way the meeting is being run.

Speech Vocabulary

Match these speech terms with the definitions on top of page 534.

1. parliamentary procedure
2. chair
3. bylaws
4. orders of the day
5. new business
6. adjourn
7. amend

8. minutes
9. reconsider
10. quorum
11. executive session
12. order of precedence
13. privileged motion
14. call for the question

a. person in charge of a meeting
b. business discussed for the first time
c. motion to close a meeting
d. system for ranking motions
e. minor motion to correct an urgent problem
f. official written record of a meeting
g. kind of meeting closed to outsiders
h. motion to take a vote

i. agenda for a meeting
j. minimum number of members needed to conduct business
k. to change or modify a motion
l. set of rules based on British example
m. motion to look again at a motion
n. rules a group agrees to abide by

Academic Vocabulary

Use a print or online dictionary to find the definition of each term. Then match the term on the left with the correct explanation on the right.

1. parliament
2. innumerable
3. clique
4. railroad
5. painstakingly
6. agenda
7. restate
8. germane
9. suspend
10. preamble

a. exclusive group
b. in an extremely careful way
c. list of things to be done
d. national legislative body
e. repeat in a new form
f. related or pertinent
g. to interrupt or stop
h. to push through hastily
i. too many to be counted
j. introduction to a formal document

To Remember

Answer the following based on your reading of the chapter.

1. Parliamentary procedure protects two vital democratic rights: the right of the majority to _____ and the right of the minority to _____.
2. The most important guidebook for parliamentary procedure is called _____.
3. The first principle of parliamentary procedure, _____, helps groups stay on task.
4. Issues left over from a previous meeting are called _____. Issues that come up for the first time during a meeting are called _____.
5. The secretary keeps a record of each meeting. This record is called _____.
6. How many members must be present at a meeting for there to be a quorum?
7. A special kind of main motion, usually written with a preamble, is called a _____.
8. Why must a motion be seconded?
9. The highest-ranking privileged motion is _____.

To Do

1. Contact your state legislature and inquire about its specialized rules, or bylaws. What are some of these rules, and what is the purpose of each?
2. Watch newspapers and magazines for stories about people who have broken the rules (whether official, social, or ethical). Clip these articles out, bring them to class, and discuss them with your classmates.
3. Find out what it takes to start a new club at your school.

To Talk About

1. Discuss whether and to what degree the rules of parliamentary procedure for large, formal gatherings like those of state legislatures and the U.S. Congress are suited for everyday use.
2. What danger exists if one person in a meeting knows the rules of parliamentary procedure better than everyone else present?
3. What power does knowledge of the rules of parliamentary procedure give a person?

To Write About

1. Write an essay about rules that apply in a democratic society. Consider the legal system; the unwritten "social system," which tells us how we should treat each other in public; codes of ethics; and value systems. To what extent do these systems protect us from our own worst instincts?
2. Obtain a copy of the minutes of a recent meeting of any organization. Reconstruct the meeting in the form of a play.

Related Speech Topics

British parliament

Thomas Jefferson and the Declaration of Independence

Qualities of a good leader

Henry Robert, author of *Robert's Rules of Order*

The presidential nominating process

Election campaigns

Election reform

UNIT

6

The Person Revisited

UNIT CONTENTS

CHAPTER 21
BUILDING LEADERSHIP

The very essence of leadership is that you have to have a vision.

—Theodore Hesburgh

Learning Objectives

After completing this chapter, you will be able to do the following.

- Define the terms leadership and leader and then effectively apply these terms to intrapersonal and interpersonal communication.
- List the specific components of leadership.
- Understand the correlation between leadership skills and self-confidence.
- Realize the importance of effective speaking in leadership.
- Implement leadership skills in your daily life.

Chapter Outline

Following are the main sections in this chapter.

1. Leadership and Learning Styles
2. The Planks of Leadership

Speech Vocabulary

In this chapter, you will learn the meanings of the speech terms listed below.

leader
leadership
learning styles

vision
conflict management

Academic Vocabulary

Expanding your academic vocabulary will help you become a more effective communicator. Listed below are some words appearing in this chapter that you should make part of your vocabulary.

culmination
entrepreneur
facilitate

harmoniously
forfeiting
simulated

The comedian John Belushi once said, "Everyone is in some way a leader. Large or small, we all have an influence on somebody. The leaders gain the glory," he noted, "but they also feel the pain." The purpose of this chapter is to offer you some tips on what it takes to make Belushi's leadership "glory" a real-world possibility.

The following pages should make you more aware of how to come out on top, and what steps to take if you wish to bypass leadership problems.

The first step is to examine leadership and learning styles—and to find out how to understand not only those who lead but also those who are led. The next step is to analyze the planks of leadership and examine what qualities must be studied and then practiced by the effective communicator who wishes to lead and direct others.

You are a leader. You might lead in some classes, with certain friends, in certain clubs or organizations, or in your family. What is your style? It is important for you to realize that just as it takes hard work and planning to construct a house, it takes dedication and thought to lead others. Let's put your words to work!

Introduction

What do the words *leader* and *leadership* mean to you? Is a leader the person who is the "boss"? The authority figure? The biggest? The loudest? Generally speaking, a **leader** is a person who directs or who is in charge of others, while **leadership** focuses on the talents, qualities, and skills that a leader uses to influence people. But all leaders aren't the same.

Psychologist Dean Keith Simonton noted that many historical leaders were very different from one another. Beethoven's musical genius and leadership came with a price: he was rude to his friends and servants. George Washington was a talented military leader, but he was a poor public speaker.

Simonton added that one characteristic of leadership was undeniable: a genuine passion for the task at hand.

Speech and leadership work together. At some time in your life, by choice or otherwise, you will find yourself in a position that demands your

An effective leader has a genuine passion for the task at hand.

leadership. Your spoken words and the way you use them will then become your credibility.

The nationally recognized Hugh O'Brien Leadership Conference explains that for some people, endowed with magnetic personalities, leadership comes naturally. For most people, though, the conference believes that leadership is the *culmination*, or the result, of a number of individual qualities that should be examined and then put into practice.

The first two chapters of this book compared the building of a good speaker to the building of a well-made house. Now, in the final chapter, we come to the roof. The roof is the top of the house and is the last part of the construction. Isn't the roof an extension of the construction below it? Similarly, leadership is the "extension" that can result when you add a constructive, confident attitude to a solid sense of personal integrity. And the "planks of leadership" make up the "roof," or final step, in completing our "house of effective oral communication."

© Digital Vision/Alamy

Leadership and Learning Styles

A line from the popular musical *The Music Man* declares that when it comes to selling, "Ya gotta know the territory." In other words, you need to know the makeup of your target people and what makes them tick if you want to sell your product. Every leader is, in a sense, a salesperson. He or she is selling an idea or a course of action, asking others to buy in and follow. But what style works? Is there a sure-fire approach that will be effective in any territory? The answer, unfortunately, is no—for when it comes to leadership, unlike clothes you can buy, one size does *not* fit all. Different people are swayed or influenced by different leadership approaches. Let's look at three leadership styles, as suggested by Patricia Pitcher in her book *The Drama of Leadership*: the technocrat, the artist, and the craftsman. After reading, decide which leadership style is most attractive to you; consider the positives and negatives of each, and choose one you might be tempted to follow.

Technocrats are no-nonsense leaders, often more interested in numbers than in people.

Leadership Styles

The Technocrat. The technocrat leads by having a strong sense of the bottom line—often spending more time figuring out numbers and strategy than figuring out people. This leadership style, says Pitcher, is no-nonsense. It is a "my way or the highway"

What makes a good leader?

"The Voice of Hispanic America"

Maria Elena Salinas is not only one of the most influential Hispanics in the country; the Emmy Award–winning co-anchor of *Noticiero Univision* is the most recognized Hispanic journalist in the United States. During her 25-year career, Salinas has interviewed some of the most powerful leaders in the country and the world. In addition, she has become an important advocate for Hispanics.

According to Salinas, "There are issues I feel passionate about, such as immigration, education, health care and the political empowerment of Latinos. The needs of our community are many, and that is why my work as a journalist has given way to multiple public service projects throughout the years in which I have worked with the U.S. Departments of Education and Health and Human Services, the World Health Organization, as well as several non-profit organizations in providing information that will improve the lives and well-being of Latinos."

As a journalist, she feels it is her job to not only inform the community, but reach out to them to help improve their lives: "There's a tremendous responsibility being the voice and image of the Hispanic community."

Though many Americans may never have heard of Salinas, for millions of Hispanics, she is their voice, their role model, and their champion.

approach to motivating others. The only voice that the technocrat wishes to hear is his or her own, and people often follow because they are afraid not to do so. The technocrat values logic over emotion. The technocrat is intense, detail oriented, and hard headed, refusing to compromise. The main objective for the technocrat is to get the job done, and he or she focuses only on that goal.

The Artist. The artist leads by imagination and intuition. Even though he or she doesn't know how all of the pieces fit together, the artist has a distinct vision of the big picture. This leadership style actively invites others to share ideas and isn't afraid to show emotion and laughter. The artist, though sometimes unpredictable, is a daring *entrepreneur*—one who goes after new ideas and sees things from a different perspective. The artist can be found in any social or professional setting where creativity is important. Sometimes we are fascinated by the artist and go along with him or her just to share in the unique possibilities that might result from this type of leadership.

The Craftsman. The craftsman (male or female) leads by common sense and integrity. He or she is trustworthy, well balanced, and excellent at listening. This leadership style draws followers because the craftsman is a caring, logical person who values getting the job done but refuses to sacrifice people and their views and feelings in the process. The craftsman is liked because he or she is predictable and seems to have it together. Such a leader

Walter Cronkite, second from left, represents the total craftsman. He is considered one of the twentieth century's finest broadcast journalists.

LEADERSHIP

What qualities make these people leaders?

Colin Powell

Hillary Rodham Clinton

Cesar Chávez

Condoleezza Rice

George W. Bush

Oprah Winfrey

isn't afraid to venture into creative thinking, but he or she is always aware of the real world and what is reasonable. The craftsman is skilled at decision making and strategically avoids making others feel like winners or losers.

The Answer Is in the Blending These are three leadership profiles that you may have encountered somewhere in your life. Which style is the best? Patricia Pitcher states that there are times when the technocrat is needed—when the tough, "just give me the facts" approach is smart. When Thomas Buckley first ran for auditor of Massachusetts in 1941, his speech consisted of only seven words: "I am an auditor, not an orator!" He continued to run (and win!) for years after, each time campaigning with these same seven words. Needless to say, Buckley was all business. However, Pitcher's research shows that the technocrat leadership style is on the way out. More and more, those in charge are realizing that people *need* people—and that social and professional success sometimes depends more on effective communication that fosters teamwork and collective problem solving than it does on a dictatorial approach based on intimidation that stresses everyone out. The best leadership style, Pitcher concludes, is a blending of the artist and the

These attorneys are doing research before presenting their arguments in court.

The best speakers, teachers, and leaders are those who can use their words to communicate with the greatest number of people. To do that, you need to be familiar with people's **learning styles**—the ways that they learn most effectively. We examine four learning styles here: discussion, logic, design, and emotion.

Learning Style 1: Discussion Some people learn best through meaningful discussion. They want to be actively involved in the oral communication process, with lots of dialogue and feedback. They appreciate face-to-face communication. Getting everyone's opinion is important to them, and they love to brainstorm, or throw many ideas onto the table. They enjoy discussing each item before making a decision. They are alert and involved when they have the opportunity for verbal interaction.

craftsman—a combination of creativity and genuine enthusiasm with levelheadedness, compassion, and collaboration.

Learning Styles

A good leader knows that before there can be effective motivation, there must be effective communication. Obviously, if you know how people learn best, you increase your chance of getting and keeping their attention.

Perhaps when you read the sentence "A leader knows that people learn differently," you think it is referring only to classroom teachers. Not so. All leaders are teachers in some way. They teach specific strategies and lessons. They teach and promote certain attitudes. They teach about people and life.

Learning Style 2: Logic Others learn best when things are presented logically, with a "just the facts" approach. Discussed in Chapter 10, logic stresses analysis, organization, and an approach focusing on good sense. Some members of this group, not impressed by a lot of talk, are genuinely interested when they hear a direct, logical, to-the-point plan of action.

Learning Style 3: Design Some people learn best when they can see and hear how the big picture fits together. People in this category might include engineers and other builders and designers. They are encouraged when the leader presents a clear picture of relationships and shows how the different parts are all going to work together as a smooth-running unit.

Learning Style 4: Emotion For many people, the best communication is a hands-on approach, one in which the leader is energetic and fired up. As you have probably heard before, enthusiasm is contagious. Often, a leader who shows the group that he or she is emotionally involved with a specific project or idea will quickly attract highly involved and committed followers.

Do any of these methods sound familiar? Which would work best for you? Knowing about learning styles can help a leader communicate with others. There are other ways of categorizing learning styles, but keeping these four types in mind should help when you are thinking about using your words to reach everyone. If you know how people learn—what approach excites them—you improve your chance of communicating effectively with them.

Hands-on leaders like this fix-up volunteer will likely appeal to your emotions.

SECTION 1 REVIEW

Recalling the Facts

1. List the three leadership styles given in this section. Which one sometimes puts numbers ahead of people and their feelings?
2. Which leadership style depends on imagination and intuition?
3. What do you call combining leadership styles to get the best overall approach to leadership?
4. List the four learning styles given in the section. Which one stresses a knowledge of the big picture? Which one involves enthusiasm and a fired-up presentation?

Thinking Critically

One leadership style is that of the technocrat. It is said that this type of leader is on the way out, because the future will call for a great deal more team building and consensus building. However, think about class projects, work that has to be done on the job, or even balancing a checkbook. In such cases, mightn't some qualities of the technocrat be useful? When else?

Unfortunately, leaders can take the technocratic approach too far. Give some examples of how this approach might turn followers off.

Taking Charge

Analyze and evaluate leadership styles shown in the media. What television programs depict people who lead differently? What about your favorite movie characters? People in the news? List the three different leadership styles. After each, list individuals who might fall in each category. You should have at least *two* for each category. Be prepared to explain your reasoning, based on the definition for each leadership style in this section.

The Planks of Leadership

According to a study by management specialist Thomas Peters, history makers from Martin Luther King Jr. to Thomas Jefferson have had these "top ten" things in common:

1. commitment
2. focus
3. passion
4. willingness to take risks
5. creativity or distinctiveness
6. honesty
7. imperfection
8. sensitivity to followers' needs and aspirations
9. skill at what they did
10. indifference to making some people angry

Obviously, leaders are people who aren't afraid to give power and authority to others. In addition, they have the power and the drive to make things happen.

As you read the following discussion, pay attention to the specific communication strategy at the end of each plank. It will show you how to demonstrate a quality of leadership by using an appropriate verbal, nonverbal, or listening strategy to promote both individual and group communication effectiveness.

Plank 1: A Leader Has a Sense of Vision

On July 20, 1999, the United States celebrated the thirtieth anniversary of the first moonwalk. When scientists proposed the idea of a human being in outer space, let alone a person walking on the moon, few thought it was possible. But a sense of vision, as well as follow-through, turned this idea into a reality. Such a sense of vision is one key trait of a leader.

Simply put, **vision,** as it applies to leadership, means the ability to see more than just the obvious.

Leaders with a sense of vision can often "solve the puzzle" because they have the ability to see a situation in its entirety and then focus on what really matters. Often, vision enables a leader to spot a need that must be met, to create a product or program that has tremendous possibilities, or to see how the pieces in the big picture could better fit together within a plan or an organization.

There's a difference, however, between making random predictions and displaying a true sense of vision. Consider the following predictions, which were made in the 1960s by people who thought they had a sense for what would occur at the turn of the millennium. According the *New York Times,* in 1966, Arthur C. Clarke predicted that by the

Vision drove workers at the National Aeronautics and Space Administration (NASA) to make the first moonwalk happen.

NASA Johnson Space Center (NASA-JSC)

year 2001, inventors would develop construction materials stronger than steel but lighter than aluminum. These materials would enable houses to fly. As he said, "Whole communities may migrate south in the winter." In 1967, *Science Digest* predicted that by the turn of the century, "Discarded rayon underwear will be bought by chemical factories and converted into candy." Obviously, these predictions failed to come true; their "vision" was, to say the least, a little clouded. But such failures shouldn't stop the rest of us from trying to discover what a true sense of vision is.

To develop this sense, a leader must have insight, a long-term perspective, and an ability to ponder the big picture. As Anil Nanji, a successful California businessman, points out, vision is not only a picture of the way things should be, but also a guiding light that helps one channel the decisions and actions that accompany that vision.

Specific Communication Strategy: As a leader, practice creative thinking skills, but also seek out the ideas of others so that you can truly grasp the big picture. Look at a situation and then take a step back and consider another perspective. Use your intrapersonal and interpersonal communication skills. Ask yourself and others, What are the parts and how do they fit together to form the whole? What do we want to accomplish? What are our goals? What do we dare to dream? How can we best realize our vision? Sharing plans with others and opening the door to dialogue often results in more-effective long-range planning. A good leader recognizes the importance of gathering and using accurate and complete information as the basis for making communication decisions.

Plank 2: A Leader Is Willing to Act

Novelist Sinclair Lewis was invited to give a lecture to aspiring authors. He began his lecture by asking, "How many of you really intend to be writers?" Everyone in the room raised a hand. "In that case," responded Lewis, "my advice to you is to go home and write." With that, he left the room.

Now, Lewis may have been overly blunt in his approach, but his point was clear. Leaders are doers. They take action. They believe in getting the job

Novelist Sinclair Lewis spoke little but wrote volumes. He exemplifies the doer.

done and getting it done well. After all the talking, analyzing, and pondering, it is the leader who says to the rest of the group, "OK, let's get started. Let's do something *now!*"

While speaking at a leadership seminar, a university professor said that it was time for students to quit thinking and talking about success and to start acting. Unlike Sinclair Lewis, he offered more-detailed advice. He suggested that the students map out a specific plan of action and then start working to realize their goals. The seminar, which was titled "Now Is the Time to Start Thinking and Growing Rich," dealt with both personal and material success. It stressed that personal leadership begins with a philosophy of action. What follows is an example of what can happen when an individual is determined to take positive action to achieve success.

This individual was the last of several brothers to leave Germany for the United States. The year was 1847, and he was only eighteen years old. His brothers, who owned a dry goods business in New York, soon put him to work. He learned English quickly and proved to be an excellent salesman.

In 1853 he opened his own dry goods business in California to take advantage of the gold rush. One day he received a letter from a tailor in Nevada who regularly bought cloth from him. The tailor wrote about a customer who had complained that the pockets of the work trousers the tailor had made him kept ripping. The tailor had come up with a solution: put metal rivets in the pocket corners. Now his riveted trousers were becoming so popular that he wanted to take out a patent on them, but he lacked the money for the application fee. He was writing his cloth supplier in California to propose that the two men form a partnership and take out the patent together. The dry goods businessman saw the potential for this product and agreed.

What was this businessman's name? Levi Strauss. And May 20, 1873—the day he and his partner received the patent—is considered the birthday of blue jeans.

Before long, workingmen were buying up the innovative trousers, which came to be known simply as Levi's, and word spread about their ruggedness. In response, Strauss expanded his line of work wear to include shirts, jackets, and other clothing. Why? He saw a need, he saw a market, he saw an opportunity.

Levi Strauss saw an opportunity and acted on it. Today, Levi's jeans are known worldwide.

Today Levi's is a household name around the globe because, back in the 1870s, Levi Strauss had the nerve to act. Levi Strauss was a leader! You can learn a valuable lesson from this story. Allow your vision to work for you, and then get in there and get your hands dirty. While luck might sometimes *facilitate* positive results, it is leadership that will most often bring those results.

Specific Communication Strategy: When leadership is needed, take charge. Make statements to the group such as these: "Here's what we need to do now." "Now let's make a list specifying who's responsible for what. We'll report back tomorrow on our progress." "It's time that we quit talking and start doing!" Let your spoken words show that you are not afraid of a challenge and that you will act to get the task completed.

Plank 3: A Leader Makes Good Decisions

Nothing will kill the credibility of a leader more quickly than being perceived as indecisive. However, there is a world of difference between simply making a decision and making the right decision. Your decisions should show intelligence, but they should do more. They should reflect ethical communication, showing that you feel a sense of social or professional responsibility to your group. Let's look at three specific questions that a good leader might answer before making a final decision.

Question 1: Am I knowledgeable about the issues and the people involved? Good leaders do their homework, learning the facts that might affect their decision on an issue. Once again, it is important to gather accurate and complete information. Are statistics about the issues needed? What is the history of the issues? What does the current literature say about them? Knowing all you can about the issues can give you the scope to make a good decision and can add credibility to your position as a decision maker.

In addition to knowing about issues, you need to know about people. How will the group react to your decision? Do you have the group's best interest in mind? Are you considering what they will think, as well as how they will feel? What will be the long-range effect on everyone involved? A good leader remembers that people are the most important consideration in making any decision!

Researching the issues makes you a more credible leader.

Question 2: Am I making decisions in the correct order? A good leader has to know how to prioritize decisions, putting what is most important first. A school committee that spends hours on getting a big-name band to entertain the hundreds of people who will attending an end-of-the-year dance before it decides on a location large enough to accommodate all of those people might run into problems later. A good leader decides on the larger issues first and then moves down the list, realistically considering needs versus wants before prioritizing. Are you working with something that is essential or something that would be a luxury? How will one decision affect another? Making a correct decision can be a big job; making the decision when it should be made is equally important.

Question 3: Am I aware of the risks involved? While a good leader should be informed and able to prioritize, she or he must also be willing to take a chance if the situation seems to call for it. You can't always act according to what has been done before. Sometimes risk taking shows creativity, insight, and progress.

In taking risks, however, a good leader is never caught off-guard. You consider the potential consequences of your decision. Is the risk a smart one, or might it be too costly? The pilot of a commercial aircraft would be foolish suddenly to disregard the instructions of an air traffic controller and strike out on her or his own. The pilot would be putting the lives of everyone on the plane in jeopardy. As an effective leader and decision maker, you must sometimes use your instincts, but you must also use your common sense and sound judgment when the well-being of others is at stake.

If you consider each of the three questions in this section when making important decisions in your personal, professional, school, community, and family life, then you may find stepping to the front and leading others less daunting and more productive.

Specific Communication Strategy: When sharing your final decision with others, try to focus your communication on three terms: *what*, *why*, and *how*. If others clearly understand what your decision is, why you made it, and how you believe it can be carried out, then they are more apt to respect the decision. Even if they disagree with it, they will respect the time, energy, and thoroughness that went into making it. And if you include how you plan to implement the decision, others will gain confidence in the decision's workability. Also, remember to tell the members of the group that you appreciate their input and that you seriously considered it before making the final decision. A decision tends to meet with more approval when people understand rather than assume why the decision was made.

Plank 4: A Leader Can Handle Conflict

Of all the qualities of a leader, none ranks higher than the ability to work *harmoniously* with other people and make them feel good both about themselves and about the group's objectives. A fact of life for anyone in charge of a group, however, is that things don't always run smoothly. Problems arise and personalities clash. This is why a leader must work diligently to solve problems, manage conflicts, and build consensus in the group.

How should a problem be handled? First of all, good leaders know that intense arguing and emotional outbursts won't help. All that happens when emotions are allowed to run wild is that communication takes a back seat to confrontation, which gets in the way of what both the leader and the group are after. Cool heads must prevail. An awareness of the principles of conflict management can help. **Conflict management** is the ability to turn a potentially negative situation into a positive one.

A speech consultant working with a group of business supervisors and executives to improve communication and public speaking offered the following plan for conflict management. This plan, which has worked for him and countless others, includes four steps:

Shut up!
Look up!
Hook up!
Chill down!

1. *Shut up!* A good leader doesn't always have to be the one doing the talking. If you are having a problem with another person, keep quiet and listen to what that person is saying. Don't interrupt! Allow the person to finish speaking before you talk.

2. *Look up!* Establish eye contact with the person. Don't look off to the side or down at the floor. Let the person know that you are genuinely involved in what he or she is saying by looking at the person and showing an understanding, responsive attitude.

3. *Hook up!* It is important to hook up emotionally with the person, to try to understand her

Air traffic controllers must be acutely aware of risks, using their specialized training to keep airspace safe.

or his point of view. You may need to see the situation from another perspective and understand why someone else might not feel as you do.

4. *Chill down!* When you do verbally respond to the person, make your comments rational, sensitive, and constructive. Don't permit your temper or the heat of the moment to control a situation and allow it to escalate into an even larger problem.

Try this four-point plan in your dealings with other people. Your conflict management skills may not only improve the situation but also increase your confidence in how you communicate with others every day. It's worth a try!

Closely associated with conflict management is a leader's willingness to get along with others. Even though getting along often takes hard work, it's worth the effort. After all, you can't make it all alone. But a leader who won't strive to create a harmonious working environment might find that he or she has to do all of the work alone.

One way to create a harmonious working environment is to praise people's efforts. Studies have shown that people like to be told when they are doing things right. It fosters group rapport and increases productivity. In complimenting people, vary the words that you use. Words lose their impact if they are used insincerely or are repeated over and over. Here are some words you could use to compliment and encourage others: *great, wonderful, outstanding, excellent, perfect.* Also, try to verbalize praiseworthy traits, using words such as *hard-working, dedicated, detail-oriented, trustworthy, responsible, caring, considerate, loyal, dependable, honest,* and *friendly.* What terms can you add to either list?

Specific Communication Strategy: Tactfully summarize for others what they have said to you so they know that you were paying attention to them.

Being a good leader means keeping people focused in the midst of conflict or exciting situations.

Also, pay careful attention to how you say something. You can add to your effectiveness as a leader by being aware of the tone of your voice and the nonverbal signals that you are giving. Body language speaks just as loudly as words, so convey through body language a message that shows people, "I take seriously what you have to say, and I am really listening!"

Plank 5: A Leader Works to Avoid Pitfalls

You have probably heard the saying "Forewarned is forearmed." It means that being conscious of a potential problem ahead of time might help you stop it before it gets started. With this in mind, be alert to the following four pitfalls of leadership and work to avoid them.

Pitfall 1: Being Afraid to Fail Leaders don't like to make mistakes. A good leader tries to be conscientious and show the group that she or he can be counted on to do things correctly. However, a leader should not always play it safe. If, as a

COMMUNICATION *BREAKTHROUGH*

Special Olympics athlete

Special Olympics

Eunice Kennedy Shriver, a sister of John F. Kennedy, had a sister, Rosemary, who had mental disabilities. After visiting many hospitals for people with such disabilities, Shriver was appalled at the crowding and understaffing she saw. She was also appalled that the patients were never encouraged to exercise and thus were in poor physical condition. Hospital staff told her that running, jumping, and playing could injure the patients. Shriver decided to take matters into her own hands. In 1962 she started an exercise class and constructed a playing field for people with mental disabilities—in her own backyard! By 1968 this class had evolved into the Special Olympics movement.

Special Olympics provides athletic training and competition for children and adults with mental disabilities. Events include basketball, bowling, cycling, gymnastics, judo, skating, soccer, swimming, tennis, and volleyball. Today more than 10,000 communities around the world offer Special Olympics programs; more than a million athletes participate in the United States alone.

Special Olympics has two major objectives: (1) to promote the physical and emotional growth of people with mental disabilities, through friendship and family support, and (2) to offer people with such disabilities opportunities for achievement and courage through athletics. Eunice Kennedy Shriver was a leader because she saw a need and then acted to meet it. What was one result? Special Olympics has become a symbol that communicates to the entire world that people really do care about each other.

Most of the work for Special Olympics is done by volunteers—more than 700,000 of them worldwide. And perhaps one of the most rewarding volunteer jobs is to be a "hugger"—someone who hugs an athlete when he or she completes an event. Every athlete has a hugger.

Says one volunteer mother, "Everyone involved with the Special Olympics is a leader because when all of the voices are heard laughing and cheering together, we all feel inspired and understand that each of us is depending on the other person. That makes me feel good inside!"

Questions

1. What do you think the volunteer mother means by her statement? Why could it be true that "Everyone involved with the Special Olympics is a leader"?

2. Why is it noteworthy that most of the work for Special Olympics is done by volunteers?

leader, your attitude is, "I'd like to try that, but I'm afraid that I'll fail," then you might be *forfeiting* some of the creativity and personal vision that the group counts on you to provide.

Don't be afraid of what your instincts and personal intuition might be telling you to do. Of course, you have to make sure that you are not being reckless, but you should also keep in mind that many great leaders failed at one time or another. The baseball great Babe Ruth was a home-run king, but he also led the major leagues in strike-outs. The explorer Christopher Columbus left Europe to find the East Indies; he failed to find them, but he found America. The inventor and genius Thomas Edison had an interesting philosophy about failure. He said that when his work produced 99 failures in a row, he then knew 99 ways that didn't work and was closing in on the solution. Abraham Lincoln lost five elections before he eventually became president.

Babe Ruth was never afraid to fail!

As a leader, don't live with a fear of failure. If your group knows that you have its best interests at heart, it will most likely support your efforts. Go for it!

Pitfall 2: Not Paying Attention to Details Of course, a leader should focus on the big picture, but he or she should also pay attention to the small things. A good leader is aware that paying attention to details early will help clarify the big picture later.

Details matter! If handled correctly, they can make you appear organized and competent to your group. If handled incorrectly, they can make you appear foolish and inept. In 1987, for example, the Nobel Prize Committee for Science and Economics notified Donald O. Cram that he had won the Nobel Prize in chemistry. The problem was that Donald O. Cram was a California rug shampooer. The award was really meant for Donald J. Cram.

Ignoring details or dismissing them as trivial often results in projects that don't work or organizations that fall apart. It was a detail—the seemingly insignificant O-ring—on the space shuttle *Challenger* that ultimately caused the loss of seven lives and a huge setback for the U.S. manned space program.

Pitfall 3: Forgetting People and the Original Objectives A major pitfall for any leader is to forget the human factor in decision making or to lose sight of what it was that the group was originally after. As a conscientious leader, you need to ask yourself these questions: "What exactly were we trying to accomplish?" "Who played key roles and worked hard right from the start?" It can be easy for those in charge to get detoured. Stay on track. Also, reward group members who deserve special consideration for being there when times were tough.

Pitfall 4: Not Listening to Others It is important to listen to others, for a variety of reasons. Not only is it a nice thing to do, but it is also smart. By listening to others, you can gain new insights, stimulate new ideas, and build on the input of others. Seeing other perspectives and synthesizing different viewpoints enables leaders to have a better understanding of a situation. As the owner of Motivation Media, a broad-ranging corporate communications

Planetary Emergency

On October 12, 2007, former vice president Al Gore was awarded the Nobel Peace Prize for his efforts to inform the public about global warming and work toward a solution. According to the Norwegian Nobel Committee,

> Al Gore has for a long time been one of the world's leading environmentalist politicians. He became aware at an early stage of the climatic challenges the world is facing. His strong commitment, reflected in political activity, lectures, films and books, has strengthened the struggle against climate change.

After his defeat in the presidential race of 2000, Gore began focusing on the natural environment and ways to change human behavior before it's too late. This cause has been important to him since he was in college. In 2006 Gore starred in the Academy Award–winning documentary *An Inconvenient Truth*, based on the best-selling book he coauthored. The book and movie expose myths about global warming and present theories about how to stop it.

Many experts and leaders have criticized Gore's theories and the fact that he won the Nobel Prize. Some experts also question whether global warming is even a legitimate concern. However, others feel that the award legitimizes the view that global warming is one of the most serious threats facing us today.

Upon receiving the award, Gore said:

> We face a true planetary emergency. The climate crisis is not a political issue; it is a moral and spiritual challenge to all of humanity.

A mechanic pays attention to small details to keep a car running smoothly.

company, explains, "In some ways, I think I never have my own idea. What I have is an ability to synthesize the thinking and contributions of others." The company credits its success to its ability to listen to customers and then incorporate findings so that service is always top-notch.

People also appreciate the opportunity to be heard. This does not mean that every idea has equal merit or will be acted on immediately, but it does mean that leaders gain respect and support from others by establishing a rapport that includes openness to input. This input may take the form of brainstorming or evaluating, or it may involve venting feelings or simply expressing concerns. If handled in an atmosphere of mutual respect, such interactions will lead to a happier, more comfortable, more successful group of people.

Specific Communication Strategy: This is a good time to make use of your intrapersonal communication skills and remind yourself of some important points. Give yourself a good talking-to and consider all of your options. What are the risks? Have you thought through all of the details? What was the primary issue and who were the people

Leaders must know how to motivate. This young woman encourages her peers to volunteer.

there from the start? Did you listen to others before making a decision? Answer such questions to yourself. This activity can help you avoid a few of the pitfalls that signal, "Beware: Danger Ahead!"

Plank 6: A Leader Knows How to Motivate

When the U.S. women's soccer team won the World Cup in 1999, its victory over the top-rated team from China rocked the sporting world. Certainly, this accomplishment resulted from great skill, but it also resulted from a tremendous desire to win, to beat the odds, to reach new heights of success. From star goalkeeper Brianna Scurry to Brandi Chastain, who scored the winning goal,

the team was filled with leaders who were motivated to excel.

Recall from Chapter 1 that to motivate means to inspire either yourself or others to act. The subject of motivation comes up near the end of this chapter for a reason: it is the consequence of all that has been discussed. Motivation may be created by any number of factors:

- The honesty and integrity that you show
- The strong work ethic that you exhibit
- The discussion that you promote
- The logic and intelligence that you put forward
- The plan of action that you offer
- The emotion that you share
- The creativity that you lend
- The confidence and decisiveness that you exhibit

Wanted: Leader

Must be able to see the big picture; solve problems through analysis and discussion, followed by action; teach people according to different learning styles (discussion, logic, design, and emotion); make good decisions, based on knowledge, priorities, and awareness of risks; manage conflict; avoid pitfalls like being afraid to fail, not paying attention to details, and forgetting original objectives; and motivate self and others.

Motivation is a very personal thing. What motivates some won't motivate others. Thus, the job of a good leader is to know his or her group well enough to know what will work with whom. No textbook can specifically prescribe how every leader can motivate every group member. In the end, motivation results when the people in your group trust you enough to follow your advice.

Specific Communication Strategy: Read the advice given for Planks 1–5. Work on making both your verbal and your nonverbal communication clear and meaningful. At the same time, leave room for the creativity and spontaneity that often come when leader and group are functioning cooperatively as one productive unit.

So there you have the six planks of leadership. To be a good speaker and a good leader, you must work from the inside out and establish a strong value system that will anchor your words and give them substance.

True leaders, contrary to what some might believe, are everywhere. They include both females and males, young and old, rich and poor, and they represent various ethnic groups. It is our job to recognize the tremendous leadership potential that people have. In the tragic shooting that took place at Columbine High School in Colorado in April 1999, one girl, who was trapped in a small, hot band room with scores of other students, told how three or four "geeks," the "not-real-popular kids," took charge and articulated a well-organized plan of escape through the overhead heating and cooling ductwork. Their leadership saved lives.

Everyone has leadership potential. Your ideas might not be great when it comes to literature and writing plays, but what about your thoughts on writing music? Your ideas about a trade such as carpentry? About cars? About kids and teaching?

These JROTC cadets from Chicago marched in a Memorial Day tribute honoring the many military who died serving our country.

Share your ideas. Listen to the ideas of others. You just might uncover some real eye-opening solutions and discoveries.

Being a good leader can be tough, but people who use their communication skills to inspire others, to promote smart problem solving, and to help all of us get along better with each other are certainly building a bright future and are destined to end up—like the roof on our house of communication—at the top!

These students participated in clean-up work that helped collect twenty four metric tons of abandoned fishing lines and ghost nets in the Northwestern Hawaiian Islands.

(t)US Army photo by Sgt. 1st Class Marisol Hernandez;(b) NOAA 200th Anniversary Postcards from the Field, NOAA/Dept. of Commerce

SECTION 2 REVIEW

Recalling the Facts

1. One of the planks of leadership says that a leader can handle conflict. List the four steps that a speech consultant gave to businesspeople that also might work for you.
2. Which one of the planks was based on the idea that leaders are doers? What person from history whose name appears on a popular brand of jeans was definitely a doer?
3. Which plank is often a result of all of the others?

Thinking Critically

The book *21-Day Countdown to Success* by Chris Witting talks about some examples of people who didn't give up when faced with initial failure. For instance, a newspaper once fired a young cartoonist because he didn't "have any good ideas." It was Walt Disney. Basketball icon Michael Jordan was cut from his junior high basketball team. News personality Katie Couric flopped in her first TV job because she had a "squeaky voice." Yet, none of these three gave up.

Why is it important that leaders be able to bounce back from adversity? Think of a person (or people) in history or current events who wasn't afraid to fail and who achieved personal or professional success. What qualities did she or he exhibit that you might want to apply to your own life?

Taking Charge

Several leadership pitfalls are listed in this chapter. What are your own leadership problems? List two pitfalls that you find difficult to overcome when attempting to lead. Try not to use the ones listed in the book; think of your own. Katie Couric, when told that her voice was a problem on the air, took voice lessons. What can you list as some possible solutions or action steps that you might use to solve your leadership problems? Jot them down and then be prepared to discuss them with the class. Be ready for a small group discussion or an informal oral presentation.

Looking Back

Listed below are the major ideas discussed in this chapter.

- Leadership involves your ability to motivate yourself and others.
- A leader is a person who puts leadership skills into action.
- Leadership styles vary. There is the technocrat, the artist, and the craftsman.
- The best leaders often blend styles to reach a broader group.
- The planks of leadership provide a framework for leadership.
- A good leader has a sense of vision and sees how the big picture fits together.
- A good leader is a doer who will take charge of a situation and get things done.

- A good leader is aware that people learn differently and adjusts his or her leadership style to meet the demands of the group.
- A good leader knows not only how to make decisions but also the order in which to make them.
- A good leader knows conflict management skills.
- A good leader is aware of body language and the impact of nonverbal communication.
- A good leader is aware of pitfalls to avoid.
- A good leader can effectively do whatever it takes to motivate others.
- The spoken word should always be used constructively.

Speech Vocabulary

leader
leadership
learning styles
vision
conflict management

1. Write the definition of each term as given in the chapter, and give the number of the page where it is defined. For each term, write an original sentence showing the term in action.

2. Prepare a quiz. On the left side of your paper, list the new speech terms, leaving out some of the letters of each word. (Example: -e-der-hi- for *leadership*.) On the right side of your paper, list the definitions of the terms in a different order. Have a classmate take your quiz by matching each term with the correct definition. Be sure to have an answer key.

Academic Vocabulary

culmination
entrepreneur
facilitate
harmoniously
forfeiting
simulated

1. Define each academic vocabulary term and use it in an original sentence.

2. Write a story titled "The Day I Had to Take Charge of the Class and Become the Leader." Select at least three new speech terms and at least three general vocabulary terms and use them effectively in the story. Be sure that your story is at least one page long and makes sense when read aloud.

To Remember

Answer the following questions based on your reading of the chapter.

1. A leader who has a sense of _____ can see a situation in its entirety and keep both details and the big picture in perspective.
2. A leader must be willing to _____ if anything is ever going to get done!
3. Because people have different _____, leaders should use a variety of strategies to connect with followers.
4. If you can handle a stressful situation and turn a potentially negative situation into a positive one, then you have excellent _____ skills.
5. Often, your nonverbal communication, or your _____, will convey more to people than the words that you speak.
6. List the four leadership pitfalls.
7. As discussed in the Communication Breakthrough, people who _____ —that is, donate their time and efforts—can accomplish great things for humanity.
8. The planks of leadership illustrate six characteristics of a good leader. List the first five.
9. A tragedy took place at Columbine High School. Based on what you read, describe the students who took charge and led others to safety.

To Do

1. Construct a chart on a large sheet of paper. On one side of the chart, make a heading that says, "What a Leader Does." On the other side of the chart, make a heading that says, "What a Leader Doesn't Do." Now fill in the chart. Be sure to make your work colorful and attractive, and be sure that you include some original ideas on leadership in addition to what the chapter taught.
2. Interview a leader. The person can be in your school, your community, or your family. Find out that person's views on (a) why leadership is important, (b) where leadership is most needed in our society, (c) why some people are afraid to lead, and (d) how best to motivate others. Be ready to present your findings to the class. Also, note why you selected the person and why you consider her or him a noteworthy leader.
3. Make a collage—"an artistic composition of materials pasted over a surface, often with a unifying theme." The theme is "Leadership Around the World." Cut out pictures, words, and phrases that you can use to portray this theme. Your collage should have many words and pictures if you are going to create the impact that you want. With your teacher's permission, you may work with a partner. Be neat and complete in your work.
4. According to a study of leadership styles by Korn and Ferry, "A combination of so-called feminine and masculine traits is needed for leadership in the 21st century." Survey respondents perceived men as risk taking, self-confident, and very competitive. They perceived women as stronger at listening, building relationships, and being able to share power and information. Survey the other students in your class. See if they agree with the findings of this study. Ask them to give examples to validate their reasoning. Write the responses, and be ready to make a class presentation.

To Talk About

1. Why in today's world are people often skeptical about many of their leaders? Why don't they trust some of them? Use newspapers, magazines, radio, and television to give specific examples of what you mean. What lessons can you learn about your own leadership from what you see some other leaders doing?

2. A leader often sees a need and then takes the initiative to fill that need. In Japan, productivity and efficiency are primary concerns. This has created grueling work schedules, reducing the time workers have to spend with their families. A company called Japan Efficiency has made it possible for busy workers to "rent" people to take their place in family visits. Sons and daughters who don't have the time to visit their family can hire professional actors or actresses (at $1,150 for three hours) as substitutes. Said one Japanese reporter, "The parents are aware of what's going on, but they just want to hold a child or give advice to the younger generation." What is your reaction to this whole situation? What do you think of this company, Japan Efficiency? What do you think of what the children are doing? What about the parents?

3. The quality of leadership is often dependent on the quality of "followership." Why are followers important? What are some important responsibilities that followers should have, and why is "followership" a vital element in a democracy?

To Write About

1. An Illinois girl wishes to be on the all-male wrestling team. Does she have the right? If allowed to join, what problems might she encounter? What positive outcomes might there be? Write your responses to these questions in complete sentences. Be sure to make your reasoning clear.

2. Why is it important to get along with others? In an essay at least one page long, give your own three- or four-point plan for conflict management, and the steps that you would take to handle a stressful situation. Give examples, if possible, and explain your reasoning.

Related Speech Topics

How I can be a leader in the classroom, at work, in my home, and in the community

Why the United States needs the volunteer

Why getting along with people matters in leadership

The person in the news that I most admire as a leader

Why parents must be leaders at home

Why a leader must sometimes be a follower

How nonverbal communication can make or break a leader

Why self-discipline is important to a leader

The elements of leadership that people tend to forget

Why everyone is a leader at one time or another

Celebrities as leaders: do they shine or not?

GLOSSARY

A

abstract word—a word that names an intangible, such as a quality, an attribute, or a concept

accommodation—a negotiation strategy in which differences are minimized, smoothed over, or suppressed (lose-win approach)

acronym—a word formed from the initial letter of each of the major parts of a compound term

active listening—a listening role in which the listener participates and shares in the communication process by guiding the speaker toward common interests

adjourn—to close a meeting

advance organizer—in a speech, introductory statements that forecast what an audience may expect

affirmative— an expression meaning "yes" or "true"; in debate, the side that upholds the proposition

affluent—having a generously sufficient—and typically, an increasing—supply of material possessions

after-dinner speech—an entertaining speech that follows a banquet or other meal

agenda—orders of the day; a list of things to be done

aggressive tone—a pushy or brash way of communicating, which considers only one point of view, leaving little or no room for compromise or discussion

alienate—to make hostile, unfriendly

allegory—the use of symbolic, fictional figures and actions (as in a story or painting) to express generalizations about human existence

alliteration—the repetition of the same sounds—usually consonants at the beginning of words—in words that are close together

allusion—an indirect reference to a well-known person, place, thing, or idea

almanac—an annual publication that provides statistics and general facts

ambiguous—capable of being understood in more than one way

amend—in parliamentary procedure, to change a motion by adding and/or removing words

analogy—an illustration in which characteristics of a familiar thing or idea are used to explain or describe characteristics of an unfamiliar thing or idea

analysis—the separation of a thing into the parts or elements that compose it; an examination of a thing to determine its parts or elements; a statement showing the results of such an examination

analytical—marked by the ability to separate a thing into the parts or elements that compose it, or by the ability to examine a thing to determine its parts or elements

anecdote—a brief story used to illustrate a point

anthology—a collection of selected literary pieces or passages

anthropologist—one who studies human beings, including their physical characteristics and environmental, social, and cultural relations

antithesis—a contrasting of ideas by means of parallel arrangement of words, phrases, and so on; the opposite

apathetic—having little or no interest or concern (indifferent); having or showing little or no feeling or emotion

apoplectic—affected with, inclined to, or showing symptoms of stroke

appreciative listening—a listening style used to enjoy pleasurable sounds, as in music or nature

appropriateness—being suitable or compatible

argument—a reason for favoring one side of a proposition and the facts that support that reason

articulation—the crispness and distinctness of an utterance

assert—to state or declare positively and often forcefully and aggressively

assertion—a positive declaration

assertive tone—a direct yet tactful communication approach

assonance—the repetition of the same or similar vowel sounds between different consonants of words that are close together

atlas—a publication that includes maps and other geographical information

attribution—the act of crediting a work (such as a piece of literature or art) to a particular author or artist

audience analysis—the process by which a speaker considers the needs and expectations of the audience that will be listening to a speech

auditory—relating to or experienced through hearing

aural—relating to the sense of hearing

avarice—excessive desire for wealth or gain; greediness

avoidance—a negotiation strategy in which an individual tries to resolve a conflict by withdrawing or by denying that a problem exists (lose-lose approach)

B

barter—to trade by exchange of goods

begging the question—an argument that assumes the truth of whatever the argument is trying to prove

bias—an insufficiently grounded judgment in favor of or against someone or something

body—in a speech, the part containing the content and analysis that prove the thesis statements

body language—the way one uses his or her body to send messages

bombard—to assail (attack violently with blows or words) persistently

braille—a system of writing for the blind that uses characters made up of raised dots

brainstorming—a process in which group members offer their ideas—as many as possible, as quickly as possible—to encourage creative thought and solutions

brash—lacking restraint and discernment; tactless

bridge—a transition from one answer to another

brief—an outline that summarizes specific case arguments

briefing—a speech informing members of a group of changes in policy or procedure

burden of proof—a term used in formal debate and in law to refer to the responsibility to prove something

burgeoning—growing and expanding rapidly

bylaws—a set of special rules agreed upon by the members of a group

C

cadence—the measure or beat of a rhythmic flow of sounds in language

call for the question—in parliamentary procedure, a proposal to take an immediate vote on a motion

canned—prepared in advance in standardized form for nonspecific use or wide distribution; lacking originality or individuality

captive audience—an audience that has been forced to attend

case—a debater's ideas and evidence organized into a position supporting one side of a resolution

case study—the analysis of a "typical" example in great detail, in order to draw general conclusions

catalog—a complete list of materials in a library collection, briefly describing each and indicating where it can be found

causality—a claim that one event is the result of another event

cause-effect pattern—a pattern of organization that arranges elements of an argument in a "this caused this" sequence

chair—the presiding officer of a meeting or an organization

chalk talk—a speech in which the speaker uses a visual aid, such as a chalkboard or whiteboard—to convey information

chauffeur—a person employed to drive an automobile

chronological pattern—a pattern of organization that arranges elements in time sequence, or in the order in which they happened

circumstantial evidence—the evidence at hand—evidence that may suggest a conclusion but does not prove it

climactic pattern—a pattern of organization that arranges elements in order of importance

clique—a narrow, exclusive group of persons—especially one held together by common interests, views, or purposes

cognizant—having knowledge of something through personal experience; mindful, aware

cohesion—a quality of group discussion in which members have respect for each other, share similar values, and rely on one another for support

collaboration—a negotiation strategy that focuses on resolving a conflict by recognizing and valuing the experience, expertise, and perceptions of both parties (win-win approach)

combustion—an act or instance of burning; a slow oxidation; a violent agitation

commemorative speech—an inspiring speech recalling heroic events or persons

commencement address—a speech given during a graduation ceremony

common ground—a shared goal or interest

communication—the process of sending and receiving messages

communication barrier—any obstacle (whether attitudinal, social, educational, cultural, or environmental) that gets in the way of effective communication

comparative—considered as if in comparison with something else

compelling—forceful; demanding attention

compelling insight—an understanding, or seeing into, a situation in a way that is forceful or demands attention

compendium—a brief summary of a larger work or a field of knowledge

competency—an ability to get something done

competition—a negotiation strategy that focuses on defeating or outshining another person rather than resolving a problem (win-lose approach)

competitive—(1) marked by rivalry; (2) the burden of a negative counterplan to show that neither the affirmative proposal nor the negative proposal should be adopted

composure—a calm, controlled manner

compression—the act of reducing size or volume by squeezing or pressing together (usually to achieve simplicity)

compromise—a negotiation strategy in which each individual gives up something to meet in the middle (win-lose win-lose approach)

concise—expressing much in few words

concrete—naming a real thing or class of things; not abstract or theoretical

concrete word—a word that names a thing that can be perceived through the senses

confidence—awareness of, faith in, or reliance on one's ability to do the right thing in a specific situation

conflict management—the ability to turn a potentially negative situation into a positive one

connotation—the range of meanings and feelings associated with a word by an individual, based on personal experience

conscience—the sense of the moral goodness or blame-worthiness of one's own conduct, intentions, or character—together with a feeling of obligation to do right or be good

consensus—a nearly unanimous agreement among group members about a particular solution

consonance—the repetition of the same or similar consonant sounds preceded by different vowel sounds in words that are close together

constructive—in debate, a speech in which arguments are initially advanced and defended (from construct—"to build something")

constructive conflict—a situation in which group members use their differences to discover the best ideas

content—the information or topics presented in a work; a work's meaning or significance; what, as opposed to how, something is expressed

conversational quality—a distinguishing feature of spontaneous-sounding speech

converse—something reversed in order, relation, or action

covert—not openly shown or engaged in; covered over

conviction—a strong belief in one's message and a determination to convey that message to one's audience

cooperative—marked by a willingness of group members to work together toward a common end or goal

correlated—involving two or more events that are related in some way

courtesy—politeness, manners, and respectful consideration for others

credentials—qualifications

credibility—a person's ability to inspire belief

criteria—a set of standards that a solution must meet

critical listening—a listening style used to analyze and assess a message for logic and value

criticism—an evaluation or judgment (often negative)

crooned—sang in a soft, gentle, and intimate manner

cross-examination—a period following each speaker's constructive during which the speaker who has just spoken is questioned

crystallize—to cause to take a definite form

culmination—climax or fulfillment

cultural literacy—the information that an average citizen can be expected to know

cutaway—a model that shows the inner workings of an object

D

database—a collection of related information

debate—a method to solve problems; a formal contest of skill in reasoned argument

dedication—a desire to practice and be committed to one's speech

deduction—a form of reasoning in which one argues from generalizations to a specific instance

deficit—a deficiency, especially in revenue relative to expenditures

definition—an explanation of a term—reflecting, in a speech, the speaker's intended meaning or specialized use

degraded—reduced from a higher to a lower rank or degree

delivery—the mode or manner that a speaker uses to transmit words to an audience

demeaning—degrading, debasing; lowering in status, esteem, quality, or character

demographics—the statistical characteristics of human populations

denotation—the basic and generally understood meaning of a word found in the dictionary

diagram—a visual aid used by a speaker to explain a process

dialogue—conversation between actors, persons, or groups

dignitary—a person of high position or honor

dire—warning of disaster; desperately urgent

disclaimer—a speaker's attempt to explain what is not to be inferred from the speech; an acknowledgment of incomplete knowledge of a subject

disconcerting—confusing, upsetting

discriminative listening—a listening style used to single out a particular sound from a noisy environment

discussion—a cooperative exchange of information, opinions, and ideas

disintegration—the act of breaking apart or decomposing; loss of unity

disruptive conflict—a conflict that divides people into competing sides, which refuse to compromise, to the point that group discussion cannot achieve a decision

distal—apart from the point of attachment

distinction—the difference between words, objects, ideas, or the like—explained by saying what something is and, especially, what it is not

distortion—a twisting out of the true meaning; a false or unnatural appearance

diverse—varied, differing from one another, unlike

download—to transfer data from one computer's memory to the memory of another, usually smaller, computer

dramatic interpretation—a speech contest event in which a speaker memorizes and performs a relatively serious work of literature

dramatic monologue—a first-person narration in which a single character speaks

E

eloquent—having or showing clear and forceful expression; vividly or movingly expressive or revealing

emancipation—the act of freeing from restraint, control, or the power of another

embalm—to treat something (such as a corpse) to protect it from decay

emotional appeal—a persuasive technique that involves "striking an emotional chord"; the use of issues and values such as patriotism, family, and honor to win an audience's favor

empathic listening—a style of listening that encourages people to talk freely, without fear of embarrassment

empathy—a sincere understanding of the feelings, thoughts and motives of others

emulated—strived to equal or excel; imitated

enhanced—added or contributed to, improved

enthusiasm—the energy, both intellectual and physical, a speaker transmits to inspire an audience

entrepreneur—one who organizes, manages, and assumes the risks of a business or other enterprise

epitomize—to serve as a typical or ideal example of

equilibrium—a state of balance between opposing elements; a state of intellectual or emotional balance; poise

equitable—fairly distributed

erudite—marked by extensive learning or scholarship

ethical (personal) appeal—a persuasive quality based on a speaker's natural honesty, sincerity, and commitment to what is right and good

ethics—a person's sense of right and wrong

ethnicity—a quality related to one's racial, national, or cultural background

ethos—the Greek word for *character*—associated with Aristotle's personal (ethical) appeal

etiquette—the forms of conduct or procedure prescribed by custom or authority to be observed in social, official, or professional life; decorum

etymology—the history of words, as shown by tracing their development and relationships

eulogy—a speech praising or honoring someone who has died

euphemism—an expression substituted for another expression that may be offensive or distasteful

evasive—tending or intended to elude or avoid, usually by dexterity or stratagem

evidence—anything that establishes a fact or gives cause to believe something

evoking—calling forth or up; to bring to mind or recollection

exaggerate—to enlarge something (as in a statement) beyond normal bounds or the truth

excursion—digression (the act of turning aside from the main subject of attention); a pleasure trip

executive session—a kind of meeting or part of a meeting open only to group members

expedient—adapted for achieving a particular end; governed by self-interest

extemporaneous—not planned or rehearsed

extemporaneous method—a delivery method in which the speaker refers only to notes or a brief outline

eye contact—a device used by speakers that involves looking directly into listeners' eyes to emphasize a point or to show how strongly the speakers feel about something

F

facilitate—to make easier

factual proposition—a proposition that is either true or false

fallacy—an error in reasoning or a mistaken belief

false analogy—a comparison of two things that do not really have similarities

false comparison—a comparison of unlike things

false premise—an erroneous assertion; a premise that is faulty and will lead to an error in deduction

faltering—hesitating in speech, purpose, or action

fear—a biological process that activates our emergency energy system so that we can cope with danger; unpleasant, often strong, emotion caused by anticipation or awareness of danger

feedback—a reaction that a receiver gives to a message offered by a sender

fever chart—an infographic resembling the pattern that might result from recording the varying temperatures of someone with a fever by plotting points and connecting dots (especially useful for showing financial information or change over time)

fiasco—a complete failure

filter—to use emotional barriers (based on background and personality) to absorb information selectively

fireside chat—a speech in which a leader informally addresses the concerns, worries, and issues of a group

first affirmative constructive (1AC)—in Lincoln-Douglas debate, a speech prepared before the round in which the affirmative speaker presents the affirmative case

first affirmative rebuttal (1AR)—in Lincoln-Douglas debate, the speech made by the affirmative speaker that responds to the negative case and rebuilds the affirmative case; in policy debate, the speech that responds to the negative block and extends the argument the second affirmative rebuttal will need to win the debate

first negative constructive (1NC)—in Lincoln-Douglas debate, the speech in which the negative speaker presents the negative case and refutes the affirmative constructive; in policy debate, the negative position the first negative speaker presents

first person—referring to the person speaking (I, me, we, us)

flippant—lacking proper respect or seriousness

flowsheet—a record of the words or arguments written during a debate

follow-up question—a question that helps an interviewer pursue topics that come up unexpectedly during an interview

foreshadowing—giving a hint or suggestion of beforehand

forfeiting—losing, or losing the right to, by some error, offense, or crime

format—(1) a programming style or specialization (2) the general organization established for the conduct of a debate, specifying the amount of time and the order in which each debater is allowed to speak

forum—a post-panel discussion in which panel members invite questions and comments from the audience

friendliness—a warm, congenial attitude

G

germane—pertinent, applicable

gesture—body language involving hand or arm movement

gigantic—exceeding the usual or expected (as in size or force); enormous

gluttony—excess in eating or drinking

goodwill—a genuine interest or concern

graph—a visual aid used by a speaker to demonstrate a statistical relationship

groupthink—a tendency to go along with a group, even at the cost of abandoning one's personal beliefs

grovel—literally, to creep with the face to the ground to show subservience; to abase (humble or degrade) oneself

H

handout—printed material (such as fliers, brochures, or information sheets) prepared and duplicated before a speech and supplied to the audience for reference

haphazardly—in a manner marked by lack of any plan, order, or direction

harmoniously—in a manner marked by agreement or by accord in sentiment or action

hasty generalization—a faulty argument based on incomplete or unrepresentative information

haven—a place of safety, or a place offering favorable opportunities or conditions

hoke—(used with *up*) to make corny or phony

house—(1) in parliamentary procedure, a group during its meetings (2) the area in which an audience sits

humorous interpretation—a speech contest event in which a speaker memorizes and performs a funny work of literature

hyperbole—a method of saying more than what is true, or exaggerating, for the sake of emphasis

I

ignoring the question—a speaker's attempt to divert the attention of the audience from the matter at hand

illustration—an example that clarifies a point or adds a human note

imagery—language that communicates sense experience (creating mental pictures, for example) or that calls to mind emotions or ideas that tend to go with certain sensations

I-message—a statement that emphasizes what one wants

impression—how an audience perceives a speaker, based on the way the speaker presents himself or herself and his or her ideas

impromptu—made or done as if on the spur of the moment; having little or no preparation

impromptu method—a delivery method that is completely unrehearsed, using no notes and relying on the speaker's ability to offer an immediate verbal response

incidental motion—in parliamentary procedure, any proposal to change how a meeting is being run

incorrigible—incapable of being corrected, amended, or reformed

indented—set in from a margin (as are subordinate or supporting ideas in an outline)

index—in a book, an alphabetical list found in the back, indicating the exact page or pages on which a reader can find particular information

indifferent audience—an audience that is apathetic or uninterested in the speaker and his or her topic, often because the audience does not find the topic relevant to their personal situation

induction—a form of reasoning in which specific cases are used to prove a general truth

inflection—the altering of a speaker's tone or pitch to create emphasis

infographic—an illustration created by using graphic arts software, such as Adobe Illustrator or Freehand

informal debate—any debate conducted without specific rules

inhibition—an inner check on free activity, expression, or functioning

innovation—a new idea, method, or device

innuendo—hint, insinuation—especially a veiled reflection on character or reputation

innumerable—too many to be numbered

insinuated—introduced gradually or in a subtle, indirect, or artful way; implied in a subtle or devious way

instinctively—in a manner marked by spontaneity, independence from judgment or will, or by a natural, inherent attitude, impulse, or capacity

integrate—to form, coordinate, or blend into a functioning whole

integrity—a strong sense of right and wrong; adherence to a code of values

intensification—the act of making more acute or sharp; enhancement

interior monologue—a first-person narration in which the narrator is speaking to himself or herself

interlibrary loan—a cooperative system by which libraries lend specific materials to one another; something lent, or a grant of temporary use, through such a system

internship—a position as an unpaid volunteer working to gain experience

interpersonal communication—transmittal of messages between two or more people

interviewer—the person who asks the questions in an interview

intimacy—close association, contact, or familiarity

intimate distance—the distance used primarily for confidential exchanges (within eighteen inches), almost always reserved for close friends

intimidation—the act of making timid or fearful, to frighten; compulsion or deterrence by or as if by threats

intrapersonal communication—dialogue conducted with oneself to assess one's thoughts, feelings, and reactions

introduction—the beginning of a speech, containing the attention-getter, the link statement, the thesis statement, and frequently a preview statement

introspective—marked by reflectively looking inward, examining one's own thoughts or feelings

intuition—quick and ready insight; the power or faculty of knowing things without reasoning

irony—a figure of speech using words that imply the opposite of what they seem to say on the surface

irrational—not governed by reason; lacking normal mental understanding or coherence

J

jargon—the specialized vocabulary of people in the same profession or other group

jeopardy—exposure to loss; peril, hazard, risk

jump on the bandwagon—persuasive technique based on the need to conform

justification—the act of proving to be just, right, or reasonable; such proof

L

label—a descriptive or identifying word or phrase

leader—a person who guides, directs, or has charge of others

leadership—the ability to motivate and unite others to work together to accomplish a specific task; the position of leader; the act of leading

leading question—a question that puts words in a subject's mouth

learning styles—the different ways in which people learn most effectively

Lincoln-Douglas debate—a competitive type of formal debate, addressing propositions of value, practiced at high schools across the nation

link—(1) in debate, an explanation by the negative team demonstrating that the affirmative plan has a direct link to its disadvantage (2) in a speech, the statement in the introduction that comes between the attention-getter and the thesis statement and logically connects the two

listening spare time—thinking time created by the ability to listen faster than people can speak

logic—the science of reasoning which uses a system of rules to help one think correctly

logical appeal—the use of sequence, analysis, organization, and evidence to prove a point and persuade

logos—a Greek word for *logic* and *reason*—associated with Aristotle's logical appeal

M

main heading—in a speech, one of the major divisions, areas, or arguments of the purpose statement

main motion—in parliamentary procedure, a proposal that asks the group to take action

manipulate—to influence, especially with intent to deceive; to manage or use skillfully

manipulating—influencing, especially with intent to deceive

mannequin—a lifeless form representing the human figure

manuscript method—a delivery method in which the speaker writes and subsequently reads the speech, word-for-word

map—a visual aid used to demonstrate a geographical relationship

mediation—an intervention between conflicting parties to promote reconciliation, settlement, or compromise

mediator—a neutral person to whom discussion participants can turn when disagreements threaten to get out of control

memorized method—a delivery method in which the speaker memorizes and then gives the speech word-for-word without using notes

mesmerized—hypnotized, spellbound, or fascinated

message—that which is sent or said

metaphor—a figure of speech that compares two unlike things by saying that one thing is the other thing (without using an expression such as *like* or *as*)

meter—a measure of the rhythm in a line of poetry

methodically—in an orderly manner

microcosm—a little world, community, or unit that is a typical or an ideal example of a larger one

miffed—in a state of ill humor (as from a trivial quarrel)

mimic—to imitate closely

minstrel—a wandering performer, known as a rhapsode in ancient Greece, who read his or her works aloud (often accompanied by music) in public competitions

minutes—the written record of an organization's meetings

mock trial—a kind of discussion that imitates a court trial

model—a miniature representation of something

moderator—the person in a group who leads discussion—getting it started, keeping it on track, and bringing it to a close

monopolize—assume complete possession or control of

monotone—a tone in which words are delivered at the same rate and pitch, without variation

mood—the overall feeling or atmosphere created or expressed in a work

motif—a dominant idea or central theme

motivation—an inner drive, need, or impulse that causes a person to act

multimedia presentation—a speech supplemented by special software, which allows the speaker to combine several kinds of visual and audio aids

N

name calling—to give someone a negative label without any evidence

narrative—a story or the telling of one

narrowing—limiting and more closely defining a topic

nectar—the drink of the Greek and Roman gods; any delicious drink; a sweet plant secretion that is the raw material for honey

negative—an expression meaning "no" or "false"; in debate, the side that contradicts the proposition

negative rebuttal (NR)—in Lincoln-Douglas debate, the final speech made by the negative speaker, summarizing the debate and attempting to shut down the anticipated arguments in the affirmative speaker's rebuttal

negotiation—the act of conferring with another person or other people to settle a matter

new business—subjects brought up for the first time in a meeting

newness—an original or unique approach to a topic

nonassertive tone—a communication approach that lacks vitality, seeming uninterested and uninvolved

nonverbal communication—facial expressions or body movements used to express attitudes or moods about a person, situation, or idea

nonverbal message—something communicated without words, as through facial expressions and body language

notes—a listing of ideas in brief, outlined form

nuclear family—a family group that consists only of mother, father, and children

GLOSSARY

O

offstage focus—a technique used in Readers Theater in which readers use scripts and envision the scene out in the audience

old business—business not completed in a previous meeting

omniscient—relating to a third-person point of view in which the narrator of a story is all-knowing and moves freely in and out of the minds of the various characters

online—connected to, served by, or accessible through a system—especially a computer system; done by connecting to such a system

open-ended question—a question that allows a subject to decide how best to answer. It encourages a comprehensive, in-depth response and discourages a yes-no or true-false response.

opposed audience—an audience that is hostile to a speaker or to the speaker's topic or position

oral cavity—the mouth

oral interpretation—the art of communicating works of literature by reading aloud

oral (or verbal) communication—communication that is primarily spoken

orator—a person who delivers a public speech—especially a person known for doing this skillfully

oratory/rhetoric—the art or study of public speaking

order of precedence—in parliamentary procedure, the relationship of motions to each other

orders of the day—an agenda or list of topics to be discussed during a meeting

organization—in a speech, a structure or form that enables an audience to follow along easily

original oratory—a speech contest event in which contestants write and speak on a topic of their choice

ought—a person's concept of the ideal; a moral obligation based on a sense of duty

outline—in a speech, a logically organized framework that shows how the speech will progress

overhead projector—a visual aid used to project transparencies (often charts and graphs) onto a blank wall or screen

oxymoron—a literary device that places words that are in opposition directly beside one another, as in *cruel kindness*

P

pace—the rate, or speed, at which a person speaks

painstakingly—in a manner that shows diligent care or effort

palatable—agreeable or acceptable to the mind or taste

panacea—a remedy for all difficulties or ills

panel—an informal discussion that takes place before an audience

parallelism—the use of the same grammatical form to express ideas that should logically be treated equally (often involving the repetition of words or phrases)

paraphernalia—articles of equipment, accessory items, personal belongings

paraphrase—to repeat in one's own words

paraphrasing—rewording an original passage

parliament—an assembly that constitutes the supreme legislative body of a (usually) major political unit, such as the United Kingdom

parliamentary procedure—a system of rules followed in formal meetings, based on ideas developed in the British parliament

passive listening—a listening role in which the listener does not share in the responsibility for, or involve himself or herself in, the communication process

pathos—the Greek word for *feelings* and *emotions*—associated with Aristotle's emotional appeal

pause—a lull in conversation, often providing a good opportunity for an interviewer to convey more information

people skills—the ability to work well with others by using polite communication procedures

perception—how one sees things

performance anxiety—a specific stage fright, often associated with musicians, actors, and other entertainers

periodical—a publication such as a newspaper, magazine, or journal that is published at regular intervals

periodical index—a listing of articles published in periodicals

peripheral—outside one's direct field of vision and hearing; relating to outer bounds or a border area

persona—the fictional speaker of a work to be interpreted

personal distance—the distance comfortable for conversation between friends (a foot and a half to four feet)

personal space—a comfort zone each person maintains around himself or herself, where intrusions would usually be unwelcome

personification—giving human characteristics to non-human things

persuasive speaking—speaking that influences others to believe or think something, or to take action

pervasiveness—the state of being diffused (spread out) through every part of something

phobia—a persistent, irrational fear that causes a person to avoid specific situations

phonation—voice production

picturesque—resembling a picture; bringing about mental images

pie chart—an infographic in the form of a circle with individual wedges, each representing a different component (especially useful for showing relative proportions of a whole)

pitch—the vocal notes (highs and lows) that a speaker reaches while speaking

plagiarism—copying or imitating another person's language or ideas and passing them off as one's own original work

platform movement—walking or stepping in a directed manner from one spot to another while speaking

polarizing—dividing group members into competing sides that refuse to compromise

policy proposition—a proposition that focuses on the desirability of a particular course of action

pollster—one who questions people to obtain information or opinions to be analyzed

portfolio—a selection of work, such as a job candidate's best school assignments, used to show and help assess one's performance

posture—the position of the body when it is still

power source—the origin of the energy needed to make things go

preamble—an introductory statement—especially the introductory part of a constitution or statute that usually states its reasons and intent

premise—an assertion that serves as a basis for argument

prep time—in debate, the preparation time allotted during rounds for organizing responses and preparing questions

prerequisite—something that is necessary to an end or to carrying out a function

prescriptive—relating to what is laid down as a guide or rule of action (In a speech, a prescriptive topic requires the speaker to prescribe—lay down as a guide or rule—specific policy suggestions.)

preview statement—in a speech, the statement at the end of the introduction that presents an overview of the major areas that will be discussed in the body

prioritizing—arranging in order of importance

privileged motion—in parliamentary procedure, a proposal to resolve an urgent problem other than the main motion

problem-solution pattern—a pattern of organization that presents a problem and then provides possible solutions

procession—a group of individuals moving along in an orderly, often ceremonial way

professional communication—communication that takes place on the job or is related to a career

pronunciation—use—especially the correct use—of the organs of speech to say something

proof—specific evidence that establishes the truth of something

propaganda—ideas, facts, or allegations spread to further or oppose a cause—often distorting the truth or deceiving an audience in the process

proposition—a statement of the point to be debated

prospective—relating to or effective in the future; likely to come about

proxemics—the study of spatial communication; in oral communication, the physical distance between the speaker and the audience

proximal—next to or nearest the point of attachment

proxy—one who acts as a substitute for another

public distance—the distance maintained between strangers (normally twelve feet or more)—a distance at which people need barely acknowledge each other's presence

public lecture—a lecture delivered to a community or school group

puff ball—an easy, open-ended question

purpose statement—in a speech, a statement that presents the selected topic and the speaker's specific purpose in speaking

Q

qualm—a sudden feeling of doubt, fear, or uneasiness

questions of evaluation—questions that ask group members to agree or disagree on possible solutions and to make value judgments

questions of fact—questions that ask group members to recall information that pertains to the questions at hand

questions of interpretation—questions that ask group members to give their opinions on what the information means

quorum—in parliamentary procedure, the minimum number of members that must be present in order for a group's decisions to take effect

quotation—the repetition of someone else's exact words

R

railroad—to put through something (such as a law) hastily

rapport—a shared feeling of trust and cooperation

rate—the speed at which a person speaks

reasoning—the process of thinking, understanding, and drawing conclusions about some evidence

rebuffed—rejected or criticized sharply

rebuttal—the act of countering an opponent's attacks to one's argument and thereby rebuilding the argument

receiver—a person who intercepts a message and then decodes it

reciprocal—mutually corresponding or communicating

recitation—delivery before an audience, usually of something memorized

reconsider—in parliamentary procedure, a motion to reexamine a main motion that has already been passed or defeated

refrain—a regularly recurring phrase or verse

refute—to prove, using evidence, that something is wrong or false

regurgitating—throwing out, back, or up

reiterate—to state or do over again or repeatedly

renowned—widely acclaimed and honored; celebrated, famous

repetition—the act or process of repeating

reprimanded—reproved (scolded or corrected) sharply, usually from a position of authority

reputation—the overall quality or character of someone or something as perceived by people in general; the general recognition of a particular characteristic or ability

resolution—(1) a formal statement of opinion (2) in parliamentary procedure, a special type of main motion that begins with an explanation of why the motion should be passed

responsible—answerable or accountable for one's actions

restate—to say again or in another way

retention—the mind's ability to hold onto experience, or remember—making recall and recognition possible

rhapsode—a wandering minstrel in ancient Greece that would read his or her works aloud in public competition

rhetorical—(1) relating to the art of speaking or writing effectively (2) asked merely for effect, and thus not requiring an answer (3) relating to tricks of language, such as testimonials, false comparisons, and "jump on the bandwagon" suggestions

rhetorical question—a question asked merely for effect, and thus not requiring an answer

rhyme—most commonly, the repetition in different words of the last stressed vowel and of any sounds following that vowel, usually at the end of lines of verse

rhythm—the natural flow of stressed and unstressed syllables in language—most strongly marked and patterned in verse

rife—widespread, prevalent, abounding

rigorous—harsh, severe, or strict; scrupulously accurate or precise

roundtable—a special panel discussion in which a small group of participants talk about a topic of common concern while sitting around a table, or in an open circle

S

sanctity—the quality or state of being holy or sacred; holiness of life and character

scanner—a device that methodically examines an image or a document to obtain data, especially for display or storage by a computer

scenario—a sequence of events, especially when imagined; an account or a synopsis of a possible course of action or a series of events

scene setting—a technique oral interpreters use to focus a scene they are describing, on an imaginary stage in front of them

search engine—a Web site with software that allows users to search for specified information on the World Wide Web

second affirmative rebuttal (2AR)—in policy debate, a speech that summarizes the affirmative position and clearly explains why the major issues in the debate have gone affirmative

second person—referring to the person spoken to (you)

segregation—a cutting off from others—especially a separation by race, social class, or ethnic group

self-esteem—respect for oneself, often realized through self-discovery

sender—a person who transmits a message

senile—relating to old age—especially to a loss of mental abilities that is associated with old age

sequential—following in sequence, making a continuous or connected series; following in a chronological order

serendipity—making a pleasant discovery by accident

sign—a type of inductive reasoning in which one draws conclusions about a situation based on physical evidence

signposting—a preview of arguments to be made later in a speech

simile—a figure of speech that compares two unlike things by using an expression such as *like* or *as*

simulated—given a close imitation of the effect or appearance of; faked

sincerity—the quality of being honest or genuine

slang—nonstandard words associated with certain groups

sloth—laziness

social communication—the communication that occurs in one's personal and community life

social distance—the distance generally maintained between people in most social and business exchanges (four to twelve feet)

sound bite—a brief statement that sticks in the mind, as often heard on television and radio broadcasts

sounding board—a person or group on whom one tries out an idea or opinion as a means of evaluating it

sparkler—information (especially in the form of an analogy, story, anecdote, or quotation) given during a response that makes the point come alive

spatial pattern—a pattern of organization that arranges the elements on the basis of spatial or situational relationships

speech of acceptance—a brief speech given by a person receiving a gift or an award

speech of presentation—a brief speech presenting a person with an award or a gift

spellbound—held by or as if by a spell; fascinated

spontaneity—the quality or state of being spontaneous; doing or producing freely and naturally; impulsive, instinctive

stack the deck—to present unbalanced evidence that only presents one side

stage fright—the nervousness felt by a speaker or performer in front of an audience

status quo—the existing conditions or the way things are

status report—a report summarizing a group's achievements and goals

stereotyping—making a distorted mental image of someone or something on the basis of an oversimplified opinion, a prejudiced attitude, or an unexamined judgment held in common by members of a group

stoic—not affected by passion or feeling—especially, showing indifference to pain or distress

stress—to emphasize the most important word or words in a sentence

subject—the person who answers the questions in an interview

subordination—ranking in terms of importance

subsidiary motion—in parliamentary procedure, a proposal to adjust or fine-tune a main motion

suffice—to meet or satisfy a need

summarize—to cover the main points in a compact manner, without wasted words

superficial—of or relating to the surface or appearance only; shallow

supporting materials—information that supports and reinforces the main headings of a speech (not to be confused with details, which are more specific)

supportive audience—an audience that likes a speaker and what the speaker has to say—and thus may be willing to support and promote the speaker's ideas

GLOSSARY

suppress—to restrain from the usual course of action; to keep from expressing

surrogacy—the act of taking the place of another; the substitution of one for another

suspend—to stop temporarily; to make inactive for a time

syllable—a unit of spoken language consisting of an uninterrupted utterance; a commonly recognized division of a word

syllogism—a form of deductive reasoning made up of two premises and a conclusion

symbol—(1) anything that stands for an idea and is used for communication (2) an image of a person, place, thing, or action that calls to mind some other, usually broader, idea or range of ideas

sympathetic—showing a capacity to enter into and share feelings or interests of another; expressing sorrow for another's loss or misfortune

symposium—a formal discussion in which several experts present, in the form of short speeches, a variety of points of view (after which an open discussion between experts and audience may follow)

synonymous—alike or nearly alike in meaning or significance

systematic—having a regular method or order

T

table a motion—in parliamentary procedure, to set aside a motion for the time being

table of contents—the outline of a book's general plan or organization—normally found at the beginning of the book and listing the main sections and chapters

tact—diplomacy in dealing with others

talk show—a discussion format in which a host or hosts lead a discussion on a particular topic, interview guests who have knowledge on the topic, and may allow the audience to ask questions

tangible—that which one is aware of through the senses, especially touch

tedium—boredom

temperament—characteristic or habitual inclination or mode of emotional response

testimonial—a celebrity or expert endorsement of a message

testimonial speech—a speech of praise or celebration honoring a living person

theme—the central idea of a work

thesis—a statement defining or expressing the purpose of a speech

thesis statement—the statement that presents the overall purpose of a speech

third person—referring to a person or thing spoken of (he, him, her, she, it, they, them)

timbre—distinctive tone

tone—a combination of the pitch and timbre of a speaker's voice, pauses, rhythm, and unique pronunciation—often a reliable clue to the speaker's feelings

tone of voice—the pitch and timbre (distinctive tone) of a person's voice

topic-specific—characteristic of a speech whose introduction is directly connected to the rest of the speech

town hall meeting—traditionally, a discussion in which a group of citizens meets in a public place to discuss community problems and vote on possible solutions

transformation—the process, the act, or an instance of changing in composition, structure, outward form, or appearance

transition—a word or phrase in a speech that connects one part of the speech to the next

trivia—unimportant matters

U

ubiquitous—existing everywhere at the same time; widespread

unbiased—free from all personal, unreasoned judgment and favoritism; fair

uncommitted audience—an audience that is neutral or has not made up its mind about a speaker's topic

understatement—the use of "reverse exaggeration" for emphasis, especially to draw attention to an absurdity

unobtrusive—not bold or aggressive; inconspicuous

V

value—a standard used to judge whether something is right or wrong, good or bad

value criteria—in debate, concepts that provide further standards of judgment for determining whether the value premise has been realized

value premise—in debate, a supposition that provides a standard of judgment for determining whether a resolution is true

value proposition—a type of proposition, involving philosophical judgments, for which there is no right or wrong answer

verbatim—word-for-word

vested—fully and unconditionally guaranteed as a right, benefit, or privilege. (as in a vested interest, to which the holder has a strong commitment)

vicariously—in a manner that shares someone else's experience by using imagination or sympathetic feelings

vision—the ability to see more than the obvious—to look beyond and ahead for answers and possibilities

vocal process—the system that produces sound

vocalized pause—a meaningless utterance—such as *you know, uh,* or *and a*—used to fill moments when a speaker is not sure what to say next

volume—the loudness or softness of a speaker's voice

vouchers—a form or check indicating a credit against future purchases or expenditures (as in school vouchers)

vulnerable—susceptible; having little resistance to; open to attack or damage

W

written communication—any communication that must be read

Y

yes-no question—a question that may be answered with a simple yes or no—thus allowing a subject to answer without elaborating

Z

zinger—in a speech, a concluding statement that is a powerful reminder of the rightness of the speaker's position

GLOSARIO

A

abstract word—abstracto palabra una palabra que describe un intangible, tal como una cualidad, atributo y concepto.

accommodation—acomodo estrategia de negociación en la que las diferencias se minimizan, se atenúan o se suprimen (enfoque pierde-gana).

acronym—sigla palabra formada por la letra inicial de cada una de las partes principales de un término compuesto.

active listening—escuchar activamente una forma de escuchar en la cual el que escucha participa y comparte en el proceso de comunicación al dirigir a la persona que habla hacia intereses comunes.

adjourn—clausurar levantar la sesión.

advance organizer—resumen inicial discurso de introducción que da una idea de lo que puede esperar la audiencia.

affirmative—afirmativo expresión que significa "sí" o "verdadero"; en un debate, la persona que defiende la proposición.

affluent—acaudalado que tiene mucho más que suficiente y típicamente, disponibilidad creciente de posesiones materiales.

after-dinner speech—discurso de sobremesa un discurso entretenido que sigue a un banquete o comida.

agenda—agenda órdenes del día, lista de cosas a realizarse.

aggressive tone—tono agresivo forma prepotente o insolente de comunicarse, que considera un solo punto de vista, y no deja nada o casi nada de espacio para discutir o llegar a un arreglo.

almanac—almanaque publicación anual que recoge datos y hechos principales

alienate—enajenar tornarse hostil, poco amistoso.

allegory—alegoría uso de figuras de ficción o acciones simbólicas (como en un cuento o cuadro) para expresar generalizaciones sobre la existencia humana.

alliteration—aliteración la repetición de sonidos, normalmente consonantes, al comienzo de dos palabras que están cerca una de la otra.

allusion—alusión una referencia indirecta a una persona, lugar, objeto o idea bien conocida.

almanac—almanaque publicación anual que recoge datos y hechos principales.

ambiguous—ambiguo capaz de ser entendido en más de una forma.

amend—enmendar en procedimientos de parlamentarios, modificar una moción por añadir y/o quitar palabras.

analogy—analogía una ilustración en la cual las características de un objeto o una idea familiar se utilizan para explicar o describir las características de un objeto o una idea desconocido.

analysis—análisis separación de un todo en las partes o elementos que lo componen; examen de un todo para determinar sus partes o elementos—también el informe que muestra los resultados de tal examen.

analytical—analítico marcado por la habilidad de separar un todo en las partes o elementos que lo componen, o por la habilidad de examinar un todo para determinar sus partes o elementos.

anecdote—anécdota relato breve que se usa como ilustración

anthology—antología una colección de pasajes o obras de la literatura.

anthropologist—antropólogo persona que estudia a los seres humanos, incluyendo sus características físicas y sus relaciones ambientales, sociales y culturales.

antithesis—antítesis un contraste de ideas mediante el uso paralelo de palabras, frases, etc.; lo opuesto.

apathetic—apático que no tiene ningún interés o preocupación (indiferente), que tiene o demuestra muy escaso o ningún sentimiento o emoción.

apoplectic—apoplético afectado por, con tendencia a, o que muestra síntomas de una apoplejía.

appreciative listening—escuchar apreciativamente un estilo de escuchar que se utiliza para gozar y saborear sonidos placenteros tales como la música o la naturaleza.

appropriateness—apropiado ser especialmente apto o compatible.

argument—argumento una razón para favorecer una parte de una propuesta y los hechos que respaldan dicha razón.

articulation—articulación la claridad y precisión de una oración.

assert—aseverar afirmar o declarar positivamente y a menudo en forma enérgica y agresiva.

assertion—aseveración enunciación positiva.

assertive tone—tono asertivo comunicar los planteamientos en forma directa, pero con tacto.

assonance—asonancia la repetición de sonidos de vocales que son iguales o parecidos.

atlas—atlas publicación que incluye mapas y otra información geográfica.

attribution—atribución acto de reconocer una obra (como ser, de arte o literaria) a un artista o autor determinado.

audience analysis—análisis de la audiencia el proceso mediante el cual un orador considera las necesidades y expectativas de la audiencia que estará escuchando el discurso.

auditory—auditivo relacionado o experimentado a través del oído.

aural—auditivo relacionado con el sentido del oído.

avarice—avaricia deseo excesivo por la riqueza, o las ganancias; codicia.

avoidance—evasión estrategia de negociación en la cual un individuo trata de resolver un conflicto retirando o negando la existencia de un problema (enfoque pierde—pierde).

B

barter—trueque comerciar mediante el intercambio de bienes.

begging the question—dar por sentado lo que queda por probar un argumento que asume que lo que sea que está tratando de probar ya es cierto.

bias—sesgado prejuicio sin suficiente fundamento o a favor de o en contra de algo o alguien.

body—cuerpo en un discurso, la parte que proporciona el contenido y análisis que prueba las afirmaciones de tesis.

body language—lenguaje corporal la forma en que uno usa su cuerpo para enviar mensajes.

bombard—bombardeo asalto (ataque violento de palabras o golpes) persistente.

Braille—Braille sistema de escritura para los ciegos que utiliza caracteres formados por puntos sobresalientes.

brainstorming—lanzar ideas proceso en el cual un grupo de miembros expone sus ideas, lo más rápido y variado posible para estimular el pensamiento creativo y las soluciones.

brash—descarado que carece de restricción y discernimiento, sin tacto.

bridge—puente la transición de una respuesta a otra.

brief—escrito una reseña que resume los argumentos específicos del caso.

briefing—sesión informativa discurso que se comunica los cambios de política o de procedimientos a los miembros de un grupo.

burden of proof—peso de la prueba un término utilizado en un debate formal y en el derecho para referirse a la responsabilidad de probar algo.

burgeoning—floreciente que crece y se expande rápidamente.

bylaws—estatutos un conjunto de reglas especiales acordadas entre los miembros de un grupo.

C

cadence—cadencia medida o compás de un fluido rítmico de los sonidos de lenguaje.

call for the question—llamar a voto en los procedimientos parlamentarios, una propuesta para tomar un voto inmediato sobre una moción.

canned—envasado preparado de antemano en forma estandarizada para uso no específico o amplia distribución, carente de originalidad o individualidad.

captive audience—público cautivo un público que ha sido forzado a asistir.

case—caso las ideas y evidencias de la persona que participa en el debate, organizadas en una postura que apoya un lado de una resolución.

case study—estudio de casos el análisis en gran detalle de un ejemplo "típico," con el propósito de obtener conclusiones generales.

catalog—catálogo lista completa de materiales en las colecciones de una biblioteca, que brevemente describe cada uno y cómo localizarlo.

causality—causalidad la declaración de que un evento es el resultado de otro evento.

cause-event pattern—patrón causa efecto un patrón de organización que ordena los elementos de un argumento en una secuencia de "debido a que esto sucedió, esto resultó."

GLOSARIO

circumstantial evidence—evidencia circunstancial la evidencia a la mano. Podría sugerir una conclusión, pero no la comprueba.

climactic pattern—patrón culminante un patrón de organización que ordena los elementos en orden de importancia.

clique—camarilla exclusivo grupo de personas, especialmente aquéllas que se mantienen unidas por intereses, puntos de vista o propósitos comunes.

cognizant—conocedor que tiene conocimiento de algo por experiencia personal, atento, informado.

cohesion—cohesión cualidad de una discusión de grupo en la cual sus miembros se respetan mutuamente, comparten valores similares y cuentan con apoyo mutuo.

collaboration—colaboración estrategia de negociación que se centra en resolver el conflicto; la experiencia, pericia, y percepciones de ambas partes son reconocidas y valoradas (enfoque gana—gana).

combustion—combustión acto o instancia de quemarse, oxidación lenta, agitación violenta.

commemorative speech—discurso conmemorativo un discurso emotivo que recuerda eventos o personas históricas.

commencement address—discurso de graduación un discurso que se da durante una ceremonia de graduación.

common ground—interés mutuo una meta o un interés compartido.

communication—comunicación el proceso de enviar y recibir mensajes.

communication barrier—barrera a la comunicación cualquier obstáculo (ya sea de actitud, social, educacional, cultural o del medio ambiente) que se entromete en una comunicación efectiva.

comparative—comparativo considerado como si estuviera comparado a otra cosa.

compelling—apremiante fuerte, que demanda atención.

compelling insight—percepción apremiante comprensión o percepción de una situación de una manera muy fuerte que demanda atención.

compendium—compendio breve resumen de una obra más extensa o de un campo del conocimiento.

competency—habilidad la habilidad de lograr algo.

competition—competencia estrategia de negociación que se centra en derrotar u opacar a la otra persona más bien que en resolver el problema (enfoque gana—pierde).

competitive—competitivo (1) caracterizado de rivalidad (2) también, la carga de un plan alternativo negativo, para demostrar ni las proposiciones afirmativas o ni las negativas se deben adoptar.

composure—compostura un comportamiento calmo, controlado.

compression—compresión acto de reducir el tamaño o volumen comprimiendo o apretando (normalmente para lograr simplicidad).

compromise—transar una estrategia de negociación en la cual cada individuo sacrifica algo para llegar a un acuerdo (trade-offs— intercambios) (enfoque ganar—perder).

concise—conciso expresar mucho en pocas palabras.

concrete—concreto lo que nombra una cosa real, o categorías de cosas; no abstractas o teóricas.

concrete word—palabra concreta una palabra que nombra algo que se percibe a través de la frase.

confidence—confianza conocimiento de fe o confianza en uno mismo y en su habilidad de hacer lo correcto en una situación específica.

conflict management—manejo de conflictos la habilidad de convertir una situación potencialmente negativa en una positiva.

connotation—connotación los distintos significados y sentimientos asociados a una palabra por una persona, basado en experiencia personal.

conscience—conciencia sentido de corrección moral, o de merecimiento de culpa por la propia conducta, intenciones o carácter unida a un sentimiento de obligación de hacer lo correcto o de ser bueno.

consensus—consenso acuerdo casi unánime entre los miembros de un grupo sobre una solución en particular.

consonance—consonancia la repetición de sonidos consonantes, ya sean iguales o parecidos, precididos por sonidos de vocales distintos en palabras que están cerca una a la otra.

constructive—constructivo un discurso en el cual los argumentos se presentan y defienden desde el inicio (viene de construir—"edificar algo").

constructive conflict—conflicto constructivo situación en la que un grupo de miembros usa sus diferencias para descubrir las mejores ideas.

content—contenido información o tópicos presentados en una obra y la esencia, el significado e la importancia de ella; qué se expresa, a diferencia de cómo.

conversational quality—calidad coloquial una característica que destaca el discurso que aparenta ser espontáneo.

converse—inverso algo que tiene el orden, relación o acción invertida.

conviction—convicción un fuerte convencimiento respecto de nuestro mensaje y la determinación de comunicar dicho mensaje a la audiencia.

cooperative—cooperación caracterizado por una disposición de los miembros del grupos a trabajar unidos para lograr un fin o meta común.

correlated—directamente relacionada involucrar dos o más eventos relacionados de alguna forma.

courtesy—cortesía urbanidad, buenos modales y respetuosa consideración hacia los demás.

covert—solapado que no se muestra abiertamente, intereses ocultos, encubierto.

credentials—antecedentes calificaciones.

credibility—credibilidad la habilidad de una persona de inspirar que las personas lo crean.

criteria—criterio conjunto de normas que se deben tomar en cuenta para llegar a una solución.

critical listening—escuchar críticamente una forma de escuchar utilizada para evaluar y analizar un mensaje buscando su lógica y su valor.

criticism—crítica evaluación o juicio—generalmente negativo.

crooned—canturreo cantar en forma suave, dulce e íntima.

cross examination—contrainterrogatorio el período que sigue a la intervención de cada orador en el cual se interroga al orador.

crystallize—cristalizar hacer que tome una forma definitiva.

culmination—culminación clímax o realización.

cultural literacy—alfabetismo cultural la información que se puede esperar que conozca el ciudadano promedio.

cutaway—recortado un modelo que muestra la composición interior de un objeto.

CH

chair—presidente la persona a cargo de la reunión o una organización.

chalk talk—presentación ilustrada un discurso en el cual el orador utiliza ayuda visual—una pizarra o tablero en blanco—para transmitir información.

chauffeur—chofer persona empleada para conducir un automóvil.

chronological pattern—patrón cronológico un patrón de organización que ordena los elementos en una secuencia de tiempo o en el orden en que estos sucedieron.

D

database—base de datos una colección de información relacionada.

debate—debate un método para solucionar problemas; una competencia formal de habilidades en un argumento razonado.

dedication—dedicación el deseo de practicar y comprometerse con su propio discurso.

deduction—deducción una manera de razonar en la cual uno argumenta desde generalizaciones hasta una instancia específica.

deficit—déficit deficiencia en cantidad, especialmente por excesos de gastos en relación con los ingresos.

definition—definición la explicación de un término que refleja el significado deseado por el orador o el uso especializado en el contexto de un discurso.

degraded—degradar rebajar de un rango o grado más alto a uno más bajo.

delivery—presentación el modo o manera que un orador utiliza para transmitir palabras a una audiencia.

demeaning—rebajar degradar, desvalorizar; bajar la condición, aprecio, calidad o carácter.

demographics—demografía características estadísticas de las poblaciones humanas.

denotation—denotación el significado básico y generalmente conocido de una palabra contenida en un diccionario.

diagram—diagrama una ayuda visual utilizada por un orador para explicar un proceso.

dialogue—diálogo conversación entre actores, personas o grupos.

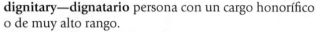

dignitary—dignatario persona con un cargo honorífico o de muy alto rango.

dire—de mal agüero advertencia de desastre, sumamente urgente.

disclaimer—aclaración el intento del orador de explicar lo que no se infiere por el discurso o el reconocimiento de una falta de conocimiento de la materia.

disconcerting—desconcertante desorientante; perturbador.

discriminative listening—escuchar en forma discriminada un estilo de escuchar utilizado para aislar un sonido en particular de un entorno ruidoso.

discussion—debate intercambio cooperativo de información, opiniones e ideas.

disintegration—desintegración acto de romper o descomponer, pérdida de la unidad.

disruptive conflict—conflicto disociador conflicto que divide a personas en dos bandos en pugna, los que se niegan a hacer concesiones hasta el punto en que no se puede alcanzar una decisión de grupo.

distal—distante del centro lejos del punto de unión.

distinction—distinción diferencia entre palabras, objetos, ideas, etc. que explica diciendo lo que es una cosa y, más especialmente, lo que no es.

distortion—distorsión deformación del verdadero significado, apariencia falsa o anormal.

diverse—diverso variado diferente de otra, distinto.

door opener—invitación una frase utilizada por la persona que escucha para invitar e instar a que la persona que habla continúe.

dossier—historial inventario personal de vida, incluyendo información laboral.

download—descargar transferir datos de la memora de una computadora a la memoria de otra computadora, normalmente más pequeña.

dramatic interpretation—interpretación dramática un evento competitivo de discursos en el cual el orador memoriza y representa una pieza de la literatura de una naturaleza relativamente seria.

dramatic monologue—monólogo dramático unrelato en la primera persona en la cual un solo personaje habla.

E

eloquent—elocuente que posee o muestra una expresión clara y vigorosa, expresándose o revelando los hechos en forma vívida y conmovedora.

emancipation—emancipación acto de liberarse de las restricciones, control o poder impuesto por un tercero.

embalm—embalsamar tratar algo (tal como un cadáver) para protegerlo de la descomposición.

emotional appeal—apelación emocional una técnica de persuasión que involucra "tocar un punto emocional"; el orador utiliza temas y valores tan variados como el patriotismo, la familia y el honor para ganarse el favor de la audiencia.

empathic listening—interlocutor enfático estilo de escuchar alentando a las personas a hablar libremente sin temor o vergüenza.

empathy—empatía una sincera comprensión de los sentimientos, ideas y motivaciones de los demás.

emulated—emulación esforzarse por igualar o superar, imitación.

enhanced—intensificar agregar o contribuir a, mejorar.

enthusiasm—entusiasmo la energía, tanto intelectual como física, que transmite el orador para inspirar a su audiencia.

entrepreneur—empresario alguien que organiza, administra y asume los riesgos de un negocio u otra empresa.

epitomize—epitomar servir como el ejemplo típico o ideal de algo.

equilibrium—equilibrio estado de balance entre elementos opuestos, estado de equilibrio intelectual o emocional: serenidad.

equitable—equitativo distribuido justamente.

erudite—erudito marcado por un amplio conocimiento o ilustración.

ethical (personal) appeal—apelación ética (personal) una cualidad persuasiva basada en la honestidad, sinceridad y compromiso natural del orador a lo que es correcto y bueno.

ethics—ética el sentido de lo correcto y de lo incorrecto en una persona.

ethnicity—étnicidad una cualidad relacionada con la nación, raza o etnia de una persona.

ethos—ethos palabra griega para el carácter; se asocia con el atractivo personal (ético) de Aristóteles.

etiquette—etiqueta formas (de conducta o proceder) determinadas por la costumbre o la autoridad que se deben observar en la vida social, oficial o profesional: decoro.

etymology—etimología historia de las palabras que se muestra siguiendo su desarrollo y relaciones.

eulogy—elogio un discurso alabando u honrando a alguien que a muerto.

euphemism—eufemismo una expresión que se sustituye por otra expresión que puede ser ofensiva o de mal gusto.

evasive—evasivo con tendencia o intención de eludir o evitar, usualmente por medio de habilidad o estratagema.

evidence—evidencia cualquier cosa que establece un hecho o da causa a creer en algo.

evoking—evocación recuerdo, llamado; traer a la mente, rememorar.

exaggerate—exageración agrandar algo (una aseveración) fuera de lo normal, que sobrepasa límites y vá más allá de la verdad.

excursion—desviación digresión (acto de alejarse del principal sujeto de atención), viaje de agrado.

executive session—reunión ejecutiva tipo de reunión o parte de reunión que está abierta solo a los miembros del grupo.

expedient—conveniente adaptado para lograr un fin en particular; gobernado por el propio interés.

extemporaneous—improvisado sin planificar ni ensayado.

extemporaneous method—método extemporáneo un método de presentación en la cual el orador se refiere solo a apuntes o a una breve reseña.

eye contact—contacto visual una característica utilizada por los oradores mediante la cual miran directamente a los ojos del que lo escucha a fin de enfatizar un punto o demostrar lo serio que ellos consideran este asunto.

F

facilitate—facilitar hacer más fácil.

factual proposition—proposición fáctica proposición que es o verdadera o falsa.

false analogy—falsa analogía una comparación de dos cosas que no son realmente parecidos.

false comparison—comparación errónea una comparación entre dos cosas diferentes.

false premise—premisa falsa una declaración errónea; una premisa que es fallida y que resultará en un error de deducción.

faltering—vacilar titubear en el discurso, propósito o acción.

factual proposition—propuesta objetiva una propuesta que es verdadera o falsa.

fallacy—falacia un error de razonamiento o una convicción equivocada.

fear—temor proceso biológico que activa nuestro sistema energético de emergencias de modo que podamos manejar el peligro; emoción desagradable, a menudo fuerte, causada por la sensación o conciencia de peligro.

feedback—retroalimentación la reacción que el receptor entrega a un mensaje ofrecido por el transmisor.

fever chart—cuadro de fiebre infografía que presenta un patrón parecido a lo que resulta de medir la temperatura variable de una person con fiebre, trazando los datos (es muy útil para representar datos fiancieros o cambios a lo largo del tiempo).

fiasco—fiasco fracaso completo.

filter—filtrar usar barreras emocionales (basadas en antecedentes y personalidad) para absorber selectivamente la información.

fireside chat—conversación junto al hogar un discurso en el cual e líder se dirige al grupo de manera informal respecto de las preocupaciones, temores y problemas del grupo.

first affirmative constructive—(1AC)—primera afirmación constructiva en el debate Lincoln-Douglas, discurso que se prepara antes de una ronda en la cual el orador afirmativo presenta un caso positivo.

first affirmative rebuttal—(1AR)—primera refutación afirmativa en el debate Lincoln-Douglas, el discurso pronunciado por el primer orador afirmativo que responde al caso negativo y vuelve a construir el caso afirmativo; en un debate sobre políticas, el discurso que responde al bloque negativo y amplía el argumento que la segunda refutación afirmativa necesitará para ganar el debate.

first person—primera persona refiérese a la persona que habla (yo, nosotros).

first negative constructive—(1NC)—primera negación constructiva en el debate Lincoln—Douglas, el discurso mediante el cual el orador negativo presenta el caso negativo y refuta la aserción constructiva; en un debate sobre políticas, la posición negativa que el primer orador negativo presenta.

flippant—impertinente que carece de un adecuado respeto o seriedad.

flowsheet—hoja de flujo un registro escrito de las palabras o argumentos presentados durante un debate.

follow-up question—pregunta complementaria una pregunta que ayuda al entrevistador a perseguir temas que surgen en forma inesperada durante el curso de una entrevista.

foreshadowing—presagiar dar una pista o sugerencia con antelación.

forfeiting—enajenar pérdida o pérdida de derechos, por algún error, ofensa o crimen.

format—formato (1) un estilo de programación o especialización. (2) la organización general establecida para la conducción de un debate. Especifica la cantidad de tiempo y el orden en el cual se permitirá hablar a cada participante.

forum—foro debate que viene a continuación de un panel en el cual los panelistas participantes invitan a la audiencia a formular preguntas y hacer comentarios.

friendliness—amigable una actitud cálida, agradable.

G

germane—pertinente relativo, aplicable.

gesture—gesto lenguaje corporal que emplea movimiento de la mano o del brazo.

gigantic—gigantesco que excede lo usual o esperado (como en tamaño o fuerza); enorme.

gluttony—gula exceso en la comida o bebida.

good will—buena disposición un interés o preocupación genuino.

graph—gráfico una ayuda visual utilizada por un orador para demostrar una relación estadística.

group think—pensamiento de grupo tendencia de estar de acuerdo con el grupo aún a costa de tener que renunciar a sus propios principios.

grovel—arrastrarse literalmente, arrastrarse con la cabeza en el suelo para demostrar sumisión; rebajarse (humillarse o degradarse) a sí mismo.

H

handout—volante material impreso (tal como volantes, folletos u hojas informativas) preparadas y duplicadas con antelación a un discurso y proporcionadas a la audiencia como material de referencia.

haphazardly—al azar en una manera caraterizado por la falta de planificación, orden o dirección.

harmoniously—armoniosamente de acuerdo; marcado por una concordancia en sentimiento o acción.

hasty generalization—generalización apresurada un argumento fallido basado en información incompleta o poco representativa.

haven—asilo lugar seguro o un lugar que ofrece oportunidades o condiciones favorables.

hoke—falsificar (utilizado con "up") trillar, imitar.

house—sala (1) en procedimientos parlamentarios, un grupo durante sus reuniones. (2) el área en el cual la audiencia toma asiento.

humorous interpretation—interpretación humorística un concurso de hablar en público en el cual un orador memoriza y representa una obra literaria de naturaleza ligera.

hyperbole—hipérbole un método de decir más de la verdad o de exagerar a modo de énfasis.

I

ignoring the question—ignorar la pregunta el intento por parte del orador de desviar la atención de la audiencia del asunto en discusión.

illustration—ilustración un ejemplo que aclara un argumento o que introduce un elemento humano.

imagery—imaginería lenguaje que comunica una experiencia sensorial (crear imágenes en la mente, por ejemplo) o que hace recordar emociones o ideas que acompañan ciertas sensaciones.

I-message—mensaje yo enunciado que enfatiza lo que desea una persona.

impression—impresión cómo percibe la audiencia al orador basado en la forma en que se presenta a sí mismo y a sus ideas.

impromptu—impremeditado elaborado o hecho en ese momento, con muy poca o ninguna preparación.

impromptu method—método improvisado un método de entrega sin ensayo previo, en que el orador no utiliza apuntes y depende de su habilidad para ofrecer una respuesta verbal inmediata.

incidental motion—moción incidental una propuesta para cambiar la forma en que se está conduciendo una reunión.

incorrigible—incorregible incapaz de ser corregido, enmendado o reformado.

indented—sangría dispuesto con un espacio desde el margen (tal como las ideas subordinadas o de apoyo).

index—índice en un libro, una lista en orden alfabético ubicada al final de un libro que informa de la página o las páginas exactas en las cuales el lector puede encontrar información en particular.

indifferent audience—audiencia indiferente una audiencia apática o no interesada en el orador y en su tema, a menudo porque la audiencia no encuentra que el tema es relevante para su situación personal.

induction—inducción una forma de razonamiento en la cual se utilizan casos específicos para probar una verdad general.

inflection—modulación el cambio en el tono o volumen de voz por parte del orador con el objeto de crear énfasis.

infographic—gráfico informativo ilustración creada utilizando un programa de arte gráfico de una computadora como ser el Freehand o el Adobe Illustrator.

informal debate—debate casual cualquier debate realizado sin reglas específicas.

inhibition—inhibición freno interno impuesto a la libertad de acción, expresión o funcionamiento.

innovation—innovación una nueva idea, método o dispositivo.

innuendo—indirecta sugerencia, insinuación, especialmente una reflexión velada sobre el carácter o la reputación.

innumerable—innumerables demasiados para ser contados.

insinuated—insinuado introducido en forma gradual o de modo sutil, indirecto o astuto implícito en forma insidiosa o tortuosa.

instinctively—instintivamente en una manera marcado por espontaneidad e independencia del juicio o voluntad; o por una actitud, impulso o capacidad natural e inherente.

integrate—integrar formar, coordinar o mezclar en un todo funcional.

integrity—integridad fuerte sentimiento de bien y de mal; adhesión a una escala de valores.

intensification—intensificar acto de hacer más agudo o intenso; un realce

interior monologue—monólogo interior una narración en primera persona en la cual el narrador se está hablando a sí mismo.

interlibrary loan—préstamo interbiblioteca un sistema de cooperación mediante el cual las bibliotecas se prestan libros entre sí; algo prestando, o un permiso para uso provisional, por medio de tal sistema.

internship—práctica puesto de voluntario sin sueldo que trabaja para adquirir experiencia.

interpersonal communication—comunicación interpersonal transmisión de mensajes entre dos o más personas.

interviewer—entrevistador la persona que hace las preguntas durante una entrevista.

intimacy—intimidad relación estrecha, contacto o familiaridad.

intimate distance—distancia íntima la distancia que se utiliza principalmente para intercambios confidenciales, casi siempre reservada para amigos cercanos (una dieciocho pulgadas).

intimidation—intimidación el acto de hacer volver tímido o temeroso, asustar, forzar o disuadir por medio de amenazas reales o aparentes.

intrapersonal communication—comunicación intrapersonal diálogo interal que se lleva para evaluar pensamientos, sentimientos y reacciones propios.

introduction—presentación el inicio de un discurso; contiene el llamado de atención, la declaración de vínculo, la declaración de la tesis y frecuentemente, una declaración de antecedentes.

introspective—introspectivo marcado por mirar hacia adentro de manera relfectiva para examinar sus propios pensamientos o sentimientos.

intuition—intuición percepción rápida y espontánea; el poder o facultad de saber las cosas sin raciocinio consciente.

irony—ironía una expresión que utiliza palabras que sugieren lo opuesto de lo que parecen decir en la superficie.

irrational—irracional no gobernado por la razón; carente de comprensión o coherencia mental normal.

GLOSARIO

J

jargon—jerga el vocabulario especializado de personas en la misma profesión o en un mismo grupo.

jeopardy—riesgo expuesto a pérdidas; peligro, albur, riesgo.

jump on the bandwagon—hacer suya una causa triunfante técnica persuasiva basada en la necesidad a pertenecer.

justification—justificación acción que prueba la justicia, corrección o racionalidad; tal prueba

L

label—rótulo palabra o frase descriptiva o de identificación.

leader—líder una persona que guía, dirije o está encargada de otras.

leadership—liderazgo la habilidad de motivar y unir a otros para que trabajen unidos para lograr una tarea específica; la posición de ser líder; el acto de dirigir.

leading question—pregunta capciosa una pregunta que "pone palabras" en la boca del sujeto.

learning style—estilo de aprendizaje las diferentes maneras en que las personas aprenden con eficacia.

Lincoln–Douglas debate—debate Lincoln–Douglas tipo competitivo de debate formal, que se ocupa de proposiciones de valores y se practica en las escuelas secundarias del todo el país.

link—vínculo (1) en un debate, una explicación por parte del equipo negativo que demuestra que el plan afirmativo tiene un vínculo directo con su desventaja. (2) en un discurso, la declaración en una introducción que viene entre el llamado de atención y la declaración de la tesis y que conecta a los dos de una forma lógica.

listening spare time—tiempo de sobra para escuchar tiempo para pensar creado por la habilidad para escuchar más rápido de lo que la gente puede hablar.

logic—lógica la ciencia de razonar que utiliza un sistema de reglas para ayudar a la persona a pensar correctamente.

logical appeal—apelación lógica el uso de la secuencia, el análisis, la organización y la evidencia para probar un punto y persuadir.

logos—logos una palabra griega que significa lógica y razón; se asocia a la apelación lógica de Aristóteles.

M

main heading—encabezado principal en un discurso, una de las principales divisiones, áreas o argumentos de la declaración de propósito.

main motion—moción principal en procedimientos parlamentarios, una propuesta que pide al grupo que tome acción.

manipulate—manipular influenciar, especialmente con la intención de engañar, manejar o utilizar hábilmente.

manipulating—manipulando influenciando, especialmente con la intención de engañar.

mannequin—maniquí forma sin vida que representa a la figura humana.

manuscript method—método de manuscrito un método de entrega en la cual el orador escribe y posteriormente lee el discurso palabra por palabra.

map—mapa una ayuda visual para demostrar una relación geográfica.

mediation—mediación intervención entre partes en conflicto para promover una reconciliación, un acuerdo o un compromiso.

mediator—mediador persona neutral al que se puede recurrir los que participan en una discusión, para resolver disputas fuera de control.

memorized method—método de memoria un método de entrega en la cual el orador memoriza y luego presenta el discurso palabra por palabra sin el uso de apuntes.

mesmerized—hipnotizado hipnosis, mantener embelesado o fascinado.

message—mensaje aquello que se envía o dice.

metaphor—metáfora una expresión que compara dos cosas distintas al decir que una es la otra (sin el uso de las palabras igual a o como).

meter—metro medida del ritmo en una línea de poesía.

methodically—metódicamente con una maneraordenada.

microcosm—microcosmo mundo pequeño, comunidad o unidad que constituye un ejemplo típico o ideal de uno más grande.

miffed—irritable en un estado de mal humor (como resultado de una pelea sin importancia).

mimic—mimo imitar fielmente.

minstrel—trovador uno, los itinerantes, que en la Grecia antigua eran denominados "rapsodas", que leían sus obras en voz alta (frecuentemente con acompañamiento musical) en competencias públicas.

minutes—acta el registro escrito de las reuniones de una organización.

mock trial—juicio simulado clase de discusión que imita un juicio en tribunal.

model—modelo una representación en miniatura de algo.

moderator—moderador miembro de un grupo que dirige un debate (inicia el debate, lo mantiene dentro del tema y cierra el debate).

monopolize—monopolizar asumir el control o posesión total.

monotone—monótono un tono en el cual las palabras se entregan a la misma velocidad y entonación sin variación.

mood—ambiente el tono emocional creado o expresado en una obra.

motif—motivo idea dominante o tema central.

motivation—motivación una fuerza, necesidad o impulso interior que causa que la persona actúe.

multimedia presentation—presentación con medios múltiples discurso complementado con programas software, que permite al orador combinar varias clases de medios auxiliares visuales y/o auditivos.

N

name calling—insultar dar a alguien una etiqueta negativa sin tener evidencia.

narrative—narración una historia o el contar una historia.

narrowing—enfocarse limitarse y definir un tema de manera más precisa.

nectar—néctar el brebaje de los dioses griegos y romanos; cualquier bebida deliciosa, secreción dulce de una planta que constituye la materia prima de la miel.

negative—negativo expresión que significa "no" o "falso"; en un debate, la persona que contradice la proposición.

negative rebuttal—(NR)—refutación negativa en un debate Lincoln–Douglas, el discurso final pronunciado por el orador negativo que hace un resumen del debate y trata de "callar" los argumentos que se pueden prever de la refutación hecha por el orador afirmativo.

negotiation—negociación el acto de conferenciar con otro (u otros) para llegar a un arreglo sobre alguna materia.

new business—nuevo asunto asuntos presentados por primera vez en una reunión.

newness—novedoso un enfoque original o único hacia un tema.

nonassertive tone—tono no asertivo forma de comunicación que carece de vitalidad y aparece como carente de interés e indiferente.

nonverbal communication—comunicación no verbal las expresiones faciales o movimientos corporales utilizados para expresar actitudes o sentimientos respecto de una persona, situación o idea.

nonverbal messages—mensajes no verbales algo comunicado sin palabras, tal como las expresiones faciales o movimientos corporales utilizados.

notes—apuntes un listado de ideas escritas en forma breve y ordenada.

nuclear family—núcleo familiar grupo familiar consistente solamente en un padre, una madre y sus hijos.

O

offstage focus—enfoque hacia fuera del escenario técnica utilizada en reader's theater en el cual lectores utilizan libretos y se imaginan la escena afuera, entre la audiencia.

old business—asuntos pendientes asuntos que no fueron concluidos en reuniones anteriores.

omniscient—omnisciente relacionado con un punto de vista de tercera persona en la cual el narrador de una historia lo sabe todo y se desplaza con libertad dentro y fuera de las mentes de los distintos personajes.

online—en línea conectado con o acesible por un sistema—especialmente un sistema de computador; hecho por medio de una conexión a tal sistema.

open-ended question—pregunta abierta una pregunta que permite que el sujeto decida cuál es la mejor manera de responder. Fomenta una respuesta integral y profunda y trata de evitar una respuesta sí o no, verdadero o falso.

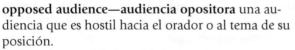

opposed audience—audiencia opositora una audiencia que es hostil hacia el orador o al tema de su posición.

oral cavity—cavidad oral la boca.

oral interpretation—interpretación oral el arte de comunicar obras de la literatura mediante una lectura adecuada en voz alta.

oral, (or verbal) communication—comunicación oral o verbal comunicación que es principalmente hablada.

orator—orador una persona que presenta un discurso público—en particular una persona conocida por hacerlo con destreza.

oratory or rhetoric—oratoria o retórica el arte o el estudio de hablar en público.

order of precedence—orden de prioridad en procedimientos parlamentarios, la relación de las mociones entre sí.

orders of the day—orden del día una agenda o lista de temas que se discutirán durante la reunión.

organization—organización en un discurso, un sistema de estructura y forma que permite que la audiencia pueda seguir fácilmente.

original oratory—oratoria original concurso de discurso en que los concursantes discursan y escriben sobre un tema de su propia elección.

ought—deber idea o concepto que tiene una persona de un ideal—obligación moral basada en un sentimiento de deber.

outline—reseña en un discurso, un marco lógicamente organizado que indica la forma en que progresará el discurso.

overhead projector—proyector de transparencias una ayuda visual para proyectar transparencias (frecuentemente cuadros y gráficos) hacia una pared o telón.

oxymoron—oxímoron un dispositivo literario que une palabras que están en directa oposición, tal como "bondad cruel."

P

pace—ritmo la velocidad a la habla una persona

painstakingly—esmeradamente en una manera que demuestra un esmerado cuidado o esfuerzo.

palatable—apetitoso agradable o aceptable a la mente (o al gusto).

panacea—panacea remedio para todas las dificultades o enfermedades.

panel—panel de expertos discusión informal que tiene lugar ante una audiencia.

parallelism—estructura paralela o paralelismo el uso de la misma forma gramatical para expresar ideas que debieran, lógicamente, ser tratadas con igualdad (frecuentemente involucra la repetición de palabras o frases).

paraphernalia—pertrechos equipo, accesorios, bienes personales.

paraphrase—paráfrasis repetir en sus propias palabras.

paraphrasing—parafrasear expresar un segmento original con palabras diferentes.

parliament—parlamento asamblea que constituye el cuerpo legislativo supremo de una unidad política (normalmente), tal comoel Reino Unido.

parliamentary procedure—procedimiento parlamentario un sistema de normas observado en reuniones grupales basado en ideas desarrolladas en el parlamento británico.

passive listening—escuchar pasivamente una forma de escuchar en la cual la persona que escucha no comparte la responsabilidad ni se involucra con el proceso de comunicación.

pathos—pathos la palabra griega para sentimientos y emociones; el término se asocia a la apelación emocional de Aristóteles.

pause—pausa una brecha en la conversación. Frecuente-mente proporciona una buena oportunidad para que el entrevistado (sin ser inducido) ofrezca mayor información.

people skills—habilidad con la gente habilidad para trabajar bien con otras personas por medio de una cortés comunicación.

perception—percepción cómo uno ve las cosas.

performance anxiety—ansiedad ante el público una forma de miedo al escenario, a menudo asociado a músicos, actores y otros artistas.

periodical—revista publicación como un periódico diario o académico, o una revista de moda o de noticias, que se publica a intervalos regulares.

periodical index—índice periódico un listado de artículos que se han publicado en revistas.

peripheral—periférico fuera del campo directo de visión y audición; relacionado con los límites externos o una área límite.

persona—persona el relator ficticio de la obra que será interpretada.

personal distance—distancia personal la distancia cómoda para una conversación entre amigos (entre un pie y medio a cuatro pies).

personal space—espacio personal una zona de comodidad que cada persona mantiene a su alrededor y en la cual una intrusión no sería bienvenida.

personification—personificación asignar características humanas a objetos no humanos.

persuasive speaking—oratoria persuasiva oratoria que influencia a otros a creer o pensar en algo o a tomar acción.

pervasiveness—capacidad de penetración el estado de se difundio (esparcido) por todas partes.

phobia—fobia un miedo persistente e irracional que hace que una persona evite situaciones específicas.

phonation—fonación la producción de la voz.

picturesque—pintoresco semejante a un cuadro, que produce imágenes mentales.

pie chart—gráfico circular infografía en forma de círculo que tiene sectores en forma de cuña, que corresponden a un componente distinto (muy útil para representar las partes como un procentaje del total).

pitch—tono las notas vocales (agudas o graves) que el orador alcanza cuando habla.

plagiarism—plagio copiar o imitar el lenguaje, ideas o pensamientos de otro o pasarlos como el trabajo original de uno.

platform movement—movimiento escénico caminar o desplazarse de manera dirigida desde un punto a otro mientras se habla.

polarizing—polarización división de los miembros de un grupo en dos bandos rivales que rehusan hacer concesiones.

policy proposition—propuesta de políticas propuesta que se enfoca hacia la conveniencia de un plan de acción determinado.

pollster—encuestador persona que hace preguntas a la gente para obtener información u opiniones para análisis.

portfolio—carpeta una selección de trabajo, por ejemplo los trabajos escolares ejecutados por un candidato que entrevista por un puesto de trabajo, que se utiliza para mostrar y analizar el rendimiento de uno.

posture—postura la posición del cuerpo cuando está quieto.

power source—fuente de poder el origen de la energía necesaria para que las cosas funcionen.

preamble—preámbulo en un debate, la declaración introductoria, específicamente la parte introductoria de una constitución o estatuto que normalmente formula las razones y la intención de la ley.

premise—premisa una aserción que sirve como la base para un argumento.

prep time—tiempo preparatorio el tiempo preparatorio permitido en cada ronda para organizar las respuestas y preparar las preguntas.

prerequisite—prerequisito algo que es necesario para un fin o para llevar a cabo una función.

prescriptive—prescripción relacionado con lo que se establece como guía o norma de ación (en un discurso, un tópico de prescripción requiere que el orador "prescriba"—establezca como guía o norma—indicaciones de políticas específicas).

preview statement—declaración previa en un discurso, la declaración al final de la introducción que presenta una vista general de las principales áreas que se discutirán en el cuerpo.

prioritizing—prioridad arreglar en orden de importancia.

privileged motion—moción privilegiada en procedimientos parlamentarios, una propuesta para resolver un problema urgente distinto a la moción principal.

problem-solution pattern—patrón de solución de problemas un patrón de organización que presenta un problema y luego ofrece posibles soluciones.

procession—procesión grupo de individuos que se mueven en un orden determinado, a menudo en forma ceremonial.

professional communication—comunicación profesional la comunicación que tiene lugar durante el trabajo o que está relacionada a una carrera.

pronunciation—pronunciación el uso—en particular el uso correcto—del aparato vocal para decir algo.

proof—prueba evidencia específica que establece la verdad de algo.

GLOSARIO

propaganda—propaganda ideas, hechos o alegaciones para deformar o oponer una causa—que a menudo distorcionan la verdad o engañan a la audiencia durante el proceso.

proposition—proposición una declaración del punto a ser discutido.

prospective—perspectivas relativo a o efectiva en el futuro, probable de acontecer.

proxemics—proxémica el estudio de la comunicación espacial; en la comunicación oral, se refiere específicamente a la distancia física entre los oradores y la audiencia.

proximal—próximo más cercano al punto de unión.

proxy—apoderado alguien que actúa como substituto de otro.

public distance—distancia pública la distancia que se mantiene entre extraños (normalmente doce pies o más). Una distancia a la cual las personas apenas si reconocen la presencia del otro.

public lecture—conferencia pública una conferencia realizada a la comunidad o a un grupo académico.

purpose statement—declaración de propósito en un discurso, una declaración que presenta temas selectos y el propósito específico del orador al hacer la presentación.

puff ball—pregunta suave una pregunta abierta fácil de contestar.

Q

qualm—desasosiego sentimiento súbito de duda, temor o intranquilidad.

questions of evaluation—preguntas de evaluación preguntas que se formulan a los miembros de un grupo solicitando su opinión negativa o positiva con respecto a posibles soluciones y la emisión de un juicio de valores.

questions of fact—preguntas pertinentes preguntas formuladas por los miembros de un grupo que guardan relación con los hechos en discusión.

questions of interpretation—preguntas de interpretación preguntas que solicitan a los miembros de un grupo que den sus opiniones sobre el significado de la información.

quorum—quórum en procedimientos parlamientarios, el número mínimo de miembros que deben estar presentes a fin de que se aprueben las medidas del grupo.

quotation—cita la repetición de las palabras exactas de otra persona.

R

railroad—apresurar aprobar algo (como una ley) muy precipitadamente.

rapport—afinidad sensación compartida de confianza y cooperación.

rate—ritmo la velocidad a la cual habla una persona.

reasoning—razonamiento el proceso de pensar, comprender y sacar conclusiones respecto de alguna evidencia.

rebuffed—denegar agudo rechazo o crítica.

rebuttal—refutación el acto de contrarrestar el ataque de un oponente al argumento de uno y de esa manera reconstruir el argumento.

receiver—receptor una persona que intercepta un mensaje y luego lo decodifica.

reciprocal—recíproco correspondencia o comunicación mutua.

recitation—declamación recitación ante una audiencia, generalmente de algo memorizado.

reconsider—reconsiderar en procedimientos parlamentarios, una moción para reexaminar la moción principal que ya ha sido aprobada o rechazada.

refrain—refrán frase o verso que se repite regularmente.

refute—refutar probar, utilizando evidencia, que algo es equivocado o falso.

regurgitating—regurgitar devolver hacia fuera, atrás o hacia arriba.

reiterate—reiterar decir o hacer otra vez una cosa, o en forma repetida.

renowned—renombre aclamado y honrado universalmente; célebre, famoso.

repetition—repetición el acto o proceso de repetir.

reprimanded—reprimenda reprobar (regañar o corregir) severamente, generalmente desde una posición de autoridad.

reputation—reputación la cualidad o característica de alguien o algo tal como se percibe los demás en general; el reconocmiento de una característica o habilidad.

resolution—resolución (1) una declaración formal de opinión. (2) en procedimientos parlamentarios, un tipo especial de moción principal que comienza con una explicación de porque la moción debe ser aprobada.

responsible—responsable responsabilidad y reconocimiento de las consecuencias de sus acciones.

restate—volver a exponer volver a exponer (decir) lo mismo o en otra forma.

retention—memorizar habilidad de la mente para retener experiencias, o recordar, lo que hace posible el reconocer y el recordar.

rhapsodes—rapsoda trovadores itinerantes de la antigua Grecia que se reunían para leer sus obras en competencia pública.

rhetorical—retórico (1) relativo al arte de la oratoria o de escribir en forma efectiva; (2)pregunta que se ha creado por un efecto y que no requiere de respuesta; (3) relacionado con las tretas del lenguaje como los testimonios, las falsas comparaciones y las sugerencias de "subirse al carro de la victoria".

rhetorical questions—preguntas retóricas preguntas que se hacen por un efecto y que no necesitan de una respuesta.

rhyme—rima comunmente, la repetición, en distintas palabras, de la última vocal tónica y de los sonidos que la siguen, normalment al final de las estrofas de un verso.

rhythm—ritmo el flujo natural de sílabas acentuadas y no acentuadas en lenguaje—más destacadamente en verso.

rife—corriente difundido, frecuente, abundante.

rigorous—riguroso duro, severo o estricto, escrupulosamente exacto o preciso.

round table—mesa redonda debate especial de panelistas en el cual un pequeño grupo de participantes conversa sobre un tópico de interés común sentados alrededor de una mesa o en un semi círculo.

S

sanctity—santidad la cualidad o estado de ser santo o sagrado: santidad de vida y carácter.

scanner—explorador dispositivo que metódicamente examina un imágen o documento para obtener datos, en particular para que lo visualize o almacene un computador.

scenario—escenario secuencia de eventos, especialmente cuando son imaginarios; un relato o resumen del curso proyectado o posible de eventos o acciones.

scene/setting—escena/situación técnica que usan los intérpretes orales para concentrar la escena descrita en un escenario imaginario frente al lector.

search engine—motor de búsqueda sitio Web con software que permite a los usarios buscar información específica en la red mundial.

second affirmative rebuttal—(2AR)—segunda refutación afirmativa en un debate de políticas, este discurso resume la posición afirmativa y hace una presentación clara explicando por qué los principales puntos del debate se han tornado afirmativos.

second person—segunda persona refiérese a la persona a la cual se le habla (usted, tú).

segregation—segregación separación del resto, especialmente una separación debido a la raza, clase social o grupo étnico.

self-esteem—autoestima el valor por sí mismo, a menudo logrado a través del auto descubrimiento.

sender—transmisor la persona que envía un mensaje.

senile—senil relacionado con la edad avanzada, especialmente a la pérdida de la habilidad mental que se asocia con la vejez.

sequential—secuencial seguir una secuencia, hacer una sucesión continua o relacionada; seguir un orden cronológico.

serendipity—buena suerte descubrir algo agradable por casualidad.

sign—signo un tipo de razonamiento inductivo en el cual uno saca conclusiones sobre una situación basado en la evidencia física.

signposting—ideas clave revisión previa de los argumentos que se van a desarrollar con posterioridad en un discurso.

simile—símil una expresión que compara dos cosas distintas utilizando una expresión como "igual" o "como".

simulated—simulado que tiene el efecto o apariencia de, falsificado.

sincerity—sinceridad la cualidad de ser honesto o genuino.

slang—jerga palabras no convencionales asociadas a ciertos grupos.

GLOSARIO

sloth—holgazanería pereza

social communication—comunicación social la comunicación que tiene lugar en la vida personal y comunitaria.

social distance—distancia social la distancia que generalmente se mantiene entre las personas en la mayoría de los intercambios sociales y comerciales (entre cuatro y doce pies de distancia).

sound bite—"mordida de sonido" pequeños trozos de entrevistas que se recuerdan fácilmente, muchas veces se transmiten por televisión y transmisiones de radio.

sounding board—"junta de resonancia" persona o grupo de personas en las cuales se prueba una idea u opinión como medio de evaluación.

sparkler—chispa información (en particular en forma de analogía, cuento, anécdota o cita) que se entrega durante el curso de una respuesta que hace que el punto tome vida.

spatial pattern—patrón espacial un patrón de organización que ordena los elementos sobre la base de relaciones de espacio o de situación.

speech of acceptance—discurso de agradecimiento breve discurso dado por una persona que recibe un regalo o un premio.

speech of presentation—discurso de premiación un breve discurso para entregar un premio o un regalo a una persona.

spellbound—hechizado atrapado por o como por un hechizo; fascinado.

spontaneity—espontaneidad la cualidad o estado de ser espontáneo—hacer o producir libre y naturalmente, impulsivo, instintivo.

stack the deck—asegurar el resultado para presentar evidencia no equilibrada que solo presenta un lado de las cosas.

stage fright—miedo al público el nerviosismo que siente un orador o artista frente a una audiencia.

status quo—status quo las condiciones existentes o la forma en que están las cosas.

status report—informe de situación un informe que resume los anteriores logros de un grupo y sus metas futuras.

stereotyping—asignar estereotipos formar una idea mental distorcionada de algo o alguien basado en una opinión muy sencilla, un prejuicio, o un juicio no examinado que llevan los miembros de un grupo.

stoic—estoico no afectado por la pasión o los sentimientos, especialmente la demostración de indiferencia ante el dolor o la angustía.

stress—subrayar, acentuar dar énfasis a la palabra o las palabras mas importantes de una oración

subject—sujeto la persona que responde a las preguntas del entrevistador.

subordination—subordinación catalogar de acuerdo a la importancia.

subsidiary motion—moción auxiliar en procedimientos parlamentarios, una moción para ajustar o mejorar una moción principal.

suffice—suficiente que cumple o satisface una necesidad.

summarize—resumir que cubre los puntos principales en forma compacta sin derroche de palabras.

superficial—superficial de o relativo a la superficie o solamente a la apariencia, trivial.

supporting material—material de apoyo información que apoya y refuerza el encabezado de un discurso. (No debe confundirse con los detalles, que son más específicos.)

supportive audience—audiencia sustentadora una audiencia a la cual le agrada el orador y lo que éste tiene que decir—y por eso está dispuesta a apoyar y promover las ideas del orador.

suppress—suprimir restringir el curso normal de acción; evitar la expresión.

surrogacy—subrogancia el acto de tomar el lugar de otro, o la sustitución de uno por otro.

suspend—suspender parar temporalmente, mantener inactivo por un tiempo.

syllable—sílaba unidad de lenguaje hablado consistente en una sola pronunciación, división comúnmente aceptada de una palabra.

syllogism—silogismo una forma de razonamiento deductivo compuesto de dos premisas y una conclusión.

symbol—símbolo (1) cualquier cosa que represente una idea y que se utilice en la comunicación; (2) imágen de una person, un lugar, una cosa o una acción que hacer recordar otra ideas o serie de ideas, normalmente más generales.**sympathetic—simpatía** que demuestra la capacidad de entender y compartir los sentimientos o intereses de un tercero, de expresar dolor por la pérdida o desgracia de otra persona.

symposium—simposio debate formal en el cual varios expertos presentan un conjunto de puntos de vista mediante discursos breves; los discursos pueden dar lugar a un debate entre los expertos y la audiencia.

synonymous—sinónimo similar en sentido y significado.

systematic—sistemático tener un método u orden regular.

T

table a motion—archivar una moción en procedimientos parlamentarios, una propuesta para postergar momentáneamente una moción.

table of contents—tabla de contenido el esbozo del plan general u organización de un libro. Generalmente se encuentra al inicio del libro, y es una lista de las principales secciones y capítulos del libro.

tact—tacto diplomacia en el trato con los demás.

talk show—programa de entrevistas formato de discusión en que el presentador o los presentadores dirigen una discusión sobre un tema particular, entrevistan a invitados que tienen conocimiento del tema, y pueden permitir que el público haga preguntas.

tangible—tangible aquello que podemos percibir a través de los sentidos, especialmente por medio del tacto.

tedious—tedioso cansador a causa de lo largo o aburrido.

tedium—tedio aburrimiento

temperament—temperamento característica o inclinación habitual, o forma emocional de respuesta.

testimonial—testimonio el patrocinio de un mensaje por parte de una celebridad o experto.

testimonial speech—discurso testimonial un discurso de elogio o celebración en honor de una persona en vida.

theme—tema la idea central de una obra.

thesis—tesis una declaración que presenta o expresa el propósito general de un discurso.

thesis statement—declaración de tesis la declaración que presenta el propósito general de un discurso.

third person—tercera persona refiérese a la persona o cosa sobre la cual se habla (él, ella, eso, ellos).

timbre—timbre tono distintivo.

title card—tarjeta de título un sistema de catalogar libros mediante el uso de tarjetas organizadas por título.

tone—tono la combinación del volumen y el timbre de la voz, pausas, ritmo y pronunciación única de una persona. Frecuentemente es un indicio seguro de los sentimientos del orador.

tone of voice—tono de voz el diapasón y timbre (tono distintivo) de la voz del orador.

topic-specific—tópico específico característica de un discurso cuya introducción está directamente conectada al resto del discurso.

town hall meeting—reunión de alcaldía tradicionalmente, un debate en que un grupo de ciudadanos se reúne en un lugar público para discutir sobre problemas de la comunidad y votar sobre posibles soluciones.

transformation—transformación el proceso, acto o instancia de cambiar la composición, estructura, configuración externa o apariencia.

transition—transición una palabra o frase en un discurso que une una parte del discurso con la siguiente.

trivia—trivialidades asuntos sin importancia.

U

ubiquitous—ubicuo existir en todas partes al mismo tiempo; diseminado.

unbiased—imparcial libre de todo juicio y discriminación personales e infundados; justo.

uncommitted audience—audiencia no comprometida una audiencia que es neutral (o que aún no se ha decidido) hacia el tema del orador.

understatement—declaración exageradamente modesta el uso de "exageración al revés", particularmente con el propósito de dar énfasis—para llamar la atención a un absurdo.

unobtrusive—discreto que no es osado o agresivo; indiscernible.

V

value—valores normas que se usa para para juzgar si algo está bien o mal, correcto o incorrecto.

value criteria—criterio valórico en un debate, conceptos que proporcionan normas adicionales de juicio para evaluar si se ha efectuado una premisa valórica.

value premise—premisa valórica en un dabate, suposición que proporciona normas de juicio para evaluar si una decisión es cierta o no.

value proposition—propuesta de valores tipo de propuesta que involucra juicios filosóficos para las cuales no existen respuestas correctas o incorrectas.

verbatim—verbatim el recuento de una entrevista palabra por palabra.

vested—establecido completa e incondicionalmente garantizados, como un derecho, beneficio o privilegio. (tal como un interés, al cual el tenedor tiene un fuerte compromiso.)

vicariously—indirectamente en una manera que comparte la experiencia de otro usando la imaginación o sentimientos de simpatía.

vision—visión la habilidad de ver más allá de lo obvio; buscar más allá y al futuro para encontrar las respuestas y posibilidades.

vocal process—proceso vocal el sistema que produce sonidos.

vocalized pause—muleta pausa, palabras sin significado, tales como "tú sabes," "aaaa," y "este", utilizadas para llenar los vacíos cuando el orador no está seguro de lo que dirá a continuación.

volume—volumen el nivel de la voz del orador.

voucher—recibo un formulario o cheque que indica un crédito contra futuras compras o gastos (como en el caso de los recibos escolares).

vulnerable—vulnerable susceptible; que tiene poca resistencia; expuesto a un ataque o a daños.

W

written communication—comunicación escrita cualquier comunicación que deber ser leída.

Y

yes-no question—pregunta sí o no una pregunta que puede ser respondida con un simple "sí" o "no" y que permite que el sujeto responda ala pregunta sin elaborar.

Z

zinger—comentario cáustiscoen un discurso una aseveración final que constituye un poderoso recordatorio de la rectitud de la posición del orador.

INDEX

policy, 446
value, 446
Prose, oral interpretation of, 379–380, 387
Proxemics, 285–286
Psychoneuroimmunology, 337
Public distance, 87
Public domain, 323
Public forum debate, 437
Public lectures, 303
Public libraries. *See* libraries
Public officials, interviewing, 120, 132, 140
Public speaking, 13, 23. *See also* Speeches
    Dale Carnegie course on, 214
    Washington, G., and, 500
Public utterance, rhythms of, 384
Puff balls, 135
Purpose statement, 205, 206

Q

Queener, Donald, 344–345
Question(s). *See also* Interview questions
    anticipating, 124, 135, 325
    asking, 50, 106, 123–127, 197, 216
    begging the, 231
    calling the, 477–478, 487
    to consider before speaking, 14
    for decision making, 508–509
    embarrassing, 59
    of evaluation, 160
    for extemporaneous speeches, 358, 359, 408
    of fact, 160
    for group discussion, 155, 159–161, 164
    ignoring the, 230
    of interpretation, 160–161, 164
    for leadership, 508–509, 513
    listening and, 59, 60
    motion to table a, 486–487
    of privilege, 488
    by receiver of message, 6
    research, 173, 176
    responding to, in L-D, 459
    rhetorical, 197, 244–245
"Quickie words," 118
Quintilian, 13
Quorum, 479–480, 484
Quotations
    as attention-getters, 198–199, 216
    for conclusions, 39

extemporaneous speech and, 358
as impromptu speech topics, 364
in L-D, 451, 452, 454
for original oratory, 408
plagiarism and, 186–188
research and, 184
for supporting thesis, 315–316

R

Radio
    interviews, 118
    as news source, 184
Railroading, 472, 473
A Raisin in the Sun (Hansberry), 8
Rand McNally Goode's World Atlas, 183
Rapport, 121, 511, 514
"Rapport talk," 57
Rate, of speech, 52, 276, 277
    in characterization, 387
    feelings and, 80
"Rate gap," 52
Rather, Dan, 12
Reaching Up program, 17
Reader's Guide to Periodical Literature, 182, 466
Readers Theater, 388–389
Reading
    group, 388–389
    interpreting and. *See* Oral interpretation
    listening *vs.*, 56
    of multimedia presentations, 325
    research and, 174
Reagan, Ronald, 233, 404
Reasoning
    by analogy, 225–226
    circular, 231
    deceptive, 64
    deductive, 226–227, 237
    defined, 222
    emotional appeals *vs.*, 230, 234
    inductive, 223–227, 237
    logic and, 220–237, 340–341, 448
    by sign, 224, 226, 227, 229
Rebuttals, 435, 458, 460–461
Receiver, 5–6, 51. *See also* Listening
Recess, 486, 488
Reciprocal respect, 14
Recitations, poetry, 374, 375
Reconsidering motions, 482

S

Sadness, 79
Safire, William, 404
Salinas, Maria Elena, 502
Sallust, 234
Sandberg, Jared, 178
Satire, 317, 397–398
Scanners, 323
The Scarlet Letter (Hawthorne), 282
Scene setting, in oral interpretation, 386–387
Scholarships, 133–138, 336–337, 410
Schools/colleges
   organization in, 194
   recruiters, 172
   thoughts during college lecture, 58
Scobey, Sally, 63
Scotese, Peter, 424
Scott, Dred, 445
Scott, Willard, 27
Scurry, Brianna, 515
Search engines, 178–181
Seating, 148–149, 166, 326
Second affirmative rebuttal (2AR), 458, 461
Second-person narrations, 379
"Second signature," walking as, 76, 92
Secretary, of organizations, 476, 478–479
See It Now (TV series), 430
Seinfeld, Jerry, 25–26
Self-communication, 12
Self-concepts, 54
Self-doubt, 12
Self-esteem, 33–34, 99, 188
Self-perception, 32–34
Sender, in communication process, 5–6
Senses, 62, 243
September 11, 2001, terrorist attacks, 109
Sequence, 15, 37, 150
Sergeant-at-arms, 479
Seuss, Dr., 372
The Seven Habits of Highly Effective
   People (Covey), 61
Sexist language, 259–260
Shakespeare, William, 377
  on brevity, 107, 308
  facts about, 313–314
  and hyperbole, 250
  and listening, 50, 56
  oral interpretation of, 385

quoting, for rhetorical effect, 361
  rhythm of language and, 384
Shaw, George Bernard, 395
Shell Oil, 195
Shetty, Shilpa, 86
Shields, Brooke, 131
Shocking language, 260–261
Should, ought *vs.*, 448
"Should Prozac Be Banned?" (Mallory), 358–361
Showmanship, 388
Shriver, Eunice Kennedy, 512
Shulman, Max, 234
Sign language, 263
Signposting, 359, 451
Signs
  of greeting, 84–85
  "hook'em, horns," 75
  OK, 75
  "peace," 8
  "rabbit ears," 74
  reasoning by, 224, 226, 227, 229
  thumbs-up, 8, 83
  "V," 6, 74
Silence
  in interviewing, 130
  "sounds of," in poetry, 380
Silent language, 75
Silent listener, 64
Silent Messages (Mehrabian), 366
Similes, 246–248
Simon, Carly, 27
Simonton, Dean Keith, 500
Simple Fun for Busy People (Krane), 337
Simplicity, 363
The Simpsons, 356, 372
Sincerity, 345
Six Cs (clear, concise, complete, correct,
   concrete, connect), 304–305, 307–309
Skepticism
  of leaders, 520
  trust and, 16
Slang, 101, 259, 261
Slavery, 445, 467, 474
Slides, 319
Sliming, 460
Smiling
  body language and, 76, 80, 81, 290
  confidence and, 38
  at humor, 76